Still the most comprehensive,
authoritative go-to reference for:

- ✦ Coping with crying and colic

- ✦ The hows and whys of choosing when and what to feed
  your baby or older child

- ✦ How to give your baby a bath

- ✦ What to do about issues such as thumb-sucking or
  nail-biting

- ✦ Sports and sun safety

- ✦ Common household dangers you need to be aware of

- ✦ What to include in a home first-aid kit

- ✦ How to handle problems at school

BOOKS BY DR. BENJAMIN SPOCK

DR. SPOCK ON PARENTING

DR. SPOCK'S THE FIRST TWO YEARS
(edited by Martin T. Stein, MD)

DR. SPOCK'S THE SCHOOL YEARS
(edited by Martin T. Stein, MD)

Published by Pocket Books

DR. SPOCK'S BABY AND CHILD CARE

10TH EDITION

by Benjamin Spock, M.D.

Revised and updated by
Robert Needlman, M.D.

G

Gallery Books

New York   London   Toronto   Sydney   New Delhi

The ideas, procedures, and suggestions in this book are intended to supplement, not replace, the medical advice of trained professionals. All matters regarding your child's health require medical supervision. Consult your physician before adopting the medical suggestions in this book, as well as about any condition that may require diagnosis or medical attention.

The authors and publishers disclaim any liability arising directly or indirectly from the use of this book.

G

Gallery Books
An Imprint of Simon & Schuster, Inc.
1230 Avenue of the Americas
New York, NY 10020

This Gallery Books trade paperback edition October 2018

GALLERY BOOKS and colophon are registered trademarks
of Simon & Schuster, Inc.

For information about special discounts for bulk purchases,
please contact Simon & Schuster Special Sales at 1-866-506-1949
or business@simonandschuster.com.

The Simon & Schuster Speakers Bureau can bring authors to your live event. For
more information or to book an event, contact the Simon & Schuster Speakers
Bureau at 1-866-248-3049 or visit our website at www.simonspeakers.com.

Interior design by Davina Mock-Maniscalco
Illustrations by Grace Needlman

Manufactured in the United States of America

10   9   8   7   6   5   4   3   2

Library of Congress Cataloging-in-Publication Data is available.

ISBN 978-1-5011-7533-6

ACKNOWLEDGMENTS

The book you are reading was first published more than seventy years ago. When it came out in 1946, *The Common Sense Guide to Baby and Child Care* by Dr. Benjamin Spock revolutionized parenting and changed the lives of a generation. The children of that generation are the grandparents and great-grandparents of this one. Maybe they are *your* parents. So, in a way, you might be "a child of Spock." I know I am.

Dr. Spock's warm and wise advice still makes sense today. The book has changed with the times. When Gloria Steinem, the groundbreaking feminist, told Spock that he was a sexist, he listened and changed. Later, he embraced a vegetarian diet and went on to live to ninety-four.

Before he died, Dr. Spock worked on the seventh edition of *Baby and Child Care* with a gifted pediatrician, Steven Parker, who was also one of my own most influential teachers. So when I revised *Baby and Child Care* for its eighth and ninth editions, I owed a huge debt to both Dr. Spock and Dr. Parker. Marty Stein, who also worked on the seventh edition, has been a leader in Developmental and Behavioral Pediatrics for years, and I've relied on his insights and writings throughout my career.

For this tenth edition, I have turned for help to a team of experts including Nazha Abughali, Kim Burkhart, Jessica Chupnick, Abdulla Ghori, Reema Gulati, James Kozik, Jackie Miller, Gloria Needlman, Mary O'Connor, Nancy Roizen, Susan Santos, Lenore Skenazy, Terry Stancin, Marty Stein, and Martha Wright. They, and many other friends and colleagues, have greatly enriched this edition of *Baby and Child Care,* although, of course, the responsibility for the finished product and any errors it contains is mine.

Mary Morgan, who was married to Dr. Spock for twenty-five years, has been an enormous source of guidance and support. Writing a book, like raising a child, is an act of faith. Thanks, Mary, for having faith in me. Thanks also to Daniel Strone, Katie Robinson, and Nicole Robson at Trident Media Group; and to Marla Daniels, Polly Watson, and Sarah Wright, our editors at Simon and Schuster; and to Alicia Brancato, Lisa Litwack, and Davina Mock-Maniscalco for production and design; and to Grace Needlman for the illustrations.

Finally, thanks to my family: to Grace, for teaching me to look to the future, and to Carol, for your good sense and even better heart. Without you, I couldn't even start, let alone finish, a project like this book.

Dr. Spock's newest and fully updated guide to *Baby and Child Care* reminds parents to trust themselves *and* their children. Along with ever-useful information on sleeping, feeding, and diapering, this comprehensive tenth edition helps parents deal with some of the most pressing issues of today:

✦ Child care in an era of exploding information and growing anxiety

✦ Promoting success without overstressing competition

✦ Electronic media and the obsession with electronic games

✦ Nutrition: how to prevent obesity and other chronic illnesses, and enrich happiness

✦ Diversity in cultures, families, parenting beliefs, and sexuality

✦ The newest thinking on children with special health and developmental needs

✦ Common problems: ADHD, autism spectrum disorders, anxiety, depression, and more

CONTENTS

Acknowledgments   *v*

Preface   *xxv*

Trust Yourself and Your Children   *1*

    Trust Yourself   1

    Parents Are Human   3

    Nature and Nurture   6

    Different Families, Different Challenges   7

SECTION I

YOUR CHILD, AGE BY AGE

Before Your Child Is Born   *13*

    Babies Develop; Parents, Too   13

    Prenatal Plans and Decisions   16

    Choosing Your Baby's Doctor   20

    Planning the Homecoming   22

    Helping Siblings Cope   24

    Things You'll Need   26

Your Newborn, Birth to About Three Months   *35*

    Your Baby at Birth   35

    Enjoy Your Baby   36

Parents' Early Feelings   40

Caring for Your Baby   44

Feeding and Sleeping   46

Crying and Comforting   50

Diapering   55

Bowel Movements   58

The Bath   61

Body Parts   64

Temperature, Fresh Air, and Sunshine   68

Common Newborn Concerns   72

The First Year, Four to Twelve Months   *77*

A Time of Firsts   77

Caring for Your Baby   79

Feeding and Growth   80

Sleeping   82

Crying and Colic   84

Spoiling   89

Physical Development   92

Learning About People   99

Clothes and Equipment   101

Common Physical Issues in the First Year   104

Your Toddler: Twelve to Twenty-Four Months   *115*

What Makes Them Tick?   115

Help Your Toddler Explore Safely   117

Fears at Around One Year   122

Challenging Behaviors   124

Sleep Issues   126

Eating and Nutrition   128

Toilet Training and Learning   130

Your Two-Year-Old   *133*

    Being Two   133
    Worries at Around Two   136
    Challenging Behaviors   140
    Diet and Nutrition   143
    Toilet Learning   144

Your Preschooler: Three to Five Years   *145*

    Devotion to the Parents   145
    Romantic and Competitive Feelings   147
    Curiosity and Imagination   150
    Sleep Issues   151
    Fears at Around Three, Four, and Five   152
    Worries About Injury and Body Differences   156
    Preschool   159

School Age: Six Through Eleven Years   *169*

    Fitting into the Outside World   169
    Social Lives   172
    At Home   176
    Common Behavior Concerns   177
    Success in School   182
    Problems in School   191
    The Unpopular Child   194

Adolescence: Twelve to Eighteen Years   *197*

    Challenges of Adolescence   197
    Puberty and Growth   198
    Early Adolescence: Twelve to Fourteen   202
    Middle Adolescence: Fifteen to Seventeen   206
    Late Adolescence: Eighteen to Twenty-One   210

College   211
General Strategies for Dealing with Teens   220
Adolescent Health Issues   224

SECTION II

FEEDING and NUTRITION

Feeding in the First Year   *231*

When to Feed   232
Getting Enough and Gaining Weight   236
Vitamins, Supplements, and Special Diets   238
Self-Feeding   241
Changes and Challenges   244

Breastfeeding   *247*

Benefits of Breastfeeding   247
Getting Started   249
Is Your Baby Getting Enough?   256
The Nursing Mother's Physical Condition   258
Breastfeeding Techniques   263
The Working Mother   267
Manual Expression and Breast Pumps   269
Breastfeeding Challenges   270
Breast-and-Bottle Combinations   274
Weaning from the Breast   275

Formula-Feeding   *279*

Choosing and Preparing Formula   279
Formula Refrigeration   283
Washing and Sterilization   284
Giving the Bottle   285

Bottle-Feeding Problems   286
Weaning from the Bottle   291

Starting Solid Foods   *297*

Healthy from the Start   297
When and How to Begin   297
Solid Foods, Six to Twelve Months   307

Nutrition and Health   *311*

What Is Good Nutrition?   311
Building Blocks of Nutrition   312
Dr. Spock's Diet   320
What to Cook   326
Simple Meals   332
Tips for Happy Eating   335

SECTION III

HEALTH and SAFETY

General Medical Issues   *343*

Your Child's Doctor   343
Telephone Calls to Your Doctor   345
Fevers   349
Diet During Illness   355
Giving Medicine   358
Isolation for Contagious Diseases   360
Going to the Hospital   362
Caring for a Sick Child   366

Immunizations   *369*

A Historical Perspective   369

How Vaccines Work   369
Risks of Immunization   373
The Immunization Schedule   375
Coping with Shots   378

Preventing Injuries   *381*

   Keeping Children Safe   381

Part 1: Safety Inside the Home   **383**
Dangers at Home   383
Drowning and Water Safety   384
Fire, Smoke, and Burns   386
Poisons   389
Lead and Mercury   392
Choking   395
Suffocation and Strangulation   397
Guns in the Home   397
Falls   398
Toy Safety   400
Home Safety Equipment   400

Part 2: Safety Outside the Home   **401**
Riding in Cars   401
Streets and Driveways   405
Bicycle Injuries   407
Playground Injuries   409
Sports Safety   410
Cold and Hot Temperatures   414
Sun Safety   416
Bugbites   418
Preventing Dog Bites   420
Fireworks and Trick-or-Treat   421

First Aid and Emergencies   *423*

    Cuts and Scratches   423

    Splinters   424

    Bites   424

    Bleeding   426

    Burns and Electrical Injuries   428

    Skin Infections   430

    Objects in Nose and Ears   430

    Objects in the Eye   431

    Sprains and Strains   431

    Fractures   432

    Neck and Back Injuries   434

    Head Injuries   435

    Swallowed Objects   435

    Poisons   436

    Allergic Reactions   438

    Convulsions or Seizures   439

    Choking and Rescue Breathing   439

    Home First-Aid Kit   444

Dental Development and Oral Health   *447*

    Tooth Development   447

    Teething   449

    What Makes Good Teeth?   450

    Early Dentist Visits   452

    Tooth Decay   453

    Brushing and Flossing   454

    Dental Varnish and Sealants   456

    Dental Injuries   456

    Preventing Mouth Injuries   457

Common Childhood Illnesses **459**

Colds 459
Ear Infections 467
Sore Throats and Strep Throats 473
Croup and Epiglottitis 476
Bronchitis, Bronchiolitis, and Pneumonia 479
Influenza (The Flu) 481
Asthma 482
Snoring 485
Nasal Allergies 486
Eczema 488
Other Rashes and Warts 491
Head Lice 495
Stomachaches 495
Constipation 501
Vomiting and Diarrhea 505
Headaches 510
Seizures 511
Eye Problems 514
Joints and Bones 516
Heart Problems 518
Genital and Urinary Disturbances 520
Hernias and Testicle Problems 523
Sudden Infant Death Syndrome (SIDS) 524
Acquired Immune Deficiency Syndrome (AIDS) 526
Tuberculosis 527
Reye's Syndrome 528
West Nile Virus 528
Zika Virus 529

SECTION IV

RAISING MENTALLY HEALTHY CHILDREN

What Children Need **533**

Love and Limits 533
Early Relationships 534
Sex Roles 537
Fathers 541
Self-Esteem 543
Beyond Parenting 545
Raising Children in a Troubled Society 549
The Natural World 550
The Importance of Risk 553
Learning in the Brain 555
How Children Think 558
Reading Aloud 566

Child Care **579**

Parents Work 579
When to Return to Work 579
Child Care Alternatives 581
Choosing a Child Care Program 588
After-School Care 590
Babysitters 591
Time with Your Child 593

Discipline **597**

What Discipline Is 597
Reward and Punishment 601
Tips for Setting Limits 611
The Problem of Permissiveness 616

Manners   621
Parents' Angry Feelings   622

Grandparents   *627*

Sexuality   *631*

The Facts of Life   631
How Sexuality Develops   637
Talking with Teens about Sex   642
Gender Nonconformity and Sexual Preferences   645

The Media   *651*

Different Types of Families   *661*

Adoption   661
Single-Parent Families   669
Stepfamilies   672
Gay and Lesbian Parents   675

Children with Special Needs   *679*

Coping within the Family   680
Taking Action   684

Stresses and Traumas   *687*

The Meaning of Stress   688
Terrorism and Disasters   690
Domestic Violence   692
Physical Abuse and Neglect   693
Sexual Abuse   695
Death   698
Separation from a Parent   701
Divorce   703

SECTION V

COMMON DEVELOPMENTAL AND BEHAVIORAL CHALLENGES

Acting Out   717

   Temper Tantrums   717
   Swearing and Back Talk   722
   Biting   725

Messiness, Dawdling, and Whining   729

   Messiness   729
   Dawdling   731
   Whining   734

Habits   737

   Thumb-Sucking   737
   Other Infant Habits   742
   Rhythmic Habits   743
   Nail-Biting   744
   Stuttering   745

Toilet Training, Soiling, and Bed-Wetting   749

   Readiness for Toilet Training   749
   A Gentle Training Approach   754
   Bladder Control   760
   Setbacks in Bowel and Bladder Control   764
   Soiling   765
   Bed-Wetting   766

Sleep Problems   773

   Night Terrors and Sleepwalking   773

   Insomnia   774

Disorders of Feeding and Eating   777

   Feeding Problems   777

   Needing to Be Fed   783

   Gagging   785

   Thin Children   786

   Obesity   788

   Eating Disorders   793

Sibling Rivalry   799

   Jealousy and Closeness   799

   The Many Faces of Jealousy   802

   Jealousy of the New Baby   806

   Siblings with Special Needs   811

Anxiety and Depression   813

   Anxiety   813

   Depression   818

Hyperactivity (ADHD)   823

Learning Disabilities   833

Intellectual Disability   843

Autism   849

Down Syndrome and Other Genetic Disorders   857

Getting Help   *861*

   Why People Seek Help   861
   First Steps   861
   Types of Therapy   862
   Choosing a Professional   863
   Working Together   867

Common Medications for Children   *869*

Glossary of Common Medications   *873*

Resource Guide   *887*

Index   *901*

To Allen and Gloria Needlman,
my first and best teachers

PREFACE

About This Tenth Edition of
Dr. Spock's Baby and Child Care

The first edition of *Baby and Child Care* arrived with a boom, the postwar baby boom, a time of rapid change and bracing optimism. Now, more than seventy years later, the optimism seems to be replaced by anxiety. The world is objectively safer, but it feels more dangerous. We walk around with unlimited information in our pockets, but that only makes it harder to know what to believe. Everywhere one looks, there are new ideas; but which of these are actually better, and which are fads, or worse?

Baby and Child Care is now a classic. But Dr. Spock, who ran for president while opposing the Vietnam War, was a radical in his parenting philosophy. "Spare the rod, spoil the child" was (and is) a time-tested belief that Dr. Spock notoriously rejected. In its place, he maintained that children are *people* who want to learn, get along, and ultimately become happy, strong adults; people who will act respectfully if they themselves are respected. Respect for children begins with getting to know them, appreciating the challenges they face in growing up and the remarkable strengths they bring to the task. This book tries to be respectful in that way, to both children and their parents, to convey both what's *new*, and also what's *true*.

Baby and Child Care is not a book of rules. It's more like a travel guide, highlighting the major attractions as well as some of the less obvious landmarks. It can help you choose a path (breastfeeding or formula), or get around an obstacle (colic or constipation); it gives you a feel for the terrain in some of the more forbidding regions (ADHD, autism). Dr. Spock trusted parents to chart their own course with love and common sense, and a little expert guidance. If the information in this book helps you navigate parenthood with a little more confidence, it will have done its job.

A word on wording. There are many places in this book where I suggest that you talk with your child's doctor. By "doctor" I mean to include not only pediatricians and family doctors but also nurse practitioners who provide medical care for many children. When talking about children I try to use "he" and "she" at random, except in those few instances that apply only to one or the other (care of the penis, for example). I know that binary gender distinctions don't do justice to the full variety of human nature, but I haven't figured out a way to reflect that understanding in language that isn't terribly awkward sounding.

Along similar lines, when I talk about "parents" I usually mean to include mothers, fathers, stepparents, grandparents, and other grown-ups who play a similar role. In most places, I don't make any distinction between adoptive parents and biological parents. Parents are the people who take primary responsibility for loving and raising children.

If I use "mother" and "she" most of the time, it's because doing so uses fewer words than "mother and/or father," and switching around might be confusing. "Fathers" refers to male partners (often husbands), but also in some places to female partners in families where there are two mommies. For example, in the section on breastfeeding, the "mother" is the one whose breasts are making the milk; the "father" refers to the other parent, male or female!

It's messy. I haven't yet gotten comfortable with making everyone "parents" and "partners." And even then, the words won't reflect the diversity and complexity of relationships in families. So I have to trust you, my readers, to make it past all these confusions to the intended meaning.

TRUST YOURSELF AND YOUR CHILDREN

TRUST YOURSELF

You know more than you think you do. You want to be the best parent you can be, but it's not always clear what's best. There's so much information out there, it's hard to know what to listen to. Everyone has an opinion. What made sense a generation ago may not work anymore.

Don't take too seriously what your friends and family tell you. Don't be awed by the experts. Trust your own common sense. Bringing up your child doesn't have to be complicated if you take it easy and rely on your instincts. The natural loving care that parents give their children is a hundred times more important than knowing how to make a diaper fit tightly or just when to start solid foods. Every time you pick your baby up and feed her, change her, smile at her, she's getting the feeling that she belongs to you and that you belong to her.

The more people study different methods of bringing up children, the more they learn that what good mothers and fathers naturally feel like doing for their babies is usually best after all. All parents do their best job when they feel easy and confident. Better to relax and make a few mistakes than to try too hard to be perfect.

It's important to respond to a baby's cries. But if you don't always get there instantly, it gives your baby a chance to soothe herself. If you lose your patience with your toddler (and every parent does at times), it teaches your toddler that you have feelings, too. Children need to learn that people can get angry and then get over it.

Children are driven from within to grow, explore, experience, and build relationships with other people. A lot of parenting lies in just letting your child follow these urges. Children are resilient. They make mistakes and suffer setbacks, then keep on growing. So trust yourself, and remember to trust your child, too.

How you learn to be a parent. Books and blogs can help, but we learn most about parenting from the way we were brought up ourselves. A child who is raised in an easygoing way is likely to be the same kind of parent; likewise for a child raised by strict or controlling parents. We all end up at least somewhat like our parents, especially in the way we deal with our children. The moment may well come when you are talking to your child and you hear your mother's or father's voice coming from your own lips with almost the same tone and maybe even the same words.

Think about your own parents. What did they do that you now see as positive and constructive? What did they do that you never want to repeat? Think about what made you the kind of person you are today and what kind of parent you would like to be. These insights can help you understand and trust your own parenting instincts.

We also learn how to be parents through the experience of caring for our children. With a baby, finding that you can feed, change, and bathe successfully, and that your baby responds contentedly, builds confidence and familiarity. These feelings grow in time; you probably won't feel this way right off the bat.

As parents, we expect to influence our children. But you may be surprised to discover that it's a two-way street; that being a parent becomes the most important step in your own growth as a person.

Think about your goals. What kind of adults do you want your children to become? Is doing well in school the top objective? Is the ability to have close relationships important? Do you want them to compete and win, always, or do you want them to learn to cooperate and sometimes defer to others? Do you want them be rule followers, or people who think for themselves?

Some parents get so caught up in the difficult day-to-day issues of *how* they are parenting that they lose perspective about *why* they are doing it. Take a moment, now and then, to look at the big picture. I hope that raising your children will help clarify what's truly important to you.

PARENTS ARE HUMAN

Parents have needs, too. Books about child care, including this one, put so much emphasis on the child's needs—for love, for understanding, for patience, for consistency, for firmness, for protection, for comradeship—that parents sometimes feel physically and emotionally exhausted just from reading about what is expected of them. They get the impression that they are meant to have no life of their own apart from their children. They can't help feeling that any book that seems to be standing up for children all the time is going to be critical of parents when anything goes wrong.

To really be fair, this book should have an equal number of pages about the genuine needs of parents: their frustrations (both inside and outside the home), how tired they get, and their need to hear once in a while that they are doing a good job. An enormous amount of hard work goes along with child care: preparing food, washing clothes, changing diapers, cleaning up messes, stopping fights and drying tears, listening to stories that are hard to understand, joining in games and reading books that aren't very exciting to an adult, trudging around zoos and museums, responding to pleas for help with homework, being slowed down in housework and yard work by eager helpers, going to parent-teacher association meetings on evenings when you are tired, and so on.

The fact is that child-rearing is a long, hard job, the rewards are not always obvious, the work is often undervalued, and parents are just as human and almost as vulnerable as their children.

Of course, parents don't have children because they want to be martyrs. They have them because they love children and want to raise their very own. Taking care of their children, seeing them grow and develop, gives most parents—despite the hard work—their greatest satisfaction in life. It is a creative and generative act on every level. Pride in other accomplishments usually pales in comparison.

Needless self-sacrifice and excessive preoccupation. Many people facing the new responsibility of parenthood feel that they are being called on to give up all their freedom and all their former pleasures, not as a matter of practicality but almost as a matter of principle. Others simply become obsessed with parenting, forgetting all their other interests. Even if they do occasionally sneak off to have some fun, they feel too guilty to get full enjoyment. They come to bore their friends and each other. In the long run, they chafe at the imprisonment and can't help but unconsciously resent their babies.

Total absorption in a new baby is normal. But after a while, usually by two to four months, your focus needs to broaden again. In particular, pay attention to sustaining a loving, intimate relationship with your partner. Carve out some quality time with your husband, wife, or significant other. Remember to look at each other, smile at each other, and express the love you feel. Make an effort to find enough privacy and energy to continue your sexual relationship. Remember that a close, loving relationship between parents is the best way children learn about how to be loving with others. One of the best things you can do for your child, as well as for yourself, is to let your children deepen, not inhibit, your relationship with your partner.

NATURE AND NURTURE

How much control do you have? All this talk about parenting and choices could give you the impression that how your child turns out is entirely up to you: Do a good job, and you'll have a good child. If your child learns to talk later than other children or has more temper tantrums, then of course it's your fault.

Except that it isn't. The truth is, some children are simply more difficult to soothe, more fearful, more reckless, more intense, or in other ways more challenging for parents. If you are lucky, your baby will have a temperament that fits well with your expectations and personal style. If not, then you may need to learn special skills in order to help your child thrive. For example, you may need to learn how to calm a colicky baby, or how to help an extra-cautious child begin to take small risks.

But special skills are not enough. First, you'll need to accept your child for who he is. Children need to feel valued *as they are*. Only after that can they work together with their parents to handle themselves in more effective ways.

Accepting the child you have. One gentle couple might be ideally suited to raise a boy with a sensitive nature but unprepared for an energetic, assertive one. Another couple may handle a spunky daughter with joy, but feel disappointed with a quiet, thoughtful one.

Being human, parents can't help feeling let down if their real child doesn't match the child of their dreams. What's more, as children become a little older they may remind us, consciously or unconsciously, of a brother, sister, father, or mother who made life hard for us. A father may be excessively bothered by timidity in his son and never connect it with the fact that he himself had a terrible time overcoming his shyness as a child.

What matters most is how well your expectations for your children fit with their inborn talents and temperaments. If the fit doesn't come easy (and there is no rule that it must!), then it is up to you to adapt. You can't change your child's nature, but you can change how you respond to it. If you are disappointed that your child is not a math whiz or sports star and if you push to make him what he is not, then you will both suffer unnecessarily. On the other hand, if you accept your child for who he is, then your life together is bound to be smoother. More important, your child will grow up accepting himself.

DIFFERENT FAMILIES, DIFFERENT CHALLENGES

There's no one right way to raise children, and there's no one best kind of family. Children can thrive with a mother and father together or apart, or with a mother or father alone; with two mothers or two fathers; with grandparents or foster parents; or as part of large extended families. Most of the time, in this book, I just use "mother" or "father" to save words.

Families that don't fit the standard mother-father mode may need to do some special planning. For example, in families with same-sex parents it may take planning to ensure that the children have a chance to develop close relationships with both men and women. In families with children adopted from overseas, parents may need to make special efforts to learn about their children's cultures of origin (the children, at

some point, are likely to want to know). Parents who hold different religious beliefs need to figure out how their children can grow up with a connection to tradition (or sometimes, traditions) and community. Children whose parents come from different parts of the world or have different racial identifications need to learn to embrace their multiple heritages. Good parenting means planning for your children's needs; that's true in *all* families.

Global mobility. Some parents find themselves in countries far from where they grew up. It's stressful to leave behind everything familiar—family, language, culture, land—particularly when it comes to raising children. Things that were important in a parent's own childhood may simply not exist in this new place; what was good parenting at home might even be considered neglectful or abusive here. No wonder parents often feel unsure of themselves, worried, or angry.

The key to success is flexibility, the ability to hold on to traditions and values and also take part in mainstream society. To be successful, children may need to learn to speak different languages at home and at school and to switch back and forth between two sets of social rules. Parents need to find ways to support their children as they shuttle back and forth between worlds, to embrace tradition and newness at the same time. The same tensions pull at all families, not just migrant ones, because the world children grow up in now is so different from the world of just a generation ago.

Special challenges. Children with special health and developmental needs make extra demands. All the trips to the doctor for testing, the days and nights in the hospital, things you wish you could do with your child but can't: It can be overwhelming. But somehow parents rise to the challenge, finding joy in moments and milestones that others take for granted.

The challenges can also come from the past. Violence and fear can leave scars. If you had a difficult time in your own childhood, if your parents were cruel or had to battle emotional problems or addiction, then it's easy, as a parent, to fall into the same pattern. Making the choice to do things differently is hard.

You can make that choice. Parents from all kinds of backgrounds, facing all kinds of challenges, find the wisdom and courage to give their children what they need. In turn, their children give those qualities back to the world.

SECTION I

Your Child, Age by Age

BEFORE YOUR
CHILD IS BORN

BABIES DEVELOP; PARENTS, TOO

Fetal development. Think of all the amazing changes that turn a fertilized egg into a baby! By the time a woman misses her period, about five weeks after the last one, the embryo is a little disk with three layers. Over the next two to three months, the inner layer will transform into the main internal organs; the middle into muscles and bones; and the outer into skin and brain. These transformations take the form of an intricate dance, with tissues ballooning, dividing, wrapping around each other, and fusing, all precisely orchestrated by genes and hormones. It's miraculous that things go right as often as they do. At ten weeks, the fetus looks almost human, but tiny: only about two inches long and roughly a third of an ounce.

Four or five months into the pregnancy—just about halfway—is when you probably first feel your baby moving. If an ultrasound hasn't already been done, those little kicks and nudges might be the first proof that there really is a baby in there—a thrilling moment!

During the third trimester, after about twenty-seven weeks, the baby's length doubles and the weight triples. The brain grows even more quickly, and new behaviors appear. By twenty-nine weeks, an unborn baby will startle in response to a sudden loud noise. But if the noise repeats every twenty seconds or so, the baby learns to ignore it—an early sign of memory.

Babies remember pleasant sounds, too. After birth, they prefer their mother's voice over that of a stranger. If you have a favorite piece of music that you play over and over, chances are your baby will love it, too. Your baby is getting to know you, your sounds, smells, tastes, and rhythms.

Mixed feelings about pregnancy. There is a myth that every woman is overjoyed when she finds that she is going to have a baby. She spends the pregnancy dreaming happy thoughts; love is instantaneous, bonding like glue. In reality, most pregnant women have some negative feelings, too, starting with nausea and vomiting. Loose clothes become tight; tight clothes unwearable. Athletic women find that their bodies don't move as they once did. Feet and backs may ache.

The first pregnancy spells the end of carefree youth. Social life and the family budget get spread thinner. After you have had one or two, the arrival of one more child may not seem like such a drastic change. But a mother's spirit may rebel at times during any pregnancy. A particular pregnancy may be strained for obvious reasons: Perhaps it came unexpectedly, or at a time of disharmony between the parents or serious illness in the family. Or there may be no apparent explanation.

A mother who truly wants another child may still be disturbed by sudden doubts about whether she will have the time, the physical energy, or the unlimited reserves of love that she imagines will be called for. Or the inner doubts may start with the father. Each parent may feel needier and have less to give the other. Sometimes normal fears take the form of disturbing dreams of babies born sick or deformed.

These reactions are some of the normal mixed feelings during pregnancy, and most often they are temporary. In a way, having mixed feelings during your pregnancy is a good thing, since it gives you a chance to work them out before the baby actually arrives. Even some of the most wonderful parents can tell you about the negative thoughts and emotions they endured.

It's okay if you don't feel love for your unborn baby. Many pregnant women find it hard to love a baby they've never held. For some, love starts with the first ultrasound that shows a beating heart; for others, it's feeling the baby move for the first time; for others it's not until later. There is no "normal" time to fall in love with your baby. Love may come early or late, but it comes.

Most of us have been taught that it's unwise to hope for a girl or a boy, in case it turns out to be the opposite. But most expectant parents have a sex preference during each pregnancy, in part because it's hard to imagine a future baby without picturing it as being one sex or the other. So enjoy your imaginary baby, and don't feel guilty if you learn that your baby is not the sex you had envisioned.

Fathers' feelings during pregnancy. Fathers may feel proud, protective, and connected to their partners in a deeper way, but they also can have mixed feelings. Many worry they won't be good enough. There can also be, underneath, a feeling of being left out, which may be expressed as crankiness toward the mother, wanting to spend more evenings with his men friends, or flirtatiousness with other women.

These reactions are normal, but they are no help to a woman who needs extra support at a vulnerable time. When fathers are able to talk about their negative feelings, they often find that the fear and jealousy shift aside, allowing the excitement and connection to come forward.

Tragically, some expectant fathers become emotionally or physically abusive. If you feel threatened or afraid, or if you have ever been hurt or forced to have sex, you owe it to yourself and your baby to get help. Talk to your doctor, or call (800) 799-SAFE, the national domestic violence hotline.

A generation ago, most fathers would never have dreamed of reading a book about raising babies. Now it almost goes without saying that fathers participate at every stage. They go to prenatal visits, attend childbirth classes, and support their partners in labor and delivery. They aren't lonely, excluded onlookers anymore.

PRENATAL PLANS AND DECISIONS

Before you conceive. It's a good idea to consult with a doctor before you start trying to become pregnant, especially if you have concerns about your health or questions about fertility or genetic disorders. As soon as pregnancy is even a possibility, start taking folate. A daily multivitamin or supplement with 400 micrograms of folate, started three months or more before conception, lowers the risk of serious spinal cord defects.

This is also the time to limit your exposure to chemicals that can affect the baby's developing brain. The brain is most vulnerable very early on, even before most women know they are pregnant. So, it's important to take steps *before* you know.

The short list of harmful substances includes cigarette smoke and air pollution in general; insecticides; lead and other heavy metals; flame retardants in some furniture and bedding; phthalates in some plastics and cosmetics; and of course alcohol. It might seem overwhelming, but your choices still make a difference. For example: Instead of eating fish that are high in mercury, such as sea bass and swordfish, you can choose farm-raised trout, wild Pacific salmon, Pacific sardines, anchovies, or fish sticks. Learn more about avoiding harmful chemicals at Project TENDR (www.projecttendr.com).

Certain infections pose prenatal risks. Mosquitoes can carry Zika (see page 529). Young children often carry cyto-megalovirus (CMV). Women who work in preschools need to know whether they have immunity to CMV (most adults do) to avoid catching it during pregnancy. Toxoplasmosis is carried by kittens. Pregnant women should wear gloves and a mask when changing the kitty litter, or get someone else to do it!

Prenatal care. Getting prenatal care is one of the best things you can do for your baby. Simple steps—taking folate, avoiding cigarette smoke and alcohol, and getting your blood pressure checked—can make a huge difference. Routine testing can detect problems that can be treated before they harm your baby. It's best to start prenatal care early, but late is better than never.

Typically, prenatal visits happen once a month for the first seven months, once every other week in the eighth month, and weekly after that. They're an opportunity for you to get advice about common issues such as morning sickness, weight gain, and exercise. Routine prenatal ultrasounds can make a baby seem much more real, especially for fathers. And you'll have the option of learning your baby's sex.

In many communities women can choose among various providers of prenatal care, including obstetricians, family physicians, nurse midwives, certified midwives who aren't nurses, and licensed and lay midwives. Obstetricians nearly always deliver in hospitals, whereas lay midwives tend to specialize in home births.

It's important that you like and trust your doctor or midwife. Does the professional listen to you and give you clear information? Is the person you see for prenatal visits the same person who will actually do your delivery? If not, do you trust that the other professionals in the group will also provide good medical care to you? Will the hospital and the OB group accept your medical insurance?

Plan your delivery. Home or hospital? Natural childbirth or an epidural? Lying down or squatting? Home as soon as possible or extended hospital stay? Visiting nurse, lactation consultant, or both?

No single approach suits every woman, and no method is clearly best for babies. Childbirth is safer now than ever before, but it's still unpredictable. Think about your ideal delivery, but stay flexible in case of unforeseen events. Plan to ask a lot of questions and do some more reading.

Consider hiring a doula for your delivery. Doulas are women who are trained to provide continuous support throughout labor. They help mothers find the most comfortable positions and movements, and use massage and other techniques to reduce tension. An experienced doula can often reassure a woman who's feeling panicky or overwhelmed.

Doulas can help fathers, too. It's the rare father who can soothe a laboring woman's pain and anxiety as well as a trained doula, especially when the father is anxious himself. A doula frees up the father to be with his partner in a loving way rather than as a coach. Most fathers feel supported by the doula, not replaced.

Research has proven the beneficial effect of doulas. Doulas reduce the need for cesarean sections and epidural (spinal) anesthesia. (Spinal anesthesia, although often a godsend, does have some risks; for example, it increases the risk that the baby may run a fever and therefore need to be given antibiotics after delivery.) If doulas were pills instead of people, they'd be prescribed for every birth! For more information about doulas, see www.dona.org.

How you'll feed your baby. It's worth giving this some thought ahead of time. It's a personal decision, and either way can work. Breastfeeding offers many health benefits; bottle-feeding may be easier for some parents (especially women who work outside the home). Formula costs money and often needs mixing and warming, and bottles need cleaning; breastfeeding takes effort, sometimes it hurts, and it can feel uncomfortable in public places. Some mothers love the closeness that comes from feeding their babies from their bodies. Some prefer the freedom to let their partners give bottles in the middle of the night. Breastfeeding helps mothers regain their prepregnancy body shapes sooner. Some women fear that breastfeeding will make their breasts less attractive, but it's the pregnancy itself (not the nursing) that changes breast shape the most.

Many women choose formula because they plan to return soon to school or work. But even a short period of breastfeeding is better, medically, than none at all. And breastfeeding often can continue during hours at home, even after work or school resumes.

There is so much to say about the hows and whys of breastfeeding and formula-feeding that each has its own chapter later in the book (see pages 247 and 279).

CHOOSING YOUR BABY'S DOCTOR

Pediatrician, family doctor, or nurse practitioner? While you are pregnant, you can find a doctor for your baby, if you don't already have one. Who should it be and how can you tell if the person will work out? Some parents get along best with a doctor who is casual and not overly fussy. Others want to be given directions down to the last detail. You might prefer an older, seasoned professional or one who is more recently trained. Start by talking with other parents. Obstetricians and midwives often can give good recommendations, too.

Nurse practitioners are registered nurses with extra training that allows them to function like doctors in many ways. They work with doctor backup; how much the doctor is actually involved varies from practice to practice. Doctors often have more experience managing complex sicknesses; nurse practitioners may have more time scheduled for checkups and usually provide excellent preventive care. I wouldn't hesitate to use a nurse practitioner who comes highly recommended. (I'll say just "doctor" from now on, to keep things simple.)

The "getting to know you" visit. If this is your first baby or if you are moving to a new area, it's wise to schedule a doctor visit a few weeks before your due date. There's nothing like actually meeting someone to know if she makes you feel comfortable enough to talk about whatever is on your mind. You can learn a great deal from a pre-birth visit and come away confident that your child's medical care is all set.

When you visit the office, is the staff pleasant and courteous? Are there things for children to do in the waiting room? Are there picture books? Ask practical questions: How many physicians and nurse practitioners are there in the practice? How are phone calls handled? What happens if your baby becomes ill after office hours? What if you have an emergency during the day? How much time is allotted for well-child checkups? (Fifteen minutes is about average nowadays.) Find out about insurance and fees, and what hospital the practice uses.

A key issue is continuity of care. Will your child have one particular doctor, or do patients in the practice see whoever happens to be available? Health care for children works best when parents and doctors work as a team. It may be easier to work with one particular doctor, rather than with every doctor in the practice.

When you talk with the doctor, choose a couple of issues to discuss that are important to you, such as the doctor's views on breastfeeding, on allowing you to be present if your child needs to have a painful procedure, and on issues such as sleep arrangements or toilet training. Pay attention to how the interview makes you feel. If you feel comfortable, listened to, and unrushed, you've probably found the right doctor; if not, you may want to visit some other practices.

Prenatal breastfeeding consultation. If you are unsure whether or not to breastfeed it can be helpful to discuss the issue with your baby's doctor, or a lactation consultant. You may want to attend breastfeeding classes, offered by many hospitals and large practices. Knowing more will help you feel comfortable with your decision. A prenatal consultation can help you anticipate any problems and deal with them ahead of time.

PLANNING THE HOMECOMING

Arranging for extra help in the beginning. Try to get someone to help you during the first few weeks. It's exhausting to do everything by yourself. Most expectant parents feel a little scared at the thought of taking sole charge of a helpless baby. Feeling scared doesn't mean that you won't do a good job. But if you feel really panicky, you'll probably handle things more comfortably with a supportive relative by your side.

Your baby's father may be a great support person, if he's not feeling too anxious himself. A grandparent may be an ideal helper, if you get along easily; otherwise it's probably better if grandparents visit but don't stick around. It helps to have a person who has taken care of babies before, but it's most important to choose someone you like having around.

You might consider hiring a housekeeper or doula for a few weeks. Many doulas offer their services after birth as well. Or maybe pay someone to come in once or twice a week to do the laundry, help you catch up on the housework, and perhaps watch your baby for a couple of hours. It makes sense to keep your helper around for as long as you need the help and can afford it.

Nurse home visits. Many hospitals and health plans offer nurse home visits one or two days after you take your baby home, particularly if the hospital stay has been less than forty-eight hours. The visiting nurse can look for medical problems, such as jaundice, and can help deal with breastfeeding or other issues. If nothing else, the nurse can reassure you that everything is going well.

Visitors. The birth of a baby brings relatives and friends flocking, but it's okay to say no. It's normal to be tired during the first weeks with a new baby, and visitors can be a further drain on your energy. It makes sense to limit visits to the few people you really want to see. Everyone else should understand.

Most visitors want to hold the baby, waggle their heads at her, and keep up a streak of baby talk. Some babies can take a lot of this treatment, but others—especially premature babies—get overstressed. Pay attention to how your baby responds, and stop things if you need to. Relatives and friends who care about you and your baby won't be offended.

Anyone who picks up your baby should wash well first, until your baby is at least three or four months old. Young children, in particular, often carry viruses that can make newborns quite ill. So keep young cousins and other relatives at a safe distance.

Preparing your home. If your home was built before 1980, there's a good chance it contains lead paint. You can remove loose paint chips and paint over exposed, weathered patches. But don't use a scraper, sander, or heat gun, because lead dust and vapors can raise your own lead level, which might affect your baby. It's best to hire a professional. Check the basement for black mold, and have any moldy walls repaired.

If you are using well water, it's important to have it tested for bacteria and nitrates before the baby arrives. Nitrate salts in well water can cause blueness of the baby's lips and skin. Write or call your county or state health department for assistance. Well water won't contain added fluoride, so you'll need to discuss fluoride supplements with your doctor (see page 451).

HELPING SIBLINGS COPE

What to say while you're pregnant. Young children, like everybody else, find pregnancy fascinating. Once your body begins to change and the risk of an early miscarriage has passed, it's good to open the discussion. A child might need time to get used to the idea of being an older brother or sister. Even toddlers can pick up reassurance from your tone of voice; older children need to hear—many times!—that they are loved as much as ever. Be positive, but don't overdo your enthusiasm or expect your child to be thrilled.

The arrival of the baby should change an older child's life as little as possible, especially if he has been the only child up to that time. Emphasize the concrete things that will stay the same: "You'll still have your same favorite toys; we'll still go to the same park to play; we'll still have our special treats; we'll still have our special time together."

Make changes ahead of time. If your older child isn't yet weaned, it will be easier to do it a few months *before* you deliver, and not when she is feeling displaced by the new baby. If her room is to be given over to the baby, move her to her new room a few months ahead so that she feels that she is graduating because she is a big girl, not because the baby is pushing her out. The same applies to advancing to a big bed. If she is to go to preschool, she should start well before the baby arrives, if possible. Nothing sets a child's mind against preschool as much as the feeling that she is being banished to it by an interloper. Also, a child who has friends at school often feels less threatened by the new arrival at home.

During and after delivery. Some parents hope to strengthen family togetherness by including their children in the delivery itself. But watching one's mother go through labor can be upsetting for a young child who might think that something awful is happening. Older children can also be disturbed by the stressful effort and the blood that are part of even the smoothest deliveries. From the mother's point of view, labor is tough enough all by itself without having to worry about how a child is handling it. Children can be included by being nearby, but not actually in the delivery room.

Later, when things have calmed down, siblings can be encouraged to visit as much as they like; to see, touch, and talk with the new baby. Parents sometimes try to tell their children how they should feel about the new baby. Instead, it's wiser to *ask* them, and reassure them that whatever feelings they have are okay.

Bringing your baby home. It's usually hectic when you come home after giving birth. You're tired and preoccupied. The father is scurrying about, being helpful. If the older child is there, he stands around feeling left out, thinking warily, "So this is the new baby!"

It may be better for the older child to be doing something out of the house, if this can be arranged. An hour later, when the baby and the luggage are in place and you're at last relaxing, you can give your older child some undivided attention. Since children appreciate concrete rewards, it's nice to bring a present home, like a baby doll or a wonderful new toy. Let your child bring up the subject of the new baby when he's ready, and don't be surprised if his comments are unenthusiastic or hostile.

Actually, most siblings handle the first days of a new baby pretty well. It often takes several weeks before they realize that the competition is there to stay, and several months before the baby is old enough to start grabbing their toys and bugging them. The section on siblings has more on how you can help siblings get along (see page 799).

THINGS YOU'LL NEED

Buying things ahead of time. Some parents don't feel like buying anything until they have their baby. The idea that planning ahead of time might jinx the pregnancy is common in many cultures. Parents may not want to tempt fate.

The advantage of arranging things ahead of time is that it lightens your burden later. Many parents feel exhausted after delivery, and even little chores can seem overwhelming. It can be comforting to know that you have the basics on hand.

What do you really need? The sections that follow should help you decide what to buy ahead of time and what you might buy later (or never). I'd suggest you check the most recent copies of magazines such as *Consumer Reports* for the latest information on safety, durability, and practicality.

CHECKLIST

Things You'll Need Right from the Start

✓ A safety-approved car seat.

✓ A crib, cradle, or bassinet with a firm mattress and tight-fitting sheets. (See page 49 about sleep safety.)

✓ A few swaddling blankets.

✓ T-shirts or onesies; in cooler climates, a couple of warm fleece sleep sacks.

✓ Wipes and diapers, either disposable, cloth that you wash yourself, or cloth from a diaper service. Cloth diapers come in handy, even if you mainly use disposables.

✓ Nursing bras and a breast pump. (If you plan to bottle-feed, add formula, bottles, nipples.)

✓ A cloth sling or front-pack baby carrier.

✓ A diaper bag with places for diapers, wipes, ointment, a folding plastic changing pad, and nursing supplies.

✓ A digital thermometer and a child's nose syringe with bulb suction.

Car seats. Babies need to be in car seats for every trip, even the first ride home from the hospital (see page 401 for car safety). Some car seats double as baby carriers (but it's easier to carry a baby in a sling or a front pack). Other infant seats can be turned around to face forward once your baby is large enough. Be sure that the seat meets government safety standards. Find guidelines on seat choice at www.safercar.gov. Buy your seat new. A hand-me-down may fail in a crash, because plastic weakens over time. Even if it looks okay, a seat that has been through one crash may not hold up in a second one. See page 401 for more on car seats and their installation; it's harder than you think!

A place to sleep. You may long for a beautiful bassinet lined with silk, but your baby won't care. Go for safety over style. Choose a crib, cradle, or bassinet with a firm, well-fitting mattress—one that doesn't show a dent when the baby is picked up. As radical as this may seem, babies don't need blankets. Sleep sacks, wearable blankets, and "onesies" are safer, because they can't get wrapped around an infant's head (page 70).

Your baby's crib should be sturdy, with the mattress support firmly attached to the headboard and footboard. It should have childproof side-locking mechanisms, at least twenty-six inches from the mattress to the top of the rail, and slats no more than 2⅜ inches apart. Any cutout openings should also measure 2⅜ inches or less.

Look out for sharp edges and corner posts that stick up more than one-sixteenth of an inch (high enough to snag an article of clothing, which could then trap or strangle a baby). If you're buying a new crib, look on the box to see that it meets federal safety standards. For used cribs and family heirlooms, *you* have to be the safety inspector. Before 1980, cribs were painted with lead-containing paints; they aren't safe unless all of the old paint has been stripped off. Crib bumpers don't add protection and they do pose a risk of suffocation. Special mattresses or other features advertised to make cribs safer aren't proven, and are probably a waste of money at best.

Equipment for bathing and changing. You can give your baby a bath in the kitchen sink, a plastic tub, a dishpan, or a washstand. Molded plastic bathing tubs with contoured pads or liners are useful and generally inexpensive. A spraying faucet is great for rinsing the baby's hair.

The water should be lukewarm but *not hot*. You can use a bath thermometer, but it's best to rely on your own hand to test the water temperature. Fill the tub and test the water before you put your baby in. For added protection against scald burns, set the temperature setting on your hot water heater at 120°F or lower.

You can change and dress your baby on a low table or the bathroom counter or on the top of a bureau. A changing table with safety straps is convenient but not necessary. Wherever you change your baby (except on the floor), it's important to keep one hand on him at all times: You can use the safety straps, but don't trust them.

Seats, swings, and walkers. An inclined plastic seat with safety straps and a handle is useful. It lets your baby sit facing you, or watch the world go by. Make sure the base is larger than the seat so that your baby can't tip it over when she's excited. A cloth seat can be inexpensive, light, and equally comfortable. If you put a baby seat on a countertop or table, be aware that your baby's movements could inch the seat off the edge.

Baby seats are often overused. A baby needs physical contact. Hold your baby for feeding, comforting, playing, and dancing. Plastic baby seats are also not the best for carrying babies: Your baby will be happier and more secure in a cloth sling or front pack, and you will have both arms free with less strain on your shoulders.

Young babies usually love motion, and swings can be calming. (Strap-on baby carriers do the same thing, with more human contact.) Babies don't actually become "addicted" to swinging, but too many hours of the same hypnotizing motion probably isn't best for them.

Infant walkers don't help with walking, and they're dangerous. It only takes an instant for a baby to propel his walker down a flight of stairs. Don't buy a walker. If you already have one, take off the wheels or throw it away. You can buy infant seats that bounce, swivel, or rock. They're much safer for children.

Strollers, carriages, and backpacks. Strollers are best once babies can hold their heads up steadily. Newborns and little infants do better in a cloth front pack, where they can look up into their parent's face and listen to her heartbeat. A folding umbrella stroller can be easily carried on a bus or in a car; be sure it's a sturdy one, and use the safety straps.

A carriage (pram) is like a bassinet on wheels; it's nice to have for the first few months if you plan on taking long strolls with your baby, but hardly necessary. An alternative, after your baby has outgrown the cloth carrier, is a backpack, preferably with a metal frame and padded hip belt so you can carry a large baby or toddler without much strain. Your baby can look over your shoulder, chat with you, play with your hair, and fall asleep with her head nestled into your neck.

Play yards (playpens). Some parents and psychologists fear that imprisoning a child in a playpen may stifle the child's spirit. Children deprived of human contact for hours on end do suffer, but an hour here and there in a playpen gives a baby a chance to learn to entertain himself. A young infant can be left safely in her cradle or crib, but once your baby starts crawling, it's very helpful to have a confined place where she can play safely while you do other things. There are play yards designed to fold into compact travel-size cases, which are great for going on visits (good for children up to thirty pounds or up to thirty-four inches tall).

If you are going to use a play yard, you should put your baby in it each day starting at around three months. Some babies tolerate play yards well, some poorly. If you wait until a baby starts to crawl (six to eight months), the play yard will surely seem like a prison and will be met with persistent howls.

Clothing. Babies grow very rapidly during the first year, so buy clothing to fit loosely. For most newborns, you can start with three- to six-month-size clothes. As a rule, babies don't need more in the way of clothing than adults, and babies who are overdressed are often uncomfortable.

For little babies, nightgowns are practical day and night. The mittens on the ends of the sleeves, which keep babies from scratching themselves, can be worn open or closed. Long gowns make it harder for babies to kick off their coverings; short ones may be better in hot weather. Buy three or four, more if you can't do laundry every day.

Undershirts come in three styles: pullover, side-snap closing, and "onesies" that slip over the head and snap around the diaper. Medium weight and short sleeves should be fine unless your home is unusually chilly. The most comfortable fabric for children is 100 percent cotton. Start with the one-year-old size or, if you are fussy about fit, the six-month size. Buy at least three or four. If you cut off the tags, they won't irritate your baby's neck.

By law, all sleepwear from nine-month size to size 14 must either be tight-fitting, or treated with flame-retardant chemicals. Given that some flame retardants can damage the developing brain, it's probably wisest to go with untreated sleepwear designed to fit snugly. Be sure to look at the labels, which are required by law. For onesies with feet, check inside the feet for threads, which can wind painfully around your baby's toes.

Sweaters are useful for extra warmth, but they can be hard to get over a baby's head, unless there are shoulder snaps, buttons, or zippers up the back.

Knitted acrylic or cotton caps are all right for going outdoors in the kind of weather that makes grown-ups put on caps, or for sleeping in a chilly room. Avoid caps that are too large, because they can cover a baby's face as she moves around while sleeping. For milder weather, caps are unnecessary; most babies don't like them anyway. You don't need booties and stockings, at least until your baby is sitting up and playing in a cold house. A sun hat with a chin strap to keep it on is useful for the baby who will tolerate it.

Some parents find that quality used clothes or hand-me-downs are a good choice for rapidly growing children. Watch for scratchy lace close to the face and arms; it can make even an adult irritable. Headbands are cute, but if they're too tight or itchy (or if a ponytail or braids are too tight), they can cause the head to hurt. Most important, be on the lookout for any loose buttons or decorations that could pose a choking hazard, and for ribbons and cords that could get wrapped around a baby's arms or neck.

Toiletries and medical supplies. Any mild soap will do for the bath; in fact, for all but the most soiled body parts, plain water works fine. Liquid baby soaps and deodorant soaps often cause rashes, and antibacterial soaps contain chemicals that may be unsafe for babies. Cotton balls are useful at bath time for wiping the baby's eyes. Baby lotion isn't really necessary unless your child's skin is dry, but it's pleasant to rub it on and babies love a massage. Look for creams and lotions with no added scent or color. Baby oils are fine for dry or normal skin. Mineral oil may cause a mild rash on some babies.

Under the diaper, an ointment containing lanolin and petrolatum (petroleum jelly) protects the skin. Talcum powder can damage the lungs if inhaled; cornstarch-based powders are safer.

Infant nail scissors have blunted ends, though many parents find infant nail clippers easier to use. I prefer using a nail file: There's no chance of drawing blood, and files don't leave sharp edges.

You'll need a fever thermometer. Digital thermometers cost about $10 and are fast, accurate, easy, and safe. High-tech ear thermometers are less accurate and more expensive. Old-style thermometers that contain mercury aren't safe. If you have one already, don't just throw it in the garbage; call the sanitation department for advice on proper disposal, or bring it to the doctor's office.

A child's nose syringe with bulb suction is helpful to remove mucus during colds if the mucus is interfering with feeding.

Feeding equipment. For breastfeeding you may not need any equipment other than yourself. But you might want a breast pump (see page 270). After pumping you'll need at least three or four bottles (look for BPA-free plastic bottles or, to be safest, glass) to store the milk, and nipples to go with them.

If you know that you're going to bottle-feed, buy at least nine of the eight-ounce bottles and a bottle brush. Buy a few extra nipples, in case you are having trouble making the nipple holes the right size. There are all kinds of specially shaped nipples, but no proof for the claims made by their manufacturers. Some nipples withstand boiling and wear and tear better than others. Be sure to follow instructions as to when to replace old nipples. You don't need to buy a bottle warmer. A pan of warm water works well, and babies don't mind room-temperature formula. A few terry-cloth bibs are handy.

Pacifiers. Many babies like sucking, and use it to calm themselves down. A pacifier before sleep may even reduce the risk of crib death. Three or four pacifiers should do to start. (The practice of blocking up a baby bottle nipple with cotton or paper and using it as a pacifier is dangerous. The contraption tends to fall apart, leaving little pieces that are easy to choke on.) Breastfed babies should suck on breasts, not pacifiers, at least for the first few months.

YOUR NEWBORN, BIRTH TO ABOUT THREE MONTHS

YOUR BABY AT BIRTH

Emotional responses to labor and delivery. For some women, labor is a profoundly moving rite of passage; for others it's a painful experience to be endured and forgotten about. However you respond is okay; there's no one right way. Some will push with each contraction for endless hours; others will get discouraged and demand that the doctor pull the baby out. Some exhausted women scream at their well-meaning husbands to get out of the delivery room and never come back. One new mother feels an instant flood of love for her baby; another, after hearing that the baby is okay, just wants to sleep. Both turn out to be wonderful parents.

If your labor and delivery experience is not what you expected, it's normal to feel bad, even guilty. If you go in hoping for a natural birth and end up with a cesarean, it's natural that you might feel that somehow you were to blame (you weren't), or that your baby has been harmed by the experience (almost never the case).

The first minutes after birth are a special time for mothers and babies to fall in love with each other. Whenever possible, doctors now get out of the way and let bonding take place. But if that can't happen, if babies or mothers need immediate medical attention, all is not lost. Bonding can happen in spite of separations. It's a strong force. Instead of instant bonding, the process is often a gradual one. It can take days or weeks.

For many women, even after the best of deliveries there can be a letdown when the baby actually arrives. Parents may expect to recognize the baby immediately as their own flesh and blood and respond with an overwhelming rush of maternal and paternal feelings. But often this doesn't happen in the first day or even in the first week. Completely normal negative feelings pop up.

A good and loving parent may have the sudden thought that making a baby was a terrible mistake—and then feel instantly guilty for having felt that way. If you know that mixed feelings are normal, you don't have to be afraid of them. They normally fade in the first month. If they persist, talk about them with your doctor, or the baby's.

ENJOY YOUR BABY

Challenges of the first three months. Once the exhaustion of delivery has worn off a bit, you'll probably find that caring for your new baby is a lot of work; wonderful, but still work. Newborn babies rely on parents to manage their basic life functions—eating, sleeping, filling diapers, and keeping warm. Your baby can't tell you what she needs from moment to moment. It's up to you to figure out what to do.

Many parents find that, for a time, all of their energy is taken up fine-tuning their babies: helping them eat when they're hungry and stop when they're full, stay awake more during the day and sleep more at night, and feel comfortable in a world that can be overstimulating. Some babies seem to take these challenges in stride. Others have a harder time. But by two or three months, most babies (and their parents) have the basics figured out.

Meeting your baby's needs. From what some people say about babies demanding attention, you'd think that they come into the world determined to get their parents under their thumbs by hook or by crook. This isn't true. Your baby is born to be a reasonable, friendly—though occasionally demanding—human being.

Don't be afraid to feed her when you think she's truly hungry. If you are mistaken, she'll simply refuse to take much. Don't be afraid to love her and enjoy her. Every baby needs to be smiled at, talked to, played with, and fondled—gently and lovingly—just as much as she needs vitamins and calories. That's what will make her a person who loves people and enjoys life.

Don't be afraid to respond to other desires of hers as long as they seem sensible to you. When she cries in the early weeks, it's because she's uncomfortable for some reason— maybe it's hunger or indigestion, fatigue, or tension. Being held, rocked, or walked may be what she needs. Spoiling doesn't come from being good to a baby in a sensible way; it happens when parents are too afraid to use their common sense.

All parents want their children to turn out to be healthy in their habits and easy to live with. Children want the same thing. They want to eat at reasonable hours and later learn good table manners; to develop a regular pattern of sleep; to move their bowels according to their own healthy pattern, which may or may not be regular. Most children will sooner or later fit into the family's way of doing things because they want to.

Babies aren't frail. "I'm so afraid I'll hurt her if I don't handle her just right," a parent may say about her first baby. You don't have to worry; there are many ways to hold her. If her head falls backward by mistake, it won't hurt her. The soft spot on her skull (the fontanel) is covered by a tough membrane that isn't easily injured.

The system to control body temperature works quite well in most babies if they're covered sensibly. They inherit good resistance to most germs. During a family cold epidemic, the baby is apt to have it the mildest of all. If a baby gets her head tangled in anything, she has a strong instinct to struggle and yell. If she's not getting enough to eat, she will probably cry for more. If the light is too strong for her eyes, she'll blink and fuss, or just close them. She knows how much sleep she needs, and takes it. She can care for herself pretty well for a person who can't say a word and knows nothing about the world.

Babies thrive on touch. Before birth not only are babies enveloped, warmed, and nourished by their mothers, but they participate in every movement their mothers make. In many parts of the world, little babies stay closely attached to their mothers, who carry them in cloth slings next to their bodies. Our society puts much more distance between mothers and their babies. We strap them into infant seats so that they don't have to be held; there are even car seats that can be snapped right onto the stroller so parents barely have to pick their babies up at all. Compare this treatment to the best cure for the hurts, slights, and sadness of infants, children, and adults—a good hug.

Physical touch releases hormones in the brain—both the baby's and the parent's—that heighten feelings of relaxation and happiness. When babies have their heels pricked for routine blood tests, they cry much less if their mother is holding them skin to skin; premature infants who have daily skin-to-skin time grow faster.

Bonding. New mothers spend a lot of time touching their babies. Birthing hospitals have learned that mothers and babies need to be together right from the start. Ideally, newborns straight from the womb are dried and placed on their mothers' chests, where they snuggle in and often begin to nurse. Early bonding supports long-term emotional closeness and security. When hospital policies or medical emergencies interfere, it's harder for many parents and children to feel as connected.

But bonding has also been widely misunderstood. There's a fear that if bonding hasn't taken place in the first twenty-four or forty-eight hours, it never will. The truth is, bonding occurs over time, and there is no deadline. Parents bond with children they adopt at any age. Bonding happens *despite* child-rearing practices that separate parents from their infants.

Early return to a job. Many mothers have to go back to their paid jobs too soon. The U.S. is particularly harsh in this respect; other advanced societies provide paid maternal leave for much longer, in many cases up to a year. Here, mothers often worry about the effects of early separation on their babies, and grieve because they feel they are losing the precious first months of their babies' lives. (See page 267 on maintaining breastfeeding after starting back at a job.)

If too-early return to work weighs on you, you might feel yourself pulling back emotionally, preparing yourself for the separation. This is a natural response, but painful. It might help to know that babies form strong emotional bonds with mothers and fathers, even when they are cared for by others during the day. Loving care provided in the mornings and evenings, on weekends, and (of course) in the middle of the night is enough to cement the bond. You can trust your child to connect with you, as long as you remain open to connection yourself.

If you can control when you return to your job, try to listen to your heart. If there is any way you can stretch your maternity leave, even if it means a loss of income, you may end up glad you made that choice. By about four months, most mothers feel much better about resuming outside jobs, having had a chance to truly connect with their babies.

PARENTS' EARLY FEELINGS

Being scared. You might feel anxious, as well as just plain exhausted. You worry when your baby fusses and cries, when she sneezes or gets a rash. When she's sleeping you tiptoe into her room to be sure she's still breathing. If she had any medical issues in the newborn period—a low Apgar score, or maybe jaundice—your worries grow. It's probably instinctive for new parents to be overly protective, but those fears can still be unsettling. Early worries often fade by two or three months. Be sure to ask your baby's doctor for reassurance, if you need it.

The blue feeling. You may find yourself feeling discouraged early on, even if there isn't anything definitely wrong. You just weep easily, or you may feel bad about certain things.

Feelings of depression may appear soon after delivery or several weeks later. Often it is when a mother comes home from the hospital. It isn't just the work that gets her down. It's the feeling of being responsible for the household, plus the entirely new responsibility of the baby. A woman who was used to going to work every day is bound to miss the companionship of colleagues; she's tired and physically sore, and she has the idea that she's *supposed* to be blissful.

Baby blues are common and normal. Sometimes you can chase them away by doing things that cheer you up: going for a walk, working out, hanging out with friends, doing creative things like writing or painting. Sometimes you have to give yourself time to feel better.

Talk with your partner about your feelings and be prepared to listen, too. Many new fathers feel strangely down just when they think they should feel the opposite. Overwhelmed and uncertain about their new role, they might withdraw emotionally or become whiny and critical. This reaction couldn't come at a worse time from the standpoint of a mother, who might respond by feeling angry, sad, or depressed. Good communication is essential to avoid this kind of vicious-circle misery.

If your mood does not lift within four to six weeks, or if it is getting worse, you may be suffering from postpartum depression. The "baby blues" almost always pass within two months, but postpartum depression can go on and on. True depression happens after up to one in five pregnancies. If you or your partner have a severe mood change at any time, but especially after pregnancy, get medical help right away. No one knows exactly what causes postpartum depression, but women who have faced depression before are more vulnerable to it.

This is not the sort of problem that you can fix by just cheering up or going for a run, but there is help. You can start with your doctor, who might refer you to a mental health professional. The good news about postpartum depression is that it is *treatable*. Both talk therapy and antidepressant medication can work. No mother should have to suffer with this problem alone.

The father's feelings early on. A father shouldn't be surprised if he has mixed feelings toward his wife and baby. Resentments and regrets, wishes to be "free," or simply a lack of expected joy can arise during the pregnancy, in the hospital, or later. Often these uninvited visitors show up just when mothers are neediest themselves for understanding, appreciation,

affection, and help with children and chores. Mothers sometimes make things worse by criticizing and complaining. Even
so, when fathers understand how much they are needed, they
can put their negative responses aside and instead choose to
play their crucial supporting role. This choice can clear a space
that allows joyful feelings to return.

Sexual relations after delivery. Pregnancy, labor, and delivery usually dampen sex. Near the end of pregnancy, intercourse may become uncomfortable or at least physically
challenging. After delivery, physical pain, normal preoccupation with the baby, the demands of breastfeeding, and lack of
sleep can crowd out sex for days, weeks, even months. This
can also be a tough time for a man's libido. For some, the shift
in perspective of their partner from lover to mother interferes
with sexual feelings. All manner of emotions arise.

Knowing that sexual intercourse may be slow in returning, you won't need to be too alarmed at its temporary absence. Taking a break from intercourse doesn't mean stopping
all sexual relations. Cuddling, hugging, kissing, and romantic
words and glances are as meaningful and important as ever,
maybe even more so.

In time, most parents get back on track sexually. What
makes the biggest difference is that you keep in mind how
much you love and care for each other, and make a conscious
effort to express that love through words and touch. You
might enjoy reading poetry aloud to each other, going for
walks together, exchanging warm-oil massages, meditating together, having quiet meals together, and sharing lots of hugs
and kisses.

CARING FOR YOUR BABY

Being with your baby. Be quietly friendly with your baby. All the time that you're feeding him, burping him, bathing him, dressing him, changing his diaper, holding him, or just sitting in the room with him, he's getting a sense of how much you mean to each other. When you hug him or make noises at him, when you show him that you think he's the most wonderful baby in the world, it makes his spirit grow, just the way milk makes his bones grow. That must be why we grown-ups instinctively talk baby talk and make faces when we greet a baby, even grown-ups who are otherwise dignified or reserved.

I don't mean that you need to entertain your baby all day long, constantly joggling or tickling him. That would tire him out, and in the long run might make him tense. You can be quiet much of the time. Gentle, easygoing companionship is good for him and good for you. It's the comfortable feeling of your arms when you hold him, the fond, peaceful expression on your face when you look at him, and the gentle tone of your voice.

Your newborn's senses. All of your baby's senses work at birth (and, indeed, were working *before* birth), although to different degrees. The senses of smell, touch, and motion are already well developed. Babies detect odors in the amniotic fluid before birth, and they prefer the smell of their mothers' bodies. They're calmed by being swaddled, held, and rocked.

Newborns can hear, but their brains process sound slowly. If you whisper in a baby's ear, it may take several seconds before the baby responds by looking for the source of the sound. Because of the way the inner ear develops, babies hear higher-pitched sounds better and prefer speech that is slow and musical—the way parents seem to naturally talk to them.

Babies also can see, but they are very nearsighted. Their eyes focus best at nine to twelve inches, about the distance to the mother's face when nursing at the breast. You can tell when a baby catches you with her eyes: If you slowly move your face from side to side, her eyes follow you. Babies prefer looking at faces. Their eyes are sensitive, so they tend to keep them closed in normal light but open them when the lights are low.

Your baby is an individual. Newborn babies have their own personalities. Some are calm; others are more excitable. Some are regular in their eating, sleeping, and bowel habits; others are more erratic. Some can handle lots of stimulation; others need a quieter environment. When babies have their eyes open and a look of concentration on their faces, they are taking in information about the world around them. One baby may stay in this alert, receptive mode for several minutes; another baby may shift in and out, alternating with periods of drowsiness or fussing.

As you take care of your baby, you'll begin to figure out how to do enough talking, touching, and playing to keep your baby interested, but not so much that he gets stressed. You'll notice when he looks away, hiccups, or fusses—all signs of stress—and you'll give him a chance to regroup. Your baby will also become more skillful in letting you know when he wants more and when he has had enough.

FEEDING AND SLEEPING

What feeding means to your baby. Think of a baby's first year this way: She wakes up and cries because she's hungry and wants to be fed. She is so eager when the nipple goes into her mouth that she may shudder. When she nurses, you can see that it is an intense experience. Perhaps she breaks into a sweat. If you stop her in the middle, she may cry furiously. When she has had as much as she wants, she is usually groggy with satisfaction and falls asleep. Even when she is asleep, she sometimes looks as if she is dreaming of nursing. Her mouth makes sucking motions, and her whole expression looks blissful.

This all adds up to the fact that feeding is her great joy. She gets her first ideas about people from those who feed her, and she gets her early ideas about life from the way feeding goes. When you feed your baby, hold her, smile at her, and talk with her, you are nurturing her body, mind, and spirit. When it's working well, feeding feels good for your baby and you. Some babies feed well right from the start; others take several days before they begin to catch on. When feeding problems last longer than one or two weeks, even with help from family members and experienced friends, it's wise to get professional help. There is much more on feeding—getting to a regular schedule, knowing how much to give, and so on—in later sections.

Sorting out day and night. Your newborn couldn't care less if it's night or day, so long as he's fed, cuddled, and kept warm and dry. This shouldn't be too surprising. It was pretty dark in the womb, and he was probably more active when you were quietest, at night.

How do you help him sleep better at night? Talk and play with your baby more during the daytime. After dark, feed him efficiently and without much fanfare; don't wake him to feed unless there's a medical reason to. Let him learn that daytime is fun time and nighttime is kind of low-key and boring. By two to four months, most babies have started to get it straight.

How much should a baby sleep? The baby is the only one who can answer this question. One baby needs eighteen hours of sleep, another only about twelve. As long as babies are well fed, get plenty of fresh air, and sleep in a cool place, you can trust them to take the amount of sleep they need.

Most babies in the early months sleep from feeding to feeding if they are getting enough to eat and not having indigestion. There are a few babies, though, who are unusually wakeful right from the beginning, and not because anything is wrong. If you have this kind of baby, try to let some of the awake times be more stimulating—talking, playing, looking at things together—and let other periods be calm ones.

As babies get older, they gradually stay awake longer and take fewer naps during the day. You're apt to notice more wakefulness first in the late afternoon. Each baby develops a personal pattern of wakefulness and tends to be awake at the same times every day.

Sleep habits. Newborns sleep wherever they are. But by about three or four months, it's a good idea for them to get used to falling asleep in their own beds. This is one way to prevent later sleep problems. A baby who gets used to being held and rocked to sleep tends to need the same attention for months or even years; when she awakens in the night, she expects the same treatment.

Babies can get used to either a silent home or a noisy one, so there is no point in tiptoeing around the house. An infant who is used to ordinary household noises usually sleeps right through a visit by talking, laughing friends or a TV turned to a reasonable volume. Some infants, however, appear to be hypersensitive to sounds. They startle easily at the least noise and appear to be happiest when it's quiet. If your baby is like this you'll probably need to keep the house quiet while she sleeps, or else she will constantly wake and fuss.

Where should a baby sleep? Babies are safest when they sleep in their parents' room, but *not* in their parents' bed. Even though co-sleeping is traditional in many parts of the world, this arrangement carries a higher risk of crib death (sudden infant death syndrome, or SIDS) than if babies have their own crib, cradle, or bassinet next to the parents' bed. Overly warm rooms and secondhand cigarette smoke (even if it drifts in from a different room) also increase the risk of SIDS.

Babies can sleep well alone, but it's comforting to them to have a parent nearby. Parents also tend to sleep better if they don't have to be constantly aware of a tiny person right next to them. Still, most find it comforting to be able to look up and see their babies lying safely nearby.

If your child starts out sleeping in your room, a good age to move her to her own is usually three to four months. By six months, a child who regularly sleeps in her parents' room may feel uneasy sleeping anywhere else. After that, it's harder to move a child to her own room, although never impossible.

On back or stomach? Today, everyone knows that "back to sleep" is certainly safest. All infants should be put to sleep on their backs (faceup), with only rare medical exceptions. Sleeping faceup has cut the number of deaths from crib death in half! Most babies easily take to sleeping on their backs if they've never gotten used to sleeping the other way. Sleeping on the side isn't as safe, since side-sleeping babies often roll facedown. Babies who spend all of their time lying faceup sometimes develop flat spots on the back of the head. To avoid this problem, give your baby time lying on her stomach *when she is awake and you are watching her.*

CHECKLIST
Sleep Safety Tips

✓ Babies should sleep alone, in their parents' room.

✓ Always put your baby to sleep faceup, even for naps.

✓ Remove blankets, pillows, and other cloth items—they increase the risk of suffocation.

✓ Use a safety-approved bassinet, cradle, or crib. If in doubt, check with the U.S. Consumer Product Safety Commission (www.cpsc.gov).

✓ Avoid overdressing—overheating increases the risk of SIDS.

✓ Protect your baby from secondhand cigarette smoke, which has many harmful effects, including increasing risk of SIDS.

CRYING AND COMFORTING

What does all that crying mean? Crying has many meanings, not just pain or sadness. Especially in the first weeks, baffling questions pop into your mind: Is she hungry? Is she wet? Is she uncomfortable? Is she sick? Does she have indigestion? Is she lonely? Parents are not apt to think of fatigue, but it's one of the commonest causes of crying.

Sometimes the answer is none of the above. By the time they are a couple of weeks old, most babies have fretful periods for no apparent reason. Fussy crying is common in healthy babies all over the world. It usually increases over the first six weeks of life, then gradually decreases over the next six weeks.

A newborn's immature nervous system and digestive system have to adjust to life in the outside world. This adjustment is harder for some babies than for others. Babies who are held close to their mothers all day cry as often as other babies, but settle down more easily.

Few things are more upsetting than a little baby who cries and cannot be comforted. So it's important to remember that excessive crying in the early weeks is usually temporary and not a sign of anything serious. If you're concerned (and who wouldn't be?), bring your baby to the doctor for an examination. We doctors are happy to reassure parents whenever we can! The other key thing to remember—and it bears repeating—is that it is *never* safe to shake a baby to make the crying stop.

Sorting out the causes. We used to think that mothers could learn to interpret their baby's cries. In reality, even excellent parents generally can't tell different cries apart by their sounds. Instead, they just try various things. Here are some possibilities:

+ Is it hunger? If your baby took less than half her usual amount at her last feeding, it may be the reason she's awake and crying an hour later, instead of after the usual three hours. If she cries soon after a full feeding, however, it's less likely that she's hungry.

+ Does she crave sucking? Sucking calms babies, even when they're not hungry. If your baby is fussy but you think she's well-fed, you can offer a pacifier or help her to find her own fingers. Most babies suck for pleasure in the early months and stop on their own sometime before age two. Early sucking does not cause long-term pacifier addiction.

+ Is she getting enough milk? A baby doesn't outgrow the milk supply all of a sudden. She will have been taking longer and longer to breastfeed or have been polishing off every bottle for several days and then looking around for more. She begins to wake and cry a little earlier than usual. In most cases, it's only after she has been waking early from hunger for a number of days that she begins crying after a feeding.

+ Does she need to be held? Young babies often need the physical sensations of being held and rocked. Some are comforted by being wrapped up snugly in a blanket. It may be that swaddling and rocking are comforting because they re-create the familiar sensations of being in the womb. White noise—the sound of a vacuum cleaner, a white-noise app, or a parent going "Shhhh"—often has a similar calming effect.

✦ Does she need motion? Some babies relax best if kept in gentle motion, by being pushed back and forth in a rocking bassinet, rocked in the carriage, or held in your arms or in a carrier and walked quietly, preferably in a darkened room. A baby swing is sometimes very helpful for this purpose. Some parents put their babies in a baby seat on top of the dryer; the sound and vibration can be comforting. (If you try this, make sure your baby is securely belted in, and use duct tape to make sure the seat cannot vibrate off the dryer onto the floor!)

✦ Infant car seats put pressure on the stomach, making GERD worse (see page 53). Convertible car seats are less likely to do this.

✦ Is she crying because she's wet or has had a bowel movement? Check the diaper and try changing it (it can be hard to tell if it's wet). If she wears cloth diapers, check the safety pins; one may be poking her. Also check for hair or threads wrapped around a finger or toe.

✦ Is it indigestion? The occasional baby who has a hard time digesting milk may cry an hour or two after a feeding. If you are breastfeeding, you should consider changing your own diet—cutting down on cow's milk or caffeine, for example. If you are bottle-feeding, ask your doctor if a formula change is worth a try. Some studies have found that switching to a hypoallergenic formula reduces crying; other experts disagree with this tactic, unless there are other signs of allergy such as rash or a family history of food allergies.

+ Is it heartburn? Most babies spit up without even noticing. A few of them experience pain when stomach acid comes up into the esophagus. Babies with heartburn usually cry soon after feeding; they look uncomfortable, grimace, and may arch their backs. You can try burping your baby again, even though you got a burp before. If this kind of crying happens often, talk with your doctor about gastroesophageal reflux disease, or GERD.

+ Is the baby sick? Sometimes babies cry because they just aren't feeling well. Irritability may be an early symptom, followed later by fever, rash, diarrhea, or vomiting. If your baby is crying inconsolably and has other symptoms of illness, take her temperature and call her doctor.

+ Is she spoiled? Though older babies can be spoiled, you can be sure that in the first few months your baby is not crying because she's spoiled. Something is bothering her.

+ Is it fatigue? Some young babies can't drift peacefully into sleep. Their fatigue at the end of every awake period produces a tension that is a hump they must get over before falling asleep. They have to cry. Some of them cry frantically and loudly; then, gradually or suddenly, the crying stops and they are asleep.

✦ Is she overstimulated? When young babies have been awake an unusually long while or when they have been stimulated more than usual, they may react by becoming tense and irritable. Instead of it being easier for them to fall asleep, it may be harder. If the parents or strangers then try to comfort them with more play or more talk, it only makes matters worse. So if your baby is crying at the end of a wakeful period and after she has been fed and had her diaper changed, you can assume that she's tired and put her to bed. If she continues to cry, you can try leaving her on her own for a few minutes (or as long as you can stand) to give her a chance to settle down on her own.

CHECKLIST
Tips for Comforting a Crying Baby

✓ Offer a feeding or a pacifier.

✓ Change the diaper.

✓ Hold, swaddle, and rock or vibrate (never shake).

✓ Play white noise.

✓ Darken the room and reduce stimulation.

✓ Reassure yourself that your baby is fine and you've done all you can. Then take a break (maybe drink some warm herbal tea) and give your baby time to calm down on her own.

DIAPERING

Cleaning your baby. You don't need to wash your baby when changing a wet diaper, but it's nice to let the skin air-dry. After a bowel movement, you can use plain water on cotton balls or a washcloth, baby lotion and tissues, or diaper wipes. Premoistened wipes are handy, but some contain perfumes and other chemicals that can irritate the skin. With girls, always wipe from front to back. For boys, put a spare diaper loosely over the penis until you're ready to fasten the diaper, so you won't get sprayed. Always wash your hands with soap and water after changing a diaper.

When to change. Most parents change the diaper when they pick their baby up for feeding and again before they put him back down. Or you may be able to save time by changing only after the feeding, after your baby has passed a bowel movement. Most babies don't mind a wet diaper, but a few are extra-sensitive and have to be changed more often. You'll probably go through about twelve diapers a day, or about eighty a week.

Disposable versus cloth. Why would anyone choose cloth diapers? Cloth diapers reduce the consumption of wood pulp and the clogging of landfills. The companies that sell disposables claim that disposables aren't any worse for the environment, but that has never made sense to me. Disposable diapers made from bamboo, rather than petroleum-based materials, are a little more expensive than conventional disposables, but are less damaging to the environment (which is, after all, where your baby is going to be living!). Look online for deals, and let your conscience and your wallet be your guides.

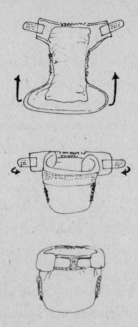

Cloth diapers and disposables cost about the same if you use a diaper service; if you wash your own, you cut the cost in half but it's a lot more work. Carrying bulky blocks of disposable diapers home from the store is a chore. Diaper services deliver clean diapers to your door each week.

Disposables absorb more urine, so they can seem dry when they're full, but they still need changing about as often as cloth. (Occasionally a superabsorbent diaper splits open, releasing some of its gelling material. Some parents mistake this material for insects or even for a rash, but it's quite safe.) Cloth diapers are handy for wiping up spit-up, so it's good to have some around in any case.

Many parents choose pre-folded cloth diapers that close with Velcro. Here's how to fold a diaper for a full-size newborn: (1) Fold lengthwise so that there are three thicknesses (see picture). (2) Fold about one-third of the end over. Half of the folded diaper now has six layers; the other half has three layers. A boy needs the double thickness in front. A girl needs the thickness in front when she's lying on her belly (not to sleep, of course, but for playing), and in back when she lies on her back to sleep. When you put in the pins, slip two fingers of your other hand between the baby and the diaper to prevent sticking the child. The pins slide through the cloth more easily if you keep them stuck into a bar of soap.

In the past, parents put their babies in waterproof plastic pants to protect the sheets (and themselves). Modern diaper wraps made out of high-tech, breathable materials allow more air to circulate around the baby's bottom, a real help in reducing moisture and the resulting rashes. But they tend to leak a bit. An alternative is to use two diapers. The second one can be pinned around the waist like an apron, or folded into a narrow strip down the middle.

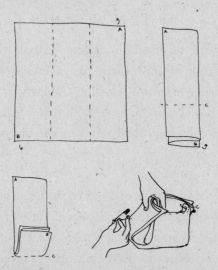

Cloth diaper images courtesy of Green Mountain Diapers

Washing diapers. With a diaper service, there's no washing. Just toss the diaper and all its contents into the plastic pail supplied by the diaper company; the company picks up the pail and leaves you a big bag of nice, clean diapers. If you're doing the washing yourself, first scrape the contents of the diapers into the toilet (a high-pressure sprayer that attaches to the toilet makes rinsing faster and easier). Next, put the diapers into a covered pail partially filled with water, with one-half cup of borax or bleach per gallon. Clean the diaper pail each time you do a diaper wash. Wash the diapers with mild soap or detergent and rinse two or three times, more if your baby has sensitive skin.

If the diapers are becoming hard, nonabsorbent, and gray with soap deposit, you can soften them by using a water conditioner. Don't use a fabric softener; these leave a coating that makes diapers less absorbent.

BOWEL MOVEMENTS

Meconium. For the first day or so after birth, the baby's bowel movements are a greenish-black goo called meconium. After that they change to brown or yellow. A newborn should have at least one bowel movement, or BM, before leaving the hospital; if your baby hasn't had a BM by the end of the second day, tell the doctor.

Early BMs. Most babies poop after they eat, because a full stomach stimulates the intestinal tract all the way down. Some breastfed babies begin to strain almost as soon as they start nursing; they produce nothing, but may strain so hard while the nipple is in their mouths that they can't nurse. You have to let their intestines quiet down for fifteen minutes and try again.

In the first weeks, breastfed babies usually have several BMs every day. The BMs can be light yellow in color; watery, pasty, or seedy; or they may have the consistency of thick cream soup. Rarely are they hard. After two or three months, many breastfed babies shift to one BM a day or less, because breast milk is so thoroughly digested that there isn't enough stuff left over to make up a good-size BM. Don't let this pattern alarm you; it's entirely normal as long as your baby is comfortable and the BMs are soft, not pebbles.

Most formula-fed babies start out having one to four BMs a day; some have as many as six. After a few weeks, the number tends to decrease to one or two a day. The BMs are usually pasty, pale yellow or tan; sometimes they're darker or greenish. Some young babies always have BMs that are more like soft scrambled eggs (curdy lumps with looser material in between). The number and color aren't important if the consistency is soft but not watery and your baby is comfortable and gaining weight well. Some babies on cow's-milk formula have overly hard BMs.

Straining with stools. A baby may push and strain a lot, grimacing and grunting, but then produce a soft bowel movement. This isn't constipation, which always causes hard stools. Rather, the problem is poor coordination. The baby is pushing out with one group of muscles and holding back with another. The net result is that nothing happens. Finally the holding-back muscles relax, and things go well after that. The problem goes away as the baby's nervous system matures.

For overly hard BMs which are pebbly or like a large ball,

two ounces of prune juice once a day often does the trick, or two to four teaspoons of pureed and strained prunes, even though the baby doesn't otherwise need solid food yet. Try to avoid laxatives, enemas, or suppositories. If, however, your baby continues to have hard and painful BMs or blood in the BM from straining, this is a sign of constipation. Constipation in young babies can sometimes be a symptom of a medical problem (see page 501), so it's reasonable to consult the doctor if simple remedies don't work.

Changes in the color of the stool. Brown, yellow, or green—it simply doesn't matter. Healthy BMs come in many colors. Do call the doctor if the BMs turn red, black, or white. Red stools may be caused by blood from the intestines, or from beets and red juices. Black stools may be due to bleeding from the stomach. Pale or white stools can be due to blockage of bile.

Mucus in the BMs. Don't worry about mucus in the BM, as long as your baby seems to be healthy. Some babies form a great deal of mucus in the early weeks. Mucus in the BM can also come from higher up—from the throat and bronchial tubes of a baby with a cold.

With mild intestinal infections, the BMs typically become loose, more frequent, and greenish, and the smell changes; with more serious infections, you might see blood and mucus mixed in with the BM. Babies with serious intestinal infections usually have poor feeding, fever, sleepiness, irritability, vomiting, and/or swollen, tender bellies. Call the doctor if you see any of these signs.

Another possibility is cow's-milk-protein sensitivity. Certain proteins in formulas made from cow's milk can cause inflammation in the intestines, leading to blood and mucus in BM. The same problem can occur in nursing babies, if cow's-milk protein from the mother's diet gets into the breast milk. Babies with protein sensitivity usually look healthy, although they can be colicky. The treatment is a switch to a special formula, or putting the nursing mother on a dairy-free diet. Most babies grow out of the problem by about a year of age.

Blood in the BMs: Streaks of blood on the outside of a BM usually come from a crack in the skin around the anus (like the cracks at the corners of the mouth). The cause is overly hard BMs. The bleeding is not serious in itself, but you need to deal with the constipation (see pages 106 and 501). Larger amounts of blood in the movement are rare, but a potentially serious sign.

THE BATH

First bath. If you're nervous about giving your baby a tub bath, you can give sponge baths until you feel more secure. Many babies love tub baths, but they aren't actually necessary. A thorough sponge bath, with attention to the diaper area and around the mouth and nose, is just as good. (Most doctors advise avoiding tub baths until the navel is dried up. But nothing awful happens if the navel gets wet; just dry it off well.)

You can give a sponge bath with the baby on a table or in your lap. You'll want a piece of waterproof material under the baby. If you are using a hard surface like a table, there should be some padding over it (like a folded blanket or quilt) so that your baby won't roll too easily. Rolling frightens young babies.

Wash the face and scalp with a washcloth and clear warm water. Lightly soap the rest of the body when and where needed, with the washcloth or your hand. Then wipe the soap off by going over the whole body at least twice with the rinsed washcloth, paying special attention to creases.

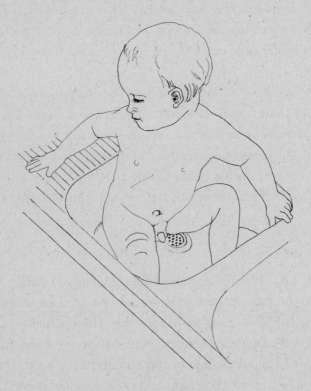

Getting ready for a bath. Before starting, be sure you have everything you need close at hand. If you forget the towel, you'll have to go after it holding a dripping baby in your arms. Take off your wristwatch or your Fitbit. An apron can protect your clothes. Choose a mild, hypoallergenic soap or moisturizing bar; some so-called "pure baby soaps" are actually harsh on sensitive skin. Have at hand:

- ✦ Soap

- ✦ Washcloth

- ✦ Towel

- ✦ Absorbent cotton for nose and ears if necessary

- ✦ Lotion

- ✦ Diapers, shirt, nightie

The bath can be given in a washbowl, dishpan, kitchen sink, or plastic tub. Some tubs have sponge cutouts to support and position the baby properly. For your own comfort, you can put a dishpan or tub on a table or on something higher, like a dresser. You can sit on a stool at the kitchen sink.

You can also use a regular bathtub. This will be hard on your back and legs, unless you get into the bath yourself, then have your partner give you your baby. Your lap is a perfect baby bath. Remember, though, that babies need warm, *but not hot*, water.

Giving a tub bath. The water should be about body temperature (90–100°F). Always test the water temperature with your wrist. It should feel comfortably warm but not hot. Use only a small amount of water at first, an inch or two deep, until you get the knack of holding your baby securely. A tub is less slippery if you line it with a towel or diaper each time.

Hold your baby so that her head is supported on your wrist, and the fingers of that hand hold her securely by the armpit. Wash the face first, with a soft washcloth without soap, then the scalp. The scalp needs to be soaped only once or twice a week. Wipe the soap suds off the scalp with a damp washcloth, going over it twice (if the washcloth is too wet, the soapy water may get into the eyes and sting). Then you can use the washcloth or your hand to wash the rest of your baby. Wash lightly between the outer lips of the vagina. When you use soap, it's easier to soap your hand than a washcloth. If the skin gets dry, try omitting soap except for once or twice a week.

Use a soft bath towel for drying, and blot rather than rub. If you begin giving the tub bath before the navel is completely healed, dry it well after the bath with cotton balls. Avoid baby powder containing talcum, because it is harmful to the lungs if inhaled. Cornstarch-based powder works almost as well and is safer.

Lotion. It's fun to apply lotion to a baby after a bath, and your baby will like it, too. Babies don't really need lotion, but it may help when the skin is dry or if there is a mild diaper rash. Baby oils and mineral oil work as well, but sometimes they cause a mild rash.

BODY PARTS

Skin. Newborn babies develop all sorts of spots and rashes, most of which fade or disappear on their own. Rashes *may* be signs of a serious medical condition, however, so it's sensible to ask the doctor to look at any new rash. (Also, see page 107 for milia and other common newborn rashes.)

Ears, eyes, mouth, nose. You need to wash only the outer ear and the entrance to the canal, not inside. Use a washcloth, not a cotton swab (which just pushes the wax further in). Wax is formed in the canal to protect and clean it.

The eyes are bathed by tears constantly, not just when your baby is crying. This is why it is unnecessary to put any drops into healthy eyes.

The mouth ordinarily needs no extra care.

The nose has a beautiful system for keeping itself clear. The cells lining the nose are covered with a fringe of whiplike projections that beat constantly, moving the mucus down toward the front of the nose. The mucus collects on the nose hairs, tickling the baby until she sneezes or rubs it away. When you are drying your baby after the bath, you can first moisten and then gently wipe away any balls of dried mucus with the corner of the washcloth. Don't fuss at this too long if it makes your baby angry.

Sometimes, especially when the house is heated, enough dried mucus collects in the nose to interfere with a baby's breathing. You can tell if this is happening because each time she breathes in, the lower edges of the chest are pulled inward. An older child or adult would breathe through the mouth, but most babies can't do this. A nasal spray of salt water (saline) helps loosen dried mucus.

Nails. The nails can be cut easily while your baby sleeps. Clippers may be easier than nail scissors. Use a nail file to get rid of sharp edges. If you file every day, you might not need to clip. Sing a song while you file, and nail care can become a pleasant part of your routine.

The soft spot (fontanel). The soft spot on the top of a baby's head is where the bones of the skull have not yet grown together.

The size of the fontanel at birth varies. Large ones are fine but take longer to close. Fontanels can close as early as nine months or as late as two years; the average is twelve to eighteen months.

Don't worry about touching the soft spot. It's covered by a tough membrane and there's no risk of hurting a baby there with ordinary handling. If the light is right, you can see it pulsating.

The navel. After birth, the doctor clamps the umbilical cord and cuts it off. The stump that's left dries up and drops off, usually in about two or three weeks.

When the cord falls off, it leaves a raw spot, which takes a number of days or weeks to heal over. The raw spot should be kept clean and dry. A scab covers it until it is healed; it doesn't need a dressing and will stay drier without one. There may be a little bleeding or drainage a few days before the cord falls off and until the healing is complete. If the scab on the unhealed navel gets pulled by clothing, there may be a drop or two of blood. Don't worry about this.

It's best to keep the diaper below the level of the unhealed navel, so that it doesn't keep the navel damp. If the unhealed navel becomes moist and produces a discharge, use a cotton swab dampened with alcohol to clean between the cord stump and the skin. If healing is slow, the raw spot may become lumpy with what's called granulation tissue. The doctor may apply a chemical that will hasten drying and healing.

If the navel and the surrounding skin become red or tender, call the doctor right away. Infections of the navel are rare, but can be serious.

The penis. Boy babies often have erections, especially when their bladder is full or during urination, or for no apparent reason. It's normal.

The foreskin is a sleeve of skin that covers the head (glans) of the penis. The opening of the foreskin is large enough to let urine out, but small enough to protect the tip of the penis from diaper rash. As the baby grows, the foreskin normally separates from the glans and becomes retractable. By age three or four, most foreskins can be pulled back to expose the glans all the way, but for some boys this change may only occur in their teen years. This is no cause for concern.

At the end of your baby's foreskin you may see a white, waxy material (smegma). This is perfectly normal. Smegma is secreted by the cells on the inside of the foreskin as a natural lubricant between the foreskin and the glans.

Wash the penis when you give your baby a bath. You don't have to do anything special to the foreskin; just wash gently around the outside to remove any excess smegma. If you want, you can clean beneath the foreskin by pushing it back very gently, just until you meet resistance. Never forcibly retract the foreskin. This hurts, and could lead to infections or other complications. In time, the foreskin normally becomes looser.

Circumcision. When a penis is circumcised, the foreskin is cut off. This operation provides modest medical benefits. Circumcised boys get fewer bladder and kidney infections during childhood. Circumcision reduces the spread of HIV (but so do condoms). There are also risks: pain, bleeding, and infection, though rarely.

In Judaism and Islam, circumcision has religious significance. In some other cultures it's a puberty rite, marking a boy's passage into adulthood. Some parents worry that it will upset their uncircumcised son to look different from his circumcised father or older brothers (I've not known this to happen).

Circumcision hurts. Most doctors now use injections to numb the area; others give babies sugar water, which relieves the pain at least a little. In the Jewish tradition, babies suck on a cloth soaked with wine. Still, many babies take a day to recover from the stress of the operation.

The glans will be red and tender at first. Wrapping it with gauze saturated with petroleum jelly keeps it from sticking, painfully, to the diaper. A spot of blood or several spots on successive diaper changes merely means that a small scab has been pulled off. The penis is bound to be tender for a week or so, but if there is oozing of blood or swelling, or your baby seems to be in pain, talk with the doctor.

TEMPERATURE, FRESH AIR, AND SUNSHINE

Room temperature. A room temperature of 65°F to 68°F for eating and playing is right for babies weighing over five pounds, just as it is for older children and adults. Smaller babies have a harder time controlling their body temperature, and may need to be kept warmer and dressed in extra layers. Very small babies control their body temperature best when they're right next to their parents, ideally skin to skin. Avoid cold or hot drafts in front of air conditioners and heat vents.

In cold weather, the air outside tends to contain very little moisture. When this dry air is taken into a house and warmed up, it acts like a dry sponge, sucking up moisture from the skin and nose. Dried mucus can make it hard for babies to breathe and may lower children's resistance to infections. The warmer the room temperature, the more drying the air becomes. Humidifiers help.

Inexperienced parents sometimes feel that they need to keep their baby overly warm. They keep the room too hot and the baby too wrapped up. Under these conditions, some babies even develop heat rash in winter. Overheating also increases the risk of crib death.

How much clothing. A normal baby has a good internal thermostat, as long as he isn't covered in too many layers. Babies and children who are plump need *less* covering than adults. More babies are overdressed than underdressed. This isn't good for them. People who are always too warmly dressed lose their ability to adjust to changes and are more likely to become chilled. So, in general, put on too little rather than too much and then watch your baby. Don't try to put on enough to keep the hands warm, because most babies' hands stay cool when they are comfortably dressed. Feel the legs or arms or neck. The best guide is the color of the face. Babies who are getting cold lose the color from their cheeks, and they may begin to fuss, too.

In cold weather, a warm cap is essential because babies lose lots of body heat from their heads. A sleeping cap should be of knitted acrylic, so that if it slips over the face your baby can still breathe through it.

Sweaters on and off. When putting on sweaters and shirts with small openings, remember that a baby's head is more egg-shaped than ball-shaped. Gather the sweater into a loop; slip it first over the back of your baby's head, then forward, stretching it as you bring it down past the forehead and nose. Then put your baby's arms into the sleeves. When taking it off, pull your baby's arms out of the sleeves first. Gather the sweater into a loop as it lies around the neck. Raise the front part of the loop up past the nose and forehead while the back of the loop is still at the back of the neck, then slip it off toward the back of the head.

Practical coverings. A young infant is safest in a sleep sack (see page 28), because blankets come untucked and can pose a suffocation risk. In a warm room (over 72°F) a baby only needs cotton covering. In a cooler room (60°F to 65°F) an all-acrylic bag gives the best combination of warmth and washability. When your baby is awake, a knitted shawl tucks and wraps easily, and lets you easily adjust the amount of covering to the temperature. Avoid coverings that are heavy, such as solid-feeling quilts.

Fresh air. Changes of air temperature help tone up the body's system for adapting to cold or heat. A bank clerk is much more likely to become chilled in winter than a lumberjack. A baby living continuously in a warm room usually has a pasty complexion and may have a sluggish appetite. An eight-pounder can certainly go out when it's 60°F or above. The temperature of the air is not the only factor. Moist, cold air is more chilling than dry air of the same temperature, and wind is the greatest chiller. Even when the temperature is cooler, a twelve-pound baby can be comfortable in a sunny, sheltered spot if dressed appropriately.

If you live in a city and have no yard to hang out in with

your baby, you can push him in a carriage. If you get in the habit of transporting your baby in a carrier on your chest or back, you will be wonderfully conditioned as he gets bigger. Your baby will love riding where she can see your face, hear your voice, look around, or nap.

Sunshine. While it's good for babies to spend time outdoors, sunlight contains ultraviolet (UV) rays, which can lead to skin cancer years later. Infants are especially vulnerable, because their thin skin contains relatively little melanin, the pigment that protects against UV damage. Dark-skinned babies are safer; those with pale skin and blond or red hair are most at risk. Beaches, pools, and boats are especially hazardous, because the UV rays reflect up from the water as well as shine down from above.

Children and adults should use sunscreen with a sun protection factor (SPF) of at least 15; higher for those with more sun-sensitive skin. Creams and lotions work equally well. Choose one that smells and feels good to you, so you'll apply it often.

Babies less than six months old are apt to find any sunscreen irritating, so cover them up if they're going to be out for more than a few minutes, in a hat with a wide brim, and pants and a long-sleeved top made out of material that will block the sun's rays. Even then, a fair-skinned baby should not sit poolside for long. Sunbathing—exposure to UV light for the purpose of getting a tan—is unhealthy at any age.

Babies can't rely on sunlight to make the vitamin D they need. Breastfed babies should take vitamin D drops. Infant formulas have enough D added.

COMMON NEWBORN CONCERNS

Birthmarks. It's the rare newborn who has no birthmarks. Doctors may or may not remember to reassure you about every spot. If you have questions, be sure to ask them.

Stork bites and angel's kisses. Many newborns have a collection of red, irregularly shaped spots on the nape of the neck (stork bites), on the upper eyelids (angel's kisses), or between the eyebrows. These birthmarks are clumps of little blood vessels that have grown because of exposure to the mother's hormones in the womb. Most disappear gradually, and nothing needs to be done for them.

Hyperpigmented spots. These slate-blue patches used to be called Mongolian spots, but they occur in babies of all nationalities, especially those with darker skin. They're usually around the buttocks but may be scattered anywhere. They are simply areas of increased pigment in the top layer of the skin, and almost always disappear completely in the first two years.

Moles. Dark brown spots should be checked by your doctor, especially if they grow or change color. There is a small risk that they might develop into skin cancer later in life.

Strawberry marks. These are fairly common, though they usually show up later in the first year of life. They start as pale areas, but over time change to raised marks of a deep crimson color and look like shiny strawberries. They usually grow for a year or so, then shrink until they disappear. The general rule is that half are completely gone by age five, 70 percent by age seven, and 90 percent by nine years. They rarely need medical treatment.

Sucking blisters. Babies are sometimes born with little blisters on their hands or wrists from sucking in the womb.

Some develop white dry sucking blisters in the middle part of their lips, which can peel. These always clear up with no special treatment.

Blue fingers and toes. The hands and feet of many newborns look blue, especially when cool. Some babies with pale skin also show a bluish mottling all over their bodies. These color changes are caused by slow blood circulation in the skin and are not a sign of illness. Bluish lips in an active baby are normal, but blueness of the gums or of the skin around the mouth sometimes signals low blood oxygen, especially if there is also difficulty breathing or feeding. If you see this, call your doctor.

Jaundice. Many newborn babies develop a yellow tinge of the skin and eyes. The color comes from bilirubin, a substance produced by old red blood cells. Bilirubin gives BMs their brownish color.

A little jaundice is normal. It goes away over the first few days as the liver and intestines become more active. If the bilirubin level rises too fast, doctors use special lights to get it back to the safe range. If your baby seems yellow in the first week of life, let the doctor take a look.

Sometimes jaundice persists beyond the first week or two, usually in a breastfed baby. Some doctors advise mothers to stop breastfeeding for a day or two; others recommend continuing or even increasing breastfeeding. In either case, the baby almost always does well.

Breathing problems. New parents often worry when their baby's breathing is irregular or so shallow that they can't hear it or see it. They may worry, too, the first time they hear their baby snoring faintly. These things are normal. Still, if anything at all concerns you about your baby's breathing, it's always right to ask the doctor. Persistently rapid or labored breathing is a sign of illness.

Umbilical hernia. Many babies have navels that stick out in a squishy lump that can be small (the size of a grape) or larger. Underneath the lump there is a soft spot in the strong fibers that make up the belly wall. You can push down on the lump and feel a ring of fiber, about the size of a dime. (It's perfectly safe to do this, and your baby won't mind.) When the baby cries, a small bit of intestine may push up through this umbilical ring, causing the navel to puff out. Small and medium-size rings usually close by themselves in a few weeks or months. Large ones may need a simple surgery, which usually can wait until after the baby's first birthday.

It used to be thought that taping a coin across the navel would make an umbilical hernia close faster; it doesn't. Keeping a baby from crying is impossible, and also doesn't help. Very, very rarely, a loop of bowel gets trapped in the hernia and becomes swollen, hard, and painful. This condition is a medical emergency.

Swollen breasts. Many babies, both boys and girls, have swollen breasts for some time after birth, and a little milky fluid might run out. This is all normal, caused by hormones that passed from the mother to the baby in the womb, and goes away in time. The breasts should not be massaged or squeezed, since this irritates them and may lead to infection.

Vaginal discharge. Girl babies often have a vaginal discharge at birth, with white, thick, sticky mucus. This condition is caused by the mother's hormones (the same ones that cause swollen breasts) and goes away on its own. At a few days of age, many girl babies have a little bit of bloody discharge for a day or two, caused by the dropping-off of maternal hormones after delivery. If a bloody discharge persists after the first week, have it checked out by the doctor.

Undescended testicles. Testicles form inside the abdomen and move down into the scrotum just before birth. Occasionally they don't make it all the way. Many of these undescended testicles do come down into the scrotum soon after birth. Other testicles hide: There are muscles that can jerk them back up into the groin. A light touch or even chilling of the skin from being undressed may be enough to trigger this protective reflex. A good time to look for them is when your baby is in a warm bath. Doctors are trained to hunt for testicles. If a testicle can't be found by six to nine months, a surgeon may need to look.

Startles and jittery movements. Newborn babies often startle at loud noises and sudden changes in position. Some very sensitive babies nearly jump out of their skins when their own arm and leg movements cause their bodies to rock around. For this reason, they may hate the bath, and prefer to be washed in their parent's lap and then rinsed while held securely in both hands. They gradually get over this uneasiness as they grow older.

The trembles. Some babies have trembly or jittery moments in the early months. Their chins may quiver or their arms and legs may tremble, especially when they're excited or just after being undressed. This is normal and it goes away in time.

Twitching. Some babies twitch occasionally in their sleep; once in a while there is a baby who twitches frequently. This, too, usually disappears as the baby grows older. Tell the doctor if twitching continues even while you are holding the limb; this could be a sign of a seizure.

THE FIRST YEAR, FOUR TO TWELVE MONTHS

A TIME OF FIRSTS

Discoveries in the first year. The first three months of life are about getting basic systems working smoothly. Months four through twelve are all about discovery. Infants discover their own bodies and gain control of muscles large and small. They explore the world and begin to figure out the basics of cause and effect. And they learn to read other people's feelings and predict how their own actions will affect those feelings. These momentous discoveries take infants to the very threshold of language.

The meaning of milestones. It's exciting to watch your baby hit the big milestones: rolling, sitting, standing, walking, first words. But don't focus too much on the timing. Being fast or slow doesn't matter in the long run. Development is not a race.

There are developmental timetables you can consult to see if your child is doing what she is "supposed" to be doing at each age. Such charts have never been part of this book. First off, every child's pattern of development is unique. One may be very advanced in her strength and coordination, a sort of infant athlete, yet she may be slow in doing skillful things with her fingers or in talking. Children who turn out later to be smart in schoolwork may have been slow to talk in the beginning. Likewise, children of average talent may have shown advanced early development.

It's a mistake to compare your baby to an average timetable. Development is bumpy. There are often small backward slides just before forward moves. You don't need to push for forward progress or worry too much about small regressions. There is no evidence that making a concerted effort to teach a child to walk or talk or read early has any real long-term benefit. Children need an environment that allows for the next developmental achievement but doesn't push them into it.

Most pediatricians and family doctors now use standardized questionnaires to detect children with developmental delays. This is a good practice, because it takes some of the pressure off parents and makes it possible for children to get special services if they need them. If you have concerns, of course, ask your child's doctor.

Autism concerns. Autism is common now. As you care for your baby, pay attention to specific behaviors that go *against* autism. If your baby meets these milestones, you can relax:

At four months, your baby should love "talking" with you—that is, looking at your face, listening to your voice, and responding with noises and excited facial expressions of his own. By nine months, he should be babbling, making a variety of word-like sounds. By one year, he should be pointing with one finger to show you something interesting, and by fifteen months he should have at least one meaningful word.

If you are concerned that your child is not meeting these milestones, talk with your baby's doctor or with the child development agency in your county. With early identification, more and more children with autism are growing up connected, communicative, and much more content.

CARING FOR YOUR BABY

Companionship without spoiling. During his play periods, it's good for a baby to be near his parents and other family members so that he can see them, make noises at them, hear them speak to him, and now and then have them show him something. But it isn't necessary or sensible for him to have someone amusing him all the time. He can enjoy being around people and still learn how to occupy himself. When new parents are so delighted with their baby that they hold him or make up games for him all day long, he may come to depend on these attentions and demand more and more of them.

Things to watch and things to play with. Beginning at around three or four months, babies like looking at bright-colored things and things that move, but mostly they enjoy looking at people and their faces. Outdoors, they are delighted to watch leaves and shadows. Indoors, they study their hands and shadows and pictures on the wall. There are bright-colored crib toys that you can hang between the top rails of the crib. Place them just within arm's reach—not right on top of your baby's nose—for when she begins reaching. Be careful to keep any strings short, however, so they can't become strangulation hazards if your baby pulls them down.

Toward the middle of her first year, a baby's greatest joy is handling and mouthing objects: collections of plastic objects linked together (made for this age), rattles, teething rings, animals and dolls of cloth, household objects that are safe in the mouth. Don't let your child have objects or furniture that may be covered in paint containing lead, small glass beads and other small objects that can be choked on, or thin plastic toys that can be chewed into small, sharp pieces.

Electronics in the first year: If a screen is on, a baby will stare at it. This is not a sign of advanced development; more likely, the baby is just mesmerized by the shifting colors. Screens entertain at a cost. Young children easily become dependent on them and lose some of their natural drive to explore. A child with a plastic cup and spoon, a few wooden blocks, and a board book can think up fifty creative ways to use those objects; a child in front of a screen can only watch and respond to preprogrammed prompts. The richest developmental stimulation comes in playing and talking with a real person—you!—who responds with empathy and shared pleasure, something no screen can do.

FEEDING AND GROWTH

Feeding decisions. Breast milk is the best nutrition for babies through the first twelve months of life, with spoon foods added at around six months, and finger foods at around nine months. Any amount of breastfeeding is better than none. These days, about eight out of ten mothers start out breastfeeding.

But it is your decision. Babies who have taken formula from birth or starting before six months can also thrive. Decisions about breastfeeding need to take into account the needs of babies *and* of their parents. (See the Feeding and Nutrition section, page 231, for details on breast-, bottle-, and spoon-feeding, and on when to introduce specific foods, including peanuts).

If you choose not to breastfeed, a commercial infant formula is much safer than homemade or low-iron formulas. Regular cow's milk isn't safe for babies under twelve months. (See page 240 for concerns about cow's milk in general.)

Feeding is about more than food; it's a time for emotional sharing and closeness. Hold your baby, talk with her, try to "read" the signs she sends with her eyes and body. Turn off your phone or take it off the hook; turn off your electronics; focus on your baby and the experience of being together.

Mealtime behavior. Once babies can reach, they love to play with food. They learn a lot about the physical world by slinging squash and poking peas; and a lot about relationships by opposing and provoking parents. Skillful parents allow the experimenting, but set limits: "You can pick up your mashed potatoes, but if you throw them, dinner is over." Feeding is going well if both you and your baby come away happy. But if mealtimes regularly leave you tense, worried, or angry, talk with your child's doctor.

At around nine months, a baby may start showing signs of independence in feeding. He wants to hold the spoon himself, and he turns his head away if you try to do it for him. He's developing a will of his own, which is a good thing, even if trying at times. By the way, you can handle the spoon issue by giving your baby one spoon to use as best he can, while you use a second spoon to actually get some oatmeal into his mouth (the "two spoon" method).

Growth. Babies roughly double their birth weight by three to five months, and triple it by a year. Doctors plot children's weight, length, and head size on growth charts that show how big average children are at different ages, and also the range of normal. Whether your child is one of the smallest, one of the largest, or more in the middle, a healthy growth pattern is a good sign that your baby is getting the right amount to eat and that the main body systems are working well.

Bigger is not necessarily better, and while a growth curve at the ninety-fifth percentile means that a child is likely to be one of the largest in his preschool class, it doesn't mean much more than that.

SLEEPING

Bedtime rituals. Many of us have our own bedtime habits. We like our pillow just right and the covers to fit a certain way. Babies are the same. If they learn to fall asleep while being held by Mommy or Daddy, this can become the *only* way for them to nod off. Then, when they wake up in the middle of the night, Mommy or Daddy has to wake up, too.

There is a better way. If your baby can learn to fall asleep while lying alone in his crib, then he can do the same thing in the middle of the night (and you can keep on sleeping). So, once your baby is three or four months old, put her to bed while she's awake and let her learn to get herself to sleep. You may hear her awaken in the middle of the night (all babies do this), but she won't have to cry until you get up and rock her; she'll just fall back asleep.

Early waking. Some parents like to get up with the sun and enjoy early mornings with their babies. But if you prefer to sleep, you probably can teach your baby to sleep later or to be happy in bed in the morning. In the middle part of the first year, most babies become willing to sleep a little later than the uncivilized hour of 5:00 or 6:00 a.m. You just need to give your child a chance to go back to sleep. If your child murmurs or fusses a little, it's okay to wait without responding; he'll let you know if he truly needs attention.

Changes in sleep. By about four months, most babies sleep mainly at night, perhaps waking up once or twice to nurse, with two or three naps during the day. Toward the end of the first year, most are down to two naps a day. Some babies sleep as few as ten or eleven hours out of twenty-four, others as many as fifteen or sixteen. Total sleep time gradually decreases during the first year.

At around nine months of age, many babies who have been good sleepers start waking up in the middle of the night and demanding attention. Many have also just discovered that a toy or other object that disappears under a cloth or behind your back actually still exists: They are grasping the idea of "object permanence." From your baby's point of view, it means that out of sight is no longer out of mind.

Now when your baby wakes up and finds herself alone, she knows that you are nearby even though out of sight. So she cries for company. Sometimes a simple "Go to sleep" will be enough; other times you might need to pick her up. If you put her back down before she is completely asleep, she'll learn to fall back to sleep on her own.

Sleep problems. Many babies develop problems falling asleep or staying asleep, often after a minor illness such as a cold or ear infection. The baby, who feels miserable at night, feels a lot better in the parents' bed. But once the illness is over, the baby doesn't want to leave!

The solution is to reestablish the baby's habit of falling asleep in her own bed. It's easiest to do this in two steps: (1) Mommy or Daddy stays by the child's bed until the child is asleep; (2) the parent gradually moves away, while the child is on the brink of sleep, until the child can fall asleep without a parent in the room. A comforting ritual—stories, prayers, kisses—helps a great deal. Do this at bedtime and in the middle of the night, too, if necessary. Patience is essential.

Parents who work late shifts sometimes struggle with bedtime. I often hear, "I get home at seven and bedtime is eight, so we don't have any time together." In this case, a baby's sleeplessness is not so much a problem as a solution, a way to have time together. A change in the parent's schedule, if possible, may do the trick.

CRYING AND COLIC

Normal crying versus colic. All babies cry and fret sometimes, and it's usually not too hard to figure out why. The section on crying in newborns (page 50) also applies to babies through the first year of life. Crying tends to increase until a baby is about six weeks old and then, mercifully, begins to diminish. By three or four months, most babies fuss for a total of about an hour a day.

For some babies, however, the crying just goes on and on, hour after hour, week after week, no matter what the well-

meaning and frantic parents do. A standard definition of colic
is inconsolable crying for more than three hours a day, more
than three days a week, and lasting more than three weeks. In
reality, any crying or fussing that lasts much longer than expected in an otherwise healthy baby qualifies as colic. Colic
refers to pain from the intestines, but there are many causes
for excessive crying.

There seem to be two distinct patterns. The usual colicky
infants cry mainly in the evening, typically between 5:00 and
8:00 p.m. (but they could do so at other hours, as well).
During the rest of the day they're mostly content and easy to
soothe. It's not clear what makes the evening hours especially
uncomfortable. Other infants cry at any and all times of day
or night. Some of these babies also seem to be generally tense
and jumpy. Their bodies don't relax well, and they startle easily at slight noises or after quick changes of position.

Responding to colic. It's tough to be the parent of a fretful, colicky, irritable baby. Your baby may be soothed when
you first pick her up, but after a few minutes she's apt to be
screaming harder than ever. She thrashes with her arms and
kicks with her legs. Not only does she refuse to be comforted,
but she acts as if she were angry at you for trying. As the minutes go by and she acts angrier and angrier, you feel that she
is spurning you as a parent, and you can't help feeling mad at
her. But getting angry at a tiny baby makes you ashamed of
yourself, and you try hard to suppress the feeling. This makes
you tenser than ever.

There are various things you can try to help the situation,
but first I think you have to come to terms with your feelings.
All parents feel upset, afraid, and frustrated if they can't calm

their infant. Most feel guilty, especially if it is their first baby, as if the baby is crying because the parents are doing something wrong (which is not true). And most parents also get angry at their babies. This is normal. Give yourself a break. It isn't your fault that your baby is crying and that you're reacting emotionally. It just means that you truly love your baby; otherwise you wouldn't be so upset.

Never shake a baby. Feelings of desperation and anger drive some parents to shake their babies in a last-ditch effort to get them to stop crying. But the result—a real tragedy—is often severe, permanent brain damage, or even death. Before you get to the point where shaking seems to be a solution, get help. Your baby's doctor is a good place to start. Most cities and towns also have parent-support hotlines that you can call at any hour of the day or night (call 411; look in the community services listings in the phone book; or see Parents Anonymous in the Resource Guide, page 893). It's important to make sure that *all* of the adults who take care of your child—including grandparents, babysitters, and friends—know that it is *never* safe to shake a baby.

Medical evaluation. If you have a baby with colic, the first thing to do is have her examined to make sure there is no obvious medical cause. If your baby is growing and developing normally, that should be reassuring. (A colicky baby who is *not* growing normally deserves a very thorough medical evaluation.) Sometimes repeated doctor visits are necessary.

Once you know that your baby just has colic, you can rest assured that colicky babies don't grow up to be any more or less happy, smart, or emotionally healthy than other babies.

The trick for you is to get through the next few months with your confidence and good spirits intact.

Help for your baby. First, look again at the list of remedies for crying on page 54. There are several other things you can try for a colicky infant: All of these approaches work some of the time, but none works all of the time.

✦ Offer a pacifier between feedings.

✦ Swaddle your baby snugly in a receiving blanket.

✦ Rock her in a cradle or carriage.

✦ Use a front carrier for long walks.

✦ Take her for a ride in the car.

✦ Try an infant swing.

✦ Play music, soothing or raucous.

Many babies often do best on a low-stimulus regime: quiet room, few visitors, low voices, slow movements in handling them, a firm hold in carrying them, a big pillow (with a waterproof cover) for them to lie on while being changed and sponge-bathed so that they won't roll, or by being swaddled in a receiving blanket most of the time while awake.

Give your baby a belly massage with lubricating lotion. Place a warm-water bottle on her belly. (Make sure it is not too hot: You should be able to rest the inside of your wrist against the warm-water bottle without discomfort. As an extra precaution, wrap it in a diaper or towel.) Lay your baby across your knees or across a warm-water bottle and massage her back.

Change what she drinks: Try a formula change (this may help as often as half the time), or a little chamomile or mint tea. If you're breastfeeding, stop drinking milk, coffee, and tea with caffeine, and stop eating chocolate (which also contains caffeine) and foods that cause gas, such as cabbage.

If none of these methods work and if your baby is not hungry, wet, or sick, then what? I think it's best to put your baby down in his crib, let him cry for a while, and see if he can calm himself. It's hard to listen to a crying infant without trying to do something, but realistically, what else is there for you to do? Some parents can go out for a little walk while they let their baby cry (as long as there is another adult to watch the baby); others can't bear to leave the room. Do whatever feels right for you, because there is simply no right or wrong way to handle this situation. Many babies fall asleep within ten to twenty minutes. If your baby is still crying after this time, pick her up and try everything again.

Help for yourself. Many parents get worn out and frantic listening to a baby cry, especially when it's their first and they're with the baby constantly. It can really help to get away from home and your baby for a few hours at least twice a week, more often if it can be arranged. If you can, hire a sitter or ask a friend or neighbor to come in and relieve you.

If you're like many parents, you may hesitate to do this: "Why should we inflict our baby on somebody else? Besides, we'd be nervous being away for so long." But you shouldn't think of time off like this as just a treat for you. It's very important for you, your baby, and your whole family that you not get exhausted and depressed. If you can't get anyone to come in, take turns with your partner one or two evenings a week. Your baby doesn't need two parents at a time to listen to her. Invite friends to come in and visit you.

Remember that everything that helps you keep a sense of balance also helps your baby in the long run. Also, even though it may seem awkward, remember to *make sure to talk with anyone who watches your baby about the dangers of shaking.*

SPOILING

Can you spoil a baby? This question comes up naturally in the first few weeks at home if a baby is fussing a lot between feedings instead of sleeping peacefully. You pick him up and walk him around and he stops crying, at least for the time being. Lay him down, and he starts all over again. It might feel like your baby is running the show, but it's more likely that such a young baby is simply feeling miserable. If he stops fussing when picked up, it's probably because the motion and the warm pressure on his abdomen from being held make him forget his pain or tension at least temporarily.

The answer to the spoiling question really depends on what lessons you think babies are learning in the first months of life. Young infants live entirely in the here and now; they can't anticipate the future. They also can't formulate the thought "I'm going to make life miserable for these people until they give me everything I want."

What infants do learn during this period is what to expect. If their needs are met promptly and lovingly, they come to feel that good things generally happen and that unhappiness passes with the help of special people they come to know as parents. This sense of basic trust in what to expect colors the child's attitude toward people and to life's challenges for a long time, maybe for life.

So the answer to the question "Can a young baby be spoiled?" is no, not until six to nine months of age. A better question is, How can you help your baby develop a sense of basic trust? The answer is to try to figure out his needs, and meet them.

Spoiling after six months. You can be a little more suspicious by six or seven months. By then, colic and other causes of physical discomfort are usually done. With a very young baby, you try hard to meet his needs; with an older baby, toddler, and child, you help him to understand that needs and wants are different things: Needs get met, wants *sometimes* get met. An older child can play by himself for a few minutes, and wait a bit for your attention.

Naturally, some babies who were held and walked a great deal during the early months have become accustomed to constant attention. Take the example of a mother who can't stand to hear her baby fret, even for a minute, and who carries him most of the time he's awake. By the age of six months, the baby cries immediately and holds out his arms to be picked up as soon as his mother puts him down. Housework has become impossible. The mother can't help resenting her enslavement, but she can't tolerate the indignant crying, either. The baby is likely to sense the parent's anxiety and resentment and may respond by becoming even more demanding.

How do you "unspoil"? It takes willpower and a little hardening of the heart to say no to your baby. To get yourself in the right mood you have to remember that, in the long run, being unreasonably demanding and excessively dependent is worse for babies than for you, and gets them off-kilter with themselves and with the world. So you are reforming them for their own good.

Make a schedule for yourself, on paper if necessary, that requires you to be busy with housework or something else while your baby is awake. Go at it with a great bustle—to impress your baby and impress yourself. Say you are the mother of a baby boy who has become accustomed to being carried all the time. When he frets and raises his arms, explain to him in a friendly but very firm tone that this job and that job must get done this afternoon. Though he doesn't understand the words, he does understand the tone of voice. Stick to your busywork. The first hour of the first day is the hardest.

One baby may accept the change better if his mother stays out of sight a good part of the time at first and talks little. This helps him become absorbed in something else. Another adjusts more quickly if he can at least see his mother and hear her talking to him, even if she won't pick him up. When you bring him a plaything or show him how to use it, or when you decide it's time to play with him, sit down beside him on the floor. Let him climb into your arms if he wants, but don't get back into the habit of walking him around. If you're on the floor with him, he can crawl away when he eventually realizes you won't walk. If you pick him up and walk him, he'll surely object noisily just as soon as you start to put him down again. If he keeps on fretting indefinitely when you sit with him on the floor, remember another job and get busy again.

What you are trying to do is to help your baby begin to

build frustration tolerance—a little at a time. If she does not begin to learn this gradually between six and twelve months, it is a much harder lesson to learn later on.

PHYSICAL DEVELOPMENT

Body control starts with the head and gradually works down to the arms, hands, trunk, and legs. At birth a baby knows how to suck, and if something touches his cheek he tries to reach it with his mouth. After a few days he's more than ready to do his part in nursing. If you try to hold his head still, he becomes angry right away and twists to get it free. (Probably he has this instinct to keep from being smothered.)

All on his own, he follows objects with his eyes, usually by about one month if not before. By three or four months, he waves his arms when he sees things, as if to reach for them. By five or six months, he can reach accurately. By seven or eight months, he can grab.

Using their hands. Some babies can put their thumbs or fingers in their mouths from day one. Ultrasounds show them doing it in the womb. But most can't get even their hands to their mouths with any regularity until they are two or three months old. And because their fists are still clenched tight, it usually takes them longer to get hold of a thumb separately.

At about two or three months, many babies love to look at their hands. They bring them up until, surprised, they bang themselves in the nose—only to stretch their arms out and start all over again. This is the beginning of eye-hand coordination.

The main business of hands is to grab things. A baby

seems to know ahead of time what he's going to be learning next. Weeks before he can actually grab an object, he looks as if he wants to and is trying. At this stage, if you put a rattle into his hand, he holds on to it and waves it.

Around the middle of the first year, he learns how to grab something that's brought within arm's reach, and how to transfer an object from one hand to the other. Gradually he handles things more expertly. Starting at around nine months, he loves to pick up tiny objects, especially those you don't want him to (like specks of dirt), carefully and deliberately.

Right- and left-handedness. Most babies use either hand equally well for the first year or two and then gradually become right- or left-handed. A strong hand preference in a very young baby could mean that the *other* arm is weak; the doctor should check it out. About 10 percent of all people are left-handed. Handedness tends to run in families. Handedness is inborn, so it's a mistake to try to force a left-handed child to become right-handed; it just confuses the brain.

Rolling over and falling off. The age at which babies roll over, sit up, creep, stand up, or walk is more variable than the age at which they get control of their head or arms. A lot depends on temperament and weight. A wiry, energetic baby is in a great rush to get moving. A plump, placid one may be willing to wait until later.

A baby should never be left unwatched on a table for even as long as it takes you to turn your back. Since you can't be sure when that first roll will happen, it's safest to always keep a hand on your baby when she's up high. Once she can roll, it's not safe to leave her even in the middle of an adult's bed. It is amazing how fast a baby can reach the edge, and many do fall from an adult bed to the floor, which makes a parent feel very guilty.

If a baby cries immediately after a fall from a bed, then stops crying and regains his normal color and activities within a few minutes, he probably has not been injured. If you notice any change in behavior in the next hours or days (the baby is fussier, sleepier, or not eating, for example), call your doctor and describe the event; in most cases, you will be reassured that your baby is well. If your child has lost consciousness, even for a short time, you need to call the doctor promptly.

Sitting up. By seven months, most babies can sit steadily without support after being helped up. But before babies have the coordination to succeed, they want to try. When you take hold of their hands, they attempt to pull themselves up. This eagerness raises the question, at what age can you prop your baby up in the high chair? In general, it's better not to prop babies straight up until they can sit steadily by themselves for many minutes. This doesn't mean that you can't pull them up to a sitting position for fun, or sit them in your lap, just as long as the neck and back are straight. It's a curled-over position that's not good for long periods.

High chairs are great for letting your baby eat meals with the rest of the family, but falling out of one is bad news. If you are going to use a high chair, get one with a broad base so that it doesn't tip over easily, and always use the strap to buckle your baby in. Don't ever leave a baby alone in a high chair.

Squirming while being changed. Babies rarely lie still while being changed or dressed. It goes completely against their nature. From the time they learn to roll over until about one year, when they can be dressed standing up, they may struggle against lying down or cry indignantly as if they have never heard of such an outrage.

There are a few things that can help. One baby can be distracted by a parent who makes funny noises, another by a small bit of cracker or cookie. You can have an especially fascinating toy, like a music box or a special mobile, that you offer at dressing time only. Distract your baby just before you lay her down, not after she starts yelling.

Creeping and crawling. Creeping, when your baby begins to drag himself across the floor, can begin anytime between the ages of six months and one year. Crawling on hands and knees usually starts a few months later. Occasionally, some perfectly normal babies never creep or crawl at all; they just sit around until they learn to stand up.

There are a dozen different ways of creeping and crawling, and babies may change their style as they become more expert. One first learns to creep backward, another sideways, like a crab. One wants to crawl on her hands and toes with her legs straight, another on his hands and knees, still another on one knee and one foot. The baby who learns to be a speedy creeper may be late in walking, and the one who is a clumsy creeper, or who never learns to creep at all, has a good reason for learning to walk early.

Standing. Standing usually comes in the last quarter of the first year, but an ambitious and advanced baby may stand at as early as seven months. Occasionally you see one who doesn't stand until after one year but seems to be bright and healthy in all other respects. Some of these are plump, easygoing babies. Others just seem to be slow getting coordination in their legs. These children almost always turn out just fine. It's reassuring if the doctor finds them healthy and they seem bright and responsive in other ways.

Quite a number of babies get themselves into a jam when they first learn to stand up, because they don't yet know how to sit down again. One poor thing stands until she is frantic with exhaustion. The parents unhitch her from the railing of her playpen and sit her down. But instantly she forgets all about her fatigue and pulls herself to her feet again. This time she is crying within a few minutes. The best a parent can do is give her especially interesting things to play with while she's sitting, wheel her in the stroller longer than usual, and take comfort in the fact that she'll probably learn how to sit down within a week. One day she tries it. Very carefully, she lets her behind down as far as her arms reach and, after a long moment of hesitation, plops down. She finds that it wasn't such a long drop and that her seat is well padded.

As the weeks go by, she learns to move around while hanging on, first with two hands, then with one. This is called cruising. Eventually she has enough balance to let go altogether for a few seconds when she is absorbed and doesn't realize what a daring thing she's doing. She is getting ready for walking.

Walking. Babies walk alone when they're ready to. Inheritance probably plays the largest role, followed by ambition, boldness, heaviness, and how well they can get places by creeping. A baby who is just beginning to walk when an illness lays her up for two weeks may not try again for a month or more. One who is just learning and has a fall may refuse to let go with her hands again for many weeks.

Most babies learn to walk at between twelve and fifteen months. A few start earlier, and some a little later. In otherwise healthy babies, the age of walking doesn't have much to do with other developmental attainments. An early walker is no more likely to be bright intellectually than a late one. You don't have to do anything to teach your child to walk. When her muscles, her nerves, and her spirit are ready, you won't be able to stop her. (The devices called "walkers" don't help babies learn to walk sooner, and they're dangerous, see page 399.)

Bowlegs, toeing in, toeing out. A parent of an early walker may worry that it's bad for the baby's legs. For the most part, though, children's physiques are able to stand whatever they're ready to do by themselves. Babies sometimes become bowlegged or knock-kneed in the early months of walking, but this happens with late walkers as well as with early walkers. Most babies toe out to some degree when they start to walk. One baby starts with the feet sticking right out to the sides, like Charlie Chaplin, and ends up toeing out only moderately. The average baby starts toeing out moderately and ends up with the feet almost parallel. The baby who starts out with feet almost parallel is more apt to end up toeing in. Toeing in and bowlegs often go together.

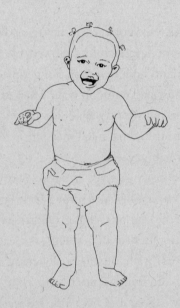

The straightness of legs, ankles, and feet depends on several factors, including a baby's inborn pattern of development. Some babies seem to have a tendency to knock-knees and ankles that sag inward. The heavy child is more apt to develop these conditions. Other babies—especially active, athletic ones—seem to be born with a tendency to bowlegs and toeing in. Another factor may be the position babies keep their feet and legs in. For instance, you occasionally see a foot that becomes turned in at the ankle because the baby always sits with that foot tucked under him.

Doctors examine hips, knees, ankles, and feet regularly; if weak ankles, knock-knees, bowlegs, or toeing in develop, corrective measures may be recommended, but most of these conditions resolve themselves over time.

LEARNING ABOUT PEOPLE

Changing reactions to strangers. You can get an idea of how your baby goes from phase to phase in development by watching his reaction to strangers at different ages. This is how it goes in a doctor's office for a typical baby until he's about a year old: At two months he doesn't pay much attention to the doctor. As he lies on the examining table, he keeps looking over his shoulder at his mother. The four-month-old is the doctor's delight. He breaks into a body-wiggling smile just as often as the doctor is willing to smile and make noises at him. By five or six months, the baby may have begun to change his mind; by nine months he is certain that the doctor is a stranger and therefore to be feared. When the doctor approaches, he stops his kicking and cooing. His body freezes as he eyes the doctor intently, even suspiciously, maybe for twenty seconds. Finally his chin puckers and he begins to shriek. He may get so worked up that he cries long after the exam is over.

Stranger anxiety. The nine-month-old baby isn't only suspicious of the doctor; anything new and unfamiliar makes him anxious. What has changed to make your baby go from loving everyone to being a suspicious worrywart?

Before about six months of age, babies remember when

they have seen something before (we know, because they tend to stare longer at such things). After six months, they start to get the idea that what is unfamiliar might be dangerous. So the first thing they do when a new person approaches is check in with their parent.

By twelve to fifteen months, babies are better at predicting the future: "Maybe I don't know who this person is, but nothing awful has happened in the past, so I can handle this stranger without panicking."

Cautious babies. When babies see something new or unexpected their hearts beat fast for a few moments. In some babies, the heart rates go up more and stay high longer. These babies often grow into cautious children. They tend to hang back in a new situation before joining in, and get upset if you rush them. This temperament trait is called "slow to warm up." It's not caused by anything parents do, but sensitive handling helps.

If you have a baby who responds intensely to new people, let well-meaning strangers know to take things slow, but don't keep strangers away altogether. With repeated exposure, things that were strange become more familiar, and children who are slow to warm up become more comfortable.

CLOTHES AND EQUIPMENT

Shoes: when and what kind? There's usually no need to put anything on a baby's feet until he is walking outdoors. Indoors, babies' feet stay cool just the way their hands do, so they aren't uncomfortable barefoot. They don't need knitted booties or soft shoes in the first year unless the floor is cold.

After a baby is standing and walking, there's real value in leaving the child barefoot most of the time when conditions are suitable. The arches are relatively flat at first. Your baby gradually builds the arches up and strengthens the ankles by using them vigorously in standing and walking. Walking on an uneven or rough surface also fosters the use of the foot and leg muscles.

Of course, a child needs shoes outdoors in cold weather and when walking on hazardous surfaces. But it's good for a child to continue to go barefoot (or with socks) indoors till the age of two or three, and outdoors, too, in warm weather at the beach, in the sandbox, and in other safe places.

Semisoft-soled shoes are best at first. They should be big enough so that the toes aren't cramped, but not so big that they almost slip off. Stiff shoes with extra support are expensive and useless. Canvas sneakers are just fine. The feet are pudgy the first couple of years, and as a result, low shoes sometimes do not stay on as well as high-top shoes. There isn't any other reason for ankle-high shoes; the ankles don't need extra support. It's helpful to have a nonskid sole. You can rough up a smooth sole with coarse sandpaper.

Small children outgrow their shoes fast, so get into the habit of checking every few weeks to make sure they are still large enough. As a child walks, the toes push forward with each step, so there needs to be plenty of space in front. Check with your child standing: If you press with your thumb, you should be able to feel about one-quarter of an inch of empty space in the toe of the shoe.

Playpens. A playpen in the family room, kitchen, or home office lets a baby be near the action without the danger of being stepped on or spilled on. When babies are old enough to stand up, the playpen gives them a railing to hold on to and a firm foundation under their feet. In good weather they can sit safely in the playpen on the porch and watch the world go by.

If you are going to use a playpen, it's best if your baby gets accustomed to it at three or four months, before he has learned to sit and crawl and before he has had the freedom of the floor. Otherwise he might consider it a prison from the start. By the time he can sit and crawl, he has fun going after things that are a few feet away and handling larger objects like cooking spoons, saucepans, and strainers. When he becomes bored with the playpen, he can sit in a bouncing chair or a chair-table arrangement. It's good for him to have some free creeping time, too.

Even if they are willing, babies should not be kept in playpens all the time. They need time to explore, with an adult watching. Every hour or so they should be played with, hugged, and perhaps carried around in a front pack for a spell. Between twelve and eighteen months, most babies tolerate the playpen for shorter and shorter periods.

Swings. Swings are useful after babies have learned to sit and before they learn to walk. Some have motors, some are for use in doorways, and some have springs for bouncing. The springs should have covers to prevent finger injury, or the coils should not be more than one-eighth of an inch apart. One baby is happy swinging for a long time, while another soon grows bored. Swings keep babies from getting into trouble, but babies also need lots of opportunities to creep, explore, stand, and walk.

Walkers. You might think that walkers would help babies walk. They actually interfere, because all babies have to do to get around is thrash their legs. Different skills are needed to walk, and the baby who uses a walker may be less motivated to learn them.

Walkers are dangerous. They raise the baby's height so that she can reach objects that may hurt her; they make it easier for her to tip over; and they allow her to move forward at an amazingly fast rate. Terrible injuries have come from babies falling down stairs in their walkers. Baby walkers should be banned. If you already own one, you can take the wheels off so it can't roll, or just throw it out.

COMMON PHYSICAL ISSUES
IN THE FIRST YEAR

It's best to consult your doctor promptly about any change in your baby's health. Don't try to diagnose it yourself, because it's easy to miss little signs that sometimes signal serious illness. Once the doctor has made the diagnosis, it helps to know a few things:

Hiccups. Most babies hiccup pretty regularly after meals (many babies hiccup in the womb). Try extra burping or a sip of warm water. If hiccups go on and on, ask the doctor.

Spitting up and vomiting. When a small amount of curdled milk spills gently out of the baby's mouth, that's spitting up. When the stomach contents are ejected with enough force to propel them several inches, that's vomiting. In general, spitting up and vomiting are not serious, as long as a baby is gaining weight well, isn't bothered by coughing or gagging, and is happy. When in doubt, check with the doctor.

Babies spit up because the muscle that closes off the entrance to the stomach hasn't fully developed. Anything that increases stomach pressure—squeezing too tightly, laying the baby down, or just the digestive motions of the stomach itself—causes stomach contents to flow in the wrong direction. Babies who overfill their stomachs spit up to feel better. Extra burping can sometimes help.

Most babies do a lot of spitting up during the early months. Some spit up several times after every feeding. Milk sometimes comes out of their noses, because the nose and the mouth are connected in back. (Milk stains come out of sheets and clothing more easily if they are first soaked in cold water.) Spitting up usually slows down after babies can sit up, although sometimes not until they're walking. Teething may make it worse for a while.

Vomiting tends to alarm parents, but a baby who is otherwise thriving who vomits now and then is probably fine. If a baby vomits what seems like a whole feeding and seems happy enough, don't feed her until she acts very hungry. The stomach may be a little upset, and it is better to give it a chance to quiet down. Remember that the amount vomited usually looks larger than it actually is. There are babies who you would swear are vomiting most of every feeding but who still go on gaining weight satisfactorily. It doesn't matter if the spit-up is sour or curdled. Normal stomach acid curdles milk.

Formula-fed babies sometimes do better with a change in formula (see page 88), but in most cases spitting up or vomiting goes right on, no matter how you change the feedings. When should you call the doctor?

- ✦ Spitting up along with irritability, crying, gagging, arching of the back, coughing, or poor weight gain. These can be signs of gastroesophageal reflux (GERD, page 506).

- ✦ New onset of vomiting (more than one or two episodes), especially if it is forceful or if what comes up looks yellowish or greenish, or very dark.

- ✦ Vomiting along with fever or a change in activity (sleepier, less playful, irritable), or other signs of illness.

- ✦ Vomiting or spitting up that is concerning to you for

any reason. Even if it turns out to be plain old spitting up, it's never wrong to seek reassurance from your baby's doctor.

Constipation. Constipation refers to hard, dry stools that are difficult to pass. It's not the number of BMs each day that determines whether or not a baby has constipation. Passing hard stools can cause small streaks of red blood on the stool; it's usually not serious, but ask the doctor.

Constipation sometimes starts when a breastfed baby starts solid foods. It's as though his intestine has had such an easy time with the breast milk, it doesn't know what to do with different foods. The baby develops firm, infrequent stools and seems uncomfortable.

You can offer a little sugar water (one teaspoon of granulated sugar to two ounces of water); prune, apple, or pear juice (start with two ounces; ask the doctor before giving more than four ounces); or stewed prunes (start with two teaspoons a day). Some babies get cramps from prunes, but most don't. For formula-fed babies, four ounces a day of water or prune juice often loosens things up.

If these cures don't work, or if constipation is severe, it's important to ask the doctor. Some parents feel that the iron in infant formula causes constipation (I don't think it really does). But in any case, iron is critical for brain growth, so low-iron formula is not a good solution.

Diarrhea. A baby's intestines are sensitive during the first year or two. A viral infection, a new food or medicine, or too much fruit juice can result in a couple of extra stools that are looser than usual, greenish, and unusually smelly. The baby may have a mild decrease in appetite or a stuffy nose. As long as she's playful and active and making normal amounts of urine, things usually get better in a couple of days without any special treatment. A baby's BMs can take on various colors, which usually mean nothing serious (see page 60).

Treatment for diarrhea is better and simpler than it was a few years ago. We used to stop breast milk, formula, and food, and gave babies a "clear diet" of apple juice, flat soda, or Jell-O water. But this strategy actually makes diarrhea worse. Instead, feed your baby normally (except for any new food you think is upsetting her stomach) and let her eat as much as she wants. If the diarrhea lasts more than two or three days consult the doctor, even if your baby continues to act healthy.

Rashes in general. It's always good to show a new rash to the doctor. Rashes can be hard to describe in words, and some innocent-looking rashes are signs of illnesses that need prompt medical attention.

Common diaper rash. The diaper area stays moist, even with the most absorbent diapers. That's why the best treatment for almost any diaper rash is to let the baby go diaperless for a few hours a day. A good time is right after a bowel movement, or during "tummy time." Fold a cloth diaper underneath your baby or put him on a towel (boys are apt to spray, so keep some paper towels handy). Almost all babies develop a few spots of diaper rash from time to time. If it is slight and goes away as fast as it came, no special treatment is necessary except air drying.

Don't wash the diaper area with soap while there is a rash, because soap can be irritating. Use plain water instead of dia-

per wipes. You can give the skin a protective coating by slath-
ering on petroleum jelly or any of the diaper ointments. Some
diaper services use special rinses in the case of diaper rash. If
you wash the diapers at home, try adding half a cup of white
vinegar to the last rinse.

A diaper rash caused by yeast (also called candida) will
have bright red spots or an area that is solidly red, bordered by
the red spots. The treatment is a prescription antifungal
cream. A rash with blisters or pus (especially with fever, but
even without) is likely to be caused by bacteria and should be
seen by a doctor.

Rash from diarrhea. Diarrhea can cause a very sore rash
around the anus, or a smooth, bright red rash on the buttocks.
The treatment is to try to change the diaper just as soon as it is
soiled—which is no small task. Then clean the area very gently
or rinse it with lukewarm water, pat dry with a soft towel, and
apply a thick covering of a protective ointment (one brand is as
good as another). If this doesn't work, leave diaper off and the
bottom exposed to the air. As long as the diarrhea is flowing,
nothing you do may help much. Once the diarrhea is over,
the rash will cure itself.

Rashes on the face. Milia are shiny white pimples without
any redness around them. They look like tiny pearls in the
skin. They develop when glands in the skin make oil, but the
glands haven't opened up yet, so the oil packets just sit there.
Over the next weeks or months, the oil ducts open and let the
oil out.

Some babies have a few smooth pimples on the cheeks
and forehead. They look like acne, and that's exactly what

they are. These may last a long time, or they may fade and then get red again. Different ointments don't seem to do much good, but these spots always go away eventually.

Another common rash goes by the frightening name *erythema toxicum*, although it is quite safe. It looks like splotchy red patches that are one-quarter to one-half inch in diameter, some with a tiny white pimple head; in darker-skinned infants, the splotches can be purplish in color. They come and go on different parts of the face and body. Eventually, they go and stay gone. Larger, pus-filled blisters or pimples could be infections and should be reported promptly to the doctor.

An irritated rash with scaling and flaking on the cheeks may be eczema; it often runs in families, and is worse in winter. Babies develop other minor skin changes too, which don't have names, and usually mean nothing. When in doubt, ask the doctor.

Rashes on body and scalp. *Prickly heat* is common in hot weather. It looks like clusters of very small pink pimples surrounded by blotches that are pink in light-skinned babies and may be dark red or purplish in dark-skinned ones. Tiny blisters form on some of the pimples. When they dry up they can give the rash a slightly tan look. Prickly heat usually starts around the neck; it may spread down onto the chest and back and up around the ears and face, but it seldom bothers a baby. You can pat this rash several times a day with a mixture of one teaspoon bicarbonate of soda in one cup water. Another treatment is dusting with cornstarch powder. Don't use talcum powder, which can irritate the lungs. Most prickly heat goes away on its own. It is more important to try to keep the baby cool. Don't be afraid to take off the baby's clothes in hot weather.

Cradle cap (seborrhea) appears as greasy yellow patches or reddish crusts on the scalp and face, in the diaper area, and elsewhere. Try oiling the patches to soften them and then wash with a mild dandruff shampoo and brush out the scales. Don't leave the oil on for too long. Medicated shampoos and prescription medication can also help. Cradle cap rarely persists beyond the first six months.

Impetigo is a bacterial infection of the skin. It's usually not serious, but it is contagious. It starts with a delicate blister that contains yellowish fluid or white pus and is surrounded by reddened skin. The blister breaks, leaving a small raw spot. It does not develop a thick crust in infants as it does in older children. Impetigo starts in a moist place, such as at the edge of the diaper or in the groin or armpit, and can spread. Over-the-counter antibacterial ointments and air drying help. Disinfect sheets, towels, clothing, and cloth diapers using ordinary bleach in the wash. If the problem doesn't clear up promptly, call the doctor. Prescription antibiotics may be needed.

Mouth troubles. *Thrush* is a common mild yeast infection. It looks like patches of milk scum stuck to the cheeks or tongue or roof of the mouth, but it doesn't wipe off easily. If you do rub it off, the underlying skin looks red and may bleed slightly. Thrush can make babies' mouths sore, and they may fuss when nursing. A prescription medication applied several times a day usually cures the problem, although it may come back later. If there is a delay in getting medical advice, it is helpful to have your baby drink half an ounce of water after nursing to wash the milk out of the mouth and give the thrush fewer nutrients to live on. Don't be fooled by the color of the inner sides of the gums where the upper molar teeth are going to be. The skin color here is normally very pale and is sometimes mistaken for thrush by parents who are on the lookout for it.

Cysts on the gums and the roof of the mouth. Some babies have one or two little pearly white cysts on the sharp edges of their gums. They may remind you of teeth, but they are too round and they don't make a click on a spoon. Similar cysts can often be seen on the roof of the mouth, along the ridge that runs from front to back. They have no importance and eventually disappear.

Eye troubles. Many babies develop a mild redness of the eyes a few days after birth. It usually clears up by itself.

Blocked tear duct. The tear duct is a tiny tube that carries tears from the inner corner of the eye into the nose. When this duct is blocked, tears can't drain off fast enough; they well up in the eye and run down the cheek. The lids keep getting mildly infected because the eye is not being cleansed well by the tears. The eye waters and tears excessively, particularly in windy weather. White crud collects in the corner of the eye and along the edges of the lids. This discharge may keep the lids stuck together when your baby first wakes up.

The usual treatment is gentle massage of the tear ducts to try to open them up; your doctor will show you how to do this. Antibiotic drops or ointments may be needed, too. When the lids are stuck together, you can soften the crust and open the eye by gently applying warm water (not hot—the eyelid skin is very sensitive to temperature) with your washed fingers or a clean washcloth.

Conjunctivitis. Yellow or white pus in an eye that looks pink or bloodshot or "beefy" under the lower lid could mean a more serious infection. Call the doctor promptly. Swelling of the eyelid or around the eye also calls for medical attention.

Crossed eyes. Sometimes parents think their baby's eyes are crossed when they are really straight: This illusion is caused by the base of the nose being wider in babies; a doctor will know what to look for. It's also not uncommon in a newborn baby for the lid of one eye to droop a little lower than the other, or for one eye to look smaller. In most cases, these differences become less and less noticeable with time.

One reason babies' eyes sometimes appear crossed is that when they are looking at something in their hands they have to converge (cross) the eyes a lot to focus on it, because their arms are so short. Their eyes won't get stuck that way. Parents often ask whether it is safe to hang toys over the crib, since the baby sometimes is cross-eyed looking at them. Don't hang a toy right on top of a baby's nose; hang it a foot away or more.

It's normal for a newborn's eyes to cross now and then. After three to four months, even fleeting crossed eyes should be reported to the doctor. At any age, eyes that stay crossed need a medical evaluation. This needs to happen promptly to preserve the child's vision. When the eyes point in different directions, the brain suppresses the vision of one of them, which becomes "lazy." Over time, the loss of vision in the lazy eye can become permanent.

The treatment is to put the lazy eye back to work, usually by wearing a patch over the non-lazy eye, or by wearing special glasses. Occasionally surgery is needed to get the eyes pointing in the same direction.

Breathing troubles. Babies sneeze easily. Sneezing gets rid of dust and dried mucus that collect in the nose; it doesn't mean a cold unless the nose begins to run, too.

Noisy breathing is common and usually unimportant; still, a baby with noisy breathing should be examined by a doctor. Many babies make a soft snoring noise in the back of the nose. It's just like a grown-up snoring, except that babies do it while they are awake; it goes away.

A common type of noisy breathing is caused by under-development of the cartilage around the voice box. As the baby inhales, the cartilage flops together and rattles, causing a noise called *stridor*. It sounds as if the baby is choking, but she isn't. If your baby has stridor, by all means talk with your doctor. The new onset of stridor always needs attention, because it can be due to something the baby choked on. Mild stridor goes away as the baby grows older.

Noisy breathing that comes on suddenly in an infant or child may be due to croup, asthma, or other infection, and requires prompt medical attention (see page 347).

Breath-holding spells. Some babies get so furiously angry when they are frustrated that they cry and then hold their breath and turn blue. When this first happens, it's bound to scare the wits out of you. But your baby won't die. In the worst-case scenario, a baby holds her breath for so long that she blacks out; at that point, the body assumes control and starts breathing again. Rarely, a baby not only blacks out but also makes seizure-like movements. This is terrifying to watch but not actually dangerous. A different sort of breath-holding spell occurs when a baby is startled or suddenly in pain, cries once, then passes out.

Talk with your doctor about any breath-holding episodes. Sometimes iron drops can help. Once you're reassured that there's nothing medically wrong, there isn't much else to do. You can try to divert your baby's attention when she starts to fuss, but this won't work all the time. Remember, breath-holding spells aren't truly dangerous and usually go away in a few years.

YOUR TODDLER: TWELVE TO TWENTY-FOUR MONTHS

WHAT MAKES THEM TICK?

Feeling their oats. One year is an exciting age. Babies are changing in lots of ways—in their eating, in how they get around, in how they understand the world, in what they want to do, and in how they feel about themselves and other people. When they were little and helpless, you could put them where you wanted them, give them the playthings you thought suitable, and feed them the foods you knew were best. Most of the time they were willing to let you be the boss. It's more complicated now. They're human beings with ideas and wills of their own.

By fifteen to eighteen months, your child's behavior makes it clear that she's heading for what is often called the "terrible twos." The term is slanderous, because two years is a marvelous age. When you suggest something that doesn't appeal to her, she feels she must assert herself. Her nature tells her to. It's the beginning of the process called individuation, when she begins to become a person in her own right. To become her own person she needs to push back against your control.

Toddlers say no in words or actions, even to things they like. Some call this negativism, but if babies never disagreed with their parents, they would never learn to think for themselves and make their own decisions.

Independence and outgoingness. A baby grows more independent and more dependent at the same time. This sounds contradictory, but that's how babies are. A parent complains about her eighteen-month-old, "He's begun to cry every time I go out of the room." This doesn't mean that he is developing a bad habit. Rather, he's growing up and realizing how much he depends on his parents. It's inconvenient, but a good sign. Yet at this very age he is also becoming more independent: He is developing the urge to be on his own, discover new places, and befriend unfamiliar people.

Watch a baby at the crawling stage when his parent is washing dishes. He plays contentedly with some pots and pans for a while. Then he gets a little bored and decides to explore in the dining room. He creeps around under the furniture there, picking up little pieces of dust and tasting them. After a while, he feels the need for company again and suddenly scrambles back into the kitchen. At one time you see his urge for independence getting the upper hand; at another, his need for security. He satisfies each in turn.

As the months go by, he becomes bolder and more daring. He still needs his parents, but not as often. He is building his independence, but part of his courage comes from knowing he can get security when he needs it.

Independence comes from security as well as from freedom. A few people get that twisted around backward. They try to train independence into children by leaving them in a room by themselves for long periods, even though they are crying for company. But when parents force the issue this hard, the child learns that the world is a mean place, which makes him even more dependent in the long run.

At around a year old, your baby is at a fork in the road. Given a chance, she will gradually become more independent: more sociable with outsiders (both grown-ups and children), more self-reliant, and more outgoing. Stranger anxiety, so intense at nine months, begins to wane. If she's kept away from others and used to having only her parents around, it may take longer for her to become sociable outside the home. The most important thing is for a toddler to have a strong attachment to consistent caregivers. With a solid foundation of emotional security, outgoingness will eventually come.

HELP YOUR TODDLER EXPLORE SAFELY

The passion to explore. Toddlers are determined explorers. They poke into every nook and cranny, shake a table or anything else that isn't nailed down, want to take every single book out of the bookcase, climb onto anything they can reach, fit little things into big things, and then try to fit big things into little things. In short, they are into everything.

Curiosity is a two-edged sword. On the one hand, it's the way your child learns. He has to find out about the size and shape and movableness of everything, and test his own skill before he can advance to the next stage. His endless exploration is a sign that he's bright in mind and spirit. On the other hand, this can be exhausting for you, requiring your constant attention to let him to explore but at the same time keep him safe.

Exploration and risk. Some children are content to sit quietly in a playpen, but others need to move. Once your baby consistently demands to be let out, listen to her! Sooner or later she must be let out to roam around, if not at ten months, at least by fifteen months. And she's not going to be any more reasonable or easier to control then. At whatever age you give her the freedom of the house, you will have to make adjustments, so it's better to do it when she is ready.

Once she's walking well, it's time to let her out of her stroller, too. Never mind if she gets dirty; she should. Keeping an able-bodied walking baby tucked in her stroller may keep her out of trouble, but it also hinders her development and dampens her spirit.

Try going to parks or other places where you don't have to chase after her every minute and where she can get used to other children. If she picks up cigarette butts, you have to jump up, take them away, and show her something else that's fun. You can't let her eat handfuls of sand or earth, because it will irritate her intestines. If she puts everything in her mouth, try giving her a hard cracker or some clean object to chew on to keep her mouth busy.

You can't prevent every small injury. If you were careful enough or worried enough to succeed, you would only make your child timid and dependent. Every child needs to get some cuts and bruises as a natural part of their active, healthy play.

Safety at home. How do you keep a one-year-old baby from hurting herself? Arrange the rooms where she'll be so that she's allowed to play with most of the things she can reach. If there are plenty of things she *can* do, she's not going to bother so much about the things she can't do.

Practically speaking, this means taking breakables off low tables and shelves; taking valuable books off the lower shelves of the bookcases and putting old magazines there instead, or jamming the good books in tight so that your baby can't pull them out. In the kitchen, put the pots and pans and wooden spoons on the shelves near the floor and put the china and food out of reach. Put a lock on the cabinet under the sink where cleaning supplies are, and lock up all true poisons far from anywhere your baby can reach. Fill a lower bureau drawer with old clothes, toys, and other interesting objects and let the baby explore it, empty it, and fill it to her heart's content.

Setting limits. Even after you babyproof, there will always be a few things that your toddler will have to leave alone. After all, there have to be lamps on tables; she mustn't pull them off by their cords or push the tables over. She mustn't touch the hot stove, turn on the gas, or crawl out a window.

You can't stop a toddler just by saying no, at least not in the beginning. Even later it will depend on your tone of voice, how often you say it, and whether you really mean it. Saying no is not a method to rely on heavily until she has learned from experience what it means—and that you mean it. Don't say no in a challenging voice from across the room. This gives her a choice. She says to herself, "Shall I be a wimp and do as she says, or shall I be mature and grab this lamp cord?" Remember that her natural instinct is egging her on to try things and to balk at directions. Chances are she'll keep on approaching the lamp cord with an eye on you to see how angry you get. It's much wiser, the first few times she goes for the lamp, to go over promptly and whisk her to another part of the room. You can say no at the same time to begin teaching her what it means. Then quickly give her a magazine or an empty box, anything that is safe and interesting.

What if she goes back to the lamp a few minutes later? Remove her and distract her again, promptly, definitely, cheerfully. Say, "No, no," at the same time that you remove her. Sit down with her for a minute to show her what she can do with the new plaything. If necessary, put the lamp out of reach this time, or even take her out of the room. You are cheerfully but firmly showing her that you are absolutely sure in your own mind that the lamp is not the thing to play with. You are keeping away from choices, arguments, cross looks, and scoldings—which may not do the job and which are likely to make her irritable.

You might say, "But she won't learn unless I teach her it's

naughty." Oh yes she will. In fact, she can accept the lesson more easily if it's given in this matter-of-fact way. When you disapprovingly waggle a finger from across the room at babies who haven't yet learned that no really means no, your crossness rubs them the wrong way. It makes them want to take a chance on disobeying. And it's no better if you grab them, hold them face-to-face, and give them a talking-to. You're not giving them a chance to give in gracefully or forget. Their only choice is to surrender meekly or to defy you.

Take the example of a baby who is getting close to a hot stove. A parent doesn't sit still and say, "No-o-o," in a disapproving voice; he jumps up and gets the baby out of the way. This is the method that comes naturally if a parent is really trying to keep a child from doing something, and not just engaging in a battle of wills.

Harness or wrist lead? Many toddlers can follow the rule to stay nearby or hold a parent's hand in the supermarket or mall. Others, more active and adventurous, see something interesting and take off to investigate. The parents of such a young explorer either have to keep one eye on their child at all times, keep their child in the stroller or shopping cart, or keep their child tied to them in some way. A harness that buckles around the upper body or a wrist lead can be a practical solution. Will some people give you disapproving stares for leashing your child? Possibly. Should that worry you? No. Anything that helps your toddler to stay safe while out in the world and at the same time allows you to relax and enjoy your child is a good thing.

FEARS AT AROUND ONE YEAR

Fear of separation. Many healthy toddlers develop a fear of being separated from their parents. It's the same instinct that makes lambs follow their mothers around and bleat when apart. Separation anxiety kicks in as children develop the ability to wander away. Some bold, busy children show very little separation anxiety; others show a lot. This difference is more a reflection of inborn temperament than of parenting.

At around eighteen months or so, many children who have been happy explorers start acting clingy. They now can imagine being apart from their parents, and it's scary! This period of anxious clinging usually fades away sometime around age two or two and a half.

Frightening sounds and sights. Your toddler may become fascinated with one thing for several weeks on end—the telephone, for instance, or electric lights. Remember that he learns best by touching, smelling, and tasting things, and that as a little scientist, he needs to conduct his experiments over and over again. Toddlers also begin to develop fears of certain things: things that move suddenly or make noise, such as the opening of an umbrella, the sound of a vacuum cleaner, a siren, even rustling branches. We all fear what we don't understand. In the second year of life, that's a lot!

If the vacuum cleaner bothers him, tell him when you're about to turn it on, let him see how you do it, and allow him to push the switch a few times. If he's still scared, try not to use the vacuum for a while if he's nearby. Always be comforting and sympathetic. Don't try to convince him it's a ridiculous fear; his terror makes perfect sense to him at his level of understanding.

Fear of the bath. Between one and two years, your child may become frightened of the bath. She may fear slipping underwater, getting soap in her eyes, or even seeing and hearing the water go down the drain. How can you help her feel more comfortable while she cleans up?

Don't force her into the bathtub. You can try using a plastic dishpan, or just give sponge baths for a few months until her courage returns. Then start with just an inch of water and remove her before you let the water out. Let her play with putting small things into larger containers and large things into small containers, so that she can come to understand that she is too big to go down the drain. To avoid soap in the eyes, soap her face with a washcloth that is not too wet and rinse several times with a damp (not dripping) washcloth. Use baby shampoo that won't sting her eyes.

Leeriness around strangers. A toddler's nature tells him to be leery and suspicious of strangers until he has had a chance to look them over. But then he wants to get closer and eventually make friends—in one-year-old fashion, of course. He may just stand close and gaze, or solemnly hand something to the newcomer and then take it back, or bring everything movable in the room and pile it in the person's lap.

Savvy adults know to give a small child time to size them up. You may want to tell visitors in the beginning, "It makes him shy when you pay attention to him right away. If you ignore him for a while, he'll try to make friends sooner."

Give your toddler plenty of chances to get used to seeing strangers. Take him to the grocery store, and to places where other small children play (parks in summer; libraries in winter). He won't be very interested in actually playing with them, but at times he'll want to watch, getting ready for more cooperative play when the time comes, at between two and three.

CHALLENGING BEHAVIORS

Dawdling. The mother of an eighteen-month-old boy walks with him every day to the grocery store. But instead of walking right along he wanders across the sidewalk and climbs the front steps of every house they pass. The more she calls to him, the more he lingers. She is afraid he is developing a behavior problem.

This toddler doesn't have a behavior problem; he's just too young to keep the grocery store in mind. His natural instincts say to him, "Look at that sidewalk to explore! Look at those stairs!" Every time his mother calls to him, it reminds him of his newly felt urge to assert himself.

What can the mother do? If she has to get to the store promptly, she can take him in his stroller. But if she's going to use this time for his outing, she should allow plenty of extra time and let him make his side trips. If she keeps moving slowly, he'll want to catch up to her every once in a while.

Trouble stopping fun activities. It's time to go in for lunch, but your small daughter is digging happily in the dirt. If you say, "Now it's time to go in," in a tone of voice that means, "Now you can't have any more fun," you will get resistance. But if you say cheerfully, "Let's go climb the stairs," you may give her a desire to go.

But suppose she's tired and cranky that day, and nothing

indoors has any appeal. Just pick her up casually and carry her indoors, even if she's squealing and kicking. Do this in a self-confident way, as if you were saying to her, "I know you're tired and cross, but when we have to go in, we have to." Scolding her won't make her see the error of her ways. Arguing with her won't change her mind; you will only get yourself frustrated. A small child who is feeling miserable and making a scene is comforted underneath by sensing that the parent knows what to do without getting angry.

Young children are very distractible, and that's a big help. They are so eager to find out about the whole world that they don't much care where they begin or where they stop. If they're absorbed in a ring of keys, you can make them drop it by giving them an empty plastic cup. If your baby fights against having the food washed off his face and hands with a cloth after meals, set a pan of water on the tray and let him dabble his hands while you wash his face with your wet hand. Distractibility is one of the handles by which wise parents guide their children.

Dropping and throwing things. At around the age of one year, babies learn to drop things on purpose. They solemnly lean over the side of the high chair and drop food on the floor, or toss toys, one after the other, out of the crib. Then they cry because they haven't got them. Are they deliberately trying to annoy their parents? No. They aren't even thinking about their parents. They are fascinated by a new skill and want to practice it all day long, the way an older child wants to ride a new two-wheeler. If you pick up the dropped object, they realize it's a game that two can play and are even more delighted.

Unless you want to play this game *a lot,* it's better not to get in the habit of picking up dropped toys right away. Instead, simply put your baby on the floor when he gets in this dropping mood. If you don't want him throwing food off the high chair, take the food away when he starts dropping, and put him down to play. You can say, "Food is for eating, toys are for playing," but there's no need to raise your voice. Trying to scold a baby out of dropping things doesn't help.

Temper tantrums. Between one and three years, nearly all children have temper tantrums; some children start as early as nine months. They've gotten a sense of what they want, and when they can't have it they feel angry. Children need to experience frustration in order to learn how to cope with it. You don't have to solve every problem for your child, but do step in if you sense that he's becoming overwhelmed. See page 141 for more on tantrums in two- and three-year-olds, and a longer discussion of tantrums on page 717.

SLEEP ISSUES

Shifting naps. Nap times tend to shift around age one. One baby whose nap was at 9 a.m. wants it later and later, then is wide-awake at bedtime. Another refuses the morning nap altogether and is exhausted and cranky by 4:00 p.m. The schedule may change from day to day. You have to put up with these inconveniences as best you can, realizing that they are temporary.

With some babies you can give them some quiet time in their cribs around 9 a.m. even if they don't fall asleep. Of course, another kind of baby only gets furious if put to bed when she's not sleepy, and nothing good is accomplished.

If a baby becomes sleepy just before noon, try moving lunch up to 11:30 or even 11:00 for a few days. Then the long nap will come after lunch. But for a while, after cutting down to one nap a day, whether morning or afternoon, the baby may get frantically tired before suppertime.

Not all babies give up their morning nap in the same way. One is through with it at nine months; another needs it as late as two years. Often, two naps are too many and one is not enough. You can help babies through this period by giving them supper and putting them to bed for the night a little earlier for the time being.

Bedtime routines. While you need to be a little flexible around sleep issues, it's also very helpful to have a bedtime routine. When things happen in the same way every day, it gives a young child a comforting sense of control. Bedtime routines can include stories, songs, prayers, hugs, and kisses. What's important is that the same things happen in roughly the same order. Television, videos, and other electronics tend to keep children awake, as does roughhouse play. These activities are best left out of the bedtime routine.

Keep bedtime agreeable and happy. Remember that it is delicious and inviting to the tired child, if you don't turn it into an unpleasant duty. Have an air of cheerful certainty about it.

EATING AND NUTRITION

Changes at around one year. After the first birthday, growth normally slows down and with it the toddler's appetite. Some actually eat *less* than they did a few months before. But if your child's growth plots out well on the standard growth curve at the doctor's office, you can be assured that he is getting enough. If you make the mistake of showing your toddler that you want him to eat more, he may eat less just to show you who's in charge. A better strategy is to give your toddler small helpings, so he can enjoy demanding more. Don't worry about how much goes in. Instead, make sure that your child is happy and full of energy, and pay attention to the growth chart, as the doctor will.

Early in the second year, many parents wean their babies from the breast or the bottle. Unless you are giving your toddler a nondairy diet, the drink of choice should be whole cow's milk. Toddlers need the high fat content of whole milk (or full-fat soy or almond milk) to build their brains. Wait till after age two to switch to low-fat milk to prevent adult heart disease.

Eating is a learning experience. For children to approach eating in a reasonable and healthy manner, they need to learn to pay attention to the body signals that tell them when they are hungry and when they've had enough. They need confidence that food will be there when they're hungry, and that when they're not hungry they won't be forced to eat. To help your toddler learn these important lessons, make good food available but leave it up to your child to decide how much to eat.

Table manners are also important. Every toddler experiments with mixing and smearing food, and tests the limits of what is acceptable. When your toddler crosses the line— throwing mashed potatoes, for instance—all you need to do is tell her firmly but calmly that food is for eating. Then move her from the table and help her find a ball or a cloth toy to throw. When eating turns to playing and it's clear your child isn't hungry anymore, then it's time for the meal to end. Twenty minutes or so is usually long enough.

Meals are also important times for socializing. Talk with your toddler, even if she can't talk back and probably doesn't understand much; she will in time. Talk about what you're both doing and feeling in the moment; that's what makes most sense to a young child.

TOILET TRAINING AND LEARNING

Readiness to train. Before about eighteen months, most toddlers aren't ready for toilet training. They don't seem to notice when they have to go, and don't understand why they should sit on the potty instead of just filling up their diapers. Toddlers find their bodily productions interesting, not disgusting. They don't see what all the fuss is about if the contents of their diaper get smeared around a bit.

Of course, there are some toddlers who train early and make all the *other* parents think their children are slow. But for most children, training before age eighteen months is bound to be difficult and unsatisfying. By two to two and a half, most children can master the potty without a fuss. If you do start earlier and things don't go well, you haven't caused any long-term psychological damage, assuming you didn't use harsh punishment or abuse.

There is a fast approach described in the book *Toilet Training in Less Than a Day*. But the instructions are fairly complicated and if you don't follow them to the letter—or if your child doesn't cooperate—you may both end up frustrated.

Toilet learning. While most one-year-olds aren't ready for *training,* they can certainly *learn* about the potty. If you let your child into the bathroom with you and there happens to be a child-size potty there, your toddler might sit on it or even pretend to use it, just as she mimics vacuuming and other adult activities. This early interest doesn't necessarily mean she's ready to take the next step. If you pressure her or overdo the praise, there's a good chance she'll balk.

Part of using the toilet is handwashing afterward, and many toddlers are happy to have an excuse to get their hands wet and soapy. It's helpful if you talk about what you're doing as you do it, so your child learns the words. I favor simple, factual terms like "pee" and "poop" rather than cutesy baby talk or euphemisms ("wee-wee" or "number two," for example). By talking in a straightforward way, you let your child know that toileting is simply a fact of life—not something secret, shameful, or mysterious.

YOUR TWO-YEAR-OLD

BEING TWO

A tumultuous time. Some refer to this period as the "terrible twos," but it's really terrific. Your child is beginning to come into her own and learning what it's like to be an independent person. Her language skills and imagination are increasing at a breathtaking pace. But her understanding of the world is still so limited that many things can seem scary.

Two-year-olds live in contradictions. They are both independent and dependent, loving and hateful, generous and selfish, mature and infantile. They stand with one foot in the warm, cozy past and the other in an exciting future full of autonomy and discovery. With so much going on, it's no wonder that two is a challenging age for parents and children alike. But terrible it isn't. It's really pretty amazing.

Two-year-olds learn by imitation. In a doctor's office, a two-year-old girl solemnly places the stethoscope bell on different spots on her chest. Then she pokes the otoscope in her ear and looks a little puzzled because she can't see anything. At home she follows her parents around, sweeping with a broom when they sweep and brushing her teeth when they do. It's all done with great seriousness. She is making giant strides forward in skill and understanding by means of constant imitation.

Imitation is a powerful teacher. For example, when you treat others politely, your two-year-old learns to be polite. It's okay to tell a two-year-old to say "please" and "thank you," but it's much more effective to let him hear *you* use those words in appropriate circumstances. (Don't expect to see politeness until about four or five, however.) If your child sees you constantly checking your cell phone, she'll demand access to the phone as well, and giving it to her is a bad idea, as I argue below. Young children who see parents using hurtful language or threats often develop similar problem behaviors. That doesn't mean that parents can't ever argue or disagree. But a steady diet of angry conflict is harmful to children, even if they are just bystanders.

Communication and imagination. One two-year-old makes sentences of three and four words, while another is just beginning to link two words together. A two-year-old who only says a few isolated words should have a hearing test and developmental evaluation, even though chances are good he'll simply be a late talker.

Imagination and language grow together. What starts out as simple imitation at two becomes rich make-believe play by three. To spark your child's imagination and learning, expose her to a rich mix of experiences. Let her play with blocks, dolls, musical instruments, old shoes, cookie dough, water for splashing and pouring. Play along yourself at times. Let her explore the natural world, even if it's just the neighborhood park or cracks in the sidewalk. Look at picture books together, and give your child paper and crayons. Scribbling is the first step on the way to writing.

Beware, though, of electronics. The flashing lights mesmerize young children, but that's where the learning stops. Lots of apps promise to promote child development, but the promises are empty. Two-year-olds learn language from human conversation, not just from clicking on screens; they need to use all their senses, not just sight and sound. When they play, children exert effort to focus and maintain their attention. Electronics, with their bells and bright lights, do this work for them, depriving the children of opportunities to learn. For two-year-olds, even the best apps actually impair development (see page 651).

Parallel play and sharing. Two-year-olds don't play cooperatively with each other very much. Mostly they enjoy playing *near* each other (parallel play). There is no point in trying to teach a two-year-old to share; he simply isn't ready. In order to share, a child first has to understand that something *belongs* to him—that he can give it away and expect to get it back. Refusing to share at age two says nothing about how generous a person will become when he is older.

Still, a two-year-old can begin to learn play skills. When your child grabs a toy from his companion, you can firmly but cheerfully take the toy away from him, return it to its rightful owner, and quickly try to distract him with another object of interest. Long harangues about why he should share things are wasted breath. He will start to share when he understands the concept of sharing, usually around three or four, and not before.

WORRIES AT AROUND TWO

Separation fears. By age two, some children have gotten over their toddler clinginess, but others haven't yet. A mother complains, "My two-year-old seems to be turning into a mama's girl. She hangs on to my skirt when we're out of the house. When someone speaks to us, she hides behind me." Two is a great age for whining, which can be a kind of clinging.

Here's what can happen when a sensitive, dependent child of two years, particularly an only child, is separated abruptly from the parent who has spent the most time with him. Perhaps his mother has to go out of town unexpectedly for a couple of weeks, or she has to go to work outside the home and arranges for a stranger to come in and take care of him during the day. He may not make a fuss while his mother is away, but when she returns, he sticks to her like Velcro. He becomes panicky whenever he thinks his mother may be leaving again. Other changes—a family member moving away, or a move to a new house, for instance—may also trigger clinging and whining. It's wise to take his sensitivity into account when changes in the household are being considered.

A child who is frightened by separation—or anything else—is very sensitive to whether her parents feel the same way about it. If they act hesitant or guilty every time they leave her side, if they hurry into her room at night when she cries, their anxiety reinforces her fear that there really is great danger in being apart from them.

Bedtime separations: Separation anxiety is worst at bedtime. The terrified child fights against being put to bed. If his mother tears herself away, he may cry in fear for hours. If she sits by his crib, he lies down only as long as she sits still. Her slightest move toward the door brings him instantly to his feet.

If your two-year-old child has become terrified about going to bed, the soundest advice, but the hardest to carry out, is to sit by her crib in a relaxed way until she goes to sleep. Don't be in a hurry to sneak away; that will alarm her again and make her more wakeful. This campaign may take weeks, but it should work in the end. If your child was frightened because one of you left town, try to avoid going away again for many weeks.

Give her this special care the way you'd give special consideration to a sick child. Look for signs of your child's readiness to give up her dependence, step by step, and encourage her and compliment her. Your attitude is the most powerful factor in getting her over her fear—that and the maturational forces that, with time, will allow the child to better understand and master her fears.

Making the child more tired by keeping her up later or omitting her nap may help a little but usually won't do the whole job. A panicky child can keep herself awake for hours even though she's exhausted. You need to take away her worry.

Concern about wetting the bed. Bedtime worries sometimes circle around peeing. The child keeps saying "go pee"—or whatever word he uses. His mother takes him to the bathroom, he does a few drops, and then he cries "go pee" again just as soon as he is back in bed. You might say that he uses this as an excuse to keep her there. This is true, but there is more to it. Children like this one are really worried that they might wet the bed.

They sometimes wake every two hours during the night

thinking about it. This is the age when the parents are apt to be showing disapproval when there is an accident. Maybe the child figures that if he wets, his parents won't love him so much and will therefore be more likely to go away. If so, he has two reasons to fear going to sleep.

If your child is worried about wetting, keep reassuring her that it doesn't matter if she needs a change of sheets—that you'll love her just the same.

Children may use separation anxiety to control. A child clings to his mother because he has developed a genuine fear separation. But if he finds that she is ready to do anything he wants in order to reassure him, he may begin to use his anxiety as coercion. There are three-year-olds, for instance, who are anxious about being left at preschool and whose parents not only stay at school for days but stay close to the children and do whatever they ask. After a while, you can see that such children are exaggerating their uneasiness in order to boss their parents around. A parent can say, "I think you are grown-up now and aren't afraid to be in school. You just like to make me do what you want. Tomorrow I won't need to stay here anymore."

How to help a fearful two-year-old. When it comes to the management of children's fear, a lot depends on how important it is for them to get over it in a hurry. There's no great need for children to be hurried into making friends with dogs or going into deep water in the pool. They'll want to do these things as soon as they dare.

On the other hand, children should not be allowed to come into the parents' bed every single night (unless you've decided that co-sleeping is for you). They should be comforted and soothed in their own beds so that sleeping with the parents doesn't become a habit.

Once children have started preschool, it's better for them to go regularly unless they're deeply terrified. A skillful teacher can help a child become engaged in play to make the separation easier. A child with a school-refusal problem must get back to school sooner or later; the longer it is put off, the harder it becomes to get back.

Overprotectiveness. Sometimes a child's separation fears reflect a parent's overprotective feelings. There may have been an incident, long ago, when the child truly was in danger: a serious infection, or an injury. The dread that something horrible could occur is hard for many parents to shake. TV news also exploits fear to boost ratings. In fact, statistics show children are actually *safer* in many ways now than at any time in the recent past, but you'd never guess this looking at the news.

Sometimes overprotection is fed by unexpressed anger. It's normal for parents to feel anger toward their children, even to wish at times that they'd never been born. These thoughts make some parents feel so guilty that they suppress them and instead exaggerate dangers in the world outside, such as kidnappers. If this description might fit you, consider a short course of psychotherapy. Once you make peace with your normal anger, the sense of extreme danger from outside may also recede.

If your angry feelings have led you to act toward your child in ways you wish you hadn't—for instance, yelling when it really wasn't necessary—then it's helpful to talk with your child about how you were feeling. Talking about angry feelings helps a child understand and take control of his own emotions. Use simple words. You might say, "I know how angry you feel toward me when I have to say no to you. Sometimes I feel angry, too."

CHALLENGING BEHAVIORS

Negativism. One-year-old Jenny contradicts her parents. Two-and-a-half-year-old Jenny even contradicts herself. She has a hard time making up her mind, and then she wants to change it. She acts like a person who feels she is being bossed too much, even when no one is bothering her and even when she tries to boss others. She insists on doing things just so. It makes her furious to have anyone interfere in one of her jobs or rearrange her possessions.

The child's nature urges her to decide things for herself and resist pressure from other people. Trying to fight this battle without much worldly experience seems to get her tightened up inside.

You can help by letting your child work at his own pace when possible. Let him dress and undress himself (with just a little help from you) when he has the urge. Start his bath early enough that he has time to dawdle. At meals, let him feed himself without urging. When he is stalled in his eating, let him leave the table. When it's time for bed, going outdoors, or coming in, steer him while talking about pleasant things. Get things done without raising issues. Your goal is not to let him be a little tyrant, but not to sweat the small stuff either.

Two-year-olds behave best when parents set firm, consistent, and reasonable limits. The key is to choose those limits carefully. If you find yourself saying no a lot more than yes, you're probably setting too many. A battle of wills with a two-year-old is tiring, so save the battles for issues that are truly important. Safety issues, such as sitting in the car seat, are clearly important. Wearing mittens on a cold day may not be so very important. After all, you can always stuff the mittens in your coat pocket and pull them out when your two-year-old's hands get cold.

Temper tantrums. All two-year-olds have tantrums now and then, and some healthy children have many. There are many causes: frustration, fatigue, hunger, and overstimulation (you see these tantrums all the time in busy stores). Savvy parents address the underlying problem: "You're tired and hungry, aren't you? Let's get you home and fed and to bed, and you'll feel a lot better." Fear can also cause tantrums. This happens regularly at the doctor's office. The best thing to do in these situations is to be calm and reassuring. No good comes from scolding a scared child.

Children who show their emotions intensely have more tantrums (and also more outbursts of joyful laughing). Children who are less flexible and more sensitive to changes also have more tantrums. They tend to last longer in children who are more persistent. Once these children get started doing anything it's hard for them to stop, whether they're playing, practicing walking, or screaming at the top of their lungs.

During a tantrum, it's helpful to stay nearby or hold your child on your lap so that he doesn't feel alone. Afterward, it's best to move on to a positive activity and put the upset in the past. A hug and kiss and a quick word of praise along the lines of "Nice job pulling yourself together" can let your child salvage some self-esteem and learn to recover faster the next time. Remember to praise yourself, too, for staying calm and rational—not easily done when your two-year-old is having a meltdown. For a lot more on tantrums, see page 717.

Whining. It's normal for young children to whine (puppies whine, too), but it's still annoying. With an infant you have to guess what your child needs. Once your child can use words, however, it's best to insist that she do that. A firm, unemotional "Use your words; I don't listen to whining" is all it usually takes, although you may have to repeat this message many times before it sinks in fully. Be aware, though, that if you give in to whining now and then—and the temptation is strong— it can become much harder to put a stop to it.

Favoritism toward one parent. Sometimes a young child can get along with either parent alone but flies into a rage when the other parent comes onto the scene. It may be partly jealousy, but at an age when she's sensitive about being bossed around and trying to do a little bossing herself, a child might just feel outnumbered when she has to take on two important people at once.

It's more often the father who is particularly unpopular at this period; he sometimes gets the feeling he's pure poison. He shouldn't take the child's reaction too seriously or feel hurt. It will help if he regularly cares for her by himself, doing things that are fun as well as everyday things such as feeding and bathing. That way she gets to know him as an enjoyable, loving, and important person, not just an intruder. If a child objects at first when her father takes over, the father should cheerfully but firmly carry on, and the mother should have the same firm and cheerful attitude as she leaves.

Taking turns this way can give each parent one-on-one time with the child, and time alone as well. But there is also value in being all together, even if the two-year-old acts cranky. It's good for a child (particularly a first child) to learn that her parents love each other, want to be with each other, and will not be bullied by her.

DIET AND NUTRITION

Changes in the diet. A two-year-old can eat pretty much what the family does. You still need to be aware of choking hazards—small, hard foods such as peanuts, whole grapes, carrots, and hard candies—and keep these out of your child's diet. If you've been giving your toddler whole milk, you can switch to 1 percent or skim. Brain growth slows down after age two, so a high-fat diet isn't needed, and getting used to a lower-fat diet early in childhood lowers the risk of heart disease years later. Young children can't usually wait five or six hours between meals. Three meals and three snacks is a good schedule. The best snacks are simple foods such as cut-up fruit or whole-grain crackers, not highly processed items, whether or not they claim to be healthy.

Food choices. Most two-year-olds handle cups and spoons with ease but may still need help with forks and knives. Since many young children resent getting help, even if they need it, you may want to focus on foods that can be eaten with a spoon or just fingers. Young children need practice making food choices. Peas or squash? Peanut butter sandwich with jelly or without? A couple of small choices are enough; more and bigger choices can be overwhelming. If you offer a small selection of attractive foods at each meal, any choice your child makes is a healthy one.

Food choices start with what you bring home from the store. Choose fresh vegetables instead of chips and other high-fat snacks, fruits instead of cookies and cakes, and low-fat milk or water instead of soda. If you want your child to eat healthfully, it's best to keep the house stocked with healthful foods and keep the junk food out.

Food fads and fights. One two-year-old wants only grilled cheese at every meal; another demands noodle soup. Usually such fads last a few days, then fade away, only to be replaced by new ones. In the interest of peace and harmony, you may want to give in to some extent. Five days in a row of peanut butter and jelly for lunch isn't harmful, especially if there's milk, fruit, or some green vegetable at other meals. If you think about what your child eats not just in one day but over the course of a week, you might see that the diet is pretty balanced after all.

TOILET LEARNING

Letting it happen. Most children figure out the toilet between age two and three. In their hurry to be done with diapers, parents often push, prod, or pester, but this usually just makes the process longer and more stressful. Toilet learning begins in the first year and ends several years later with a child who feels comfortable dealing with her bodily processes, knows how to wipe and wash up, and has adopted her parents' views about privacy and modesty. If you take this long view, you might feel more comfortable allowing toilet training to move forward at its own pace. See page 749 for specific techniques.

YOUR PRESCHOOLER: THREE TO FIVE YEARS

DEVOTION TO THE PARENTS

A less rebellious age. Around three, many children reach a stage in their emotional development when they feel that their fathers and mothers are wonderful people, and they want to be like them. The automatic resistance and hostility of the two-year-old often lessen after three.

The feelings toward the parents aren't just friendly now; they are warm and tender. However, children are not so devoted to their parents that they always obey them and behave well. They are still real people with ideas of their own. They want to assert themselves, even if it means going against their parents' wishes at times.

While most children between three and five are delightful, four-year-olds can be the exception. A lot of assertiveness, cockiness, loud talk, and provoking behaviors often appear around four, as children realize that they know everything; mercifully, this realization soon fades.

Striving to be like the parents. At two years of age children eagerly imitate their parents' activities. By three, the quality of their imitation changes. Now they want to be totally like their parents as people. They play at going to work, doing housework, and caring for children (using a doll or a younger child). They pretend to go for a drive in the family car. They dress up in their parents' clothes and mimic their conversation, their manners, and their mannerisms.

All of this playing has a serious purpose; it's how a child develops his or her character. This process depends more on what children observe about their parents than on what the parents try to teach using words. Basic attitudes toward work, people, and themselves all get their start this way. This is when children learn to be the kind of parents they're going to turn out to be twenty years later. You can hear their future parent voices if you listen to the affectionate or scolding way they talk to their dolls.

Gender awareness. It's at this age that a girl becomes more aware of the fact that she's female and will grow up to be a woman. She watches her mother with special attentiveness and tends to mold herself in her mother's image. The little girl is not about to become an exact replica of her mother, but she will surely be influenced by her in many ways. A boy realizes that he is on the way to becoming a man and attempts to pattern himself mainly after his father.

Of course, girls also learn a great deal from observing their fathers, and boys from their mothers. This is how the two sexes come to understand each other well enough to be able to live together. And children partly model themselves after other important grown-ups in their lives as well. But in the very early years, parents (especially parents who are the child's same sex) play a special role.

Psychological gender—the gender a child feels itself to be—usually corresponds to bodily gender, but not always.

The reasons for discordance are not well understood, but parenting seems to have little to do with it. Thankfully, we are getting better at helping children who are genderqueer, or nonbinary, to lead full and happy lives (see page 645).

Fascination with babies. Boys and girls now become fascinated with all aspects of babies. When they find out that babies grow inside their mothers, both boys and girls are eager to carry out this amazing feat themselves. They want to take care of babies and love them, the way they were cared for and loved. They will press a younger child into the role of a baby and spend hours acting as father and mother to him, or they'll use a doll.

It's not generally recognized that little boys are as eager as girls to grow babies inside themselves. When their parents tell them that this is impossible, they are apt to refuse to believe it for a long time. "I will too grow a baby," they insist, really believing that if they wish hard enough for something, they can make it happen. In a similar way, a preschool girl might announce that she is going to grow a penis. Ideas of this kind are not necessarily signs of dissatisfaction with being one sex or another. Instead, they come from the young child's belief that he or she can do everything, be everything, and have everything.

ROMANTIC AND COMPETITIVE FEELINGS

Wishes and worries. Up to this age, a boy's love for his mother has been predominantly of a dependent kind, like that of a baby. But now it also becomes increasingly romantic. These feelings aren't sexual, of course, in the same way an adolescent

or adult feels a hormone-driven attraction, but they are possessive. By the time he's four, he's apt to insist that he's going to
marry his mother when he grows up. He isn't clear on just what
marriage consists of, but he's absolutely sure who is the most
important and appealing woman in the world. The little girl
who is growing in her mother's pattern often develops the same
kind of love for her father.

These romantic urges help children to grow spiritually;
they form the deep roots of the feelings that will later bear
fruit in strong adult relationships. But there is another side to
the picture that creates unconscious tension in most children
at this age. As a little boy becomes more aware of his possessive devotion to his mother, he also becomes aware of how
much she already belongs to his father. This irritates him, no
matter how much he loves and admires his father. At times he
secretly wishes his father would get lost, and then he feels
guilty about having such disloyal feelings. Reasoning as a
child does, he imagines that his father has the same jealous
and resentful feelings toward him.

The little girl develops a similar possessive love for her father. She wishes at times that something would happen to her
mother (whom she loves so much in other respects) so that
she could have her father to herself. She may even say to her
mother, "You can go away for a long trip, and I'll take good
care of Daddy." But then she imagines that her mother is jealous of her, too—a frightening thought! If you think about
classic fairy tales like "Snow White," you can see these fantasies and worries brought to life in the figure of the wicked
stepmother.

Children try to push these scary thoughts out of their
minds, but they are apt to come to the surface in their

make-believe play. These mixed feelings toward the parent of the same sex—feelings of love, jealousy, and fear—also come out in the bad dreams that little children are so apt to have. Dreams of being chased by monsters, robbers, and other frightening figures often draw their power from angry or jealous feelings that are a part of the normal struggles at this age.

Moving past possessiveness. What happens to all of these powerful, conflicting feelings? When things work as they should, by age six or seven children become quite discouraged about the possibility of having a parent all to themselves. The unconscious fears about the parent's supposed anger turn their pleasure in dreaming about romance into an aversion. Now they shy away from kisses from the parent of the opposite sex. Their interests turn with relief to impersonal matters such as schoolwork and sports. More and more they try to model themselves after other children of their own sex, and after adults other than their parents.

Parents can help by gently keeping it clear that they do belong to each other. When a girl declares that she is going to marry her father, he can act pleased with the compliment, but also explain that he's already married and that when his daughter grows up she'll find a man her own age to marry.

When parents are being companionable together, they needn't and shouldn't let a child break up their conversation. They can cheerfully but firmly remind her that they have things to talk over, and they can suggest that she get busy, too. Their tactfulness will keep them from prolonged displays of affection in front of her, just as it would if other people were present, but they don't need to spring apart guiltily if she comes into the room unexpectedly when they're hugging or kissing.

When a boy is being rude to his father because he's feeling jealous, or to his mother because she's the cause of his jealousy, the parent should insist on politeness. The converse is equally true if a girl is being rude. But at the same time the parents can ease the child's feelings of anger and guilt by saying that they know the child is cross at them sometimes.

A father who realizes that his young son sometimes has feelings of resentment and fear toward him does not help the boy by trying to be too gentle and permissive. It's no help, either, for the father to try to avoid making his son jealous by pretending that he (the father) doesn't really love his wife very much. In fact, if a boy becomes convinced that his father is afraid to be a firm father and a normally possessive husband, the boy will sense that he is having his mother too much to himself and will feel really guilty and frightened. And he will miss the inspiration of a confident father, which he must have in order to develop his own self-assurance.

In the same way, a mother best helps her daughter to grow up by being a self-confident mother who doesn't let herself be pushed around, who knows how and when to be firm, and who isn't at all afraid to show her affection and devotion to her husband.

CURIOSITY AND IMAGINATION

Intense curiosity. At this age, children want to know about everything they encounter. They put two and two together and draw their own conclusions, which are often wrong. They connect everything with themselves. When they hear about trains, they want to know right away, "Will I go on a train someday?" When they hear about an illness, it makes them think, "Will I have that?"

A gift for imagination. Preschool children are virtuosos of imagination. When children of three or four tell a made-up story, they aren't lying in our grown-up sense. Their imagination is vivid to them. They're not sure where the real ends and the make-believe begins. That is why they love to hear stories, and why they are scared of violent TV programs and videos and shouldn't see them.

You don't need to scold your child or make him feel guilty for making up stories. You can simply point out that what he said isn't actually so, although he may *wish* it were so. In this way, you're helping your child learn the difference between reality and make-believe.

An imaginary friend who shows up now and then, perhaps to help with a particular adventure—daring to go into the basement alone, for example—is a sign of a normal, healthy imagination. But sometimes a child who feels lonely will spend hours each day telling about imaginary friends or adventures, not as a game but as if he believes in them. When you help such a child to make friends with real children, the need for fantasy playmates lessens.

SLEEP ISSUES

Most children give up their naps sometime before age four but may still need quiet time in the afternoon. If they sleep much less than ten hours a night, they're bound to be overtired, although some need as little as eight hours, and others need twelve or thirteen. Sleep problems that began earlier in life, such as excessive bedtime stalling or frequent waking, often continue through the preschool years, and new sleep problems may arise, even for children who have been good sleepers. Nightmares and night terrors are common (see page 773).

Sleep problems can develop out of the normal feelings of possessiveness and jealousy described above. The child wanders into the parents' room in the middle of the night and wants to get into their bed because (without putting these thoughts into words) he doesn't want them to be alone together. If he is allowed to stay, he might end up literally kicking his father out of the bed. It's much better for everyone if his parents firmly, but not angrily, take him back to his own bed.

FEARS AT AROUND THREE, FOUR, AND FIVE

Imaginary worries. New types of fear often crop up—fear of the dark, of dogs, of fire engines, of death, of crippled people. Children can now put themselves in other people's shoes and picture dangers that they haven't actually experienced. They want to know not only what causes everything but also what these things have to do with them. They overhear something about dying, and they want to know what dying is. As soon as they get a dim idea they ask, "Do I have to die?"

Some children are born with a tendency to respond to anything new or unexpected with anxiety or fear. Fears are also more common in children who have been made tense from battles over such matters as feeding and toilet training, in children whose imaginations have been overstimulated by scary stories or videos, in children who haven't had enough opportunity to develop their independence, or in children whose parents have overplayed warnings about the dangers "out there."

This is not to say that every child who develops a fear has been handled mistakenly in the past. The world is full of things young children do not understand, and no matter how lovingly they have been raised, they sense their own vulnerability.

Helping your child cope with fears. Your job as a parent is not to banish all fears from your child's imagination; it's to help your child learn how to cope with those fears. You can help your child deal with particular fears, whether about dogs or bugs or monsters, by lowering the level of tension in general. Avoid scary TV and violent video games. Call off any battle that you might be engaged in about eating or staying dry at night. Keep her behaving well by firm guidance rather than by letting her misbehave and then making her feel guilty about it afterward. Never threaten her with monsters or policemen or the devil; she is afraid enough of her own mental creations. Arrange to give her a full, outgoing life with other children. The more she is absorbed in games and plans, the less she will worry about her inner fears.

One of the most powerful ways a young child combats fear is through make-believe play. You might see her pretending to give her doll a shot or beating up a pretend monster. You'll know when she's conquered the fear, because her playing will shift to other topics. Sometimes a child will become stuck in a particular fear, and her playing about it only makes her more and more anxious. In these cases, guidance from a children's mental health professional can help. In the end, your child is the one who needs to overcome her fears; even so, your confidence that she'll be able to do it eventually is very important.

Fear of the dark. Reassuring your child is more about your manner than your words. Don't make fun of her or try to argue her out of her fear. If she wants to talk about it, as a few children do, let her. Give her the feeling that you want to understand but that you are absolutely certain that nothing bad will happen to her. Leave her door open at night if that is what she wants, or leave a dim light on in her room. It's a small price to pay to keep the goblins out of sight. The light, or the conversation from the living room, won't keep her awake so much as her fears will. When her fear subsides, she will be able to stand the dark again.

Fear of animals. Preschool children often develop a fear of certain animals, even if they have never had a bad experience with them. It doesn't help to drag a scared child toward a dog to prove that nothing bad happens. The more you pull, the more the child will feel he has to pull in the opposite direction. As the months go by, the child will try to get over his fear and approach a dog, and he'll do it faster by himself than you can ever persuade him to.

Fear of the water. It's almost always a mistake to force a child into the ocean or a pool. Yes, occasionally a child who is forced in finds that it is fun and loses the fear abruptly, but in more cases it works the opposite way. Remember that the child is longing to go in, despite the dread she feels.

Fear of talking. Young children are often quiet around strangers until they feel more comfortable. A child who talks normally at home but refuses to say a word at preschool, even after days or weeks, may have *selective mutism*. An experienced child psychologist can help.

Questions about death. Questions about death are apt to come up at this age (see page 698). Try to be matter-of-fact. You might say, "Everybody has to die someday. Most people die when they get very old and sick, and their body just stops working completely." Remember that behind your young child's question about death in general, there is almost always a very specific concern that *you*, Mom or Dad, could die. Since time flows differently for a child than for an adult, saying that you'll be alive for a long, long time may not give much reassurance; for a child, "a long time" could mean "until tomorrow." Instead, you can reassure your child that you will be very old and your child will be old and grown-up, with children of his own, and only then will it be time for you to die.

Choose your words carefully. For example, "We lost Uncle Archibald" can strike terror into the heart of any child who himself has gotten lost. This is the age when children take everything quite literally. One child I know became terrified of flying after hearing death spoken of as "going to our home in the sky." It's especially important not to refer to death as "going to sleep," because many children will become terrified of bedtime, or they'll wonder why somebody doesn't just wake Uncle Archibald up.

It's much better to explain as simply as possible—and without sugarcoating the facts—that death is what happens when the body stops working completely. Children who spend time in nature have a chance to see many examples of things that die; they can begin to understand death as part of the larger pattern of the world.

It's important, too, to convey your family's beliefs about death, religious or otherwise. With this and other sensitive topics, it's important to be open to questions and to answer them simply and truthfully, but don't give more information than your child is asking for. Children have a way of knowing when they have heard enough; it's best to honor that intuition. No important topic gets talked about all at once; there are always other opportunities.

WORRIES ABOUT INJURY AND BODY DIFFERENCES

Why these worries arise. Preschool children want to know the reason for everything. If they see a person in a wheelchair, they first want to know what happened to that person; then they put themselves in the person's place and wonder if the same thing might happen to them.

They have a great interest in what bodies can do, such as hop, run, and climb. So body intactness is important. This explains why a young child can get so upset about a broken cookie, refusing a cookie that's in two pieces and demanding a whole one.

Body differences. Some young children also worry about the differences between boys and girls. If a boy of around the age of three sees a girl undressed, it may strike him as odd that she doesn't have a penis like his. He's apt to say, "Where is her wee-wee?" If he doesn't receive a satisfactory answer right away, he may jump to the conclusion that some accident has happened to her. Next comes the anxious thought, "That might happen to me, too." The same misunderstanding may worry the little girl when she first realizes that boys are made differently. First she asks, "What's that?" Then she might want to know, "Why don't I have one? What happened to it?" That's the way a three-year-old's mind works. Children may be so upset that they're afraid to ask their parents.

This worry about why boys are different from girls shows up in different ways. Here are some examples: A boy of just under three, with an anxious expression, keeps watching his baby sister being bathed and telling his mother, "Baby is boo-boo," his word for "hurt"; at about the same time, he begins to hold on to his own penis in an anxious way. A little girl becomes worried after she finds out about boys, and keeps trying to undress different children to see how they are made. A boy of three and a half first becomes upset about his younger sister's body and then begins to worry about everything in the house that is broken, such as a broken toy. Everything that is damaged seems to remind him of his fears about himself.

It's wise to realize ahead of time that normal children this age are likely to wonder about things like bodily differences. It's no use waiting for them to say, "I want to know why a boy isn't made like a girl," because they won't be that specific. They may ask some kind of question, or they may hint around, or they may just wait and get worried. Don't think of this as an unwholesome interest in sex. To them it's just like any other important question at first. You can see why it would work the wrong way to shush them, scold them, or blush and refuse to answer. That would give them the idea they are on dangerous ground, which is not what you want to convey.

On the other hand, you don't need to be solemn, as if you were giving a lecture. It's easier than that. It helps, first of all, to bring the child's fear out into the open by saying that he probably thinks a girl had a penis but something happened to it. Then you try to make it clear, in a matter-of-fact, cheerful tone, that girls and women are made differently from boys and men; they are meant to be that way. A small child understands an idea more easily from examples. You can explain that Johnny is made just like Daddy, Uncle Fred, and Mr. Smith (listing all the individuals that the child knows best), and that Mary is made like Mommy, Aunt Helen, and Mrs. Jenkins.

A little girl needs extra reassurance, because it's natural for her to want to have something that she can see. (One little girl complained to her mother, "But he's so fancy and I'm so plain.") It will help her to know that her mother likes being made the way she is, and that her parents love her just the way she is. This may also be a good time to explain that girls when they are older can grow babies of their own inside them and have breasts with which to nurse them. That's a thrilling idea at three or four.

PRESCHOOL

Preschool is school. The term "preschool" means, literally, "before school." But preschool isn't something that occurs before school; it *is* school. The focus of preschool should be not on preparing a child to succeed at "real" school later but on her educational needs right now.

Good preschools expose young children to a range of experiences that nurture sensitivity, creativity, and competence. These include dancing and making rhythmic music, painting pictures, finger painting, clay modeling, building with blocks, vigorous outdoor play, and playing house, which is really playing family. Ideally, there are quiet corners for individual play and for those times when a child feels the need to rest.

Preschool tries to nurture a broad variety of capabilities— academic, social, artistic, musical, and muscular. The emphasis is on initiative, independence, cooperation (discussing and sharing play equipment instead of fighting over it), and incorporating the child's own ideas into play.

Preschool is different from child care. Of course, a lot of what goes on in a preschool classroom involves taking care of a child's physical and emotional needs, and a lot of what goes on in a good child care setting is, in fact, educational. The difference is the philosophy, which sees early childhood as a time of intense learning, not just a phase to pass through while waiting for the real learning to start.

Readiness for preschool. Everything you do to keep your child safe and healthy, to teach reasonable behavior, and to have fun with others prepares your child to succeed in school. Beyond this, the qualities that make a child ready for school include basic listening and speaking skills, and an eagerness to find things out. It also helps to have a familiarity with letters and their sounds, a love of stories, and an interest in the printed word.

Good preschools welcome children at different levels. Not every child has to be verbally precocious, artistically gifted, or extraordinarily well behaved. Skilled preschool teachers are trained to work with children who have different strengths and needs.

At the beginning of preschool, many children use simple three- to five-word sentences. They can express their needs and tell what happened in the recent past. They understand most of what's said to them. They can listen to a story for several minutes, then talk about it. However, they are prone to misunderstanding. For example, if you say you are "hungry enough to eat a horse," a three-year-old might point out seriously that there aren't any horses around.

At age three, children often mispronounce words. In general, you should be able to understand at least three-fourths of what they say. Children who have articulation problems or who stutter may become frustrated when people don't understand them. A patient teacher can be very helpful, as can a skilled speech therapist.

Some preschools require children to be comfortable using the toilet before starting in school, but not all do. Being around peers who go to the bathroom like grown-ups is a huge incentive for children who still rely on diapers. Most work hard and master toilet skills within a few weeks. Many young children still need help with wiping, or at least a reminder to wipe well and wash their hands. Preschool teachers understand that being able to use the toilet independently is a major milestone, and gladly work with parents to help children achieve this goal.

Eating is part of preschool. By age three, children are usually able to manage finger foods and drinking from a cup, and they understand basic table manners. Children with developmental disabilities may need individual help during meals and snacks as part of their educational program.

Preschool children learn basic dressing and undressing: putting on a coat, for example, and slipping on boots. Teachers expect to help with buttons, zippers, and snaps. It's also okay if some children need more assistance for a while.

What a good preschool looks like. A good preschool teacher is many things: a nurturing caregiver, an instructor sowing the seeds of learning, a physical education coach, and a guide to the creative worlds of art, music, and literature. The more you understand about what a preschool teacher actually does, the better able you'll be to look for excellence and to appreciate it when you find it.

A preschool classroom shouldn't look like a classroom for older children. Instead of desks or tables in regular rows, there should be areas for different activities: painting, block building, make-believe, reading, and playing house. Children should have ample opportunities to move from space to space according to their interests. An important part of their education is to learn how to decide on an activity, and then stick with it for a while. Good teachers keep tabs on their students— where they are in the room and how engaged they are in their activities. If a child is having a hard time choosing, the teacher helps him settle into an activity. If a child is stuck in the same activity for too long, the teacher helps him make another choice.

Many aspects of the room also change daily. One day the art area features finger paints. A day or two later, there may be an assortment of materials for mosaics. Another day there are sheets of paper stapled together to make books. How long an activity lasts depends on the children's interest. In addition to the regular activity areas, some parts of the room reflect projects or special areas of focus for the class. One month there is a grocery store, with children shopping, making change, and taking inventory; the next month, a post office appears; after that, it might be a bakery.

The different areas in the room connect with other things

the class is doing. For example, after a visit to a pizza parlor, the children might transform a part of the room into a restaurant. These special areas also reflect the values and concerns that the children are developing: a focus on the environment, perhaps, featuring an indoor garden and items collected on a nature walk around the neighborhood. In planning and making these changes, the teacher listens to the children. She understands that the classroom is not hers, but rather is theirs. As the children think and talk about their space and how they use it, they are learning important lessons about negotiation and cooperation.

The teacher arranges the environment outside the classroom as well. All preschools need to have outdoor spaces for active play. A thoughtfully designed yard has safe areas for running, climbing, riding, and make-believe play. The teacher keeps track of each child, noticing who is doing what and for how long. She offers direction where needed and sometimes joins in the play, but she also knows when to observe quietly.

The teacher makes creative use of the neighborhood and beyond. A walk around the block becomes an opportunity to observe the different shapes of leaves, the materials buildings are made of, street signs and what they mean. These observations then feed into discussions and further projects back in the classroom. (I know all this because for many years my mother was a lead preschool teacher at the University of Chicago's Laboratory Schools, one of the premier educational institutions in the country. All of the things I describe above were part of my mom's classroom. You can read more about it in her book, *It's Not Forsythia, It's for Me.*)

The first days at preschool. An outgoing four-year-old takes to preschool like a duck to water. It may be quite different with a sensitive three-year-old who still feels closely attached to his parents. If his mother leaves him at school the first day, he may not make a fuss right away, but after a while he may miss her. When he finds she isn't there, he may become frightened. The next day he may not want to leave home.

With a child like this, it helps to introduce him to school gradually. For several days, his mother might stay nearby while he plays and then take him home again after a time. Each day, the mother and child stay for a longer period. Meanwhile, he is building up attachments to the teacher and other children that will give him a sense of security when his mother no longer stays.

Sometimes a child seems quite happy for several days, even after his mother has left him at school. Then he gets hurt and suddenly wants her. In that case, the teacher can help the mother decide if she should come back for a number of days. When a mother is staying around the school, she ought to remain in the background. The idea is to let the child develop his own desire to enter the group, so that he forgets his need for his mother.

Sometimes the mother's anxiety is greater than the child's. If she says good-bye three times over with a worried expression, he may think, "She looks as if something awful might happen if I stay here without her. I'd better not let her go." It's natural for a mother to worry about how her small child will feel when she leaves him for the first time. Teachers can often provide good advice in this situation; they've had lots of experience with it. A parent-teacher conference before the beginning of school gives the teacher a head start in getting to know the child and in collaborating with the parents.

A child who starts with some genuine anxiety about separating may learn that this gives him control over a highly sympathetic parent. In this situation, it's usually best for the parents to act confident and firm and explain that everybody goes to school every day. If the child's anxiety results in a day at home with Mom or Dad, the anxiety is bound to grow. But if a child goes to school despite some anxiety, the anxiety will shrink and eventually disappear, as the child learns that school is actually safe and fun. If a child's terror is extreme, the situation should be discussed with a children's mental health professional (see page 861).

Reactions at home. Some children find the early days and weeks of preschool to be hard work. The large group, the new friends, and the new things to do get them keyed up and worn out. If your child is too tired at first, it doesn't mean that she can't adjust to school, only that you have to compromise for a while until she is used to it. Discuss with her teacher whether it would be wise to cut down her school time temporarily. In one case, coming to school in the middle of the morning is the best answer. Taking the easily tired child home before the end of the school day works less well, because she hates to leave in the middle of the fun.

The problem of fatigue in the early weeks is further complicated in an all-day school by the fact that a certain number of children are too stimulated or nervous to sleep at naptime. Keeping the child at home one or two days a week may solve this temporary problem. Some small children starting preschool preserve their self-control in school in spite of fatigue but let loose on the family when they come home. This calls for extra patience and a discussion with the teacher.

A well-trained preschool teacher ought to be, and usually is, a very understanding person. A parent shouldn't hesitate to talk over the child's problems with the teacher, whether or not those problems are connected with school. A teacher sees things from a different angle, and has probably faced the same problems before.

Pressures in preschool. Education can be competitive, and preschools are not immune. Ambitious parents may regard the right preschool as the prelim to an Ivy League diploma. Some preschools incorporate academic structure and teaching practices. Children are taught to memorize the alphabet, spell simple words, and solve math worksheets. There is regular "seat work," which means staying in your chair and concentrating on an assigned task. All of these efforts are intended to prepare children for the next rung of the educational ladder.

What's wrong with this approach? Most young children are eager to please their teachers. Given a set of letters to recite, they dutifully obey and actually learn some letters. After a lot of drilling, they can even read several words by sight. Some of the more advanced will be able to sound out simple words. They'll be impressive when they start in kindergarten.

However, by the end of second grade they won't be exceptional. They will have invested a lot of effort with no lasting payoff. Many will have learned that reading is something you do to please your teachers; others will conclude that it is hard and boring, and best avoided whenever possible.

This is not to say that letters and numbers shouldn't be taught, only that they need to be taught in a way that is meaningful for the children. For example, rather than doing drills with alphabet flash cards, children can listen to stories and incorporate elements of them into their own dramatic play and art. If they make up their own stories, the teacher might write them down and read them back to the class. If things in the classroom are labeled, they learn to recognize those words.

Preschool teachers know how to call attention to the writing and counting that are part of almost any activity. For example, if the classroom has a pet hamster, every child will know how to read the animal's name on the sign above the cage. The teacher might make a calendar showing feeding times, then invite the children to sign up to be the feeder on a particular day, counting the days until it's their turn. Another problem with an overly academic approach to preschool is that it gets in the way of play, which is the way children *really* learn, develop social skills, and exercise their creativity. A skill-and-drill approach to preschool education teaches young children that learning is something you do out of a sense of duty or obedience. A play-centered approach teaches children to love learning itself.

SCHOOL AGE: SIX THROUGH ELEVEN YEARS

FITTING INTO THE OUTSIDE WORLD

After about five or six, children turn into *kids*. Unlike little children, who focus mostly on a small circle of important adults, kids care a lot about what other kids say and do. They care how they measure up and where they fit in. They get interested in academic subjects and acquire skills in art, music, and sports. They begin to pay attention to popular culture, and soon know more about the latest hits than their parents do. Toward the end of elementary school, some take notice of issues such as presidential politics and global warming and develop strong opinions. In little ways at first, and more and more over time, they become independent of their parents, even impatient with them. They begin to take their places within their schools and communities, and the bigger world.

Rules and order. School-age children become strict about some things. They're no longer so interested in make-believe without any plan. They want games that have rules and require skill. In video games, and in games like hopscotch and jump rope, you have to do things in a certain order, which becomes harder as you progress. If you miss, you must penalize yourself and start over again. It's the very strictness of the rules that appeals to children.

This is the age for starting collections, whether it's stamps or cards or stones. At this age, children have the desire to put their belongings in order. Suddenly they neaten their desk, put labels on the drawers, or arrange their piles of comic books. They don't keep their things neat for long, but you can see that the urge must be strong for them to take on this daunting task.

Independence from parents. Children after age six go on loving their parents deeply underneath, but they usually don't show it so much on the surface. They're often cooler toward other adults, too. They no longer want to be adored for their cuteness; they don't want their cheeks pinched! They're gaining a sense of dignity as individuals and want to be treated as such.

They turn to trusted adults outside the family for ideas and knowledge. If they mistakenly get the idea from an ad-

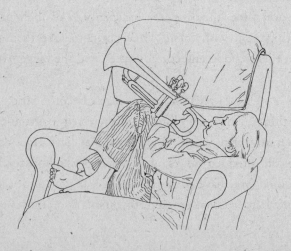

mired science teacher that red blood cells are larger than white blood cells, there's nothing their parents can say that will change their minds. The ideas of right and wrong that their parents taught them have sunk in so deeply that kids now think of them as their own creations. They're impatient when their parents keep reminding them of what they ought to do, because they know already and want to be considered responsible.

Bad manners. Kids often pick up a little tough talk, along with the style of clothes and hair that other kids have. They may lose some of their table manners, come to meals with dirty hands, slump over their plates, and stuff too much food into their mouths. Perhaps they kick the leg of the table absentmindedly. They throw their coats on the floor. They slam doors or leave them open.

Without realizing it, they are accomplishing three things at once. First, they're looking to children of their own age as models of behavior. Second, they're declaring their right to be more independent of parents. Third, they're keeping square with their own conscience, because they're not doing anything that's morally wrong.

These bad manners and bad habits are apt to make parents unhappy. They imagine that children are forgetting all that they so carefully taught. Actually, these changes are proof that the children have learned what good behavior is—otherwise they wouldn't bother to rebel against it. When they feel they have established their independence, they will probably start following their family's standards of behavior again. This can take several years.

Not every kid has to be a troublemaker. One who gets

along happily with easygoing parents may show no open re-
belliousness at all. But if you look carefully, you will see signs
of a change of attitude: a willingness to make suggestions,
question ideas, and voice criticism.

What do you do about the disruptive or obnoxious signs
of growing independence? You may be able to overlook some
of the minor irritating ways, but you should be firm in matters that are important to you. When you have to ask them to
wash their hands, try to be matter-of-fact. A lighthearted, hu-
morous approach can help, too. It's the nagging tone, the
bossiness, that children find irritating and that spurs them on
to rebel even more.

SOCIAL LIVES

Importance of peers. For kids, being accepted by peers is a
matter of greatest importance. The children in any classroom
can tell you who is popular and who is "weird." For the unpopular ones, school can be a lonely and demoralizing place.
It's no wonder, then, that school-age children often go to great
lengths to fit in, even if it means breaking some family rules.

A parent's power is limited here. You can tell your child to
ignore what all the other kids think and do, but few children
can follow this advice. On the other hand, if your child is unable or unwilling to fit in at all, your coaching him to "be
cool" is also likely to fail (although some professional counseling may help a little). Maybe the best you can do is to look
around for groups that match your child's interests and style,
and that fit with your values. It could be a chess club, an art
class, a theater group, or a sports team with an understanding
coach.

Priming the popularity pump. If a boy is having trouble making friends, it helps for the teacher to arrange things so that he can use his abilities to contribute to class projects. This gives the other kids a chance to notice his good qualities. A teacher can also raise a child's popularity by putting him in a seat next to a popular child, or letting him partner with that child in activities. A well-liked teacher can raise a child's popularity by showing that she thinks highly of him.

As a parent, you can raise your child's popularity by making your home welcoming and fun. Encourage your child to invite friends to meals and serve the dishes that they like. When you plan fun weekend things, like picnics or going to movies, let your child invite someone he want to be friends with (who might not necessarily be the one *you* would have chosen!). Children, like adults, have a mercenary side, and they are more apt to feel friendly toward a child whose parents provide treats for them.

Naturally, you don't want your child to have only bought popularity; that kind won't last anyway. What you are after is to prime the pump, to give him a chance to break into a group that may be shutting him out because of the natural clannishness of this age. Then, you hope, he can take over from that start and build real friendships of his own.

Clubs and cliques. It seems to help children, when they're trying to be grown-up, to get together in groups. A number of kids who are already friends decide to form a secret club. Given a chance, they sit together at lunch, play with each other at recess, and go over to each other's houses after school; they fix up a secret meeting place and develop their own rules for governing themselves; or they use cell phones or social networking sites to connect with each other.

A main function of groups is to define who is "in" and who is "out." Such line-drawing is natural. But if it leads to cruel teasing, ostracism, cyberbullying, or physical attacks, then parents and teachers need to step in.

As children enter middle school, at around age ten or eleven, the pressure to belong intensifies. Tickets into cliques include physical attractiveness, athletic or academic ability, money, the right clothes, the right talk, etc. A child without these desirable traits might find herself lonely and miserable. A sympathetic and skillful teacher or guidance counselor can sometimes help turn things around; at other times, a psychologist or other professional can help a child learn the social skills she needs.

Bullies. There was a time when bullying was considered normal, a tough part of growing up, like getting shots, that kids just have to put up with. But bullying causes real harm. Children who are bullied often develop stomachaches, headaches, and other signs of stress or depression. They might withdraw to their room or act out in angry ways. Bullies tend to target the most vulnerable kids, those with few friends. For these children, being bullied adds fear and humiliation to their everyday experience of loneliness—a terribly destructive mix.

The bullies suffer, too. Although they may enjoy a kind of social success during their school years, the long-term prospects are less positive. Having learned to prosper through intimidation, they often have difficulty keeping relationships and jobs, and keeping out of trouble with the law.

The first line of defense against bullying is adult supervision in the places where it typically takes place—hallways, bathrooms, the playground. Parents have the right to demand schools that are safe for children to attend. It does not help much to tell a child to ignore the attacks or to fight back. Although some children benefit from exercise or martial arts training, the idea is not to make the child a better fighter but to build her self-confidence so that she is less easy to intimidate.

The key to preventing bullying is education. Effective school-wide programs insert anti-bullying education into every class throughout the year so that the culture of the school changes. Children learn to stand up against the bullies, not give their silent approval by acting as an audience, and actively to take care of each other. Principals, parents, and teachers need to make preventing bullying a priority, because bullying undermines the security of every child in the school, and children need to be safe to learn.

AT HOME

Work and chores. In many societies school-age children work on farms or in businesses. In the United States, school is the only occupation of most children. But they, too, need to feel that they can contribute meaningfully to their family's well-being. A six-year-old can help set and clear the table; an eight-year-old can help with pulling weeds; a ten-year-old can do simple cooking.

Chores teach children about doing their share. Although chores often conform with stereotyped sex roles—cooking for girls, lawn work for boys—it's better to let children experience a full range of jobs so they can take a broader view of their capabilities.

The best way to get your child to do chores is to be consistent and matter-of-fact about his responsibilities. Don't make lots of exceptions or let him get away without finishing his tasks. Assign chores that your child *can* do, and take the attitude that they *will* be done every day.

Allowance and money. Most kids begin to understand about saving and spending at about age six or seven, so that's a good time to start giving a weekly allowance. An allowance lets a child make small decisions about money. For these decisions to be meaningful, parents need to resist the temptation to simply buy their children things whenever they feel generous, or when their children plead extra hard. Kids need the opportunity to learn from their choices.

Of course, parents must still set limits on how the money is spent. If you have a rule against guns in your home and your child wants to spend his saved-up allowance on a toy gun, your rule still holds. Allowance shouldn't be used as payment for routine chores. The reason to do chores is "because everyone in the family helps out." However, refusal to do chores might result in a loss of some privileges, including the privilege of an allowance.

An allowance teaches children how to delay gratification, plan ahead, and use math. Young kids can learn basic skills of counting and grouping (ten pennies equals a dime). Older kids apply more complex operations: If you have $2.75 saved, then add this week's $2, then spend $1.25 on candy, will you still have enough for a pack of trading cards that costs $5? If you want a computer game that costs $35, and you get $5 a week, how long will it take you to save enough for the game?

COMMON BEHAVIOR CONCERNS

Lying. Younger children often lie simply to escape the consequences of their misdeeds. Did they take those cookies? Well, they didn't really *mean* to, they just sort of did it, so in a way, perhaps the answer is no—or so the child may think. Children need to learn that saying something is so does not *make* it so. They also need to learn that it's better to own up early, rather than make things worse by lying. They learn through moral stories told by parents and teachers, and also through experience.

Why does an older child lie? Everyone, grown-up or child, gets in a jam occasionally when the only tactful way out is a small lie, and this is no cause for alarm. But if your child tells a lie to deceive, the first question to ask yourself is: "Why does my child feel she has to lie?"

Children aren't naturally deceitful. A child who often lies is under too much pressure of some kind. As the parent, your job is to find out what is wrong and help find a better solution. You might say gently, "You don't have to lie to me. Tell me what the trouble is and we'll see what we can do." Often, though, a child won't be able to tell you right away. For one thing, she may not understand the situation well enough to explain in words. But even if she can name some of her worries, she may be afraid to talk about them. Helping her to express her feelings and worries takes time and understanding. Sometimes you'll need the help of a teacher, school psychologist, guidance counselor, or other professional.

Cheating. Young children cheat because they don't like losing. A six-year-old thinks that the point of playing is to win. He's gleeful as long as he's on top, miserable if he starts to fall behind. Learning to lose gracefully takes years. Eventually most kids figure out that everyone has more fun when everyone plays fair. They don't learn this from grown-ups as much as from each other.

A group of eight-year-olds is likely to spend more time arguing about *how* to play a game than they do actually playing it. A tremendous amount of learning takes place during these debates. At first, children see the rules as something fixed and unchangeable. Later, as their concepts of right and wrong become more mature and flexible, they realize that rules can be changed, as long as all the players agree.

Kids can also enjoy games where no one loses and everyone wins. Playing noncompetitive games may help a child realize that the object is to have fun, not to beat your opponent (see page 655).

Screen dependence. A child who stays glued to a video game, tablet, or phone, and who becomes furious when told to stop may be developing an unhealthy dependence (see drspock.com).

Compulsions. The tendency toward strictness becomes so strong in many kids that they develop nervous habits. You might remember them from your own childhood. The most common is stepping over cracks in the sidewalk. There's no sense to it; you just have a feeling that you ought to. Other examples are touching every third picket in a fence, making numbers come out even in some way, and saying certain words before going through a door. If you think you have made a mistake, you must go way back to where you were absolutely sure that you were right, and start over again.

Compulsions may be a response to anxious feelings. One source of anxiety might be hostile feelings toward parents. Think about the childhood saying, "Step on a crack, break your mother's back." Everyone has hostile feelings at

times toward the people who are close to him, but his conscience would be shocked at the idea of really harming them and warns him to keep such thoughts out of his mind. And if a person's conscience becomes excessively stern, it keeps nagging about such unacceptable thoughts even after he has succeeded in hiding them away in his subconscious mind. He still feels guilty, though he doesn't know what for. It eases his conscience to be extra careful and proper about such a senseless thing as how to navigate a crack in the sidewalk.

Mild compulsions are so common in kids eight to ten years old that they shouldn't be a concern, particularly in a child who is happy, outgoing, and doing well in school. On the other hand, if a child has compulsions that occupy a lot of his time, or if he is tense, worried, or unsociable, then it's sensible to seek professional help. Severe compulsiveness, like many other anxiety-related disorders, often has a genetic cause. A strong family history of anxiety problems should be a tip-off to consult a doctor or mental health professional sooner rather than later.

Tics. Tics are nervous habits such as eye blinking, shoulder shrugging, grimacing, neck twisting, throat clearing, sniffing, or dry coughing. Like compulsions, tics occur most commonly around the age of nine, but they can begin at any age after two. The motion is usually quick and repeated roughly in the same form each time.

A tic may last off and on for weeks or months and then go away for good or be replaced by a new one. A tic such as dry coughing may start with a cold but continue after the cold is gone. Shoulder shrugging may begin when a child has a

new loose-fitting garment that feels as if it were falling off. Children may copy a mannerism from another child with a tic, especially from a child they look up to.

Tics often appear without any obvious cause, as part of the sequence of brain development in some children. They tend to get worse when a child is tense or under pressure. Sometimes the problem is a parent who is overly critical or controlling, sets standards that are too high, or fills a child's days with too many planned activities. If the child were bold enough to fight back, he might be less tightened up inside.

A child's tics are out of his control, even if he can suppress them for a short time. Scolding only makes the problem worse. The best strategy is to make life at home and in school as relaxed and pleasant as possible, minimizing nagging and conflict. About one child in ten has mild tics that usually go away by themselves. About one in a hundred has multiple tics that persist for over a year. Such a child may have *Tourette's syndrome,* and should be seen by a doctor.

Posture. People who are buoyant and sure of themselves show it in the way they sit, stand, and walk. Many children slouch because of a lack of self-confidence, too much criticism, or loneliness. The natural impulse of parents is to harp on posture: "Remember the shoulders," or "For goodness' sake, stand up straight." But the posture of children who are stooped over because they feel beaten down won't be improved by more nagging.

Instead, children often do better with posture work through dance or other body movement classes, or via a physical therapist. In these places, the atmosphere is more businesslike than at home. The parents may be able to assist a boy in carrying out his exercises at home, if he wants help and if they can give it in a friendly way. But their main job is to support the child's spirit by aiding his school adjustment, fostering a happy social life, and making him feel adequate and self-respecting at home.

There are also physical causes to consider. Some children are born with relatively relaxed muscles ("low tone"). Many spend too many hours hunched in front of screens. Being overweight can exaggerate swayback, knock-knees, and flat feet. Chronic illness and chronic fatigue (from any cause) can cause children to slump and sag. A child with poor posture should have a thorough medical evaluation.

SUCCESS IN SCHOOL

What school is for. A dedicated school principal once said to me, "Every child has gifts; it's our job to help discover and nurture them." I think this comes close to defining the heart of education. In fact, the word "education" stems from Latin words that mean "to lead out"—that is, to draw out the child's inner qualities and strengths. That is very different from the notion that teachers are there to pour knowledge into children, as if they were empty jars waiting to be filled.

School teaches children how to get along in the world: how to do work, respond to authority, manage complex peer relationships, and handle competition, challenges, and success. Good teachers try to understand each of their pupils and help each one along. For children who lack self-confidence, they find avenues for success. For children who find it hard to be flexible and accommodating, they assign work in groups.

For children who seem unengaged, they look for creative ways to spark their curiosity.

In the old days, it used to be thought that all a school had to do was teach children how to read, write, figure, and memorize a certain number of facts about the world. Now the curriculum is more about understanding different texts (factual, fictional), asking probing questions, thinking critically, and putting together ideas. Many of the facts a child learns in grade school will be obsolete by the time she graduates from high school, so the emphasis has shifted from accumulating knowledge to learning how to think.

Educational disparities. It's a sad fact that the United States has some of the worst educational outcomes in the world, as well as some of the best. As a general rule, the quality of a community's schools parallels the income of its residents. Children who grow up in economically disadvantaged neighborhoods often go to poor schools, and grow up to join the nearly 45 percent of U.S. adults whose literacy skills are so low that they can't get a decent-paying job. And so the cycle of poverty and educational disadvantage propagates itself.

One response has been that many schools for lower-income children focus relentlessly on the basics: reading, spelling, math. A no-nonsense approach like this has its benefits; everyone knows what's expected of them. But children still need a chance to cultivate their curiosity, to think creatively and critically, and to have fun. I know an inner-city school that boasts of pass rates on the statewide standardized tests that rival those of wealthy suburban schools. The children at this school work hard to meet high expectations. But they also have time to play, create, reflect, and explore areas of interest. A key to this success is that the parents all buy in to the high expectations, and convey these to their children.

Discipline is an issue in every school. Children have to feel safe before they can learn. Many schools in lower-income areas have a jail-like atmosphere, with metal detectors and armed guards. But you can't snap discipline onto children from the outside, like handcuffs; it's something that children have to develop inside, by first understanding the purpose of their work and feeling a sense of responsibility to others in how they perform it. Effective schools convey core values in every aspect of their operations: high expectations for effort, respect for others, mutual support, and personal responsibility. When parents and schools work together to build these values into children's everyday experiences, the children thrive.

Linking school with the world. A school wants its pupils to learn firsthand about the outside world so that they will see the connection between their schoolwork and real life. A class that is studying food may have an opportunity to observe some of the steps in growing, harvesting, transporting, and marketing vegetables. A class that is studying government might visit city hall and sit in on a session of the city council.

Another thing that a good school needs to teach is democracy, not just as a patriotic ideal but as a way of living and getting things done. A good teacher knows that she can't teach democracy out of a book if she's acting like a dictator in her classroom. She encourages her pupils to decide how to tackle certain projects and overcome the difficulties they run into. She lets them figure out among themselves how to divide up the tasks. That's how they learn to appreciate each other and get things done, not just in school but in the outside world, too.

When a teacher tells her pupils what to do every step of the way, the children may work while she is in the room. When she leaves, though, a lot of them will start fooling around. They figure that lessons are the teacher's responsibility, not theirs. Children who help to choose and plan their own work and cooperate with each other in carrying it out accomplish as much when the teacher is out of the room as when she is present. They know the purpose of their work and the steps to accomplish it. Each one wants to do a fair share because each is proud to be a respected member of the group and feels a sense of responsibility to the others. This is the very highest kind of discipline. It's what makes the best citizens and the most valuable workers.

How school helps a child with difficulties. A structured curriculum is important, but so is flexibility. Consider this example: A girl in fourth grade was struggling with reading and writing. She had fallen behind, and felt ashamed about being a failure. Outwardly, she wouldn't admit anything except that she hated school. She had never gotten along easily with other kids, even before her school troubles began. It made matters worse that the other children saw her as stupid, or so she thought. She had a chip on her shoulder. Once in a while she would show off to the class in a smarty way. Her teacher used to think that she was just trying to be bad. Of course, she was simply trying to gain some kind of attention from the group. It was a healthy impulse to keep herself from being shut out.

She transferred to a school that was interested in helping her not only to read and write, but also to find her place in the group. The teacher learned from her mother that she used tools well and loved to paint and draw. The children were painting a large picture of life in a prehistoric village, and constructing a scale model of an archaeological dig. The teacher arranged for the girl to have a part in both these projects. Here were things she could do well without nervousness.

As the days went by, she became more and more fascinated with ancient civilizations. In order to paint her part of the picture and make her part of the model correctly, she needed to find out more from books. Now she wanted to learn to read, and she tried harder. Her new classmates didn't look down on her because she couldn't read. They thought more about how she was such a good painter and model builder, and often asked her to help them. She began to warm up. She had been aching for recognition and friendliness for a long while, and as she felt more accepted, she became more friendly and outgoing.

Learning to read. The best way to teach reading has been controversial. Early on, the teaching of reading consisted of memorization, repetition, copying, drills, and more drills. In the 1960s, researchers discovered that many very young children learned a lot about literacy simply by observing their parents, the same way they learned talking and other basic skills. They loved scribbling and played at making letters and words; they noticed familiar words on cereal boxes and street signs and learned what they meant. Some even taught themselves to read. For a time, experts thought that these *emergent literacy* skills might make formal reading instruction unnecessary.

In recent decades, educational research has come back to the idea that most children need to be taught how the alphabet works: how letters stand for sounds, and how those sounds come together to form syllables, and then words. This emphasis on phonics has not replaced the insights of emergent literacy. Instead, we know that children need exposure to both kinds of learning. They need to be read to; they need to make up their own stories and dictate them to parents and teachers, then read them back; they need lots of time to play with letters and words. These are the lessons of a landmark 1998 report from the National Research Council, *Preventing Reading Difficulties in Children.* This report finally ended the battle between the emergent literacy and phonics approaches: Both are important.

Physical education. In the past, the focus of PE classes was to train children to participate in competitive sports. More recently, the focus has shifted to developing healthy habits and fitness. The hope is that children will make regular physical activity part of their lives. Regular physical activity improves children's attention and moods. Exposure to a variety of different physical activities—such as swimming, running, gymnastics, and other sports—helps children discover the activities that most appeal to them. With increasing coordination and endurance, they tend to enjoy the activities even more and are more likely to continue them.

In PE classes, children learn how to be part of a team; they learn how to win and lose, and how to support classmates who aren't as skilled as they are. For children who have academic difficulties or learning disabilities, physical education provides a welcome opportunity to participate, and perhaps excel. Vigorous, skillful physical activity can provide an important avenue for self-expression. Children benefit greatly from a PE teacher or coach who understands this emotional side of physical activity and sports.

The role of parents in schools. Children learn best when parents and teachers work together. When parents show respect to teachers, children respect their teachers more. It's easy to maintain a positive relationship with the school when your child is doing well, but it's even more important when your child is struggling or when there are things about the school that need improvement.

Parent-teacher conferences are certainly important. If you can, get to know your child's teachers. Volunteer to help in the classroom; participate in field trips and special events. Teachers communicate more easily with involved parents. If your child has any academic, behavioral, or social difficulties, you'll hear about them early on, when they're easier to fix. The best solutions almost always include both parents and teachers. Parent groups such as the PTA make great contributions to schools. Parents can provide vital feedback to schools about the lives of the students. What concerns do their children voice at home? Which parts of the school experience are strong, and which could be stronger? Parents who give time and effort to the PTA gain standing in the school community. The teachers and the school principal are more likely to see you as an ally.

Parents as advocates. When a child is having difficulties in school, either academic or social, it's often hard for parents to know how to make things better. Some parents feel helpless in the face of an educational system that seems impersonal. Other parents feel empowered to take a leadership role when it comes to their children's education. Leadership doesn't necessarily mean being completely in charge, however. Effective parents know that they need to work together with teachers and principals, and sometimes with doctors or therapists. They know how to be pleasant and thoughtful, but also persistent and vocal. They know their rights and join with other effective parents. They become a force for the positive education of their children. Not all school personnel are thrilled about these empowered parents, but they generally respect them and work hard to meet their expectations.

As a parent, your point of reference is bound to be your own school experience. If you were lucky enough to go to a good school, you may have very high standards. If not, then it's important to remain open-minded and optimistic that your child can have a better experience. Your active, committed, thoughtful cooperation with the school can help bring that about.

Homework. In the early grades, the purpose of homework is to get children used to the idea of doing schoolwork at home, and to help build time-management and organization skills. Later, homework has three main goals: to give children practice in using skills or concepts they learned in class; to prepare them for the next class; and to give them an opportunity to work on a project that is time-consuming or requires outside resources (such as the library, the Internet, or you, the parents).

There are no hard-and-fast rules about how much homework is the right amount. The National Education Association and the National PTA recommend about twenty minutes a night in the early elementary grades (first through third), about forty minutes in fourth through sixth grade, and about two hours in seventh through ninth.

Children who do homework score better on standardized tests. It stands to reason that when teachers set high expectations for learning, including relatively high homework demands, children learn more.

More isn't necessarily better, however, especially in elementary and middle school. Beyond a certain point, homework squeezes out other valuable activities, such as play, sports, music lessons, hobbies, and relaxation. And it becomes a source of stress for the child and the family.

If your child routinely needs to spend much more time on homework than you think she should, talk with the teacher. The homework expectations may be unrealistic, or your child may be experiencing special difficulties that need to be addressed. Certainly if you find yourself dreading homework, or coming away each night with a headache, talk with the teacher and maybe with your child's doctor. Homework shouldn't be torture.

Helping with homework is fine, as long as you don't complete the assignment yourself. Some parents struggle because they don't really understand the work. This happens a lot with Common Core math, which uses a vocabulary unfamiliar to most parents. While you may be tempted to reject the new approach out of hand, you might find that with effort it actually does make sense (go to drspock.com for help with understanding Common Core math). But even if you feel comfortable with the subject, you may still have a hard time tutoring your child, either because you're impatient or because lots of kids just don't want to learn school stuff from their parents. Public libraries and other community institutions often provide home-work help either free or at low cost. If you can, coordinate your efforts and the tutor's with your child's teacher so you're all working as a team.

PROBLEMS IN SCHOOL

We should view school problems with the same urgency with which we view a high fever: It's an indication that something is wrong and that steps should be taken promptly to fix it. Whatever the cause, when problems persist, a child is bound to believe the worst about himself. Once a child becomes con-vinced that he is stupid, lazy, or bad, it becomes much harder for him to move ahead.

Causes of school problems. Many different problems, alone or in combination, may undermine a child's ability to make it in school. An average student may struggle in a class that is too high-powered and pressured; a bright student may find herself bored and unmotivated in a class that moves too slowly. A child who is being bullied may develop a sudden aversion to school and her grades may drop. Hearing or vision difficulties, chronic illness, learning disabilities, and ADHD (see page 823) may all lead to serious problems. Children with sleep disturbances may fail to pay attention because they are chronically overtired. An unforgivably high number of chil-dren still go to school hungry. Among psychological causes are worries about ill or angry parents, divorce, or physical or sexual abuse.

It's rare for a child to fail solely because of laziness, and a child who has given up trying isn't lazy. Children are naturally curious and enthusiastic. If they have lost their eagerness to learn, it's a sign that there is a problem that needs to be addressed.

School problems are not just a matter of grades. A child who gets all A's but is so perfectionistic and anxious that his stomach hurts and he dreads going to school has a problem. A child who gets B's only by working so hard that she has no time for friends or fun may also need help.

Sorting it out. Have a friendly discussion with your child about her school problem. Don't ask, "Why?" Children rarely can give a sensible answer to this question, and usually hear it as scolding. Instead, ask for details about specific events: What happens when Mrs. Smith calls on you to read? What thoughts do you have then? What feelings do you have? What happens when it's time to line up for recess?

Meet with the teacher and principal. Think of them as collaborators, not the enemy. Assume that they are on your side, caring about your child.

Talk with your child's doctor and make an appointment with a developmental and behavioral pediatrician, a child psychologist, or another professional who has experience in the area of school problems. There should be one doctor—either your child's primary care doctor or a specialist—who helps you to put all of the information together to come up with a better idea of what the problem is and where to go next.

It may be helpful for a child who is immature to repeat kindergarten or first grade. After that, however, simply repeating a grade is not an effective treatment for serious school problems. More often, it is a painful disaster. Unless whatever went wrong in the first place is specifically addressed, the problem is likely to repeat itself, and the blow to the child's self-esteem often causes him to sour on school altogether.

Helping children outside school. There is much that a parent can do outside the school setting to help a child who is having serious academic problems. Most children are curious about the world around them. When you share and encourage that curiosity, the child's interest in learning grows. Make regular excursions to parks, libraries, and museums. Look in the local newspapers and check bulletin boards in libraries or on a nearby college campus for free concerts and lectures. Listen for signs of interest on your child's part, and follow those up with more exploration.

When school is frustrating for a child, it is even more crucial that the child love learning and develop other skills and talents that can be of use later in life. A child who loves fixing things can cultivate that skill and later find work at a bike shop, and later as a mechanic. A child who loves art could eventually make a living in design, animation, or any of a dozen related fields. For a child who struggles academically, it's terribly important to have an area of satisfying competence.

Relations between parents and teachers. It's easy to get along with a teacher if your child is the star of the class. But if your child is having trouble, the situation is more delicate. It's natural for parents and teachers to blame each other. Each, no matter how reasonable, secretly feels that the child would be doing better if only the other would handle him differently. It's helpful to the parents to realize at the start that the teacher is just as sensitive on this point as they are, and that they will get further in a conference by being friendly and cooperative.

Some parents are afraid of facing a teacher, forgetting that just as often the teacher is afraid of them. The parents' main job is to give a clear history of the child's past, what his interests are, and what he responds to well or badly, then to work with the teacher on how best to apply this information in school. Don't forget to compliment the teacher on those parts of the class program that work with your child.

Occasionally a child and teacher simply dislike one another. When this happens, the best response may be to work with the principal to move the child to a different classroom. In any case, it's never productive for parents to criticize a teacher out loud. A child who hears her parents badmouthing her teacher may feel empowered to act out in class and blame others for her problems. It's more helpful for the parents to be sympathetic without laying blame: "I know how hard you are trying," or "I know how unhappy it makes you when your teacher raises her voice." Learning to get along with an unreasonable authority figure is difficult, but it is a valuable life lesson.

THE UNPOPULAR CHILD

For most children, what matters most in school is having friends. Nearly every child has days when he comes home and announces, "Nobody likes me." But for the child who feels this way day after day, every day becomes torture. He's belittled and teased, the last to be picked for any game. He's apt to feel isolated, down on himself, and depressed.

The unpopular child doesn't know how to fit in, or simply can't. He might not be aware of how his behavior comes across to the other children. His efforts to make friends are often clumsy and drive his peers away even more. He gets labeled as "weird" or "unfriendly," even though he desperately wants friends. The other children, of course, don't understand this. From their point of view, he simply doesn't know how to play, won't follow the rules, or always insists on having things his way. An unpopular child may have a developmental disorder such as ADHD (page 823) or autism (page 849), or a physical difference (he might be unusually large or small, for example), or be intellectually or artistically gifted, or may simply not have the "right" clothes. Anything that sets a child apart can set her up for being outcast.

Helping the unpopular child. If your child is very unpopular, don't shrug it off as unimportant. Watch him interact with the other children. It can be difficult and painful to assess your child's behavior objectively, so talk to his teachers and other caring adults who will be honest with you about what they see as well. If you're concerned, seek a professional evaluation by a child psychiatrist or psychologist sooner rather than later. A thorough evaluation will pinpoint not only your child's areas of difficulty but also his strengths.

As a tuned-in parent, you can do a lot to help your child make friends. Get involved in the school and get to know some of the other children and their parents. Ask the teacher to find a classmate who seems inclined to be friendly and seat him next to your child. Invite this classmate to your home to play, or to go with your child to a park, a movie, or some other place of mutual interest. Taking just one friend prevents your child from being the odd kid out. Make the play dates short at first so there's less time for things to go wrong. Remind your child ahead of time how to play nicely. You might say, for example, "Remember, ask Johnny what he wants to play with; that way, he'll have a good time and want to come back." Watch your child and praise him afterward for any positive behaviors he showed. If you have to, step in to get things back on the right track.

The unpopular child always is treated better when adults are around to supervise. For this reason, enroll your child in group activities such as sports, religious events, or dance classes. Talk with the group leader ahead of time so she can give extra support. Your child's predicament will not be new or unusual to anyone who works with children.

When your child is having serious difficulties being accepted by other children, be available and listen empathetically; don't scold or reprimand. Every child needs comfort, love, and support; an unpopular child needs these most of all. An experienced doctor or psychologist can help figure out if there is a diagnosis such as ADHD or depression that needs specific treatment. A therapist can help an unpopular child develop the skills needed to make and keep friends.

ADOLESCENCE: TWELVE TO EIGHTEEN YEARS

CHALLENGES OF ADOLESCENCE

Adolescents have a lot to cope with. Puberty reshapes their bodies in ways that change how they feel about themselves and how the rest of the world responds to them. Sexual urges both exhilarate and terrify. Society adds to the turmoil by sending mixed messages about adolescent sexuality, on one hand idolizing it and on the other treating it as a dangerous force that needs to be quelled. School is a haven for some teens but can feel like a prison to others. The ability to think abstractly leads many teens to question the adult world that they are preparing to join. Idealism can be a powerful force for good, or can lead to acts of violence.

Faced with challenging teen behavior, parents need to remember that the fundamental values they taught their children have not disappeared. Most teens hold to their family's core beliefs, even if they dye their hair a color never seen in nature or get tattoos. By focusing on the long-term goal—a healthy, well-functioning young adult—you may be better able to sort out behaviors that are truly concerning from those that are signs of growing independence, or merely annoying.

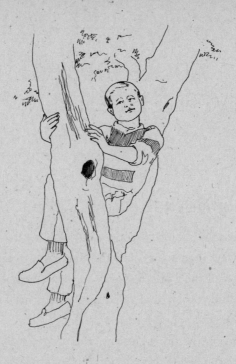

Underneath their cocky exteriors, teens feel unsure about themselves. It helps them when parents have faith in their ability to make it. At the same time, the dangers are real. Risky sex, substance abuse, and self-destructive behaviors can have long-term consequences, and many mental health problems emerge in the teen years. So parents also need to be willing to step in before their teens get into real trouble.

PUBERTY AND GROWTH

The physical changes of puberty span two to four years. In girls, breast growth usually starts around age ten, although it can start as early as eight or as late as thirteen. Menstrual periods usually begin about two years after the first breast changes, normally by age fourteen or fifteen. On average, boys start puberty about two years later than girls, between age ten and about fourteen. If puberty starts much earlier or later, it's important to make sure that there is no medical condition causing the unusual timing.

Puberty first starts in the brain. Hormones flowing from the brain's pituitary gland rev up the testicles and ovaries, which in turn make testosterone and estrogen, which cause all the other changes. What exactly sets the brain into action in the first place, no one knows for sure. Globally, improved nutrition has lowered the age of puberty considerably over the last century. But it's also possible that some less healthful factors, such as pesticides in food or other chemicals in the environment, may mimic the brain's internal signals to make puberty occur earlier in life.

Puberty in girls. Let's trace what happens in the case of the average girl. Early in elementary school she was growing at two to two and a half inches a year. By around age eight her growth had slowed to one or two inches a year. Suddenly, at about ten, she begins to shoot up at three to three and a half inches a year. Instead of putting on five to eight pounds a year, as she used to, she now gains between ten and twenty pounds a year and her appetite jumps up too.

Her breasts begin to develop. A hard lump forms under one nipple, sometimes raising worries about breast cancer, until the other breast also declares itself. The breasts are cone-shaped for the first year or two, rounding out into hemispheres as the first menstrual period approaches. Occasionally one breast begins to develop months before the other. This is nothing to worry about, although the earlier-developing breast tends to stay larger throughout puberty and sometimes beyond.

Pubic hair starts to appear soon after the first breast changes, followed by armpit hair and changes in skin texture. The hips widen and extra fat rounds out the body. The first menstrual period usually comes around age twelve or twelve and a half. After that, growth in height slows down. Many girls have irregular and infrequent periods for the first year or two. This is not a sign that something is wrong; it only means that full maturity was not reached by the first period. There are other normal variations: In some, pubic hair appears months before breast buds, and once in a while armpit hair is the earliest sign of change.

Healthy development can be faster or slower than the average. Parents who were late developers are more apt to have children who are late developers, and vice versa. A girl who begins puberty at eight may feel self-conscious when she finds herself the only girl in her class who's shooting upward. A girl who begins puberty at seven should be seen by her doctor. Early puberty causes early bone growth, making the children tall at first. But because their bones also *stop* growing early, they end up being extremely short as adults. Medical treatment can prevent this outcome. A thirteen-year-old who has shown no signs of pubertal development doesn't need to worry—she just needs to wait. A girl who hits fourteen without any of those signs, or who has been physically mature for over two years without having a period, should be evaluated by her physician.

Puberty in boys. The average boy begins puberty at twelve, though early developers may begin at as young as ten. Plenty of slow developers start at as late as fourteen, and some wait longer.

Pubic hair appears, the testicles enlarge, and finally the penis begins to grow, first in length and then in diameter. All these changes start before the growth spurt, so that early on the boy himself may be the only one who notices. (Body odor, alas, often announces puberty to the world; boys, for some reason, seem less interested in dealing with it than girls.) Boys are often very aware of their more frequent erections and are certain that everyone around them notices as well.

During puberty, boys may grow twice as fast as before. Height usually increases first, along with arm length and shoe size, creating a gangly, uncoordinated look. The muscles fill in later. The hair in the armpits and on the face grows thicker and longer. Growth in the larynx makes the voice crack and deepen. Some boys notice changes in their breasts, with a small area under one or both nipples swelling and becoming tender; this is normal. The breasts themselves may enlarge, especially in obese boys, often causing shame. Weight loss and exercise help, as may breast reduction surgery (though this is rarely necessary).

After about two years puberty is nearly done. Boys keep on growing, more slowly, until around age eighteen. Late-developing boys may grow into their early twenties. Early pubertal development in boys is seldom upsetting. For a couple of years, an early-developing boy may be the tallest and strongest in the class (very early development, before age ten, should be evaluated medically). Late development, on the other hand, can be very upsetting. A boy who is on a slow timetable, who is still a "shrimp" at fourteen, usually needs reassurance, and sometimes counseling, to help him cope. Size, physique, and athletic ability count for a lot at this age.

Some parents, instead of reassuring their son, hunt for a doctor to treat him with hormone shots. But these treatments may cause a boy to end up shorter than he normally would have been by stopping his bone growth prematurely, and there is no evidence of long-term psychological benefits. For the rare child with too little growth hormone production, a pediatric endocrinologist should be consulted. See page 200 for talking with boys about puberty.

EARLY ADOLESCENCE: TWELVE TO FOURTEEN

Changing bodies and minds. Early on, the main challenge for teens is to come to terms with rapidly changing bodies— their own and their peers'. These years see the widest variation in physical development. The average girl is nearly two years ahead of the average boy, towering over him in height and dwarfing him in sophistication. She may be interested in going to dances and being treated as if she were glamorous, while he is still an uncivilized boy who thinks it would be shameful to pay attention to her. Social functions that include a range of age groups may work more smoothly, because kids can find peers of different ages whose interests match their own.

Early adolescents are acutely self-conscious about their bodies. They exaggerate and worry about any defects, and think that everyone else is focused on them. A child whose body is shorter, taller, rounder, or thinner than most may easily conclude that he is abnormal. Freckles, ears that stick out, glasses, uneven teeth, braces, breasts that are too small or too large, or any other physical difference can seem to the adolescent like a glaring flaw.

Early adolescents may not be able to manage their new bodies with as much coordination as they used to, and the same is true of their new feelings. They are apt to be touchy and easily hurt when criticized. At one moment they feel like grown-ups and want to be treated as such. The next moment they feel like children again and expect to be cared for.

Separating from parents. A central problem for adolescents is to figure out what kind of people they are going to be, doing what work, living by what principles. Some seem to follow a direct path; others head down many side roads before they find their way. The first step is to separate themselves emotionally from their parents. It's hard, because they've been patterning themselves after them all their lives.

Now they must pry themselves apart. A usual first step is to find fault with everything parental. One parent lamented, "Oh, to be only half as wonderful as my child thought I was, and only half as stupid as my teenager thinks I am."

Friendships. Adolescents often become ashamed of their parents for a few years, particularly around their friends. In trying to establish their own identity, early adolescents often make intimate ties with friends of the same age. Close friendships support teens while they work on creating identities of their own. One boy mentions that he loves a certain song, hates a certain teacher, or prefers a certain article of clothing. His friend exclaims with amazement that he has always felt the very same way. Both are delighted and reassured. Each has lost a degree of his feeling of aloneness and gained a sense of belonging. This is one reason teens spend so much time talking with each other, texting and posting on social networking sites.

The importance of appearance. Many adolescents help to overcome their feelings of aloneness by slavishly conforming to the styles of their classmates—in clothes, hair, language, reading matter, music, and entertainers. These styles have to be different from those of their parents' generation. If they irritate or shock their parents, so much the better. That's why it rarely works for a parent to simply express revulsion or distaste. You can issue a simple ban ("No navel rings in my house!"), but you're probably asking for a fight, one you may well lose.

Instead, if you can get past your gut reaction, you might actually be able to speak reasonably with your teen. You might point out, for example, that a certain style in hair or clothes proclaims an association with a subgroup—skinheads or prostitutes, for example—that your child actually does not endorse. You might point out a real-life constraint, such as "They won't let you into school wearing that miniskirt." If you can persuade your teen rather than simply overrule her, you can both win.

On the other hand, if you have an open discussion with your teenager, you might end up being persuaded yourself. We adults tend to be slow to accept new styles. What horrifies or disgusts us one day may later become quite acceptable for us as well as for our children. This was true with the long hair and blue jeans introduced by youths in the 1960s, the pants for girls that so upset school authorities at one time, fluorescent hair colors, and tattoos. The challenge is to hold on to your core values while you keep an open mind.

Early teen sexuality. Most teens fantasize and dream about sex; many experiment with kissing and petting; a minority experience actual intercourse. Masturbation, a nearly universal behavior, may be a cause for shame and self-reproach, or simply a fact of life. Most boys also experience ejaculation of semen during sleep (wet dreams). One boy takes these in stride; another worries there might be something wrong with him.

Sexual preferences. Sexual feelings and experimentation during the teen years may be directed toward the opposite sex, same sex, both, or neither. It's not unusual for early teens to engage in same-sex genital touching, then wonder what this means about their sexuality, especially in communities where homosexuality is still taboo. Although society has come a long way toward acceptance, intolerance is still the rule in many places. It can take the form of teasing and put-downs, backed up by the threat of ostracism or frank persecution.

Sexual intolerance makes it difficult for teens to show affection for same-sex friends, let alone talk about feelings that might hint at same-sex attraction. A sensitive doctor can sometimes provide information and reassurance. Creating a space for such conversations is one reason teens should have a chance to talk confidentially with their doctors without a parent present, at each annual visit.

It helps if a child has grown up with parents who talk about sexuality in nonjudgmental and accepting tones. It's important for parents to take notice of insulting jokes and prejudiced comments and speak out against them; to talk about homophobia and why it's as wrong as racism or any other form of discrimination; and to introduce children to books, videos, and music that are created by openly gay, lesbian, or bisexual artists, or that deal with those themes. In these ways, parents send the message that it is safe for their teens to open up about their own sexual feelings. Parents who convey intolerance only close off the conversation and risk adding to their children's isolation.

MIDDLE ADOLESCENCE:
FIFTEEN TO SEVENTEEN

Freedom and its limits. Increasingly, middle teens want more freedom than their parents give them. It's natural for children approaching adulthood to insist on their rights, but you don't have to take every complaint at face value. Teens who are unsure about themselves may perceive that it is their parents who are blocking their way, rather than their own fears. They reproach their parents indignantly or blame them when talking with friends.

You can suspect this unconscious maneuver when your teen suddenly announces a plan for some escapade that is way beyond anything he's done before. For example, he and some friends—boys and girls—are planning to go camping for a weekend without any parents along. Teens who come up with such schemes may be asking to be stopped.

They are also on the lookout for evidence of hypocrisy in their parents. To the extent that their parents are obviously sincere about their rules, their children feel obligated to continue to adhere to them. But if they can uncover hypocrisy in their parents—parents who warn against alcohol but regularly get drunk themselves—this relieves them of the moral duty to conform and offers a welcome opportunity to reproach their parents. At the same time, however, it may undermine their sense of safety.

Taking risks. Teens tend to see themselves as invulnerable; we now know that this illusion is partly due to specific structures in the adolescent brain. It's hard to talk teens out of this perception. Appeals to logic often fall on deaf ears.

Risk-taking serves a purpose; every discovery and advance involves risk. Mistakes, as long as they are not too serious, are great teachers. A teen who bicycles across the country or spends hour after hour practicing skateboard jumps is gaining skills, building self-esteem, and learning to exercise judgment. Some risks, however, can be costly. The child who experiments with cigarettes may end up addicted. Teen drinking all too often ends tragically when a drunk teen gets behind the wheel of a car. Risky sex and drug experimentation can also have permanent consequences.

The challenge for parents is to help teens take risks *sensibly*. Education about risks and risky behavior needs to start before the teen years and can't be left entirely to the schools. Effective parents find many opportunities to talk with their children about values and choices; even more important, they teach by example. They also avoid putting their children in situations where the temptations are too great. Allowing a sixteen-year-old to stay late working on the school newspaper conveys trust and encourages responsibility. Leaving her home alone for a weekend invites risky behavior.

Should parents confess? Parents often ask if they should tell their children about their own histories of teenage risk-taking. They don't want their teens to think they are being given permission to misbehave. On the other hand, the truth tends to come out anyhow, and teens resent being manipulated. They also need to be able to rely on their parents as sources of information. It's more helpful for teens to trust their parents than to perceive them as paragons of virtue.

Of course, parents are under no obligation to confess everything to their children. If your child asks you about something that you really don't feel comfortable talking about, it's best to say just, "I really don't feel comfortable talking about it."

Even though many teens push back against their parents' values, they do care what their parents think. Let your teen know that your top priority is that he or she is safe. Above all, he must never get into a car driven by someone who is drunk or less than completely alert, because the consequences can be sudden and final. After that, you expect him to stay away from alcohol, cigarettes, and drugs, because these too could be harmful. Your messages about risky behaviors will ring true especially if you have been talking reasonably with your child all along about staying safe and healthy.

Jobs and work. Middle adolescence is when many teens first take jobs outside of the occasional babysitting or yard work. In moderation, wage work can build self-esteem, responsibility, and independence. It can allow teens to widen their social contacts and explore fields that may eventually lead to careers. Many teens, however, spend so much time on the job that they don't have time to relax or do homework, and they are chronically overtired and cranky. Also, many jobs carry significant health and safety risks. Parents may need to step in to keep work from getting out of hand.

Sexual experimentation. Middle adolescence is when many teens explore sex. Kissing and petting are almost universal, oral-genital sex happens frequently (although many teens don't think of this as "real" sex), and in the middle teen years many adolescents experience sexual intercourse. Romances are often brief, with relationships taking a backseat to attraction and experimentation. This is not to say that middle-adolescent romances are all superficial or of no consequence. The emotions— joy and misery, elation and dejection—can be intense.

Parents can only control their middle adolescents' sexuality to a point. Educational programs stressing abstinence may have obvious appeal to parents but don't actually reduce teen pregnancy, according to most studies. If teens are intent on sexual experimentation, the rules laid down by parents may not stop them; they might even make sex seem more attractive because it is off-limits. It's more effective for parents to keep communication open, let their children know how they feel about sex, avoid obvious temptations (for example, no unchaperoned sleepovers), and trust their teens to act responsibly.

Feelings, freedoms, and limits need to be a regular topic of conversation. Parents should talk with their teens about sex many times, rather than having "the talk." A trusted doctor can often help open these lines of communication.

Homosexuality and sexual questioning. Middle teens who are questioning their sexuality or who have identified themselves as homosexual may need extra support (see page 646). Despite societal gains, there is still a high rate of suicide and attempted suicide related to sexual and gender questioning. Parents might seek professional counseling to help their child and themselves to deal with the concerns and challenges that often accompany non-mainstream sexuality or gender. A trusted pediatrician or family doctor would be a good place to start. Organizations such as Parents and Friends of Lesbians and Gays, which have chapters all across the country, provide information and advice, and hold events (go to drspock.com). Most cities and large towns have gay and lesbian switchboards or hotlines that can connect you to help.

LATE ADOLESCENCE: EIGHTEEN TO TWENTY-ONE

Tasks of the age. At this age, conflicts between adolescents and their parents tend to cool down a bit, as young adults focus on choosing a career direction and making more meaningful emotional relationships. In the past, older teens prepared to go off to college or to a job that would allow them to live independently. Recently, many have either chosen or felt compelled to continue living in their parents' homes. As society and the economy continue to change, the challenges of late adolescence will change, too.

Idealism and innovation. With increased knowledge and independence comes the desire to make discoveries, rethink conventions, and right wrongs. Many scientific advances and masterpieces of art have been created by individuals just on the threshold of adulthood. They were no smarter than the older people in their fields, but they were biased in favor of the new and the untried, and willing to take risks.

Finding their way. It sometimes takes young adults several years to craft their identities. They may decline to take ordinary jobs as their parents did and adopt unconventional lifestyles. These decisions might seem like evidence of vigorous independence to them, but they don't yet add up to a positive stand on life or a constructive contribution to the world.

Other young people who are idealistic and altruistic may take a sternly radical view of things for a number of years—in politics, the arts, or other fields. Various tendencies of this developmental stage operate together to draw them into these extreme positions: a heightened need to criticize, intolerance of hypocrisy and compromise, courage, and a willingness to sacrifice.

A few years later, having achieved a satisfactory degree of emotional independence from parents and having found out how to be useful in their chosen field, they are more tolerant of the frailties of their fellow human beings and more ready to make constructive compromises. Many remain progressive, some remain radical, but most become easier to live and work with.

COLLEGE

The process of choosing. For many adolescents, choosing a college is the first major life decision in which they have a real say. It's an important opportunity for them to examine their goals and weigh their priorities. Teens should take the decision seriously, but not so seriously that it becomes overwhelming.

To help your teen get organized, start with a calendar of application deadlines from the high school guidance office. Your teen will know how to find out everything about any college online. The standard college guidebooks—available in many high school guidance offices and most public libraries—provide information about courses, students, faculty, and financial aid for more than two thousand institutions.

What if your child makes a mistake? Although choosing the right school can make for a happier, more successful college experience, choosing the wrong school can be a learning experience as well. In fact, many students start out at one school and complete their degree at another. Changing schools is inconvenient, but it's not the end of the world.

Factors to consider. The main question when choosing a college is, "What do I want to get out of college?" It helps to break down this big question into smaller, more manageable pieces. The list that follows is intended to introduce you to the range of issues involved in college selection and to help you in discussions with your teen.

What type of school? Most students choose a four-year college leading to a BA (bachelor of arts) or BS (bachelor of science) degree. But there are other options, such as shorter programs offered by many community colleges and vocational schools. A four-year college offers the greatest amount of flexibility in future education and careers, but even so, it's not always the best choice for every student. Also keep in mind that your child's decision is not carved in stone: students who initially earn an associate's degree can later decide to transfer to a four-year program.

How big? Big universities may take pride in their famous professors, but the average student may only get to see them in large lecture halls, while most of the hands-on teaching is done by graduate students. Smaller schools may deliver less star power but more access. Big schools offer more extracurricular and social activities, but it may be easier to get to know classmates at smaller campuses. Some students feel lost at a big school; others feel confined at a small one.

Cost. In principle, financial aid is intended to make all colleges accessible to all students. But going to a more expensive school may involve greater financial sacrifices. From a strictly financial point of view, state universities may seem to be an obvious bargain compared with most private schools, which can cost three times as much (or more). However, if a student qualifies for a substantial scholarship or another type of financial incentive at a private college, it might actually end up being affordable, perhaps even cheaper than a state school.

Location. Some students thrive on the excitement of a big city; others immerse themselves in their studies and don't pay much attention to the world outside. Your teen may have strong feelings about which part of the country she wants to live in. If she loves skiing, that might eliminate a lot of territory. If she's prone to seasonal depression, a place with long, cloudy winters may be out. Closeness to family is another key issue. How important is it to you and to your teen to be able to spend time together more than once or twice a year?

Academic majors. While many teens enter college without a clear academic major in mind or change majors during the course of their schooling, most have at least a general idea of what they're interested in. A school that is strong in humanities but weak in natural sciences may be perfect for a student whose passion is Renaissance poetry. On the other hand, it's not unheard of for a poetry lover to switch to pre-med and develop a sudden interest in physics and chemistry. A college with all-around strengths gives students more flexibility to change their minds without having to change schools.

Extracurricular activities. Students who are committed to a particular athletic or extracurricular activity often are tempted to choose a school that excels in that area. It's better, however, if there are several areas where the school's strengths and the student's interests overlap. Otherwise, he may find himself unhappy for the many hours of each day when he's not involved in his favorite pursuit.

Religious identification. Some students know, without any hesitation, that they will attend a school with a specific religious identity. Others need to decide how important it is to them to combine religious training with secular studies. They may decide that having an active religious community within a secular university is what they need. Or religion may not factor into their choice at all.

Diversity. One of the virtues of a college education is the opportunity for students to learn from and about each other.

Counterbalancing the benefit of diversity is the support some students derive from being surrounded by peers with similar values and worldviews. This consideration applies equally to racial or ethnic diversity, income diversity, geographic and political diversity, and sexual diversity.

Reputation. Some colleges have a reputation for being party schools; others see themselves as serious or politically progressive. It may be hard to determine this sort of information from the college catalog, but many guidebooks note each school's special flavor—and this is one of the main things to look for on a campus visit.

Other questions. Here are some useful factual questions:

+ How many students apply, and how many of these are accepted?

+ What are the grade point averages and average (or minimum) SAT or ACT scores?

+ How many applicants receive financial aid, and what is the typical or average aid package?

+ What does the typical aid package consist of in terms of grants, loans, and work-study programs?

+ How safe is the campus? Colleges are required to report campus crime statistics.

+ What does the campus look like? Architecture that is inspiring to some may be gloomy to others.

+ How is the campus housing? Some schools require freshmen to live in dorms; some have mandatory meal plans. It can be hard to assess the appearance of dormitories without actually visiting.

+ Are fraternities and sororities an important part of college life?

+ What is the availability and cost of off-campus housing?

+ How many students enroll, and how many complete their degrees in how many years, on average?

+ How many who look for jobs in their chosen field get them? Ask about specific jobs, too.

+ How many who apply to graduate schools are accepted? Ask this about specific majors, too.

Guidance counselors. A good high school guidance counselor can help your teen assess her life goals and plan an academic course to reach them. Based on her goals, the counselor can help your child select the right courses and extracurricular activities, and can help her ask the questions and find the facts she needs to make the best choice. If this sounds precisely like the sort of help you yourself are planning on giving your child, it is. Precollege counseling shouldn't replace a parent's input; it should supplement it.

At the same time, your job is to help your child keep the whole process in perspective. Yes, it's important to think and plan ahead. But it's also important to enjoy life as you're living it. A high school student needs to follow his interests even if they don't lead to a fatter CV, and he has to have some fun, too. He shouldn't sacrifice his adolescent years at the altar of college admissions.

Entrance exams. Our competitive culture puts a tremendous value on high test scores. It's no wonder, then, that college entrance examinations—the SAT, ACT, and others—so often cause intense anxiety in teens. Many parents pay hundreds or even thousands of dollars for private coaching in hopes of higher scores.

The different names of the tests can be confusing. SAT used to stand for Scholastic Aptitude Test; ACT originally stood for American College Testing. But the nonprofit companies that produce the tests decided that the tests' official names would be simply the SAT and the ACT, not standing for anything.

To further confuse the issue, there are now the SAT and the SAT Subject Tests. The SAT and the ACT are aptitude tests. The SAT Subject Tests are achievement tests. (Before the name was changed, the SAT Subject Test was called the SAT II; before that, it was called the Achievement Test.) Even as test prep companies have multiplied, the tests themselves have come under fire. Many experts argue that both the SAT and the ACT discriminate against women and minorities. For example, women as a whole score lower than men on the SAT, but earn higher grades their freshman year.

Most admissions officers put more weight on high school grades than on the standardized test scores. They also take into account the difficulty of a student's high school courses, the application essay or personal statement, and recommendations from teachers and coaches.

Many colleges no longer require SAT or ACT test scores. (For a listing, see www.fairtest.org.) Instead, students can submit a report or an essay that they wrote for a high school course, which allows the admissions office to see both the quality of the student's work and the toughness of the school's grading.

Nonetheless, most colleges still rely on standardized tests, so your child may have to take them even if you're philosophically opposed. To find out which tests are required at which schools, look in college catalogs, college guidebooks, or online.

Test preparation. The College Board (which produces the SAT, the SAT Subject Tests, and the high school AP [Advanced Placement] tests) maintains that coaching doesn't raise SAT scores very much—only twenty-five to forty points, on average. However, critics of the SAT argue that students who can afford extensive coaching do raise their scores significantly, giving an unfair edge to well-to-do students.

Both sides agree that taking the test more than once does raise scores, although admissions officers often look down on students who make more than two attempts. For motivated students, public libraries often can provide free and low-cost opportunities to practice test-taking skills. Children who have learning disabilities may qualify for additional time or other accommodations; if you think this might be important, plan to apply early to the College Board and other testing companies.

Saving for college. The purpose of financial aid is to make college affordable to everyone. However, most financial aid— some 60 percent of it—comes in the form of loans, which means that many students finish college with a load of debt to go with their diploma.

The key to college savings is to start putting money away early on to take advantage of compound interest. In assessing a student's financial need, the federal government calculates that approximately 5 percent of parents' savings should go toward college expenses each year; therefore, the estimated financial need—and thus the value of financial aid you receive—is reduced by that amount. The government does not count savings in the form of home equity or any savings at all if a family's income is less than $50,000 a year.

In one sense, if you qualify for financial aid, having money in the bank costs you, because the federal government counts it against your financial need. On the other hand, if you don't save ahead of time, you may have to take out more student loans. If you do, you or your child may end up paying more in interest than it would have cost to have saved the money in the first place.

Putting money away in your child's name may save money in taxes, because your child's tax rate is likely to be lower than yours. However, money saved in your child's name dramatically reduces any financial aid award. This is because the federal government considers that 35 percent of a child's savings is available to pay for college in a given year. So, saving money in your child's name probably makes sense only if you are sure that you earn too much to qualify for financial aid.

There are also several government-sponsored savings plans that offer tax incentives for college savings. See drspock.com for information on these and other programs that can help with college savings, scholarships, and loans. Even though college is expensive, financial aid and loans should make it possible for every child to afford a college education.

GENERAL STRATEGIES FOR DEALING WITH TEENS

Make rules about safety. Most adolescents are bound to feel rebellious at least sometimes, whether or not the parent is being reasonable. But teens need guidance and limits from their parents, no matter how much they argue against them. Their pride won't let them admit the need openly, but in their hearts they often think, "I wish my parents would make definite rules for me, like my friends' parents do." They sense that it is one aspect of parents' love to want to protect their children from getting into trouble through inexperience, and from real danger.

Parents need to know when children will come home from parties and dates, where they are going and with whom, and who is to drive. If your child asks why you want to know, you can answer that good parents feel responsible for their children. "Suppose there is an accident," you can say. "We ought to know where to inquire or to search." Or you can say, "If there were a family emergency, we would want to be able to reach you." Likewise, you should tell your children where you are going and when you expect to be home.

Show respect, and expect it in return. Adolescents want to discuss the issues on what they feel is an adult-to-adult basis. An overbearing or preemptory approach by parents only sparks indignation. Parents need to try to listen, if they are to persuade.

If the argument ends in a draw, though, the parents shouldn't be so scrupulously democratic that they assume the child is as likely to be right as they are. The parents' experience should be presumed to count for a lot. In the end, the parents should confidently express their judgment and, if appropriate, their explicit request. They owe their child this clarity and certitude.

Parents should indicate, without necessarily saying so in words, that they realize the young person will be out of their sight most of the time and will therefore comply because of her conscience and respect for her parents, not because the parents can make her obey or because they can watch her at all times.

Young people never have been willing to be guided beyond a certain point by their parents, but that doesn't mean that they haven't benefited from discussions. Many parents conceal their own opinions and refrain from criticizing adolescent tastes and manners for fear of seeming old-fashioned or oppressive. It's more helpful, however, for parents to talk freely about their views and their own experiences growing up, but to do so as if they are talking to a respected adult friend, not as if they are laying down the law or as if they think their opinions are right simply because they are parents.

Deal with defiance. But, parents ask, what if the child openly defies a request or quietly disobeys? In the early years of adolescence, if the child-parent relationship is sound and the rules or limits are reasonable, few children defy or disobey when it comes to serious matters, although they may protest loudly. Don't let the protest or back talk distract you from the issue at hand.

In the later years, parents may choose to support their teen's decision, even if it goes against the parents' best judgment. For example, a seventeen-year-old might have her heart set on becoming a chef, but her parents think law school is a better direction. In such cases, an older teen needs to follow her own path even if it turns out to be a mistake. When parents know and accept their children, they are better able to see the world through their eyes. They may then come to embrace their children's choices, or succeed in persuading them to rethink their decisions.

Even when an older adolescent defies or disobeys a parental direction, this does not mean that the direction did no good. It certainly helps inexperienced people to hear all sides. If they decide not to take their parents' advice, they may be making a reasonably sound decision, perhaps possessing knowledge or insights that the parents lack. Certainly as they progress into adulthood, they must be prepared to reject advice on occasion and take responsibility for their decisions. If young people reject their parents' counsel and get into trouble, they'll gain greater respect for their parents' judgment, though they may not admit it.

Use your best judgment. Suppose you don't know what to say or think about some issue. For example, your teen wants to go to a concert that's scheduled to last until 2:00 a.m. You can discuss it with other parents, but don't feel bound in advance to follow their advice. In the long run, you can do a good job only if you are convinced you are doing the right thing. And what is right for you is what you feel is right, after hearing the arguments.

Some questions to ask yourself when deciding whether or not to allow a specific behavior: Is it safe? Is it legal? Does it undermine a core moral principle? Has your child considered the consequences? Is your child acting freely, or is someone else (a teacher, a peer) exercising undue influence? By focusing on such questions, you may be able to chart your own best course of action, and may also be able to help your teen make a wise decision.

If your teen is doing something that seems dangerous or unwise, it's more effective to let her know that you are concerned than simply to criticize or lay down the law. "You always seem unhappy after you go on a date with Jim" is likely to be more effective than "Jim's a stinker!" When a teen is engaged in seriously dangerous activity, parents have to do whatever they can to keep their child safe; generally that involves getting professional help.

Contract for safety. Let your teen know that you'll pick him up anytime, from anywhere, no questions asked. As unpleasant as this sounds, it is far better than having to deal with injuries or legal problems that result from driving while intoxicated, for example. Teens also need access to confidential medical care so that they are free to discuss any questions that they may not feel comfortable sharing with their parents. Good medical care doesn't make teens promiscuous: just the opposite.

Take reasonable precautions against suicide. Most important, do not keep guns at home; overwhelmingly, guns in the home *increase* the risk of injury and death, rather than the opposite (see page 397). If your teen seems sad, down, or distant, if he loses interest in things that he used to love, or if his grades drop off suddenly, keep the possibility of depression in mind and seek help.

Expect civil behavior and participation. Individually and in groups, adolescents should be expected to behave civilly to people and to be cordial to their parents, family friends, teachers, and the people who work with them. At times it is natural for youths to have at least a mildly hostile attitude toward adults. But it does them no harm, and much good, to have to control this hostility and be polite anyway.

Adolescents should also have serious obligations in helping their families by doing regular chores and special additional jobs. This benefits them by giving them a sense of dignity, participation, responsibility, and happiness, and it helps the family as a whole.

You can't enforce these expectations with threats or by yelling, but you are entitled to express them in discussions with your children. It helps adolescents to hear their parents' principles, stated in calm and sensible terms, even if they don't always conform.

ADOLESCENT HEALTH ISSUES

Acne. With puberty, the skin becomes coarser and the pores enlarge and secrete more oil. Some of the pores become clogged with a combination of oil and old skin cells that turn black, resulting in a blackhead. Bacteria living harmlessly on the skin may infect these plugged pores, causing a pimple (a whitehead).

Nearly everyone has acne during puberty. It's not caused by dirt, sexual fantasies, masturbation, or eating chocolate. However, hair oil can trigger acne on the forehead, as can oil misting up from deep fryers. Squeezing pimples—a temptation many find hard to resist—really does tend to make them worse. Most pimples are small and near the surface, but there is a deeper, scarring type of acne that tends to run in families and needs medical treatment.

What can you do about acne? Vigorous daily exercise and fresh air seem to improve many complexions. And it's generally a good idea to wash the face with a mild soap or soap substitute and warm water in the morning and again at bedtime. There are soaps and topical medications that contain 5 to 10 percent benzoyl peroxide that can be purchased without a prescription. And there are many water-based cosmetic preparations (the oil-based ones should be avoided) available for covering up pimples and blemishes while nature takes its course.

If these measures fail, look into medical treatment. Children are entitled to all the help they can get with pimples, for the sake of improving their present spirits and to prevent permanent scars.

Diet in adolescence. The best way to encourage healthy eating for teens, as for younger kids, is to offer good food at pleasant meals, and let your child decide what and how much to eat. Teens who are active and growing quickly can eat huge portions and need every calorie. You can also assume that there will be a certain amount of eating whatever their peers are eating, just to fit in.

This is not the time to micromanage your child's intake.

If you try, your teen may feel compelled to score points by eating whatever you say she shouldn't. In fact, most teens care about their bodies and are eager to understand the connections between what they eat and how they feel. If food is not a battleground for control, a teenager may enjoy learning about different foods with and from her parents. It's best to keep your mouth closed when your teen opens hers.

Adolescent idealism often touches food. Many teens experiment with vegetarianism, for ethical or environmental reasons, if not for health. Vegetarian diets that include dairy and eggs can easily provide complete nutrition without any special supplements, and do offer many advantages, both in personal health and for the health of the planet (see page 320). Of course, if you've raised your child as a vegan, there's a pretty good chance that, as a teen, he'll have a fling with a hamburger or two. It's not the end of the world, as long as you don't make it so.

For the most part, a healthy mix of grains, vegetables, fruits, and, if you choose, lean meats is all a teen needs to thrive. Fast-growing teens need an adequate intake of milk or (for vegans) nondairy sources of calcium. In regions with long dark winters or lots of cloud cover, a daily supplement containing 400 to 800 IU of vitamin D makes sense.

Be alert for concerning changes. Sharp increases in consumption, especially of sweets and salty snacks, sometimes follow stress or depression, and can lead to weight gain that intensifies the emotional upset. On the other hand, a loss of appetite and preoccupation with being "fat" can signal anorexia nervosa (particularly in a tense or driven teen). Laxative abuse and binge eating with vomiting are other reasons to go for professional help (see page 793).

Sleep. Teens need sleep. The average ten-year-old can get by with eight hours a night, but the average teen needs nine or ten. Both biology and culture drive teens to shift bedtime and wake-up time later. But school interferes, forcing teens to get up early even though they stayed up late. Sleep-deprived teens typically get sleepier or crankier from Monday to Friday, then catch up by sleeping till Saturday afternoon. The cycle begins again on Monday. The consequences can include poor school performance, irritability, symptoms of depression, and excessive weight gain.

When teens realize that sleep deprivation is making them suffer, they are usually willing to join with parents in seeking a solution. Although it can be tough for busy teens to make time for sleep, a bedroom ban on cell phones, video games, and TV can often help (see page 653).

Exercise. Many teens sit too much and move too little. Regular exercise, through sports, dance, martial arts, or other pursuits, helps teens maintain energy, avoid obesity, and prevent depression. It may even boost IQ. More is not always better, however. Compulsive exercise can be a sign of an eating disorder (see page 793).

Contraception. This is an important topic for many teens, male and female, even if they have not begun having intercourse (see page 642). Oral contraceptive pills (OCP, or "the pill") can be used to treat irregular periods or severe acne, as well as to prevent pregnancy, but of course only condoms can prevent sexually transmitted diseases. More and more teens and young women are using various forms of long-acting, reversible contraception (LARC). Intrauterine devices earned a bad reputation for causing serious infections that could cause infertility, but modern IUDs are much safer, and more effective than the pill without any effort. They go in quickly with minimal if any pain, and are easy to take out.

Most parents would prefer their teenage children not to have sex, but many teens go ahead regardless. You might be inclined in this case to "lay down the law," but open discussion might help your teen make better, safer choices.

Feeding and Nutrition

FEEDING IN THE FIRST YEAR

Feeding decisions. You want to feed your baby, and your baby wants to be fed. Both of you come with strong instincts about how to get the job done. There are also plenty of other people—friends and family, the media, and of course doctors—telling you what to do. It's fine to listen to everybody, but in the end, you have to do what your heart, or your gut, tells you is best. Perhaps the most important person to listen to is your baby.

A baby knows a lot about diet. She knows how many calories her body needs and what her digestion can handle. If she's not getting enough, she'll probably cry for more. If there's more in the bottle than she feels like eating, she'll probably stop. Take her word for it. Feeding usually works best when you follow your baby's cues: Let her fill up when she feels empty and stop when she feels full. That way, you'll be nurturing her self-confidence, her joy in life, and her love of people, as well as her body.

Your main job, then, is to understand your baby's hunger cues. Some babies are fairly easy to read. They feel hungry on a predictable cycle and feel comfortable once full.

Other babies are more difficult. They cry at odd intervals, sometimes from hunger, sometimes from other discomforts. Babies like this put parents' patience and self-confidence to the test. If it feels like you can't make sense of your baby's signals, don't blame yourself, but do ask for help from experienced friends and family members and from your baby's doctor.

The important sucking instinct. Babies nurse because they're hungry and because they love to suck. Some babies feel the sucking urge more than others. Bottle-fed babies sometimes end up overeating because they just keep on sucking and the formula keeps on flowing. When they overfill their stomachs, they spit up or pass large, watery stools. Some breastfed babies have the same problem. If you think your baby is full, try a pacifier; if she's still hungry, she'll let you know.

WHEN TO FEED

Feeding schedules. A hundred years ago, experts told parents to feed their babies every four hours by the clock. This plan works well enough for many babies, but babies who have trouble adjusting to a regular schedule or whose stomachs can't hold four hours' worth of milk are miserable.

Babies who are fed on demand usually fall into a pattern of six or seven feeds a day at more or less regular intervals. Usually breastfed babies start out feeding quite often (every hour is not unusual), but then settle down into a more humane pattern. Smaller babies tend to eat more frequently than bigger babies. Breastfed babies on average eat more often than bottle-fed babies, because breast milk is digested more quickly than formula. All tend to gradually lengthen the interval between feedings as they grow bigger and older.

The intervals between feedings may vary within each twenty-four-hour period but tend to have some consistency from one day to the next. At some times of the day, babies are apt to want to eat more frequently. They may have a stretch of fretfulness lasting several hours, which usually occurs in the early evening. During these hours, a breastfed baby may want to nurse almost continually, crying if she is put down. A bottle-fed baby may act hungry but not take much if offered a bottle, though she may suck avidly at the pacifier. The evening fussiness gradually improves over the first few months—though it may seem to take forever.

By one, two, or three months of age, babies come to realize they don't need the middle-of-the-night feeding and will give it up. Somewhere between the fourth and twelfth month, they will be able to sleep through the feeding at the parents' bedtime, too.

Helping your baby get on schedule. Individual babies differ widely in how soon they can comfortably settle down to regular schedules. If you wake your baby during the day four hours after the last feeding, it helps him to establish regular daytime eating habits. If, when he stirs and whimpers a couple of hours after the last feeding, you hold back for a few minutes and give him a chance to go to sleep again or offer a pacifier, you are helping his stomach adjust to a longer interval. If, on the other hand, you always pick him up and feed him as soon as he stirs, even though it's shortly after the last feeding, you keep him accustomed to short intervals and small feedings.

Most babies who are good feeders can be eased into a reasonably consistent schedule and will give up the middle-of-the-night feeding a couple of months after birth. On the other hand, if a baby is a listless, sleepy feeder at first, or a restless, fretful waker, or if the breast milk supply is not yet well established, it will be more comfortable for all concerned to go more slowly. But even in these cases, it's reasonable to work gently toward more regular feedings, with an average interval of two to three hours for breastfed babies and three to four hours for bottle-fed ones.

If a baby who generally can go three or four hours awakens after two or two and a half and seems really hungry, it is all right to feed her then. But if she wakes up after only an hour, it's more likely that she has indigestion. Try burping her again, or see whether she will be comforted by a couple of ounces of water or a pacifier. You don't always have to feed a baby every time she cries. If she is crying at the wrong times, you have to study the situation (see page 50).

Middle-of-the-night feedings. The easiest rule for night feedings is not to wake your baby but to let him wake you. A baby who still needs that feeding usually wakes surprisingly close to the hour of 2:00 a.m. Then some night, probably when he's between two and six weeks old, he will sleep through until 3:00 or 3:30 a.m. Feed him then. The next night he might wake still later. Or he might wake but cry in a drowsy way, and go back to sleep if he is not fed right away.

If a two- or three-month-old baby weighs at least twelve pounds, it's reasonable to try convincing her to give up the middle-of-the-night feed. Take your time responding to her fussing; she may just fall back to sleep. When babies get ready to give up the middle-of-the-night feeding, they usually do it within two or three nights. In the case of the breastfed baby, he may nurse longer at his other feedings. In the case of the bottle-fed baby, you can increase the amount in his other bottles to make up for the bottle he's given up, if he wants that extra amount. Night feedings should be given quietly in a darkened room, in contrast to daytime feedings, which can be accompanied by more stimulation.

For those babies who are already off the middle-of-the-night feeding but are still quite irregular about their daytime feeding hours, I'd continue to wake them at 10:00 or 11:00 p.m., provided they're willing to be fed. This at least ends the day on schedule, helps very much to avoid a feeding between midnight and 4:00 a.m., and tends to encourage them to sleep until 5:00 or 6:00 the next morning.

GETTING ENOUGH AND GAINING WEIGHT

Average weight gain. No baby is average. One baby is meant to be a slow gainer, and another is meant to be a fast gainer. When doctors talk about an average baby, they mean only that they have added together the fast, slow, and medium gainers.

On average, babies weigh a little over seven pounds at birth and double their weight by three to five months. Babies who are small at birth tend to grow faster, as if trying to catch up. Babies who are born big often grow more slowly at first. The average weight gain in the first three months is roughly one ounce a day, or nearly two pounds a month. By six months the average gain drops to about one pound a month; by nine months that drops again to just two-thirds of a pound; and by age two it's down to about a half pound a month.

Weight gain also varies from week to week, especially after the first month or so. Teething or illness may take the appetite away for several weeks, and babies may hardly gain at all. When they feel better, their appetite revives and their weight catches up with a rush.

If you find that your baby boy has gained only four ounces in the past week, whereas before he had always gained seven, don't jump to the conclusion that he is starving or ill. If he seems happy and satisfied, wait another week to see what happens. He may show a large gain that makes up for the small one. For the breastfed baby, wetting the diapers at least six to eight times a day, being alert and happy when awake, and sleeping well are good indications that he's getting enough to eat.

How often to weigh. Most babies get weighed only when they go to see their doctor, which is often enough. When a baby is happy, weighing more often than once a month serves no purpose. On the other hand, if your baby is colicky or irritable, or doing a lot of vomiting, more frequent weighing at the doctor's office may help you and the doctor decide what the matter is. For example, crying in a child who is gaining weight rapidly usually signals colic, rather than a need for food.

Slow weight gain. Many healthy babies gain weight more slowly than the average. However, if they often seem hungry, that is a pretty good sign that they are meant to be gaining faster. Once in a while, slow gaining means that a baby is sick, so check in with the doctor.

Some laid-back babies gain weight slowly and don't seem too hungry. But if you give them more to eat, they take it quite willingly and gain more rapidly. In other words, not all babies yell when they are being fed too little.

Fat babies. It seems hard for some people to change their feeling that fatness in babies is attractive and desirable. But babies who carry around a lot of fat are no happier or healthier than leaner ones, and they tend to develop rashes where their fat folds rub together. Fatness in infancy does not necessarily mean that the baby will be fat for life, but it's not a kindness to babies to fatten them up too much.

Refusal to nurse in later months. Once in a while a baby between four and seven months old acts oddly at feeding time. The mother will say that her baby nurses hungrily at the breast or bottle for a few minutes. Then he becomes frantic, lets go of the nipple, and cries as if in pain. He still seems very hungry, but each time he goes back to nursing he becomes uncomfortable sooner. He takes his solid food eagerly.

It may be that this distress is caused by teething. As the baby nurses, the suction engorges his painful gums and makes them tingle unbearably. You can break each nursing period into several parts and give the solid food in the intervals, since the distress comes on only after a number of minutes of sucking. If he is on a bottle, you can experiment with enlarging the hole in a few nipples so that he finishes the bottle in a shorter time with less strenuous sucking. If your baby's discomfort is excessive as soon as he begins to suck, you could, for a few days, give up the bottle altogether. Give him his milk from the cup if he is skillful enough, or from a spoon, or mix a large amount of it with his cereal and other foods. Don't worry if he doesn't get his usual amount.

An ear infection may cause enough pain in the jaw joint that babies will refuse to nurse even though they can eat solids pretty well. Occasionally a baby will refuse to nurse during the mother's menstrual periods. Offering the breast more often during those days may help the baby take at least a little. Pumping or expressing the milk manually may help to relieve the fullness and keep the supply going until baby and mother can return to business as usual.

VITAMINS, SUPPLEMENTS, AND SPECIAL DIETS

Extra water. Some babies like water; others don't. It isn't necessary; there is enough fluid in breast milk or formula to meet a baby's ordinary needs. Babies may need extra water in very hot weather or when they're running a low fever. Babies who ordinarily refuse water often take it at these times. Dark yellow urine is a sign a baby needs more fluid, which could be more breast milk. If you are giving extra water, it's important to continue giving the regular amount of formula or breast milk as well. Babies given *only* water can become quite ill. (See page 356 for water to treat diarrhea.)

Vitamin D. Breast milk, although wonderful in many ways, contains very little vitamin D. Breastfed babies need an extra 400 IU of D every day. One dropperful of an over-the-counter baby multivitamin provides this amount. Bottle-fed babies normally get enough vitamin D from their formula, but one dropperful a day of a multivitamin won't hurt.

Many adults have low vitamin D themselves. It's worth getting your vitamin D level checked if you live in a region with limited sunlight, if you stay indoors all day, or if your skin tone is darker (which increases the amount of sun exposure needed to make the vitamin). Mothers with low D throughout pregnancy give birth to babies with low D. Babies born prematurely start life with low stores of vitamin D and need extra D in their diets to prevent serious problems.

Other vitamins. Mothers and children who consume eggs and dairy products daily should get plenty of B_{12} in their diet without needing a supplement. Breastfeeding mothers who are vegan should take a multivitamin with B_{12}; their infants will get additional B_{12} from their daily multivitamin drops. After weaning, children who are being raised on vegan diets also need a vitamin B_{12} supplement.

The best source of vitamins for you and your child is fresh or frozen fruits and vegetables and other wholesome foods. If you're giving your baby a multivitamin to prevent vitamin D or B_{12} deficiency, you're covered for all the rest.

Iron. Iron is essential for growth and healthy brain function. Breast milk provides iron in an easily absorbed form. Store-bought infant cereals are usually iron-fortified. But if you're giving your baby mostly homemade foods and breast milk, you may need to add iron drops. One dropperful a day of a baby's multivitamin with iron usually takes care of any iron needs. Babies should have their blood tested for iron at around the age of twelve months and again around twenty-four months.

All infant formula should be iron-fortified. Low-iron formulas lead to iron deficiency, and shouldn't be used. (For iron and constipation, see page 106.) Cow's milk provides very little iron, and it can also cause iron to be lost in the stool. For these reasons, babies under a year of age should *not* be given cow's milk.

Fluoride. If your child drinks fluoridated water, there is no need for extra fluoride. If your water has less than 0.6 parts per million (ppm) of fluoride, ask your baby's doctor how much you should give. Vitamin drops with extra fluoride are sold over the counter, but too much fluoride causes its own problems, so check with the doctor first before using these.

Low-fat diets. Children need fats in their diet for energy and brain development, especially in the first two years of life when brain growth is fastest. The typical North American diet is very high in fat; most children over the age of two (and most of us grown-ups) would be better off taking in far less. But babies are different. Low-fat diets for children under age two can cause serious growth problems and even long-term learning problems. Of course, if your baby has a special medical condition, you should follow the doctor's advice.

The healthiest fats are found in foods such as soy products, peanut butter, other nut butters, and avocados. Children who eat meat and full-fat dairy products usually get plenty of fat, too.

SELF-FEEDING

Making messes. When babies become bored with trying to eat and start stirring or slopping the food, it's time to move the dish out of reach, perhaps leaving a few crumbs on the tray for them to experiment with. Even when they're trying very hard to feed themselves correctly, they make plenty of accidental messes, and this you've got to put up with. If you're worried about the rug, put a big plastic tablecloth under the high chair. Children's spoons with wide, shallow bowls and short, curved handles work well. Or use a regular teaspoon.

Early practice. Some babies can use a spoon skillfully before their first birthday; some two-year-olds can't yet. The age at which your baby masters self-feeding depends largely on how soon you let her start trying. Babies start getting ready at six months when they hold their own bread crusts and other finger foods. Then at around nine months, they want to pick up each little morsel and put it in their mouths. Babies who don't have a chance to finger-feed are apt to be delayed in spoon-feeding.

By nine to twelve months, most babies want to control the spoon, and try to yank it out of their parent's hand. Don't think this has to be a tug-of-war. Give your baby that spoon and get another one to use yourself. Your baby will soon discover that feeding himself is more complicated than just getting possession of the spoon. It may take weeks for him to learn how to get a speck of food on the spoon, and weeks more to learn not to turn it upside down between the dish and his mouth.

Giving up control. When your one-year-old can feed herself, let her take over completely. It isn't enough to let her have a spoon and a chance to use it; you've got to gradually give her more reason to use it. At first she tries because she wants to do things for herself. But after she sees how complicated it is, she might give up the whole business if you keep on rapidly feeding her anyway. When she begins to be able to get a speck to her mouth, give her a few minutes with the food at the beginning of the meal, when she's hungriest. The better she gets at feeding herself, the longer she should have at each meal to do it.

By the time she can polish off her favorite dish in ten minutes, it's time for you to get out of the picture. This is where parents often go wrong. They say, "She can eat her own cereal and fruit, but I still have to feed her the vegetable and potato." This attitude is a little risky. If she's able to manage one food, she has skill enough to manage the others. If you go on feeding her the ones she doesn't bother with, you build up a sharper and sharper distinction between the foods she wants and the foods *you* want her to take. In the long run, this takes away her appetite for your foods. But if you serve a well-balanced diet from among the foods she is presently enjoying and let her feed herself entirely, the chances are great that she will strike a good balance from week to week, even though she may slight this or that food at certain meals.

The point is to let your child learn to self-feed somewhere around a year because this is when he'll most likely *want* to try. Suppose a parent keeps a baby from doing it at this age, and then at twenty-one months declares, "You big lummox, it's time for you to feed yourself." Then the child is apt to take the attitude "Oh, no! It's my custom and my privilege to be fed." At this more advanced stage, trying to manage a spoon is no longer exciting.

CHANGES AND CHALLENGES

Table manners. Babies want to eat more expertly, more neatly, all by themselves. They want to graduate from fingers to spoon and from spoon to fork as soon as they feel equal to the challenge, just as they want to try all the other difficult things that they see others doing.

This doesn't mean that you should expect perfect table manners from a toddler. Babies around a year old have a powerful urge to dip their fingers into the vegetable, squeeze a little cereal in their hands, and stir a drop of milk around on the tray. This isn't fooling around; they need to experiment with the feel of food. But if they try to turn the dish over, hold it down firmly. If they insist, keep it out of reach for a while or end the meal.

Slowing down after six months. A baby may take solids eagerly at first, and then rather suddenly lose a lot of his appetite. It may be that he is simply not growing as fast; or he may be bothered by teething. One baby wants to leave out a lot of his solid food; another turns against his formula or breast milk. After six months, some babies refuse to be fed. If you let them have finger food while you're offering food in a spoon, it often will solve this problem. Going to three meals a day may help. If you are in doubt, the doctor can make sure that your baby is growing normally.

Refusing vegetables. If your one-year-old daughter suddenly rejects the vegetable that she loved last week, let her. You don't gain anything by forcing the issue. If you pressure her, you might turn a temporary dislike into a permanent hate. If she turns down the same vegetable twice in succession, leave it out for at least a couple of weeks. If she turns down half her vegetables for a while, as is common in the second year, serve her the ones that she does like. If she turns against all vegetables for a while but loves her fruit, let her have extra fruit. If she is taking enough fruit, milk, and good-quality grains, she is not missing any of the nutrients in vegetables.

Becoming choosy. Somewhere around a year old, babies become choosier and less hungry. This is not surprising. Appetite naturally varies from day to day and from week to week. We grown-ups know that one day we grab a big glass of tomato juice and another day soup looks better. Children are the same. The reason you don't see this variation more often in younger infants is that most of the time they are too hungry to turn anything down.

Fed up with cereal. Many babies get tired of cereal, especially for supper. Don't try to push it in. Offer bread or pasta instead. Even if they give up all starches for a few weeks, it won't hurt them. Expect your baby's tastes to change from month to month. If you don't make a battle of it, your child will probably eat a reasonably balanced diet from week to week. If it stays unbalanced for weeks, however, ask your child's doctor.

Fooling around at meals. Children play around when they're not really hungry, so it's reasonable to take the food away and let them do something else. It's right to be firm, but you don't need to get mad. If your child immediately whimpers for the meal, give him one more chance. If he gets really hungry between meals, give him a little more at snack time, or give the next regular meal early. If you always stop the meal casually when he loses interest, he'll do his part by paying attention when he's hungry.

BREASTFEEDING

BENEFITS OF BREASTFEEDING

Health benefits. When commercial infant formulas first came out, they were advertised as being the scientific way to feed a baby. But science has found just the opposite: With few exceptions, breast milk is more healthful than formula. Breast milk contains substances that fight infections; protect against allergies, eczema, obesity, and other chronic illnesses; and promotes optimal brain growth. Breast milk is so chemically complex that no formula manufacturer can fully reproduce it. For mothers, breastfeeding lowers the risks of breast cancer and ovarian cancer, and of heart attacks later in life.

The American Academy of Pediatrics recommends breastfeeding for at least the first twelve months of life; the World Health Organization recommends two years. Any breastfeeding is better than none.

Practical and personal benefits. It costs less to breastfeed. There is no formula to buy, carry home, and mix, and no bottles to warm and wash. Breastfeeding can help mothers lose weight after pregnancy (it takes a lot of calories to make milk). When the baby nurses, the mother's body releases oxytocin, a hormone that causes feelings of contentment and happiness and helps the uterus return to its prepregnancy size.

Breastfeeding does wonders for a young mother and her relationship with her baby. Intimate physical closeness, several times a day, creates an enduring emotional connection that runs in both directions. Breastfeeding mothers have the satisfaction of knowing that they are providing their babies with something no one else can give them.

Mixed feelings. Some women feel uncomfortable about breastfeeding. It may seem immodest; they may fear failure, the embarrassment of breastfeeding in public, or that breastfeeding will cause their breasts to lose their shape (it doesn't). All of these feelings are normal and understandable. But these outside pressures don't have to have the last word. Many mothers choose to breastfeed in spite of the barriers society erects. They see it as their choice, alone.

Fathers (or non-breastfeeding partners) can also have mixed feelings. They might feel shut out or jealous. It helps if they remember that they play an important supporting role. Breastfeeding can be tiring. Everything a partner does to make the mother's life easier—bringing a pillow or a glass of water, looking after the other children, rocking the baby and changing diapers—makes the breastfeeding that much more successful.

Sexual feelings. Most nursing mothers describe powerful feelings of love and connection while nursing. Some also experience pleasurable sensations in their breasts and in their genital region similar to the sensations they experience during sexual excitement. These are the normal response to oxytocin, a hormone produced in the brain during breastfeeding.

Some mothers and fathers are embarrassed by milk leaking during lovemaking, while others find this arousing. So you can see that it's really important for parents to try to openly discuss their feelings about nursing. Sometimes having this discussion with a doctor or lactation consultant present can help parents realize that there's nothing wrong with feeling the way they do.

GETTING STARTED

Tips for success. Some babies seem to know how to breastfeed from the first try, and for others it may take two to three weeks before breastfeeding is comfortable for both mother and baby. Three things make a big difference: breast stimulation, avoiding formula, and not getting discouraged. It is not always easy to get breastfeeding started. It helps to have a supportive coach, either a trained lactation consultant or a woman with a lot of experience breastfeeding. While books help, too, there's no substitute for hands-on assistance. Most postpartum nurses, midwives, pediatricians, and obstetricians know the best breastfeeding coaches in town. Ideally, you will find your coach before you deliver.

First days. Breastfeeding naturally starts at delivery. A newborn baby who is dried and laid naked on her mother's abdomen will often wriggle up to the breast and begin to nurse even before she is an hour old. Nobody has to tell her; she already knows what to do! All newborns should have this skin-to-skin experience within the first hour after birth, or after the mother is awake. Birthing hospitals that are accredited as "baby friendly" include postpartum skin-to-skin time as standard practice.

Keep your new baby with you as much as possible. Continuous rooming-in from birth on is best. Holding your baby to your chest, skin to skin, stimulates milk production. You won't make much milk for the first few days, but your baby won't need much, either, just a teaspoon at each feeding.

Let your baby feed as often as she wants until nursing and your milk supply are well established. With practice, babies become more and more skilled at latching on and sucking. The more your baby nurses, the more milk you'll make. If you have pain when you first start breastfeeding, let your nurse know. Coaching from an experienced nurse or lactation consultant can usually solve the problem.

Avoid early formula. It's normal for babies to be thirsty in the first days while the breast milk is coming in. Babies who fill up on formula are less motivated to put effort into nursing. The best policy is to avoid formula until breastfeeding is well established, and avoid pacifiers and rubber nipples, too.

Listen to your supporters. Seek out and listen to friends and family members who have breastfed successfully. Don't let others discourage you. A mother who chooses to breastfeed may occasionally be subjected to skepticism from friends and relatives who are otherwise quite sympathetic. There are remarks like: "You aren't going to breastfeed, are you? Why in the world are you trying to do that? With breasts like yours, you'll never succeed. Are you trying to starve the child to prove a point?"

Comments like these can really hurt, unless you recognize that they are really a reflection of the other person's fears or regrets. Listen to yourself, and to people who support your decision. Your mother or mother-in-law might be a key ally, or you may want to connect with community resources that support breastfeeding (see page 252).

Milk supply concerns. It is normal for mothers to worry that they aren't making enough milk. Sometimes a mother becomes discouraged just as her milk is coming in, or perhaps a day or two later, because she isn't producing very much. This is no time for her to quit. She hasn't given herself half a chance.

Be sure you are getting enough to eat and drink, and as much rest as possible. Drinking several glasses of water a day is crucial: Without plenty of water, the body can't produce much milk. (Juice is fine, too, if you prefer, but stay away from too much coffee, tea, and other caffeine-containing drinks.) Put your baby to the breast often, at least eight to twelve times in a twenty-four-hour period, even if she seems uninterested at first. With increased breast stimulation, milk production goes up. If you're concerned about your milk supply, call your baby's doctor or the lactation specialist.

Middle-of-the-night feedings are especially important at first in giving the breasts regular stimulation. Young babies are often more awake—and therefore more effective nursers—in the middle of the night. Plan to sleep when your baby naps during the day. If your baby isn't taking much to begin with and your breasts feel full, it helps to empty them after each feeding. Your hospital nurse should teach you hand expression before you and the baby go home, or you can use a breast pump (see page 269).

Newborns normally lose about up to one-tenth of their body weight in the first week; after that they should gain steadily, about one ounce per day. They usually return to their birth weight by two weeks of age. The baby's weight-check visit is a good time to get help and reassurance.

Getting help. All new babies should see the doctor within one to three days of leaving the hospital for a weight check. Many hospitals have lactation consultants who counsel breastfeeding mothers. (An International Board Certified Lactation Consultant may have the initials IBCLC after her name.) The La Leche League is composed of mothers who have succeeded at breastfeeding and who are eager to support inexperienced mothers (www.llli.org). The International Childbirth Education Association instructors in your community and peer counselors in WIC, the federally funded Women, Infants, and Children nutrition program, can provide support and usually can refer you to a lactation consultant. See the Resource Guide, page 889, for more.

When the milk comes in. At first the breast makes colostrum. It looks thin but it's high in nutrients and infection-fighting substances. The milk most often comes in on the third or fourth day, just as many babies become more wakeful and hungry. If you had a cesarean-section birth, your milk supply may increase more slowly. It usually comes in gradually, but sometimes it's so sudden that a mother can name the hour.

Starting on day three or four, most breastfed babies want to nurse up to ten or twelve times a day. Frequent nursing doesn't mean that the breast milk supply is inadequate. It's just that the baby is now settling down to the serious business of eating and growing. At the same time, the breasts receive the strongest stimulation from the hormones. Supply and demand don't always match. At one time the breasts may be too full; at another, there isn't enough milk to satisfy the newly hungry baby. Still, the system works remarkably well. After the first week, the baby's hunger teaches the breast how much to produce.

How long to nurse at each feeding. In the past, doctors advised starting with short periods and gradually working up. That advice was wrong. When babies are allowed to nurse for as long as they wish, they take their time to latch on properly, thus avoiding nipple soreness. The letdown reflex, which moves milk to the front of the breast, takes time to kick in. Longer nursing from the start allows the letdown reflex to come into play.

All this means that a new mother who wants to breastfeed needs to prepare herself for doing that, and not very much else. Other adults in the family need to take up the slack, to allow the nursing mother to focus on meeting the needs of her newborn.

How often can you nurse? Nurse when your baby is hungry. Every two to three hours is typical, but each baby is different, and some nurse as often as every half hour on some days. Try putting your child to the breast before she gets so hungry that she's crying: It's easier to get a calm baby latched on than a crying one. Babies show signs of hunger by rooting, turning their head when their cheek is touched, or bringing their hands to their mouths. Most babies are hungry when they first wake up. It's the hunger that wakes them!

If your baby has nursed and starts crying soon after, check the diaper. It's also okay to let a baby fuss a bit in the hope that she'll go back to sleep. Sometimes if the father takes the baby and holds her against his bare chest, the warmth and smell, different from the mother's, will be soothing; sometimes swaddling or rocking can help. But if none of these things works, go back to feeding.

A baby who sucks and sucks and never seems content may not be getting much milk. Listen for swallowing sounds; check that your baby is having several loose, yellow, seedy stools a day and wetting frequently; let the doctor check that her weight gain is good. Get help from a lactation consultant early, before the problem becomes severe.

One or both breasts? A simple, reliable method is to let your baby finish one breast first, then offer the other. You'll know when your baby is finished when he lets go. He might take a little from the second breast, or a lot; the choice is his. Letting your baby decide guarantees that he ends the feeding full but not too full. Start the next feeding with the breast you *finished on* last (so, if you started on the right last time, start on the left the next time). That way both breasts get emptied equally.

Nursing patterns. Different babies approach nursing differently. Knowing your baby's pattern will help you adapt to it.

Eager beavers avidly draw the breast in and suck vigorously, but they may clamp down too hard on the nipple. You may have to start again, to make sure they open wide enough to get the full areola into their mouths.

Excitable babies may become so agitated that they keep losing the breast and then, instead of trying again, they scream. They may have to be picked up and comforted for several minutes before they are calm enough to try again. After a few days they usually settle down.

Procrastinators can't be bothered to nurse the first few days; they are waiting until the milk comes in. Prodding them only makes them stubborn. They do well when the time comes.

Tasters must, for a little while, mouth the nipple and smack their lips over the drop of milk they taste, before they settle down to business. Efforts to hurry them only make them angry.

Resters want to nurse a few minutes and then rest a few minutes before starting again. They can't be rushed. They usually do a good job in their own way, but it takes them longer.

Difficult nursing behaviors. Some babies never seem to nurse very vigorously and fall asleep soon after starting; then they may wake and cry again a few minutes after they're put back to bed. If your baby gets sleepy or restless after a few minutes at one breast, try unwrapping her; she may be too warm and comfortable. You can also try shifting right away to the other breast, to see if the easier flow of milk will help. You'd like her to nurse ten to fifteen minutes on one breast to be sure that it is well emptied, but if she won't, she won't.

Other babies react with irritation when they find they can't get enough milk. They jerk their heads away from the breast and yell, try again, then get mad again. This behavior often raises a mother's anxiety, which interferes with milk letdown. Anything that can help a mother relax—music, a magazine, whatever—can help interrupt this vicious cycle.

When a baby refuses the breast, a mother can't help feeling rejected and frustrated. She shouldn't let her feelings be hurt by this inexperienced but apparently opinionated new-comer. If she can keep trying for a few more feedings, the chances are that the baby will figure out what it's all about.

IS YOUR BABY GETTING ENOUGH?

Weight gain and satisfaction. Breastfed babies should have a weight and breastfeeding check at the doctor's office one to three days after hospital discharge (or by three to five days of age). A second doctor's visit should occur about two weeks after that. After the first week or so, average weight gain is about an ounce a day; some healthy babies gain faster, others more slowly.

Along with weight gain, it's important how a baby looks and feels. A contented baby is probably getting enough even if the weight gain is slower than average. Many babies are happy through the day but cranky in the evening. Nursing more frequently toward the end of the day—even every hour or less—may take the edge off this late-in-the-day hunger. If this doesn't help and the weight gain is good, the cause could be colic (see page 84).

Help for poor weight gain. A baby who is gaining very slowly and acting hungry most of the time is probably not getting enough. He may act either unusually upset or lethargic. He'll have fewer than six wet diapers a day, his urine will look dark or smell strong, and he'll have infrequent bowel movements. If you see these signs, ask the doctor.

Some miss out on feeding because they sleep too much. These babies may need to be woken up every three to four hours during the night and put to the breast. Diaper changes often help wake babies up. Babies who are sleepy at the breast can be encouraged to feed by being burped and switched to the other breast before they fall asleep. If this routine is repeated four or five times during a feeding, most babies will be gaining weight and nursing more vigorously within a week.

Hard to tell how much. The question of how much the baby is getting often baffles new mothers. You certainly can't tell from the length of time the baby nurses. She goes on nursing after she's already gotten most of the milk—sometimes for ten more minutes, sometimes for thirty—because she's still getting a trickle of milk, or because she enjoys sucking and being close to her mother.

Most mothers with experience say that they cannot tell how much milk is in a breast from how full it feels. In the first week or two, the breasts are noticeably full and firm as a result of hormonal changes, but after a while they normally become softer and less prominent, even though the milk supply is increasing. A baby can get six or more ounces from a breast that to the mother does not seem full at all. You can't tell anything from the color and appearance of the milk, either. Breast milk always looks thin and bluish compared to formula.

Crying and hunger. When babies fuss or fret, mothers often worry that their milk supply is failing. But many babies, whether formula or breastfed, have fretful spells, usually in the afternoon or evening. Babies who are getting all the milk they can possibly hold have crying spells just the same as babies who are receiving less. A mother who understands that fussing in the early weeks is not always caused by hunger won't be so quick to lose confidence in her breast milk supply.

Hunger is more likely to wake a baby a little earlier for the next feeding than to bother her in the first hour or two after the last feeding. If she's hungry, it may be because she's in a growth spurt, or it may possibly mean that her mother's milk has decreased slightly because of fatigue or tension. In either case the answer is the same: Accept that she will wake and want to nurse more frequently for a few days, and then she will probably go back to her previous schedule.

For a fretful baby, the key is to give breastfeeding a good chance to work. Let your baby nurse as often as she wants, for as long as she wants. If she makes a reasonable weight gain in a week or two, put off consideration of formula again for at least two more weeks.

Sometimes, though, it can be too stressful to nurse a fussy baby. If you feel this way, it may be best to give the nursing a break. You can pump, and your partner or other helper can give the breast milk by bottle. Once you've had a chance to relax, you can get back to nursing with renewed energy.

THE NURSING MOTHER'S
PHYSICAL CONDITION

General health. Take good care of yourself when you're nursing: Turn off the phone, nap when your baby naps, let the housework go, forget outside worries, keep visitors down to one or two comfortable friends, and eat and drink well. Most medications are safe during breastfeeding, but if you take medication for a chronic medical condition or an acute illness, check with your obstetrician or your baby's doctor.

Breast size. Breast size shouldn't limit nursing success. Larger or smaller breasts contain the same milk-producing glands; the rest is fatty tissue. The milk glands enlarge during pregnancy and call for more blood flow, so the veins become prominent. Women with very large breasts may want to talk with a lactation consultant for advice about special techniques to make breastfeeding easier.

Flat or inverted nipples. The areola is the ring of darker skin surrounding the nipple. Gently compressing the areola between a finger and thumb causes the nipple to stick out more. If your nipples retract or sink back in (inverted nipples), plan to work with a lactation consultant once your baby is born.

Exercise. Regular exercise helps to tone the body, lift the spirits, and control weight. For aerobics, try a thirty-minute walk several times a week with the baby in a carrier. Weight training builds strength and increases the metabolic rate, burning calories faster. A lot can be accomplished with cheap hand weights, an exercise book from the library, and just a few minutes each day. If you love sports, play them! It won't affect your milk supply, as long as you drink enough liquids.

Changes in breast shape. Some mothers shy away from breastfeeding because they are concerned it will cause droopy breasts. Breast shape depends on the character of the supporting tissue of the breasts, which varies from person to person. There are women who never breastfeed but whose breasts flatten after pregnancy; others may breastfeed several babies with no effect on their figures, or may end up liking their bodies more.

It's important to have well-fitting bras that support your breasts during the last part of pregnancy, when they are enlarging, to prevent skin stretching. Buy nursing bras that you can open in front using one hand.

The mother's diet during nursing. Most nursing mothers can eat what they want. Some babies react to certain foods with gas, fussiness, or a rash. For example, if a mother drinks cow's milk, some of the proteins pass into the breast milk and may irritate the baby's stomach. Caffeine and chocolate can also cause problems. If you get the sense that a particular food bothers your baby, try going without it for a few days, then try it again.

A nursing mother needs to take in what she's putting out, plus a bit more. Breast milk contains lots of calcium for the baby's fast-growing bones. If you normally drink little milk or have chosen a nondairy diet, you can get plenty of calcium from calcium-supplemented juices or soy or almond milk, or from calcium supplements in tablet form.

Nursing mothers also need vitamin D. Sources include milk, some yogurts, and vitamin supplements, including prenatal vitamins. Mothers with darker skin, and those who live in less sunny places, usually need to take vitamin D pills to get enough. Nursing babies also need to take vitamin D, 400 IU per day. If a doctor prescribes a very high dose of vitamin D to the mother (much more than usual), the baby may get enough in the breast milk and thus not need the drops.

There is no good to be gained from drinking more fluid than feels comfortable, because the body promptly pees out the excess water. On the other hand, a busy new mother may forget to drink as much as she needs and go thirsty through absentmindedness. A good time to drink something is when your baby drinks.

Your diet should include plenty of vegetables, especially green leafy vegetables like broccoli and kale; fresh fruit; beans, peas, and lentils; and whole grains. These foods are rich in vitamins, minerals, and fiber. Meat can be a good source of zinc and iron. (See page 321 for more on vegetarian and vegan diets.)

During breastfeeding, it makes sense to limit your intake of heavy metals and pesticides, because these may be passed to your child. It's reasonable to avoid fish, such as tuna, that concentrate heavy metals in their flesh, and choose organic produce whenever possible, as these contain less pesticides. Also, look for organic ingredients in processed foods such as tofu and soy milk. Conventionally grown soybeans and many grains and other bulk crops often contain a dangerous pesticide called glyphosate.

Smoking, drinking, and drugs. Of course, smoking is unhealthy for mothers and children at any time. But even if you smoke, breastfeeding is still healthier for your baby than formula. (For help quitting, call 1-800-QUIT-NOW, or 1-800-784-8669.)

A nursing mother who drinks a glass of wine or beer a day is not harming her baby. But the first months of having a new baby are stressful, and a new mother might easily have one drink to relax, then another, and another. So if there is alcoholism in your family or if you think you could possibly develop that problem, you're wisest to avoid alcoholic beverages. If you do drink too much on a particular occasion, you can pump and discard the milk that was in your breasts at the time, then go back to regular nursing.

Check with your baby's doctor about any prescription drugs, and stay away entirely from recreational ones. If you have a drug habit, seek professional help so you can stop safely and for good.

Does nursing tire the mother? You occasionally hear that nursing takes a lot out of a woman. Many women do feel fatigued in the early weeks of breastfeeding, but so do many who feed with formula.

A mother who is nursing has to spend several hours each day sitting down. Formula-feeding mothers may feel compelled to do household chores, while a nursing mother has an excellent reason to let someone else worry about the laundry.

Nursing certainly is tiring for the mother who has to wake up three times a night. A willing father or partner can't take over that chore entirely, of course, but he or she can hand the baby to the mother, change the diaper if need be, and return the baby to the crib. Once the nursing is well established, if the father wants to offer a bottle of breast milk during a nighttime feeding, there's no harm in that. If the mother nurses at nine and goes to sleep, the father can give a bottle around midnight, and the mother can be reasonably well rested in time for the 3:00 a.m. feeding. With luck, both parents can look forward to stopping the nighttime feedings within the first four to six months.

Menstruation and pregnancy. Some women never have a period while nursing; others menstruate regularly or irregularly. Once in a while, a nursing baby will be mildly upset during the mother's period or temporarily refuse to nurse.

Fertility does go down while breastfeeding. If the baby is less than six months old, taking only breast milk, and not going more than five hours between feedings, and if the mother is *not* having periods, there is a very small chance (about 2 percent) that she will become pregnant, even without using any other contraception. Even so, condoms add a margin of safety. Check with your doctor about when to resume another family planning method.

BREASTFEEDING TECHNIQUES

Relaxation and letdown. Feelings affect milk flow. A conscious decision to relax pays off in general well-being and easier nursing. Take some slow breaths and let your muscles loosen, one set at a time: shoulders, forearms, neck, jaw, face. Give yourself a few minutes before you expect your baby to wake to enjoy something, whether it's shutting your eyes, reading, or perhaps listening to music.

After a few weeks, you may notice a distinct letdown feeling as the milk comes in at nursing time. It might give you a pins-and-needles feeling in the breasts. Your body is responding to a surge of oxytocin, which activates both the breasts and the pleasure centers in the brain. Milk may start leaking from your breasts when you hear your baby begin to cry in the next room. Not all mothers seem to notice a letdown, even though the nursing is going fine.

Positioning. Any of these positions can work: sitting in a chair, or lying on your side with your baby lying across your lap, or tucked under an arm. You should be comfortable, with one hand free to hold your baby and the other to steer the breast. For women with large breasts, it's helpful to have a supportive nursing bra to hold the breast up; it's too difficult to hold up a heavy breast *and* a heavy baby.

There are two things to avoid when putting babies to the breast. The first is holding the head with both hands when trying to direct it toward the breast. Babies hate to have their heads held; they fight to get free. The other is squeezing the cheeks to get the mouth open. Babies have an instinct to turn toward anything that touches their cheeks. This reflex helps them find the nipple. When you squeeze both cheeks at the same time, it confuses them.

For the positions that follow, I'll assume you're starting with your left breast; when you switch sides, you change hands, too.

Sitting position (cross-cradle hold). Nestle your baby's bottom in the crook of your right elbow with his back supported by your forearm and his head supported by your right hand. His face, chest, stomach, and knees should be facing you. A pillow under him and another under your elbow will provide good support. With your left hand, support your left breast by placing your four fingers under it and your thumb on top, well behind the areola.

Lying on your left side (left breast). You may prefer this position, especially if you've had stitches. Have someone help you position pillows behind your back and between your legs. Your baby should lie on his side facing you. You can use pillows under your baby and under your own head and shoulder to bring the nipple to the right height. Curl your left arm around your baby in the cradle hold and use your right hand to get the nipple in position.

The football hold. Sit in a comfortable chair (most prefer a rocking chair) or in bed with plenty of pillows keeping you upright. Rest your left arm on a pillow and tuck your baby's trunk and legs between your left elbow and your body; his legs will point straight up the back of the chair or the pillows behind you. You can steer your baby's head using your left hand, and position the breast using your right. This position works well if you had a cesarean section, or to nurse a small baby, or just for a change.

Skin to skin. This is probably the easiest and most natural approach: Have your baby (with just a diaper on) lie on your chest while you are reclining and while you have your bra off. Let your baby rest and gently stroke her and talk to her. Now you can both relax. After a little while your baby may begin slowly moving her head toward one breast. You can help guide her to the breast and help her to latch on. When she is finished with the first breast, repeat the same thing and she'll move to the opposite breast.

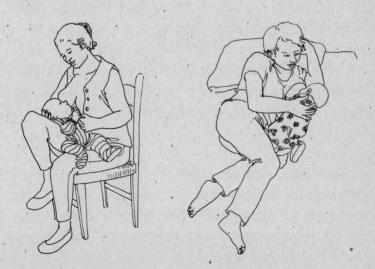

Latching on. Once you're both in position, the next step is latching on. The key here is patience and knowing what to wait for. With a good latch, the baby takes the whole nipple and much of the areola into her mouth; she doesn't just chomp on the nipple! A baby latching on does the same thing you do when you eat a really fat sandwich. You can help by holding the breast a little bit like that overstuffed sandwich, too, squeezed down between your thumb and forefinger.

Gently tickle your baby's lower lip with your nipple until he opens his mouth very wide. (This sometimes takes a few minutes.) Then pull your baby in close so his mouth is over the nipple with most or all of the areola inside. The nipple should be pointing toward the roof of the mouth. His nose will be touching your breast. If his breathing seems obstructed, pull his bottom closer to you or lift up your breast gently with your lower fingers. This will make the extra space he needs to nurse without his nose being blocked.

Some babies latch on easily; others need help. Breastfeeding may be a little uncomfortable at first, but it should never be painful. If there is pain, it means your baby is not latching properly. If you feel your nipple being pinched, use a finger to pull your baby's cheek near the corner of his mouth to break the suction, free your nipple, reposition your baby, and start over. For babies who have trouble latching on, help from a lactation consultant can make a big difference.

Sucking. Milk is made in glands throughout the breast, then collects in the milk ducts, each of which leads to a separate opening in the nipple. Babies don't just suck on the nipple. They use their gums to squeeze the milk ducts under the areola, causing the milk to squirt out. To nurse effectively, babies have to have most of the areola in their mouths. The baby's tongue keeps the areola drawn into the mouth and gets the milk from the front of the mouth back into the throat.

Babies who take just the nipple into their mouths get very little milk. And if they clamp down on the nipple, it hurts! If your baby starts to clamp down on the nipple, slip your finger into the corner of his mouth to break the suction before pulling the breast out (if you just pull the breast out without breaking the suction, it's likely to hurt.) Then help your baby latch on again, this time with the areola well into the mouth. If your baby persists in clamping onto the nipple, stop that feeding.

Care of the nipples. Breasts don't need any special care during pregnancy. After the baby is born and begins to nurse, glands in the areola secrete a lubricating substance. It helps to allow a small amount of breast milk to dry on them after a feeding. A purified lanolin made especially for breastfeeding, such as PureLan or Lansinoh, can be soothing. Wear a bra that has an absorbent lining, so that the nipple is not constantly damp.

Cracked, sore nipples are a sign of problems, which a lactation consultant can help fix. With good technique, nursing should be a comfortable experience, not an ordeal.

THE WORKING MOTHER

Nursing and working. Many women hesitate to breastfeed, because they know they will have to return to their jobs in a month or two. But it should be possible to hold a job and also breastfeed, although it's not always easy. Mothers who work outside the home can breastfeed their babies all day long on their days off, and express milk every few hours while at work. This helps to keep up a good milk supply, and the baby can take the expressed breast milk from a bottle the next day.

By law, employers have to allow nursing mothers breaks for pumping, and a place to do it, not just the bathroom. (An obstetrician colleague of mine, Marjorie Greenfield, provides her patients with a letter for their employers explaining the benefits of pumping on the job, including less stressed and more productive workers, healthier babies, and fewer work days lost.)

Breast milk in the bottle. You can give your baby breast milk from a bottle during the workday. Wait until she is three to four weeks old, if possible, before introducing the bottle. By this time she should be used to nursing efficiently, and your milk flow should be well established.

One fast way to express and store milk is to nurse your baby on one breast and use the breast pump on the other (this may take some practice). The letdown reflex caused by the nursing makes the pumping more efficient. Or you can pump one hour after a feeding to build up your milk supply, just as if you were feeding another baby.

Breast milk keeps five to six days in the refrigerator and four to five months in most freezers (longer in stand-alone freezers). You can smell and taste it to be sure it's not sour before giving it to your baby. Once you start a bottle of stored breast milk, it's good for only about two hours. Never add warm milk to a bottle of cold or frozen milk; doing so encourages spoilage.

Before you return to work, let your baby get used to taking milk from a bottle. Start with one bottle of breast milk three times a week. Warm milk works best, since that's what breastfed babies are used to. Many babies won't take the bottles from their mothers—they know the difference—so the father, an older sibling, or a sitter may need to take over. You might need to leave the room or even the house. Or, try holding your baby in a non-nursing position when you offer her the bottle. For example, she can be lying in your lap with her feet toward you and her head toward your knees.

MANUAL EXPRESSION AND BREAST PUMPS

Nursing mothers need a way to empty their breasts that doesn't rely on baby power. Engorged breasts may be too hard for infants to handle. A small number of babies cannot nurse because of prematurity, cleft palate, or another medical condition. Manual expression—using the fingers to squeeze the milk out of the breast—is a handy skill to acquire.

Manual expression. The best way to learn manual expression is from an experienced person while you are in the birthing hospital. A visiting nurse or a lactation consultant can teach you at home later on, if necessary. It can seem like an awkward business at first, but don't be discouraged.

The finger-and-thumb method. Massage the breast to bring the milk toward the areola. Place the tips of your thumb and index finger on opposite sides of the areola, just at the edge of the darker skin. Then press thumb and finger in deeply toward the ribs. In this position, squeeze them rhythmically together, while sliding the fingers forward slightly, to push the milk along. Use one hand to express the opposite breast, and the other hand to hold the cup that catches the milk. The main thing is to press in deeply enough and at the edge of the areola. Don't squeeze the nipple itself. After a bit, shift the thumb and finger partway "around the clock," to be sure that all the milk storage areas are being pressed. If the finger and thumb become tired—and they will at first—you can switch hands.

Breast pumps. Mothers who express their milk regularly usually prefer to use a breast pump. High-quality electric pumps work best and may be covered by health insurance. Hand-operated pumps with ergonomic handles also work well and are less expensive, although they tend to be slower. Many hospitals have low-cost rental programs, and WIC provides good pumps to support breastfeeding.

BREASTFEEDING CHALLENGES

Biting the nipple. You can't blame a baby for trying a few bites when her gums are tingling during teething or when a couple of teeth have come in. Babies can be taught quickly not to bite. Instantly slip your finger between her gums and gently say no. If she does it again, put your finger in again, say no, and end the feeding. It's usually late in the feeding anyway when a baby starts to bite.

Fussing at the breast. Occasionally a baby who has been nursing well for four or five months will start to cry or fuss a few minutes after starting to nurse. Teething pain might be the cause. See page 449.

Pains during nursing. Early on you may feel cramps in your lower abdomen as soon as your baby starts nursing. Nursing releases oxytocin, which causes the uterus to contract. The cramps disappear once the uterus gets back to its nonpregnant size. Sharp pains in the nipple that last a few seconds after the baby begins to nurse are very common in the first few weeks, and mean nothing.

Sore or cracked nipples. If soreness starts to develop, check the nursing position and latching-on (pages 263 and 266). Nurse more frequently to empty the breasts better and prevent your baby from becoming too hungry. Change nursing positions so that the baby's gums squeeze different parts of the areola. Use ice packs to lessen engorgement and make it easier for your baby to latch on correctly.

If pain persists, look carefully for a cracked nipple. The physician or nurse practitioner may prescribe an ointment or dressing such as hydrogel. Sometimes, when nipples are very sore, the only thing to do is to pump and give the baby a bottle so the nipples can rest. This is a situation where help from an experienced lactation consultant can be the key.

Flat nipples. If a mother's nipples are flat or retracted (drawn back into the breast by the supporting tissue), it may complicate getting a baby started at the breast, especially if the baby is the excitable type. If she searches around and can't find the nipple, she may cry angrily and pull her head back.

There are several things you can try. If possible, nurse your baby when she first wakes up, before she gets too cross. If she starts crying at the first attempt, stop right away and comfort her before trying again. Take your time. Sometimes a nipple can be made to stand out better if you massage it lightly with the fingers first. Using manual expression or an efficient breast pump can help draw the nipples out. This will also squeeze some of the milk out, so that the areola will be softer and more compressible. Then press the areola into a more protruding shape, between thumb and finger, when putting it into the baby's mouth.

Breast shields are still sold, but there's little evidence that they actually work.

Breast engorgement. A breast that is overfull with milk becomes firm and uncomfortable. When engorgement is severe, the whole breast is enlarged, surprisingly hard, and very painful. This can happen if a baby starts sleeping longer at night or if the mother returns to work or is away from the baby and does not express her milk. The usual mild case can be relieved by having the baby nurse more often or by pumping. It may be necessary to soften the areola first by manual expression, so that the baby can get it into her mouth.

More severe engorgement usually occurs, if at all, in the latter half of the first week, and usually lasts only a couple of days. It's rare after that. Try massaging the entire breast, starting at the outer edges and working toward the areola. Do this in a warm shower; the water is relaxing, and there's no mess when milk squirts all over. You can massage your breasts once a day, or several times; or let a helper do the massaging. Applying a warm, damp cloth helps prepare the breasts for massage. Between nursings or treatments, wear a well-fitting bra to give firm support. Acetaminophen (Tylenol) and ibuprofen (Motrin) can help with the pain. You can apply an ice bag or hot-water bottle for short periods, or try cool cabbage leaves.

And, most important, feed your baby frequently, before your breasts become firm and painful.

Plugged ducts. Sometimes only one part of the breast feels firm, hard, or like a lump. When one of the milk ducts is plugged, the milk made behind it cannot drain. Plugged ducts typically occur after the hospital period. Treatment is similar to that for whole-breast engorgement, including:

+ Nursing with the baby's nose pointing toward the blocked segment, because the suction is strongest right in the middle, under the baby's nose.

+ Massage of the hard area by a helper while breastfeeding (this takes three hands).

+ Applying a warm damp cloth or hot-water bottle, followed by massage of the engorged area; an ice bag or hot-water bottle between treatments; increased frequency of nursing; frequent changes of the baby's nursing position.

Breast infection (mastitis). A breast infection often begins as a sore spot within the breast. The skin may become red over the spot, and fever and chills may develop. Headache, achiness, and other flu-like symptoms may be early signs. Take your temperature and call the doctor; you may need antibiotics. While you take them, it is important to continue feeding your baby to empty your breasts. Your doctor should give you an antibiotic that is safe for both you and your baby.

When the mother is ill. In ordinary illnesses, you can nurse as usual. Nursing doesn't increase the chances your baby will get what you have. Babies usually have milder colds than older members of the family, because they've gotten antibodies from their mothers before birth and get more in the breast milk. Some mothers notice a decrease in milk supply when they're sick, but it comes right back with increased nursing.

BREAST-AND-BOTTLE COMBINATIONS

A bottle now and then. Once your milk supply is well established, you can safely offer your baby a bottle of expressed breast milk now and then without worrying that she will reject the breast. As much as one bottle per day should be fine; more than that and some babies will begin to turn up their noses at the breast, and because they are not suckling enough, the milk supply decreases.

If you plan to wean your baby from breast to bottle sometime between two and six months, it's a good idea to offer a bottle at least once a week, even though you could nurse just as well. The reason is that some babies become so set in their ways during this age period that they will refuse to take a bottle of breast milk or formula if they are not used to it, and this can cause quite a struggle. A baby rarely gets this opinionated before the age of two months, and after six months she can be weaned directly to the cup, if you prefer, and she is likely to accept it readily.

WEANING FROM THE BREAST

Weaning over time. Just as breastfeeding is a partnership between you and your baby, so is weaning. Both of you need to agree to wean. If the baby is very upset about weaning, maybe this is not a good time to wean, and you need to slow down the weaning process or put it off for a month and try again.

Weaning usually starts with the introduction of solid foods at around four to six months and continues over the next several months, depending on the baby and the mother. A mother who loves nursing her baby may feel mildly depressed after she stops, as if she has lost some of her closeness to her baby. It helps to take it slow. Breastfeeding doesn't have to be all-or-nothing: A woman can nurse one or two times a day until her baby is two years old or older.

From breast to bottle. How long is it important to nurse? The decision is personal. The biological benefits of breast milk are strongest in the first six months, but continue well after that. The emotional benefits do not cease at any definite point either.

If you have been producing a good amount of milk, start at least two weeks before you want weaning to be complete. First, omit one breastfeeding a day, the one when your breasts are the least full. Instead, give a bottle or cup of expressed breast milk, formula, or whole milk (if your baby is one year old or older). Let your baby take as much or as little of this as she wants. Wait two or three days until your breasts become adjusted to the change, then omit another breastfeeding and substitute a second daily bottle or cup. Again, wait two or three days and then omit another breastfeeding. You'll probably need to wait three or even four days each time before omitting these last two nursings. Anytime your breasts become uncomfortable, you can use a breast pump for a few minutes or express some milk in a warm shower, just enough to relieve the pressure.

If the baby won't take the bottle. A baby of four months or more may refuse completely. For one week try offering a bottle once or twice a day, before the breast or solid food. Don't force it; don't get her angry. Take the bottle away if she refuses, and give her the rest of her meal, including the breast. In a few days' time she may change her mind.

If she's still adamant, omit an afternoon breastfeeding altogether and see if this makes her thirsty enough that she will try the bottle in the early evening. If she still holds out, you will probably have to give her the breast, because you will be uncomfortably full. But continue to omit an afternoon nursing for several days. It may work on a subsequent day even though it didn't on the first. If your baby is six months or older, she may accept a cup better than a bottle.

The next step is to try omitting every other breastfeeding over a twenty-four-hour period and reduce the amount of solid foods so that she's pretty hungry—or omit solids altogether. You can use a breast pump or manual expression just enough to relieve the pressure and discomfort.

If you need to wean quickly. Rarely, a woman has to stop breastfeeding suddenly. Manual expression will relieve the pain, and you can gradually decrease the amount you express over several days. Avoid pills that promise to dry up the milk; they're expensive, have side effects, and often produce a rebound effect that increases the pressure in the breasts.

Weaning from breast to cup. After six months it may be easiest to wean from breast to cup, omitting the bottle altogether. Most babies start showing signs that they need to nurse less about that time. They may stop several times during a feeding and want to play. They can often learn how to take more and more from the cup and will switch over completely in a few weeks, without any sign of regret.

It's a good idea to begin offering sips of expressed breast milk, formula, or water from the cup from the age of six months, so that your baby gets used to it before she is too opinionated. By nine months, encourage her to hold the cup herself. If by nine months she is nursing for shorter periods, she may be ready for gradual weaning. Now offer her the cup at all her meals and increase the amount as she shows her willingness to take more, but continue to breastfeed her at the end of the meal.

Next, leave out one of her daily breastfeedings, the one that she seems the least interested in, and give her only the cup. This is usually at breakfast or lunch. Then omit one breastfeeding each week or so. Willingness to be weaned may not progress steadily. If your baby feels miserable from teething or illness, she may want to go back to nursing a little more. This is natural, and it's fine to accommodate her.

Hesitation to wean. Many mothers find that they are reluctant to end breastfeeding, and some will put off weaning week after week. As with the decision to breastfeed in the first place, you're wise to listen to yourself, and respect your feelings. You don't have to stop at any particular age.

Sometimes a mother will be afraid to wean because the baby is not taking as much from the cup as he used to take from the breast. This may postpone the weaning indefinitely. It's safe to stop the nursing once a baby is taking an average of four ounces from the cup at each meal, or a total of twelve to sixteen ounces of formula or milk a day. After that, he'll probably increase the amount he takes from the cup up to a total of sixteen ounces or more. This is usually enough with all the other things he's eating.

FORMULA-FEEDING

CHOOSING AND PREPARING FORMULA

Why formula? Even though mother's milk is better, many babies grow up healthy on formula. The decision to go with formula is usually a personal one; only rarely is there a medical reason for it. For example, breastfeeding is not recommended for women with HIV/AIDS, nor for those taking certain medications; and infants with rare metabolic conditions may need medically designed formulas. But on the whole, doctors and even formula manufacturers agree, "Breast is best" (see page 247).

That said, there are nonmedical reasons you might want to bottle-feed. One of the best, I think, is that your partner wants to take a more active role in nourishing your baby. (Pumped breast milk works well for this, of course, but it takes more effort on your part.) A less good reason is fear of failure. With support, almost every woman can breastfeed. On the other hand, if you just don't want to (it's *your* decision!), don't be swayed by the fear that bottle-feeding will somehow harm your baby; it won't. And don't give too much weight to the approval or disapproval of friends or relatives (or even doctors).

BOTTLE BASICS:

+ Mix the formula according to the instructions. Only add as much water as they say, no more.

+ Most cities and towns have clean water. You can use this right from the tap, and put bottles and nipples in the dishwasher. Otherwise, you'll need to boil the water and sterilize the bottles and nipples.

+ Hold your baby close and lift the bottle so the formula fills the nipple. Touch; talk or sing; burp; repeat. Follow your baby's cues. Give as much as he wants, and expect that to change from day to day. Try a pacifier if you think your baby is full but wants to suck more.

How many bottles? During the first week, bottle-fed babies often want to nurse six to ten times in a twenty-four-hour day. Most babies start off slow and then become more wakeful and hungry after three or four days, so don't be surprised. After that, the number of bottles you need will depend on how fast your baby grows, which changes from week to week, and how much other food she eats. Start with four ounces in a bottle. Your baby will let you know when that is no longer enough. In the first month of life, most babies will want between twenty-one and twenty-four ounces a day.

Which brand? If you've chosen formula, your next decision is, which one? Standard infant formulas are made from cow's milk that has been processed to make it safe for babies. The manufacturers replace the butterfat with vegetable oils, lower the protein content, and add carbohydrates, vitamins, and minerals. Most formulas now also contain essential fatty acids, substances that play a role in brain development.

Infant formulas are regulated by the U.S. Food and Drug Administration (FDA), so all brands have to meet basic nutrient requirements. Many brands make claims to special properties (for gassy babies, for sensitive stomachs, for toddlers), but the evidence for real advantages is scant. Your baby may prefer the taste of one brand over another. Some brands claim to be organic or free of BPA (see page 34), and in general I'd go with one of these. Cost is also a consideration. You'll want to shop online and in the bigger wholesale stores; the corner drugstore is likely to be more expensive.

Do-it-yourself formulas. Cow's milk itself—as opposed to cow's-milk *formula*—is *not* safe for infants under a year of age. The protein and sugar mix is wrong, there isn't nearly enough iron, and infants fed straight cow's milk are likely to become seriously ill. In the past, some mothers made up their own "formulas" using evaporated milk, but these homemade mixtures aren't safe. Likewise, soy milk—as opposed to soy-based formula—is unsafe for babies, because it does not have the right mix of nutrients for rapidly growing infants.

Soy and other special formulas. Formulas made from soy protein and from chemically modified proteins (so-called elemental, or predigested, formulas) offer no advantage for most babies. They should be used on doctor's advice only. Some babies have allergic reactions to proteins in cow's milk, but about half of these babies also have allergies to soy. For these children, breast milk is the way to go, if at all possible. Premature infants weighing less than about four pounds at birth should not be fed soy formulas in any case.

Some experts are concerned that aluminum, which is used in the processing of infant formulas, may increase the long-term risk of Alzheimer's. Others have speculated that chemicals called phytoestrogens in soy may interfere with normal hormone functions. There's still debate on these points, and enough evidence to at least raise the question.

Liquid, concentrate, or powder. The basic nutritional content is the same for all three. Powder costs the least, lasts longest on the shelf, and has lower concentrations of BPA (page 34). Ready-to-drink and concentrate are convenient. It's fine to use some of each—powder for everyday feedings, ready-to-drink in single-serving bottles for trips. With powder or concentrate, it's important to follow the mixing instructions carefully, since formula that is too concentrated or too diluted can make babies quite sick.

Mixing and diluting. For powder, the standard recipe is one level, unpacked scoop of powder for every two ounces of water, using the scoop that comes in the box. For a single bottle, first fill with eight ounces of water, then add four scoopfuls of powder. Cap and shake gently to mix. For concentrate, you usually add an equal amount of water (four ounces of concentrate plus four ounces of water). Read the instructions on the package.

If you're sterilizing (see page 284), bring the water to a full boil for a minute, then let it cool. Don't boil more, since that will only concentrate any lead or other mineral impurity. Test to make sure that the formula isn't too hot, by dripping some on the underside of your wrist.

Iron-fortified or low-iron. Babies need iron to make red blood cells, and for brain development. Iron deficiency in early infancy can cause lifelong learning disabilities. Some mothers think that iron-fortified formula causes constipation, but research hasn't found this to be true. Even if it were, I'd still argue for iron-fortified formula. There are ways to manage constipation, but the ill effects of iron deficiency can be dire. Low-iron formula shouldn't be sold.

FORMULA REFRIGERATION

Saving formula. If you use less than a full can of concentrated liquid formula or ready-to-use formula, you can save what is left for the next day. Leave it in the can, cover the top, and keep it in the refrigerator. Use it all up the next day, or discard what's left. Never keep an open can longer than the time specified on the label.

The same rule applies if you make a quart jar of formula or fill all the day's bottles in one batch: Keep it in the refrigerator and use it all up the next day or discard what's left. Never keep bottled formula more than twenty-four to forty-eight hours, as specified on the label.

How long after a bottle has been taken out of the refrigerator can you still use it? To be on the safe side, don't give your baby a bottle that has been out of the refrigerator for more than two hours. (An unopened bottle that was filled and sealed in the factory can sit at room temperature for months, of course.)

If you know that you'll be away from home for more than a couple of hours, you can carry an insulated bag with an ice pack in it, or you can carry powdered formula to mix with water when you need it. If you can't keep the baby's bottles cold until feeding time—for instance, if your electricity goes off—you can use single-serving, ready-to-feed bottles (keep some on hand) and discard anything that remains after feeding. Or use powder and mix it up one bottle at a time.

WASHING AND STERILIZATION

Washing. Careful washing of the bottles, nipples, screw rings, disks, and jars is important. Rinse these out soon after each bottle-feeding, before any leftover formula dries. Later, you can use dish soap and a brush, or use a dishwasher. (Nipples tend to deteriorate in the dishwasher, so it's best to wash them by hand.)

A bottle brush is a must for washing the insides of the bottles. To get the inside of the nipples clean, use a nipple brush; then twist a needle or toothpick in each nipple hole and squirt water through the holes.

If you have the kind of bottle with a disposable liner, you still need to wash the nipples and caps. The ounce marking on these bottles aren't accurate enough for diluting the formula, however, so it's harder to mix up one bottle at a time.

If you need to sterilize. In most cities and towns, the water is clean enough that you don't have to sterilize baby bottles; just wash them. If you use well water or for any other reason have any question about your water supply, check with your doctor, public health nurse, or health department to see whether or not you have to sterilize, and up to what age. Lead in drinking water continues to be a concern in many places. Ask your health department. Sterilizing doesn't remove lead; you'll need bottled water, or special filters.

Sterilizers usually come with all the racks, bottles, disks, nipples, and rings that you'll need to get started, along with bottle and nipple brushes and tongs. You can buy a stovetop sterilizer (which is basically a large kettle) or an electric sterilizer that turns itself off at the right time.

If you're filling a day's bottles at once, it's convenient to sterilize the bottles and the formula in them all at the same time (*terminal sterilization*). Follow the directions for using your stovetop or electric sterilizing kit. (For more details on sterilizing, see drspock.com.)

GIVING THE BOTTLE

Warming the bottle. Many parents warm up the bottles because breast milk is warm. But most babies enjoy formula right out of the refrigerator, and it's just as good for them as formula that's room temperature or warmer. Most babies do insist, though, that the formula come at the same temperature at each feeding.

If you warm the bottle, do it in a saucepan, a pitcher of hot water, or a washbasin. If there is no hot-water faucet near the baby's room, it's more convenient to use an electric bottle warmer. Body temperature is the right temperature to aim for. The best way to test this is to shake a few drops on the inside of your wrist. If it feels hot, it is too hot.

Warning about microwave use. It's *never* safe to heat a baby's bottle in a microwave. The contents can be hot enough to burn the baby even though the bottle feels cool to your touch. Microwaves aren't suitable for sterilizing bottle equipment or formula, either. If you do resort to the microwave sometimes (and many parents do, no matter what the experts say), it is *very important* that you *stir the formula well with a spoon* so that there are no hot spots in the formula. Then feel the temperature of the formula with your finger or drop a few drops onto your wrist before offering it to your baby. If the formula feels hot, it's hot enough to burn your baby's mouth.

Getting into position. Angle the bottle so that the air pocket inside the bottle is well above the nipple; this way your baby doesn't swallow a lot of air. If the air bubble in her stomach gets too big, a baby feels uncomfortable and might stop nursing. A few babies need to be burped two or even three times in the course of a bottle, others not at all. You will soon find out what works for your baby.

Feeding with love. Fill your child with love, as well as formula. Gaze at your baby, talk soothingly about anything at all, and especially about your baby; hum, sing, caress. Turn off electronics, silence the phone. Take time to enjoy loving and being loved in the complete and simple way that babies love.

BOTTLE-FEEDING PROBLEMS

Bottle propping. Hold your baby during bottle-feedings rather than propping the bottle. You want your baby to connect the joy of eating with your face, your touch, and the sound of your voice. Babies who take their bottles lying flat on their backs sometimes develop ear infections when the formula runs down the eustachian tube into the middle ear.

Overfeeding and spitting up. Most babies thrive on about twenty-four ounces in twenty-four hours; only very rarely more than thirty-two. Babies sometimes use the bottle more for comfort than for nutrition. When babies overfeed, they tend to vomit to relieve the uncomfortable stomach pressure. A pacifier or another comforting technique may help (see page 50).

Bottle-feeding makes some parents overly concerned with getting a certain amount in at each feed. Some babies do want the same quantity at every feeding of the day, but there are others whose appetites are much more varied. Breastfed babies may get as much as ten ounces at the morning nursing and as little as four ounces at the evening feeding and be perfectly happy with each. If you can trust breastfed babies to take what they need, you can trust your bottle-fed baby.

Nipple holes too small or too large. Small nipple holes force babies to suck harder. They may fuss because they're getting too little; or swallow lots of air, causing gassiness; or become tired and go to sleep before finishing. With holes that are too large, babies may choke or get indigestion, and may get too little sucking satisfaction and do more thumb-sucking. Gulping formula too quickly also increases swallowed air and gassiness.

For most babies, the right speed is when the bottle takes about twenty minutes of straight sucking time. The holes are generally right for a young baby if, when you turn the bottle upside down, the milk comes out in a fine spray for a second or two and then changes to drops. If it keeps coming in a spray, the holes are probably too large. If it comes in slow drops from the beginning, the holes are probably too small.

The holes in many new nipples are too small for a young

baby but are right for an older, stronger one. If they are too small for your baby, enlarge them carefully as follows: Stick the dull end of a fine (no. 10) needle into a cork. Then, holding the cork, heat the needle point in a flame until it's red-hot. Stick it a short distance into the top of the nipple. You don't have to poke it into the old hole. Don't use too large a needle or poke it in too far, until you can test your results; if you make the holes too large, you'll have to throw the nipple away. You can make one, two, or three enlarged holes. If you have no cork, you can wrap a piece of cloth around the dull end of the needle or hold it with a pair of pliers.

Nipple holes clogged with scum. If you have trouble with clogged nipple holes, you can buy nipples that have a small crosscut in the tip instead of having holes. You can make small crosscuts in your regular nipples with a clean razor blade.

Getting babies to take more. Quite a number of children develop feeding problems. They may lose the natural appetite that they were born with because parents try to get them to eat more than they want to.

When you succeed in getting a child to take a few more mouthfuls than she is eager for, it looks to you as if you have gained something. But this isn't so. She will only cut down at her next feeding. Urging children doesn't get you anywhere, and after a while it begins to take away the child's appetite, and makes her want to eat less than her system really needs.

In the long run, urging robs children of some of their positive feeling for life. Babies are meant to spend their first year getting hungry, demanding food, enjoying it, and reaching satisfaction. This lusty success story nurtures self-confidence, an outgoing nature, and trust in their parents. But if mealtime becomes a struggle, if feeding becomes something that is done *to* them, they go on the defensive and build up a balky, suspicious attitude toward meals and toward people.

This doesn't mean that you have to snatch the bottle away for good the first time your baby pauses. Some babies like to rest a bit several times during a feeding. But if she seems indifferent when you put the nipple back in her mouth (and she doesn't need to be burped), then she's satisfied, and you should be too.

Babies who wake in a few minutes. What about babies who go to sleep after they've taken four of their five ounces and then wake up and cry a few minutes later? Waking like this is more apt to be due to an air bubble or colic than to hunger. Babies won't notice a difference of an ounce, especially if they've gone to sleep. In fact, babies will often sleep just as well when they've taken only half their usual amount, though they may wake a little early.

It's perfectly all right to occasionally give the rest of the formula a little later, if you feel sure that your baby's hungry for it. But it's better to assume first that she's not really hungry and give her a good chance to go back to sleep, with or without a pacifier. In other words, try to postpone the next feeding for two or three hours, but if your baby is truly hungry, feed her.

The young baby who only half finishes. A mother may bring her baby home from the hospital and find that he stops taking his bottle and falls asleep when it's still half-full. Yet they said in the hospital that he was taking it all. The mother keeps trying to rouse him, to wedge another quarter of an ounce in, but it's slow, hard, frustrating work. What's the trouble? He may be a baby who hasn't quite "come to" yet. (An occasional baby stays sluggish like that for the first two or three weeks and then comes to life with a bang.)

The constructive thing to do is to let the baby stop when he wants to, even if he's taken only an ounce or two. Won't he then get hungry long before it's time for the next feeding? He may or he may not. If he does, feed him. "But," you say, "I'll be feeding him all day and all night." It probably won't be that bad.

The point is that if you let a baby stop feeding when he feels like it and let him come to feel his own hunger, he will gradually become more eager for his feedings and take larger amounts. Then he will be able to sleep for longer periods. You can help him to learn to wait longer and be hungrier by trying to stretch out the interval between feedings to two, then two and a half, then three hours. Don't pick him up as soon as he starts fussing. Wait a while. He may go back to sleep. If he gets to crying hard, though, you'll have to feed him. Sluggishness and refusing to eat can also be signs of illness in a young baby. If you are concerned, have your baby seen by the doctor. It is never wrong to ask for professional advice, especially with a new infant.

Fussing or falling asleep. The baby who fusses soon after starting a bottle or who promptly goes to sleep may be frustrated by a nipple hole that is clogged or too small. See if the milk comes out in a fine spray when the bottle is first inverted. Try enlarging the nipple hole a little anyway as an experiment (see page 288).

Bottles in bed. Once babies' teeth come in, it's important that they do not fall asleep with a bottle of formula. Formula left on the teeth promotes the growth of bacteria, which causes tooth decay. It's not uncommon to see babies whose top front teeth are completely eaten away: This is a serious health problem. Falling asleep with milk in the mouth can also lead to ear infections.

After six months, many babies want to sit up, take the bottle away from the parent, and hold it themselves. Practical parents, seeing they're not much use, may put such babies in their cribs, where they drink their bottles and put themselves to sleep all in one operation. This may seem like a handy way to put babies to sleep, but in addition to causing tooth and ear problems, it makes it impossible for some of them to go to sleep without a bottle. When the parent tries to withhold a bedtime bottle at nine, fifteen, or twenty-one months, the baby will cry frantically and be unable to fall asleep for a long time. So if you want to prevent bedtime problems later on, let your baby hold her own bottle, but keep her in your lap (or the high chair, if that's what she'd prefer).

WEANING FROM THE BOTTLE

When to wean. Some parents are eager to get their babies weaned to the cup by a year. Others feel strongly that all babies are entitled to the bottle for two years. The decision depends partly on the parents' wishes and partly on the baby's readiness.

Babies often show less interest in sucking by five or six months. Instead of nursing eagerly for twenty minutes, as they used to, they stop after five minutes to flirt with their parents or play with their bottle or with their own hands.

These are the early signs of readiness for weaning. These babies go on being somewhat casual toward the bottle at eight, ten, or twelve months, though in most cases they'll take it as long as it's offered. They also like formula from the cup, and they continue to do so once the bottles stop coming.

The main reason for weaning babies from the bottle by one year is that this is when they'll accept the change most easily. By this age most babies will be holding their own bottles at feeding time, and it's best to let them take over. You can help them be more grown-up by getting them started with a cup.

Weaning by a year also prevents some problems. Toddlers who sip milk or formula on and off during the day are prone to develop tooth decay, because the sugary fluid coats the teeth, promoting the growth of bacteria. Toddlers who take frequent sips of milk may eat poorly, because the steady trickle of milk takes the edge off their appetite, and their growth may suffer. Or they may put on too much weight.

Sipping by five months. By five months old, most babies can take a sip from the cup each day. You aren't going to try to wean them to the cup right away. You only want to get them accustomed to the idea that formula comes in cups, too.

Pour half an ounce of formula into a small cup. Your baby probably won't want more than one sip at a time, but she'll think it's fun. Once she's comfortable taking formula from the cup, offer her water and diluted juice from the cup, too. This way she'll learn that different liquids can come in a cup.

Getting used to the cup. Once the cup has been introduced, offer it matter-of-factly once or twice at each solid meal, holding it to your baby's lips. Keep the cup in sight so he can indicate if he'd like more. (If you usually give him a bottle at the end of his meal, keep it out of sight until then.) He'll also be interested in anything you're drinking, and you can hold your glass to his lips and let him have a taste if the contents are suitable.

You can let him try his own skills, too. Suppose he's six months old and wants to grab everything and put it in his mouth. Give him a small, narrow, empty plastic glass or cup that he can hold easily by himself, or a baby's mug with two handles. When he does it fairly well, put a few drops of formula into the cup. Increase the amount as he gains in skill. If he gets balky or loses interest, drop the matter for a meal or two. Remember that in the early months of cup drinking, he'll probably want only one swallow at a time. Many babies don't learn to take several gulps in succession until they are one to one and a half years old.

Sippy cups. Cups with a lid and spout are easy for babies to handle. Some babies become attached to their sippy cups, carrying them around and sipping on and off like they did with their bottles, with the same risk of tooth decay. For these babies, the transition to a regular cup can be hard. In the long run, it's probably less trouble to skip the sippy cup.

Wean gradually. Take it easy and follow your baby's lead. Perhaps your baby is around nine months old and is becoming a little bored with her bottle and likes formula from the cup. Gradually increase the amount in the cup and offer the cup at every meal. This leaves less and less in the bottle. Then leave out the bottle that she takes the least interest in. In a week, give up the second bottle and then the third. Most babies love their supper bottle most and are slowest in giving it up. Willingness to be weaned doesn't always increase steadily. Misery from teething or a cold often makes babies want more of the bottle for the time being. Follow your baby's needs.

The reluctant weaner. Babies who are reluctant to give up the bottle at nine to twelve months may take one sip from the cup and push it away impatiently. Or they may pretend they don't know what it's for; they let the formula run out at the sides of their mouths, smiling innocently. They may relent a little at twelve months, but it is more likely that they'll remain suspicious until fifteen months or even later.

Put an ounce of formula in a small plastic cup and just set it on the tray every day or so. Don't force it. If one sip is all they take, don't even try to give them two. Act as if it doesn't make any difference to you. Once they start with sips, it will probably take several more months before they are ready to give up the bottle altogether. This applies particularly to the supper or bedtime bottle.

If your child is suspicious of the old cup he has always been offered, he may be delighted with a new cup of a different shape or color. Offering cold milk may change his mind. Adding a little cereal to the cup of milk may make it different enough to be acceptable for drinking. You can remove the cereal gradually a few weeks later.

Preventing weaning problems. Babies can get emotionally attached to their bottles. If they regularly take a bottle in bed, it becomes a source of emotional comfort. This doesn't happen when children take their bottles in their parent's lap, because the real parent is right there. So, hold your baby for her bottles, and don't let her take them to bed.

If your baby already has a bedtime bottle attachment, it's important to change what's in the bottle from formula to water. That way, cavities ("bottle mouth") won't be such a problem (see page 454). If you water down the nighttime bottles bit by bit, you should be able to get your baby to accept straight water at night without too much of a fuss. From there, it may be easier for your baby to give up the nighttime bottle altogether.

Parents' weaning worries. Sometimes it's the parent who is worried about weaning. A baby may take less from the cup than she did from the bottle. She may want a bottle even after she's pushed the cup away. But as long as her daily total is sixteen ounces or more, she really doesn't need that bottle.

A bottle may calm a child down. She's taking it for emotional comfort, not because she's thirsty. A parent can play into this problem by always offering a bottle for every upset. The baby may end up taking much more milk than she needs, and losing her appetite for actual food. A baby shouldn't be drinking more than thirty-two ounces (a quart) a day.

If you have to wean. If you decide that you need to take the bottle away because your child has become overly dependent on it or it's interfering with your baby's health, just do it. You can expect your child to be upset, angry, or even sad for a bit. But you don't have to worry about lasting psychological damage; children are tougher than that!

STARTING SOLID FOODS

HEALTHY FROM THE START

Food tastes form early and tend to last. Young children who develop a taste for salt often grow into salt-loving adults who are prone to high blood pressure. The love of sugar seems to be universal, but young children who get sugary foods as rewards have an extra reason for overconsuming. On the other hand, those who start out enjoying fruits, vegetables, whole grains, and healthy proteins reap the benefits for the rest of their lives.

WHEN AND HOW TO BEGIN

Spoon food. A baby's first solid foods aren't solid, they're mushy. The main thing is, they arrive on a spoon and can't just be sucked down. Babies have to learn how to move the mush around with their tongues; it's hard to do at first.

Most doctors advise starting spoon food between four and six months (the official AAP recommendation is to wait until six). Babies take to the idea more easily then than when they are older and more opinionated. Breast milk or formula supplies all the nutrients most babies need for the first six months; solid foods add important minerals after that.

There's no rush. Some parents start solid foods earlier because they don't want their baby to be one day later than the baby up the street. But with eating, earlier does not mean better. If you pay attention to your baby's signs, you can pick up cues to tell you when starting spoon foods is developmentally right for him: Can he hold his head up well? Is he interested in table foods, grabbing for yours? How does he respond when you put a small amount of food on his tongue?

Young infants have a reflex that causes them to thrust out their tongue in response to mushy foods. It's frustrating to try to feed a baby who still has an active tongue thrust reflex. If your baby sticks out his tongue as soon as any little bit of food touches it, don't force the issue. Instead, wait a few days, then try again.

Give your baby time to learn to like each new food. Start with a teaspoonful or less and work up gradually to two or three tablespoonfuls if your baby wants it. Give just a taste for several days, until your baby shows signs of enjoying it.

Solids before or after the milk? Most babies who are not used to solids want their milk first. They become indignant if offered a spoonful of something mushy instead. So let your child nurse a while before offering the spoon. A month or two later, when your baby has learned that solid foods can ward off starvation just as well as milk, you can experiment with moving the solids up to the middle or beginning of the meal. Eventually, almost all babies are happy to take all their solid food first and then top it off with the beverage, the way many adults do.

What kind of spoon? A teaspoon is pretty wide for a small baby's mouth, and most spoons have a bowl so deep that the

baby can't scoop all the contents out. A spoon made especially for babies is the better option. Some parents like to use
a flat butter spreader; others prefer a wooden tongue depres-
sor, the kind that doctors use (find them at drugstores). There
are spoons with rubber-coated bowls for teething babies who
want to bite. For babies who are feeding themselves, wide-
bowled, short-handled spoons work well.

How to introduce solid foods. Start with just one meal of
solids a day until you're both used to it. Take your time. It's
probably best to give solids at no more than two meals a day
until your baby is six months old, because the breast milk or
formula is so important in the early months.

Pick any meal you like to start. It works best if your baby
is hungry but not ravenous or overtired. A good time might
be an hour or so after a regular breast- or bottle-feeding. Your
baby should be wide awake, in a good mood, and ready for an
adventure—and so should you. It helps for the baby to be sitting in a sturdy high chair, wearing a bib.

A baby girl taking her first teaspoonful of solid food is
quite funny and a little pathetic. She looks puzzled and disgusted. She wrinkles up her nose and forehead. You can't
blame her. After all, the taste is new, the consistency is new,
the spoon may be new. When she sucks on a nipple, the
milk gets to the right place automatically. She's had no training in catching hold of a lump of food with the front of her
tongue and moving it back into her throat. She just clacks
her tongue against the roof of her mouth, and most of the
cereal gets squeezed back out onto her chin. You will have to
scrape it off her chin and scoop it back into her mouth.
Again, a lot will ooze out, but don't be discouraged—some

goes down inside, too. Be patient until she is more experienced.

Which food first? The exact order isn't important. Parents often give rice cereal first (look for brown rice cereal, which is more nutritious than the traditional white). You can mix it with either expressed breast milk or formula, whichever your baby is used to. Some babies prefer starting with a vegetable; that's fine, too. Hold off on fruits, though, because babies who love the sweetness are prone to reject everything else. There is some advantage in getting a baby used to variety, but it's wise to introduce only one new food at a time.

Cereals. Most parents begin with one of the precooked cereals made especially for babies. They are ready to eat as soon as they're mixed, which is a great convenience. Most are fortified with iron, which babies need. You can also give your baby the same cooked cereals you serve the other members of the family. But these grown-up cereals shouldn't be the mainstay of your baby's diet, because they do not have enough iron in them.

It's a good idea, if you are starting with cereal, to mix it a little thinner than the directions on the box say. It will seem more familiar to the baby and be easier to swallow. Also, babies and small children dislike food with a sticky consistency.

You will know within a few days how your baby is going to take to cereal. Some babies seem to decide, "It's weird, but it's nourishment, so I'll eat it." As the days go by, they'll grow more and more enthusiastic.

But there are other babies who decide on the second day of cereal that they don't like it at all. And on the third day they dislike it more than on the second. If your baby feels this way, be careful. Take it easy. If you try to push the cereal into your baby against his will, he will get more and more rebellious. In a week or two he may become so suspicious that he will balk at the bottle also. It's best to not get into an argument with a baby about his first solid food.

For babies who reject cereal, go slow. Give only enough to cover the tip of a teaspoon, once a day; add a little fruit to see if he likes it better that way. If in two or three days he is getting more set against it, then stop altogether for a couple of weeks. Or try vegetables or fruit instead. At first, babies are puzzled by these foods, too. But within a day or two, practically all of them decide they love them. By the end of two weeks they are ready to assume that anything that comes on a spoon is wonderful. Then you can add cereal, too. If all this fails, ask your baby's doctor.

Vegetables. If you give vegetables before fruits, your baby won't expect everything to taste sweet. Start with string beans and peas. Squash, carrots, beets, and sweet potatoes can come next; they're sweet, but not as sweet as most fruits. Give each one for a few days, to be sure that your baby doesn't develop a rash.

There are other vegetables—such as broccoli, cauliflower, cabbage, turnips, kale, and onions—that are so strong-tasting some babies don't like them. If your family likes these foods, try straining them and serving them to your baby perhaps mixed with a little apple juice to counteract their strong taste. Hold off on corn at first, because the large husks on the kernels can cause choking.

You can serve your baby fresh or frozen vegetables,

cooked and strained or pureed in a food processor, blender, or grinder. Store-bought baby vegetables in jars are fine, too. Buy the straight vegetables rather than mixtures. Only feed your baby out of the jar if you plan to use the whole jar, because saliva can spoil foods. Work up to several tablespoonfuls or half a baby jar, as desired. The rest, if refrigerated, can be given the next day. Cooked vegetables spoil fairly rapidly.

Babies are more likely to be choosy about vegetables than about cereals or fruits. You will probably find one or two vegetables that your baby doesn't like. Don't push them, but try them again every month or so.

It's common for undigested vegetables to appear in bowel movements when the baby first starts those foods. This is not a bad sign so long as there is no looseness or mucus. Increase the amount of each vegetable slowly until the baby's digestion learns to handle it. If a vegetable causes looseness or much mucus, omit it for the time being and try a very small amount after another month.

Beets may color the urine or show up red in the bowel movement. This is nothing to worry about if you remember that it is caused by beets and not blood. Green vegetables often turn the bowel movement green. Spinach can cause chapping of the lips and irritation around the anus in some babies. If this occurs, omit spinach for several months and then try again. Babies who eat a lot of orange or yellow vegetables, such as carrots or squash, often develop an orange or yellow tinge to their skin. This condition is not dangerous, and it goes away once the baby cuts back on those vegetables.

Fruits. Apples, peaches, pears, apricots, and prunes are usually good first fruits. For the first six or eight months of a baby's life, the fruit is stewed, except for raw ripe banana. If you buy baby food, look at the label to make sure it is all fruit. (Fruits packed in syrup can be useful if your baby's bowel movements are hard, however.) It's also easy to make your own. Just stew the fruit in a pot until it's soft, then mash it up or use a blender. Make sure it's smooth, with no lumps to choke on.

You can give fruit at any feeding, once or twice a day. Increase each fruit gradually as your baby learns to like it. Prunes, prune juice, and sometimes apricots are mildly laxative for almost all babies. This makes them doubly valuable if your baby tends to have hard stools. You can give puréed prunes or prune juice at one feeding and some other fruit at another feeding each day.

If your baby's bowels become loose, you will probably want to omit prunes and apricots for a couple of months and give other fruits only once a day.

After age six months or so, you can begin adding or substituting other raw fruits besides bananas: scraped apple, pear, avocado. One main concern is the risk of choking: It's safest to wait with berries and seedless grapes until your baby is two, and then cut them up or mash them until your child is past age three.

High-protein vegetarian foods. Once your baby is familiar with cereals, vegetables, and fruits, you can introduce other foods. Try very well-cooked beans and legumes, like lentils, chickpeas, and kidney beans.

Start with small amounts of cooked beans. If you notice that your baby develops an irritated bottom and you see bits of undigested bean in his bowel movement, wait a few weeks before reintroducing beans, and make sure they are very well cooked. Tofu is also a good choice. Many babies happily eat it in small cubes or mixed with applesauce, other pureed fruits, or vegetables.

For beans and legumes, it's easy and economical to buy them dried. Simply soak a bowl of them overnight, then boil them until they are as soft as you want. (This takes planning, but it is otherwise rather easy.) If you use canned beans, put them in a strainer and rinse them well to remove some of the sodium; still, they'll never be as salt-free as the beans you boil yourself.

Meat. Beef, pork, and poultry are good sources of concentrated nutrition, and many parents add servings of well-cooked, mashed, or pureed meat soon after their babies have mastered cereals, fruits, and vegetables. But there are disadvantages: Children who become used to meat during their early years may pay a price in adulthood for the saturated fat and animal proteins these foods contain (see page 311). Another growing concern is contamination by bacteria, such as *E. coli*, that can cause serious infections. Infants are especially at risk. Most store-bought meat is processed in large factories where these bacteria spread. Meats must always be thoroughly cooked so that there is no pinkness at all, and any surfaces or utensils touched by raw meat must be thoroughly cleaned with soap and water. Fish, such as cod or haddock, are a healthier and safer source of meat, as long as they're well cooked and all the bones have been removed.

Foods that trigger allergies. We used to tell parents to delay introducing peanuts, eggs, dairy, soy, nuts, fish, and shellfish because these are the most common food allergy triggers. Now we know that early exposure, by six months of age or before, actually *lowers* the risk of food allergies. This makes sense if you consider that early on the baby's immune system is learning what is safe and what is not.

An infant who takes grains, vegetables, and fruits without developing diarrhea or a rash will probably also do fine with peanut and other allergenic foods. For infants who did have negative reactions to first foods, or who have moderate or severe eczema (page 488), or if food allergies run in the family, it's best to ask the doctor first before starting allergenic foods. But don't put it off thinking you're avoiding the problem; this is one time when delay is not the safest policy. Once a baby starts with these foods, around six months, regular reexposure helps prevent allergies.

Straight peanut butter is too sticky for little babies, and poses a choking hazard. It and other nut butters are safer mixed into pureed sweet potatoes or squash. Add cow's milk to soups or give Greek yogurt off the spoon. (Cow's milk isn't safe as the main drink for infants under a year, but a bit mixed into soup or other foods won't hurt.) Grind up fish and shellfish to a fine consistency.

Eggs. Egg yolks supply healthy fats, calories, vitamins, and iron. The body absorbs the iron best if the yolks are eaten along with a source of vitamin C, such as oranges or other citrus fruit, tomatoes, potatoes, or cantaloupe. It's wise to wait until your baby accepts these foods before adding egg yolks. Yolks are high in cholesterol, but it's not clear that this is a bad thing. Whites cause allergies in some babies, so *do* introduce them early, following the guidance above.

Mixed dinners. There are a variety of "dinners" in jars for babies. They usually consist of small amounts of meat and vegetable with a larger amount of potato, rice, or barley. If you buy vegetables, grains, beans, and fruits in separate jars, it's easier to know how much of each food your baby is getting. When there is a tendency to allergy, these ready-made mixtures may be problematic unless the baby has already taken each of the foods included in the mixture without reaction.

Making your own baby food. Preparing food for your baby lets you control the ingredients and saves money. You can use fresh, organically grown foods. It's easier than you might think.

Make a large batch of any healthy food you choose, then puree it. Add water, expressed breast milk, or formula to get the consistency right for your baby. Freeze serving-size portions in ice cube trays or on cookie sheets and then store them in plastic freezer bags until they're used. When you reheat the food, be sure to stir it well to avoid hot spots. Otherwise, one spoonful might be cool and the next one scalding, especially if you used the microwave.

Don't add sugar or salt. The earliest experiences with food set a child's idea of what tastes good, and high sugar and salt intake are serious health concerns in later years. Commercial baby foods often add sugar and salt, because it makes the food taste better to grown-ups!

Commercial baby foods. When you buy baby food in jars, read the fine print. When the large print says "creamed beans," the fine print may say "beans with cornstarch." Choose plain fruits or plain vegetables to be sure that your baby is getting enough of these valuable foods and is not being overloaded with refined starches.

Steer clear of cornstarch puddings and gelatin desserts. They don't have the right food values, and they contain a lot of sugar. Instead, give your baby plain strained fruits. A baby who has never been exposed to refined sugar will find plain fruit to be delightfully sweet.

SOLID FOODS, SIX TO TWELVE MONTHS

Two or three meals a day. By six months your baby may take one, two, or three meals of solids a day. A moderately hungry baby might have cereal for breakfast, vegetable and tofu or beans for lunch, and cereal and fruit for supper. A baby who tends to be constipated can have prunes every night along with her cereal, and another fruit at breakfast or lunch. You may want your baby to have beans and vegetable at supper with the rest of the family, the cereal and fruit at lunch. Let your baby be your guide, and do what's convenient for you.

Lumpy and chopped food. At around six months, you'll want your baby to get used to lumpy or chopped foods. Even without teeth, babies can mush up lumps of cooked vegetables or fruit and pieces of whole-wheat bread or toast with their gums and tongue. If your baby is squeamish about lumps, go slowly, but keep offering so he has a chance to overcome his original resistance.

Make the change to chopped foods gradually. At first, mash them up pretty fine with a fork; gradually mash less and less. Give small spoonfuls. Babies can't stand to have a whole spoonful of lumps dumped into their mouths when they're not used to it.

Finger foods. By six or seven months, babies can grab food whole-handed. And once babies *can* do this, they *want* to do it. Hand-to-mouth feeding prepares babies to spoon-feed themselves at about a year.

A traditional first finger food is a crust of stale whole-wheat bread or toast or a dry bagel, especially if babies are teething. As the bread or toast dissolves off into their mouths, it makes them feel they're getting somewhere, even though most of it ends up in their hair. Teething biscuits often contain extra sugar. It's better to let your baby get used to enjoying things that aren't so sweet.

By eight or nine months, most babies can nab small objects with their fingers. You can start putting pieces of fruit or cooked vegetable and tofu chunks on your baby's high chair tray for her to pick up. (And be sure to check around for choking hazards. A good rule of thumb is, if something can fit inside a toilet paper tube, it's a choking hazard.) If your baby is especially interested in the food on your plate, you can take a bit at a time and move it to where your baby can reach.

With or without teeth, by their first birthdays almost all babies can handle the same foods as the rest of the family, as long as the pieces are cut up small enough and hard foods that are choking hazards are avoided.

Choking on solid foods. All babies choke a little while getting used to eating lumpy foods, just as they fall when they're learning to walk. Foods little children often choke on include:

- ✦ Hot dogs

- ✦ Round candy

- ✦ Peanuts

- ✦ Grapes

- ✦ Cookies

- ✦ Meat chunks or slices

- ✦ Raw carrot slices

- ✦ Peanut butter

- ✦ Apple chunks

- ✦ Popcorn

You can make grapes, apples, and meat safer by cutting or breaking them up into little pieces. Peanut butter is safer spread on bread than eaten off a spoon or finger. But it's best to avoid hot dogs and hard round candies altogether: There's no way to make them safe, and they're not good for children (or adults) anyhow.

Nine times out of ten, babies who are choking easily bring the food up or down without any assistance. If you feel like your help is needed, you can pull the food out with your fingers, if you can see it. If that doesn't work, put the baby over your lap with her head down and her bottom up. Hit her firmly between the shoulder blades a couple of times with the palm of your hand (see page 440). This virtually always solves the problem.

Even after your child can feed himself independently, it's best if you sit down with him and talk and (sometimes) eat together. Meals are more fun that way, more nourishing in a holistic sense, and also safer.

NUTRITION AND HEALTH

WHAT IS GOOD NUTRITION?

It's natural to give your children the foods you remember from your childhood. On the other hand, some diets are healthier than others. If you've thought about changing your own diet for health reasons, you may want to consider changing your child's as well.

The typical North American diet is high in animal fats and refined sugars (pizza with a soda), which are linked to obesity, high blood pressure, heart disease and stroke, diabetes, cancer, and more. These adult diseases often have their roots in childhood. By age three, many American children already have fatty deposits in their arteries, and by age twelve, 70 percent of children have these early signs of blood vessel disease; by age twenty-one, virtually all young adults have them.

It's easy to get confused about good nutrition. But most experts agree on some basics: People should eat less saturated fat and refined sugar, and more unsaturated fat, complex carbohydrates, and lean protein. If children learn to enjoy simple foods—whole grains, fruits, and vegetables—they can enjoy a complex mix of nutrients that support health during childhood and throughout life.

Children who are cheerfully and regularly offered a variety of healthful foods learn to prefer these foods. The trick is to make them a regular part of the family diet without putting too much emphasis on the fact that they are "good for you" (with the clear implication that "nobody really likes to eat this stuff"). Telling a child, "If you eat your broccoli, I'll give you some dessert," just makes him hate broccoli. If healthful foods are part of the family routine, children accept most of them naturally.

BUILDING BLOCKS OF NUTRITION

Calories. Calories aren't nutrients, they're a measure of the energy content of food. Proteins and carbohydrates contain about 4 calories per gram (113 calories per ounce); fats and oils contain more than twice as many: 9 calories per gram (255 calories per ounce). A small amount of fat goes a long way.

Children need calories to grow and to fuel their bodies. Young children (age one to three) need as few as 900; a moderately active young man may need 3,900—more if he's an athlete. Women and children at different ages fall in between. But counting calories is usually a waste of time; the body does a good job of figuring out when it needs more energy and when it's had enough.

Children should get about 50 percent of their calories from carbohydrates, about 30 percent from fats, and about 20 percent from proteins.

Sugars and starches. Refined sugar, honey, and syrup provide quick energy, but they don't stave off hunger for very long. Starchy foods release their energy more slowly, because the body first has to break the starch down into sugar. Vegetables and whole grains (whole wheat, brown rice) deliver fiber and protein along with the starch, which makes them even better at keeping people full over time. Highly processed sugar and starch in soda, candy, and white bread provide calories with few other nutrients ("empty calories"). The body remains hungry for the nutrients it isn't getting.

Sugars and starches get broken down into glucose, which is the energy source for the brain and every cell in the body. Sugary foods drive up the level of glucose in the blood and brain, creating a "sugar high," but the body quickly counters with insulin, which sends the glucose level crashing back down. This cycle fuels sugar cravings, which can develop into an addiction. Young children who sip juice all day are budding sugar addicts. Better for them—and for their teeth—to drink water and eat less-processed foods.

Fats. Fats and oils (liquid fat) supply long-term energy and the raw material for the walls of every cell, and for key parts of the brain. *Saturated* fats are the more solid fats found mainly in meat and dairy products. *Unsaturated* fats are the more liquid fats found mainly in plant-based foods, especially nuts, seeds, and oils, and also in fish. Polyunsaturated fats are more unsaturated than mono-unsaturated fats, and generally healthier. *Trans* fats aren't found in nature; they're manufactured by heating vegetable oil in the presence of hydrogen gas. Another term is "hydrogenated vegetable oil." These fats show up in many margarines and commercial baked goods and are a major cause of heart disease.

A healthy diet provides about 30 percent of its calories as fat, with twice as much unsaturated fat (20 percent) as saturated fat (10 percent), and no trans fat at all. Diets with even less saturated fat are probably even better, since saturated and trans fats—both fats that are solid at room temperature—contribute to hardening of the arteries, while polyunsaturated fats have the opposite effect. The term "fatty acid" just means "fat."

The body is able to make most of the fats it needs. But a few varieties of fatty acid are *essential,* meaning that they can't be made, they have to be eaten. These include omega-6 and omega-3 fats, which include linoleic acid (LA) or alpha-linolenic acid (ALA). The body uses these to make a long list of chemicals, including DHA and EPA, which are important in the brain and elsewhere (the initials stand for long chemical names that pretty much nobody can pronounce). Good sources of essential fatty acids include fish oils, soy products, nuts and seeds, and many green leafy vegetables. ALA is particularly high in fish and also in flaxseed, walnuts, and canola oil. (You can find ground flaxseed in most natural food stores; it tastes especially good in smoothies, salads, and breakfast cereals.)

Cholesterol. Bodies need cholesterol for cells and hormones. It comes in different varieties. One kind (LDL) carries cholesterol to blood vessel walls, where it builds up; hence LDL is called "bad cholesterol." Another kind (HDL) carries the cholesterol away from the blood vessels back to the liver, where it gets broken down; hence HDL is "good cholesterol." High blood levels of LDL are a warning sign for high blood pressure, stroke, and heart attacks.

Most of the cholesterol in the body is made in the body itself, but diet is also important. Diets that are high in cholesterol tend to promote high levels of LDL and thus high rates of heart disease. You can lower cholesterol in your diet by eating less meat and dairy. Only animal products contain cholesterol. Plants don't make cholesterol at all. Any food that is entirely made from plants contains zero cholesterol. It's that simple.

Proteins. These are the body's main building material for muscles and organs, and for the enzymes that make the machinery run. Proteins in the diet get broken down into amino acids, then reassembled into our own proteins. We use twenty-two different amino acids to make proteins. If certain ones are in short supply, the process of protein making slows down and leftover amino acids are burned for fuel, stored as fat, or dumped in the urine. That's why, in a growing child, each day's intake should provide all the necessary amino acids.

Foods that provide all of the necessary amino acids are called "complete" or "high-quality." Meats and soy foods are complete proteins, as are combinations of any whole grain and a legume (peanut butter on whole wheat bread, for example). An advantage of nonmeat protein is that it comes with less saturated fat and no cholesterol.

How much protein a child needs depends on her body composition, activity level, and rate of growth. A ballpark figure is about one gram of protein per kilogram of body weight per day; but no sensible parent would try to go by the numbers. The amount of meat needed in a meal is only the size of a deck of cards or what fits in the palm of one hand. Children, being smaller, need less. If you offer a reasonably small amount of a high-quality protein food, you can trust your child to eat what she needs.

Fiber or roughage. Plants contain a lot of material that our bodies can't readily digest. This stuff—fiber or roughage—passes into the intestines and absorbs water, making soft bowel movements. A person on a low-fiber diet—say, a child who only eats pizza, french fries, and peanut butter and jelly on white bread—is apt to become constipated. Fiber found in beans and oats (soluble fiber) also helps lower cholesterol levels.

The best sources of fiber are vegetables, fruits, whole grains, and legumes. Leafy greens, broccoli, green beans, and cabbages are mainly composed of fiber and water. Starchy vegetables like potatoes and green peas are less roughage-rich. Granulated sugar, corn syrup, and refined grains such as white flour contain little if any fiber; meat, dairy products, fish, and poultry contain no fiber at all.

Minerals. All natural, unrefined foods contain a variety of necessary minerals, such as calcium, iron, zinc, copper, magnesium, and phosphorus.

Calcium. Bones and teeth are mostly made up of calcium and phosphorus. Over the years, doctors have counseled children and teens to consume plenty of calcium to prevent thinning of the bones in old age (osteoporosis). Dairy foods provide lots of calcium, hence the national advertising campaign urging everyone to drink more milk. But some experts question whether children really need this much calcium. The key, these doctors argue, is not how much calcium is *taken in*, but how much is *retained*. Physical activity that puts stress on bones (e.g., running, jumping rope) makes bones retain calcium. Certain foodstuffs (e.g., salty foods and meat) cause the kidneys to dump calcium. Active children with low meat intake can build stronger bones than sedentary children who drink lots of milk. (See page 324 for other health benefits of getting calcium from nondairy sources.)

Iron. Hemoglobin, the oxygen-carrying substance in red blood cells, requires iron. So do key enzymes in the brain. Even a mild iron deficiency in early childhood can cause long-term learning problems. Breast milk contains a highly absorbable form of iron; infant formulas have extra iron added for the same reason. (Regular cow's milk is not safe for infants because it contains too little iron and also blocks the absorption of iron from the intestines.) Iron-fortified cereals and other iron-rich foods become important after about six months of age. Meats and egg yolks are iron-rich, as are green leafy vegetables like kale. Most children's multivitamins contain iron as well.

Zinc. Cell growth depends on zinc. The cells that line the intestines, heal wounds, and fight off infections are especially vulnerable to zinc deficiency. Babies absorb zinc well from breast milk, and from meat, fish, and dairy. Legumes, nuts, and whole grains also have zinc. But since plant-based zinc is not easily absorbed, children on vegan diets should take a daily multivitamin with zinc for extra insurance.

Iodine is used in the thyroid gland and the brain. Iodine deficiency is rare in industrialized countries because iodine is added to table salt. Elsewhere, though, iodine deficiency is a major cause of cognitive disability in children. Children who do not eat meat and only eat sea salt or kosher salt might need an iodine supplement.

Sodium. The kidneys control the level of sodium in the blood, and diets that are very high in sodium put a strain on the kidneys, and can lead to high blood pressure and loss of calcium. Table salt is about one-third sodium by weight, and many processed foods are extremely high in it.

Vitamins. A well-rounded diet provides plenty of vitamins. For vegans and children who shun vegetables and fruits, a daily multivitamin ensures adequate intake. Breastfed infants also need extra vitamins (see page 260).

Vitamin A. Vegetables and fruit, particularly yellow and orange ones, supply all of the vitamin A children need. Excess vitamin A from overuse of supplements is harmful, but this won't happen from eating a lot of vegetables.

B vitamins. The most important B vitamins are thiamine (B_1), riboflavin (B_2), niacin (B_3), and pyridoxine (B_6). Many foods contain B vitamins, and deficiencies are rare. Cobalamin (B_{12}) is plentiful in meats and dairy foods but absent from plant-based foods, so vegans need to take a multivitamin to be sure they get the B_{12} they need. A crucial vitamin for making DNA and red blood cells is folic acid (vitamin B_9). Folate is especially critical for young women who might become pregnant, since folate deficiency can lead to serious birth defects involving the spinal cord (e.g., spina bifida). Folate also plays a role in making DNA and red blood cells. Fortified flour and baked goods, spinach, broccoli, turnip greens, whole grains, and fruits such as cantaloupe and strawberries are good sources.

Vitamin C (ascorbic acid). Bones, teeth, and blood vessels need vitamin C, as do many other body functions. Bruising, rash, painful bleeding of the gums, and joint pain can be signs of vitamin C deficiency, which is rare in North America. Good sources include oranges, lemons, grapefruit, raw and properly canned tomatoes and tomato juice, raw cabbage, and other fruits and vegetables. Vitamin C is easily destroyed in cooking. Megadoses of vitamin C do not prevent or cure the common cold.

Vitamin D. The body makes this vitamin in response to sunlight. Vitamin D deficiency leads to weak bones, sleep problems, moodiness, and perhaps obesity. It's common in cold and cloudy climates, and in people who spend too much time indoors. People with dark skin tone are more at risk, because skin pigment blocks some of the D-making rays. Daily vitamin D supplements help in these cases. Mothers need extra vitamin D during pregnancy and breastfeeding. A daily vitamin D supplement of 400 IU is important for every breastfed child, starting at two months; infant formula has vitamin D added.

Vitamin E. One role of vitamin E is to help the body deal with harmful chemicals that may contribute to aging or cancer. However, taking extra vitamin E doesn't seem to help, and it *is* possible to overdose. Vegetarian diets are naturally rich in vitamin E. Children who avoid vegetables might benefit from a daily multivitamin that contains E.

Vitamin toxicity. Very high doses of vitamins (megadoses) are sometimes suggested for treating or preventing certain conditions; more often, though, these high doses don't do any good or actually cause harm. Vitamins A, D, and K are the ones most likely to cause serious problems with toxicity, but other vitamins such as pyridoxine (B_6) and niacin (B_3) can also cause severe negative effects. Before you give your child higher-than-usual doses, be sure to check with your child's doctor.

Phytochemicals. This refers to a large number of beneficial chemicals that are made by plants. They protect against oxidation (destruction) of proteins, reduce inflammation and blood clots, prevent bone loss, and fight off certain cancers. Plants grown in healthy soils without pesticides tend to make more of these beneficial chemicals; cooking tends to degrade them (but one, lycopene, is best absorbed from cooked tomatoes). Food manufacturers sometimes add antioxidants, but the best sources are fruits and vegetables themselves.

DR. SPOCK'S DIET

There's no question that the typical U.S. diet is too rich in fat, sugar, and salt. Everybody agrees that children should eat more vegetables and whole grains. Dr. Spock's nutritional philosophy went several steps further. He believed that the healthiest diet was plant-based, without meat, eggs, or dairy products. This approach is not as far-out as it may seem. The American Dietetic Association published a scientific review in 2009 that concluded that vegan diets confer significant health benefits compared to diets that include dairy and meat, including lower rates of heart attacks, high blood pressure, diabetes, obesity, cancer, osteoporosis, dementia, diverticulitis, and gallstones. Imagine being able to protect your child from these plagues!

Dr. Spock wrote, "I have personally been on a nondairy, low-fat meatless diet since 1991, when I was eighty-eight years old. Within two weeks of beginning this diet, my chronic bronchitis went away after years of unsuccessful antibiotic treatments. . . . I no longer recommend dairy products after the age of two years."

Where does that leave you as a parent? No one answer is best for everyone. A diet based on the U.S. Department of Agriculture's recommendations, including small portions of meat, low-fat milk, eggs, and a variety of plant-based foods is a common choice for many children. On the other hand, a diet that's mostly or completely free of milk, eggs, and meat, while it requires some thought, can be equally delicious and may offer even more long-term health benefits to you and your children.

Vegetarian diets. A diet that excludes all animal flesh is vegetarian. Lacto-ovo vegetarians eat dairy products and eggs; vegans don't. Lots of people consider themselves vegetarians but eat a little meat now and then. There's no point in being too picky about the terminology.

Children who eat a variety of whole grains, fruits and vegetables, legumes, nuts and seeds, dairy products, and eggs don't need any special diet planning or supplements to be healthy. Children who don't eat dairy and eggs should make sure to take supplemental vitamin B_{12} and maybe vitamin D. A daily multivitamin and time in the sun will do the trick.

Vegetarian diets tend to be lower in calories than diets that include fatty meats. That may be a challenge for young children, who need lots of calories for growth. Nuts and nut butters, seeds, avocado, and different oils are among the foods that pack a lot of energy into a small volume. If vegetarian eating is new to you, you may need guidance from a good cookbook or, better yet, from friends who can show you what to do. Your child's doctor will follow weights, heights, and the usual blood tests to monitor for any nutritional problems. But you shouldn't expect any.

Getting started eating better. It's better to eat smaller portions of meats than larger ones. Lower-fat cuts of meats are best; high-fat meats like baloney and salami are worst. Chicken and pork have just as much cholesterol as beef and almost as much fat. The fat in fish is healthier. Cooking meat at high temperatures creates cancer-forming chemicals. This is bad news for lovers of barbecue!

Your first step toward a healthier diet may be finding one or two meatless recipes you like. Make these a part of your weekly menu, and add new meatless dishes every month or so. Explore different products that take the place of meats, such as meatless burgers and hot dogs.

Tofu is a versatile, inexpensive, cholesterol-free protein source. If you can't imagine any way to make it appealing, go out to a vegetarian or Asian restaurant for inspiration, or let a friend who has already taken the plunge show you the way.

Iron without meat. Iron is important for growing children, and red meat is a good source of it (providing about 2.5 mg per serving, about twice as much as chicken or pork). Ounce for ounce, canned sardines are right up there with beef, and canned clams have nearly 10 times as much! Vegetarian foods can be rich in iron as well. The iron from nonmeat sources is less easily absorbed, so children need more. But more is what they get: 7.0 milligrams in a half cup of cooked fortified oatmeal, 6.7 milligrams in a half cup of tofu, 3.3 milligrams in a half cup of cooked lentils. Other good sources include whole-wheat bread, hard-boiled eggs, kidney beans, prunes, and raisins. Iron deficiency is no more common among vegetarian children than it is among meat eaters.

Concerns about cow's milk. Most of us grew up being told that milk was good for you, so it's hard for us to imagine that it might actually pose health risks. Whole milk, cheese, and ice cream are rich in the saturated fats that block arteries and cause heart attacks. In fact, milk is the number one source of fat in children's diets in the United States—higher than burgers, fries, and chips. (A cup of whole milk has 4.6 grams of saturated fat, more than four slices of bacon; a tablespoon of butter has 7.3 grams.) Doctors recommend whole milk for toddlers from age one to two, because the rapidly growing brain needs fat. But the omega-3 fatty acids that are essential for brain development are found in vegetable oils; cow's milk is very low in these healthy fats.

There are other concerns about dairy products, too—even the low-fat ones. They can impair a child's ability to absorb iron and can cause blood loss from the intestines in small children and in children who have milk allergies. These problems, combined with the fact that cow's milk has little iron of its own, can lead to iron deficiency. For sure, children under a year of age should not drink cow's milk.

Allergic reactions to the proteins in cow's milk are common. If asthma or eczema runs in the family, a dairy-free diet sometimes eliminates these problems. Sensitivity to cow's milk can trigger constipation, ear infections, and even (rarely) diabetes.

As children grow up, many develop stomachaches, bloating, diarrhea, and gas caused by undigested lactose (milk sugar). The ability to digest milk sugar disappears for many people in late childhood. Other mammals don't drink milk after infancy, and that's probably the normal pattern for humans, too.

Experts disagree about the role of cow's milk in a variety of adult diseases, including cancers of the prostate, ovary, and breast. Concern focuses on the hormones dissolved in the milk fat. Choosing skim milk and fat-free milk products should, in theory, lower this risk.

Cow's milk and calcium. Everyone knows that milk is an important source of calcium, but scientists debate the pluses and minuses of cow's milk when it comes to bone health. For example, several well-done studies found *no* connection between the amount of cow's milk children drink and the amount of calcium they store in their bones. That really is a remarkable finding. If drinking cow's milk is crucial for bone growth, then you'd expect that people who drink more milk would have stronger bones. But they don't. In fact, the United States has very high per capita milk consumption and also very high rates of osteoporosis. Calcium intake is just one of many factors that influence bone density (see page 316).

Almond milk, now widely available, delivers the same amount of calcium and vitamin D as cow's milk. Soy and rice drinks also have added calcium. Calcium is easily absorbed from many leafy vegetables and beans, which also provide vitamins, iron, complex carbohydrates, and fiber. Here is a list of calcium-rich foods:

CALCIUM SOURCES

(approximate number of milligrams per serving)

100 mg

1 cup kale, cooked or fresh

1 cup navy beans
3½ ounces tofu
1 cup cottage cheese
1 tablespoon blackstrap molasses
1 English muffin
1½ cups boiled sweet potato

150 mg

1 cup cooked broccoli
1 ounce mozzarella or feta cheese
½ cup cooked collard greens
1 cup soft-serve ice cream
5 medium figs, dried

200 mg

1 cup beet or turnip greens
1 ounce cheddar or jack cheese
3 ounces canned sardines or salmon with bones

250 mg

1 ounce Swiss cheese
½ cup firm tofu
1 cup rhubarb

300 mg

1 cup cow's milk
1 cup yogurt
½ cup ricotta cheese
1 cup enriched soy or rice milk (but check the label;
some brands may vary)
1 cup calcium-fortified orange or apple juice

Sources: Jean A. T. Pennington and Judith Spungen, *Bowes and Church's Food Values of Portions Commonly Used* (New York: Harper & Row, 1989).

WHAT TO COOK

We used to think of vegetables, grains, and beans as side dishes. Now we know better. These foods take center stage in a healthy diet. Children can certainly thrive on simple foods, cooked simply. Here are some ideas.

Green leafy vegetables. Broccoli, kale, collards, watercress, Swiss chard, Napa cabbage, Chinese cabbage, bok choy, spinach, and other green vegetables are loaded with absorbable calcium, iron, and vitamins; the darker the color, the richer the nutritional value. Leafy greens should be steamed or stir-fried quickly, some just one or two minutes, so that they come out bright green. They can be seasoned with a little salt and pepper when your child is older, but it's best to avoid added salt for younger children so that they don't develop a taste for very salty foods.

Other vegetables. Squashes of all sorts, including pumpkin, are good baked or used in soups and stews, along with carrots, rutabagas, potatoes, and other roots. Baked sweet potatoes (yams are the same thing) and beets are naturally sweet. Peppers of all varieties are vitamin-rich. Green beans provide vitamins and fiber.

Wait until two years to serve kernel corn. Young children don't chew it; it passes through them unchanged. Use only tender corn. When cutting it off the cob, don't cut too close; then each kernel will be cut open. When your child is three or four and you start to offer corn on the cob, slice down the center of each row of kernels so that they are all split. Corn off the cob can be served either warm or frozen, right from the bag; children often enjoy picking up the crunchy kernels one at a time.

Beans and legumes. Red beans, black beans, black-eyed peas, chickpeas, and lentils are rich in protein, calcium, fiber, and many other nutrients. They are also a good source of calories. Tofu and tempeh, both made from soybeans, work well in salads, stews, stir-fries, and soups. A meal that includes beans and brown rice—or any bean-and-grain combination—delivers a complete protein with no cholesterol and little saturated fat.

Peanut butter is a terrific food, cheap, tasty, and nutritious. Most brands, however, are made with lots of added sugar. Look at the ingredient list on the jar. It should read simply "peanuts" or "peanuts and salt."

Whole grains. Brown rice, barley, oats, millet, whole-wheat noodles and pasta, and whole-grain bread provide complex carbohydrates for sustained energy as well as protein, fiber, and vitamins.

Many people worry about gluten, a protein in wheat, barley, and rye. Gluten can trigger celiac disease, a very serious condition (see page 509). A different condition, *non-celiac gluten sensitivity,* has been connected with problems of learning and behavior, low energy, and abdominal discomfort. There is no lab test that can confirm or rule out non-celiac gluten sensitivity. The only way to tell is to elimi-nate gluten entirely. Gluten-free foods are easy to find, if sometimes costly, but keeping a child on this diet can be dif-ficult. It may mean, for example, no eating at a friend's house unless that house is also gluten-free. If you do put your child on a gluten-free diet (other than for celiac dis-ease), it's worthwhile to check a few months later to see if you can reintroduce gluten without symptoms coming back. Often, you can.

Meats. Quality matters here: Animals that graze on grass pro-duce meat that is lower in saturated fat than conventionally raised meat, and these animals usually are given fewer hor-mones and antibiotics. High-quality meat costs more, but you can save money by using less of it. An adult serving is only three ounces; a child-size portion is smaller yet. Ground beef is a special concern because modern production methods mix beef from many animals in a single package, increasing the risk of bacterial contamination. To be safe, it has to be cooked so that no pink remains; rare burgers shouldn't be on the menu anymore.

Fish. Fish is a good source of unsaturated fats, including omega-3 fatty acids. Many experts suggest two or three serv-ings of fish a week, but you can get plenty of omega-3 fatty acids from vegetarian sources (see page 314). Contamination of fish with mercury and other heavy metals is a concern, par-ticularly for pregnant women (page 395). Farm-raised fish may not be the same nutritionally as their wild-caught cous-ins; it depends on what they have been fed. Wild-caught fish is expensive; frozen is cheaper, and no less nutritious. Small, short-lived fish such as sardines provide healthy fats without heavy metals. Sardines from the Atlantic and Mediterranean are seriously overfished, but sardines from the Pacific are still okay to eat; check www.seafoodwatch.org for updates. A taste for sardines is worth acquiring!

Fats and oils. The healthiest oils contain the least saturated fat. Canola oil is good (7 percent saturated), followed by corn, peanut, and olive oils (all about 14 percent). Lard is bad (39 percent saturated); butter worse (50 percent). Margarine and spreads in tubs contain 10 percent to 40 percent saturated fat, depending on the brand. Margarine used to be very high in synthetic trans fats, but these unhealthy substances have now been largely phased out (see page 313).

Any healthy oil can work as the base for a salad dressing or brushed on the bottom of a skillet for stir-frying. Tofu or sweet potato slices sprayed lightly with oil, then baked in a hot oven, come out with a crispy top. Try Dijon mustard or salsa on steamed vegetables for a spicier taste. Jam and cinnamon work well on toast without the layer of butter in between.

Fruits, seeds, and nuts. These foods make delicious treats. Locally grown fruits in season are fresher and often cheaper. Baking or stewing makes fruits sweeter and easier to digest. Drying makes them easy to pack as snacks. Seeds and nuts can be roasted and eaten alone or in salads.

Dairy. Whole milk (4 percent fat) is best for babies age one to two years, who need the fat for brain growth. Change to low fat (2 percent) at age two, and skim (1 percent) at age three. Milk is a good source of calcium and vitamin D (many nondairy milks are fortified with these nutrients to the same level as cow's milk, or higher). Yogurt is great with fruit, or in smoothies. A slice of cheese with sprouts and avocado makes a great sandwich filling, but a diet high in cheese is also likely to be high in saturated fat.

Eggs. Egg whites are a great source of protein, fat-free, and low in calories. Egg yolks are good sources of vitamin B_{12} and other nutrients. They're high in cholesterol but low in saturated fat, containing about the same amount as a tablespoon of olive oil. Some people eat only the whites, avoiding the yolks. Eggs are safe for babies. An egg yolk whipped with canola oil and a bit of lemon juice makes mayonnaise. Whipped egg whites, of course, make meringue.

Sugar. Brown sugar and raw sugar are nutritionally the same as white sugar (that is, pretty bad). Soda and candy are packed with sugar, but so are many prepared foods that you wouldn't expect to be. Look for "modified corn starch" on the label. See drspock.com for the 100 other names for sugar. Once you take sugar out of the diet, you'll begin to notice the real taste of fruits and sweet vegetables such as pumpkin, corn, squash, and carrots.

Salt. Most processed foods are very salty, which makes food with a normal amount of salt taste bland. It's better to cook food yourself and use salt sparingly. Table salt is fortified with iodine, an essential nutrient. If you remove all table salt and processed foods from your child's diet, you may need to think about other sources of iodine; however, iodine deficiency is very rare in the United States.

Juice and water. Most of the juice marketed to children is just sugar water with flavoring, coloring, and maybe some vitamins. Even 100 percent pure juices are packed with sugar. A large glass of 100 percent orange juice, for example, delivers all of the sugar of a half-dozen oranges, but none of the fiber. It has lots of vitamin C, true, but most of that just gets excreted by the kidneys. A child would be better off just eating one whole orange. A child who loves orange juice might equally adore watered down juice, which still delivers refreshment and vitamin C, with less sugar.

The beverage children really need is pure, clean water. In most places, water from the tap is perfectly safe. Let the cold run for a couple of minutes until the water is icy so that it's coming from the water main, and hasn't been sitting in the pipes in your home (see page 392 for concerns about lead, and page 23 about well water). Fill a glass container with cold water and put it uncovered in the refrigerator. Any chlorine in the water will evaporate off, leaving delicious cold water. For variety, add some lemon juice, cucumber, or herbs.

Herb teas, warm or cold, are healthy and cheap. Be aware of caffeine in coffee, of course, but also in black and green teas, and in many popular soft drinks marketed to children. (Chocolate also contains a fair amount of caffeine.)

Sweets. You don't have to be so worried about refined sugars that you stop your child from eating sweets altogether. Cookies, cake, or ice cream now and then do no harm. It's a steady diet of such foods that deprives children of nutrition. There is no reason to train your child to expect a rich dessert after every dinner. You don't need to keep your home stocked with store-bought cookies or ice cream. Instead, make a batch of cookies with your child, enjoy the process and the product, and when the cookies are gone, enjoy other sweet things (fruit, for example). Artificial sweeteners avoid the problems of sugar, but they're so sweet that they make naturally sweet things taste bland by comparison. Children are better off with a little real sugar now and then.

SIMPLE MEALS

The whole business of diet sounds complicated, but it needn't be. Roughly speaking, the following foods are required every day:

+ Vegetables, green or yellow, three to five servings, some cooked, some raw.

+ Fruit, two or three servings.

+ Legumes (beans, peas, and lentils), two to three servings.

+ Whole-grain bread, crackers, cereals, or pasta, two or more servings.

+ A little fish or meat, optional.

Suggested meals. If some of these suggestions seem odd or unusual, that's the point. If you want to change what you and your children eat, you need to be willing to try different things. Keep an open mind and see what works for you.

Breakfast

✦ Fruit or green leafy vegetables, or both

✦ Whole-grain cereal, bread, toast, or pancakes

✦ Scrambled tofu with greens

✦ Almond milk (or soy or rice milk)

✦ Vegetable soup

Lunch

✦ A filling dish such as baked beans; whole-wheat or oat cereal, millet, or barley soup with vegetables; whole-grain bread or sandwiches with tofu spread or nut butter; potato; soup with crackers or toast; steamed, boiled, or stir-fried leafy greens

✦ Vegetable or fruit, raw or cooked

✦ Dry-roasted sunflower seeds

✦ Milk (almond, soy, rice), caffeine-free tea, water

Dinner

✦ Green leafy vegetables, briefly cooked with a little water

✦ Beans or bean products such as tofu or tempeh

✦ Whole-grain rice, whole-wheat bread or pasta, or other whole grains

✦ Raw fruits or applesauce

Variations. Many parents complain that they don't know how to vary lunch. A good rough rule is to serve three items:

1. A filling dish with plenty of calories

2. A fruit or vegetable

3. A green leafy vegetable (kale, broccoli, collards, scallions) cooked in any one of a variety of ways

Breads and sandwiches of several kinds can be the filling dish as children approach the age of two. Use whole-wheat bread to start with. Mustard makes a good spread for sandwiches and potatoes. Ketchup is loaded with sugar, but salsa can be equally delicious. Sandwiches can be made with a wide variety of other foods, plain or in combination: raw vegetables (lettuce, tomato, grated carrot, cabbage), stewed fruit, chopped dried fruit, peanut butter, or tofu.

A fairly substantial dish is a broth or soup with lots of barley or brown rice; or a vegetable soup, plain or creamed, with a couple of handfuls of whole-wheat toast cut into small cubes to toss in. Lentil, split-pea, and bean soups are a good balance with a grain dish and a green vegetable.

Simple unsalted whole-grain crackers can be served plain or with one of the spreads mentioned above. A baked potato can be topped with vegetables, baked beans, mustard, black pepper, or salsa. A small amount of salsa (or ketchup) entices many a child to eat a greater variety of vegetables.

Cooked, precooked, or dry cereal can be made more exciting by adding sliced raw fruit, stewed fruit, or chopped dried fruit. Instead of a filling first course followed by stewed or raw fruit, you can start with a cooked green or yellow vegetable, or a vegetable or fruit salad. A banana makes an excellent and filling dessert.

Whole-wheat pasta, hot or cold, is a good source of complex carbohydrates and fiber. Some children don't seem to like grains and pasta. They will do just fine nutritionally on fruits, vegetables, and beans. Their taste for grains will develop later if it's not forced on them early on. You can add noodles to a stir-fry or have noodles in a broth with greens added.

TIPS FOR HAPPY EATING

Have fun with foods. Serve foods with different colors, textures, and tastes. When you can, let your children help you choose and prepare the food, set the table, and clean up. All of these activities can be joyful.

Make mealtimes times for conversation by turning off the TV and cell phones. Parents themselves often find the no-phone rule hard to follow: All the more reason to have it! Some families say grace or meditate for a few minutes, which can establish a spirit of thankfulness and togetherness for the meal. Scoldings should not be part of the dining experience, despite the inevitable spills and lapses of manners, and despite any misdeeds committed earlier in the day.

Keep a balanced attitude about food. Even though it's

good to have a general awareness of calories, vitamins, protein, carbs, fiber, sugar and fat, you don't need to calculate grams and percentages. Just offer well-balanced meals. Remember that not all essential foods need to be eaten at every meal. What's important is what is taken in over the course of a day or two.

You can't go wrong if you stick with variety and avoid overfocusing on any particular food or nutrient. Serious-minded parents who have the mistaken idea that vitamins are the whole show and that starches are inferior may serve their child carrot salad and grapefruit for supper. The poor child can't get enough calories out of that to satisfy a rabbit. A plump mother from a plump family, ashamed of her son's scrawniness, may serve him only rich foods, crowding out vegetables, beans, and grains. In the process, he is apt to be deprived of minerals and vitamins.

An overall goal is to help your child learn how to regulate his own food intake. It's an important life skill. If a child is underweight or overweight, self-regulation is even more important.

You can teach self-regulation by setting out a reasonable selection of options at each meal, then letting your child decide how much of each to eat. Children learn to eat sensibly the way they learn to walk: by doing it. As a parent, your job is set up a safe learning environment, then let your child do the rest.

Temporary substitutes for vegetables. Suppose a child has refused vegetables in any form for weeks. Will her nutrition suffer? Fruits can provide many of the nutrients found in vegetables, as can whole grains. So if your child refuses to eat vegetables for a period of time, don't make a big issue out of it. Continue to keep mealtime relaxed and fun. If you are really concerned, give your child a daily multivitamin. Her taste for vegetables will return—unless you turn eating them into a power struggle, in which case she may refuse to eat them just to show you who's boss.

Some experts advocate disguising vegetables or hiding them in other foods. On principle, I'm not a fan of deceiving children, even in a little matter like this. They always catch on eventually, and then find it hard to believe you on other matters, and to tell the truth themselves when it's inconvenient or uncomfortable.

Taming a sweet tooth. The love of sugar and fat is probably human nature; the expectation that every meal ends in dessert is learned. When parents say, "You can't have your ice cream until you finish your vegetables," they are using junk food as a bribe, and teaching that the best rewards are sugary. Teach your young child, instead, that a banana or peach is the greatest treat of all.

Children tend to eat what their parents eat. If you drink a lot of soda, eat a lot of ice cream or candy, or have chips around all the time, your children will want these things too. Sweets brought by a grandparent who visits occasionally can be regarded as a special treat. Grandparents who always bring sweets need to find other ways to show love to their grandchildren, such as games, walks, or stories.

Snacks. Many young children and some older ones want a snack between meals; others never snack. If it's the right kind of food, given at a sensible hour, and presented in the right way, a snack shouldn't interfere with meals or lead to dietary problems. When the regular meals contain plenty of carbohydrates in the form of grains and vegetables, children are much less likely to feel ravenous between meals.

A snack shouldn't contain too much fat or protein. Fruits or vegetables are the best bet. Milk often takes away the child's appetite for the next meal. Occasionally, though, you see children who can't eat enough at one meal to hold them over till the next. But with richer, more caloric snacks, they have a better appetite for the next meal because they're not exhausted.

For most children the snack is best given midway between meals, no closer than an hour and a half before the next one. A few children, though, have a snack in the middle of the morning but still get so hungry and cranky before lunch is ready that they pick fights and refuse to eat. A small glass of orange or tomato juice may improve their disposition and their appetite, even though it is twenty minutes before lunch.

Parents sometimes complain that their child eats badly at meals but is always begging for food between meals. This problem doesn't arise because the parents have been lenient about offering snacks between meals. Quite the contrary. More often, the parents have been urging or forcing the child to eat at mealtimes and holding back food at other times. It's the pushing that takes away the appetite at meals. After months of it, the very sight of the dining room is enough to make the child's stomach revolt. But when the meal is safely over (though little has been eaten), the stomach feels natural again. Soon it's acting the way a healthy empty stomach is meant to act—it's asking for food. The treatment, then, is not to deny children food between meals, but to let mealtime be so enjoyable that their mouths water then, too.

More often, children want to snack too much because they've been brainwashed. The food industry spends billions of dollars a year on marketing to children. Snack foods are the main advertisers on children's TV. The more your child watches, the more you'll be bombarded by demands for brightly packaged, highly processed products. Noncommercial public TV is much healthier in this regard. Cable and streaming services can be commercial-free options, or not.

Feeding a child between meals is a matter of common sense and doing what suits your individual child. Children have preferences and moods like everyone else; some days they may feel like apples, other days like celery. As a parent, you decide when snacking happens, and you set the boundaries of what's acceptable based on your own ideas about nutrition, cost, and convenience. Your child should have a say in what gets served, and more or less complete control over how much she puts in her mouth. That way, she'll grow up with a love of healthy foods, and an ability to regulate her own intake.

Health and Safety

GENERAL MEDICAL ISSUES

YOUR CHILD'S DOCTOR

Children get health care from pediatricians, family doctors, nurse practitioners, and sometimes physicians' assistants (PAs). To keep things short, I'll refer to all of these professionals simply as doctors.

Routine checkups. With babies, it helps to get regular doses of reassurance. A quick checkup within two to five days after delivery is standard, followed by visits at one, two, four, six, nine, twelve, fifteen, eighteen, twenty-four, thirty, and thirty-six months, and yearly thereafter, as recommended by the American Academy of Pediatrics. If you'd like additional visits, by all means ask for them.

These visits allow you to get to know and trust your child's doctor and to ask questions. If you have worries (most parents do!), this is a good time to voice them. The responses you get should be sympathetic but objective.

Each checkup should include measurements (height, weight, head circumference for the first three years, and blood pressure); screening for development; testing of hearing and vision at certain ages; and a complete physical exam. You can also expect questions about behavior, nutrition, and safety;

advice about development in the coming months; and usually immunizations. Yearly blood tests looking for iron deficiency and lead poisoning, and skin testing for tuberculosis exposure, may be indicated.

Asking questions. The doctor is the medical expert, but you know your child best, so be a partner in your child's health. The doctor's advice depends on the information you supply and the questions you ask.

Some parents hesitate to ask questions that they think might be too simple or silly. But if there's any kind of question on your mind, you're entitled to an answer. Most doctors are happy to answer any questions they can, the easier the better. If you write down your questions before each visit, you won't worry about forgetting any of them.

It often happens that a parent asks about a problem and the doctor explains part of it, but gets sidetracked before having answered the most important part. It's best to be bold and make clear exactly what you want to know. Often, on getting home from an office visit, parents find that they forgot to bring up their most important questions and are embarrassed to call back so soon. But doctors are not bothered by these calls; they are quite used to them.

Questions also come up between visits. If you are certain that the question can wait, then by all means wait. But if not, you should call or, if you can, send your question electronically. Even if you are pretty sure that the problem is trivial, it's better to ask and be reassured than to sit and worry.

Disagreements with the doctor. In most cases parents and doctors soon come to know and trust each other. But occasionally, since they are all human beings, there are misunderstandings and tensions. Most of these can be cleared up. It's best to lay your feelings on the table. If you are unsatisfied with your doctor's advice or care, you should bring the problem out into the open right away in the most matter-of-fact manner you can.

Sometimes a parent and doctor find that they can't get along, no matter how frank and cooperative they try to be. In this case, it's better all around to admit it openly and find a new doctor. All health professionals, including the most successful, have learned to accept that they don't suit everybody.

Asking for a second opinion. If your child has a condition that worries you intensely, it's always your right to ask for a second opinion. Many parents worry about expressing a lack of confidence in their doctor. But second opinions are a regular part of the practice of medicine, and doctors should take them in stride. Doctors, like any other human beings, sense uneasiness, and it makes their job harder. A second opinion clears the air for them as well as for you.

TELEPHONE CALLS TO YOUR DOCTOR

Phone policies. Ask about your pediatric practice's phone policy. When is the best time to call about a new illness? Sick children often show their first definite symptoms during the afternoon, and most doctors would like to know about them as early as possible so that they can plan accordingly.

Most practices have a nurse during the workday who decides if the child needs to see a doctor. On nights and weekends, you should be able to reach an answering service, which notifies the doctor or nurse who is on call that night.

When to call, in general. It's simple: If you're concerned, you should call, even if you think the call might be unnecessary. If you need to reassure yourself—"It's probably nothing"—then *call,* and let a professional help reassure you. It's better to call too much, especially in the beginning, than to not call and worry.

By far, the most important rule is to consult the doctor promptly, at least by telephone, *if a baby or child looks or acts sick.* Pay attention to signs such as unusual tiredness, drowsiness, or lack of interest; unusual irritability, anxiousness, or restlessness; or unusual paleness. These general signs of illness apply to all children. They are particularly important in the first two or three months of life, when a baby can be seriously ill without fever or other specific symptoms and signs of illness.

Specific symptoms to call about. A child who is playful, bright-eyed, and active is probably healthy. However, there are a few symptoms that should trigger a call to the doctor, no matter what else is going on.

Fever. Under three months of age, a temperature above 100.4°F is concerning. Young infants don't usually run fevers, and they can become very sick very fast. If your newborn seems sick, don't let a normal temp reassure you: *Call!*

Past three months, there is room for waiting and watching. If your baby seems otherwise happy and is only running a low fever, you can probably wait until morning to call. After the age of three or four years, a fever up to 102°F or even

103°F can accompany a mild infection, so temperature alone is not a great sign. You have to rely on your judgment: If your child seems sick to you, call the doctor.

Rapid breathing. Children breathe faster than adults. Healthy infants breathe up to forty times a minute, young children up to thirty, and children ten years and above up to twenty. Count the number of breaths in sixty seconds, with each in-out being one breath. Fever and pain drive up the respiratory rate, as do illnesses such as pneumonia and asthma. A pattern of several seconds of rapid breathing followed by slow breaths is usually normal in young infants. Sustained rapid breathing is usually a sign that there's something seriously wrong.

Labored breathing. Difficulty moving air in and out of the lungs will cause a child to pull with the muscles in the stomach, chest, and neck. You can see the skin suck in over the collarbones and between and under the ribs. Other signs are flaring of the nostrils or grunting sounds with each breath. Doctors call this "respiratory distress," and it's often a sign of serious illness.

Noisy breathing. A high-pitched sound when the child breathes out is wheezing. A coarse sound when the child breathes in is called stridor. These are often signs of asthma or infection. Mucus in the nose can also cause noisy breathing. If it's not obvious to you, let the doctor listen. The stethoscope can often distinguish between a snotty nose and a more serious blockage farther down in the windpipe or lungs. Noisy breathing means that at least some air is moving in and out. If a child has labored breathing *without* noise, call right away; it could be an emergency.

Pain. Pain is the body's internal alarm that something is

wrong. If the pain is not severe and there are no other symptoms (such as fever), you can probably safely wait and watch. If the pain seems severe, if the child cannot be consoled, or if he seems quite ill, then by all means call the doctor. When in doubt, call.

Vomiting of any unusual type should be reported promptly, especially if the child looks sick or different in any other way. This does not apply to the spitting up after meals that is so common in young infants. Bright yellow or green vomit is sometimes a sign of blocked intestines; this needs medical attention right away.

Diarrhea of the more serious sort, such as bloody diarrhea and unusual quantities of loose or watery stools in infants, should be reported to the doctor immediately. The usual runny stools can wait. Look for signs of dehydration (tiredness, decreased urine output, dry mouth, and decreased tears). Call right away for blood in the bowel movements or urine, or bloody vomit.

Injury to the head should be reported if your child loses consciousness. Other concerning signs: Your child isn't happy and healthy-looking within fifteen minutes, begins to look more lethargic and dazed as time goes, or begins to vomit. Any of these changes after a head injury merits a call to the doctor. Also, call for *any* head injury in an infant under one year of age.

Ingestion of poisons. If your child has eaten anything that might possibly be dangerous, call the poison control hotline immediately, (800) 222-1222.

Rashes. If a child seems sick and has a rash, or if a rash is extensive, you should call the doctor right away. Any rash that could be from bleeding into the skin—either large purplish blotches or small red spots that don't go away when you stretch the skin over them—should be looked at right away.

Remember, this is only a partial list of situations when you should call your doctor. When in doubt, call!

Before you call. To get the most accurate phone advice when you have a sick child, be ready to answer the following questions (and answer them, whether or not the doctor or nurse asks!):

1. What are the troubling symptoms? When did they start? How often are they occurring?

2. What are your child's temperature and breathing rate? How is her skin color—pale or flushed?

3. How sick does your child appear to be? Is she alert or lethargic? Bright-eyed or dazed? Happy and playful, or miserable and crying?

4. Does your child have any past medical problems that could relate to your current concern?

5. Is your child on any medications? If so, what are they? What have you tried so far? Has it worked?

6. How worried are you about the situation?

FEVERS

What's fever and what isn't? The first thing to realize is that a healthy child's body temperature doesn't stay fixed at the "normal" temperature of 98.6°F (37°C). It is always going up and down a little, and depends on the time of day and what the child is doing. It's usually lowest in the early morning and highest in the late afternoon, but only slightly. The change between rest and activity is greater. A temperature of 99.6°F or even 100°F is normal in small children right after they have been running around.

Up to three months of age, any temperature over 100.4°F could be a sign of serious illness and should be reported to the doctor. This is one of the few facts that you really must remember to keep your baby safe. A serious infection could include bacteria in the blood, bones, kidneys, brain, or elsewhere; these infections need to be taken very seriously. There is one exception: If your baby has been wrapped up overly snugly, unwrap her a bit and take her temperature again in a few minutes. If it's normal and stays normal, and if your baby acts healthy, she was probably just overheated.

In an older child, a temp of 101°F or higher probably means illness. In general, the higher the fever, the more likely the illness is serious, as opposed to just a cold or other viral infection. But some children with mild infections run high temps, and some children with serious infections run lower ones. Fever itself only becomes harmful to a child at temperatures of 106°F or more—higher than most children ever go.

Fever is apt to be highest in the late afternoon and lowest in the morning—but don't be surprised if a fever is high in the morning and low in the afternoon. There are a few diseases in which the fever, instead of climbing and falling, stays high steadily. The most common of these are pneumonia and roseola. An infant who is very sick may also have a below-normal temperature. Slightly low temperatures (as low as 97°F) sometimes occur at the end of an illness, and also in healthy babies and small children in the morning. This is no cause for concern as long as the child is feeling well.

What causes fever with illness? Normally, body temperature is controlled by a part of the brain called the hypothalamus. The system works like the thermostat for the furnace in a house: When the body becomes too warm, the hypothalamus calls for sweating to cool it down; too cold, and it calls for shivering to heat it up.

In response to an infection, the immune system releases chemicals that turn up the thermostat. So even though body temperature may be 100°F, if the new thermostat setting is 102°F, the child feels cold and may even shiver (shaking chills). Medicines like acetaminophen work by blocking these fever-inducing chemicals, allowing the body's thermostat to return to normal. As the fever breaks, the child may sweat, a sign that the brain now recognizes that the body is overheated.

Taking the temperature. Experienced parents can tell a child's fever with the back of their hand or by touching their lips to the child's forehead. The problem, of course, is that it's impossible to communicate to a doctor (or anyone else) just how warm the child feels.

Today's digital thermometers are fast, accurate, and easy. With a digital thermometer, all you do is wipe it off, turn it on, and pop it in. A friendly beep lets you know when it's time to read the temperature. For infants, it's most accurate to take a rectal temperature. Use a little petroleum jelly, lay your baby over your knee or hold your baby's legs up with one hand, and slide the thermometer tip in about half an inch. After age five or six, most children can cooperate by holding the thermometer under their tongue with their lips closed for a minute or so. You can also take the temperature under your child's armpit (an axillary temperature), but this is not as accurate as rectal or oral.

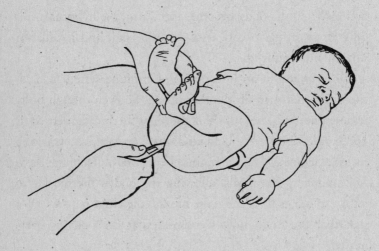

High-tech electronic thermometers that read the temperature through the ear or by scanning the skin cost more and don't offer any real advantage, except for the rare child who simply will not hold still. (If you own a glass thermometer, don't simply toss it in the garbage; give it to your child's doctor to dispose of, or turn it in to your municipal solid-waste system.)

When reporting the temperature to your child's doctor, pay attention to the decimal point. Sometimes parents say "one hundred and three" (103°F) when they mean "one hundred *point* three" (100.3°F). Clean a thermometer by washing it with lukewarm water and soap. You can then wipe it off with rubbing alcohol, but be sure to rinse it with cold water to get rid of the alcohol taste before using it again.

TEMPERATURE EQUIVALENTS

FAHRENHEIT	CENTIGRADE (CELSIUS)
98.6°	37°
100.4°	38°
102.2°	39°
104°	40°

How long to keep taking the temperature. Under most circumstances, when the temperature has stayed under 101°F for a couple of days, it's a good general rule to forget about the thermometer unless the doctor asks you to continue or unless the child seems sicker in any way. Children should be kept home from school until the temperature has been normal for twenty-four hours and they are definitely feeling better; all the cold symptoms don't have to be gone. Don't get into the habit of taking your child's temperature when she is well.

Fever is not a disease. Many parents think that fever itself is dangerous. But fever actually *helps* the body fight off infections. (Other animals, not just humans, also run fevers as a way of killing germs.) It's helpful to bring a fever down if it's interfering with the child's sleep or exhausting him. In other cases, the best thing may be to leave the fever alone.

Parents often worry that prolonged high fever can cause a convulsion or seizure. But it's actually the quick rise in temperature at the onset of an illness that can occasionally cause convulsions in small children. The reason for trying to bring a high fever down is to help the child feel less miserable, not to prevent a convulsion.

Treating a fever. If your child feels especially uncomfortable with a high fever, you can bring the temp down a little with an antifever medication such as acetaminophen (Tylenol) or, for children over six months of age, ibuprofen (Advil, Motrin). These come as tablets or liquid forms, and in rectal suppositories (very helpful for children who are also vomiting). Follow the directions on the package for the correct dose based on age and weight.

WARNING:

Never give aspirin to a child or teenager for fever, cold, or flu symptoms unless the doctor prescribes it. Use only acetaminophen, ibuprofen, and other nonaspirin products. Aspirin can make a child susceptible to Reye's syndrome, an uncommon but very dangerous condition (page 528).

It's best to talk with the doctor's office before you give repeated doses of antifever medicine. You don't want to overlook a serious illness because you have lowered the fever with medication. Even though ibuprofen and acetaminophen are sold without prescription, they are not harmless; a large overdose of either can be quite dangerous. So be sure to keep these medications safely locked up, out of your child's reach, and in childproof containers (see page 392).

When a child's fever is very high and he is flushed, use only light covers at ordinary room temperature, perhaps as little as a sheet. Your child will be more comfortable that way, and it may help his temperature come down. A tepid (luke-warm, not cool) bath can also help.

Wiping all over with a warm, damp cloth brings the blood to the surface, and evaporation cools the skin. Alcohol has traditionally been used in a wet rub, but this is not rec-ommended, because it can be absorbed through a baby's ten-der skin and cause alcohol poisoning. Warm water works just as well and is safer. These methods provide only tempo-rary relief, however, because the body's thermostat remains set at a higher temperature and will quickly cause the fever to return.

DIET DURING ILLNESS

What to eat and drink. Children often lose their appetite when they're ill. Once they're better, they eat extra to catch up. It usually doesn't help to push food on an unwilling child; but offer nutritious foods that your child loves, and let her eat what she wants. Sugars are easily digested and provide quick energy (particularly helpful when children feel sick); foods with more protein and fat deliver long-lasting energy the body needs to heal.

Drinking is another matter. Children lose fluid through fever, fast breathing, and diarrhea. Dehydration makes chil-dren feel awful, and can become a serious problem in its own right. The best fluid is whatever your child wants; the right amount is whatever she'll take. If your child is peeing regu-larly and the urine is light colored, she's drinking enough. Dark urine is a sign to increase fluids; if it persists, call the doctor.

If dehydration is a concern (page 348), there are special drinks that maximize the body's intake of fluids. Store-bought rehydration solutions are often covered by insurance, or you can make your own (see below). Plain water alone isn't as effective, because it doesn't replace the minerals that are typically lost in dehydration.

When your child is ill, don't restrict sugar. Popsicles and ice cream are soothing ways to provide calories and fluids. Dairy products may cause problems with thick mucus in some children; but if all your child wants is milk, go ahead and give that. If your child has mouth sores, citrus drinks might be irritating. Believe it or not, chicken soup—a traditional remedy in many cultures—actually helps. Small amounts, sipped frequently during the day, seem to work best.

In the past, doctors prescribed complicated food and drink regimens for diarrhea and vomiting. Now we know that the most important thing is intake, especially fluids. Children with diarrhea who drink and eat do put out more stools, but they also retain more fluid and heal faster. See page 348 for more on vomiting and diarrhea.

Children with chronic illnesses. Nutrition can be a critical issue for children with chronic illnesses such as diabetes, celiac disease, or cystic fibrosis, particularly when they have an infection on top of their underlying condition. It's best in these situations to work closely with a doctor, and often with an experienced nutritionist or dietician as well.

Feeding problems at the end of illness. If a child has a fever for several days and wants little to eat, he naturally loses weight. This worries parents the first time or two that it happens. When the fever is finally gone and the doctor says it's all right to begin working back to a regular diet, they are impatient to feed the child again. But it often happens that the child turns away from the foods that are first offered. If the parents urge him to eat, meal after meal and day after day, his appetite may never pick up.

Such a child has not forgotten how to eat, nor has he become too weak to eat. At the time the temperature went back to normal, there was still enough infection in his body to affect his stomach and intestines. As soon as he saw those first foods, his digestive system warned him that it was not ready for them yet. When food is pushed or forced onto a child who already feels nauseated because of illness, his disgust builds up more easily and rapidly than if he had a normal appetite. He can acquire a long-lasting feeding problem in a few days' time.

As soon as the stomach and intestines recover from the effects of the illness, children's hunger comes back with a bang—and not just to what it used to be. Children are usually ravenous for a week or two in order to make up for losses. You sometimes see such children whimpering for more food just two hours after a large meal. By age three, they may demand specific foods that their starved system craves most.

The best thing to do at the end of illness is to offer your child only the drinks and solids she wants, without any urging, and wait patiently but confidently for signals that she is ready for more. If her appetite has not recovered in a week, talk with the doctor again.

GIVING MEDICINE

Check with the doctor. It's always safest to check with a doctor before giving any medication. Parents who have treated colds, headaches, or stomachaches a few times in the same way come to feel like experts—which they are, in a way. But they're not trained, as a doctor is, to first consider carefully what the underlying illness could be, and to recognize sometimes subtle signs that indicate a more serious illness. It can be hard to tell a typical stomachache from appendicitis, especially if you don't know precisely what to look for.

People whose children have been treated by a doctor with an antibiotic (such as amoxicillin) are sometimes tempted to use it again for similar symptoms. But the medicine may not be effective any longer, or the child may need a different dosage or a completely different medication; the antibiotic may interfere with diagnosis when the doctor is finally consulted; there is always a risk of a rare but serious allergic reaction; and unnecessary use of antibiotics sets children up to get harder-to-treat drug-resistant infections in the future.

If you do have medication left over after a course of treatment, the best thing to do is throw it out. For the same reasons, you should never give a neighbor's, friend's, or relative's medicine to a child.

Getting the medicine in. Getting a child to take medicine can be quite tricky. The first rule is to slip it into her in a matter-of-fact way, as if it has never occurred to you that she won't take it. If you go at it apologetically with a lot of explanation, you convince her that she's expected to dislike it. Talk about something else when you put the spoon into her mouth. Most young children open their mouths automatically, like baby birds in their nest. With babies, it often works to draw up the medicine in an oral syringe (available from drugstores) and gently squirt it into the mouth alongside the cheek, toward the back.

Tablets that don't dissolve can be crushed to a fine powder and mixed with a good-tasting food like applesauce. Mix the medicine with only one teaspoon of the applesauce, in case she decides she doesn't want very much. Bitter pills can be mixed in a teaspoon of applesauce, rice syrup, or rice milk. (Some foods interfere with the absorption of certain medicines; check with a pharmacist before you give your creativity free rein.)

When giving medicine in a drink, choose one that your child doesn't take regularly, such as grape juice or prune juice. If you give your child strange-tasting orange juice, it might make him suspicious of OJ for months. Mix the meds in a small amount so that your child finishes the entire amount all at once, and gets the whole dose.

Pill-taking fears. Children who gag at the very thought of swallowing a pill can sometimes overcome their fears by practicing with small candies or mints. (Children under about four or five shouldn't try this, because of the risk of choking.) You can also try special plastic cups that have a spout that holds the pill. When your child takes a drink from the cup, the pill gets washed down. Bribes sometimes work, too. But it's best not to get into a fight with a fearful child about taking pills if there is any other way to get the medicine in.

Over-the-counter medicines. Just because a medicine is sold without a prescription does not mean it is safe. Decongestants and other cold medicines in particular have caused many serious reactions and are no longer regularly recommended for children.

Eye ointments and drops. These can sometimes be applied during sleep. For a child who is not sleeping and not cooperating, try placing him on your lap with his legs around your waist and out of kicking range. Place his head gently but firmly between your knees and hold it with one hand while applying the medicine with your other hand. (This position is also good for suctioning the nose or inserting nose drops.)

Generic prescriptions. A generic prescription is one that doesn't use the trade name for a medicine but uses the chemical name instead. In most cases, generics are cheaper and exactly the same medicine. You should ask your doctor about using generic prescriptions. Most—but not all—of the time, it's a good idea.

ISOLATION FOR CONTAGIOUS DISEASES

It's a good idea to keep a sick child in the house until he no longer has a fever and the doctor says that he's no longer contagious. Keep the amount of intimate contact (kissing, hugging, and cuddling) to a minimum, except for people who are taking care of the sick child. These precautions keep the disease from spreading, and keep your child from picking up new germs to complicate his illness.

Family members are generally not restricted from going to their jobs or school when a child or sibling has a contagious disease. But it's wise to limit unnecessary contact. For example, even though a sibling seems healthy, you might stop him from going over to his healthy friend's house to play, because it's possible your son could transmit an infection even before he's developed symptoms of it.

Handwashing and nose blowing. The best way to limit the spread of disease is through frequent, thorough handwashing. Teach your child to wash between each finger and all the way up to her wrists, scrubbing for twenty seconds or more—long enough to sing "Happy Birthday" twice or the ABCs once. A step stool makes it easier for a child to reach the sink comfortably; small bars of soap, like the bars in hotel bathrooms, are easy for little hands.

Many soaps are now advertised as "antibacterial," but it's not clear that these work any better than regular soaps, and the disinfectants in these soaps may pose health risks of their own. It's the rubbing and running water that really get rid of the germs. Between trips to the sink, alcohol-based hand sanitizers help to limit the spread of germs. You need to use a good amount with each application, work it into all the crevices, and rub it around for about ten seconds or longer.

Put boxes of tissues around the house to inspire frequent nose blowing, and place paper garbage bags nearby so that used tissues don't end up on the floor.

GOING TO THE HOSPITAL

A child who ends up in the hospital after a sudden illness or trauma is bound to be disoriented and scared. Having a parent or other close family member nearby at all times makes a huge difference psychologically. Children who go to the hospital for planned procedures, such as surgery to remove enlarged tonsils and adenoids, can become terribly anxious in anticipation of what will be done to them. A chance to voice their fears and get reassurance can help tremendously. Children with chronic illnesses and special health care needs may be hospitalized frequently. For all of these children and families, the expertise of child life specialists—professionals who are trained to help children cope with hospitals and medical procedures—can be invaluable.

Why the hospital is upsetting. Children between the ages of one and five years worry most about being separated from their parents. The illness itself will be upsetting, as will the needles and any other painful procedures, but having a trusted parent right there is tremendously comforting.

After age five, a child is apt to be most fearful about what's going to be done to him—the injury to his body, and the pain. It won't do for the parents to promise that the hospital will be a bed of roses. Children need, above all, to be able to trust their parents. On the other hand, it doesn't help to give children a long list of everything bad that might happen.

The most important thing is for the parents to show all the calm, matter-of-fact confidence they are capable of, without forcing it so much that it sounds false. Unless the child has been a hospital patient before, he is bound to fear the worst. The parents can set his mind at rest better by describing hospital life in general, rather than by arguing with him about whether it's going to hurt a lot or just a little.

It also helps for parents to mention some of the fun things about the hospital—the books and toys brought from home, the TV right over the bed, the button that calls the nurse. Many children's units also have playrooms stocked with all sorts of games and toys. You don't have to avoid discussing the medical program altogether, but let the child see that it's a small part of hospital life.

More and more hospitals have hospital preview programs for children whose hospitalization is planned ahead of time. The child and parents come to the hospital a few days before the admission or procedure, look around, and get their questions answered. A slide show or puppet show might explain what the hospital experience is going to be like. Individual tours with a child life specialist may be available. The specialist knows how to use developmentally appropriate language, toys, and pictures to reassure the child and to coach the parents in what comfort items will likely to be most helpful.

Let them tell you their worries. It's important to give your child the opportunity to ask questions and tell you what's on his mind. Young children view illness and doctors in ways that would never occur to adults. They often think they have to be operated on or taken to the hospital because they have been bad—because they haven't worn their boots, haven't stayed in bed when sick, or were angry with their mom or little sister. A child may imagine that his neck has to be cut open to remove his tonsils, or his nose removed to get to the adenoids. So make it easy for your child to raise questions. Be ready to hear about strange fears, and try to reassure him.

When and what to tell your child. If there is no chance of his finding out, I think it is kinder to wait to tell a small child until two or three days before it's time to leave. It won't do him any good to worry for weeks. On the other hand, children pick up on overheard discussions and often know more than their parents think they do. If your child seems worried or starts acting differently ahead of a planned hospitalization, it's likely she knows something is going to happen.

With a child of seven or older who can face things reasonably, it may be fairer to begin the discussion some weeks ahead. It's always wise to give a child bare-bones information and then answer the child's questions. Well-meaning parents often make the mistake of saying too much. Instead, try to follow your child's lead. Certainly don't lie to a child of any age, and never lure a child to a hospital pretending it's something else.

Anesthesia. If your child is going to have an operation, see if you can discuss the matter of anesthesia with the doctor. How a child accepts the anesthesia is apt to make the biggest difference in whether or not he becomes emotionally upset by an operation. If there is an anesthetist who is particularly good at inspiring confidence in children, it's worth a lot to have that person on the team. It's usually less frightening to the child to start with gas instead of an intravenous line. Naturally the doctor is the one who has to make the decision, but if there is an equal choice medically, the psychological factor should be considered. Children who have had a chance to play at anesthesia, pretending they are the doctor or the patient, often find the real event less stressful.

It matters what you say: The expression "put to sleep" can make children think of a dog or cat who was euthanized; it can also lead to a child's developing sleep problems after surgery. Instead, explain that the anesthesia causes a special kind of sleep, from which the anesthetist will awaken the child as soon as the operation is over. Let your child know that he won't feel or remember anything that happens during the operation. Try to stay with your child until he is under. Having a parent present when the anesthesia is given makes a child much less frightened and nervous about the surgery and reduces the need for calming medication.

Visiting. Stay with your child if at all possible. Most hospitals now have facilities so that you or another trusted adult can stay overnight in your child's room.

When parents are able to visit only intermittently, it can be upsetting for the child. The sight of the parents reminds him how much he has missed them. He may cry heartbreakingly when they leave or even cry through the entire visiting period. But this doesn't mean that the parents should stay away: The child gets security from realizing that his parents always come back when they leave. If you have to go, it's best to act as cheerful and unworried as possible. If the parents have an anguished expression, it makes the child more anxious.

A child's crying when his parents are present often tells a deeper truth. Young children frequently act calm when their parents are out of sight, even though they feel sick or must undergo painful procedures, because they are too scared to show their emotions. When the parents return and they feel safe, their real feelings come out.

Late reactions to hospitalization. A young child may seem to pull through a hospitalization all right, only to show disturbing behaviors once back at home—either clinging and being excessively fearful or acting out in aggressive ways. These are normal, if unpleasant, responses. Patience and reassurance are often all a child needs to recover psychologically. Many children, though, continue to want or need to play at being a doctor or nurse (see page 364) in order to master their medical-related fears and feelings.

CARING FOR A SICK CHILD

Special care without spoiling. When children are sick, it's natural to give them special care and consideration. You don't mind preparing drinks and foods for them at frequent intervals, or even putting aside a drink they refuse and making another kind right away. You are glad to get them new playthings to keep them happy and quiet.

A child can easily get used to this arrangement, and may start bossing his parents around and expecting instant service. Fortunately, most children are on their way to recovery within a few days. As soon as the parents stop worrying, they stop putting up with the child's unreasonable demands. After a couple of days, things are back to normal.

With longer illnesses, the persistent high level of concern and special treatment may have a bad effect on a child's spirits. He's apt to become demanding. If he's too polite for that, he may just become excitable and temperamental. It's easy for him to learn to enjoy being sick and receiving sympathy. His ability to make his own way agreeably may grow weaker, like a muscle that isn't being used.

Getting back to normal. It's wise for parents to get back into a normal routine with the sick child as soon as possible. This means little things such as having a friendly, matter-of-fact expression when entering the room rather than a worried one. Ask him how he feels today in a tone of voice that expects good news rather than bad, and perhaps ask only once a day. When you find out by experience what he wants to drink and eat, serve it up casually. Don't ask timidly if he likes it, or act as if he is wonderful to take a little. Keep strictly away from urging unless the doctor feels it is necessary. A sick child's appetite is more quickly ruined by pushing and forcing.

If you are buying new playthings, look particularly for the types that encourage children to take an active role and use their imaginations: blocks and building sets; sewing, weaving, and bead-stringing kits; painting, modeling, and stamp-collecting supplies. You can also have fun with things you find around the house. For example, you can cut pictures out of old magazines and make scrapbooks; sew bean bags and doll clothes; or build farms, towns, dollhouses, or spaceships using cardboard boxes and masking tape. Bring out toys and activities one at a time, so they're fresh and not overwhelming. Some children may want to use their time in bed to indulge in unlimited electronic gaming. That's probably a bad idea, because too much staring at screens can make children feel listless.

If a child is going to be laid up for a long time but is well enough to study, start him on his schoolwork again for a regular period each day as soon as possible. It's fine to spend time keeping your sick child company, but you don't need to be there every minute. It's healthy for a child to know that there are times when his parents will be busy elsewhere, as long as they are available for any emergency. If the child has a disease that isn't catching and the doctor lets him have company, invite other children in regularly to play and stay for meals.

The hardest part can be when the child is over his illness but not yet fully back to his old self. You have to use your best judgment about how much special consideration he still needs. The best policy is to let your child lead as normal a life as possible under the circumstances. You should expect reasonable behavior toward you and the rest of the family, and avoid worried talk, looks, and thoughts.

IMMUNIZATIONS

A HISTORICAL PERSPECTIVE

Dr. Spock recalled, "I grew up in a time when every parent was worried sick about their child contracting polio, a paralytic virus. This illness killed about twenty-five thousand people, mostly children, each year. We were warned not to drink from drinking fountains, to avoid crowds in the summer, and to fret about every viral infection. But no more. There has not been a naturally occurring case of polio in the United States since 1979. The rest of the world is a little behind us, but on the same track. Smallpox has been totally eradicated from our planet. The elimination of these illnesses is nothing less than a medical miracle, one of mankind's proudest achievements, and it came to pass because of vaccines."

HOW VACCINES WORK

The immune system remembers the germs it has defeated and combats the same infection even more effectively in the future. Vaccines work through the same mechanism. They stimulate the body to produce antibodies that recognize particular bacteria and viruses and destroy them before they can cause disease.

Illnesses prevented by vaccines. Children in the United States are protected against sixteen different diseases by the time they are twelve. Many of these diseases are rare now, precisely because of the vaccines. Whenever vaccination rates decline, however, diseases can spring back like weeds in an untended garden.

- *Diphtheria,* in which a glue-like material coats the throat and blocks off the air supply.

- *Pertussis* (whooping cough), which causes coughing spells so bad that a child can't eat, sleep, or breathe well for weeks.

- *Tetanus* (lockjaw), which causes muscles spasms, seizures, paralysis, and sometimes death.

- *Measles,* which can produce high fever, pneumonia,

and brain infection in addition to the well-known rash.

✦ *Mumps,* which can cause fever, headaches, deafness, swollen glands, and painful swelling of the testes and ovaries.

✦ *Rubella* (German measles), which is usually mild in children, but can cause severe birth defects when contracted during pregnancy.

✦ *Polio,* which causes paralysis or severe weakness. Even if children recover, symptoms can return decades later.

✦ *Hib* (short for *Haemophilus influenzae* type B, and not to be confused with influenza), which can infect the brain (meningitis), leading to deafness or seizures, or can cause swelling around the vocal cords, leading to suffocation.

✦ *Meningococcal disease,* which can cause a sudden, often fatal brain infection (meningitis), and can also cut off blood flow to hands and feet, resulting in loss of limbs. It often affects college students living in dorms.

✦ *Hepatitis B,* which can result in liver failure and sometimes liver cancer.

✦ *Hepatitis A,* a common cause of severe (but brief) diarrhea.

✦ *Rotavirus,* another cause of serious and easily spread diarrhea.

✦ *Pneumococcal disease,* which causes many cases of ear
  infections, but can also cause meningitis, pneumonia,
  and other severe infections.

✦ *Varicella* (chicken pox), which often causes an itchy,
  uncomfortable rash, and can also lead to severe pneumonia, brain swelling, or Reye's syndrome.

✦ *Influenza* (flu), which normally causes fever with aching
  muscles, headache, and vomiting but can also lead to severe pneumonia, which can be fatal. Unlike all the other
  vaccines, flu vaccine has to be given each year, because
  each year a different strain of flu virus circulates around
  the world. Adults need an annual flu vaccine, too.

✦ *Human papillomavirus (HPV),* which is responsible for
  many cases of cervical cancer, genital warts, and cancer
  of the throat. The vaccine greatly reduces the risk of a
  woman developing cervical cancer, but only if she gets
  it before she is exposed to the virus. For males, the vaccine (HPV9) protects against genital warts and lowers
  the risk of transmitting the virus.

Besides providing protection for the vaccinated child,
vaccines protect other people by lowering the number of
susceptible individuals who can spread the disease. If enough
people refuse vaccines, this so-called herd immunity breaks
down, allowing more and more people to become infected.

There are special vaccines for children who have weakened immune systems, and for those exposed to diseases that
are common outside of North America. Your child's doctor
can tell you if your child has special immunization needs.

RISKS OF IMMUNIZATION

Weighing risks and benefits. A lot of information is available about the risks of immunization, though much of it is wrong. No medication is 100 percent safe, and there *are* risks to vaccines. But the benefits of vaccines far outweigh the risks. If you're not convinced, go back and read the list of illnesses vaccines prevent (page 370). In places where vaccines are not available, or not accepted, many more children suffer and die from these diseases than the few who would have had vaccine side effects. Every expert panel and every responsible physician stands behind this conclusion.

Take Hib *(Haemophilus influenzae* type B), for example. Before this vaccine was developed, Hib struck roughly twenty thousand children in the United States each year. One of my first pediatric patients was a toddler who was deaf as the result of Hib. Nowadays, most young pediatricians never see a case of Hib, thanks to the vaccine. But a few years ago, during a temporary shortage of vaccine, five children in Minnesota got the disease, and one died.

Vaccine side effects are usually mild. Injections hurt more than a pinch but less than a stubbed toe. Some children develop soreness at the injection site, and occasionally a firm swelling that can take weeks to go away. Rarely does a high fever develop. About one in a hundred thousand children shows worrisome behavior, crying for hour after hour, not responding normally, or having a seizure. These reactions are frightening, and in very rare cases do lead to serious long-term problems. But—and I can't say this too many times—without the immunizations, the diseases being prevented would be *much* more common, and much worse.

How vaccines are made. Most vaccines are made from viruses or bacteria that have been killed and either left whole or chopped up. Some vaccines are made against the poisons produced by bacteria, and a few vaccines are made from live viruses that have been changed so that they cannot cause disease in healthy children, or cause only a very mild disease. Live virus vaccines are not safe for children who have seriously weakened immune systems (such as children receiving some cancer treatments) or children who live with people who have weakened immune systems.

Vaccines are getting safer. Pertussis vaccine used to be notorious for causing pain, swelling, redness, and fever. Today's version of the vaccine is much gentler. In the past, some vaccines contained a preservative made with mercury. This preservative was never proven to be harmful. Still, just to be safe, all vaccines commonly used for children are now mercury-free. An early version of the rotavirus vaccine sometimes caused bowel obstruction, but that problem too was solved. Vaccine reactions are tracked nationally so that even very rare dangers can be flagged and avoided.

Vaccines and autism. The number of children with autism is rising, and nobody knows why. Theories and rumors have focused on the measles, mumps, and rubella vaccine (MMR), but the research that ignited those rumors was fraudulent, and no well-done studies have found a connection between MMR and autism. Children who have received MMR have the same rate of autism as those who have not. Rejecting MMR is risky. In communities where immunization rates have fallen, epidemics of measles have broken out, and measles itself can cause severe brain damage.

Vaccines have also been blamed for other diseases, including inflammatory bowel disease. Again, a lot of careful study has shown no connection at all between vaccines and this condition.

Where to learn more. Every doctor who gives vaccines is required by law to give the patient (or the patient's parent) fact sheets called Vaccine Information Statements. These sheets, created by the U.S. Centers for Disease Control and Prevention (CDC), are very clear and accurate. You can ask your child's doctor for these handouts ahead of time so that you can read about upcoming immunizations. There are also several excellent websites listed in the Resource Guide on page 890.

THE IMMUNIZATION SCHEDULE

So young, so many shots. For many vaccine-preventable illnesses, it makes sense to start immunizing as soon as possible, because the youngest children are the most vulnerable. Many vaccines are administered several times in the first year because children often need more than one exposure in order to develop a full-strength immune response.

The standard immunization schedule comes from the CDC and is approved by the Advisory Committee on Immunization Practices of the U.S. Public Health Service, the American Academy of Pediatrics, and the American Academy of Family Physicians. The schedule is updated yearly.

Alphabet soup. Many of the shots are referred to by their initials. The following glossary should help:

- *DTaP* (diphtheria, tetanus, and acellular pertussis, a three-in-one multiple vaccine combination)

- *HepB* (hepatitis B vaccine); *HepA* (hepatitis A vaccine)

- *Hib* (haemophilus influenzae type b vaccine)

- *HPV* (human papilloma virus vaccine)

- *IPV* polio vaccine (the "I" stands for inactivated, meaning that the vaccine is made from a virus that has been killed)

- *MCV* (meningococcus vaccine, against types A,C, W, and Y); *MenB* vaccine, against meningococcus type B)

- *MMR* (measles, mumps, and rubella, another three-in-one combination); *MMRV* (which includes the varicella vaccine)

- *PCV13* (pneumococcus vaccine, which covers thirteen different strains of the bacterium)

- *RV* (rotavirus vaccine)

- *Varicella* (chicken pox vaccine)

The immunization schedule. To get the maximum protection, children should get their immunizations on time. But the schedule allows some flexibility. Doctors and parents can choose to delay some of the immunizations if a child is ill or to spread out the needle sticks. (This reason doesn't make much sense to me, since the pain from two pokes in a row isn't usually much worse than the pain from one.) If children fall far behind in their immunizations, the schedule can be changed to catch them up. The rotavirus vaccine is given by mouth. The flu vaccine needs to be given every autumn, and is not listed in the schedule below.

PRIMARY SERIES

AGE	VACCINES	NEEDLES
Birth	HepB	1
2 months	DTaP + IPV + Hib (all one needle), HepB, PCV13, RV	3*
4 months	DTaP + IPV + Hib, PCV13, RV	2*
6 months	DTaP + IPV + Hib, HepB, PCV13, RV	3*
12–15 months	MMR, varicella, PCV13, Hib, HepA	4 or 5
15–18 months	DTaP, HepA	2

* Rotavirus vaccine is given by mouth.

BOOSTERS

AGE	VACCINES	NEEDLES
4–6 years	DTaP, IPV, MMRV	2 or 3
11–12 years	DTaP, HPV (2 doses), MCV	3
16 years	MCV, MenB (2 doses)	2

The immunization schedule changes slightly from year to year. Many vaccines are available as combined products that lower the number of needles. The CDC publishes updated schedules online, at www.cdc.gov: click on "healthy living" then "vaccines and immunizations."

Keep a record with you. Unless you can access your child's medical record online, it's a good idea to keep a record of all your children's immunizations, as well as any allergies to medications, and to carry it with you when the family goes on trips or changes doctors. It often happens that a child away from home receives a wound that calls for extra protection against tetanus. If the treating doctor knows precisely when the last tetanus shot was given, it can save the child a needle. Immunization records are also needed for children entering day care, elementary school, summer camp, college, and the military.

COPING WITH SHOTS

Medications. Talk with your child's doctor about medication that might lessen the pain of immunizations. Numbing with a cold spray can help; acetaminophen taken before and after immunizations can lessen the ache (although it may also lessen the effectiveness of the immunization).

Body comfort. Babies feel safe in their parents' arms. Newborn infants getting their heels stuck for blood cry less and show fewer physical signs of stress when their mothers hold them close. Sucking on a pacifier, rocking, and stroking are all effective comfort measures for babies. A good position for an older child is facing you, chest to chest, arms and legs wrapped around your body.

Use your voice. For infants, it doesn't matter what you say. The tone of your voice is comforting. For toddlers and pre-school children, fear of the shot is often the worst part. To lower the fear, tell your child what is going to happen just before it happens. For example, "Now you'll feel the alcohol wipe. How does that feel?"

The words you use matter. Talk about "vaccines" rather than "shots." For some literal-minded preschoolers, a shot sounds like something from a gun. When children are scared, they often ignore negative phrases. So, if parents say, "Don't scream," they hear "scream." If parents say, "Stop crying," they hear "crying." It's better to use only positive words: "You're okay. There, there, it'll be over soon."

Be as honest and simple in your explanations as possible, considering your child's age and understanding. Tell him that the shot will hurt a little ("like a hard pinch"), but that it will protect him from sickness that would hurt much more than the shot.

Give your child choices. Some children want to see what the nurse or doctor is doing; others don't. A child who has a choice feels more in control. Also, you can give your child permission to holler if that helps. "It's okay to yell if you want to, but you need to hold still. Why not wait till you feel the pinch?"

Distraction or alternative focus. A very effective technique for toddlers and preschoolers is to tell a story, sing a favorite song, or look at a picture book. Children have strong imaginations. A child who is imagining herself doing a favorite activity will actually feel less pain. Two powerful distraction techniques that are great for preschoolers are blowing at a pinwheel and blowing bubbles. If your child loves bubbles, bring a bottle of bubble soap and a plastic wand to the doctor's when you go for the checkup. A lot of clever doctors have their own bubble wands. Bubbles can be magical.

Helping a fearful child. If your child is afraid of shots, ask him to draw a picture of what he thinks is going to happen. Don't be surprised if the picture shows a very small person next to a huge, terrifying needle! Help your child to see that the needle is really very, very small. Children often cope with scary things through play. Give your child a toy syringe and stethoscope, and let him practice being the doctor to a doll. By giving pretend shots, your child may come to feel more control and therefore less fear. Play together with your child, so you can correct any misconceptions.

If severe fears persist, talk with your child's doctor. Many hospitals have professionals called child life specialists who are experts at helping children cope with medical procedures. It's worth a visit with one to have your child feel more comfortable. Getting a shot and coming away feeling okay helps a young child realize that he can handle things that make him afraid; this is a great lesson at any age.

PREVENTING INJURIES

KEEPING CHILDREN SAFE

Safety is every parent's first and most important job. The rest of parenting—love, limits, values, fun, and learning—depends on safety. We promise our children that we will keep them safe, and our children expect this of us. The beginning of psychological health is the deep-down belief that there is a big person out there providing security.

Our first instincts center on safety: Infants cry and parents have the urge to pick them up. It's easy to imagine how these protective responses helped our prehistoric ancestors survive. And the world is still a dangerous place. In the United States, injuries and poisoning send one child out of ten to the doctor each year, and cause more deaths in children over age one than all illnesses combined.

Parents need to protect their children, but they can't set out to eliminate every hazard. Children need to know that their parents are looking out for them, but they also need to be able to explore, make choices, and even take some risks. Children learn to balance caution and boldness by watching their parents do it.

Why not call them "accidents"? For many people, the word "accident" implies something that is unavoidable, as in "I couldn't help it, it was an accident." But many childhood injuries happen because adults tolerate the conditions that make them possible. Consider, for example, a car without a car seat. If a child riding in such a car is badly hurt in a crash, the injury is not truly accidental; most likely it could have been prevented.

A child's age determines which form of unintentional injury is most likely to be deadly. Under age one, suffocation and choking are the most common. From one to four, drowning kills more children. After five, it is children riding in cars who are most likely to die from unintentional injuries.

Other unintentional events cause injuries but not death. Falls from heights and collisions with coffee tables commonly result in cuts, bruises, and broken bones. Falls from bicycles often result in brain injury unless the child is wearing a helmet. Lead poisoning, another very common form of unintentional injury, rarely kills but regularly causes learning problems that can limit a child's life success.

Principles of prevention. It may not be possible to prevent every single injury, but we know how to lower the risks. Practice these three basic principles:

+ *Childproof your child's environment.* Certain items simply don't belong in a house with young children, such as coffee tables with sharp corners, unguarded stairs, and furniture and beds next to open windows. Use a checklist (see drspock.com) to systematically identify hazards and remove them.

◆ *Supervise your child closely.* Even in a childproofed home, children require close supervision. Toddlers take chances, lack judgment, and need protection. Of course you can't spend every waking minute keeping track of your child. If a playroom has been well childproofed, you can relax a little. But out in the big world—and in the bathroom and kitchen—you must be vigilant.

◆ *Be particularly careful during stressful times.* Injuries happen when routines change and your attention is diverted. When the in-laws come for a surprise visit or you've got a critical deadline at work, that's when you need to make yourself think about where you left the scissors, where your father-in-law put his bottle of heart pills, and whether your cup of hot coffee is sitting too near the table edge.

Safe inside and out. In planning for your child's safety, consider two settings: inside the home and outside. Of course, no list of safety topics can be absolutely complete. So you'll need to depend on your own good sense, too, and please refer to the chapters in section I of this book that describe safety precautions that apply to children at specific ages.

Part 1: Safety Inside the Home

DANGERS AT HOME

Home can be a dangerous place for children. Drowning often occurs in bathtubs and backyard pools. Burns, poisons, medications, choking, falls—it's enough to scare anyone. But don't be scared, be prepared! By childproofing your home, you can reduce your child's chance of injury and lower your own level of anxiety. Close supervision is a must, and planning ahead is also critical. (Also see pages 49 and 118 for safety tips for babies and toddlers.)

DROWNING AND WATER SAFETY

Drowning takes the lives of nearly one thousand children under age fourteen each year. For every child who drowns, four more are hospitalized after nearly drowning, many with brain damage. Children under age four drown two or three times more often than older children.

Preschoolers often drown in the bathtub. Children have been known to crawl into a dry bathtub, turn the faucet on, and drown. Never leave a child age five or younger alone in the tub, even for an instant. A child can drown in as little as one inch of water. Do not leave her in the tub in the care of another child under age twelve. If you absolutely must answer the phone or the doorbell, wrap up the soapy child in a towel and take her with you.

A toddler can fall into a toilet or a pail of water headfirst and drown in just a few inches of water. Keep bathroom doors closed, and toilet seats down and latched if possible. Empty buckets shouldn't be left outside, because they can collect rainwater and cause drowning. The standing water can also breed mosquitoes.

Water safety. Prevention of drowning requires constant parental awareness and supervision.

1. Keep your eyes on your child when she's near the water, even with a lifeguard present. At age ten to twelve, a strong swimmer who has good judgment can swim without adult supervision, but *always* with an equally capable and responsible buddy. Do not permit her to dive unless the water is at least five feet deep and an adult is present.

2. If you have a backyard wading pool, be sure to empty it and turn it upside down after use.

3. If you have a swimming pool, it must have a fence on all sides, at least five feet high, with slats no more than four inches apart (not chain-link) and a self-closing, self-locking gate. Don't consider the side of the house as part of the fence; it's too easy for a child to slip out through a door or window.

4. Don't rely on pool alarms to warn you; they don't go off until the child is in the water, which may be too late. A better warning system would be an alarm on the pool gate.

5. Keep everyone away from pools or other bodies of water during thunderstorms.

6. Stay away from frozen ponds and lakes unless the ice has been authorized safe for skating.

7. Do not allow children to sled near water. Golf courses, a popular spot for sledding, often have bodies of water that can be dangerous.

8. Wells and cisterns should be securely protected.

Swimming lessons. For children age four and older, learning to swim lowers the risk of drowning. For children as young as one, there's some evidence that swimming lessons might be helpful, especially for children who are around water a lot. But don't count on lessons alone to prevent drowning; all of the other precautions are crucial.

FIRE, SMOKE, AND BURNS

Fires kill many children; those under five are at the greatest risk. Approximately 80 percent of all fire-related deaths occur in house fires. Half of these are due to cigarettes—another good reason not to smoke! Fire can spread rapidly, so *never* leave young children alone in a house; take them with you if you have to go out. Most fire-related deaths are actually due to smoke inhalation, not burns.

The most common burn injuries result from scalding. About 80 percent are from spilled foods and liquids, the rest from too-hot tap water. Half of all scald burns are serious enough to require skin grafting.

Burn prevention. There are concrete steps you can take; check these off as you do them:

- ✓ Install smoke detectors on each floor of your home. Place them in the hallways just outside sleeping areas and outside the kitchen. Change the batteries when you reset your clocks for daylight saving time.
- ✓ Keep a dry chemical fire extinguisher in the kitchen.

✓ Turn the temperature of your water heater down to 120°F. Most manufacturers preset their water heaters at 150°F to 160°F. At this setting, a small child will receive full-thickness burns in less than two seconds. At 120°F, it takes five minutes to produce a scald burn. If you live in an apartment or condominium, ask your landlord or condominium association to turn the water heater down. You can still get your dishes clean in water temperature less than 120°F, and your energy bill will go down. Anti-scald devices can be installed in your shower, bathtub, and sink fixtures to stop the flow of water when the temperature exceeds 120°F.

✓ Space heaters, woodstoves, fireplaces, poorly insulated ovens, and easily opened broilers are dangerous. Place grilles or guards around woodstoves, fireplaces, and wall heaters. Install radiator covers to prevent burns. Keep space heaters away from curtains and furniture, or just don't use them.

✓ Put outlet covers on all electric outlets to protect children from shocks. Don't overload outlets.

✓ Replace worn electric cords. Tightly tape the connections between cords and extension cords. Don't run cords under rugs or across walkways.

You can also lower the risk of fire and scald burns through these prudent habits:

1. Always feel the temperature of bathwater right before you put your child in, even if you remember doing it earlier. Also, feel the faucets to make sure they're not hot enough to burn.

2. Don't drink hot beverages or eat soup with a small child in your lap. Keep hot drinks or food away from the edge of the table, where a small child can reach up to pull them off. Don't use tablecloths or placemats, which a small child can pull off the table.

3. Always turn pot handles toward the rear of the stove. Using the back burners is preferable.

4. Keep matches in high places that are impossible for even a determined three- or four-year-old to reach. Starting at this age, many children go through a phase of being fascinated by fire, and it's very hard for them to resist the temptation to play with matches.

5. If you use space heaters, check to make sure that they aren't in contact with curtains, bedclothes, or towels.

6. Children's sleepwear is required by law to be flame-retardant (see page 32 on benefits of tight-fitting sleepwear).

Finally, keep your children safe by teaching them what to do to prevent fires, and how to respond if one occurs.

1. Talk to toddlers about what is hot, and warn them not to touch these things.

2. Discuss fire safety with young children. Include instructions to "stop, drop, and roll" and "crawl low under the smoke."

3. Teach your children that if they smell smoke and suspect a fire, the first thing they should do is get out of the house. They can call the fire department from a neighbor's phone.

4. Make an emergency plan with two escape routes from each bedroom, and choose a designated meeting place outdoors. Have the whole family practice the plan.

POISONS

Young children put everything in their mouths. Children nine months to five years are at the greatest risk. More poisonings happen in the home than anywhere else. A child who is active, bold, and persistent is more likely to get hold of a poison, but even quiet toddlers who seem to prefer to stay in one place can find opportunities—an open bottle of pills or an irresistible houseplant—to swallow something they shouldn't.

There are over two million calls each year to poison control centers about children. Every medicine, prescription item, vitamin, and household product should be considered a potential poison. Dangerous substances that may *seem* safe include tobacco (a single ingested cigarette is dangerous for a one-year-old), aspirin, vitamin pills containing iron, nail polish remover, perfume, and dishwasher detergent. Bleach in a

white bottle looks like milk to a toddler, and causes horrible
burns in the throat. Even medicines your child takes every day
can be poisonous if taken all at once.

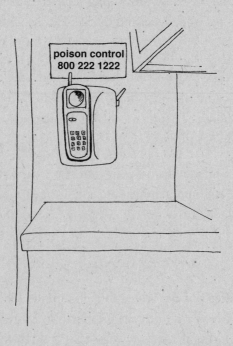

Childproofing your home. The first step is to inspect your
house with an eagle eye—or, rather, a child's eye. Then follow
these steps to childproof your home against poisoning.

1. The telephone number for the poison control hotline
   everywhere in the United States is (800) 222-1222.
   Post this number by your telephone, write it on a piece
   of paper and tape it to the phone itself, or preprogram
   it into your cell phone. If your child ever does swallow a
   poison or something that might be poisonous, the first
   thing to do is call that number for instant expert advice.

2. Store household cleaners and medications in the bathroom and kitchen way up high (with nothing nearby a child can climb on) or in cabinets with childproof locks or latches.

3. Get rid of rat poisons and insect pastes and poisons. They are just too dangerous.

4. In the basement or garage find truly safe places (ideally, locked) for turpentine, paint thinners, kerosene, gasoline, benzene, insecticides, plant sprays, weed killers, antifreeze, and car cleaners and polishes.

5. Before you discard containers, check with your city or county sanitation department for instructions on disposing of hazardous waste.

Helpful habits. Effective poisoning prevention depends on what you do every day. Here are some things to think about:

✦ Put all medicine safely out of reach immediately after each use. A cabinet or drawer with a lock or childproof latch is best.

✦ Put bold, clear labels on all medicines so that you won't give your child the wrong one. Throw out unused medicine after an illness is over.

✦ Many medication poisonings are due to children taking their grandparents' prescription drugs. Before a visit, check to be sure that the grandparents' medicines are locked away or completely out of reach.

✦ Federal and state laws now require that all medicines dispensed by a pharmacist come in childproof containers. Don't put medicine in another container. Also, don't assume that a childproof container is truly childproof.

✦ Keep cleaning supplies and other chemicals in their original containers. Don't put plant spray in a soft drink bottle, for example, or oven cleaner in a cup; this is a frequent cause of serious injuries.

Plant poisons. We think of plants and flowers as pretty. Crawling babies and small children think of them as possibly tasty. Many plants and flowers—over seven hundred of them in all—can cause illness or death. It's safest to keep plants or flowers outdoors until children are past the "eat everything" stage. At least, place plants high out of reach. Watch small children when they are around plants and flowers in the garden or away from home.

Some outdoor plants are toxic but not fatal; they can cause skin irritation and swelling of lips and tongue. Look out for poison ivy, poison oak, and poison sumac to avoid the painful irritation of an allergic reaction. Your local poison control center (1-800-222-1222) or health department can tell you whether a plant in your house or yard is safe.

LEAD AND MERCURY

The danger of lead: Lead has been removed from house paint, gasoline, and food cans, but there's still plenty of it around. At very high levels, it damages the brain and other organs. Even at very low levels, it can lower a child's IQ.

This doesn't mean you should panic if your child's lead level comes back in the mildly elevated range. Many brilliant people grew up with that much lead, or more. But, on average, even a little is measurably worse than none at all.

Who gets it, and how. Lead poisoning is mostly a problem for young children who crawl around the floor and put things other than food into their mouths. Children who are hungry or low on iron absorb more lead. Good general nutrition helps prevent lead poisoning.

The source of lead is often old paint around windows or on outside walls. As the paint deteriorates, children may ingest flakes or pick up lead-contaminated dust on their hands. People track it inside on the soles of their shoes. Other sources include pottery with lead glazes (modern machine-made pottery does not contain lead), lead in the water pipes that connect to older buildings, and some traditional medicines. Since the Flint, Michigan, crisis, lead in municipal water supplies has entered our national consciousness. Your city water department should be able to reassure you.

What to do. If you live in or around housing built before 1980, or if you live in a city where there is a lot of lead poisoning, your children should have their blood lead levels checked regularly in their early years. With very high levels, doctors prescribe medicine to remove the lead from the body; with lower levels, the main treatment is to remove the lead from the environment, make sure the child has plenty of iron, and allow the child's body to get rid of the lead on its own. Some tips for dealing with lead include:

✓ Check for peeling and cracking paint, especially around windows and doors and on porches. Remove whatever comes off easily, then cover the rest with new paint.

✓ Don't try to remove lead paint by stripping, sanding, or using a heat gun; these methods dramatically *increase* lead exposure. If you have to remove lead-containing paint, have a professional do it while you and your child are out of the house.

✓ Mop floors regularly with a lead-specific cleaning solution to pick up lead dust.

✓ Pay attention to all the places your child spends time: your home, outside, your porch, the sitter's house, the day care center, and so on.

✓ If you have older plumbing (in a home built before 1950), let the cold water run for a few minutes before using it for drinking or cooking. That way you don't use water that has been sitting for a long time in the pipes, collecting lead. (Boiling water doesn't remove lead—it makes the problem worse.)

✓ Avoid glazed pottery unless you are sure it is lead-free.

✓ Be careful about using folk medicines made from old recipes (these may be tonics your grandmother swears by, for example), because some of them contain lead.

Learn more! If you have lead in your environment, you need to know much more than there is space for here. Talk with your child's doctor. Pick up brochures from your local health department. Visit the site listed in the Resource Guide, pages 898–99.

Mercury. Mercury is like lead in many ways: Both are metals, both are common in our industrial world, and both cause brain damage and developmental problems. Mercury from factories and mines makes its way into lakes and oceans. From there, it's picked up by microscopic organisms, little fish, bigger fish, and the final consumers—us. For this reason, it's a good idea to avoid eating a lot of fish during pregnancy and early childhood. Avoid fish caught in highly polluted waters and large predator fish such as swordfish that collect mercury over their relatively long lifetimes.

Another source of mercury is the everyday mercury thermometer. It's best to treat your glass thermometer like the toxic waste it is: Bring it to your doctor's office or your local solid-waste facility for proper disposal. Then buy a cheap, accurate, safe digital thermometer.

CHOKING

Choking is a common cause of death in young children. Small children who put things in their mouths should not have little objects (like buttons, beans, or beads) within reach.

Dangerous toys. Children under age five are most at risk of choking on toys or parts of toys. A good test uses a standard toilet paper tube—if a toy is small enough to fit inside the tube, it's small enough to be a choking hazard. The

Consumer Product Safety Commission uses a similar device called a choke test cylinder that is a bit smaller than a toilet paper tube.

Look also for any small parts that might break off a toy with rough play. Try pulling off the parts yourself. Small balls or dice from games are also risky. Small magnets are particularly dangerous. Keeping an older child's toys away from a younger sibling or a young visitor to your home is a challenge!

Children often choke on balloons that have burst, sometimes while they are blowing them up. For this reason, it's best to keep latex balloons away from small children. Mylar balloons are safer.

Choking on foods. By age four or five, most children are able to handle the same foods that adults can. Before that, you have to be very careful with certain foods. Round, hard foods such as nuts, hard candies, carrots, popcorn, and grapes are especially dangerous (see page 309). Hot dogs can plug up the windpipe like a stopper in a bottle. A surprisingly dangerous food is peanut butter eaten directly off a spoon or knife; if it is aspirated, it's very hard to remove the peanut butter from the lungs. Peanut butter is safe spread thin on bread.

An excellent way to prevent choking on large pieces of food is to chew well. Children can be taught to chew properly, and if you set an example, they might follow it. Take away lollipops and ice pops if small children keep them in their mouths while running. Don't let your child lie down while eating, and never leave a baby alone with a propped-up bottle.

SUFFOCATION AND STRANGULATION

In children under age one, suffocation is a leading cause of death. An infant spends most of his time in his crib, so steps should be taken to make sure this is a safe environment (see page 48).

Toddlers can strangle themselves in cords hanging down from curtains, blinds, or appliances. Tie cords up, wrap them around cleats mounted on the wall, hide them behind heavy furniture, or use cord shorteners (little plastic devices that cords wrap tightly around). Consider replacing your blinds with cordless ones.

For older children, be aware of the risk of plastic bags. For some reason, many children have the urge to play with plastic bags by putting them over their heads, occasionally with tragic results. Keep all plastic bags stored where you have your other hazardous household materials, in a locked or inaccessible cabinet or drawer. If you have an unused refrigerator or freezer or other large appliance or are in the process of discarding one, be sure to take the doors off.

GUNS IN THE HOME

Many families own handguns or rifles. Parents often feel they need a gun for protection, but every study shows that people are more likely to be killed by a gun in their home than by a criminal who breaks into the home. Children die every day, killed by the guns meant to protect them.

Very young children play with guns, or with older children who are playing with the guns. Children showing off a gun to their friends can become shooters or victims. Adolescents, especially as they begin to experiment with drinking, may take stupid risks if a gun is accessible. They drive with them in the glove compartment, and take them out in moments of stress. Teenagers who are depressed or using drugs are at higher risk for suicide if there is a gun at home.

It's important to ask the parents of your children's playmates if they own a gun. It may seem rude, but it could be a matter of life or death.

If you own a gun, it must be stored unloaded, with the ammunition locked away in a separate place. Gun owners should complete a gun safety program offered by local police or a gun club. Safety technologies such as trigger locks or "smart" guns, which can only be fired by the gun owner, are good. But these precautions can be defeated by a curious and persistent child, or undone in a moment of carelessness. The only truly safe choice is to not have guns and children in the same home.

FALLS

Millions of children are treated in emergency rooms for falls every year, and ten times that many have injuries treated at home.

Falls occur from as many places as you can imagine: beds, changing tables, windows, porches, trees, bicycles, playground equipment, stairs, and icy sidewalks. The highest death rate due to falls is during the first year of life. Toddlers often fall from windows and down stairs; older children fall from rooftops and recreational equipment. The peak hours for falls in the home are around mealtimes, when parents are busy doing many things at once.

Stairs. Install gates at the top and bottom of stairs, including porch steps, until your children can go up and down steadily. Teach your children to use handrails, and let them see you taking the same precaution.

Falls from windows. If your child's room is above the first floor, you need a plan to keep him from falling out of the window. You can keep windows locked, of course, but that's not always feasible in summer. You can move all toys and furniture away from windows, but your child will soon be able to slide a chair over. You may be able to open windows from the top. Window screens are helpful, but they can break.

If you're good with tools, you can screw metal stopper devices or blocks of wood into the window frame to keep the window from opening more than four inches. Window guards are sturdy metal gates that have a maximum of four inches between the bars. You can place guards on all the windows in a room. But at least one window must have a guard that can be opened or removed without the use of a special key or tool, in case of fire.

Baby walkers. Once considered a necessary piece of infant equipment, the walker is now seen as a menace. Walkers give a great deal of mobility to infants who have no sense of the risks. They can easily walk right off the stairs and have no way to break their fall. All it takes is for a parent to turn his back for an instant. Many thousands of babies are hurt this way each year (see page 97).

TOY SAFETY

Every year, thousands of children are injured by their toys, and hundreds of toys are recalled because they prove dangerous. Pay attention to the age recommendations when buying toys, and use your own judgment.

Toys such as marbles, balloons, and small blocks present a choking hazard for any children who put objects in their mouths, especially children under three. Look out for sharp points or edges, and for projectiles that can injure eyes. Electric toys should only be used by children eight or older. Some toys made out of soft plastic contain chemicals called phthalates, which can cause kidney damage and other health problems. If you're unsure about whether a product contains phthalates, you can call the manufacturer.

Even your child's toy chest can be a hazard. Make sure it has a lid support, so the top can't come down fast on your child's head or neck. You can learn much more about toy safety on the Consumer Product Safety Commission website, www.cpsc.gov.

HOME SAFETY EQUIPMENT

What to buy? Gizmo makers love to sell safety equipment to nervous parents. But there are really only a few things that are absolutely necessary: working smoke detectors with fresh batteries; a fire extinguisher in the kitchen; locked cabinets for medications and other dangerous chemicals; and trigger locks and a locked storage cabinet for any guns, and another one for the ammunition. If you have stairs in your home, gates at the top and bottom can prevent tumbles. If your home is on the second floor or above, you may need window guards. A few other items are mentioned in the sections above. But remember, no item is a substitute for close adult supervision.

Part 2: Safety Outside the Home

RIDING IN CARS

Injuries to passengers. Automobile crashes top the list for unintentional injury and death. It's hard to overstate the importance of properly installed child safety seats for infants and young children, booster seats for older children, and seat belts with shoulder harnesses for everyone else. All fifty states require any child under age four to be belted into a safety seat when the car is in motion. Many states require everyone riding in the front seat to be buckled up, and children who need them to use booster seats. Some parents claim that their children refuse to be belted in. These parents need to take charge. No good parent gives a two-year-old a sharp knife to play with, and no responsible parent operates a vehicle until every passenger is secured.

Car seat choice and installation. If you can afford it, buy a new car seat. Before you get a secondhand seat, check that it has never been in a crash and is not more than a few years old. Plastic weakens over time, and a seat that has been through a crash can look okay but fall apart at the next impact.

Read all the instructions that come with the seat and do your best to install it. Then, if you can, go to an official child safety seat inspection station and get a free inspection by a certified child passenger safety technician. Inspectors find problems with three out of four seat installations. So when you show up for a free car seat check, chances are that your children will be safer when you leave than when you came.

To find the inspection station nearest you, ask at your local fire station or look on www.safercar.gov. This website, run by the National Highway Traffic Safety Administration, is the best source for reliable information about car seats, and auto safety generally.

Infant seats. When you take your new baby home from the hospital, it should be in a safety seat. While you might think that you can hold a baby safely in your lap, you simply can't. In a sudden stop from forty miles per hour, a ten-pound baby can pull away with a force of two hundred pounds or more. Placing a baby under your own seat belt is even more danger-ous, because if the car stops suddenly, your body will crush the baby against the belt.

For babies who are less than twelve months old, the only safe way to ride is in a rear-facing infant seat secured in the back seat. Keep your child in a rear-facing infant seat until she is two years old or until she is over the height and weight lim-its recommended by the car seat manufacturer. The rear cen-ter is the safest place in the car, so that's where your baby should ride. It's critically important that infants and children twelve years and under never ride in the front passenger seat of a car that is equipped with airbags (most cars now on the road). Airbags save adult lives, but they inflate outward with a force that can kill or severely injure a child.

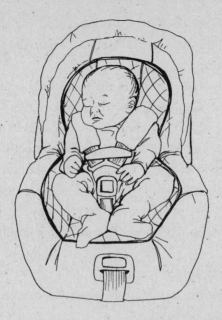

Toddler seats. Once a baby outgrows his infant seat, he's ready to graduate to a forward-facing toddler seat.

The best toddler seats use what is called a five-point harness, with straps that go over each shoulder, each hip, and between the legs. When your child is about four years old and weighs about forty pounds, it's time to move up to a booster seat. Check the instructions for the upper weight limit of your particular seat.

Booster seats. Booster seats are for children who have outgrown their toddler seats. By this time, having bought two car seats, you might be tempted to skip this stage. But booster seats are the cheapest type of car seat by far, and they make a huge difference in a child's safety and comfort. Without a booster seat, the lap belt runs across the child's abdomen. In a crash, the belt can injure the child's internal organs or spine. With the booster seat, the lap belt runs across the child's strong pelvic bones, where the worst it can do is cause a bruise.

A booster seat also makes the shoulder strap fit comfortably over the shoulder rather than against the neck, so the child is more likely to keep the shoulder belt on. In fact, booster seats *must* be used with lap-shoulder belts. With a lap belt alone, they don't do a good job of holding the child in place during a crash. Keep your child in the booster until he's tall enough to sit with knees comfortably bent, back up against the seat, and shoulder belt across the shoulders.

KEYS TO CAR SAFETY

+ Never place a child twelve years of age or under in front of a working airbag.

+ The safest place at any age is the center of the back seat.

+ A golden rule: The car doesn't move unless everyone is buckled up.

+ It isn't safe (or legal) to hold a child on your lap once the car starts moving, or to put your own seat belt around the child.

+ Even when you think you've got the car seat installed correctly, chances are you don't.

On airplanes. Children under age two can fly for free, but they don't get a seat, so you won't be able to use a child safety seat unless the seat next to you is vacant. Holding a child in your arms on an airplane is not as safe as belting a child in (but not as dangerous as doing the same thing in a car, because planes rarely make sudden stops).

Even without a safety seat, it's still safer to fly than to drive to your destination. Take your car safety seat along, whether or not you use it on the plane, so you'll have it for travel when you reach your destination. If you want to use the car seat on the plane, check to see that it is FAA approved. Another option is to buy an FAA-approved harness called CARES. Beds are available for use on airplanes by infants under two, but they can be used in the bulkhead seats only. Children over age two need tickets; check with the airline about toddler seats.

STREETS AND DRIVEWAYS

Injuries to pedestrians. Children between the ages of five and nine are at great danger of being hit and killed by cars. They think they can keep themselves safe on the street, but they really can't. Their peripheral vision isn't fully developed, and they can't accurately evaluate the speed and distance of oncoming cars. Many don't have the judgment to know when it's safe to cross.

Adults generally give their children too much credit for street smarts. The hardest job for parents is to teach children that drivers regularly ignore red lights and that crosswalks are not automatic safety zones. One-third of pedestrian injuries occur when the child is in a marked crosswalk. Parking lots are another high-risk zone, as drivers backing out of spaces may not be able to see children behind their cars.

GUIDELINES FOR PEDESTRIAN SAFETY

✦ From the time your child begins to walk on the side-walk, teach him that he can step off the curb only when you are holding his hand.

✦ Always supervise the outdoor play of preschoolers, and make sure they never play in driveways or streets.

✦ Explain to five- to nine-year-olds over and over again the rules about crossing residential streets. Model safe pedestrian behavior yourself when you walk with them. Point out how traffic lights and crosswalks work and why they need to look left, right, and left again, even when they have the traffic light in their favor and even when they are in a crosswalk.

✦ Remember that children aren't developmentally ready to cross a heavily traveled street without adult supervision until they're at least nine or ten years old.

✦ Together with your child, find the safe places to play in your neighborhood. Warn over and over about running into the street, no matter how important the game may seem.

✦ Think about where your child walks, on the way to school, to playgrounds, and to playmates' houses. Explore the neighborhood with him to find the safest route with the easiest street crossings. Then teach him that the safest route is the *only* route he should use.

✦ Try to find the time to get involved in community safety. Find out if there are enough traffic signals and crossing guards on the way to your child's school. If a new school is being built, look into the traffic pattern in that area. Will there be enough sidewalks, lights, and crossing guards?

✦ Be particularly cautious with toddlers in parking lots and insist that they hold your hand. Keep toddlers in shopping carts or put them in the car while loading bags.

Driveways. Driveways are a natural place for children to play, but they can be very dangerous. Children need to be taught that as soon as they see a car pulling in or pulling out, they must get off the driveway immediately. Drivers need to *always* walk once around their cars before backing out, to make sure there are no small children playing behind the car. Just glancing back isn't good enough, because a child can be easily overlooked.

BICYCLE INJURIES

Cycling hazards. Bicycles cause thousands of emergency room visits and hundreds of deaths every year. These injuries are especially common in the after-school hours. Sixty percent of all serious bike injuries are head injuries, which could lead to brain damage. Proper use of bicycle helmets can reduce the incidence of head injuries by 85 percent.

Choosing helmets. A helmet should have a solid, hard outer shell and a firm polystyrene liner. The chin strap should be attached to the helmet at three points: beneath each ear and at the back of the neck. Look for the label that says the helmet meets ASTM, ANSI, or Snell safety standards. You should be able to get a safe helmet for $20 or less.

The helmet must fit properly. It should sit on top of the child's head in a level position and not rock back and forth or from side to side. Measure your child's head with a tape measure and select the appropriate size according to the information on the box. Go by inches to ensure proper fit—don't just rely on the age recommendations. Replace the helmet if it is involved in any crash or serious head thump. Most companies will replace the impact-absorbing liner free if you send them the helmet.

Bike safety tips and rules. The most important rule is, "No riding without a helmet—ever." When parents ride, they must wear helmets, too. You can't expect your children to follow this rule if you break it! Children should ride only on sidewalks until age nine or ten, when judgment matures enough for them to handle traffic while riding in the street. Then teach them the basic rules of the road so they can obey all the same traffic rules that automobile drivers follow.

It's safest to get your child a tricycle or bicycle that fits her, not one that she will have to grow into. Children generally aren't ready for a two-wheeler until they're five to seven years old. Choose bikes with coaster brakes for children up to age nine or ten, when they will have developed the strength and coordination to manage hand brakes.

Put reflective materials on the bike, the helmet, and the child for better visibility. This is especially important for children who ride at dawn or dusk. Headlamps are required for any night riding, but children should be in bed at night, not riding around!

Bicycle carrier seats. Parents bicycling with a child in a carrier should follow several additional rules. Select a child carrier with headrest protection, spoke guards, and shoulder straps. Never use a backpack to carry your child on a bike. Before biking with your child, practice riding your bike with a weighted carrier in an open area, free of traffic and other cyclists, to get used to the extra weight and to gain confidence with balancing a child in a carrier. Never carry a child who's less than one year old or more than forty pounds.

A child should always wear a helmet in the carrier seat. Never leave your child unattended in the carrier. Bikes are not made to stand with loaded carriers, and many injuries are caused by falls from a standing bike. Ride on safe, uncongested bike paths, not in the street. Don't ride after dark.

PLAYGROUND INJURIES

Thousands of children end up in the emergency room each year as a result of playground injuries. Many of these injuries are severe—broken and dislocated bones, concussions, and injuries to internal organs. Now and then a loose drawstring or hood becomes caught on the climbing structure during a fall, and strangles a child. Children age five through nine are most at risk. Children are all about testing their limits and learning new skills, but they don't have the balance and coordination they need to keep from getting hurt. They need sharp-eyed adult supervision on the playground.

Making playgrounds safer. Make sure the playground equipment is well maintained and that there are impact-absorbing surfaces such as rubber mats, sand, pea gravel, or wood chips under the climbing structures and swings. Check that the surfaces have not become packed down or dispersed with use. If the playground needs improvement, talk with the local parks department or school district. If necessary, join a group of citizens to tackle the problem, or organize one. It's remarkable what people can do together.

At home, be sure any playground equipment is sturdy and well maintained. Make sure that children take off all loose clothing before going to play. Several clothing manufacturers have stopped using drawstrings in children's garments based on recommendations by the Consumer Product Safety Commission.

SPORTS SAFETY

Organized sports improve physical fitness, coordination, self-discipline, and teamwork. But injuries take a heavy toll in pain, lost practices and play, and sometimes long-term disability or worse.

Who is most at risk? Young children are especially susceptible to injury because their bodies are still growing. Before puberty, boys and girls have the same risk of sports-related injury. After puberty, boys are more frequently and severely injured than girls. Collision and contact sports have the highest rate of injury. For boys, football, basketball, baseball, and soccer top the list. For girls, it's soccer, softball, gymnastics, volleyball, and field hockey. Head injuries, though less frequent among girls, can result in more serious problems. (Cheerleading is risky for both sexes.) Children who train at the same sport year-round are prone to overuse injuries, leading to tendonitis and arthritis.

Protective gear. Equipment to protect the eyes, head, face, and mouth is a must for many sports. Mouth guards help to prevent dental injuries, which are the most common type of sports-related facial injury.

Mouth guards also cushion blows that could cause a concussion or a jaw fracture. Eye protection makes sense for ball sports, including basketball.

Specific sports.

Football. As more and more information on head injuries comes to light, it's hard to escape the conclusion that competitive football is just too dangerous for children, or anyone, to play. Consider putting your foot down, and insisting that your child choose a different sport.

Baseball. Safety includes wearing the proper gear to prevent eye, head, face, and mouth injuries. Ballplayers should wear shoes with rubber, not metal, spikes. Injuries can be reduced by using safety bases and installing safety fencing by the dugouts and benches. Youngsters should be taught to slide properly and should not be allowed to slide headfirst. Softer-than-standard baseballs and softballs can reduce the risk of impacts to the head and chest. Young players should be limited in how much they pitch, in order to prevent permanent elbow injury.

Soccer. Heading the ball is not recommended for young children just learning to play the game. It's probably no good for anyone to clobber their head over and over! Soccer goals need to be anchored to the ground so that they cannot tip over on players, and children should not be allowed to climb on movable goals.

Competitive soccer players often sustain knee injuries, as do athletes in other sports that require rapid changes in direction (basketball and lacrosse, for example). Girls, in particular, are at risk for rupture of their anterior cruciate ligament (ACL), a key structure that stabilizes the knee. ACL ruptures are devastating. They require surgery and long periods of rehabilitation, and the ligament often quickly becomes reinjured. Such an injury can leave an athlete walking in pain for life. Training programs have been designed specifically to prevent ACL injuries, and all competitive soccer teams—especially girls' teams—should use them.

Gymnastics. Many gymnasts suffer injuries to their ankles, knees, wrists, and backs. The risk of these injuries goes up as the level of competition rises. For girls in gymnastics, as well as figure skating and dance, the emphasis on having a lean body increases the risk of an eating disorder (see page 793). Coaches and parents need to set limits on the intensity of workouts, assure blocks of time to allow the body to recover, and keep alert for excessive weight loss.

In-line skating and skateboarding. These sports result in thousands of injuries each year, mostly sprained and broken wrists, elbows, ankles, and knees. These can be minimized by wearing kneepads, elbow pads, and wrist guards. Head injuries, which tend to be more serious, can be reduced by wearing a helmet. Best are multisport helmets that provide extra protection to the back of the head. The current safety label to look for on a multisport helmet is "N-94" (see the Consumer

Product Safety Commission for helmet recommendations). If your child does not own a multisport helmet, a bicycle helmet is better than nothing. Be sure your child always skates on smooth, paved surfaces without any traffic; warn her to avoid streets and driveways. Make sure she learns to stop safely using the brake pads on the heels of most in-line skates.

Sledding. Wintertime fun includes sledding down snowy hills. It is a surprisingly hazardous pastime. Before you begin, review these safety tips:

✦ Survey sledding areas before letting children use them. Look for hazards such as trees, benches, ponds, rivers, rocks, and excessive elevation.

✦ The bottom of the hill should be far from traffic or bodies of water.

✦ Inflatable snow tubes are fast and unsteerable; use extra caution when children are using them. Sleds with steering mechanisms are safer.

✦ Never allow a child under four years to sled unsupervised. The steepness of the hill should be your guide as to whether older children should be allowed to sled alone.

✦ Avoid crowded hills, and don't overload a sled with children.

✦ Do not sled alone or after dusk.

✦ If your child wears a helmet, don't let it be an excuse for recklessness.

COLD AND HOT TEMPERATURES

Cold weather. Being cold doesn't give children colds, but it does make their cheeks red and their noses run. Dress your child in multiple layers, with special attention to hands and feet when you send her out to play. But don't expect her to know when to come in. Watch the clock and use your common sense. Pain is normally a reliable indicator of bodily harm, but frostbite and hypothermia can sneak up on a child.

Frostbite most often affects the nose, ears, cheeks, chin, fingers, or toes. Signs of frostbite are a loss of feeling and color or the appearance of a white or grayish yellow patch. It can permanently damage the body, but the pain comes later, when the harm has already been done.

To treat frostbite, immerse the affected area in warm—*not hot*—water, or warm the affected area with your body heat. Skin damaged by frostbite is very delicate. Massaging, rubbing, or walking on it can cause further injury; heating it with a stove, fireplace, radiator, or heating pad can cause burns on top of the frostbite. The best treatment is prevention. Wet gloves or socks raise the risk of frostbite, so staying both dry and warm is important.

Hypothermia results from the loss of body heat due to prolonged exposure to cold temperatures. Warning signs in infants include red, cold skin and very low energy. Shivering, drowsiness, and confusion or slurred speech are danger signs in older children. If a child's temperature falls below 95°F, seek medical attention immediately and begin warming the child.

In temperatures below 40°F, little infants are safest indoors. If you need to take your baby outside for more than a few minutes, put her in a soft front carrier snuggled up against your chest, underneath your coat, with a warm hat on.

Hot weather. Infants and children up to the age of four are sensitive to high temperatures. They should drink liquids frequently through the day, wear sun hats, avoid overexertion, and stay indoors during the hottest part of the day—10:00 a.m. to 2:00 p.m.—if possible. Besides sunburn (see below), heat rash is the most common heat-related illness for young children; heat exhaustion and heat stroke are the most serious.

Heat rash is an irritation caused by excessive sweating during hot, humid weather. It looks like a cluster of red pimples or blisters. The best treatment is to clean the area with water on a soft cloth, pat the area dry, and keep it as dry as possible. Creams and ointments keep the skin moist and make the condition worse.

Heat cramps, heat exhaustion, and heat stroke often affect children under five and the elderly. But even healthy teens are vulnerable if they exercise in the heat for a long time with limited access to water. Signs of heat exhaustion include heavy sweating, paleness, muscle cramps, tiredness or weakness, dizziness or headache, nausea or vomiting, and faintness. Heat-stroke, an even more serious condition, appears as red, hot, and dry or sweaty skin along with a strong, rapid pulse, throbbing headache or dizziness, confusion, and unconsciousness.

Prevention is the key. Make sure children take frequent breaks for shade, rest, and fluids. Stop them altogether at the first signs of weakness, nausea, or excessive sweating. Be especially careful when children are dressed heavily—for example, in football uniforms, helmets, and pads—and when humidity is high.

Never leave an infant or toddler alone in a car. Even on a cloudy day, the inside temperature can rise to dangerous levels in less time than it takes to buy a tube of sunblock.

SUN SAFETY

It can feel great to be out in the sun, but the cost can be steep. Sunburns early in life increase the risk of skin cancer later. Even minor ultraviolet (UV) exposure adds up over time, causing wrinkles and spots on exposed skin surfaces, and cataracts in the eyes. If you grew up loving the sun, you may need to think about it differently now as a parent.

Who is at risk? The fairer the skin, the greater the danger. Melanin, the pigment that makes dark skin dark, protects against UV light. But even dark-skinned people need to exercise caution. Infants are especially at risk, because their skin is thin and tends to have less pigment. Activities near water double the risk of sunburn, because UV rays both stream down from above and also reflect up off the water. Snow and light-colored sand have a similar effect. What's more, you can't trust your body (or your child's) to tell you when you've had too much sun. By the time the skin begins to feel warm and look red, it's too late to prevent sunburn. You have to think ahead and limit sun exposure before any symptoms appear.

Made in the shade. First, protect your child's skin from direct exposure to sunlight, especially between 10:00 a.m. and 2:00 p.m., when sunlight is the strongest and most harmful. A good rule is that if your shadow is shorter than you are, the sun is strong enough to burn you. Remember that ultraviolet rays can damage the skin and eyes even on hazy or cloudy days.

Use an umbrella at the beach. Look for a shady tree at a barbecue. Dress your child in a long-sleeved shirt, pants, and a broad-brimmed hat, all made out of UV-resistant material (a regular summer shirt offers little protection). UV rays penetrate water, so be cautious while swimming: You can feel nice and cool while getting a sunburn.

Sunscreen is a must. Sunscreens can irritate the skin of babies less than six months old; it's best to keep them in the shade (and *not* near water, which reflects the UV rays up at them).

After six months, use a sunscreen with a sun protection factor (SPF) of 15 or more. This means that only one-fifteenth of the harmful rays get through, so that fifteen minutes of sun exposure with sunscreen is like one minute in the sun without sunscreen. The most effective sunscreens are thick white pastes that contain chemicals such as zinc oxide and titanium dioxide. These are safe, but are only practical for small areas of the body—noses, ears, shoulders, and feet.

For the rest of the body, use waterproof sunscreen: Slather it on liberally at least a half hour before sun exposure, and be sure not to miss any spots. Avoid the eyes, however; sunscreen stings. Reapply it frequently, every half hour or so. For a fair-skinned child who lives in a sunny climate, putting on sunblock cream or lotion should be part of the morning routine, with a second application in the afternoon.

Sunglasses. Everybody should wear sunglasses, even infants. Over time, UV light damages the eyes, leading to cataracts. The glasses don't need to be expensive, and the darkness of the lens doesn't matter. What's important is that the lenses are coated with a special compound that blocks UV light. Check the label. Babies look cute in sunglasses!

BUGBITES

Bites and stings are always unpleasant and sometimes dangerous. A few years back, West Nile virus had everyone frightened; now we are all aware of the danger of Zika virus. Simple precautions can lower the risk and allow your child to enjoy the outdoors without worry.

What you can do. Clothing is your first line of defense. It should cover as much skin as possible. Light-colored clothing is less attractive to bugs. Avoid heavily scented detergents and shampoos.

Use an insect repellent designed for children. Products with 10 percent DEET protect for about two hours; those with 30 percent protect up to five hours. Higher concentrations aren't safe, and DEET isn't safe at all for infants under two months. If your child is sweaty or in and out of water, you'll need to apply the repellent more often. Try to keep your child's hands free of repellent so it doesn't get in his eyes or mouth. DEET may be harmful if ingested. Wash all repellent off once your child is back indoors.

Mosquitoes. Drain standing water—in flowerpots or old tires, for example—where mosquitoes breed. Keep toddlers indoors at dusk when mosquitoes arrive in full force. Keep doors closed and repair damaged or missing screens. Be aware that the mosquitoes that spread Zika bite more during the *day* than at night.

Bees and wasps. When bees are about, avoid snacking outdoors and wash your children's hands after eating (bees love sweets). If you find a nest, it's best to have it removed professionally. Barefoot children who step on bees get stung; wearing shoes solves this problem. Bumblebees are usually unaggressive, and are fascinating to watch at work.

Ticks. Deer ticks, the carriers of Lyme disease and other diseases, are very tiny creatures—the size of a pinhead. (Wood ticks or dog ticks, about the size of a nailhead, are more common.) Lyme disease is now common across the country; you can check with your doctor or health department to find out if it is present in your region. There is lots of information on Lyme disease on the U.S. Centers for Disease Control website, www.cdc.gov; look under "L" in the A–Z index. Protective clothing and DEET-containing repellents help, but you'll still need to check carefully for ticks after your child has been playing outside, especially in tall grass or near wooded areas. If you find a tick that hasn't been attached very long, it probably hasn't had a chance to transmit disease. The best method for removing ticks is to use tweezers to grab the tick as close to the skin as possible, then pull straight out. Don't use petroleum jelly, nail polish, or a hot match to force it to back out. Wash the skin with an antiseptic, and ask your child's doctor whether your child needs to take antibiotics.

PREVENTING DOG BITES

Most people injured by dog bites are under age ten. Small children may startle or hurt the animal, provoking an attack. Never leave an infant or young child alone with any dog. (There is a series of wonderful wordless picture books about a dog named Carl who proves to be an excellent babysitter. Enjoy the books, but don't try it at home.)

When you choose a family dog, steer clear of aggressive and high-strung breeds, especially pit bulls, Rottweilers, and German shepherds. Be wary of dogs that may have been raised badly or subjected to cruelty. Spay or neuter your dog to reduce aggressive tendencies related to territorialism.

Dog rules for children. A sensitive, anxious child may need lots of reassurance before he goes anywhere near a dog. A bold, fearless child may need to be taught specific rules for dealing with dogs. Here are some commonsense ones:

+ Keep away from dogs you don't know, even if they're tied up.

+ Always ask the owner before petting or playing with a dog.

+ Never tease a dog or stare directly into the eyes of a dog you don't know. Many dogs take staring as a threat or a challenge.

+ Don't disturb a dog who is sleeping, eating, or caring for puppies.

+ If a dog comes near you, don't run away; he probably just wants to sniff you.

+ If a dog knocks you over, just curl up in a ball and stay still.

+ Beware of dogs while biking or skating.

FIREWORKS AND TRICK-OR-TREAT

The Fourth of July. Fireworks injure thousands of children each year. Most injuries are to hands, fingers, eyes, or head. Fireworks for personal use are illegal in many states, and dangerous in *every* state. Even sparklers, which seem so harmless, are a tragedy waiting to happen. Parents who insist that sparklers are an indispensable rite of childhood need to supervise closely to ensure that no one gets hurt. When you go to see fireworks, sit far away. The beautiful colors are just as nice from a distance, and the loud explosions won't scare your small child or hurt her ears.

Halloween. Nowadays, parties have become a popular alternative to trick-or-treating. But there is something about roaming the neighborhood in search of candy and donations for UNICEF that no party can match (see www.unicefusa.org).

Here are tips to make trick-or-treating *and* safe.

✓ Make sure that costumes and masks don't obstruct your child's vision. Face paint or makeup is safer than a mask.

✓ Trick-or-treaters should carry flashlights and stick to sidewalks. Shoes and costumes should fit to prevent tripping.

✓ Swords, knives, and similar implements should be made of flexible material that can't cause injury.

✓ To prevent burns, make sure costumes, masks, beards, and wigs are made of flame-resistant materials. Clothing that is very loose is more likely to come into contact with any candles (in a jack-o'-lantern, for example).

✓ Put reflective tape on bags and costumes so that drivers can see trick-or-treaters, and remind children to obey all traffic rules and not to dart out from between parked cars.

Children under eight should not trick-or-treat without the supervision of an adult or older sibling. Instruct children to travel only on well-established routes, stopping only at homes with outside lights on, and never to enter a home unless accompanied by a trusted adult.

FIRST AID AND EMERGENCIES

CUTS AND SCRATCHES

The best medicine for scratches and small cuts is lots of warm water and soap. After drying with a clean towel, cover with a bandage. Wash once a day until completely healed. An antibiotic ointment can't hurt, but thorough washing is the key to preventing infection.

Larger cuts that spread open may need stitches or a tissue adhesive to aid in healing and reduce scarring. Keep stitches clean and dry until they are removed. Inspect the wound each day for signs of infection, such as pain, swelling, redness, or drainage from the wound. A little soreness is normal.

Wounds that might be contaminated by dirt or soil, or punctures caused by dirty objects such as knives or nails, should be reported to your doctor. They can be deeper than they look. Ask about a tetanus booster. If a child got the initial series of four DTaP immunizations and a booster within the last five years, he may be protected already.

Occasionally a bit of glass, wood, or gravel may remain in a wound. Unless you can easily remove the fragments, it's best to have a doctor evaluate these wounds. An X-ray may be needed to show the foreign object. Any cut that does not heal properly or that becomes infected (with redness, pain, or drainage) may have a retained foreign object.

SPLINTERS

Try the soak-and-poke: Wash the area with soap and water, then soak it in fairly hot water for at least ten minutes. Use a hot compress if you can't cover the area with water. (You'll have to reheat your water or compress every couple of minutes.) If one end of the splinter is sticking out of the skin, grasp it with a good pair of tweezers and gently pull it out. If the splinter is entirely under the skin, you'll need a sewing needle that's been wiped with rubbing alcohol. The soaking softens the skin so that you can gently prick it open with the tip of the needle, making a big enough opening for you to grasp the splinter with tweezers. After the splinter is out, wash the area with soap and water and then cover with a clean bandage.

Don't poke at the skin too much. If you can't get the splinter out after the first soak, give it another ten minutes of hot soaking and then try again. If you still can't get it, let a professional take over.

BITES

Animal or human bites. Most human bites just cause bruising. But a bite that breaks the skin, whether human or animal, needs medical attention. Mouths are home to millions of bacteria, and different animals (dogs, cats, people) carry different germs that respond to different antibiotics. Before you get to the doctor, wash the bite with soap and lots of running water. Even if your child is receiving antibiotics, be sure to notify the doctor if you see signs of infection, such as redness, swelling, tenderness, or drainage.

With animal bites, you have to think about rabies. Rabies can be fatal and there is no cure once the infection has set in, but a special vaccine given as soon as possible after the bite can prevent the most serious illness. Many wild animals, especially foxes, raccoons, and bats, carry rabies. Pets, including dogs and cats, can also transmit the virus. You probably don't need to worry about gerbils, hamsters, or guinea pigs. If your child has been bitten, call the doctor as well as your local board of health or your state department of public health. Health officials may need to capture the animal and observe it for symptoms of rabies. If your child wakes up with a bat in the bedroom (it happens!), that's a potentially dangerous exposure, just like a bite. Call about the vaccine.

Insect bites. Most don't need any treatment, but scratching a bite can lead to infection. Look for pus, crusting, or worsening redness and pain. For itching, you can apply a paste made by adding a few drops of water to a teaspoonful of baking soda. Hydrocortisone cream (1 percent) reduces itching safely. Diphenhydramine (Benadryl) or another antihistamine can reduce itching. Antihistamines make some children tired, and others hyper. Calamine lotion is soothing, with no side effects. And it's pink!

For bee stings, check to see if the stinger is still in the skin; if it is, gently scrape the area with a credit card or other small piece of plastic. Don't use tweezers, because they can squeeze more venom into the skin. Gently clean the area, and apply ice to help with swelling.

BLEEDING

Minor wounds. A little bleeding for a few minutes helps clean the wound. Only profuse or persistent bleeding requires special treatment. To stop the bleeding, apply direct pressure while elevating the wound. Have the child lie down and put a pillow or two under the limb. Press on the wound with a sterile gauze square or any clean cloth until the bleeding stops. Clean and bandage the wound while the limb is still elevated.

When bandaging a cut that has bled a lot or is still bleeding, use a number of gauze squares (or folded pieces of clean cloth) on top of each other so that you have a thick pad over the cut. Then, when you snugly apply the adhesive or gauze roll bandage, it will exert more pressure on the cut and make it less likely to bleed again.

Severe bleeding. If a wound is bleeding at an alarming rate, you must stop the bleeding immediately. Apply direct pressure to the wound and elevate the limb if possible. Make a pad of the cleanest material you have handy, whether it's a gauze square, a clean handkerchief, or the cleanest piece of clothing on the child or yourself. Press the pad against the wound and keep pressing until help arrives or until the bleeding stops. Don't remove your original pad. As it becomes soaked through, add new material on top. A minor cut to the scalp can cause a lot of bleeding. Pressure on the wound should stop it quickly. If you have no cloth or material of any kind to press against a profusely bleeding wound, press your hands on the edges of the wound or even in the wound.

Most bleeding can be stopped by direct pressure. If not,

you might be able to use a tourniquet to shut off blood flow to a whole limb. Tie a piece of cloth around the limb upstream of the injury (closer to the body); slip a stick under the cloth band and twist to tighten. Continue to apply direct pressure and have someone call an ambulance. While you wait, have the patient lie down, keep her warm, and elevate her legs and the injured body part.

Nosebleeds. Almost every child has nosebleeds, and they are almost never dangerous. A little blood can look like a lot when it comes out of the nose. (Nosebleeds in infants are *not* common and sometimes spell trouble. They should be reported to the doctor.)

Most nosebleeds stop on their own if the child just sits still for a few minutes. Or you can gently pinch the whole lower part of the nose for five minutes. Look at your watch; five minutes seems like an eternity in these circumstances. Let go slowly. If the nosebleed continues for ten minutes, get in touch with the doctor.

Common causes of nosebleeds include dry air, nose picking, allergies, and colds. After the bleeding stops, a scab forms inside the nose; a day later the scab falls off (or the child picks it off) and the nose bleeds again. Try smearing a little petroleum jelly inside the nose a few times a day to keep the scab from drying up too quickly.

If a child has repeated nosebleeds, the doctor may offer to cauterize an exposed blood vessel or run a test to make sure the blood can clot normally. Almost always, though, the treatment of choice is patience.

BURNS AND ELECTRICAL INJURIES

Burn severity. Superficial, or first-degree, burns only affect the topmost layer of the skin, causing redness, swelling, heat, and pain (think sunburn). Partial-thickness burns (also called "second-degree" burns) involve deeper layers, and usually cause blisters. Full-thickness burns (also known as "third-degree" burns) involve the deepest layers of the skin, often with damage to the underlying nerves and blood vessels. Full-thickness burns are very serious injuries, often requiring hospitalization.

Size and location also matter. A superficial burn over much of the body (a bad sunburn or a burn from hot water) is often enough to make a child quite ill. Burns on the face, hands, feet, and genital area can cause scars or functional impairments, and should be seen by a doctor. Mild sunburns are the exception.

Sunburn. For relief of sunburn, try a cool compress and a mild nonaspirin pain reliever (ibuprofen or acetaminophen). Hydrocortisone cream (1 percent) is soothing. If blisters develop, see below; if chills and fever, call a doctor. Sunburn can be just as serious as a heat burn. Keep sunburned areas completely protected from sunshine until the redness is gone.

Other minor burns. For minor burns, hold the burned area under cold running water for several minutes, until the area feels numbed. Don't use ice; freezing can worsen the injury. Never apply any ointment, grease, butter, cream, or petroleum product. After rinsing the burn with cold water, cover the area with a bulky sterile dressing to decrease the pain.

Burns with blisters. Leave blisters alone. As long as they aren't broken, the fluid inside is sterile. Once the blister breaks, germs can get in. You can remove dead skin with a pair of nail scissors or tweezers that have been boiled for five minutes. Then cover with a sterile bandage. A prescription ointment may prevent infection. If you see signs of infection—like pus in the blister and redness around the edge—you should certainly consult a doctor. Never put iodine or any similar antiseptic on a burn unless directed by a doctor.

Electrical injuries. With electricity, the severity of injury depends on the amount of current that passes through the child. Water or moisture of any kind increases the flow of current. Therefore, no electrical device should ever be operated in a bathroom where a child is washing or bathing.

Most often, electricity gives a shock and the child pulls his hand away before any damage is done. If there is a small blister or area of redness, or a small patch of charred tissue, you can treat the injury like a burn caused by heat. An electrical current can travel through nerves and blood vessels. If your child has entrance and exit wounds, the current may have damaged nerves and blood vessels along the way. Let a doctor take a look, especially if your child has any neurologic symptoms such as numbness or tingling, or if she complains of pain anywhere other than right at the site of the electrical contact.

If a child bites into an electric cord and gets a shock, particularly if there is a small burn at the corner of the mouth, call the doctor. Your child may need special care to avoid developing a scar that could interfere with his ability to smile and chew.

SKIN INFECTIONS

Minor skin infections. Look for redness, swelling, warmth, pain, or pus. If a child has a boil, an infection at the end of his finger, or an infected cut of any type, let a doctor take a look. The best first-aid treatment is to soak the infected area in warm water or apply warm wet dressings; this softens the skin so that it can break open and allow the pus to escape, and then keeps the skin from closing over again too soon. Place a fairly thick bandage over the infection and pour enough warm water onto the bandage to make all of it thoroughly wet. Let it soak for twenty minutes, then replace the wet bandage with a clean, dry one. Repeat this wet soak three or four times a day until you can see the doctor. If you have an antibiotic ointment, you can apply it over the affected area, although this should not replace the visit to the doctor.

More serious skin infections. Signs that a skin infection is more serious include fever, a rapidly enlarging red area, red streaks starting from the site of infection, and tender lymph glands in the armpit or groin. These infections are medical emergencies. Get the child to a doctor or emergency room at once.

OBJECTS IN NOSE AND EARS

Small children often put things—beads, small pieces from toys or games, or wads of paper—into their noses or ears. If you can grasp a soft object with a pair of tweezers, go ahead and take it out. Don't try to go after anything smooth and hard; you'll probably just push it in farther. Be careful with the tweezers so that you don't cause more damage, especially if your child won't sit still. Even if you can't see the object, it may still be there. Objects that stay in the nose for several days often cause a bad-smelling discharge tinged with blood. A discharge of this kind from one nostril should always make you think of this possibility.

Sometimes an older child may be able to expel an object by blowing her nose. But don't try this with her if she's so young that she sniffs when told to blow. Other children sneeze the object out in a little while. Try squirting a little saline solution into the nose to loosen things up, and maybe suctioning with a rubber bulb syringe. If that fails, let your child's doctor take a look.

OBJECTS IN THE EYE

To remove specks of dirt or grit, try having your child blink several times while you pour water gently over the eye. If the feeling of grittiness persists for more than about thirty minutes, talk with the doctor. If the eye was hit forcefully or by a sharp object, or if it hurts, cover the eye with a damp cloth and go for help. Blood in the eye, significant lid swelling, purple discoloration around the eye, or sudden blurring of vision are all reasons for prompt medical attention.

SPRAINS AND STRAINS

Tendons connect muscles to bones; ligaments hold joints together. When muscles, tendons, or ligaments are overstretched or torn, that's a strain or a sprain. These injuries can hurt so much that you might wonder if a bone is broken, too. But in either case the first aid is the same: elevation, ice, and immobilization.

Have your child lie down for a half hour and elevate the sprained limb on a pillow. Put an ice pack (or a bag of frozen peas) over the injured area. Applying cold immediately helps to prevent swelling and decrease pain. Use an elastic bandage to wrap an ankle, knee, or wrist in order to immobilize it. Give a nonaspirin pain reliever such as ibuprofen. If the pain isn't too severe, you can watch it for a few hours or a day. If your child can resume normal movement without pain, there is no need to see a doctor.

If the area stays painful and swollen, have your child seen. Even if there isn't a broken bone, your child may require a cast or splint to allow the ligaments and tendons to heal properly. It can take a long time. If a child goes back to vigorous activity too soon, there's a risk of reinjuring the joint. It's best to follow the doctor's instructions; a physical therapist can often help with specific exercises.

Elbow injury in toddlers. A toddler may suddenly refuse to use his arm, letting it hang limply at his side. A few minutes before this the arm may have been pulled sharply, as when a parent catches the child by the hand to prevent a fall. What has happened is that one of the bones at the elbow has been pulled out of position. A physician who recognizes "toddler's elbow" can usually pop the joint back into place painlessly.

FRACTURES

Children's bones are different. Children's bones have growth plates on each end, where new bone is being formed.

A fracture at the growth plate can interfere with future growth, causing one limb to be short or bent. Children's bones are flexible, so sometimes only one side of a bone breaks (a greenstick fracture). They can also have the typical adult pattern, which is a crack all the way through a bone.

It can be hard to tell the difference between a sprain and a fracture if the only symptoms are swelling and tenderness. Bruising at the site of injury or pain that persists for days suggests a fracture. Often the only way to be sure is to take X-rays.

If you suspect a fracture, avoid further injury by immobilizing the area. Apply a splint if you can (see below), and ice. Give a nonaspirin pain reliever. Then take your child to the emergency room.

Broken wrists. A child who falls from a jungle gym or slips on the ice will often block his fall with a straight arm, and break his wrist in the process. The wrist hurts right away, but the pain might not be severe, so you might not know that there's a fracture. Days can go by, uncomfortably. An X-ray confirms the diagnosis, and a splint or cast solves the problem.

Splinting. Most broken bones should be seen in the emergency room as soon as possible. For any serious break, call an ambulance; don't try to move the child yourself unless you have to. If for some reason you can't get your child to medical attention right away, you may need to apply a splint. Splinting reduces pain and prevents further damage that could be caused by movement of the broken bones. The splint should hold the limb motionless above and below the injury. An ankle splint should reach to the knee; for a broken wrist, the splint should go from the fingertips to the elbow.

You need a board to make a long splint. You can make a short splint for a small child by folding a piece of cardboard. Move the limb with extreme gentleness when you apply the splint, and avoid any movement near the area of the injury. Tie the limb to the splint snugly in four to six places using handkerchiefs, strips of clothing, or bandages. Be sure you don't cut off the circulation. Two of the ties should be close to the break, on either side of it, and there should be one at each end of the splint.

After you apply the splint, place an ice pack over the area of the injury. Never apply ice directly to the skin; as a general rule, apply ice for no more than twenty minutes at any one time. For a broken collarbone, make a sling out of a large triangle of cloth and tie it behind the child's neck so that it supports the lower arm across the chest.

NECK AND BACK INJURIES

If you suspect a neck or back injury, don't try to move the child. Instead, keep the child comfortable, and call an ambulance. Do this for any injury that involves loss of consciousness, or any high-impact injury (a fall from a bicycle going fast, for example, or a car wreck).

Normally, the bones of the vertebral column (the spine) protect the nerves of the spinal cord. If the spinal bones break or become unlinked, even a small movement can crush the cord or cut off its blood supply. So you have to be extremely careful: Never turn the head separately from the body, and, if at all possible, wait for a health professional to move the child.

HEAD INJURIES

A baby who rolls off a bed or changing table ought to cry right away, then quickly behave as if nothing at all happened. If she's stunned, vomits, looks pale, or just isn't quite right, take her to the doctor. A swelling on a child's forehead after a fall isn't normally serious, as long as there are no other symptoms, but swellings on other parts of the skull are worrisome. Any child who loses consciousness after a fall should be seen by a doctor immediately, even if there are no other symptoms.

After a head injury, a child should be observed closely for the next twenty-four to forty-eight hours. Bleeding inside the skull can put pressure on the brain, causing symptoms that are not obvious at first but which develop over a day or two. Any change in behavior, especially increased sleepiness, agitation, or dizziness, is a red flag.

School-age children who have had a concussion—that is, a serious head injury with even a momentary loss of consciousness, confusion, or with memory loss—may develop persisting problems with concentration, memory, or mood. The treatment of concussions is complicated; a doctor should supervise.

SWALLOWED OBJECTS

Children swallow lots of things that aren't food. Small, smooth objects, like prune pits or small buttons, usually pass within a day or so, no harm done. Objects stuck in the throat can cause coughing or choking, pain or difficulty with swallowing, refusal to eat, drooling, persistent vomiting, or just the annoying feeling of something caught in the throat.

Objects sucked into the windpipe usually cause persistent coughing. Every now and then, a child who has been coughing on and off for the past few weeks turns out to have something in her windpipe, discovered when an astute doctor requests an X-ray or endoscopy.

Certain objects, including needles, pins, and coins (especially quarters), tend to cause problems. Button batteries are particularly dangerous because they can leak acid, causing internal burns. Little magnets from toys can stick together and erode holes in the intestines.

If your child shows any of the symptoms listed above or has swallowed a sharp or irregularly shaped object or *any* battery or magnet, then you need to call the doctor right away.

You might think that making your child vomit or giving a strong laxative would help flush out a swallowed object. Usually these measures don't work, and sometimes they make the situation worse. It's better to let the doctor remove the object safely.

POISONS

First aid for suspected poisoning is simple: if your child appears ill, call 911 for an ambulance, then call the national poison control hotline at (800) 222-1222. If your child appears well, call the poison hotline first. Other tips:

✦ Stay with your child and make sure she is breathing and alert. If not, call 911 or your local emergency unit for immediate help.

✦ Remove any remaining substances or solutions to prevent her from ingesting any more.

✦ Do not delay seeking help because your child seems well. The effects of many drugs and poisons—aspirin, for instance—may take hours to show. Early treatment can prevent serious harm.

✦ Call the national poison control hotline, (800) 222-1222. Tell them the name of the product your child swallowed, as well as the amount, if known.

Poisons on the skin. Medications and poisons can be absorbed through the skin. If your child's clothes or skin come in contact with a potential poison, remove the contaminated clothing and rinse off the skin with plenty of plain water for fifteen minutes. Then gently wash the area with soap and water. Place the contaminated clothing in a plastic bag, keeping it away from other children. Call the national poison control hotline at (800) 222-1222 or your doctor. If they refer you to a hospital, take the contaminated clothes with you in case they wish to test the clothes to identify the poison.

Harmful fluids in the eye. If a child is accidentally squirted or splashed in the eye with a possibly harmful fluid, try to keep the child from rubbing his eyes. Have him lie on his back and blink as much as possible while you flood the eye with lukewarm (not hot) water poured from a large glass held two or three inches above the face. Don't force the eyelid open. Keep this up for fifteen minutes; meanwhile, have someone call the poison control hotline. If you're alone, flush the eye first, then call. Some liquids can cause serious damage to the eye. Caustics, such as drain cleaners, are especially dangerous and require emergency medical care.

ALLERGIC REACTIONS

Children can have an allergic reaction to a food, a pet, a medication, an insect bite, or almost anything else. The symptoms can be mild, moderate, or severe.

Mild. Children may complain of watery, itchy eyes; sneezing or a stuffy nose; swelling of the skin that looks like large mosquito bites and itch badly (hives); or small, itchy bumps. Mild allergic symptoms are usually treated with over-the-counter diphenhydramine or another antihistamine.

Moderate. In addition to hives, the child develops wheezing and coughing. Children with these symptoms need to be evaluated by a doctor promptly.

Severe (also called anaphylaxis). Swelling in the mouth or throat, difficulty breathing due to blockage of the airway, and low blood pressure are emergencies. The treatment for anaphylaxis is epinephrine injected under the skin, followed by immediate transfer to a hospital emergency room.

A child who has had one anaphylactic reaction could have another. To prevent a serious episode, doctors prescribe a preloaded syringe of epinephrine to be carried by parents and teachers or by an older child. If a child ever uses the EpiPen, the very next place he should go is to the emergency room, even if he feels better, because symptoms may return when the epinephrine wears off.

CONVULSIONS OR SEIZURES

A generalized seizure or convulsion is frightening to witness. It's important to remain calm and realize that in most cases the child is not truly in danger. Place the child where she can't bump into anything—for example, on a rug away from any furniture. Lay her on her side so that any saliva will run out of her mouth and her tongue does not block her airway. Don't reach down her throat or stick anything into her mouth. Call 911 (see page 511).

CHOKING AND RESCUE BREATHING

Read these passages carefully, study the pictures, and imagine yourself saving a child. Better yet, get trained in emergency lifesaving. The Red Cross offers courses, as do many hospitals and fire departments. With luck, you'll never need these skills!

Choking and coughing. When a child has swallowed something and is coughing hard, give her a chance to cough it out. Coughing is the best way to clear an object from the air passages. If the child can breathe, speak, or cry, stay close by and call for help. Don't make any attempt to remove the object. Don't slap her on the back, turn her upside down, or reach into her mouth. Each of these actions can drive the object farther down the airway.

Unable to cough or breathe. When a child is choking and *no longer is able to* breathe, cry, or speak, the object is completely blocking the airway, and air is not entering the lungs. In this situation, follow the emergency steps outlined on page 440.

UP TO ONE YEAR OLD, UNABLE TO COUGH OR BREATHE
(COMPLETELY BLOCKED AIRWAY)

1. If the baby is conscious, slide one hand under her back to support her head and neck. With your other hand, hold her jaw with your forearm resting on her belly and chest.

2. Turn the child over so she is lying facedown with her head lower than her trunk. Support her with your forearm.

3. With the heel of one hand, give the baby up to five rapid blows in the middle of the back, high between the shoulder blades. *If this works, and the baby starts breathing or crying, just wait and watch!*

4. If the object was not dislodged by the back blows, turn the infant faceup while supporting her back with your forearm. The child's head should be lower than her feet. Place two fingers on her breastbone, in the center of her chest just below the level of her nipples. Give up to five quick downward chest thrusts, trying to create an artificial cough. *If this works, and the baby starts breathing or crying, wait and watch; then have the baby seen by her doctor.*

5. If back blows and chest thrusts have failed, look for the object in the back of the baby's throat by grabbing the tongue and the lower jaw between your thumb and fingers and lifting upward. If you see something, slide your little finger down along the inside of her cheek to the base of her tongue and use a hooking motion to sweep the object out. (Don't poke your finger in her mouth if you can't see anything; this could make the blockage worse.)

6. Next, reposition the baby to begin rescue breathing. Open her mouth by lifting her chin as you press back on her forehead.

7. If the baby still hasn't started to breathe, start rescue breathing (see page 443).

8. If the air does not enter the baby's lungs, her air passage is still blocked. Be sure you're lifting the chin properly and try again. Then start over with the back blows and repeat steps three through seven. Continue repeating

the sequence until the baby starts to cough, breathe, or
cry, or until help arrives.

**OVER ONE YEAR OLD, UNABLE TO COUGH OR BREATHE
(COMPLETELY BLOCKED AIRWAY)**

1. Remember, if the child is coughing, speaking, or crying, *watch but don't intervene.* If the child is conscious
   but not able to get any air in or out, do the Heimlich
   maneuver: Kneel or stand behind the child and wrap
   your arms around his waist. Make a fist with one hand
   and put the thumb of your fist just above the child's
   navel, staying well below his breastbone. Cover your
   fist with your other hand and press your fist into the
   child's abdomen with up to five quick upward thrusts.
   Be gentle with younger or smaller children. Repeat
   until the object is expelled. This should get the child to
   breathe or cough. (If this treatment stops the choking
   episode, call the doctor even if the child seems fully
   recovered.)

2. If the child still isn't breathing after the Heimlich maneuver, open his mouth by grasping both the tongue and the lower jaw between your thumb and fingers, and lift the jaw. Look in his throat for the object. If you see something, slide your little finger along the inside of his cheek to the base of his tongue, and use a hooking motion to sweep the object out. (Don't poke your finger around in his mouth if you can't see anything, or can't hook the object; this could make the blockage worse.) Repeat the Heimlich maneuver until the foreign body is removed or if the child becomes unconscious.

   If the child becomes unconscious, have someone call 911. Try the Heimlich maneuver with the child lying on his back. Kneel at his feet (or straddle the legs of a bigger child). Put the heel of one hand above his navel, staying well below his breastbone. Put your other hand on top of the first one, with the fingers of both hands pointing toward his head. Press into his abdomen with a quick upward thrust. Be gentle with smaller children. Repeat until the object is expelled.

3. If the child remains unconscious, start rescue breathing (see below).

4. If the air does not enter the child's lungs, continue to alternate rescue breathing and the Heimlich maneuver until the child resumes breathing or until help arrives.

How to give rescue breathing. Never give rescue breathing to a person who is breathing. With an adult, breathe at your natural speed. With a child, use slightly quicker, shorter breaths. Make sure each of your breaths goes into the victim.

First open the air passages by properly positioning the child's head. Do this by tilting the forehead back while lifting up on the chin with your fingers. Maintain this position every time you provide a rescue breath.

With a small child, you can breathe into the nose and mouth together. With a bigger child, breathe into the mouth while pinching the nose shut.

Breathe into the victim, using only minimal force. (A small child's lungs cannot contain your entire exhalation.) Remove your lips, allowing the child's chest to contract while you take in your next breath. Breathe into the child again.

HOME FIRST-AID KIT

An emergency is no time to look for phone numbers, bandages, and other first-aid stuff. Instead, keep a small first-aid kit in your house, stored where curious children can't reach. The following items should be included:

LIST OF EMERGENCY TELEPHONE NUMBERS

✓ How to reach an ambulance or emergency response team in your community (most communities use 911 for emergencies)

✓ National poison control hotline, (800) 222-1222 (tape this number to your telephone, or put it in your speed-dial list)

✓ Your child's doctor

✓ A neighbor to call should you need an adult to assist you

FIRST-AID EQUIPMENT

✓ Small sterile bandages

✓ Larger bandages or gauze pads

✓ An Ace bandage or a similar elastic wrap

✓ Eye patch

✓ Adhesive tape

✓ Ice pack (in the freezer)

✓ Any emergency medications your child may require

✓ A thermometer

✓ Petroleum jelly

✓ Small scissors

✓ Tweezers

✓ Antiseptic solution

✓ Antibiotic ointment

✓ Antifever medications (acetaminophen or ibuprofen)

✓ A bulb syringe

✓ A tube of 1 percent hydrocortisone cream

DENTAL DEVELOPMENT AND ORAL HEALTH

Oral health and general health are closely linked. We've stopped thinking of cavities as just a nuisance and now see them for what they are: chronic infections with serious health consequences. Tooth decay can interfere with sleep and undermine school performance. Later in life, tooth decay raises the risks of premature birth and heart attacks. Prevention is the key, and it starts even before your baby has teeth. Dr. Spock recalled, "When I was a young man, I asked a wise old gentleman what the secret to a happy life was. 'Take care of your teeth!' was his reply. It was as good advice as I ever got."

TOOTH DEVELOPMENT

Baby teeth. When will your baby's teeth appear? One baby gets her first tooth at three months, another not until eighteen months. Both are perfectly normal. The age of teething depends on a child's individual pattern. Late tooth eruption is rarely a sign of disease.

The first two teeth to appear are usually the two lower incisors, the front teeth with sharp cutting edges. The four upper incisors come in a few months later. At about one year, most babies have these six teeth. After this, there's usually a lull of several months before the next onslaught. Then six more teeth quickly appear: the two last lower incisors and all four first primary (baby) molars. The molars don't come in next to the incisor teeth but farther back, leaving space for the canine teeth.

After the first molars there's another pause of several months. Then, usually between eighteen and twenty-four months, the canines fill in the spaces between the incisors and the molars. Canines are the pointed "dog" teeth or "eye" teeth. The last four baby teeth are the second primary molars, which come in right behind the first primary molars, usually in the third year. Remember, it's normal for babies to get their teeth either earlier or later than these average ages.

Permanent teeth. Permanent teeth show up between about age six and fourteen. The six-year molars come through behind the baby molars. The baby teeth are lost in roughly the same order they appeared, beginning with the lower central incisors. The permanent incisors, pushing up underneath, come into position where the baby tooth roots have been dissolved away. Eventually all the primary teeth become loose and fall out. (Robert McCloskey's classic picture book *One Morning in Maine* is wonderful reading for all children of tooth-losing age and their parents.)

The permanent teeth that take the place of the baby molars are called bicuspids or premolars. The twelve-year molars (second permanent molars) come in behind the six-year molars. The third set of molars (eighteen-year molars, or wisdom teeth) may be impacted in the jaw and may need to be removed so they won't do any damage to neighboring teeth or the bone of the jaw. Permanent teeth often appear with jagged edges. Either they wear down or a dentist can trim them. Also, permanent teeth are yellower than primary teeth.

Permanent teeth sometimes come in crooked or out of place, but they may eventually be straightened out by the muscular action of the tongue, lips, and cheeks. If teeth don't straighten out, or if the jaw alignment is abnormal, then orthodontic treatment (braces) may be needed for bite improvement.

TEETHING

Symptoms of teething. One baby chews things, frets, drools, has a hard time getting to sleep, and generally makes life miserable for the family for a month or two as each tooth comes through. Another baby acquires teeth with no fuss at all. Most babies start to drool at around three to four months as their salivary glands become more active; it's not always about teething.

A baby who acquires twenty teeth in his first three years is pretty much always cutting teeth. So just about any minor ailment—fever, runny nose, runny poop—could sensibly be attributed to teething, just by coincidence. A few babies do have facial flushing, irritability, ear rubbing, and mildly elevated temperatures as their teeth poke through. But for the most part, what teething causes is teeth!

Help for teething. The first four molar teeth, which erupt at around twelve to eighteen months, are the ones most likely to distress a baby. What to do? First, let her chew! Provide chewable objects that are soft enough so that when she falls with them in her mouth, they won't do any damage. Rubber teething rings of various shapes are good. Avoid toys made from thin, brittle plastic, which could break and cause choking, and objects that might be coated with lead paint (that is, anything painted before about 1980, and possibly items imported from overseas). Board books are safe for babies to chew on; they're lead-free, and they get soggy but don't break into pieces that a baby could choke on.

Cold things usually help. You can wrap up an ice cube or a piece of apple in a square of cloth, or try the cool, damp cloth alone. Some parents swear by frozen bagels or frozen slices of banana. Be creative! Many babies love to have their gums firmly rubbed. And don't fret about germs on the teething ring or piece of cloth. Your baby is putting all sorts of things in her mouth anyway, none of which is germ-free. Of course, it's a good idea to wash the teething ring after it has fallen on the floor or after the dog has slobbered on it.

Ask your child's doctor before giving any medication for teething. There are lots of teething gels on the market that may offer some relief, but some contain potentially dangerous medications. (Lidocaine, the anesthetic in some gels, can turn a baby blue or, in larger doses, stop the heart.) A dose of acetaminophen can help with teething discomfort now and then, but even this safe medicine can be harmful if you give too much or for too many days.

WHAT MAKES GOOD TEETH?

Nutrition for teeth. Growing teeth need calcium, phosphorus, vitamin D, and vitamin C, starting even before birth. The plant-based, nutrition-rich diet described in the section Building Blocks of Nutrition, on page 312, supplies all of these nutrients in abundance.

What children eat after they get their teeth also matters. Young children need three meals and three snacks; for older children, one snack should be enough. Sugary foods that stick to the teeth feed the bacteria that cause cavities.

Fluoride. This naturally occurring mineral makes teeth resistant to acid. The bacteria that cause cavities use acid to break down teeth. Fluoride fights back. It only takes a little fluoride in a mother's diet during pregnancy and in the growing child's diet to make teeth decay-resistant. Where there are high levels of natural fluoride in the water, tooth decay is rare. In other places, the water department adds fluoride as a public health measure.

To fight cavities, drinking water needs to have fluoride at a concentration of 0.7 to 1.0 parts per million (ppm). To find out if your water has enough fluoride, you can ask the water department; there's a number on your bill. If you have your own well, call your county health department for advice.

If your water is low on fluoride, if your family mostly drinks bottled water, or if you use a home purification system that takes out all the fluoride and other minerals, then it makes sense for you and your children to take a fluoride supplement (drops or pills). Toothpastes and mouth rinses with fluoride help, too. Pediatricians and dentists also have fluoride preparations that they apply to the teeth.

Fluoride for babies and children. If you're breastfeeding and drinking fluoridated water, you don't need to give your baby extra fluoride. If your own fluoride intake is low, consider giving your baby an infant vitamin with fluoride. Baby formulas do not contain much fluoride, but if you are mixing the formula with fluoridated water, your child is getting plenty.

If you're giving fluoride drops, give the right amount. Too much fluoride causes ugly white and brown specks on the teeth. Your child's doctor or dentist can tell you how much to give, based on the concentration of fluoride in your water. Children who eat toothpaste (that is, *most* young children) may get too much fluoride, so use a non-fluoride-containing toothpaste until your child is old enough to spit and rinse. Up until age three, use just a tiny smear of toothpaste; after that, a small dot the size of a pea is plenty. It's wise to keep toothpaste away from a young child who might decide that it's really delicious.

EARLY DENTIST VISITS

Your child should see the dentist after her first tooth erupts, or just after her first birthday. Early preventive visits can identify problems when they can be solved easily and painlessly. Children who have good early experiences in the dentist's office look forward to coming back. With good care, most visits will be preventive in nature, rather than the "drill and fill" sessions that haunt the childhood memories of so many adults.

If you had traumatic dental experiences, it may be especially important for your child to see the dentist early. Tooth decay and gum disease are often passed from parent to child. Early care can change your child's dental fate. And if he does go on to have tooth issues, he's going to need to trust his dentist.

More and more dentists see it as their job to create a "dental home" for each child, just as pediatricians try to create a medical home. Certainly, if dental troubles run in your family, then a dental home is what your child should have.

TOOTH DECAY

What makes teeth decay? Bacteria in the mouth make a substance called plaque that sticks to the teeth and protects the bacteria. The bacteria make acid, which dissolves the minerals that make up the teeth, eventually destroying them. The more plaque, the more bacteria, the more acid, the more cavities.

Bacteria thrive on sugar and starch. Anything that keeps sugar sitting in the mouth is good for the bacteria and bad for the teeth. That's why frequent between-meal snacking, sticky sweets (lollipops, gum, dried fruits), sipping soda or juice, and munching on cookies all promote cavities.

Saliva washes bacteria away and contains substances that help teeth resist attack. Since the body makes less saliva during sleep, nighttime is when cavities are most likely to form. When children go to bed with food and plaque stuck to their teeth, the bacteria have all night long to do their dirty work. That is why it is so important to clean the teeth before bed and avoid sugary bedtime snacks.

Chewing gum. Regular chewing gum is terrible for teeth, because it keeps sugar in the mouth for long periods of time. Sugar-free chewing gum is a different story. The main sweeteners, xylitol and sorbitol, are harmful to cavity-causing bacteria. Sugar-free gum several times a day actually reduces cavities!

Parents who have bad teeth. If you have lots of cavities yourself, you're carrying millions of cavity-forming bacteria in your mouth. When you share cups or spoons with your child, bad bacteria go along for the ride.

You can stop sharing germs by getting your own teeth fixed, rinsing two or three times a day with a germ-killing mouthwash, and chewing sugar-free gum. Don't clean off your baby's pacifier in your mouth or put your baby's fingers in your mouth. Give your baby his own toothbrush.

Baby bottle tooth decay. Babies can get terrible tooth decay from sucking on a bottle all day. It's the sugar in the formula or juice that feeds the bacteria that destroy the teeth. Some parents put honey on a baby's pacifier, with the same effect (and botulism in honey can harm young children). Normally, saliva cleans off the teeth between meals. But a constant stream of sugar overcomes that defense. This problem can occur with breast milk, too, but most mothers demand time off between feedings.

The worst bottle-mouth decay happens when babies fall asleep with a bottle of milk or juice. As they sleep, the sugary fluid just sits on their teeth. Bottle-mouth decay can start even before the first birthday. Sometimes nursing caries are so severe that the infected teeth have to be removed.

The way to avoid this problem is to wean babies from the bottle after twelve months, and only give water in the bottle at bedtime (see page 295). For breastfed babies, clean off their gums and teeth with a soft toothbrush before putting them down to sleep.

BRUSHING AND FLOSSING

Effective brushing. The idea is to get rid of dental plaque before it can do its nasty work. For cleaning your baby's teeth, use a soft-bristled (not medium or firm) toothbrush. There is a myth that one should use a gauze pad or a cloth to wipe a baby's teeth and gums so as not to damage the delicate gum tissue. But those delicate gum tissues chew on table legs, cribs, coffee tables, siblings, and anything else in their way. Brush, don't wipe. Babies love it.

Teeth should be brushed after breakfast and before bedtime, with flossing between adjoining teeth before the evening brushing. If possible, an after-lunch brushing is helpful to remove food residue. Start before one year of age so your baby accepts brushing as a normal part of the day. If your child resists, insist. Brushing should be like seat belts: not optional.

Starting at about two, your child may insist on doing everything herself, but few two-year-olds have the dexterity to brush and floss well. You can let your child begin the brushing by herself from the earliest ages, but you'll need to finish up to make sure the job is done. Most children are ready to brush independently between six and ten years.

Flossing. Some parents question the need to floss a child's teeth, but teeth in the back of a child's mouth usually touch each other on the sides. Front teeth can snug up against their neighbors, too. When teeth sit close together, food and dental plaque accumulate between them. No matter how vigorously or carefully those areas are brushed, the toothbrush bristles cannot clear out the food and plaque. Dental floss dislodges all that debris so the toothbrush can sweep it away.

It's worthwhile getting your child used to gentle flossing as soon as you notice teeth touching. Your child's dentist or dental hygienist can demonstrate all the methods used to hold a child for brushing and flossing. When your child is able to brush and floss effectively without your help, she should already have well-established habits.

DENTAL VARNISH AND SEALANTS

For young children who can't be seen by a dentist, the primary care doctor will sometimes apply fluoride varnish to protect the teeth. This is a quick, safe, and painless process that can make a big difference.

Older children often benefit from sealants. Many teeth have small grooves or pitted areas in the enamel where food and plaque can build up. Dental sealants are liquid resins that flow across the tooth and fill the grooves and pits so that food can't get in. Sealants last for many years, but depending on a child's diet and oral habits, they eventually need to be repaired or replaced.

DENTAL INJURIES

Teeth take a beating. They can be cracked, displaced from their sockets, or completely knocked out. Some dental injuries may be hard to spot, so it's best to have a dentist do a full exam anytime there is significant trauma to the mouth.

Cracked teeth. Teeth have three layers: the outer protective enamel, the internal supportive structure (dentin), and the soft tissue center (dental pulp) that contains the nerves. A crack (fracture) in a tooth can affect any or all of these layers. A small fracture may only need smoothing by the dentist using a sandpaper-like tool. A more extensive crack may require a dental restoration. If a cracked tooth bleeds, the sensitive pulp might be exposed. A dentist needs to see the child as soon as possible to repair the damage and prevent loss of the pulp.

Loosened teeth. Most slightly loosened teeth reattach themselves and become stable after a few days' rest. A soft diet for a period of time helps the healing process. Teeth that are looser may need to be stabilized with a splint put on by the dentist. Antibiotics may be needed to prevent infection of the dental pulp and attachment tissues.

Avulsed teeth. If a tooth is completely knocked out of the mouth, dentists say it is *avulsed*. If a baby tooth is avulsed, it's usually best to leave it out. A permanent tooth should be reimplanted as quickly as possible.

First, make sure that the tooth is intact. Gently hold it by the crown (the part that shows in the mouth), not by the pointed roots. Rinse the tooth very gently under tap water. Do not scrub or rub the root in any way; that will damage the attached tissue, which is required for reattachment. Insert the tooth back into its normal position. If you cannot reimplant the tooth, place it in a glass of milk.

Next, take the child to the nearest dentist or hospital emergency room. Time is important with permanent tooth avulsions. After a tooth has been out of the mouth for just thirty minutes, the chances for successful reimplantation drop fast.

PREVENTING MOUTH INJURIES

Young children fall a lot, often face-first. Their teeth are perfectly located to crash into coffee tables and similar objects. As much as possible, try to crash-proof your toddler's cruising area by moving these things away. Make sure your toddler doesn't have the opportunity to bite any electrical wires. Don't let your child parade around the house with a toothbrush in her mouth. A toothbrush can do serious damage.

The risk of dental injuries rises once children begin to play sports. A Little Leaguer can be struck by a ball or bat, by a team member going after the same fly ball, or by an opposing player running the bases. Similar catastrophes happen in nearly every sport, including in-line skating, skateboarding, and martial arts. Mouth guards are crash helmets for the teeth. You can buy them at sporting goods stores or pharmacies, or your child's dentist can make a custom-fitted one.

COMMON CHILDHOOD ILLNESSES

Every parent deals with colds, coughs, and diarrhea. Thanks to vaccines, many serious infections are now rare. But new threats emerge each year or two, and chronic conditions such as asthma and allergies are on the rise. Knowing something about the common illnesses of childhood, and some of the uncommon ones, can help you feel more confident about handling problems as they arise. The information that follows, however, isn't meant to be a substitute for a doctor's judgment.

I've organized the following sections roughly by the part of the body most affected: diseases that affect the airways, from the nose and ears to the lungs; those that affect the digestive system, from the esophagus down to the rectum; those that affect the skin; and so on. Other conditions have ended up in sections on emergencies or prevention. If you don't find what you need below, please check the index.

COLDS

What common colds look like. If your baby has a cold during the first six months or so, the chances are that it will be mild. He may sneeze in the beginning; his nose will be runny or bubbly or stuffy. He may cough a little. He is not likely to have any fever. When his nose is bubbly, you might wish you could blow it for him, but it doesn't seem to bother him. On the other hand, if his nose is obstructed with thick mucus, it may make him frantic. He keeps trying to close his mouth and is angry when he can't breathe. The stuffiness may bother him most when he tries to nurse at the breast or bottle, so much so that he refuses to do so altogether at times. But after a few days he starts to get better, and within a couple of weeks he's back to normal.

Older children may have the same mild colds, or they can be more dramatic. Here is a common story. A little girl of two is well during the morning. At lunchtime she seems a little tired and eats less than usual. When she wakes up from her nap, she is cranky and her parents notice that she is hot. They take her temperature, and it's 102°F. By the time the doctor sees her, it's 104°F. Her cheeks are flushed and her eyes are dull, but otherwise she doesn't seem particularly sick. She may want no supper at all, or she may want a fair amount. She has no cold symptoms, and the doctor hasn't found anything definite except that her throat is perhaps a little red. The next day she may have a little fever, but now her nose may begin to run. Perhaps she coughs occasionally. After three or four days, the mucus from her nose may change from clear to yellow or green. Maybe she vomits once or twice. But from this point on, it's just a regular mild cold that runs its course in a week or two.

What's happening during a cold? Colds are caused by any one of about a hundred different germs. The most common culprits are viruses, including the appropriately named rhinovirus (that is, "nose virus"). These viruses don't do much damage themselves; it's the child's immune system that causes the symptoms.

Cold viruses usually enter the body through the nose or eyes, most often carried there on a child's own hands; less often they fly in, propelled by a sneeze. Once inside, they get into the cells that line the nose or throat, and start reproducing the way viruses do. The immune system responds by releasing chemicals that cause blood vessels to leak fluid into the tissues, resulting in swelling. Other immune signals trigger mucus production and fever. White blood cells rush to the scene, and the battle is on.

It's not always this exciting, however. Children and adults often acquire a cold virus but don't develop any symptoms worth noticing. But they can still pass the virus on, and the next victim might experience all the usual miseries.

When things get complicated. Colds aren't dangerous themselves, but they can lower the resistance to bacteria, which often cause more damage. Bacteria are microscopically tiny; but compared to viruses they are gigantic!

Bacteria such as strep or pneumococcus often live quietly in healthy people's noses and throats, held at bay by the immune system. It's only after the cold virus has attacked that these bacteria get their chance to invade. Their first targets are often the middle ear (otitis media), nasal sinuses (sinusitis), or lungs (pneumonia).

You can often tell when these secondary bacterial infections arise, because the child gets sicker. Her appetite and energy may fall off, and she may start running a fever. A fever on the first day of a cold isn't particularly concerning, but a new fever that begins after a cold is well under way often signals the start of a bacterial infection. Other red flags are ear pain, face pain, a worsening cough, or rapid breathing. Any of these changes should trigger a call to the doctor.

Things that look like colds but aren't. Most colds run their course in a week or two; sometimes it takes three. A runny nose that hangs on week after week may not be a cold at all but rather a nasal allergy. Itchy or runny eyes and thin, clear mucus are signs to look for. Or it could be a bacterial infection of the nasal sinuses (sinusitis), sometimes (but not always) accompanied by thick green mucus.

When coughing is especially severe, consider the possibility of whooping cough (pertussis infection). Not all people with pertussis make the classic whooping noise, especially if the person with the infection is an older child or adult.

When there is persistent dry coughing or wheezing along with the runny nose, the problem might be asthma. Cold viruses are a potent asthma trigger, as is secondhand cigarette smoke. It's important to consider this possibility, since there is effective medication specifically for asthma.

Coughing and wheezing, when severe, can also be due to other infections, such as mycoplasma, which call for specific treatment. A doctor may need to listen to your child's chest or look at an X-ray to make these diagnoses.

An illness may start with a runny nose, cough, and fever, but then the symptoms move down into the intestines, with vomiting and diarrhea for several days. These infections are often caused by different viruses (often adenoviruses), and they may be a bit more severe, because more of the body is affected. If headaches, muscle aches, fever, and a general loss of energy come on suddenly, the diagnosis may be influenza.

Treating a cold. We don't have medicines that kill cold viruses. The main point of treatment is to make your child comfortable while the immune system takes care of business.

Bulb suction. For babies and young children, start by clearing their noses with bulb suction. Use a nasal suction device with a wide plastic tip, rather than the narrow-tipped kind that usually gets sent home with a baby after birth. The wide tip makes it easy to create a tight seal against the nostril, which helps the suction work, and avoids irritating the delicate tissues inside the nose. You can buy battery-operated nasal suction devices, but there are less expensive ones that you operate by sucking on a tube (don't worry, there's a trap to keep the mucus from getting into your mouth), and these work well, too.

Nose drops. For thick mucus, put a drop or two of saline solution into each nostril. Let it sit there for about five minutes to soften the mucus before sucking it out. Babies hate this process but feel much better afterward. You can mix up a saline solution yourself: dissolve one-quarter teaspoon of salt in eight ounces of water. But it's easier to buy saline nose drops over the counter. They're cheap and come with a handy dropper.

Avoid medicated nose drops unless prescribed by the doctor. Most nose drops work by shrinking blood vessels in the nose, decreasing secretions. But they don't work for long, and after a few treatments they work less and less. After that, the nose often becomes dependent on the drops so that the secretions increase as soon as you stop using the drops. Also, these medicines produce serious side effects in some children.

Vaporizers and humidifiers. Extra moisture in the room can make secretions thinner or at least keep them from drying out so fast. How you add that moisture isn't important. In winter, the warmer you keep your home, the dryer the air becomes. A child with a cold might be more comfortable at 68°F than at 74°F. An ultrasonic humidifier can cost as little as $40. A cool-mist humidifier costing $30 or less does an adequate job. With either type be sure to clean the water reservoir at least once a week to prevent the growth of molds and bacteria; use a cup of white vinegar mixed in a quart of water.

An electric steam vaporizer uses an electric heating element to boil water. But steam isn't any better than cool mist when it comes to adding moisture to the air. And with steam, there is a danger of scalding if a child puts his hand or face in the steam or knocks the vaporizer over. If you buy one of these steam vaporizers, get a large size that holds a quart or more and turns itself off when the water boils away. Pans of water on the radiator tend to spill, and don't actually add that much moisture.

Antibiotics. The usual antibiotics (amoxicillin, for instance) kill bacteria, but not the viruses that cause colds. Taking antibiotics for a cold may not cause your child any harm right then and there, unless he has an allergic reaction or develops diarrhea. But the overuse of antibiotics breeds strains of bacteria that are resistant to antibiotics. This means that the next time your child (or someone else) is truly ill, it's more likely that the usual antibiotics won't work.

Cough and cold medicines. There never was good evidence that over-the-counter cough and cold medicines actually work; now we know that they can be dangerous, especially for infants and young children. Don't let the ads fool you. There are many different brands, but few of them do what they claim, and none is safe or effective for children under age two.

For older children, short-term (two or three days) treatment with a decongestant such as pseudoephedrine can sometimes relieve the pressure in blocked sinuses. But breathing in the vapor from a sinkful of hot water often works just as well. Antihistamines work for allergies but don't do much for colds, and they can make children drowsy and sometimes irritable and overactive. Cough medicines containing dextromethorphan (often with "DM" in the name) aren't effective. What's more, they can cause dangerous side effects and are sometimes abused by teens trying to get high. Honey is probably a better cough suppressant (but not for infants, who are susceptible to botulism).

Vitamins, supplements, and herbs. There is no proof that larger-than-normal doses of vitamin C can prevent colds or make them go away sooner. For a while zinc looked like a possible cure, but more research showed that it didn't work for otherwise healthy children. People who have low zinc levels probably do benefit from taking zinc supplements, however.

Echinacea purpurea (also known as coneflower) is an herb that lessens the severity of colds in adults and reduces the occurrence of new colds. The research in children isn't quite as strong, but points in the same direction. Be aware, though, that there are many different kinds of echinacea, and products made from them aren't regulated as medicine, so it's hard to know what you're getting. Just because it's natural doesn't mean that it's safe.

Other nondrug treatments. Chicken soup might actually contain a substance that reduces cold symptoms. Even if it doesn't, the warmth is comforting, the liquid helps keep children well hydrated, the salt may help with electrolyte balance, and the protein and fat are nourishing. Truly, it couldn't hurt. Warm liquids of any kind are helpful. Massaging the back and chest is soothing, but menthol rubs probably don't help and may even make things worse. Gently massaging the forehead and under the eyes (moving your hands down and toward the nose) may help with sinus congestion. Some people think that milk thickens secretions, and even though this belief is unproven, there's no harm in avoiding milk for a few days (unless it's all your child wants to drink). A drink of honey and lemon in warm water, with or without tea, may well be a more effective cough suppressant than any over-the-counter medicine. Children under one year shouldn't ingest honey, though, because of the risk of botulism.

Preventing colds. A typical preschooler will get six to eight colds a year; children who go to day care get even more. With each cold the child gains immunity to the particular virus that caused it, but that still leaves dozens of cold viruses that the child hasn't yet been exposed to. Over time, as the child builds immunity to more viruses, the number of colds decreases. Children who get a lot of colds early in life usually don't get as many later on.

The best thing you can do to prevent colds is to avoid close physical contact with anyone who has one (easier said than done!). Good handwashing helps (see page 763), and alcohol-based hand sanitizers kill cold viruses even better than soap and water. Children should also be taught to cough into their elbow (not their hand) and to blow their nose into tissues that then go into the garbage.

Staying inside when the weather is cold doesn't prevent colds. Just the opposite: It's because children stay cooped up inside during the winter with the windows closed that cold viruses spread so easily. Cold air does make noses run, but only viruses cause colds.

You can increase your child's ability to fight off colds by helping her to eat and sleep well and by keeping your home free of cigarette smoke. Secondhand smoke interferes with the cells in the nose and throat that are responsible for expelling mucus-coated viruses. Children exposed to secondhand smoke may not contract more viruses, but they get sicker from them. If you smoke, this is a good reason to stop.

You can also work on keeping your home as stress-free as possible: For example, keep angry yelling to a minimum. Chronic stress increases the level of cortisol, a hormone that reduces immune system function. A peaceful home is healthier for everyone.

EAR INFECTIONS

What is in an ear? To understand ear infections, you have to understand ears. The part of the ear that you can see (the pinna) collects sound waves and funnels them down the ear canal. At the end of the canal, the waves bump into the eardrum, causing it to vibrate. The eardrum can vibrate because it has air on two sides—the air in the ear canal, and the air in the middle ear space. Tiny bones connected to the eardrum pick up the vibrations and transfer them through the middle ear to the inner ear, where an amazing little organ called the cochlea turns them into nerve signals and sends them to the brain.

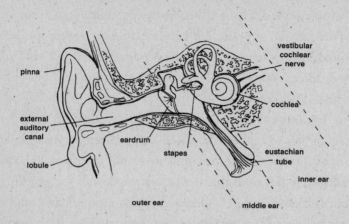

How ears get infected. The air in the middle ear is the key to understanding ear infections. The air gets there through the eustachian tubes, which connect the middle ear to the back of the throat. These tubes, alas, can let in more than air. When germs from the nose and throat get through the eustachian tubes, they can fill the middle ear with infected pus. The medical term for this condition is "otitis media," which means "inflammation of the middle ear."

Otitis media usually begins with a cold. As the body fights off the virus, tissues in the nose and throat swell up, causing stuffiness and affecting the eustachian tubes. As a result, the tubes are less able to block germs from getting into the middle ear, and less able to expel any germs that do get in.

The first germs to get in are usually the same virus that caused the cold. These viral ear infections are really just part of the cold and, like the cold, are pretty easily defeated by the immune system. Sometimes, though, the virus is followed by a second wave of attack. Bacteria that had been living peacefully in the nose take advantage of the lowered defenses to get into the middle ear and set up another, worse infection. The middle ear fills with pus, which pushes against the eardrum, causing pain. The body mounts a stronger immune response, now with a fever. Your child goes from sick to sicker.

What parents see. Usually an ear doesn't become inflamed enough to cause pain until after several days of a cold. A new fever midway through a cold together with irritability makes otitis media pretty likely. A baby may keep rubbing his ear or may just cry piercingly for several hours. He seems a little better when you pick him up, because the upright position lowers the pressure in his ear. Sometimes he vomits. A child over two may be able to tell you what the matter is. His ear hurts, and he may not hear well because the pus in the middle ear is keeping the eardrum from vibrating normally.

If there's enough pressure in the middle ear, a hole may open in the eardrum, letting the pus out. You might find dried pus and blood on your child's pillow. It sounds awful, but a ruptured eardrum often comes as a great relief to the child and speeds the healing of the infection. You can put a cotton ball loosely in the ear to soak up the pus. It is not a good idea to put anything else into the ear, because it might accidentally bump the inflamed eardrum, further damaging it. Medicated ear drops may also be helpful.

Helping with the pain. Ear infections can be painful. Keeping your child's head propped up reduces the pressure against the eardrum. A hot-water bottle or an electric heating pad may help, but small children are often impatient with them. (Don't let a child fall asleep on a heating pad; this could result in a burn.) Acetaminophen or ibuprofen in the usual doses can provide some relief. Prescription medication, given as ear drops, can deaden the ache. Antibiotics take about seventy-two hours to kick in, so a child might need pain relief around the clock for the first three days.

Over-the-counter cough and cold medicines including decongestants and antihistamines have not been shown to help ear infections, nor have any herbal or homeopathic preparations. But sugar-free gum made with xylitol may actually reduce symptoms of ear infections, because xylitol kills the bacteria that cause most ear infections. Vigorous chewing can sometimes help open up a blocked eustachian tube, as can blowing up balloons. Tender loving care (TLC) and quiet reassurance always help, of course.

Antibiotics, or not. It used to be that every ear infection got antibiotics. That has changed. Now we know that most ear infections are caused by viruses that don't respond to antibiotics and that the body can fight off on its own.

The main reason to hold off on antibiotics is that overuse of antibiotics encourages the development of resistant bacteria. When that happens, doctors have to use ever more exotic, expensive, and potentially harmful antibiotics. The more often your child takes antibiotics, the more likely she is to get sick with bacteria that those antibiotics can't kill. The solution to this problem is to use antibiotics only when they are truly necessary.

Antibiotics make sense for young children who have clear-cut ear infections with fever and other signs of severe illness, and for children who have underlying problems with their immune systems or anatomical problems such as cleft palates. In other cases, it makes more sense to wait and watch. In two or three days, the child is often better.

If the doctor does prescribe antibiotics, be sure to give every dose for the full course of treatment. Stopping early is a good way to breed resistant bacteria. If your child throws up a dose right after swallowing it, give the dose again. If your child throws up several doses or develops a rash or diarrhea, or if she is still miserable and running a fever in forty-eight hours, call the doctor. Sometimes a different antibiotic will be necessary.

Preventing ear infections. There are many things you can do: Breastfeeding boosts the child's immune system and strengthens the muscles attached to the eustachian tubes. Bottle-fed babies should take their bottles sitting in a parent's arms. Drinking while lying down allows milk to pool in the eustachian tubes, encouraging bacteria to enter. Children who stay home have fewer ear infections than those who attend large child-care centers. Protecting children from secondhand cigarette smoke lowers ear infections. Chronic allergies should be treated. Rarely, repeated ear infections are due to an underlying immune system problem; talk with your child's doctor if you think this might be so.

Middle-ear effusion. After the bacteria have been killed off, it's common for fluid (effusion) to remain in the middle ear. If you plug your ears with your fingers, you can get a sense of how things sound to a child with an effusion. Effusions can cause children to tug on their ears even after the infection has been cured (more antibiotics won't help). It can take up to three months for an effusion to go away; meanwhile, language development or a child's ability to pay attention may suffer. Think about this possibility if your child has more than three ear infections in a year, or if you think your child may not be hearing, paying attention, or speaking normally.

The first step is a hearing test. No child is too young to have one. Abnormal hearing that doesn't get better in two or three months should trigger a consultation with an ear, nose, and throat (ENT) specialist. We don't have good medicines to treat otitis media with effusion, but surgery to drain the middle ear may help.

Swimmer's ear. Most ear infections are behind the eardrum, in the middle ear. With swimmer's ear, it's the skin of the external ear canal—the part you can reach with a cotton swab—that gets infected (in Latin, *otitis externa*). These infections start with a breakdown of the skin's normal defenses, usually because of a small scratch or persistent dampness in the ear canal, or following a draining middle-ear infection. The main symptom is pain. Tugging on the ear hurts (unlike with middle-ear infections). Sometimes there is pus or an odor. A very bad odor might mean an object is stuck in the ear (see page 430). Acetaminophen or ibuprofen can help with the pain. Prescription ear drops are the main treatment.

To prevent otitis externa, teach your child to use a hair dryer to dry out her ears after swimming (caution: set the heat on low to avoid burns). A few drops of water mixed with an equal amount of white vinegar raises the acidity of the ear canal enough to discourage most bacteria from growing. Finally, don't work too hard to get all the earwax out of your child's ears. Earwax (like car wax) serves a protective function. If you clean it all out, you remove that protection and may scratch the canal in the process.

SORE THROATS AND STREP THROATS

Most sore throats are caused by the same viruses that cause colds. These infections are usually mild and get better on their own. A sore throat caused by streptococcus bacteria—that is, *strep throat*—is more serious; it can spread into the tissues of the neck, a dangerous complication; or it can cause rheumatic fever. This is a difficult-to-treat condition that can include chronic joint pains, serious heart disease, and other ailments. It's not something to fool around with. The good news is that common antibiotics remove the threat of rheumatic fever. The bad news is you have to diagnose strep before you can treat it.

Strep, or just a sore throat? A classic case of strep throat is easy to spot. The child has a high fever and throat pain so severe he can hardly swallow. He's miserable. The tonsils become fiery red and swollen, and after a day or two white spots or patches appear on them. The glands (lymph nodes) in the neck are swollen and tender. The child has a headache and stomachache, and generally lacks energy. His breath has a musty, unpleasant odor. He probably *doesn't* have a runny nose or cough, which are more often caused by viruses.

The problem with this description is, it's not always so. Any of the classic symptoms may be absent. A child with a low fever, mild sore throat, and healthy-looking tonsils *could* have strep (although he probably just has a throat virus). Young children, in particular, may be bothered surprisingly little by strep (strep throat is rare under age two). A child who has had his tonsils removed can still have strep.

Because it's hard to be certain that a sore throat isn't strep, it's wise to have a doctor evaluate any sore throat that accompanies fever of 100.4°F or higher. A throat swab and a rapid strep test can usually give the answer; a throat culture takes two or three days, but may pick up infections that the rapid test misses. If the tests come back negative for strep, your child probably just has a virus. Rest, acetaminophen or ibuprofen, and plenty of fluids help. Warm saltwater gargles and throat lozenges for children old enough not to choke (after age four or five) are also effective comfort measures.

With a positive strep test, the usual treatment is ten days of bubble-gum-flavored antibiotics, morning and night. A slightly more reliable but less pleasant treatment involves two painful injections, one in each buttock.

It used to be common practice for children to have their tonsils taken out because of frequent sore throats, until research showed that it really didn't help much. Now tonsillectomies are mostly done to treat sleep apnea (see page 485).

Scarlet fever. Although many people regard scarlet fever with dread—remember poor Beth March in *Little Women*—it's usually nothing more than a strep throat with a characteristic rash. The rash typically appears on the sides of the chest, the back, and the groin, a day or two after the child gets sick. From a distance it looks like a uniform red flush, but if you look at it closely, you can see that it is made up of tiny red spots on a reddish background. If you run your hand over this rash, it feels like fine sandpaper. It may spread over the whole body and the sides of the face, but the region around the mouth stays pale. The tongue may look like a strawberry, red with white dots.

When scarlet fever accompanies a sore throat, the treatment is the same as for a regular case of strep. Occasionally a different germ causes scarlet fever and requires different treatment; the doctor will know. Once the child recovers from scarlet fever, you may notice some peeling of skin, which gets better without any special treatment.

Other kinds of sore throat. Many people feel a slight sore throat at the beginning of every cold. Some children wake up with sore throats. They're otherwise well, and the sore throat goes away shortly. The problem is due to dry air, not illness. Runny noses can also cause sore throats, especially in the early morning, because mucus runs down the back of the throat during the night, causing irritation.

Mononucleosis. A severe sore throat, often with fever, malaise, and swollen glands, may be infectious mononucleosis (mono), usually caused by the Epstein-Barr virus. This can be a mild infection or quite severe; it usually lasts for a week or two but it can drag on. The disease is more common in teenagers; the virus spreads via saliva, giving rise to the nickname "kissing disease." There is no specific treatment for mono, but a doctor should test to make sure the diagnosis isn't strep and do a careful exam looking for an enlarged liver or spleen, which require special care.

Diphtheria. In its heyday, this bacterial infection killed thousands each year. Now, it's very rare, thanks to immunization (diphtheria is the "D" in DTaP vaccinations). The bacteria are still around, though, and threaten to come back if immunization levels drop. The signature feature of this infection is a thick glue-like coating in the back of the throat, with lots of swelling but not much fever. Death is through suffocation.

Swollen glands. Any infection in the mouth, throat, or ears can cause the lymph nodes (glands) on the side of the neck to swell up, usually to the size of a pea or lima bean, as part of a normal immune response. They can stay big for weeks or months. Occasionally the glands themselves become infected: very large, warm, and tender to touch. A doctor should evaluate all such lumps and prescribe antibiotics as needed. It's natural in these cases for parents to worry about cancer. Cancers with neck masses are rare in children, but of course you should talk with the doctor if you have any concerns.

CROUP AND EPIGLOTTITIS

What croup looks like. A two-year-old boy develops what seems to be a common cold, with a runny nose and an unimpressive fever of 100.5°F. Two days later, around 9:00 p.m., he starts coughing, making a loud, harsh barking noise. When he breathes in between coughs he makes a different, almost musical sound. The skin sucks in over his collarbones and between his ribs, showing that he is working hard to breathe. Worried, his parents bundle him into the car and drive twenty minutes to the hospital. By the time they get there, he looks much better.

This is a typical picture of croup. For some reason, it affects boys more than girls. It usually hits children six months to three years old, often in late fall or early winter. The virus moves from the nose down into the area of the vocal cords. The windpipe is normally narrow there, and the infection narrows it even further. When the child breathes out forcefully past this obstruction, the thickened vocal cords make a barking noise. When he breathes in, the swollen walls of the windpipe collapse toward each other, further blocking the airway and causing a loud noise called stridor. The cough and stridor are almost always worse at night. They can come on suddenly but also can improve almost as quickly, often after the child has been exposed to cool night air.

Croup is scary when you see it for the first time, but it's rarely as serious as it looks. It often sends children to the emergency room but seldom results in permanent harm. Some unlucky children have several bouts during their early years. In these children, the trigger may be an allergic reaction rather than a virus, a variation called *spasmodic croup*. In the last few years, we've learned of effective treatments that make the disease even less dangerous.

Emergency treatment. Stridor, the loud noise on inspiration, should always get prompt medical attention. Even though croup is rarely dangerous, there are other causes of stridor that can be quite threatening. For instance, the child may have an object lodged in his throat, or he may have *epiglottitis* (see below).

Don't panic, but do act quickly. If you cannot reach a doctor right away, take your child to the emergency room. Medicines are available that can open up the airway in croup, but these can't be given at home. Any child who is struggling to breathe should have doctors and nurses nearby, just in case.

Home treatment. If the stridor isn't too severe and your child is comfortable and drinking fluids well, the doctor may advise you to stay home. Traditionally, we've urged parents to fill the bathroom with warm mist from the shower and sit in there with their croupy child, especially if the air in your home is dry. Cool night air sometimes works even better.

Perhaps most important, try to keep your child calm. An upset, scared child breathes harder and faster, making croup worse. Probably the best way to calm your child is to stay calm yourself. A story from a book, or one you make up, can make the time pass more pleasantly.

If your child calms down promptly, she can go back into her crib or bed. You or another adult should stay awake as long as there are any symptoms of croup, and wake up two or three hours after the croup is over to make sure the child is breathing comfortably. Croup symptoms often fade away by morning, only to return the next night, and sometimes for two or three more nights after that.

Epiglottitis. This infection is now quite rare, thanks to the Hib (*Haemophilus influenza* type B) immunization. Epiglottitis looks like severe croup with a high fever. The epiglottis is a small bit of tissue that forms the trapdoor at the top of the windpipe, to keep food out. If it becomes infected and swollen, it can block off the windpipe altogether.

A child with epiglottitis becomes ill very quickly. He leans forward, drools, refuses to take any food or liquids, and will usually make no sounds at all. He may be unwilling to turn his head in any direction, because he's keeping his neck in the position that lets him breathe best. This is a true medical emergency, and everything must be done to get the child to a doctor or hospital right away, while keeping him as calm as possible.

BRONCHITIS, BRONCHIOLITIS,
AND PNEUMONIA

Bronchitis. The largest branches of the windpipe are called *bronchi*. When they're inflamed, almost always because of infection with a virus, it's called *bronchitis*. There is usually a lot of coughing and a low fever. Parents worry when they think they hear mucus vibrating in the chest. Actually, the rattling usually starts higher up in the throat, although the noise is transmitted to the chest. This sort of noisy breathing usually isn't a sign of serious illness.

A mild case of bronchitis, with no fever or loss of appetite, is only a little worse than a cold in the nose. The treatment is the same as for a bad cold: rest, fluids in moderation, honey in milk or water to soothe the cough (for children over twelve months), and tender loving care. Antibiotics don't kill viruses and don't help at all with bronchitis. Over-the-counter cough suppressants aren't effective for children and can be dangerous; it's best to avoid them altogether.

Call the doctor if your child acts sick (no energy, exhausted, dull or limp), becomes short of breath, breathes rapidly when at rest, or has a fever of more than 100.4°F. Bronchitis can mimic other, more serious infections that may require treatment with antibiotics or even hospitalization, especially in children under six months of age.

Bronchiolitis (RSV). In *bronchiolitis*, the infection has moved from the larger breathing tubes (bronchi) down to smaller air passages in the lungs (bronchioles). The "-itis" at the end of the word means "inflammation," a combination of swelling, mucus, and white blood cells that narrows and partly blocks the air tubes. Of the several different viruses that cause bronchiolitis, the most common is RSV (respiratory syncytial virus). RSV infections spread easily through physical contact, most often in the winter months,

Bronchiolitis typically hits children of between two months and two years. It starts with a cold, often with fever, followed by cough, wheezing, and difficulty breathing. When the child breathes in, his nostrils flare out, while the skin around his ribs and above his collarbone sucks inward. Doctors learn to look for these signs—flaring and retractions—as well as breathing rate as markers of severe illness. Rapid breathing is an important sign: Any child who is consistently taking more than forty breaths per minute should be assessed; faster than sixty breaths a minute (one per second) requires immediate medical attention.

For mild cases, the best treatment is the same as for colds: rest, fluids (offer, but don't force), acetaminophen or ibuprofen for fever, gentle suction to clear the nose. Comfortably humid air helps, but very high humidity only makes children damp and miserable. A child who has had wheezing problems before might respond to the usual asthma medicine (mainly albuterol), but children with bronchiolitis who are wheezing for the first time rarely do.

For severe bronchiolitis, children need to be in the hospital, where they can get extra oxygen if they need it. Premature infants and young children who have certain chronic conditions—especially heart or lung disease—should receive special injections during the winter to prevent severe RSV illness.

Pneumonia. Unlike bronchitis and bronchiolitis, pneumonia is more likely to be caused by bacteria, rather than viruses.

Bacterial infections tend to be more serious, but unlike viral infections, they respond to antibiotics.

Pneumonia usually sets in several days into a cold, although it can also start without warning. Look for a fever of over 102°F, rapid breathing (more than forty breaths per minute), and frequent cough. A child with pneumonia will sometimes make a grunting noise. Children rarely bring up mucus, so don't let the absence of phlegm fool you. Not every child with pneumonia needs to be treated in the hospital, but every child who has a fever and frequent cough needs a medical evaluation. In economically underdeveloped parts of the world, pneumonia is a leading cause of death in childhood.

INFLUENZA (THE FLU)

Flu symptoms. Influenza is tricky because the virus changes from year to year. In a usual year, it's miserable but not really dangerous. Sudden fever, headaches, and muscle aches are the hallmarks, often with a runny nose, sore throat, cough, vomiting, and diarrhea; it can last a week or two. Few children are sick enough to need hospitalization.

In an unusual year, things can be much worse. If the virus strain is especially contagious, the disease can spread fast, infecting almost everyone in its path. This was the case with the notorious H1N1 "swine flu" pandemic of 2009. (An epidemic affects a community or a country; a pandemic is a worldwide plague.) Each year there is a new vaccine, designed to protect against the strains of flu that are going around that year.

Preventing the flu. Flu spreads easily. People can pass the disease on even before they feel sick, and they stay contagious for a couple of days after the fever is gone. Sneezing shoots the virus all over the place.

Good handwashing and sneezing into one's sleeve help, but the key to prevention is vaccination. Every child six months and older should receive a yearly flu vaccination. Adults should also be immunized, especially anyone living with a baby who is too young to get the vaccine himself, as well as pregnant women.

Treating the flu. If a doctor makes the diagnosis early in the illness, there are specific antiviral medications that can make the illness shorter and less severe. Otherwise, the treatment is general support: rest, fluids, and either acetaminophen or ibuprofen for the fever and aches. Aspirin is dangerous in the setting of influenza: It may trigger a serious condition called Reye's syndrome.

Be aware, too, that a child who gets sicker midway through a bout of the flu needs to be checked again, looking for ear infections, pneumonia, or other complications that may need treating.

ASTHMA

When is it asthma? A child who has wheezing spells several times a year probably has asthma. Asthma is a narrowing of the airways in the lungs, usually in response to an allergen (pollen, for example), a virus, cold air, smoke or other fumes, or emotional upset. The wheezing happens as air whistles through the narrowed tubes. With mild narrowing, children wheeze when they breathe out; with moderate narrowing, they wheeze breathing in and out; and with severe narrowing, the wheezing stops because there isn't enough air going in or out to make a sound. Sometimes a child coughs instead of wheezing, usually at night or after exercise.

A single episode of wheezing might be the beginning of asthma, or it could be something else. For example, the child might have swallowed or inhaled a plastic toy or might be having a severe allergic reaction (see page 438). Until you are certain that your child is having a typical asthma attack, you should call the doctor for any new wheezing.

Causes of asthma. Some children inherit a vulnerability to developing asthma. Lung irritation then brings on the disease. Common irritating substances include viral infections such as RSV; secondhand cigarette smoke and other fumes; cockroaches and dust mites (see page 486); molds; and pet dander.

Young children who wheeze with every cold but not at other times may be said to have *reactive airways disease*. Basically, this is mild asthma. Often it goes away, but it sometimes goes on to become full-fledged asthma.

Treatment. Start by removing the most common triggers: cigarette smoke, dust mites and cockroaches, and mold (see above and the Asthma Control Checklist at drspock.com). An allergist can help pinpoint specific substances to target. Good nutrition, healthy sleep, and a low-stress home all help. Physical conditioning—regular aerobic exercise—can help quite a bit, too.

The first-line medications are bronchodilators. These medications open up (dilate) the bronchial tubes by causing the tiny muscles that surround the tubes to relax. We think of these drugs as "rescue medicines," because they work on tubes that have already squeezed tight—bronchial tubes in the midst of an asthma attack. If a child only wheezes every once in a while, a rescue med may be all he needs. Albuterol is the most common of these meds. For athletes, a puff or two of albuterol before a workout can often prevent tight breathing.

A child who wheezes more than once or twice a week may need an asthma controller drug, rather than relying on repeated rescues. Controller meds prevent narrowing of the tubes by reducing inflammation, a main part of the asthma response, thus dampening the response to asthma triggers.

Many children with asthma grow out of the condition, but others carry it with them into adulthood. It's hard to predict. Early, effective treatment will improve the child's physical activity, decrease the need for emergency room visits, and reduce the risk of chronic lung disease later in life, and might also increase the odds of long-term remission.

Asthma care and planning. Every child—and especially every child with a chronic illness such as asthma—deserves a medical home. Parents need a steady source of information and support in order to asthma-proof their homes and make sure that their child's other environments (schools, friends' houses, clubs) are as asthma-safe as possible. Successful treatment depends on the details: knowing how to give the medications, when to step up the intensity of treatment, and what to do if a flare-up gets worse.

Each child should have an asthma plan that the child, parents, and school understand. Teachers, especially, appreciate very clear instructions about what to look for, and what to do if they see it (go to drspock.com).

Poorly treated asthma carries a high cost in limited activities, missed school, hours in emergency rooms, and days in the hospital. With planning and steady care, however, children with asthma can live full, symptom-free lives.

SNORING

Snoring is usually just a nuisance, but sometimes it's a sign of *obstructive sleep apnea* (OSA), a serious problem. When a person falls deeply asleep, muscles that normally hold the airway open relax, causing the airway to close. Air squeezing through the narrowed airway causes the snoring sound. As the airway gets smaller, the snoring gets louder. If the airway closes altogether, the snoring stops because no air is flowing. The child begins to suffocate; blood oxygen falls; and he wakes up gasping for air.

This cycle may repeat many times during the night. By morning, the child feels as though he has barely slept, and he may have a headache. During school he's apt to be either sleepy or wound up (as some children become when overtired), and learning suffers. Over time, the low blood oxygen can damage the heart.

Anything that causes narrowing of the airway sets a child up for OSA: very large tonsils and adenoids (like tonsils, but hidden in the back of the nose), and obesity, which squeezes the airway between pillows of fat. Sleep apnea often runs in families; one or both parents might have snoring problems with chronic overtiredness.

Sometimes a child with OSA will sleep with his head up on several pillows or hanging over the edge of the bed in an effort to keep the airway open. Sometimes, though, the only symptom is snoring. Doctors test for OSA using a sleep study, or polysomnogram, which requires an overnight stay in the hospital. If the tonsils and adenoids are too large, they may need to be removed. If the child is obese, weight loss is often the main treatment. Some children need to sleep with a device that holds the airway open by blowing compressed air into the nose, a process called *continuous positive airway pressure* (CPAP). It takes some getting used to, but the relief can be life-changing.

NASAL ALLERGIES

Seasonal allergies (hay fever). You probably know people with hay fever. When pollen floats on the breeze they sneeze and their noses itch and run. In spring, the usual culprit is tree pollen; in fall, it's ragweed. (Flowers rarely cause hay fever because their pollen is too big to blow around much; it has to be carried from flower to flower by insects and other creatures.)

Hay fever runs in families. Symptoms usually start at age three or four. A doctor can confirm the diagnosis based on the symptoms, the physical exam, and knowledge of which pollens are most common in your area at different times of year.

Year-round nasal allergies. Many children are allergic to dust mites or molds (the most common culprits), pet hair and dander, goose feathers, and many other substances. Such year-round allergies can cause stuffy or runny noses that last week after week, chronic mouth breathing, and often fluid in the ears or repeated sinus infections.

The symptoms may be worse in winter, because closed windows and doors keep allergens in and fresh air out. Physical signs include dark circles and creases under the eyes and a crease across the bridge of the nose caused by pushing up the nose with the heel of the hand to wipe off the mucus, the "allergic salute." Children with chronic allergies often have difficulty paying attention in school because they're overtired, not hearing well, or simply feeling crummy.

Treating nasal allergies. For hay fever, simple steps are sometimes enough: Drive and sleep with the windows closed, use an air conditioner if possible, and stay inside when pollen counts are highest. For year-round allergies, blood tests can often pinpoint the causes; sometimes an allergist has to do skin-prick testing.

If the cause is goose feathers, you can change the pillow. If it's the family dog, you may have to find a different pet. For dust mites, some parents vacuum two or three times a week. For this to help, the vacuum has to have a HEPA (high-efficiency particulate-air) bag; otherwise the tiny allergens just shoot back into the house.

You can remove stuffed animals (where dust mites often live), or wash them in hot water every week or two. You can encase your child's mattress and pillows in plastic covers that zip shut; duct tape over the zippers seals allergens in. Keeping room humidity at less than 50 percent cuts down on dust mites and mold. An electrostatic air cleaner can also help. Some parents go as far as pulling up the carpeting and taking down the drapes, particularly in their child's bedroom.

If avoiding the triggers doesn't work, there are medications of various sorts to try. Diphenhydramine (Benadryl) blocks a key step in the allergic reaction. It's cheap and safe, but it makes some children drowsy or wired and may interfere with school. Newer antihistamines (Claritin, Zyrtec, and others) cost more, don't work any better, but sometimes have fewer side effects.

Other anti-allergy medications block different steps in the allergy response or turn down the immune response generally. Medications such as montelukast (Singulair) or fluticasone (Flonase) can be helpful, although they require close medical supervision to monitor for side effects. For severe allergies that don't respond to medication, allergy shots often can help. An allergist can help you weigh the benefits against the cost and discomfort, if you get to this point.

Preventing allergies. Allergies are more common in wealthy nations than in less developed ones, maybe because of intestinal parasites. Allergies are caused by overactivity of the same part of the immune system that fights off parasites. In places where modern sanitation has banished parasites, the immune system may turn to less serious threats such as pollen or cat dander, threats that were better ignored. We don't know if this theory—called the hygiene hypothesis—is true, although it makes sense. It may be that children need a certain amount of exposure to dirt and the things that crawl in it. If so, then preventing allergies will turn out to be another good reason for sending your children outside to play.

ECZEMA

What to look for. Eczema is a patchy, rough, itchy rash associated with very dry skin. In young babies it begins on the cheeks or the forehead, then spreads to the ears and neck. Later, around a year of age, eczema may start almost anywhere—the shoulders, the arms, the chest. The most typical spots are the creases in the elbows and behind the knees.

When eczema is mild or just starting, the color is apt to be a light red or tannish pink. If the condition becomes severe, the skin turns a deeper red. Constant scratching and rubbing cause scratch marks and weeping or oozing, which dries to form crusts. Scratched areas often become infected with bacteria, making the oozing and crusting worse. When a patch of eczema is healing, you can still feel the roughness and thickness of the skin. In darker-skinned children, healed areas may look lighter or darker than the rest of the skin for weeks or months. Not all scaly, itchy rashes are eczema. A new rash, especially in a baby, needs to be looked at by a doctor.

The allergy connection. Eczema tends to run in families, along with food allergies and nasal allergies. Together, this unpleasant threesome is known as *atopy*; another term for eczema is "atopic dermatitis." In eczema, there may be an allergic reaction to different foods or to materials like wool or silk that come in contact with the skin. In many cases, both food sensitivity and outside irritants combine to make a child miserable. In general, winter is worst for eczema, because it dries out skin that is already overly dry. Hot weather can also make eczema worse, because perspiration irritates the skin.

Particularly in severe cases, it's important to look for triggers. Among food allergies, cow's milk, soy, eggs, wheat, nuts (including peanuts), fish, and shellfish are the top suspects. A few babies can be cured only by giving up cow's milk altogether. It's best to undertake the search with the help of an experienced doctor; trying to do it yourself often results in confusion.

Treatment. Moisture is the key. A daily bath in warm water (not hot) for about five minutes allows water to soak into the skin. Don't use much soap; "pure" soap is very harsh and drying. When you have to, use a bar that's rich in moisturizers; stay away from deodorant soaps and bubble baths. Add bath oil near the end of the bath, so that it seals the moisture in. Pat your child dry with a soft towel; don't rub. Then use lots of moisturizing cream. If the skin is very dry, you can use petrolatum to seal the moisture in. Apply moisturizing cream two or three more times during the day. In the winter, run a vaporizer to keep the air in your home comfortably humid.

In order to limit skin irritation, get rid of any wool in clothing or bedding. If cold weather brings out the eczema, find a sheltered place for outings. It's important to keep the child's fingernails clipped short and filed smooth. The less the child can scratch her skin, the less the skin will itch, and the less the chance there will be of an infection getting started. For babies who will tolerate it, using a pair of white cotton mittens to cover the hands at night is helpful, since a lot of scratching can go on during sleep. Medication to reduce itching can also help.

Along with moisturizers, doctors often prescribe hydrocortisone. (Hydrocortisone is a form of steroid that is quite different from the anabolic steroids used by some athletes— and teens who want to look like athletes.) It comes in different strengths, and there are related creams and ointments (triamcinolone, for example) that are stronger yet. Antihistamines (diphenhydramine, or Benadryl, for example) can help reduce itching.

It's fine to use a moisturizer, 1 percent hydrocortisone, and diphenhydramine on your own to treat mild eczema. But for more severe eczema, it's best to work with your child's doctor or a dermatologist. If a bad patch of eczema becomes infected with bacteria, prescription antibiotics can help.

We don't have a good cure for eczema; often the best we can do is to keep it under control. Eczema that starts early in infancy often clears up substantially within a couple of years. Among school-age children with eczema, about half are free of it by their teenage years.

OTHER RASHES AND WARTS

If your child has a new rash, it's best to let a doctor see it. Rashes are hard to put into words, and it's easy to confuse them. The purpose of this section isn't to make you an expert, but only to tell you about some of the everyday rashes you can expect to see.

Dangerous rashes. A child with a minor viral infection will often develop red blotches, lacy areas, or little bumps covering the face, arms, or trunk. Recovery soon follows. What's important is that these rashes *blanch*. That is, if you use your fingers to stretch the skin where the rash is, the redness fades out. This is a good sign.

If you can't get the redness to fade by stretching the skin, beware: It may be blood that has leaked into the skin. Tiny blood vessels that break make pinpoint red dots; larger vessels that leak create irregular red or purple blotches. The situation isn't always dire. Hard coughing can sometimes cause small blood vessels to burst in the face, for example. But bleeding into the skin *can* be the first sign of a life-threatening infection or a serious blood problem. If you see red spots that don't blanch, even if your child doesn't seem very ill, call the doctor right away.

Hives (urticaria). This is an allergic reaction that causes raised red welts or blotches, often with a pale spot in the middle. Hives blanch (see above). They also itch, sometimes unbearably. And unlike most other rashes, they move around. They show up for a few hours, then fade, only to show up somewhere else.

The allergic trigger for hives may be obvious: Your child recently tried a new food or took a new medicine. (Hives, like other allergies, sometimes show up on the second or third exposure; don't be fooled.) Other triggers include heat, cold, plants, soaps or detergents, viral infections (including colds), and even strong emotions. Often, though, it's impossible to tell what set off the hives. A few children get hives repeatedly, but many have them only once or twice for no apparent reason. The usual treatment is oral diphenhydramine. Stronger medicines are available by prescription.

On rare occasions, hives occur along with swelling of the inside of the mouth and throat and difficulty breathing (anaphylaxis). If this happens, it's a medical emergency; call an ambulance right away (see page 438).

Impetigo. This often starts as a pimple with a yellowish or milky blister on top, often near the nose, but it could be anywhere. The blister breaks and a brown or honey-colored scab or crust takes its place. Any scab on the face should call impetigo to mind. The rash spreads easily, carried on the hands to other parts of the body, and to other children.

Impetigo is an infection of the skin caused by staphylococcus or streptococcus bacteria (staph or strep). Prescription antibiotics cure it. Until you can get to the doctor, try to keep your child from rubbing or picking and from sharing towels or bedding; enforce good handwashing. Untreated impetigo can lead to kidney damage, so you need to take it seriously.

Boils. A red, raised area that is painful may be a boil, an infection that forms a pus pocket in the skin. Increasingly, the cause is a form of staphylococcus called MRSA. These infections can be serious, and they need to be treated right away. A medication by mouth may suffice, or the pus pocket may need to be drained and antibiotics begun in the hospital.

Poison ivy. An intensely itchy cluster of small blisters on a base of shiny reddened skin is probably poison ivy, especially if it appears during the warm months on an exposed part of the body. The rash can look like impetigo, and sometimes a child will scratch bacteria into the skin, resulting in poison ivy *with* impetigo.

Wash the area well and scrub your child's hands, especially the fingertips. The rash caused by poison ivy is an allergic reaction to plant sap, and even a tiny bit of sap can spread the reaction to other parts of the body. Use over-the-counter hydrocortisone cream and oral diphenhydramine to combat the itching. Talk to the doctor if the reaction is extensive.

Scabies. Another itchy, bumpy rash, scabies is an allergic reaction to a mite, a tiny creature that burrows into the skin. Scabies looks like groups or lines of pimples topped with scabs, surrounded by a lot of scratch marks. It itches horribly. Scabies usually shows up in areas that are frequently touched: backs of hands, wrists, pubic area, and abdomen (but not on the back). Although scabies is not dangerous, it is highly contagious. Prescription lotion kills the mites, but the itching can continue for weeks.

Ringworm. This skin condition is caused not by a worm but by a fungus (related to athlete's foot) that infects the top layers of the skin. Look for one or more oval patches roughly the size of a nickel with heaped-up, slightly reddened borders. The outer rim is made up of little bumps or silver scales. The rash enlarges slowly over time, with clearing in the center, forming a ring. It itches a little, and it's mildly contagious. A prescription cream works well.

Ringworm on the scalp causes flaking and hair loss. Sometimes there is a large oozy swelling, as well as swollen lymph nodes at the back of the head and in the neck. Antifungal creams don't work in hairy areas; for these, treatment requires several weeks of daily medication by mouth.

Warts. Warts can be flat, mounded up, or spiky. One common type is a hard, rough mound of skin about the size of this capital "O." Warts are usually painless, but on the soles of the feet they can hurt. One variety, known by the poetic name of *molluscum contagiosum*, causes round, white or pink bumps the size of a pinhead, with a small dimple in the center. They may grow and multiply, or just sit there. Warts are caused by viruses, and usually the body fights them off eventually. Over-the-counter wart medicine can speed the process; so can (believe it or not) a daily application of duct tape. If these remedies fail, a dermatologist can freeze or cut them away; some primary-care doctors offer this service, too.

HEAD LICE

Head lice aren't really an infection; they're an infestation. The lice don't enter the body but hang around, feeding on human blood. The real problem is the itching, which can be intense. And the very idea of lice drives many people a bit crazy.

Lice pass easily from person to person, either by direct head contact (napping next to each other) or on combs, brushes, or hats. They can live for about three days away from a human body, but their eggs survive longer. Poor hygiene is not the problem.

Lice are good at hiding, so look for the eggs (also called nits): tiny, pearly white, smaller than a sesame seed, cemented to the hair, often close to the scalp. There may be itchy red pimples where the hair meets the back of the neck, especially behind the ears.

Try over-the-counter lice treatments first, but don't be surprised if the lice survive: Resistance to these chemicals is now common. Prescription insecticides usually work well. Treatments that don't work: covering the head in Vaseline or mayonnaise. One foolproof cure is to pick every single last nit off the child's head, and examine the head every few days for any new ones. Wetting the hair and using cream rinse make it easier to comb, and it becomes harder for the lice to scurry away.

STOMACHACHES

Most stomachaches are brief and mild; simple reassurance often does the trick. Fifteen minutes later, your child is back to playing normally. For any stomachache that lasts an hour or more, it's reasonable to call the doctor for advice. For severe stomachaches, don't wait even that long. There are dozens of causes of stomachaches and upsets. A few of them are serious; most are not. People are apt to jump to the conclusion that a stomachache is due either to appendicitis or to something that the child ate. Actually, neither of these causes is common. Most children have no problem digesting unfamiliar foods as well as large volumes of the foods they know and love.

Before you call the doctor, take your child's temperature and note when your child last had a bowel movement so you can relay that information. Pay attention to where on the belly it hurts: around the belly button, or more to one side; high up near the ribs, or lower down? The treatment, until you reach the doctor, should consist of putting the child to bed and giving him nothing to eat. If the child is thirsty, small sips of water are fine.

Common causes of stomachache. Young infants often have colic, which can look like stomach or abdominal pain (see page 84). If your baby has abdominal pain and is irritable or vomiting, especially if the stomach feels distended or hard, call the doctor immediately.

After the age of one year, one of the most common causes of stomachache is the onset of a simple cold, sore throat, or flu, especially when there is fever. The stomachache is a sign that the infection is disturbing the intestines as well as other parts of the body. In a young child, almost any infection may cause stomachache or abdominal pain. A small child is apt to complain that her tummy hurts when she really means that she feels nauseated. She often vomits soon after this complaint.

A common reason for repeated stomachaches is constipation. The pain may be dull and nagging or sudden and very painful (though it may go away just as quickly). It's often worse after a meal. The source of the pain appears to be cramping of the intestines as they fight to squeeze out the hard, dry bowel movements (see page 106).

Stomachaches and stress. All kinds of emotions, from fear to pleasant excitement, can affect the stomach and intestines. Stress-related stomachache is common among children and teenagers, often recurring two or more times a week. The pain is almost always in the midline, either around or just above the belly button. It is often hard for the child to describe. Since there's no infection, the child won't have fever.

A child who is under pressure to eat more or to eat different foods (vegetables, for instance) will often complain of stomachaches when he sits down to a meal or after a few bites. The parents may think the child has made up the stomachache as an excuse not to eat. But it's more likely that the pain comes from the child's tense feeling at mealtimes, and that the stomachache is real. When you lower the pressure at mealtimes, the pain slowly abates.

A child who has other worries can have stomachaches, too, especially around mealtime. Think of the child who is nervous about starting school in the fall and has a stomachache instead of an appetite for breakfast, or the child who feels guilty about something that hasn't been found out yet. Strife between parents, both verbal and physical, frequently causes stomach pain in children.

It's important to realize that the pain in these cases is real, not just something imagined or cooked up to get attention. The treatment is to attack the source of the stress—

whether it's between parents, with siblings, at school, or generated internally. A psychologist or other therapist can often help.

Appendicitis. The appendix is a little offshoot from the large intestine, about the size of a short earthworm. It becomes inflamed gradually, the way a boil does. (That's how you know that a sudden severe pain in the abdomen that lasts a few minutes and then goes away for good isn't appendicitis.) The worst danger is that the inflamed appendix bursts and spreads the infection all through the abdomen; this condition is called *peritonitis.*

A fast-moving appendicitis can reach the point of causing the appendix to burst in less than twenty-four hours. That's why any stomachache that lasts for an hour or more should be discussed with the doctor, even though nine out of ten cases will prove to be something else.

There is a classic way that appendicitis presents: first with pain around the navel, shifting to the right lower quadrant of the abdomen, then fever. The child looks ill, doesn't eat, and doesn't want to move. If you try to feel his belly, he pushes your hand away ("guarding"). That said, many times the illness follows a different script. There may or may not be right-lower pain, fever, vomiting, or an elevated white blood count. It may take an experienced doctor to make the diagnosis, often with help from an ultrasound of the belly.

It's sometimes impossible for even the most expert doctors to be absolutely certain about appendicitis. When there is enough suspicion, however, an operation is usually performed, because delay risks a ruptured appendix, which can be quite serious.

Intestinal obstruction. Rarely, a newborn is born with intestines that are blocked off, either all the time, or on and off. These babies are typically quite ill looking, and often vomit dark green bile. They need immediate medical attention.

In small children, a bit of the intestine can get pulled into the segment just below it, like a telescope folding up. The blockage that results is called an *intussusception*. In a typical case, the baby suddenly looks ill, vomits, and draws her legs up to her belly in pain. Sometimes the vomiting is more prominent; sometimes the pain is. The cramps come minutes apart; between them the baby may be fairly comfortable or sleepy. After a number of hours the baby may pass a bowel movement containing mucus and blood—the classic "currant jelly" stool. This is a sign of injury to the intestines; it's best to treat the problem before this happens.

Children between about four months through six years are prone to intussusception. The key is to suspect it and go for help. If it's caught early, the problem can often be fixed easily; if the bowel has been injured, however, surgery may be necessary.

Older children can also develop blockages of the intestines, especially if they have had abdominal surgery in the past, or if they have inflammatory bowel disease or another condition that causes inflammation in the intestines. Rarely, a birth defect involving the intestines goes unrecognized until later in life.

Intestinal parasites (worms). In less-developed parts of the world, pretty much every child has intestinal parasites. Where sanitation is better, worms are less common. Pinworms (threadworms) are an exception: They're common everywhere.

The worms look like white threads a third of an inch long. They live in the intestine, coming out at night to lay their eggs on the skin around the anus. The eggs may cause itching, disturbing the child's sleep or leading to vaginal irritation, or they can cause stomachaches, or may not be noticed at all. (In earlier times worms were thought to be the chief cause of children's grinding their teeth at night, but the connection is weak.)

Pinworms aren't harmful, but they can be hard to get rid of. A single dose of medication kills the adult worms, but the eggs can last for days or weeks outside the body. Children unknowingly pick up the eggs on their fingers and bring them to their mouths or their parents' mouths. Pinworms spread around families and child care centers, and children are often infested several times. Breaking the cycle requires careful handwashing (especially under the nails); washing of clothing, sheets, blankets, and floors; and sometimes repeated courses of medication.

Roundworms are bigger than pinworms, looking a lot like little earthworms. The first suspicion comes when one is discovered in the bowel movement. They usually don't cause symptoms unless the child has a great number of them. They're rare in developed countries. Hookworms, on the other hand, are common in some parts of the southern United States. The disease is contracted by going barefoot in soil that is infested with the larvae. Hookworms can cause malnutrition and anemia, with stunted growth and poor development.

Children born in lower-income countries and those who live in group homes often host intestinal parasites without having any symptoms at all. We find them by sending samples of stool to a laboratory for microscopic examination. Prescribed medications usually get rid of these unwanted guests.

CONSTIPATION

Constipation is common in children, and commonly misunderstood. A child who passes hard bowel movements or large painful ones is constipated, even if he goes every day. A child who passes soft BMs isn't constipated, even if he only goes every two or three days. Constipation can be a symptom of many diseases—hypothyroidism, lead poisoning, and others—but most constipated children don't have one of these conditions. Constipation itself frequently causes serious problems, both physical and psychological.

How constipation develops. Constipation usually begins with a large, hard BM that hurts on the way out. The fear of pain makes the child try to hold the next BM in. The longer the BM stays in, the drier and harder it gets. When it finally passes, it hurts again. Over time, the buildup of hard stool stretches out the intestines, weakening the muscles that normally propel the stool along. The result is even slower passage of stool through the intestines, with even more drying, hardening, and discomfort. In this way, a painful BM can give rise to a persistent problem.

Any number of things can cause the hard BM that starts the vicious cycle. It could be a passing illness with mild dehydration, such as the flu; or a reaction to cow's milk or a new food; or an emotional strain such as the birth of a sibling; or just feeling uncomfortable using the bathroom in school.

Lifestyle and constipation. Fiber-rich diets based on whole grains, vegetables, and fruits make for soft BMs. Diets rich in meat and white potatoes often provide too little fiber, making BMs harder in consistency, and harder to pass. Overweight children often have low-fiber diets and low levels of physical activity, both of which set them up for constipation. Children with ADHD, always on the go, may not sit still long enough to, well, go.

Some children react to a particular protein in cow's milk by slowing the squeezing motions of their intestines, leading to constipation. This tendency runs in families. The solution is to cut out (not just reduce) cow's milk and everything made from it. (If you try this, be sure to add other sources of calcium and vitamin D; see page 319.)

Children who don't drink enough water have harder BMs. How much is enough? Expert recommendations from the Institute of Medicine start at five cups a day for four-year-olds, and go up to eleven cups for teenage boys. Practically speaking, the idea is simply *more*, particularly if your child's stools tend toward hardness. See page 331 for tips on making water more appealing.

Problems caused by constipation. In addition to pain and bloody BMs, constipation often leads to bed-wetting and frequent daytime urination. As stool builds up in the rectum, it pushes against the lower part of the bladder, partly blocking the flow of urine. The bladder—a muscle—has to work harder to push the urine past the obstruction. As a result, it loses the ability to relax as it fills with urine, and even a relatively small amount of urine triggers bladder contractions and the urgent need to go.

Stool leakage (*encopresis*) is a terrible problem for many badly constipated children (see page 765). One of the worst things about constipation is that it draws parents too deeply into what should be, for most school-age children, their own private business. It takes a very sensitive parent to remain involved but not over-involved. When constipation has set up a power struggle between parent and child or has raised tensions in a family, it's wise to seek guidance from a psychologist, counselor, or other professional.

Constipation makes children feel rotten, and that can result in learning problems and negative behaviors. In children who don't talk (some children with autism, for example), constipation can cause aggressive outbursts directed at others, or at themselves.

Lifestyle treatments for constipation. This is the best place to start. The solution might be as easy as substituting whole-wheat for white bread, fresh oranges for orange juice, and apples for cookies. Remember that "P fruits make you poop": prunes, plums, peaches, and pears. Apricots, too. Try adding unprocessed miller's bran (available in most supermarkets) or bran cereal to muffins, applesauce, or peanut butter sandwiches. If you add bran or other dried fiber, be sure to also give your child extra water. A slurry of applesauce, bran, and prune juice is sweet and crunchy, and often works well.

It's important to make sure your child has vigorous exercise daily. Abdominal strengthening exercises (crunches, for example) help children push more effectively and gain a sense of control. Children also need time set aside each day to sit quietly on the toilet. The best time is often about fifteen minutes after dinner, because eating naturally activates the colon.

A selection of books in the bathroom can help a child sit for the fifteen or twenty minutes it takes to let things happen. A wooden stool lets shorter children plant their feet securely, which makes pushing easier.

Medication for constipation. Painfully hard bowel movements should be treated promptly, particularly in a younger child. Your doctor can recommend one of several preparations that will keep the movements soft. Treatment usually lasts for a month or more, to allow the child to become confident that the painful hardness will not recur. (Some traditional constipation cures are actually hazardous. Mineral oil, for example, can cause vitamin deficiencies or pneumonia if it is inhaled. Be aware.)

When constipation has been long-standing, the treatment needs to be more intensive. There are two phases, "clean-out" and "maintenance." No treatment can succeed if the colon stays plugged by rock-hard stool. Doctors typically prescribe large doses of oral solutions containing polyethylene glycol (MiraLax and other brands), to flush out the intestines. Children often resist, because it's boring to drink and drink, and then go and go. But they feel much better once all the hard poop is out! Other medications to unplug the intestines are also sometimes needed, so it's best to let an experienced doctor coach you through this ordeal. Sometimes a pediatric gastroenterologist needs to help.

After the clean-out comes maintenance: lifestyle changes and medication balanced to produce a soft, formed stool every day. This treatment needs to continue for six months or more, until the colon has recovered enough strength to do the job on its own. The point is to not allow the stool to build up again, restarting the vicious cycle. Children and parents have a hard time keeping up with treatment for that long, and it can take several attempts before the problem is fully controlled. Worries about the effects of long-term laxative use are reasonable, but untreated constipation is also harmful. It's important, if you find yourself in this position, to work with a doctor you trust.

VOMITING AND DIARRHEA

Infections (gastroenteritis). Most diarrhea in children is caused by viruses. These infections get called different things: stomach flu, intestinal flu, a "bug," or gastroenteritis. There may be fever, vomiting, and stomachache (usually mild). The child normally recovers in a few days, but family members or classmates often fall ill with the same bug.

There is no specific cure. Give frequent small amounts of fluid to prevent dehydration, but not fruit juices, which can make it worse. Soups and broths are good. Store-bought oral rehydration solution is effective and convenient, or you can mix your own using salt and sugar (see page 356). Let your child eat what he wants. You don't have to restrict milk or dairy products, but don't push them, either.

If your child seems quite ill, with high fever or severe cramping, or if the diarrhea contains blood or mucus, the problem could be a bacterial infection. Salmonella is one of the more common culprits, along with *E. coli,* shigella, campylobacter, and a few others. Antibiotics can treat some of these infections, but in other cases, antibiotics actually make the situation *worse.* So, bring the doctor a stool sample to send to the lab.

Salmonella, *E. coli,* and other potentially dangerous bacteria are routinely found in meat and even vegetables in grocery stores. To protect your children and yourself, follow approved practices for safely preparing, cooking, serving, and storing food: Scrub all counters and utensils with hot soapy water after preparing meat or poultry; cook meats until there is no pinkness inside; and discard foods that have been out of the refrigerator long enough to spoil (go to drspock.com for specific guidelines).

Vomiting without diarrhea. Vomiting with diarrhea often signals an infection or food poisoning. Vomiting *without* diarrhea is more concerning. It can be caused by a blockage of the intestines (especially if what comes up is yellow), a swallowed poison or medication, a serious infection almost anywhere in the body, or pressure on the brain. In short, it needs to be evaluated promptly by a doctor.

In an infant with persistent vomiting, think about gastroesophageal reflux disease (GERD). Between the esophagus and the stomach, there is a muscle that works like a valve. It opens to let food into the stomach and let swallowed air out, then closes to keep the food from squirting back up into the mouth. In babies, the nerves that control this valve are slow and the signals can get crossed. So the valve often opens at the wrong time and stomach contents—food mixed with acid—move in the wrong direction. Over time, the acid can irritate the esophagus, causing heartburn. The irritation in turn makes the valve even less effective.

Once you know the problem is GERD, the solution may be as simple as giving smaller, more frequent feedings. As a result, the stomach never gets overfilled, pressure in the stomach stays low, and food stays put. You can also thicken a baby's formula with about one tablespoon of rice cereal per eight-ounce bottle. Try laying your baby on her stomach with her head a few inches higher than her stomach, to let gravity lend a hand. (Be careful to watch your baby, and move her to her back if she falls asleep; SIDS is much less common in babies who sleep on their backs.) When GERD is not responding to these measures, medication can help lower the acid and sometimes strengthen the muscle of the valve.

A young baby who vomits forcefully after each feed could have a more serious condition called *pyloric stenosis*, a thickening of the muscle that controls the outflow from the stomach. Persistent vomiting in a young child needs medical attention.

Food poisoning. Bacteria that grow in certain foods excrete the toxins that cause food poisoning. The food may or may not taste unusual. Beware especially of pastries filled with custard or whipped cream, creamy salads, and poultry stuffing. Bacteria multiply readily in these substances if they warm up to room temperature. Another cause is improperly home-canned foods (see Food Safety at drspock.com).

Symptoms of food poisoning include vomiting, diarrhea, stomachache, and headaches. Sometimes there are chills, fever, and muscle aches. Everyone who eats the contaminated food is apt to be affected by it to some degree at about the same time, in contrast to an intestinal flu, which usually spreads through a family over a number of days. The doctor should always be called when you suspect food poisoning.

Dehydration. Many illnesses increase water loss through vomiting, diarrhea, fever, and fast breathing. Also, sick children tend to drink less. Babies and young children are especially at risk because they lose water more rapidly through their skin. Certain infections are notorious for creating dehydration. The most famous is cholera, rare in developed countries, but common (and greatly feared) when sanitation is lacking, as in natural and man-made disasters. In developed countries, rotavirus was a common culprit until a vaccine was developed.

The first sign of dehydration is that the child makes less urine than usual, and the urine is dark yellow in color. Diapers make it hard to judge urine output, especially if they are filled with liquid stool. As dehydration worsens, the child becomes listless or lethargic; his eyes look dry, and there may be no tears when he cries; his lips and mouth look parched and dry; and in a baby, the soft spot on the top of the head appears sunken.

For mild dehydration, have your child drink lots of an over-the-counter rehydration solution, or make your own (see page 356). Be aware that sports drinks aren't the same, and won't work as well, despite what the ads say. With more serious dehydration, get your child to a doctor or to a hospital as soon as possible.

Persistent diarrhea. A young child who is obviously thriving begins the day with a normal bowel movement, then has three to five soft or runny and smelly bowel movements, which may contain mucus or undigested food. His appetite remains good and he is playful and active. The problem may begin out of the blue or with a bout of stomach flu. It often gets better after the child stops drinking juice. This common problem, sometimes called *apple-juice diarrhea*, is a response to concentrated fructose in fruit juice. Children don't really need juice. Eating a whole apple or orange provides plenty of vitamins, plus fiber. A four-ounce glass of juice once a day is plenty, as a treat.

In an older child, a pattern of unexplained loose stools and cramps may be caused by *irritable bowel syndrome* (IBS). Some causes include too much caffeine (from power drinks, for example), psychological stress, and food sensitivities. A special diet that eliminates "fermentable" sugars (the FOD-MAP diet) can often help.

Serious diseases that can cause chronic diarrhea. Anytime persistent diarrhea occurs along with poor weight gain or weight loss, a doctor should look for serious diseases including inflammatory bowel disease, cystic fibrosis and other diseases of the pancreas, and celiac disease.

There are two main types of *inflammatory bowel disease* (IBD): *Crohn's disease* and *ulcerative colitis*. Symptoms include abdominal pain, bloody diarrhea, weight loss, poor appetite, pale appearance, and extreme tiredness. Typically, symptoms get worse until the diagnosis is made and treated.

In *cystic fibrosis* (CF), the pancreas stops secreting enzymes necessary to break down food. Undigested food causes diarrhea, and the child suffers from undernutrition. Children are tested for CF at birth (it's part of the heel-stick blood test), and specialized treatments are started early. There are other, less common causes of pancreas malfunction, and these can show up later, usually with chronic diarrhea and weight loss.

Celiac disease (CD) is an abnormal response to gluten, a protein found in wheat, barley, and rye. In CD, gluten causes the body to attack the intestinal cells that are responsible for absorbing nutrients. Unabsorbed nutrients cause diarrhea and bloating, while the body starves. We now have blood tests to screen for CD, but the final diagnosis usually requires a bi-opsy taken through an endoscope. Treatment is with a gluten-free diet. These days, many people who don't have CD also choose to eat gluten-free (see page 327).

HEADACHES

In young children, headaches are often early symptoms of a cold or other infection. In school-age children and teens, stress is the more common cause. Think of the child who's been memorizing a part for the school play, or the child who's been practicing extra hours for the gymnastics team. Often fatigue, tension, and anticipation combine to produce changes in the blood flow to the muscles of the head and neck, causing a headache.

An older child who has a headache can be given the ap-propriate dose of acetaminophen or ibuprofen, followed by a rest period—lying down, playing quietly, or engaging in an-other restful activity—until the medicine starts to work. Sometimes an ice pack helps.

If a headache lasts as long as four hours after the child has taken a medication, or if other symptoms of illness such as fever develop, it's worth a call to the doctor. Other concerning signs are headaches in the morning or on rising, or that awaken a child at night; headaches that follow a fall or blow to the head; headaches with dizziness, blurred or double vi-sion, nausea and vomiting; or just headaches that seem to last too long.

A child who has frequent headaches should have a thorough medical evaluation, including a check of his vision, a dental exam, a neurological evaluation, and a careful review of his eating and sleeping patterns. It's also worth considering whether something in the child's home life, school, or social activities may be causing undue stress.

Children do get migraine headaches, although not always with the classic pattern (flashing lights or other auras). A pattern of severe headaches in a child ought to raise the question of migraines, particularly (but not only) if migraines run in the family.

SEIZURES

Obvious or not. Sometimes it's obvious that a child is having a seizure. He loses consciousness and falls down; his eyes roll up; his whole body stiffens, then shakes violently. He may froth at the mouth, make grunting noises, become incontinent, or bite his tongue. After several minutes his body relaxes, but he remains sleepy or confused for a while before returning to normal. These dramatic events are described as *generalized seizures* because large areas of the brain are involved, and *tonic-clonic* because the body first stiffens, then shakes. The old term "grand mal seizure" is still used.

Other seizure types are less obvious. An infant may suddenly stare off to one side or make lip-smacking or bicycle-riding movements. A boy between ages five and eight may wake from sleep with twitching on one side of his face or body; a couple of minutes later he is okay. This kind of seizure typically goes away before the child starts eighth grade, and does not come back.

Here is another common type of seizure: A child over the

age of two, often a girl, suddenly stares blankly ahead and does not respond to her name or to being touched. After five to ten seconds she picks up again with whatever she was doing, without ever noticing the interruption. These seizures can occur repeatedly during the day, interfering with the child's learning. These events are called *absence seizures,* because the child's mind seems to go away momentarily. They respond well to medication. Yet another child carries out a complicated set of movements over and over—walking around or moving his hands in a particular way—and is unaware of his actions. This could also be a seizure.

In general, any sudden change in a child's behavior or consciousness *could* be a seizure. When in doubt, get a medical assessment.

When is it epilepsy? "Epilepsy" is the term for seizures that occur repeatedly, in the absence of fever or other obvious cause. Depending on the type of seizures and other particulars, a neurologist may diagnose a particular epilepsy syndrome. This diagnosis helps guide the treatment and informs the prognosis.

Epilepsy is upsetting for children and parents, even more than many other chronic diseases. Ignorance and fear are major hurdles. Through education, children and parents can gain control and comfort. People with epilepsy can and do lead full and rich lives.

Causes of seizures. Nerve cells are constantly firing off tiny jolts of electricity. When millions of nerves fire more or less at once, an abnormal wave of electricity can flow through the brain, causing a seizure. When a large part of the brain is affected, children lose consciousness and often have whole-body shaking, or "tonic-clonic" seizures. When a smaller area of the brain is affected, the seizure is less dramatic, such as the shaking of part of a limb, for example, without loss of consciousness. The underlying cause of the abnormal electrical pulse could be an area of scarring in the brain, or the action of a particular gene; often, though, the cause remains unknown.

Seizures with fever. By far the most common cause of seizures in young children is fever. One child in twenty-five between the ages of three months and five years has a brief tonic-clonic seizure during a fever. These children are healthy (except for the infection that is causing the fever); the seizure seems to have no long-term effect, and most of them never have another. About one-third of the children will go on to have a second seizure with fever, but again, most of them turn out to be completely healthy in the long run. Perhaps one in twenty who has a first seizure with fever will later prove to have epilepsy.

Febrile seizures often occur at the beginning of an illness such as a cold, a sore throat, or the flu. The trigger seems to be the sudden rise in temperature as the body mounts its attack on the germ. Because the seizures often come on unexpectedly, it's hard for parents to prevent them.

If your child does have a seizure with fever, follow the instructions below. Of course, you will have been scared senseless for a bit, because the normal reaction to your child having a seizure is to imagine the worst. Your child will almost certainly get over the episode long before you do.

What to do during a generalized tonic-clonic (grand mal) seizure. There is very little you need to do for a child during a convulsion except keep her from hurting herself. Move her to the floor or some other place where she can't fall. Turn her on her side to allow saliva to run out of the corner of her mouth and to prevent her tongue from blocking her airway. Make sure that her flailing arms and legs do not strike something sharp. Don't try to put anything into her mouth.

Most seizures stop by themselves. Seizures that continue past five minutes are more likely to need urgent medical intervention. Call 911. If you are there to witness the start of a seizure, make a note of when it started, because the doctor will want to know how long it lasted. After a seizure, children are usually very sleepy, and it may be an hour or more before they're truly themselves again.

EYE PROBLEMS

Reasons for seeing the eye doctor. Children need to go to an eye doctor if their eyes turn in (cross-eyes) or out (walleyes) at any age; if they are having trouble with schoolwork; if they complain of aching, smarting, or tired eyes; if their eyes are inflamed; if they are having headaches; if they hold their books too close when they read; if they cock their head to one side when looking at something carefully; or if their vision is found to be defective by the doctor. Eye charts work for most children over age three, and automated vision screeners work even with small babies. Vision screening should be performed annually. However, even if your child can read the eye chart, if she is having symptoms of eyestrain, she should be examined by an eye doctor.

Nearsightedness (myopia). Close objects appear sharp, but distant objects are blurred. The problem develops most frequently between six and ten years. It can come on quite rapidly, so don't ignore the signs (holding the book closer, having trouble seeing the blackboard at school) just because the child's vision was all right a few months before.

Conjunctivitis (pinkeye). Conjunctivitis means inflammation of the conjunctiva, which is the outer surface of the eye. It can be caused by viruses, bacteria, or allergens. If the eye is only slightly pink and the discharge from the eye is scant and clear, particularly if the child has a runny nose at the same time, the usual culprit is the same virus that's causing the cold. Viral pinkeye gets better like a cold does, without special medication.

In a child without a cold, pinkeye may be due to a bacterial infection. Thick yellow discharge, pain, or redness of the eyeball also suggest bacteria. The treatment is with antibiotic ointments or drops as prescribed by your doctor. Many other germs can cause conjunctivitis, sometimes quite severe or associated with whole-body illness. These cases need medical attention.

Conjunctivitis spreads hand-to-eye. Young children who rub their eyes, then touch other children can easily pass conjunctivitis around a classroom. Many child care centers and schools exclude children with conjunctivitis until they have had twenty-four hours of antibiotic treatment. This doesn't make sense, of course, for viral infections (mild redness, no pus) that don't respond to antibiotics anyhow. And it's often impractical to wait a week for pinkeye to completely resolve before returning to school. So teachers may need to be especially alert, and enforce frequent handwashing and limit child-to-child contact (go to drspock.com for a typical school note).

If the conjunctivitis does not clear up after a few days of medication, there may be a speck of dirt or other foreign material stuck in the eye, visible only through an ophthalmoscope. Persistent tearing of an eye, lid swelling, refusal to open the eye, or one eye that seems larger than the other all need prompt medical attention.

Styes. A stye is an infection around the root of an eyelash, caused by ordinary bacteria that live on the skin. The stye usually comes to a head and breaks, then heals. Warm compresses speed this process and reduce discomfort. A prescription antibiotic ointment also helps to promote healing. (Eyelids are very temperature sensitive, so only use warm, not hot, water.) Try to keep your child from rubbing the stye, as this can spread the infection to other hair roots. Just as with conjunctivitis, an adult with a stye should wash his hands thoroughly before caring for a baby or small child, to limit contagion.

Behaviors that affect vision. Habitually reading in poor light and a lack of time outdoors, looking at things far away, may worsen nearsightedness. Watching television, sitting too close to the set, and reading a lot in good light probably have no effect on the eyes.

JOINTS AND BONES

Growing pains. Children often complain of vague pains in their legs and arms. A child between the ages of two and five may wake up crying with pain around his thigh, knee, or calf. This happens only during the evening—the child is fine the rest of the day—but may recur each night for weeks on end. Some people believe this pain is caused by cramps in the muscles or is the aching caused by rapidly growing bones. Generally, if the pains move from place to place, if there is no swelling, redness, local tenderness, or limp, and if the child is entirely well otherwise, it is unlikely that a serious cause will be found.

Hips, knees, ankles, and feet. Hip pain always needs to be assessed medically, since the hip joint is vulnerable to injury. Pain from the hip joint is felt in the groin or along the inside of the thigh, not the area normally referred to as the hips. Limping should always be concerning, with or without hip pain, unless there is an obvious reason such as a hurt foot. Overweight children are prone to hip problems, as well as to problems in the knees, ankles, and feet.

Pain just below the kneecap, particularly in a growing adolescent, is often caused by strain on the ligament where it connects to the top of the shinbone. The pain is usually worse after sports that involve jumping. This common condition, known as *Osgood-Schlatter disease*, is an overuse injury, similar to tennis elbow. Healing requires rest and medication to reduce inflammation (ibuprofen, typically). Pain alongside or underneath the kneecap is also common and responds to rest and medication, and to exercises that strengthen the muscles that hold the kneecap in place. A physical therapist can teach these to your child.

For twisted and sprained ankles, try rest, ibuprofen, cold (ice), and elevation—that is, the combination known as RICE. Exercises prescribed by a physical therapist can speed recovery. Flat feet that don't hurt are not really a problem; painful flat feet should be evaluated, because surgery may help.

Spine. *Scoliosis* is a curvature of the spine that usually appears between the ages of ten and fifteen, more often in girls. Although the cause is unknown, it tends to run in families. Any curvature warrants an evaluation by a physician, but most cases are mild and only require monitoring. Low back pain in a child always needs evaluation, to rule out rare but serious causes. Children should avoid power lifting until their adolescent growth spurt is over, when their spines are fully matured and less vulnerable to injury.

When to worry. Any joint pain with fever could signal an infection in the joint, which is an emergency. Limping that is not explained by a recent injury also needs to be seen promptly, since it can sometimes be a sign of serious illness. Persistent aching or swelling in one or more joints, perhaps with fever or rash, may be due to arthritis. There are several different forms that affect children, some more serious than others. All need medical attention.

HEART PROBLEMS

Murmurs. A heart murmur is simply a sound made by blood flowing through the heart. Most murmurs are *innocent or functional,* which means that the heart is perfectly normal. It's good to know if your child has an innocent murmur, because then you don't have to worry every time a doctor hears it. A truly new murmur needs to be evaluated. The most common cause is anemia due to low iron intake.

When a murmur is due to a heart abnormality, the most likely cause is an opening between two of the chambers of the heart. When these openings are small, as they usually are, doctors just wait for them to close on their own. Larger openings sometimes require a procedure, often without surgery. Doctors can usually tell whether or not a murmur is innocent simply by listening. If necessary, an ultrasound can reveal the nature of any abnormalities.

Chest pain. Pain in the chest area is common in children, but it's rarely caused by problems with the lungs or heart. Most chest pain is due to acid reflux, or to emotional upset or anxiety. Teenagers are prone to inflammation of the cartilage that attaches the ribs to the breastbone. In these cases, pressing firmly on the chest brings on the pain. Ibuprofen and reassurance usually solve the problem.

Fainting. A child who stands up suddenly from a lying position, or who suffers a sudden pain or stress, may feel lightheaded. If she blacks out, it's probably a good idea to have a doctor check her. Usually, the child who has fainted is completely healthy. In rare cases, fainting is caused by an abnormal heart rhythm, detected on an EKG. A child who faints *without* any inciting pain or shock should certainly be seen by a doctor.

Any faintness or chest pain during physical exercise should be investigated, as these may be signs of *hypertrophic cardiomyopathy* (HCM), the most common cause of sudden death in athletes. HCM is one of several genetic conditions that can cause serious heart problems. If there is a history of passing out or sudden death in your family, let the doctor know.

GENITAL AND URINARY DISTURBANCES

Infections of the bladder and kidneys. Adults with bladder infections often complain of frequent, burning urination. Children sometimes have the same symptoms, but often they don't. A young child may only have belly pain or fever, or no symptoms at all; the infection is only discovered by testing the urine. If there is a lot of pus, the urine may appear hazy or cloudy, but normal urine can look the same due to ordinary minerals in it. Infected urine may smell somewhat like a bowel movement. If the infection moves into the kidneys, there is often high fever and aching or pain in the back. Children with these symptoms need prompt medical care.

After the first few weeks of life, urinary tract infections are more common among girls than boys. Wiping from back to front is a frequent cause of bladder infections in girls. Boys who have not been circumcised are somewhat more prone to urinary tract infections. It's worth keeping this in mind if your child has a fever and belly pain, or any discomfort with urination.

It's important to treat urine infections to prevent long-term kidney damage. Sometimes an underlying abnormality in the kidneys or the tubes leading from them sets a child up for repeated urinary infections. Testing for these abnormalities is important, because surgery may be needed.

Frequent urination. A sudden change in urination could be due to a bladder infection or diabetes. Constipation also causes frequent urination (see page 501).

A few individuals seem to have bladders that never hold as much as the average, and this may be the way they were made.

Other children (and adults, too) who urinate frequently are worried or high-strung. A healthy athlete may have to go to the toilet every fifteen minutes just before a race, for example. Children under chronic stress—from tensions at home or in the neighborhood, for example—may need to go to the bathroom more often.

A common story involves the timid child and the teacher who seems severe. To begin with, the child's apprehensiveness keeps his bladder from relaxing sufficiently to hold much urine. Then he worries about asking permission to be excused. If the teacher makes a fuss about his leaving the room, it's worse still.

A parent-teacher conversation may lead to a solution, for example a "secret signal" the child can use to leave the room when he needs to. This can lower the level of tension, and often the number of bathroom visits as well. It may also help to get a note from the doctor not simply requesting that the child be excused but also explaining the child's nature and why his bladder works that way.

Infrequent urination. When the body is low on water, the kidneys hold on to every drop; what comes out is scant and concentrated (dark yellow). Occasionally in hot weather, when a child is perspiring a great deal and not drinking enough, he may not urinate for eight hours or more. The same thing may happen during a fever. In these situations, children need plenty of chances and occasional reminders to drink between meals, especially when they're too little to tell you that they're thirsty.

Sore on the end of the penis. Sometimes a small raw area appears around the opening of the penis. There may be enough swelling that it's difficult for the boy to pass his urine. This little sore is a localized diaper rash. The best treatment is to expose it to the air as much as is practical. Bathing daily with a mild soap will encourage healing. If the child is in pain from being unable to urinate for many hours, he can sit in a warm bath for half an hour and be encouraged to urinate while in the tub. If this doesn't work, the doctor should be called.

Painful urination in girls. The cause could be irritation around the urinary opening from bits of bowel movement wiped the wrong way, or from various chemicals. Get rid of bubble baths, fabric softeners (including dryer sheets), and perfumed toilet paper, and use only cotton, not nylon, panties. Mix a half cup of bicarbonate of soda in a shallow, warm bath and have your child sit in it several times a day. After the bath, gently blot dry the urinary region. If these steps don't take care of the problem, the doctor should test for a bladder infection.

Vaginal discharge. A thin discharge that goes away on its own in a couple of days is not concerning. The causes and treatment are the same as for painful urination (above).

A thick, profuse discharge that is irritating, or a discharge that lasts for several days, may be caused by a more serious infection. Rarely, it's a sign of sexual abuse. Doctors are trained to ask about abuse, and to examine the genitals for other signs.

A discharge that is partly pus and partly blood is sometimes caused by a small girl having pushed some object into her vagina. If this is found to be the case, it's reasonable for her parents to ask her to please not do this again, but it's better not to make the girl feel really guilty or to imply that she might have hurt herself seriously. The exploring and experimenting she has done are not too different from what most young children do.

HERNIAS AND TESTICLE PROBLEMS

Hernias. A swelling that comes and goes in a baby's groin or scrotum could be a hernia. The swelling is caused by a loop of intestine that has slipped down through a small passageway that is normally closed. Straining or coughing pushes the intestine into this area; when the child relaxes or lies down, the bowel moves back to where it belongs.

If the bit of intestine gets stuck, the swelling becomes fixed and painful; this needs immediate medical attention. While waiting to see the doctor, try raising the baby's hips on a pillow and apply an ice bag (or crushed ice in a plastic bag in a sock). These actions may make the intestine slip back into the abdomen. Don't try to push the lump down with your fingers. Don't feed the baby by breast or bottle until you have talked with the doctor. If your baby needs an operation, it's better to go with an empty stomach.

Hydroceles. Like hernias, hydroceles cause swelling in the scrotum. Each testicle is surrounded by a delicate sac that contains a few drops of fluid; this helps it slide around. In a newborn there is often extra fluid in the sac, making the testicle appear several times its normal size. Sometimes this swelling appears later in infancy. Hydroceles usually get better on their own. Occasionally an older boy has a large hydrocele that may need to be operated on. Hernias and hydroceles may exist together; it can be confusing. Let your child's doctor help figure out what's going on.

Testicular torsion. Each testicle hangs in the scrotum on a stalk of blood vessels, and other tubes. If the testicle twists around on its stalk, the blood flow can get cut off, painfully. A suddenly swollen, tender, red or purple scrotum signals the need for urgent medical attention to save the testicle.

Testicular cancer. Teenage boys should be taught to examine their testicles once a month, feeling each one carefully for any unusual lumps or areas of tenderness. With early treatment, the prognosis is good.

SUDDEN INFANT DEATH SYNDROME (SIDS)

Nearly one in every thousand babies born in the United States dies of sudden infant death syndrome (crib death). It's usually a baby between three weeks and seven months of age. By definition, no explanation (such as an infection) is found, even when a postmortem examination (autopsy) is done.

All infants should be put to sleep on their backs, unless a doctor instructs otherwise. Having infants sleep faceup cuts the risk of SIDS in half. Other precautions such as avoiding secondhand cigarette smoke and overheating are also important (see page 48).

Responses to SIDS. The parents are in shock—a sudden death is much more shattering than one that follows a worsening illness. They may be overwhelmed by guilt, assuming that they should have noticed something or gone in to check on the child. Grief and depression can last for months. Parents may experience difficulty concentrating and sleeping, poor appetite, and heart or stomach symptoms. They may feel a strong urge to get away or a dread of being alone. Some parents need to talk; others bottle up their feelings.

If there are other children, the parents may be afraid to let them out of their sight, want to shun responsibility for caring for them, or treat them irritably. The children are also sure to be upset, whether they show ordinary grief or not. Small children may cling or behave badly. Older children may appear unconcerned, as a defense against the full force of grief and guilt. All children have resented their brothers and sisters at times, and their immature thinking may tell them that their hostile feelings brought about the death.

If the parents avoid talking about the dead baby, their silence may add to the other children's guilt. So it is good for the parents to talk about the baby, to explain that a special sickness of babies caused the death and that it was not the fault of anyone. Euphemisms like "The baby went away" or "She never woke up" simply add new mysteries and anxieties. It's particularly helpful if the parents respond in a gentle way to every one of the children's questions and comments, so that they will feel that it is all right to bring up their deeper worries. The parents should seek counseling from a family social agency, a guidance clinic, a psychiatrist, a psychologist, or a clergy member so that they can express and come to understand their overwhelming feelings.

ACQUIRED IMMUNE DEFICIENCY SYNDROME (AIDS)

AIDS is caused by the *human immunodeficiency virus* (HIV). HIV impairs the body's ability to develop immunity to other infections. Infections easily defeated by healthy people become deadly in the setting of AIDS.

HIV is not spread by touching, kissing, living in the same home, sitting in the same classroom, swimming in the same pool, eating or drinking from the same utensils, or sitting on the same toilet as someone with AIDS.

Children usually acquire HIV from their mothers during pregnancy or at the time of birth. Antiviral medications given during pregnancy can greatly reduce the chance that the baby will become infected; therefore, screening for HIV is crucial for pregnant women. Babies who are infected can survive indefinitely with proper medical care. For many people, using a combination of medications has changed AIDS into a manageable disease with a long life expectancy. There is still no known cure.

How (and why) to talk to children and teens about AIDS. Children hear about AIDS from TV, in videos and movies, and at school. Parents need to be part of the conversation. By mentioning the subject even in a casual way, you make it possible for your child to ask questions, get your reassurance and support, and learn your values.

Adolescents need to know that the greatest risk of becoming infected with HIV comes from unprotected sex with multiple partners. The greater the number of partners, the greater the chance that one of them is carrying HIV, maybe without knowing it. The surest way, of course, is to save intercourse for marriage; but simply telling teens to do this isn't a reliable strategy. Teens also need to know that latex (not lambskin) condoms provide substantial but not total protection. Other forms of birth control do not protect against AIDS. Oral sex is probably less risky, but it's not entirely safe.

Anal sex is particularly hazardous, because greater friction increases blood-to-blood mixing. Injecting drugs with shared equipment exposes people to the same risk. If these topics make you uneasy, remember that *talking* with children about sex and drugs does not make them more likely to have sex and take drugs—just the opposite, in fact (see page 642).

Dr. Spock comments, "The two greatest protections against contracting HIV, I feel, are education about safe sex techniques and a belief that the spiritual aspects of sexual love . . . are as important and as worthy of respect as the purely physical."

TUBERCULOSIS

Tuberculosis (TB). This disease is rare in the United States but still common in many developing countries. Here, the children most at risk are those who were born overseas, whose family members were born overseas, who live in low-income communities, or who are exposed to anyone with a chronic cough that could be TB.

Most people think of TB as it occurs typically in adults: with fevers, weight loss, and bloody sputum. In children, however, TB usually takes other forms. Very young children have little resistance, and the infection often spreads throughout the body. Older children may feel fine. The bacteria waits in the body, then emerges when resistance is low. The symptoms then may be vague, just unusual tiredness or a fall in appetite. Therefore, it's important to keep the possibility of TB in mind.

Anyone with suspected TB exposure should be tested, as well as any new member of the household—a caregiver or housekeeper, for example. Everyone who works in a hospital gets tested each year. A positive test in a child usually signals exposure rather than disease. Treatment with medication for several months prevents the actual disease from developing later.

REYE'S SYNDROME

This rare but serious condition can cause permanent damage to the brain and other organs. Its cause is not completely understood, but it usually occurs during a viral illness. Children and adolescents who receive aspirin when they have a viral illness, especially influenza or chicken pox, are much more likely to get Reye's syndrome than those who are given acetaminophen or another nonaspirin product.

WEST NILE VIRUS

West Nile virus frightens many people, but in fact it rarely causes severe illness in humans. The virus is carried by mosquitoes, who give it to birds as well as to humans. The best protection is to avoid mosquito bites (see page 418). The symptoms of West Nile virus are usually mild (if any) and resemble the flu. Blood tests can confirm the diagnosis, but there is no specific medicine to treat the virus; the body has to fight it off on its own.

ZIKA VIRUS

Zika virus can cause brain damage in the womb, and (rarely) neurological damage, mainly in adults. If you are pregnant or might become pregnant, check www.cdc.gov (see Zika travel information) for an updated map of regions with known Zika transmission, and advice on how to stay safe. The mosquitoes that carry Zika bite day or night, but more during the day. If you live in a Zika-infested area, you need to take special precautions to avoid being bitten (see page 418).

The virus also spreads through sexual contact, so if a partner may have been exposed to Zika, use condoms during pregnancy or (safer) avoid sex. If you think you may have been infected during pregnancy, get tested; there is also a blood test for newborns. Older children who acquire Zika usually have mild symptoms. Check with the doctor before giving any medicine.

SECTION IV

Raising Mentally Healthy Children

WHAT CHILDREN NEED

LOVE AND LIMITS

The surest way to raise mentally healthy children is to cultivate loving, nurturing, and mutually respectful relationships with them. Loving means, first of all, accepting your child as a person. Every child has strengths and weaknesses, gifts and challenges. Loving means adjusting your expectations to fit your child, not trying to adjust your child to fit your expectations.

Loving also means finding ways to be happy together, playing a tickling game, looking at picture books, going for a walk in the park, or just talking about different things. Children don't need such experiences all day long. But they do need at least some shared happiness every day.

Dr. Spock advised, "Love and enjoy your children for what they are, for what they look like, for what they do, and forget about the qualities that they don't have. I don't give you this advice just for sentimental reasons. There's a very important practical point here. The children who are appreciated for what they are, even if they are homely, or clumsy, or slow, will grow up with confidence in themselves and happy. They will have a spirit that will make the best of all the capacities that they do have, and of all the opportunities that come their way."

Children have other needs, too. Newborn babies need *everything*: feeding, changing, bathing, holding, and talking to. Over the first year of life, the experience of being nurtured creates a deep sense of trust in other people and optimism toward the world in general.

With growing abilities, children need more and more chances to do things for themselves; challenges that stretch their skills without overwhelming them; opportunities to take reasonable risks. Babies can't learn to feed themselves if they aren't allowed to make messes; children can't learn to run without skinning their knees.

Children want what they want when they want it. They need to learn the difference between wanting and needing, and that other people have needs and wants, too. They learn these lessons when parents treat them with kindness and respect and require the same in return. They learn how to handle frustration and disappointment, and what it means to be a grown-up, by watching their parents. Love is not enough. Children need love and limits, and people to look up to.

EARLY RELATIONSHIPS

Relationships and the wider world. What stimulates normal, well-rounded, emotional, social, and intellectual development? Babies and children are naturally social. Loving parents, watching and coaxing, make faces when their babies gaze at them, and smile back when their babies smile. Parents give food at times of hunger, comfort (and clean diapers) at times of misery. All of these things reinforce the child's feelings of being well cared for and connected to others.

These first feelings create a sense of trust, an optimism

about others. Even the baby's interest in the physical things of the world and her later capacity to deal with ideas and with challenges in and out of school rest on this secure base of love and trust.

A child needs to know that there is a least one loving, reliable adult to whom she belongs. This secure base gives her the confidence and motivation to follow her natural interests and master the skills that match her inborn talents. As children grow, they reach out to embrace the world, keeping part of themselves firmly rooted in the nurturing soil of their childhoods.

Early care. A child's experiences in the first two or three years of life have a profound effect on her personality. Babies and toddlers who are cared for by loving, enthusiastic parents, perhaps with the help of others, develop inner resources for coping with the inevitable challenges of growing up. By contrast, babies whose caregivers are distracted, distant, or unpredictable find it hard to keep fear and anger in check and to respond with openness and generosity. Learning is hard for them, because they can't tolerate the feeling of not knowing something yet. Their first instinct is to suspect that others are taking advantage of them, and so they try to be the ones who take advantage.

We've learned about the effects of extreme emotional neglect by studying babies and young children raised in cold orphanages where they are fed and changed but otherwise left alone in their cribs. (These places used to be common in the United States; they still exist elsewhere.) The destructive effects start showing up after about six months of age, and by twelve months they become hard to reverse, with lasting damage to language, thinking, and social relationships. Some children emerge intact, however. They are the ones who managed, even in the face of institutionalization, to develop a warm, loving relationship with one stable caregiver.

Why is a loving caregiver—whether mother, father, grandparent, or child care professional—so important to a young child's development? In the first year, a baby has to depend mainly on the attentiveness and intuition of adults to get the things that she needs. If the adults are insensitive or indifferent, she may become somewhat apathetic or depressed. If the adults are inconsistent—present one moment, absent the next—she may become wary and distrustful.

Children develop all of their core attitudes and skills through relationships. When they are treated with consistent kindness, they come to see others as loving, and themselves as worthy of being loved. Language skills, so central to a child's eventual ability to cope with emotions and the world, develop from the exciting back-and-forth exchanges between a baby and an attentive and responsive caregiver.

Whether children will grow up to be lifelong optimists or pessimists, warmly loving or distant, trustful or suspicious depends largely, although not entirely, on the attitudes of the individuals who care for them in their early years.

One person acts toward children as if they are basically bad, always doubting and scolding them. Children raised in this way may grow up doubting themselves, senselessly guilty. A person with more than average hostility finds a dozen excuses every hour for venting it on a child, and the child acquires a corresponding hostility. Other people have the itch to dominate children, and unfortunately they can succeed. These children often grow up to dominate their own children or to have such difficulty exerting authority that they can't set appropriate limits.

These are broad strokes, of course. What happens in any individual child is complicated, and much depends on the child's inborn temperament, strengths, and weaknesses. Still, how parents approach their children matters, and is something parents can think about and to some extent control.

Continuity of caregiving. From the age of a few months, babies come to love, count on, and derive their security from the one person, or at most a very few people, who provide most of their care. Even at six months, if the parent who has cared for them disappears for more than a brief time, babies can become depressed, losing their smile, their appetite, and their interest in things and people.

If a caregiver leaves, the baby may also experience a loss. It's best, therefore, if caregivers don't change suddenly during the first two or three years. If the main caregiver has to leave, it should be only after a substitute has gradually taken over. The substitute, in turn, needs to be committed to sticking with the job. In the group care of young children, if there are two or more staff people assigned to one group of children, each child should be paired up with one particular caregiver, or perhaps two, so that there will be continuity in the relationship.

SEX ROLES

Changing times, changing roles. When *Baby and Child Care* first appeared midway through the twentieth century, rigid sex roles were rarely challenged. Parents had the job of making sure that boys turned into "real men" and girls into "real women." Few parents (and no parenting experts) questioned what those designations or the assumptions behind them meant. Most doctors treated same-sex attraction as a sign of illness. The treatments for homosexuality were often as traumatic as they were ineffective.

We now know that sexual preferences and gender identity are determined by the brain, not by parenting (see pages 645–49). Gender roles, on the other hand, are defined by culture. Evolution has played a role in making the males of many species physically larger and more aggressive, humans included. But such group-level averages don't hold up at the level of individuals. For any trait, the amount of variability *within* each sex is greater than the variability *between* sexes. Which is to say, peace-loving boys are normal, as are girls who love a good fight. Despite the obvious stereotypes, plenty of normal boys love psychology and lots of normal girls love engineering.

The categories of effeminate men and masculine women hearken back to old, oppressive, stereotypes. As our culture pushes back against them, we give children permission to dress and act the way that feels most comfortable for them, free of fear. So the challenge for parents now is not "How do you make your sons and daughters into (real) men and women," but "How do you help your sons and daughters to be *themselves*?"

Mother and daughters, fathers and sons. Around three or four, the age when children really begin to take note of sex differences, a boy is likely to think about his father, "I'm going to grow up like him someday," and ditto a girl about her mother. A child's identification with a same-sex parent may be a strong force for development. Weakening sex stereotypes mean that children are now freer to emulate their *other*-sex parent, too: A girl can get her love of baseball or cooking from her dad; a boy can get his sense of fashion or appreciation of professional wrestling from his mom.

An element of competitiveness can also sneak in from the parents' side. A mother might feel a need to be more attractive than her adorable daughter; a father might feel the need to be a better athlete than his gifted son. You can imagine these competitive urges crossing sex lines, too—the father who must always be a better athlete than his gifted and driven daughter—but perhaps without quite the same energy. Competitiveness is common, and not always destructive. You might notice some of these motives in yourself, and make conscious choices about how you want to rein them in, or not.

Dr. Spock painted a sharp picture of one way competitiveness can hurt: "Sometimes a father is so eager to have his son turn out perfect that it gets in the way of their having a good time together. The man who is eager for his son to become an athlete may take him out at an early age to play catch. Naturally, every throw and every catch has its faults. If the father is constantly criticizing, even in a friendly tone, the boy becomes uncomfortable inside. It isn't any fun, and it gives him the feeling of being no good, in his father's eyes and in his own. A game of catch is fine if it's the son's idea and if it's for fun."

Apart from the gender role expectations, this vignette illustrates the balance to be struck between parents' ambitions for their children and the value of their simply having a good time together. We're ambitious for our children because we want them to have good lives, and also because successful children reflect well on us, and may gratify our own need to feel superior. If you detect this latter motivation in yourself, try to resist it. It's tough enough for children to make their own way, without having to carry around their parents' self-centered ambitions as well.

Single, or single-sex, parents. Children benefit from positive relationships with both their mothers and their fathers. But what if, as is often the case, there is only one parent available, or if the parents are of the same sex? Must the child's psychological well-being inevitably suffer?

The answer to this question is a resounding no. While it is true that children benefit from both male and female role models, they need not all live in the same home. What children need most of all is nurturing and love, someone who provides emotional support and teaches them the ways of the world. A child growing up with a single parent who delivers these necessities will be far better off than a child whose mother and father neglect his needs because of their own un-happiness. Most children from single-parent families find role models outside the home—a special uncle or aunt, perhaps, or a close friend of the family.

Children are adaptable. They don't need a perfect child-hood (as if such a thing ever existed). Given love and consis-tent care, they can thrive in all sorts of different family constellations.

FATHERS

Shared responsibility. Other than breastfeeding, fathers can do whatever mothers can, and they should. Everyone in the family benefits when parenting responsibility is shared in the spirit of equal partnership.

A father with a full-time job, even if the mother stays at home, will do best if he takes on half or more of the man-agement of the children and also participates in the house-work whenever he can. It's not just a matter of equity. Children profit from experiencing different parenting styles, and from seeing that everyone participates in run-ning the home; no one is anyone's servant; all serve each other. When a father does his share of the work at home, he does much more than simply lighten his wife's workload and give her companionship. He demonstrates that he be-lieves that this work is crucial to the welfare of the family, that it calls for judgment and skill, and that it's a shared duty. This is what sons and daughters need to see in action if they are to embrace their full range of opportunities and responsibilities.

For too long fathers have gotten away with the clever ruse that they lacked the intelligence, manual dexterity, and visual-motor skills to be capable of changing a smelly diaper! They can select clothes, wipe away tears, blow noses, bathe, put to bed, read stories, fix toys, break up quarrels, help with questions about homework, explain rules, and assign duties. Fathers can participate in the whole gamut of domestic work: shopping, food preparation, cooking and serving, dishwashing, bed making, housecleaning, and laundry.

There are increasing numbers of stay-at-home fathers whose partners, male or female, go off to full-time jobs. Children in such families grow up just as emotionally and mentally healthy as children reared in 1950s-style mom-and-pop families.

SELF-ESTEEM

Self-esteem, not self-satisfaction. Everybody, beginning in childhood, is entitled to a comfortable assumption that she is likable, that she is loved, and that doing her best is good enough. But children don't need to feel satisfied with themselves and appreciated by those around them all of the time. Parents don't have to be constantly complimenting their children, whether they really deserve it or not, in order to be sure that their children are not being deprived of self-esteem. The child who is constantly told that he is great in one way or another becomes insecure. "What if I weren't great?" he wonders. "What would happen to me then?"

Failure is part of self-esteem. It's good for a child to try something and fail, think of a way to do it better, and then try again. Failing well is a skill that can be developed. Children need at least as much practice at failing as at succeeding.

Parents are wise to praise effort, rather than results. There's no point in praising a child for being tall, or good-looking, or smart. These things just *are*. A grade of C+ that came as a result of sustained effort is more praiseworthy than an effortless A+. Praise should be reserved for the choices children make, not for their accomplishments.

That doesn't mean parents should constantly criticize, however, or assume the child has done, or is about to do, something wrong. Children who grow up under these conditions may develop a chronic sense of guilt and self-blame; their good behavior is bought at a high price.

The positive promotion of self-esteem. Children don't need compliments for every act of good behavior or for every small achievement. Take the example of the child whose parents have been encouraging him to learn to swim by praising him to the skies every time he momentarily ducks his head underwater. After an hour of this he is still demanding "Watch me swim" every minute, though he has made no real progress; he has only developed a greater appetite for praise and attention. Excessive compliments don't nurture independence (although they are much less destructive than the opposite, belittling and constant scolding).

Next to avoiding chronic scolding and belittling, the soundest way to foster self-esteem in your child is to show her an *enjoying love.* This means not just a devoted love that proves your readiness to make sacrifices for her, but an enjoyment of being with her, of hearing some of her stories and jokes, a spontaneous appreciation of some of her artwork or some of her athletic feats. You also show an enjoying love by occasionally suggesting an unanticipated treat, an excursion, or even a walk together. Effective parents also enjoy setting limits, because they understand that this is an important part of teaching their children what they need to know. It's not that they enjoy making their children unhappy by denying them things, but that they enjoy the whole process of helping a child grow and develop in every way.

Parents instill self-esteem by showing an attitude of respect for their children, such as one might show to a valued friend. This means not being rude or disagreeable, but instead being polite and gracious. There is no reason to feel free to be rude, gruff, or indifferent to our children just because they're younger than we are.

The one mistake most often made by parents who do show respect for their children is a failure to expect respect from their children in return. Children, like adults, feel more comfortable and happier when dealing with people who are self-respecting and who naturally, as a result, show that they expect respect from others. You don't have to be disagreeable to convey this expectation. When a child belches loudly at the dinner table, it's more effective to remind him to please cover his mouth than to yell at him. Respect is a two-lane street; you and your child go down it side by side.

BEYOND PARENTING

As a parent, you make choices that affect your child's life in the present and future. But many factors impact a child's mental health that are outside of any parent's reach. Realistically, you can't blame yourself for many of the hardships your child may face; nor can you honestly claim credit for the triumphs (although, really, we all do that anyhow).

Heredity. We know that many mental and emotional disorders are influenced by a person's genes. Depending on the illness, in many cases this influence can be quite powerful. For example, if both parents have manic-depressive disorder (also called bipolar), the chances are better than fifty-fifty that their child will, too. Anxiety, obsessive-compulsive disorder, schizophrenia, and attention deficit hyperactivity disorder (ADHD), are all heavily influenced by heredity, along with many other conditions.

In fact, it is likely that genes play a role in *every* mental health problem, either increasing or decreasing a child's susceptibility to stresses and temptations. Differences in susceptibility explain in part why two children raised by the same parents in the same household often follow very different mental health paths, and why identical twins raised apart often follow the same one.

Heredity also works by affecting a child's temperament, or style of behaving. One child is bubbly and outgoing; another is quiet and observant. One child seems upset by small changes in noise or light level; another barely seems to notice. One child always starts with a positive outlook; another starts with the negative and has to be won over to the positive.

Children who are often negative, intense, and persistent have been said to have a "difficult" temperament. But it's clear that temperament is either difficult or easy in relation to what is expected of a child. The temperaments of most five-year-old boys, with their high need for physical activity, are difficult in the context of a kindergarten classroom that demands a lot of desk work. You can't choose your child's temperament, but by understanding and accepting it, you can choose to respond in ways that help your child learn to function well with you, with peers, and with other adults. For example, you could look for a play-based kindergarten that builds in lots of time for physical activity.

Siblings. Parenting books often ignore the crucial role that siblings play in a child's growing up. But if you think about your own childhood, you'll probably agree that siblings—or the lack of them, if you are an only child—had a tremendous effect on your personality. Perhaps you modeled yourself after an older brother or sister who seemed to be able to do everything right, or maybe you chose to do very different things in order to stake out your own territory. If you were lucky, your siblings supported you, but if you had siblings who didn't (or don't) mesh well with your personality, you know how very difficult that can be.

There are ways for parents to take some of the edge off sibling jealousy, but whether siblings really like each other or just tolerate one another depends a lot on chance. Siblings who are close in age and compatible in temperament can be lifelong best friends. Siblings whose temperaments clash may never feel truly comfortable and relaxed together.

Parents often reproach themselves because they have different feelings about their different children. But they are expecting the impossible of themselves. Good parents love their children equally in the sense that they want the best for all of them, and will make any necessary sacrifices to achieve this. But since all children are different, no parent can feel just the same about any two of them. It is the acceptance and understanding of these different feelings, rather than feeling guilty about them, that will allow you to treat each of your children with the love and special attention he or she needs.

Birth order and spacing. It makes a difference where a child falls in the family. For example, oldest children tend to be task-oriented leaders and organizers. Youngest children are often spontaneous, self-involved, and a bit irresponsible. Middle children have less clear-cut roles and often end up finding their identities doing very different things from the other members of their families. Only children tend to combine characteristics of oldest children (high-achieving, for example), and youngest children (attention-seeking, for example).

These are only generalizations, of course. The dynamics within each family are unique. For example, if more than five years have passed between children, a youngest child might respond in some ways like an only child; if there is only about a year between children, they may act like twins. If the oldest child refuses to take over leadership of the siblings, a younger child may take on that role. A parent who is herself an oldest child might get along well with her own oldest but find her youngest child to be annoying in some ways (like her youngest sibling was). As a parent, you may be able to understand and influence these forces, but you can't really control them.

Peers and school. After age six or seven, the peer group becomes more and more important. A child's manner of speaking and dress and what he likes to talk about are all influenced by the kids in the neighborhood, at school, and on TV.

Sometimes neighborhood and peer forces can actively threaten a child's mental health. For example, children who are bullied may face a greater risk of developing long-term behavior disturbances (those who bully are also at risk). The child who has no friends at school is at high risk for depression; having even a single friend may make all the difference in the world. As a parent, you often have to step back and let your child work through the challenges of peer relationships. At other times, though, you may have to step in. One of the most important parenting decisions you ever make is the neighborhood and community you choose to live in.

RAISING CHILDREN IN A TROUBLED SOCIETY

It's hard to catalog the troubles facing American society at the end of the second decade of the twenty-first century. Our nation is wealthier than ever, but ever more plagued by uncertainty, inequality, and political division. Living standards are threatened for all but the richest, as middle-class jobs fail to keep pace with rising costs. Values of inclusion and tolerance are under fire, as are long-term commitments to the environment and international cooperation. The list of troubles goes on and on; it could fill books of its own; it *has*.

And yet, people are coming together to declare that black lives matter; that women's rights are human rights; that our communities embrace the diversity of religion, sexuality, and gender; that financial and corporate success may not be the sole measure of merit. People are coming out in numbers never seen before to raise their voices in support of their values.

Dr. Spock's comments, written decades back, called for just this change: "Children raised with strong values beyond their own needs—cooperation, kindness, honesty, tolerance of diversity—will grow up to help others, strengthen human relations, and bring about world security. Living by these values will bring far greater pride and fulfillment than the superficial success of a high-paying position or a new luxury car."

There are endless ways, large and small, to teach your children about caring for others and the world. When you drive at sixty miles per hour rather than seventy, and when you turn down the heat or turn off the air conditioner, talk about how you are saving fuel. When you see bigotry, ugliness, or injustice, speak out against it and let your children join you. Write letters to the editor. Work together with like-minded people in your community to take care of the less fortunate. Become involved politically. Some of the national groups working to improve children's lives are listed in the Resource Guide (see pages 892–99).

THE NATURAL WORLD

Watch a three-year-old explore the crack between two slabs of cement. A tiny spider crawling across a leaf fascinates her. Later she rolls down a grassy hill at the park, her face lit with pure joy.

Young children have a powerful connection to nature. Growing things of all kinds enthrall them. The slow-motion spectacle of a bean sprouting excites them. Given the chance, they gravitate to animals large and small. The moon and stars are characters in their imaginations. This special bond between children and nature suffuses many of the great works of children's literature: *Charlotte's Web, The Tale of Peter Rabbit, The Secret Garden, Goodnight Moon.*

Left to follow his own lead, a child outside naturally explores, pokes, prods, watches, and learns. He learns, among other things, to interact with a world that follows its own rules, different from the mechanical laws that define the world indoors. He learns to create his own entertainment and enjoy his own company. He locates himself in the natural world.

In an era when children lived much of their lives outdoors, these gifts of nature were often taken for granted or left to poets to describe. It's only now, when so many children live in cities, that science has begun to measure the medical and psychological benefits of nature. Compared to their indoor peers, children who regularly play outside are less prone to obesity, asthma, depression, anxiety, and ADHD. If nature could be put in a pill, doctors would prescribe it. (I am reminded that Dr. Spock's mother used to send him outside to play for hours at a time, rain or shine; she was convinced it was good for him. She was right.)

Give your children time in the woods and other wild spaces. Take walks in the parks where you live, wandering with no goal other than seeing what's there. Go to state parks on vacation and take the naturalist hikes. Find a group to go bird-watching with. Plant seeds.

The natural world can enhance your children's health and well-being. The connection runs in the opposite direction as well. Children whose love of nature is allowed to take root are apt to grow into allies of the natural world. They know why forests and rivers are worth fighting for and why it's worth-while to turn off unneeded lights and recycle aluminum cans. As a parent, you can give the world to your children and your children to the world.

THE IMPORTANCE OF RISK

Freedom, risk, and growth. If, as a child, you were allowed to roam about your neighborhood, to explore the alleys and empty lots, to cross streets to get to a friend's house, chances are you remember those times fondly. If you reflect on the experiences that were the most meaningful to you growing up, chances are they involved some risk. Maybe it was the first time you cooked dinner for your family; the first time you rode the city bus on your own; or the first time you went on an overnight camping trip with a friend.

Experiences like these allow children to see themselves as competent and independent, able to take on the world. They teach children to think and make decisions, to feel comfortable in their own company, and to figure out how to get along with their peers away from adult control. They build confidence and resilience.

In today's culture, many children are denied these experiences. As a result, they may turn to video games and online experiences that may seem to parents less risky than going outdoors (they aren't: see page 654). They become sedentary, and many become obese. Children may seek freedom and risk in other, less wholesome ways, such as experimenting with alcohol or drugs.

A false sense of danger. Contemporary parents have become so attuned to danger—from child molesters and abductors, bullies, bullets, busy streets, and children making foolish choices—that they feel they have no choice but to keep their children indoors or supervised at all times.

The reality is quite different. In all but the most crime-ridden of neighborhoods, the risks from random violence, drive-by molesters and other predators are minimal, and are no greater now than they were one or two generations ago, when children were much freer. This fact may be hard to believe; even so, it's true.

What's changed is not the risk, but our level of anxiety. In some cases, parents are swayed by sensational news stories, played over and over, that make it appear that children are being abducted from every street corner. In other cases, they're forced, by neighbors or police who perceive a child walking down the street alone or even waiting for the school bus as a child in danger, to over-supervise their children.

Letting in risk. Children need risk, within reason. This doesn't mean encouraging foolish risk-taking, such as riding a bike without a helmet or playing in traffic. It means letting children do things that might be a tiny bit dangerous, like sleeping outside in a tent, building a campfire, using a sharp knife, walking a few blocks to the library, or taking a bus downtown. As a parent, you may feel anxious at first, but your child will feel free and capable. Start with something small and simple, like cutting up an onion with a sharp knife or maybe walking to the corner store for milk. Your confidence, and your child's, can grow together.

To learn more about risk and how you can allow it into your child's life, and why you should, read *Free-Range Kids* by Lenore Skenazy.

LEARNING IN THE BRAIN

Neuroscience explains how people learn, why babies learn best when they have a chance to use their bodies and all of their senses, and why they repeat a behavior over and over, then suddenly lose all interest. We know why it's easier for them to learn certain skills at certain ages, such as picking up a second language before age ten. All thinking involves activity of the brain. As the brain acts, it changes, becoming more efficient at whatever it is doing. Experiences in the first years of life set the stage for later learning. Learning is lifelong, but the brain becomes less flexible, even as it becomes better at specialized tasks.

Genes and experience. For decades, scientists believed that the brain developed according to a detailed plan carried in the genes. Now we know that while genes draw the outlines, experience fills in the details of how the brain is wired, and therefore how it functions. Genes specify the brain areas that control basic body functions, such as breathing. Other functions, such as the ability to understand language and to speak, emerge later and are much more influenced by experience. We are born with unfinished brains. If our brains were finished at birth, they wouldn't adapt as readily to different surroundings. A child who grows up hearing Chinese develops the neural circuits required to process the sounds of Chinese and loses the ability to perceive sounds that aren't important in that language. An analogous process happens in the child who loses the ability to perceive sounds that aren't meaningful in English, including many sounds in Chinese. This kind of adaptation affects other senses as well. For example, children who grow up in modern houses become better at perceiving straight lines and squared-off angles than do children who grow up in rounded huts.

Use it or lose it. How does the brain adapt so well? A large part of the answer lies in a simple rule that governs the connections between neurons: Use it or lose it. Brain activity depends on nerve cells passing signals across tiny gaps called synapses. Each time two nerves activate a particular connection, that synapse grows stronger. As the brain develops, stronger synapses remain, while weaker ones wither away.

Early on, the brain makes many more synapses than it needs. A two-year-old baby has more synapses than a twenty-two-year-old Harvard graduate. By getting rid of unused synapses, the brain makes itself faster and more efficient. At the same time, though, it becomes harder for the brain to adapt in completely new directions. So, for example, our Harvard graduate can readily learn complicated concepts in history (an area she has studied) but has a very hard time learning the sounds of Mandarin Chinese, something that requires her brain to work in an entirely new way (and something our two-year-old can do with relative ease).

Brains exposed early to a wide range of experiences develop with the greatest flexibility. Babies need things to feel, bang, taste, draw with, build, take apart, jump on, jump off, hold, throw—a full range of stimuli. They need to hear lots of words and have the experience of being listened to. As they grow, the neural connections strengthened by their early experiences allow them to acquire all kinds of new information.

Again! Again! At ten months, a baby grabs the bars of her crib and, using all the strength in her chubby arms and legs, pulls herself up to standing. Unsure of what to do next, she lets go, bumping back down on her bottom; a minute later she is pulling up again. This continues until she starts fussing or falls asleep exhausted. This baby is not only exercising her muscles, she's exercising her brain. Each time she repeats the process of pulling up and standing, she strengthens a particular set of synapses that eventually will give her the balance and coordination she needs to stand on her own. Once she has mastered this skill, the pulling-up routine loses all interest for her and she moves on to her next project. You can see this sort of repetition in every area of development. Your baby's obsessive interest in putting blocks into a bucket is evidence that his brain is busy wiring itself up.

Learning and emotion. We're used to thinking about emotions as being very different from logic. In fact, they are closely connected. When a baby is learning, he's generally attentive, involved, and happy. Positive emotions are the fuel that powers children's exploring and learning. In another way, emotions both positive and negative make learning possible. Young children pay attention only to things that evoke positive or negative emotions. (Later, we learn to make ourselves pay attention to certain things because we know we have to, but we never learn them as well as when we're emotionally involved.) In the brain, the neural systems that produce emotions are closely connected to the systems that produce logical thought. In babies and young children, a good sign that they are learning is that they are laughing, smiling, and cooing, or simply looking with an intent, serious gaze. All of the loving you give a baby—the rocking, holding, tickling, singing, and talking—feeds her emotional growth, and at the same time strengthens her desire and ability to learn.

HOW CHILDREN THINK

Piaget's insights. How do babies and children learn to make sense of the world? Some of the earliest, and still best, answers came from a Swiss psychologist named Jean Piaget. Piaget initially developed his theories simply by making careful observations of his three young children. He then spent the rest of his life trying to prove these theories through careful scientific study, but it was watching the day-to-day development of children that got him started. You can do the same. Piaget believed that human development proceeds in stages. Through a careful description of these stages, he explained how an infant with little ability to think abstractly comes to be able to reason logically, create hypotheses about how things work, and invent new ideas and behaviors that he has never seen or heard before.

Little scientists. Piaget saw infants and children as little scientists, born with a drive to make sense of the world through constant experimentation. A four-month-old who keeps dropping food off the high chair and then looking for it is experimenting with the idea of gravity. He's also experimenting with the idea that objects continue to exist even if they're out of sight, a concept psychologists call *object permanence.*

Until a baby repeats this experiment many times, nothing really exists for him except what he is seeing and touching at that moment: Out of sight is out of mind. At three months, an infant drops her pacifier by accident and is surprised to see it on the floor a few seconds later. This happens again, and then again. Slowly, it begins to dawn on her that the object on the floor is the same one that was just in her hand. She gets the idea that if she just saw something and now it's gone, it must be on the floor. If it's not on the floor, then it probably no longer exists. It is not until the next stage, at about eight months, that her ideas about object permanence become more sophisticated and she begins to search elsewhere for missing objects.

Infants love to play peekaboo for the same reason: The face is there, then it's not, and then it is. The infant's capacity to continue this game is boundless because it is exactly one of the questions he is working on. Once he is satisfied that faces continue to exist even if he can't see them, peekaboo falls by the wayside and a new game, one that is appropriate to his current developmental questions, arises.

Sensorimotor thinking. In other words, young children learn by doing, by exercising their senses and their motor (muscle) abilities. If a baby learns to hold a rattle, she has the idea that rattles are for holding. When she shakes the rattle, bangs it on her high chair, and puts it in her mouth, she's showing that she has more ideas about rattles. If you take the rattle and hide it under a cloth, does she pull the cloth away to get at the rattle? If so, she has the idea that objects (or at least rattles) can be hidden and found. (At this point, around nine months, it becomes harder to take things away from her when you no longer want her playing with them.)

Babies are also learning about cause and effect. At four or five months, if you tie one end of a string to a baby's ankle and the other end to a mobile hanging over the crib, the baby soon learns to move his leg to make the mobile move. (Be sure you take the string with you when you go, so that it can't get wrapped around your baby's arm or neck.) Babies later learn to use objects as tools—for example, using a stick to get a toy that is out of reach. Later, they discover that hidden causes can have effects, like the springs inside windup toys. Most babies figure out how to make them work between eighteen and twenty-four months.

During the sensorimotor period, babies begin to understand words and use them to get what they want. Once toddlers start putting words together into interesting combinations, around eighteen to twenty-four months, words become a flexible tool for thinking. When that happens, the sensorimotor period comes to an end.

The key thing to understand is that thinking develops in stages. It's a mistake to rush the process, skipping over sensorimotor learning and going straight to more advanced verbal learning. All the banging, smearing, and messing around that babies do is necessary to prepare their brains to take the next step.

Preoperational thinking. Piaget used the word "operation" to mean reasoning in a logical way. He thought of preschool-age children, of between about two and four, as preoperational, because children that age don't think logically. For example, a three-year-old might think that rain falls because the sky is sad, or that she got sick because she was bad. A child in the preoperational stage mainly sees things from her own point of view. She's self-centered, but not necessarily selfish. For example, if her father is unhappy, she might bring over her own favorite stuffed animal to try to comfort him—after all, it works for her!

A young child's ideas about quantity are also illogical. Piaget showed this in a famous experiment in which he gave young children a low, wide dish full of water. Then he poured the water into a tall, narrow glass. Almost all of the children said that the glass held more, because it looked bigger. The fact that the same water could be poured back and forth between the dish and the glass didn't change the children's minds. Any poor doctor who has tried to convince a two-year-old that the needle he is about to use is really very small knows that to a child in the prelogical phase, the actual size of an object is not nearly as important as how big it *seems*. The same sort of confusion causes many young children to fear that they could be swept down the bathtub drain.

Concrete operations. Most children during the early school years, from about age six through nine or ten, are capable of logical thinking but not abstract thinking. Piaget called these early logical thoughts *concrete operations:* logical reasoning applied to things you can see and feel. This kind of thinking also shows up in children's approach to right and wrong. A six-year-old is likely to feel that a game can only be played by one set of rules. It would be wrong to change the rules, even if all the players agreed, because rules have to be followed. A nine-year-old might consider breaking a window with a wildly thrown baseball to be a more serious crime than stealing a candy bar, because the window costs more. The fact that the window breaking was completely unintentional, while the candy theft was premeditated, would not necessarily figure in this concrete-operational reasoning.

Another area where a concrete-operational child might have difficulty is in figuring out other people's motivations. It's fascinating to read a story to a young school-age child and then ask her to explain why certain characters did what they did. You'll quickly discover that what may seem obvious to you is actually very hard for your bright eight-year-old to grasp. I recommend trying this with a classic like *Charlotte's Web* by E. B. White or *Homer Price* by Robert McCloskey.

Abstract thinking. Toward the end of grade school, children begin to think more about abstract qualities such as justice or destiny. Their thinking becomes much more flexible, allowing them to imagine many different solutions to a physical or social problem. They start to reason from principles to particulars and back again. Abstract reasoning of this sort often leads teens to question their parents' teachings and values, making for sometimes heated dinnertime conversation. It can also lead teens to develop a high level of idealism, which can become a powerful political force.

Not all teens reach this state of *formal operations,* as Piaget termed it. They may use abstract thinking in some areas but not in others. For example, a fifteen-year-old who loves computers may think abstractly about firewalls and file-sharing protocols, but quite concretely when it comes to friendships with girls. In some ways, he might even be preoperational. For example, he might harbor the utterly illogical belief, common among teens, that he is invulnerable. It's what allows him to smoke cigarettes and get into cars with other teens who have been drinking.

Children are different. An understanding of cognitive development leads to an important point: Children are not little adults. They understand the world in ways that are fundamentally different from the ways most adults do. Depending on their cognitive stage, they may be more self-centered, more rigid, or more idealistic. What makes perfect sense to us may make little or no sense to a child. A parent who offers a long intellectual explanation to a two-year-old about why she should share is missing this point. Although sharing is not part of any child's way of seeing the world at that stage, that doesn't mean that it won't be later on. This same misunderstanding causes some adults to tell teenagers not to smoke because they might get lung cancer and die in forty years. It's more effective to talk about immediate consequences, like bad breath and decreased athletic performance. That's what really counts in their world.

Multiple intelligences. Piaget's theories explain a lot about children's thinking, but they don't tell the whole story. For example, we now know that very young babies are capable of feats of memory and even of simple mathematics that we never thought possible. Another advance has been the realization that the verbal-analytical intelligence Piaget talked about, which is the kind measured by the standard IQ tests, is only one of several kinds of intelligence. People display multiple intelligences, including spatial, musical, bodily-kinesthetic (movement), interpersonal (relationships with others), intrapersonal (self-understanding and insight into others), and naturalist (understanding and classifying objects in nature).

Uneven intelligence. Multiple intelligences make sense when you understand intelligence as the processing of information by the brain. Information of all sorts flows through the brain all the time—for example, information about tones and rhythms in speech or music, or about the position of one's body in space. Different parts of the brain process this information and combine it in different ways. It's possible for one area of the brain to be working quite well, while another is not. For example, people who have damage to the part of the brain that controls speech may not be able to talk, but they may be able to sing words, if the parts of the brain that house musical ability are intact.

Nobody is equally endowed with all the intelligences. One child learns best by listening, another by watching, another by holding something physical in her hand, and still another by acting out a concept with her whole body. Someone can be verbally gifted but completely at a loss when it comes to figuring out how to drive across town. When these inequalities in intelligence are very marked, they can create learning disabilities.

As you pay attention to your child's different intelligences, you may realize that some of the things you thought he was avoiding out of laziness are actually more difficult for him than you suspected. You may also recognize areas in which your child is gifted, even though these gifts may not translate to higher grades. By expanding your focus to include multiple intelligences, you can appreciate and nurture more of your child's strengths, and more of your own.

At the same time, don't put too much stock in intelligence. In the long run, success relies much more on a child's ability to persist at what's difficult than on her capacity to catch on quickly. A child who works steadily for C's deserves more praise than a child who coasts into A's.

READING ALOUD

Literacy is more than just reading and writing. Literate adults use reading to learn about things, and writing to share their ideas. Literate children view reading and writing as exciting and worthwhile in their own right. Literacy feeds their imaginations and widens their world. Often, literacy starts with a parent reading aloud. If you were lucky enough to have been read to when you were a child, you'll naturally want to share the pleasure with your child.

It's true that some children do well in school without ever having been read to. But the chances of success go way up if a child starts school already loving books. When you sit down with your child and a book, many wonderful things happen. By talking about the pictures, you expose her to lots of new and interesting words. By reading and rereading, you give her many opportunities to learn how the words come together in interesting sentences. You build up her listening and attention skills. And you help her begin to see the connections between the letters she sees and the words she hears. Most of all, it's the joyful interaction with a loving parent that brings picture books to life for children and makes being read to such a powerful experience.

Bilingual families. Children who grow up hearing two languages have a real advantage. While they often take a bit longer to start expressing themselves clearly, once they get going, they quickly become fluent speakers in both languages.

Parents should talk with their young children in the language they speak best. If they grew up elsewhere and don't speak English perfectly, they should talk and read to their children in their native language. It's much more helpful for a child to hear a language—*any* language—spoken well than to hear English spoken badly. A child who learns Spanish or Russian at home can quickly pick up English in preschool. A child who never learns to speak any language well (because he did not have the chance to hear a language spoken well) has a much harder time.

Many picture books are now available in the United States in languages other than English, and many have English and a second language printed on the same page—a great way for parents and children to learn together. How do you find these gems? Ask a librarian!

With a monolingual book, you may be able to make your own rough translation on the fly, or make up a completely new story in whatever language you want. In any language, it's much better for children to have a free-flowing back-and-forth conversation than to sit quietly and listen to words read out mechanically.

Reading to newborns. Newborns enjoy the sound of the reader's voice and the feeling of being held. Many parents start reading aloud while they're still pregnant, and their babies are born already knowing and loving the sound of their mother's and father's reading voices, which are distinct from conversational speech. Babies are hardwired to listen. Doing so calms them down. You can see their bodies relax as they focus their attention.

With newborns, it doesn't much matter what you read. Choose something that interests you—gardening, sailboats, or a novel—or something that you and your partner both enjoy. Take turns reading to each other while you cuddle with your new baby. If you choose poetry, your baby will come to love the rhythm and music of poems. Try *A Child's Garden of Verses,* by Robert Louis Stevenson (for more, go to drspock .com). And remember to sing, too!

Sharing books with babies. By six months, your baby is apt to react to a new, brightly colored book with excitement. He reaches for it, pats at it, growls, or "talks" in an excited way. He holds it, waves it about, bangs it, and chews on it. Don't be worried by this gleeful manhandling. Children learn to respect and take care of books gradually, as they come to understand their special value.

Pick board books with simple, bright pictures. Photos of other babies are a favorite. Pick some simple poetry that rhymes. If your baby likes it (and many do), read your own grown-up book out loud, stopping frequently to talk with your baby. Babies this age don't understand the words, but they like the sounds.

At somewhere around nine months of age, babies begin

to develop wills of their own. They want to feed themselves, and they often want to be in charge of their books. If reading time begins to resemble a battle, change your tactics. Try using two books, one for your baby and one for you. Read for shorter periods. It's okay to use the book as a plaything. Reading is supposed to be fun. Let your child take the book, bang it, and flip the pages. Meanwhile, you might discover a special picture now and then and show it to your baby, letting your voice convey your excitement.

Try playing peekaboo with the pictures by covering a favorite character, then asking, for instance, "Where's Clifford?" If there's a poem, read it rhythmically. Move your body (and the baby in your arms) in time with the words. If the book has pictures of babies, touch the pictures and then touch your baby in the same place.

Some babies love to listen for a long time (five to ten minutes or more). More active babies may only pay attention for a minute or less. The amount of time is not important. What matters is the shared enjoyment. If your baby seems bored, or if *you* are, pick a different book or do something else.

Toddlers and books. Between nine and twelve months of age, some babies begin to understand that things have names. Once they have this idea firmly established, they want to hear the names of everything. A picture book is the perfect vehicle for naming games. With a familiar picture book, ask, "What's that?" Pause for an instant and then give the answer. If your baby loves this game, it is because his mind is open to learning. You won't hear him saying these new words right away, but over the next year or two, you're likely to be amazed at his vocabulary.

As time goes by, toddlers pay more attention to what the pictures show. A twelve- to fifteen-month-old may be content to hold the book upside down. Starting at around eighteen months, many children will turn the book around so that the pictures are right side up.

Many younger toddlers love movement. Those who are not walking yet still love the rocking, tickling, and hugging that go along with reading aloud. Those who are walking may only sit still for a few minutes at a time, but they often enjoy listening from across the room. Mobile toddlers will often carry a book around or bring it to a grown-up to read.

A toddler who is discovering his own will may insist on picking the same book over and over, protesting if you make a different selection. To avoid a power struggle, store books on a low shelf so that your toddler can get them out and put them back herself. Put only three or four books out at a time; too many makes the choice overwhelming and just increases the number of books you'll have to pick up off the floor.

By eighteen months, many toddlers are walking steadily. A favorite activity now becomes walking while carrying some-thing, often a book. A toddler who knows that a book is a ticket to attention from parents will walk over and deposit one on a parent's lap, often accompanied by the demand, "Read!"

Reading with an older toddler. As they approach their second birthday, toddlers are making great strides in language development. Books help teach language by giving the older toddler many opportunities to name things and get feedback from a grown-up. The parent points at a picture and asks, "What's that?" Then, depending on what the toddler responds, the parent either says the name of the object and praises the child or offers a kind correction: "Nope, that's not a dog, that's a horse!"

What makes this sort of back-and-forth teaching so powerful is that it happens over and over. For a young child, repetition is a key to learning. That the same pictures come up again and again paired with the same words on the same page allows him to feel a measure of control. The child expects a particular picture or word to show up on the next page—and it does!

At the same time your toddler is mastering new words, he also is figuring out how they come together to make sentences and how sentences make stories. You may not see the results of this learning for many months. But by two and a half to three years, you may notice your child using complex story-like phrases in his play, such as "Once upon a time" or "What's gonna happen next?" The seeds of rich language are planted early through much experience with books and stories.

At this age, children are also becoming interested in the letters and words, especially if these are large and colorful. They learn that print tells the story.

The wrecking crew. Babies and toddlers are rough on books. Many bent pages can be expected, and even a tear here and there. Scribbling on the pages of a book is something almost every toddler does at least a few times in her literary career. While it looks destructive, it's a toddler's way of getting into the book.

A gentle reminder that books need tender loving care works better than scolding (which might just convince your toddler that books are too much trouble altogether). Even better, get some scrap paper and some crayons and let your toddler scribble to his heart's content on these pages. The first step on the road to writing is scribbling. If you look at your toddler's artistic creations over time, you might well start to see letter-like shapes.

Different learning styles. One toddler who is very visual in her approach to the world might spend long minutes studying the pictures or printed words in a book. Try a book with a partially hidden character. A visually oriented toddler will delight in finding the duckling on each page of Nancy Tafuri's *Have You Seen My Duckling?*.

A verbally oriented toddler will love to listen to the sound of words. Poetry is especially attractive because of the rhyme and rhythm. A story with a repeated chant ("Fee-fi-fo-fum" in "Jack and the Beanstalk") delights many toddlers, and because it is predictable, they can join in the reading.

Many young children learn best by moving their bodies and by touching. If there is motion in the story (a boat rocking on the waves, a baby on a swing, a horse galloping, or a mom stirring soup), you can act out the motion with your toddler. Talking, touching, moving, and playing make the book come alive to all of your toddler's senses.

All children learn best when they are actively involved. They love the opportunity to act out parts of the books they're listening to. So if you're reading a story about magic genies and flying carpets, you might want to dig out an old teapot and a rug or a sheet. Your child will know just what to do.

Reading with preschoolers. Preschool children have wonderful imaginations. In their minds, magic really happens. Because they don't have a lot of experience of how the world works, young children believe in many things that older children reject, like Santa Claus. In a sense, they live in a world that their imagination creates. It's natural, then, that preschoolers love storybooks.

You know that a child is caught up in the imaginative world of a book when she responds with real emotions to events in the book. Characters from the book may come alive in her play. Words from the book sneak into her vocabulary.

Preschool children want to feel a sense of control, by choosing which book to read. When a child chooses the same book over and over, it's a sign that there is something in that book that is very important to her. It may be an idea (for example, the idea of overcoming an obstacle, as in "Three Billy Goats Gruff") or a visual image (perhaps the picture of the troll under the bridge), or even just a single word. Whatever it is, once the child completely understands it, she usually moves on to a new book.

There are many ways to enjoy books and reading with your preschool child:

+ Have books all over the house—in the living room, in the bathroom, by the kitchen table, and especially in her bedroom.

+ Get a set of plastic letter magnets for the refrigerator, or foam letters for the tub.

+ Make bedtime or waking up in the morning—or both—regular times for reading together. Let your child tell you when she's had enough; also, stop when *you* have had enough. It's great if children love books, but it's always the grown-up's job to set limits.

✦ Limit TV viewing. A no-TV diet is best for preschoolers. The vivid images on TV (even, or especially, in cartoons) tend to overwhelm their sensitive imaginations, so there is no space left for the quieter but still compelling images from books (see page 151).

✦ Use your public library. In addition to a huge selection of books, many libraries offer story hours, play groups, and child-size tables and chairs for comfortable perusing. An outing to the library can feel special, even if it happens every week.

✦ Don't feel that you have to keep reading to the bitter end. If your child loses interest, the best thing to do is to stop and perhaps try a different book. It may also be that the book has touched on issues that are emotionally charged for your child. Squirming or falling asleep may be your child's way of saying, "I've heard enough for now."

✦ Invite your child to participate. Children learn most from reading aloud, and probably benefit the most emotionally, if they participate actively. That may mean making comments or even interrupting the reading to talk about an idea or feeling that comes up. Reading aloud shouldn't be a performance; it should be more like a discussion.

✦ Make up stories yourself and encourage your preschooler to help you. If you come up with a story you really like, write it down. You can make your own storybook, then read it aloud. See drspock.com for more suggestions and resources!

Reading aloud with an older child. Reading aloud doesn't have to end just because your child gets older. If it's something you both love to do together, there are many good reasons to continue. Sharing pleasant and interesting experiences makes your relationship stronger. Having a reservoir of positive feelings helps you and your child cope with disagreements and other tensions that are an inevitable part of growing up.

Reading aloud keeps interest high. Between first grade and third or fourth grade, children are still developing their basic reading skills. During that time, many of the books that are simple enough for them to read themselves are too simple for them to find interesting. But by reading aloud together, you can help your child enjoy more difficult books that are likely to keep her engaged until her reading ability catches up with her interests.

Reading aloud is especially important if your child is having difficulty learning to read. Some children find reading easy. Others, equally bright, find it quite challenging at first, often because their brains are taking longer to reach the level of maturation needed for reading. In time—most often by the end of third grade—they catch up and do just fine. But until that happens, reading is likely to be difficult, and many children sour on it. If they have parents who read to them, however, they're much more likely to continue to love books and to persist and eventually gain the skills they need for independent reading.

Reading aloud also builds listening skills. It's a good idea to stop from time to time and talk about the story with your child. First of all, you want to make sure that she is following the plot. Ask why a particular character did what he did, or ask your child what she thinks is going to happen next. When you ask open-ended questions, you strengthen your child's ability to think about what she hears and make sense of it.

Reading aloud builds vocabulary. There are words in books that you almost never hear in everyday speech. One of the best children's books of all time, *Charlotte's Web* by E. B. White, is written mostly in plain English. But even here, you find interesting words like "injustice," "terrific," and "humble." Don't be surprised if you hear your child using some of these "book words" when she speaks. Many children love to play with new words, and in the process they are building skills that will help them throughout their school careers.

Stories are the building blocks of imagination. Children take bits and pieces of the stories they hear and use them in their own make-believe. So if you want your child to have a rich imagination, let her hear lots of good stories. The same thing happens when children watch television: They build the stories into their play. But because the images on television are so vivid, children don't need to use their imagination as much. Consequently, during playtime they often simply copy what they see on television rather than creating their own stories.

Books help teach character. Many educators and psychologists believe that books are one of the best ways children learn about right and wrong. As they see how characters react in a given situation—how they treat their friends, for example, or what they do when they want something that isn't theirs—children get a clearer picture of what's admirable behavior and what's not. Stories let children live in the skin of others for a time, feeling what they feel. This experience builds empathy and understanding.

Choosing nonracist, nonsexist books. Books carry powerful messages, both in what they say and in how they say it. Books that portray respect for people of all colors, cultures, and ethnicities, and avoid sexual stereotypes help children take an accepting and positive view of themselves and the rest of humanity. Look for children's books that embrace the richness of our multicultural society.

In judging a book, look at the story line. Do people of color or females play important, leading roles? Are cultural beliefs and practices portrayed accurately? Are different lifestyles depicted in a positive light? Look at the characters. How are individual characters presented? Who has the power? Who are the heroes in the story? Who are the villains? Look at the illustrations. Are characters drawn in a way that avoids stereotypes? Do people have a variety of facial features and other physical characteristics, as well as different colors of skin?

What messages does the story send? Does it glorify violence or revenge? Stories in which the hero's only virtue is brute strength do not help children value their own positive qualities. By contrast, heroes who also show compassion, resourcefulness, and courage allow children to feel that they might be like those heroes in their own small way.

CHILD CARE

PARENTS WORK

Parents work, taking care of their children, making money, or advancing their careers. The old model with Daddy heading to the job while Mommy looks after the kids is one option; in some families these roles are reversed. Often the arrangements are complicated and change from day to day and year to year. Each family makes choices to balance everyone's needs. It isn't a simple matter of sacrificing oneself for the sake of the children: Children need happy, fulfilled parents if they are going to grow up to be happy, fulfilled adults. In what follows, "work" refers to a paying job or training, even though, of course, parenting is work, too.

WHEN TO RETURN TO WORK

How long a maternity leave should you take? It's a personal decision. Three to six months seems right for many families. This gives your baby time to settle into regular feeding and sleeping routines and to get used to the rhythm of her family. It also gives you time to adjust to your own physiological and psychological changes and to establish nursing and add a bottle or two during work hours. By about four months most babies are showing more interest in the world around them, so the process of separating for several hours a day is more acceptable to most parents.

Mixed feelings are normal, whatever month you return. After a few weeks, many parents are eager to get back on the job, if only to have adults to talk with during the day. But they often also feel sad about leaving their babies. Or they simply want more time with them. If you have the option, listen to your feelings. If you feel you need more time at home with your baby, try to take it.

Family and Medical Leave Act (FMLA). This is the federal law that sets minimum standards for maternity leave. It requires employers with more than fifty employees to allow up to twelve weeks of unpaid leave for a mother or father after the birth or adoption of a child. Many parents and children need more time together, but often feel that they don't have a realistic option to stay out for even the full twelve weeks. In many other countries, new mothers are allowed far longer with their babies before having to return to their jobs, and often continue to be paid. In Britain, for example, they receive nine months of paid leave; in India, six months for a first child; in Serbia, a full year.

Remember, fathers can also provide child care. Under U.S. law, fathers have the same right to twelve weeks of family leave that mothers do. The mother can take the first twelve weeks and then the father can take over for the next twelve weeks. That gives you twenty-four weeks before starting child care. Both parents can take leave at the same time, if you prefer.

CHILD CARE ALTERNATIVES

Arrangements in the first year. In the United States, at some point in their first year of life, most children spend at least part of their day in the care of someone other than their parents. Studies have shown that young infants can thrive in nonparental care with no harm to their intellectual or emotional development. This is true, on average, for children in child care programs that are of high quality. A particular baby, however, might have difficulty adjusting to group care; for that baby, quiet one-to-one care may be what she needs to thrive. You're the best person to decide what will work for your child.

If you have misgivings about a particular program or sitter for your child, listen to your instincts and make other arrangements.

Altered work schedules. Often the best solution is one in which the parents' work schedules can be altered so that both can work a reasonably full shift and yet one or the other can be at home for most of the day. More and more businesses are offering flexible hours, a win-win option that increases both worker satisfaction and productivity. If business slows, many companies cut hours rather than lay people off; the ability to use these hours flexibly to meet family needs can be a silver lining to the dark cloud of decreased pay.

Of course, parents need to be together during sleeping times as well as for some of the children's waking hours. A nonparent caregiver can fill in any uncovered hours. A relative with whom the parents see eye to eye may be an ideal fill-in caregiver. Another solution is for one or both parents to cut down to part-time jobs for two to three years, until the child is old enough to attend preschool or a day care center. Of course, this solution is out of reach for many families that require two full-time breadwinners to meet their expenses and provide health insurance.

In-home caregivers (sitters). Some working parents engage a caregiver to come to their home. If the caregiver works several hours a day, this person will become a formative influence on the young child's developing personality. So parents should try to find a person who shows nearly as much love, interest, responsiveness, and firmness as they do.

Far and away the most important trait is the person's disposition. She should be affectionate, understanding, comfortable, sensible, and self-confident. (Of course, a paid caregiver could be male, too.) She should love and enjoy children without smothering them with attention. She should be able to control them without nagging or severity. In other words, she should get along with them happily. It is a help when interviewing a prospective caregiver to have your child with you. You can tell how she responds to a child better by her actions than by what she says. Avoid the person who is cross, reproving, fussy, humorless, or full of theories about raising children.

A common mistake that parents make is to look first of all for a person with a lot of experience. It's natural that they should feel more comfortable leaving a child with someone who knows what to do for colic or croup. But illnesses and injuries are a small part of a child's life. It's the minutes and hours of every day that count. Experience is fine when it's combined with the right personality. With the wrong personality, it's worth very little.

Cleanliness and carefulness are more important than experience. You can't let someone make the baby's formula who refuses to do it correctly. Still, there are many rather untidy people who are careful when it's important. Better a person who is too casual than one who is too fussy.

Some parents focus on the education of a caregiver. But education is less important than a caregiver's personal qualities, especially for young children. Others are concerned that the caregiver may speak little English. But in the vast majority of cases, children are not confused by the different languages of the caregiver and parents. If the caregiver stays with the child for years, the child may reap the benefits of having learned two languages at home.

Sometimes, inexperienced young parents settle for a caregiver about whom they don't really feel right because they've decided they can't do any better, or because the person talks a good line. Keep looking until you find someone you really like. When you find the right person, pay as much as you can afford (or perhaps a bit more), so that it is hard for that person to even consider working elsewhere. When you are away at work, the knowledge that your child is in excellent hands is worth a lot.

Concerns about caregivers. If you've found a good caregiver, your child will become attached to her. When this happens, it's natural to feel jealous. But children who come to love their sitters don't love their parents any less. Try to be aware of your feelings and deal with them openly; if not, you may slip into being unfairly critical of the caregiver. On the other hand, some caregivers have a great need to take over the child, to push the parents aside, and to show that they always know best. They may be quite unconscious of this need, and they can rarely be reformed.

A common problem is that a caregiver may favor the youngest child in the family, especially one who was born after she joined the household. If she can't understand the harm in doing this, she should not stay. Favoritism of this sort is destructive to the child who is favored, as well as to the children who are not.

As the parent, you need to stay in control. At the same time, it's important to feel that you and the caregiver are partners. The most important questions for caregivers and parents are whether they can be honest with themselves, listen to each other's ideas and criticisms, keep the lines of communication open, respect each other's good points and good intentions, and cooperate for the benefit of the children.

Care by relatives. It's great if there's a relative—a grandparent, for example—who can take care of your child. But all of the issues that apply to unrelated caregivers, discussed above, also apply to family. It's very important that any family member who helps care for your child understands that you are still the parent: What you say goes. As long as you have this understanding, then care by a relative can be a wonderful alternative.

Day care centers. "Day care center" is a term used to specify a place for out-of-home group care of children during their parents' working hours, often 8:00 a.m. to 6:00 p.m. Some day care centers are subsidized by government agencies or by private companies. At its best, day care offers the advantages of the preschool: an educational philosophy, trained teachers, and full educational equipment.

The concept of the day care center in the United States originated during World War II, when the federal government wanted to encourage mothers with young children to work in war industries. It began primarily for the care of children from age two to five, but now it frequently includes younger children, including infants, as well as after-school care for kindergartners and first and second graders.

Day care centers are usually open year-round. They offer a stable, structured setting with an explicit child care philosophy that you can evaluate. However, this type of care tends to be expensive. Staff turnover tends to be high, so it's unlikely that your child will be consistently cared for by the same person. The level of training of the staff and the child-to-staff ratio are quite varied. There are great differences in the quality of day care centers. Day care centers should be licensed, showing that they meet minimal safety standards. Many are accredited as well, which is a higher quality standard.

Family day care. Family day care, where a provider and one or two assistants look after a small number of children in the provider's home, is a popular choice. In fact, many more children attend family day care than attend larger day care centers. Family day care may be more convenient and affordable than large day care centers, and more flexible in its hours. A young child may feel more comfortable in a smaller group with a family-like atmosphere. Staff turnover is usually less of a problem, so children have the opportunity to develop trusting relationships with one or two care providers—a very good thing.

On the other hand, many family day cares are unlicensed and unaccredited. Therefore, it's harder to be sure that basic health and safety measures are in place. Also, because there are fewer adults involved, the potential for abuse or neglect of children is higher. So if you choose a family day care, it's very important that you feel completely comfortable with the providers and are welcome to drop in anytime and stay as long as you want. Your child should be glad to go to the day care, and when you pick your child up, you should hear about what she did during the day. .

Is day care good for young children? There is a debate in the United States about the value or harm of day care for very young children. Some claim that group experiences are inappropriate for children in the first few years of life. They argue that every child needs one or two significant caretakers who are crazy about him, who give him their undivided attention, and who have a strong attachment to him. The opponents of day care worry that children raised at an early age by multiple caretakers will have difficulty with later interpersonal relationships. Finally, they contend that there is no better teacher for a child than an intensely involved parent.

Day care advocates tell a different story. They assert that there are many proper ways to raise a young child. They point to other cultures where infants are raised by siblings and extended family without apparent ill effects. They remind us that a decade of studies demonstrated that high-quality day care was not in any way harmful to the emotional development of children. They worry that parents who work and send their infants to day care will feel needlessly guilty that they are somehow hurting their children.

Infants are resilient creatures up to a certain point, and there is no reason why high-quality day care should harm them. Children need adults who are devoted to them, whether it's a single parent or a small group of day care teachers. They need consistency in their relationships, but this can be provided at home and in day care centers.

A few studies have looked at the differences between children who went to day care and those who didn't. Those studies show that high-quality day care—of small groups of children by carefully selected, well-trained teachers—is not harmful for most children. Exposure to caring adults and other children in a safe, stimulating environment can promote curiosity and learning. On the other hand, if large groups of children are cared for by poorly trained teachers, the experience may have the opposite effect. One study suggested that children who go to group day care for an extended period tend to be more oriented toward and responsive to their peers but less so to adults. Children who do not attend group care tend to be more oriented toward adults (often becoming the teacher's pet) and less responsive to their peers. Will this difference affect a child's later functioning in school, or persist into adulthood? Nobody knows.

Everyone does agree, though, that the *quality* of day care matters. Responsive, nurturing, stimulating, consistent care is vital and can be provided only by a stable, well-trained staff in a well-funded day care setting. Unfortunately, there are nowhere near enough day care centers with such high standards, and the few that exist may be too expensive for the average family. The only solution is unending political pressure for local and federal support for quality child care programs.

Child care as partnership. All of the adults who take part in caring for a particular child should see themselves as partners. Parents and nonparent caregivers need to share information and insights, and support each other. If your child has worked very hard in day care at a particular challenge—say, scribbling with a crayon—you ought to hear about it when you pick her up in the evening. In the same way, if your child has been up often during the night because of noisy thunderstorms, the child care provider needs to know about that in the morning.

When I was a young doctor studying child development, some of my most important lessons came from the teachers at my daughter's day care center. I would make a point of spending fifteen or twenty minutes there at the end of the day or sometimes in the morning, sitting on the floor with the teachers and children. I learned a lot about parenting by watching those very skillful professionals at work. If you can develop a relationship of cooperation and mutual respect with your child's caregiver, your child will benefit, and you'll benefit as a parent, too.

CHOOSING A CHILD CARE PROGRAM

Finding programs. First, compile a list of what's available in your community. Start with friends who can give you personal recommendations. Go online and look at the website for Child Care Aware (www.childcareaware.org) to locate the child care resource and referral organization for your area. These nonprofit organizations help parents find appropriate child care. They provide listings of programs, along with information about licensing and accreditation, group size, and other important issues.

Calls and visits. When you call a potential program, ask for the names and phone numbers of families served by the program, and ask the staff about the details of the care, including the use of discipline: Spanking should never be an option. Visit potential sites and stay for a few hours. Look for nurturing interactions between the caregivers and children. Are the children relaxed? Do they trust the teachers and turn to them for help? Do the children mostly cooperate with each other, and what happens when they don't? A good relationship between teachers and children will show in the relationships among the children.

Once your child is enrolled, plan to visit on a regular basis. Unannounced visits during the day will reassure you that all is well. Parents should feel welcome at the school, and their visits should be allowed at any time. Visits are a time to get to know the teachers, so you can communicate about the most important topic: your child.

Licensing and accreditation. If a child care center or home day care is licensed, it means that it provides a certain basic level of safety and stimulation required by the state. For example, licensed programs have to meet specific standards for fire safety and infection control. Accreditation is different. To be accredited, a program has to meet higher standards for quality of care, including training of providers, group size, space, equipment, and educational activities. A well-trained provider is more likely to understand what your child needs, and to respond in a way that supports your child's development. Accreditation is provided by national organizations such as the National Association for the Education of Young Children (NAEYC).

Group size. A key to quality is individual attention. Groups or classrooms can't be too large, and any single adult can't be responsible for too many children. The younger the child, the more attention he needs. NAEYC recommends the following maximum group sizes:

CHILD'S AGE	MAXIMUM NUMBER OF CHILDREN PER ADULT	MAXIMUM NUMBER OF CHILDREN IN ANY GROUP
Infants *(birth to 12 months)*	4	8
Toddlers *(12 to 24 months)*	4 or 5	12 (with 3 teachers) or 10 (with 2 teachers)
2-year-olds *(24 to 30 months)*	6	12
2½-year-olds *(30 to 36 months)*	7	14
3-, 4-, and 5-year-olds	10	20
Kindergartners	12	24
6- to 12-year-olds	15	30

AFTER-SCHOOL CARE

School-age children need adult supervision in the after-school hours. While family members and neighbors can fill this need, high-quality programs that also provide fun peer activities can be ideal. The same child care resource and referral agency that helps parents find quality early child care (see above) can also help with aftercare as well.

After about age eight, a mature child may be able to look after herself for an hour or so at home, if appropriate supports are in place, and everyone is comfortable with the arrangement. Supports include a trustworthy adult nearby; clear-cut rules and expectations (don't open the door for anyone, no TV, for example); and the ability to remember and carry out

safety actions (what to do if you smell smoke). Go to drspock
.com for a home-alone checklist.

For many children, though, time at home alone makes
them anxious and leaves them sad. While it's tempting to have
older children look after younger ones, this can only work
well if the older child is responsible and the younger ones are
compliant. If not, there can be a lot of tension and fighting;
you may need to make other arrangements.

It might seem that teenagers would be better able to care
for themselves after school. But in fact rates of substance use
and risky sex are higher among home-alone teens than among
peers whose time is structured and supervised. Teens (like toddlers) often feel more comfortable with firm limits on their
behavior, even if they protest. Unless you're certain that your
teen is levelheaded and rule-following, you're better off with a
structured after-school program.

Children and teens who participate in high-quality after-
school programs benefit socially and academically, and also
physically (exercise and healthy snacks). Such programs can
be expensive. Government-supported programs have proven
to be popular and cost-effective, but funding shifts with the
political winds. Advocacy by concerned parents makes a difference.

BABYSITTERS

For nighttime sitting with a baby who doesn't wake, it's enough
to have a sitter who is dependable and sensible. But for babies
who wake and for older children, the sitter should be a person the child knows and likes. It's upsetting to wake up to a
stranger. With a new sitter, stay home for the first couple of

times; watch her in action with your children to make sure
that she understands and loves children and can manage them
with kindliness and firmness. Try to find one or two reliable
sitters and stick with them.

It helps to make an instruction book for the sitter listing
the child's routine, some of the things he may ask for (in his
words), the telephone numbers of the doctor and of a neighbor to call in an emergency if you can't be reached, bedtime
hours, what the sitter may help herself to in the kitchen, how
to turn the heat up or down, and the whereabouts of linens,
nightclothes, and other things that may be needed. But most
of all, you should know your sitter and know that your child
trusts her.

Young or old? It's a matter of maturity and spirit rather than
years. There are children as young as fourteen who are extremely capable and dependable, but it's unfair to expect such
qualities in most people that age. And some adults may prove
unreliable, harsh, or clueless. One older person has a knack
with children; another is too inflexible or too anxious to adapt
to a new child.

Many communities have babysitter-training courses offered through the Red Cross or local hospitals that cover
safety and first-aid procedures. It makes sense to select a sitter
who has had this sort of training. With a young sitter—a ju-
nior high or high school student—it's also reassuring to know
that the sitter's parents are at home and available in case a true
emergency arises.

TIME WITH YOUR CHILD

Quality time. You don't have to do anything out of the ordinary to create quality time. Any activity—driving places, shopping, cooking and eating together, taking care of chores—can be an occasion for close, nurturing, and lovingly responsive interactions. If your work hours are long, you might need to make special arrangements to clear space for quality time. A preschool child might stay up late to have time with you, for example, as long as he could make up the sleep in the morning, or with a midday nap. In two-parent families, one parent could sleep while the other has quality time (the attention of one parent at a time can be quite satisfying to children).

Some parents take the concept of "quality time" to mean that *quantity* isn't important. It is. Children need to simply be around their parents, watching them in action, learning from their day-to-day example, and knowing they are an important part of their lives.

On the other hand, quantity can be overdone. Conscientious, hardworking parents may take it as an obligation to be talking, playing, and reading with their children long after patience and enjoyment have run out. Parents who regularly ignore their own needs and wishes in order to provide quality time for their children may come to resent the sacrifice, and then the spirit of friendliness evaporates. A child who senses that he can make his parent give him more time than the parent feels like giving may become pesky and demanding. The trick is to find the right balance: to spend plenty of time with your children, but not at the expense of fulfilling some of your own personal needs.

A parent who works hard all day is apt to come home exhausted. But it is just at this time that the child, who has been waiting all day to be with her mom or dad, is most demanding of attention. Rather than planning on falling straight into an armchair, feet up and eyes closed, you might instead remind yourself to *save just a little bit of energy* at the end of the day, knowing that the first thing you'll do when you get home is devote your full attention, for fifteen minutes, to your child. Then, having given your child what he needs, feel free to collapse for a bit. By making a small shift in your thinking, you can make a big difference in the quality of your evenings, and your relationship with your child.

Special time. This is a brief period—ten to fifteen minutes is usually enough—set aside every day to spend with a particular child. What's special is not what you actually do, but the fact that your child gets your undivided attention. Turn your cell phone off and the answering machine on. If there are siblings, remind them that their turn at special time is coming up, and then they will have your undivided attention.

A child deserves a little special time each day simply by virtue of being himself. If yours is a two-parent family, you can take turns doing special time. In families with lots of children, special time might have to happen less often. Parents traveling on business can have special time by telephone or by Skype or FaceTime—reading aloud from a book the child chooses, making up a story, or just talking. Special time shouldn't be taken away as a punishment. A child whose frequent misbehavior causes concern, frustration, and anger needs special time even more than an angelic one. Special time, like love, should be unconditional.

The temptation to spoil. Many working parents are inclined to shower their children with presents, bow to all their wishes, and generally let them get away with murder. Perhaps the parents are starved for their child's company; perhaps they feel guilty about having too little time with her, or afraid their child won't love them. It's tempting to substitute indulgence for physical and emotional presence, but it's a losing strategy.

It's fine for working parents to show their child as much agreeableness and affection as comes naturally, but they should also feel free to stop when they're tired, consider their own desires, avoid giving presents daily, spend only what money is sensible, and expect reasonable politeness and consideration from their children—in other words, to act like self-confident, all-day parents. The child will not only turn out better but will enjoy their company more.

DISCIPLINE

WHAT DISCIPLINE IS

Not just punishment. For many parents, disciplining a child means scolding, taking things away, making them sit in a corner, or spanking. These are all effective ways of teaching a child what *not* to do, but they don't teach children what *to* do, or why to do it. Punishments can make children outwardly obedient, if they think they might be caught, but they don't do much to strengthen inner controls. Children who are punished physically for wrongdoing are more likely to attack another child if they feel that child has acted wrongly. And harsh punishments often make children feel angry, resentful, and afraid long after the physical pain has passed.

It's better to think of discipline as training—building up the strengths and skills that children need to control their emotions, anticipate how their actions will affect others, and respond intelligently in challenging situations. For example, a well-disciplined child, when confronted with a sneering classmate, can choose from among several different responses that don't involve getting into a fight. A well-disciplined child who does something selfish or careless—well-disciplined does not mean perfect!—knows to own up to it, even though it's unpleasant to admit error. The long-term benefit of being known as an honest and forthright person is worth the brief discomfort.

"Discipline" shares a common root with "disciple." A well-disciplined child is a disciple, the follower of a parent who shows what it means to think right, say right, and do right. Discipline isn't merely about obeying rules, it's also about learning when to challenge them. Nazis on trial for genocide and U.S. soldiers responsible for civilian massacres countered that they were "just following orders." Mahatma Gandhi and Rosa Parks flouted the law in the name of justice. Which example do you want your children to follow?

Ineffective discipline. As a parent, you could create a harsh system of punishments so that, like good little robots, your children would behave perfectly—at least if they thought you were watching. But what would be the effect on their spirits and feelings toward others?

On the other hand, you could indulge their every whim and praise them regardless of their behavior. Such children might have a certain measure of happiness, but most people wouldn't want to get within ten feet of them. The challenge of discipline is to teach children the how and the why of good behavior without undermining their sense of self-worth and independent judgment.

The alternative to harsh discipline on the one hand, or spoiling on the other, is discipline that is warm, firm, and reasonable.

Why children behave. The main source of good discipline is growing up in a loving family—being loved and learning to love in return. We want to be kind and cooperative (most of the time) because we like people and want them to like us. Children gradually lessen their grabbing and begin to share somewhere around the age of three, not just because they are reminded by their parents (though that may help some) but also because their feelings of enjoyment and affection toward other children have developed sufficiently.

Another vital element is children's intense desire to be as much like their parents as possible. In the three-to-six-year-old period, they work particularly hard at being polite, civilized, and responsible. They pretend very seriously to take care of their doll children, keep house, and go out to work, as they see their parents do. If you want your child to grow up well-behaved, the first thing to do is behave well yourself, consistently.

Strict or casual discipline? This looms as a big question for many new parents, and remains a source of tension in many families. To some, a casual approach implies merely an easygoing style of management. To others, it implies permissiveness, foolishly overindulging a child, letting him do or have anything he wants. In this view, casual discipline makes for rude, spoiled children.

It turns out that strictness or casualness is not the most important issue. Good-hearted parents who aren't afraid to be firm when necessary can get good results with either moderate strictness or moderate casualness. On the other hand, a strictness that comes from harsh feelings or an excessive permissiveness that is timid or vacillating can lead to poor results. The real issue is what spirit the parent puts into managing the child, and what attitude is instilled in the child as a result.

Stick to your convictions. Parents who naturally lean toward strictness should probably raise their children that way. Moderate strictness—in the sense of requiring good manners, prompt obedience, and orderliness—is not harmful to children so long as the parents are basically kind and so long as the children are growing up happy and friendly. But strictness is harmful when parents are overbearing, harsh, and chronically disapproving, or when they make no allowances for a child's age and individuality. This kind of severity produces children who are either meek and colorless or mean-spirited.

An easygoing style can also produce children who are considerate and cooperative, as long as the parents are not afraid to be firm about the matters that are important to them. Many excellent parents are satisfied with casual manners as long as the child's attitude is friendly. These parents may not be particularly strict about promptness or neatness, but they don't hesitate to correct a child for selfishness or rudeness.

Firmness and consistency. The everyday job of the parent is to keep the child on the right track by means of firmness and consistency. Though children do the major share in civilizing themselves by loving their parents and trying to be like them, there still is plenty of work left for parents to do. In automobile terms, the child supplies the power but the parents have to do the steering. Some children are more challenging than others—they may be more active, impulsive, and stubborn than most—and it takes more energy to keep them on the right track. Their parents have to be saying, "We hold hands when we cross the street"; "You can't play with that, it may hurt someone"; "We have to leave the wagon here because it belongs to Harry and he wants it"; "It's time to go to bed so you'll grow big and strong"; and so on.

How well the guidance works depends on whether the parents are reasonably consistent (nobody can be completely consistent), whether they mean what they say, and whether they are directing the child for a good reason, and not just because they're feeling mean or bossy. The parent's tone of voice matters. An angry or belittling tone is likely to evoke anger and resentment rather than a desire to improve.

REWARD AND PUNISHMENT

Rules of behavior. A few principles of behavior apply equally to children and adults (and also to many animals). These rules aren't themselves a recipe for effective discipline, but effective parents make use of them all the time:

1. Behaviors that are rewarded happen more and more over time; those that are ignored or punished happen less and less.

2. Rewards and punishments given immediately are more effective than those that happen hours or days later.

3. Once established, behaviors persist longer if they are rewarded *some* of the time rather than *every* time.

4. If a reward stops suddenly, the behavior it was rewarding peters out, but first the behavior happens even *more* than usual.

It follows from these rules that if you want your child to start a new behavior—saying thank you, for example—you should figure out how to reward that behavior. For this, an effective reward is praise, which could be spoken ("I like how you said thank you just now"), or merely consist of an approving glance. If you want your child to stop a behavior—belching at the dinner table, for example—you could figure out a suitable punishment, and apply it every time your child belched at the table. Again, either a mild reprimand or a disapproving glance would probably work best.

Reward or punish? In general, rewards are more fun than punishments, both for parents and for children. And, happily, they often work better. Punishments tend to make children feel resentful and to undermine their motivation. Rewards tend to make children feel more like pleasing you.

You can often turn a punishment into a reward. Instead of punishing a behavior (hitting, say), reward the opposite behavior (playing nicely). Once you get into the habit of thinking this way, you'll notice that most of the behaviors you thought required punishment have opposites that you can reward. For example: rude table manners versus polite manners; being disagreeable versus being agreeable; being selfish versus being generous; being thoughtless versus being considerate. With this approach, you'll find yourself saying "no," "stop," "quit," and "don't" less often. Instead of "Stop whining," you'll say, "Tell me in words I can understand."

Effective praise. The most effective reward is usually praise or approval; the most effective punishment is usually criticism or disapproval. Effective praise has two parts. You tell your child what she did, and you tell her how you feel about it and, perhaps, what good result will come from her action. For example, "You picked up your clothes and put them all in the hamper. That makes me feel proud of you. Now we have more time to play." Just saying, "Good job!" doesn't work as well, because your child might not know what specific behavior earned the praise. Random praise for no reason at all isn't effective, either, because "being good" isn't really doing anything.

Effective criticism. Effective criticism has the same components as effective praise. It lets your child know what he did, how you feel about it, and what the consequences are. For example, "You threw your eggs on the floor. That makes me mad. Now we have to clean them up." Notice how much more information this statement conveys than simply "Bad boy!"

Discipline or behavior modification? It might sound, from the above, that I am suggesting that parents always talk to their children in a very stiff way. But after a little practice, you forget about formulas for effective praise and criticism and just begin to communicate more clearly. In reality, a lot of the communication is nonverbal, conveyed in smiles, frowns, and looks of delight or concern. Children are gifted readers of these gestures, particularly when they come from the important adults in their lives.

Teaching talk. Rewards and punishments are one way of teaching your child what he needs to know. Another way is simply talking with your child about what's going to happen and what the expectations are. If you're planning a trip to

Gramma's house, you might say, "Today we're going to Gramma's. When we get there, first we'll talk with Gramma and tell her about school or the fun things we're doing; then, after a little while, it'll be time to play." Children are much more likely to behave well if they know what to expect and what's expected of them.

Staying positive. Just as praise usually works better than criticism, expectations are almost always more effective when they are phrased in a positive way. Compare these two statements: "We're going to have a good time at the store; I expect you to listen and stay near me" and "Don't go running off in the store!" One of them paints a positive picture, the other a negative one. Children tend to act out the images: Words of negation such as "don't" or "no" don't register strongly in a child's mind, and instead the child fixes on the very behavior you're trying to prevent.

With a young child, you can often simply redirect the child from a prohibited activity (playing with the wall outlet, for example) to one that is preferred (playing with blocks). You might say something like "No, no, that's not safe," but then quickly follow up by pointing out a safe, approved activity, and physically directing your child to it, if need be.

Is punishment necessary? Most parents decide it is, at one time or another. But that doesn't prove that children themselves need a certain amount of punishment the way they need milk and vegetables to grow up right. Parents who find themselves punishing frequently should consider the possibility that the punishment is not having the desired effect. In some cases, children actually crave the added attention that comes with punishment, and act out to get it!

To punish or not to punish? A lot depends on how the parents were brought up. If they were punished occasionally for good cause, they naturally expect to have to punish in similar situations. And if they were kept in line through positive guidance alone, they are apt to find that they can do the same with their children. There are millions of poorly behaved children. The parents of some of them punish a lot, and the parents of others never do. So we can't say either that punishment always works or that lack of it always works.

Punishment is never the main element in discipline. At best, it's a vigorous reminder that the parents feel strongly about what they say. We have all seen children who were slapped and spanked and deprived plenty, yet remained ill-behaved. Other aspects of discipline—emotional warmth, reasonableness, and consistency—turn out to be more important.

When it makes sense to punish. You don't sit by and watch a small child destroy something and then punish her after the fact; you stop her and redirect her. Punishment is what you resort to when your system of positive expectations and clear communication has failed. Maybe your son, sorely tempted, wonders whether you still mean the prohibition that you laid down a couple of months ago. Or maybe he is angry and misbehaves on purpose.

The best test of a punishment is whether it accomplishes what you are after, without having other serious effects. If it makes a child furious, fearful, or worse-behaved than before, then it probably isn't working. If it seems to break the child's heart, then the cost is too high. Every child reacts somewhat differently.

There are times when a child destroys something out of carelessness. If he gets along well with his parents, he feels just as unhappy as they do, and no punishment is needed. In fact, you may have to comfort him. Jumping on a child who feels sorry already sometimes banishes his remorse and makes him angry.

Avoid threats. They tend to weaken discipline. It may sound reasonable to say, "If you don't keep out of the street with your bicycle, I'll take it away." But in a sense, a threat is a dare—it admits that the child may disobey. It will impress him more to be firmly told he must keep out of the street if he knows from experience that his parents mean what they say. On the other hand, if you see that you may have to impose a drastic penalty, like taking away his beloved bike for a few days, it's better to give fair warning; then if need be, follow through.

It quickly destroys a parent's authority to make threats that aren't or can't be carried out, such as "You're never going to watch TV again!" Scary threats, of monsters and cops who take bad children away, are never really helpful and often lead to lasting fears. Ditto for the threat to walk off and leave a dawdling child behind, because this threat undermines a central pillar of emotional security. You don't want your child to have to worry all the time about being abandoned.

Spanking. Hurting children in order to teach them a lesson is traditional in many parts of the world. Even here in the United States, many parents say that they believe in spanking.

But trends are shifting away from corporal punishment, and spanking is now illegal in many economically advanced countries.

There are several reasons to avoid physical punishment. For one thing, it teaches children that the larger, stronger person has the power to get his way, whether or not he is in the right. Some spanked children then feel quite justified in beating up smaller ones.

When an executive in an office or a foreman in a shop is dissatisfied with the work of an employee, he doesn't rush in shouting and whack him on the seat of his pants. He explains in a respectful manner what he would like, and in most cases this is enough. Children are not that different in their wish to be responsible and to please. They react well to praise and high expectations.

In the olden days, most children were spanked on the assumption that this was necessary to make them behave. In the twenty-first century, as parents and professionals have studied children here and in other countries, they have come to realize that children can be well behaved, cooperative, and polite without ever having been punished physically.

Parents often justify spanking on the grounds that they were spanked themselves and it didn't do them any harm. On the other hand, quite a few of these parents can remember having strong feelings of shame, anger, and resentment in response to spankings. I suspect that these parents were able to grow up psychologically healthy in spite of the spankings, not because of them.

Most scientific studies have found that spanking, in itself, is neither uniquely harmful nor particularly beneficial. The nature of the parent-child relationship—whether warm and loving or cold and harsh—is a much more powerful force in children's development. (See page 695 for spanking and abuse.)

Nonphysical punishments. Punishments work best if they make sense. For example, if a baby grabs his mother's nose and yanks, he gets put down on the floor. The punishment is to be separated from his mother, although he's right at her feet. Parents who use this mild form of time-out (in this case, time out from the face you just pinched) quickly teach their infants to control the urge to take hold of everything if that thing is somebody's face.

Another young child hits at her parent's face just to get attention. This behavior often gives rise to an ironic scene, with the parent slapping the child's hand while saying, "No hitting!" A more effective response is to say, "Ow! That hurts," put the child down, and find something else to be interested in for a couple of minutes. Instead of attention, the child's unpleasant behavior has earned her just the opposite.

Another form of nonphysical punishment, effective for older toddlers, is time-out in a playpen for a few minutes. Consider the toddler who insists on trying to pull the little plastic safety plugs out of the electrical outlets—a definite no-no. This persistent child has ignored your spoken limit, and when you redirect her to another activity, she gleefully runs back to the outlet. She thinks she is playing a great game. Instead of unwillingly joining the game, you can put the toddler in her playpen, say, "Time out," and leave her there for a couple of minutes. Most toddlers hate being taken away from whatever it is they are interested in, so you can expect wails of protest. But this mild form of punishment is an effective way of teaching your toddler that you mean business.

Time out. A formal time-out procedure works well for pre-school and young elementary school children. Time out means time away from attention and entertainment. At home, you can choose a time-out chair that is fairly isolated from the flow of activity—not so far away that you aren't aware of what your child is doing, but not right in the middle of things, either.

When you announce a time-out, your child needs to sit in the time-out chair until you tell him it's time to get up. You can use an egg timer, set for one minute per year of age. Much longer than that, and a young child is apt to forget why he was put in time-out and simply feel sad or resentful. But if the child gets up before the timer dings, the timer gets reset, and he has to serve his sentence again from the beginning. (Mechanical egg timers that tick seem to work better than the ubiquitous cell-phone timers; they cost a few dollars, and they're worth it.)

At the end of the time-out, you can ask your child to tell you why she needed a time-out and what she's going to do differently. If she doesn't have an idea, tell her what she did wrong, and give her another short time-out to think about it. If she got time out for avoiding a task (picking up her toys, for example), have her do the task after the time-out. This procedure makes your child responsible for learning the lesson you're trying to teach.

Some parents find that putting a child in his room and telling him that he can come out when he feels ready to cooperate works well. A theoretical disadvantage of this technique is that it may make the bedroom seem like a prison. On the other hand, it teaches the child that being around other people is a privilege that can be lost, and that when one is mad enough, a good thing to do is to find a way to be alone for a bit to calm down.

Natural punishments. When possible, let the punishment fit the crime. If a child leaves toys all over the living room after you've told him to pick them up, the toys might be put away where he can't get at them for a few days. If a teenager refuses to throw her laundry in the hamper, she may find herself without a clean shirt for school (a severe punishment for many, but not all, teens). An older teen who stays out late without calling may lose the privilege of going out until he can show that he can handle himself responsibly.

Effective punishments have a logic that even the child being punished has to acknowledge. They teach the crucial life lesson that actions have consequences.

Overreliance on punishment. When I meet a parent who says she has to punish her child all the time, I know that this is a parent who needs help. A few parents have extreme difficulty controlling their children. They say their child won't obey or that he's just bad. Often when you watch such a parent—let's say it's a mother—she doesn't appear to be really trying, even though she wants to and thinks she is. She threatens, scolds, or smacks, but is inconsistent. She makes her child obey once, but five minutes later she seems not to notice the same forbidden behavior. Or, she punishes a child's disobedience but forgets to make her child do what she said he had to do in the first place. Avoiding an unpleasant task is, for the child, a great reward! Another fed-up parent repeatedly tells the child that he's bad or rhetorically asks a neighbor, right in front of the child, whether she has ever seen a worse one.

Parents like these unconsciously expect the child's bad behavior to continue and believe that they can do nothing effective to stop it. They are inviting misbehavior without realizing it. Their scolding and punishing are only an expression of frustration. In their complaints to neighbors, they are only hoping to get some comforting agreement that the child is truly impossible. These parents need help from an understanding professional.

TIPS FOR SETTING LIMITS

You can be both firm and friendly. A child needs to feel that her mother and father, however agreeable, have their own rights, know how to be firm, and won't let her be unreasonable or rude. She likes her parents better that way. Their firmness trains her from the beginning to get along reasonably with other people.

Spoiled children are not happy creatures even in their own homes. And when they get out into the world, whether it's at age two or four or six, they are in for a rude shock. They find that nobody is willing to kowtow to them; they learn, in fact, that everybody dislikes them for their selfishness. Either they must go through life being unpopular or they must learn the hard way how to be agreeable.

Parents sometimes let their children take advantage of them for a while, until their patience is exhausted, and then become cross. Neither of these stages is really necessary. If parents have a healthy self-respect, they can stand up for themselves while they are still feeling friendly. For instance, if your daughter insists that you continue to play a game after you are exhausted, don't be afraid to say cheerfully but definitely, "I'm all tired out. I'm going to read a book now, and you can read your book, too."

Or maybe she is being balky about getting out of the wagon of another child who has to take it home now. Try to interest her in something else, but don't feel that you must go on being sweetly reasonable forever. Lift her out of the wagon even if she yells for a minute.

Angry feelings are normal. When a child is rude to his parent—perhaps because he has had to be corrected or because he's jealous of his brother or sister—the parent should promptly stop him and insist on politeness. But at the same time, the parent can say that she knows he is cross at her sometimes—all children get mad at their parents sometimes. This may sound contradictory to you; it sounds like undoing the correction. Child guidance work teaches us that children are happier, as well as better-behaved, if their parents insist on reasonably good behavior. But at the same time, it helps a child to realize that her parents know she has angry feelings and that her parents are not angry at her or alienated from her on account of them. This realization helps her get over her anger and keeps her from feeling too guilty or frightened because of it.

Making this distinction between angry feelings and angry actions works out well in actual practice. In fact, a cornerstone of mental health is to be able to recognize one's own feelings, and make reasonable decisions about whether or not to act on them. By helping your child find the words to describe her emotions, you are supporting the development of her emotional intelligence, a crucial ingredient in life success.

Don't ask if you mean to tell. It's easy to fall into the habit of saying to a small child, "Do you want to sit down and have your lunch? Shall we get dressed now? Do you want to do potty? It's time to go out now, okay?" The trouble is that the natural response of the child, particularly between one and three, is "No." Then the parent has to persuade the poor child to give in to something that was necessary anyway.

It is better not to offer a choice if what you really mean is to give a direction. With young children, a nonverbal approach works well. When it's time for lunch, lead your child or carry him to the table, still chatting with him about the thing that was on his mind before. When you see signs that he needs to go to the bathroom, lead him there or bring the potty chair to him without even mentioning what you're up to.

I'm not saying that you should swoop down on your child, and simply drag him off someplace else. It helps to be tactful. If your fifteen-month-old is busy fitting one hollow block inside another at suppertime, you can carry him to the table still holding his blocks and take them away when you hand him his spoon. If your two-year-old is playing with a toy dog at bedtime, you can say, "Let's put doggie to bed now." If your three-year-old is chugging a toy automobile along the floor when it's time for the bath, you can suggest that the car make a long, long trip to the bathroom. When you show interest in what he's doing, it puts him in a cooperative mood.

As your child grows older, he'll be less distractible and have more concentration. Then it works better to give him a little advance warning. If a four-year-old has spent half an hour building a garage of blocks, you can say, "Put the cars in soon now; I want to see them inside before you go to bed." You might advise your child to "find a good stopping spot," or offer to give him a "five-minute warning" so he'll know when to wrap it up. This approach lets your child know that his playing is important; it gives him some sense of control within the limits you set. All this takes patience, though, and naturally you won't always have it. No parent is perfect, nor needs to be.

Don't give a small child too many reasons. When your child is young, rely most heavily on distracting her from dangerous or forbidden situations in favor of something interesting and harmless. As she grows a little older and learns the lesson, remind her with a matter-of-fact "No, no" and then offer more distraction. If she wants an explanation or a reason, give it to her in simple terms. But don't assume that she wants an explanation for every direction you give. She knows that she is inexperienced. She counts on you to keep her out of danger. It makes her feel safe to have you guiding her, provided you do it tactfully and not too much.

You sometimes see a child between the ages of one and three who becomes worried by too many warnings. The mother of a certain two-year-old boy always tries to control him with ideas: "Jackie, you mustn't touch the doctor's lamp because you will break it, and then the doctor won't be able to see." Jackie regards the lamp with a worried expression and mutters, "Doctor can't see." A minute later he is trying to open the door to the street. His mother warns him, "Don't go out the door. Jackie might get lost, and Mommy couldn't find him." Poor Jackie turns this new danger over in his mind and repeats, "Mommy can't find him." It's not good for him to hear about so many bad endings. It fosters a morbid imagination. A two-year-old shouldn't be worrying about the consequences of his actions. This is the period when he is meant to learn by doing and having things happen. It's not that you should never warn your child in words, only that you shouldn't lead him out beyond his depth with ideas.

Then there is the overly conscientious father who feels he should give his three-year-old daughter a reasonable explanation of everything. When it's time to get ready to go outdoors, it never occurs to him to put the child's coat on in a matter-of-fact way and go out. He begins, "Shall we put your coat on now?" "No," says the child. "Oh, but we want to go out and get some nice fresh air." She is used to the fact that her father feels obliged to give a reason for everything, which encourages her to make him argue for every point. So she says, "Why?" but not because she really wants to know. Her father gives some reason, but she still wants to know why, and so it goes all day long. This kind of meaningless argument and explanation will not make her a more cooperative child or give her respect for her father as a reasonable person. She would be happier and get more security from him if he had an air of self-confidence and steered her in a friendly, automatic way through the routines of the day.

THE PROBLEM OF PERMISSIVENESS

When parents get unwanted results from too much permissiveness, it is not so much because they demand too little, though this is part of it, as it is because they are timid or guilty about what they do ask.

If parents are too hesitant in asking for reasonable behavior, they can't help resenting the bad behavior that comes instead. They keep getting angry underneath, without really knowing what to do about it. This bothers their children, too. It is apt to make them feel guilty and scared, but it also makes them meaner and all the more demanding. If, for example, babies acquire a taste for staying up in the evening and the parents are afraid to deny them this pleasure, the babies may turn into disagreeable tyrants who keep their mothers and fathers awake for hours. Parents are bound to dislike them for their tyranny. If parents can learn to be firm and consistent in their expectations, it's amazing how fast the children will sweeten up—and the parents will, too.

In other words, parents can't feel right toward their children in the long run unless they can make them behave reasonably, and children can't be happy unless they are behaving reasonably.

The parent who shies away from discipline. Quite a few parents shy away from guiding and controlling their children, leaving most of this work to their spouse. Mothers who aren't entirely sure of themselves may get into the habit of saying, "Just wait until your father gets home!" (Or, these days, it's the mothers who are coming home, and the fathers who are unsure!) Fathers may hide behind the paper or remain glued to the television set when a crisis occurs. When their wives reproach them, they explain that they don't want their children to resent them the way they often resented their own fathers. Instead, they want to be pals with their children.

It's good for children to have friendly parents who will play with them, but children need parents to act like parents. They will have many friends in their lifetime; but only one set of parents.

When a parent is timid or reluctant to give leadership, the children feel let down, like vines without a trellis to grow on. When parents are afraid to be definite and firm, their children keep testing the limits, making life difficult for the parents and for themselves, until the parents are finally provoked into cracking down. Then the parents feel ashamed and back off again.

The father who avoids the disciplinary role simply forces his wife to discipline for two. In many such cases, the father does not end up with the friendly relationship he seeks. Children know that adults get irritated when they keep misbehaving. When they are dealing with a father who pretends not to notice, they feel uneasy. The children may imagine that he is concealing an anger that is much more dangerous than it really is. Some children may fear this kind of father more than the one who participates freely in their management and expresses his irritation. With an expressive father, children have opportunities to learn just what his displeasure means and how to deal with it. They find out that they can survive it, and this gives them a kind of self-assurance—just as they gain confidence when they overcome their fears and learn to swim or ride a bike.

Confusion about discipline. In traditional societies, where ideas about children stay the same generation after generation, most parents have no doubt about the best way to raise and discipline their children. By contrast, in many parts of the world, ideas about children are changing so rapidly that many parents are confused. Many of these changes have been driven by science. For example, psychologists have discovered that a warmly affectionate parenting style is more likely to produce well-behaved and happy children than is a coldly controlling style. Knowing this, some parents assume that *all* that children need is love; that they should be allowed to express their aggressive feelings against parents and others; and that when children misbehave, the parents shouldn't get angry or punish them but should try to show more love.

Misconceptions like these are unworkable if carried very far. They encourage children to become demanding and disagreeable. They make children feel guilty about their excessive misbehavior. They make parents strive to be superhuman.

Another misconception, which began as a politically motivated attack against Dr. Spock for his activism against the Vietnam War, is that *Baby and Child Care* promotes permissiveness. It should be clear by now that this isn't the case, and it never was.

Guilt gets in the way. There are many situations that give rise to persistent parental guilt: the mother who returns to her nine-to-five job without first settling in her own mind whether she thinks this is neglecting her child; parents who have a child with a physical or mental disability; parents who have adopted a baby and can't get over the feeling that they have to be super parents; parents who have been brought up with so much disapproval that they always feel guilty; parents who studied child psychology in college and therefore know about all the pitfalls and feel they have to be perfect.

Whatever the cause of the guilt, it tends to get in the way of easy management of a child. The parents are inclined to expect too little from the child and too much from themselves. They often still try to be patient and sweet-tempered when their overworked patience is exhausted and the child is getting out of hand and needs some definite correction. Or they vacillate when the child needs firmness.

A child, like an adult, knows when she is getting away with too much naughtiness or rudeness, even when her parents are trying to close their eyes to it. She feels guilty inside. She would like to be stopped. But if she isn't corrected, she's likely to behave worse and worse. It's as if she were saying, "How bad do I have to be before somebody stops me?"

Eventually her behavior becomes so provoking that the parents' patience snaps. They scold or punish her. Peace is restored. But the trouble with parents who feel guilty is that they are too ashamed of losing their temper. So instead of letting well enough alone, they try to undo the correction, or they let the child punish them in return. Perhaps they permit the child to be rude to them right in the middle of the punishment. Or they take back the penalty before it has been half paid. Or they pretend not to notice when the child begins misbehaving again.

In some situations, if the child does not retaliate at all, the parent begins to subtly provoke her to do so—without realizing, of course, what she is up to. All of this may sound too complicated or unnatural to you. If you can't imagine a parent letting a child get away with murder or, worse still, encouraging it, it only shows that you don't have a problem with guilt feelings. Guilt isn't a rare problem, however. A majority of conscientious parents let a child get out of hand occasionally when they feel they have been unfair or neglectful, but most soon recover their balance. However, when a parent says, "Everything this child does or says rubs me the wrong way," it's a pretty good sign that the parent feels overly guilty and is chronically submissive and permissive, and that the child is reacting to this with constant provocation. No child can be that irritating by accident.

If parents can determine in which respects they may be too permissive and can firm up their discipline appropriately, they may be delighted to find that their child becomes not only better-behaved but much happier. Then they can really love their child better, and the child in turn responds to this.

Firmness works best when it's built on a foundation of positive, joyful, loving parent-child interactions. So, while you are thinking about how you can be more consistent, and less plagued by guilt, remember to enjoy many warm, positive interactions with your child every day. If having warm and joyful moments seems too difficult to do, for whatever reason, talk frankly about this issue with your child's doctor. Professional guidance to strengthen the emotional base of your relationship can be the first step toward happier and more effective discipline.

MANNERS

Good manners come naturally. Teaching children to say please or thank you is really not the first step. The most important thing is to have them like people and feel good about their own worth as a person. If they don't, it will be hard to teach them even surface manners.

It's important for children to grow up in a family whose members are consistently considerate of each other. Then they absorb kindness. They want to say thank you because the people they look up to say it and mean it. They enjoy shaking hands and saying please. The example of parents' politeness toward each other and toward the children is crucial.

It's also very important for your children to see you treating people outside the family with kindness and consideration, particularly people who occupy a lower social position. When you act with genuine politeness toward the person who brings you your food or who wears ragged clothing, you are teaching your child the true meaning of manners.

Manners for young children. It's best to avoid making young children self-conscious with strangers. We're apt, especially with our first child, to introduce him right away to a new grown-up and make him say something. But when you do that to a two-year-old, you make him embarrassed. He quickly learns to feel uncomfortable as soon as he sees you greeting somebody, because he knows he's about to be put on the spot.

It's much better in the first three or four years, when a child needs time to size a stranger up, to draw the newcomer's conversation away from the child, not toward him. A child of three or four is likely to watch a stranger talking to his parent for a few minutes and then suddenly break into the conversation with a remark like, "The water came out of the toilet all over the floor." This isn't Lord Chesterfield's kind of manners, but it's real manners, because he feels like sharing a fascinating experience. If that spirit toward strangers keeps up, he'll learn how to be friendly in a more conventional way soon enough.

PARENTS' ANGRY FEELINGS

Parents are bound to get cross. When your baby has been crying angrily for hours, despite all your patient efforts to comfort her, you can't go on feeling sympathetic. She seems like a disagreeable, obstinate, unappreciative creature, and you can't help feeling angry—really angry.

Or perhaps your older son has done something that he knows very well he shouldn't have done. Maybe he was so fascinated with a breakable object of yours or so eager to join some children on the other side of the street that he couldn't resist the temptation to disobey. Or maybe he was cross at you for having denied him something or angry at the baby for receiving so much attention. So he misbehaved out of simple spite.

When a child disobeys a well-understood and reasonable rule, you can't simply be a cool statue of justice. Any good parent feels strongly about right and wrong. You were taught to feel that way back in your own childhood. It's *your* rule that has been broken. It's probably your possession that has been damaged. It's your child, about whose character you care a great deal, who has done wrong. It's inevitable that you feel indignant. The child naturally expects this, and is not hurt by it if your reaction is fair.

Sometimes it takes you a long time to realize that you are losing your temper. The boy may have been putting on a series of irritating acts from the time he appeared at breakfast—making disagreeable remarks about the food, half-deliberately knocking over a glass of milk, playing with something forbidden and breaking it, picking on a younger child—all of which you have tried to ignore in a supreme effort to be patient. Then at the final act, which perhaps isn't so bad, your resentment suddenly boils over, shocking you a little with its vehemence. Often when you look back over such a series of exasperating actions, you can see that the child has really been asking for firmness all morning, and that it was your well-intentioned effort at patience that made him go from one provocation to another, looking for a check.

We also get cross with our children because of the pressures and frustrations we are feeling from other directions. A father, for example, comes home on edge from troubles that he's having in his work. He criticizes his wife, who then snaps at the older boy for something that ordinarily brings no disapproval, and the boy in turn picks on his younger sister.

Better to admit anger. So far we have been discussing the inevitability of parental impatience and resentment from time to time. But it's just as important to consider a related question: Can parents comfortably accept their own angry feelings? Parents who aren't excessively strict with themselves are usually able to admit their irritation.

A naturally outspoken good mother whose little boy has been bedeviling her may say to a friend, half-jokingly, "I don't think I can stand being in the house with him for another minute," or, "I'd enjoy giving him a thorough walloping." She isn't ashamed to admit her feelings to a sympathetic friend or to herself. It relieves her feelings to recognize them so clearly and to blow them off in talk. It also helps her to see what she has been putting up with and to be firmer in putting a stop to it.

It's the parents who set impossibly high standards for themselves who really suffer. When they detect stirrings of anger in themselves, they deny them, or feel unbearably guilty. But such buried feelings tend to pop up in other ways—as tension, for example, or tiredness or a headache.

Admitting your angry feelings helps you feel more comfortable, and it helps your child, too. When a parent believes that antagonistic feelings are too horrible to admit, the child absorbs the same dread of them. In child guidance clinics, we see children who develop fears of imaginary dangers—fear of insects, of going to school, of being separated from their parents—that prove on investigation to be a disguise for ordi-

nary feelings of anger toward their parents, which these perfectionistic children dare not recognize.

Children are happier around parents who aren't afraid to
admit their anger, because then they can be more comfortable
about their own angry feelings. And justified anger that's expressed tends to clear the air and leave everyone feeling better.

When anger is not okay. Of course, not all the antagonism
expressed toward children is justified. A loving parent who
feels angry most of the time, whether it's expressed openly or
not, is suffering from a real emotional strain and deserves help
from a mental health professional. The anger may be coming
from some entirely different direction. An ongoing state of
anger or irritation is often a sign of depression. Depression,
which affects a great many parents—particularly mothers of
young children—is a terribly painful condition. Thankfully, it
is also treatable (see page 818, and also drspock.com).

A frequent feeling of irritation toward one child in particular can make a parent feel guilty, especially if there is no obvious reason. A mother says, "This one always rubs me the
wrong way. Yet I'm constantly trying to be sweeter to her and
to overlook her bad behavior." Counseling may help this
mother better understand herself and make the changes she
knows she needs to make.

GRANDPARENTS

It's common to hear a grandparent ask, "Why couldn't I have enjoyed my own children the way I enjoy my grandchild? I suppose I was trying too hard and feeling only the responsibility."

Parents may need to be reminded from time to time of just how wonderful their children really are. Grandparents can often reassure parents that difficult behaviors are just bumps in the road. Grandparents can connect children with their family's stories and cultural heritage. At times, grandparents may be called on to step in for parents who are away at work or ill. And many grandparents take on more permanent parenting responsibilities.

Tensions are normal. Grandparents and parents care deeply about the same child, but are apt to see things at least a little differently. Disagreements, however, don't have to turn into conflicts.

A young mother who has lots of natural self-confidence can turn easily to her mother for help when she needs it. And when the grandmother offers a suggestion, the mother finds that she can accept it if it seems good, or tactfully let it pass.

But most new parents don't have that amount of assurance at first. Like almost everybody else in a new job, they are sensitive about possible inadequacies and touchy about criticism.

Sensitive grandparents try hard not to interfere. On the other hand, they have had experience, they love their grandchildren, and they can't help having opinions. For their part, young parents can keep relations most comfortable by permitting or even inviting the grandparents to voice their opinions. The parent might say something like: "I realize that this method doesn't seem quite right to you, and I'm going to discuss it again with the doctor to be sure that I'm on the right track."

Taking this tack is not the same as giving in. The parent reserves the right to make the final decision, even while recognizing the grandparent's good intentions and evident anxiety. A young parent who shows reasonableness in this way reassures the grandparent not only in regard to the present problem but also in regard to the future in general.

Some parents are sensitive about advice. More than average tension may arise if the young mother (or father) has felt a lot of parental criticism throughout her childhood. This inevitably leaves her inwardly unsure of herself, outwardly impatient with disapproval, and grimly determined to demonstrate her independence. She may take to new philosophies of child-rearing with unusual enthusiasm and push them hard; they seem like a wholesome change from what she remembers. They are also a way to show the grandparents how old-fashioned they are and to bother them a bit. Parents who find that they are constantly upsetting the grandparents should at least ask themselves whether they might be doing some of it on purpose, without realizing it.

Faced with a grandparent who is bent on controlling things,

it's very important that parents present a united front. It's a disaster if a father joins with his own mother against the baby's mother, for example. The specific issue—feeding, sleeping, bathing, whatever—is almost never as important as the principle that the parents (plural) decide.

Grandparents as caregivers. When the children are left in the care of the grandparents, whether for half a day or for two weeks, there needs to be open understanding and reasonable compromising. The parents must have confidence that the children will be cared for according to their beliefs regarding important matters. On the other hand, it's unfair to expect grandparents to carry out every step of management and discipline as if they were exact replicas of the parents. It won't hurt children to be a little more respectful to the grandparents, to have their meals on a different schedule, or to be kept cleaner or dirtier. If the parents don't feel right about the way the grandparents care for the children, they shouldn't ask them to take care of them.

Grandparents as parents. Many children are raised by their grandparents while their parents cope with mental illness or addiction. Grandparents often take on this responsibility with mixed feelings: love for their grandchildren, anger at their own children, and perhaps guilt and regret as well. The task can be wonderfully gratifying, but it is often exhausting. Grandparents in this situation may yearn for the regular relationship: that is, to "spoil" their grandkids and then go home to a quiet house.

Custodial grandparents also often worry about what will happen if their own health should give out. Government agencies that provide support for children in foster care often do not extend the same level of support to grandparents who are acting as foster parents. A supportive family and community can make a huge difference. Many cities also have grandparent groups that provide parenting tips and camaraderie (see the Resource Guide on page 894).

SEXUALITY

THE FACTS OF LIFE

Sex education starts young. Many people think that sex education means a lecture at school or a solemn talk at home. This is taking too narrow a view of the subject. Sex is about more than just how babies are made. It includes ideas about bodily sensation and romantic urges that affect how children experience other people and themselves throughout their lives.

Young children notice sexual differences and wonder about their significance. They observe romantic or sexual behaviors in older people and the media—flirting, kissing, meaningful gazes—and try to figure out what it's all about. They pay attention to different ways that boys and girls are treated, and what they're told about how they should behave. All of this is part of a child's sex education.

Sex is interwoven in family life. In earlier editions of this book, Dr. Spock emphasized the spiritual side: sexual love as the force that makes parents want to protect and care for each other, to raise wonderful children together, and (if they're religious) to include God in the marriage. Society, by contrast, treats sex as an arena for competition, as a product to sell, and as a way to sell other products. TV, billboards, and magazine

631

covers teach children about sex. Parents need to challenge these commerce-driven lessons.

Sex education for babies. Sex education starts even before children can ask questions. During bathing and changing, parents can get into the habit of talking comfortably about parts of the body, including their babies' genitals. "Now we'll wipe your vulva," or "Let's get your penis cleaned up!" Using the right words—"penis" or "vulva" rather than "wee-wee" or "thing," for example—weakens some of the taboo about the genitals that makes them seem so off-limits, and at the same time so fascinating. Talking like this early on prepares parents for more complex conversations to come.

Children start to ask questions at around age three. Children begin to get more exact ideas about the things that are connected with sex at around the age of two and a half to three. This is the "why" stage, when their curiosity branches out in all directions. They probably want to know why boys are made differently from girls. They don't think of it as a sex question; it's just another in a series of important questions. It's reasonable to handle it in a matter-of-fact way. If you react negatively or quickly change the topic, your child may get the impression that there's something bad, and perhaps dangerous, about that part of the body.

Where do babies come from? This question is also pretty sure to come up in the period around three. It's easier and better to begin with the truth rather than tell a fairy story that you have to change later. Try to answer the question simply. Young children are easily confused by too much information at one time. For instance, you can say, "A baby grows in a special place inside the mother called the uterus." You don't have to tell them more than that for the time being.

Maybe in a few minutes, maybe in a few months, they'll want to know a couple of other things. How does the baby get inside the mother? How does it get out? The first question is apt to be embarrassing to the parent, who may jump to the conclusion that the child is now demanding to know about conception and intercourse. But they are making no such demand. They think of things getting inside the body by being eaten, and perhaps wonder if the baby gets in that way, too. A simple answer is that the baby grows from a tiny seed that was in the mother all the time. It will be months before they want to know or will be able to understand what part the father plays.

Some people feel that children should be told at the time of their first questions that the father contributes by putting his seed into the mother. Perhaps this is right, especially in the case of the little boy who feels that the man is left out of the picture. But a three- or four-year-old doesn't need an exact picture of the physical and emotional sides of intercourse. It's more than he bargained for when he asked his question. All that's necessary is to satisfy his curiosity at the level of his understanding and, more important, to give him the feeling that it is all right to ask. To the question of how babies get out, a good answer is that when they are big enough they come out through a special opening that's just for that purpose, called the vagina. It's important to make it clear that it is not the opening for bowel movements or for urine.

When children ask about where babies come from, they're not only interested in the physiology and anatomy of reproduction (although this is fascinating, of course). They also need to hear their parents speak feelingly about the part played by their devotion to each other, how they want to do things for each other, give things to each other, have children together, and take care of them together, and how this goes along with the physical affection and wanting to put the seed from the penis into the vagina. In other words, parents shouldn't ever let the merely mechanical explanation of sex stand alone.

Why not the stork? The proverbial stork may be out of fashion, but many parents still feel the need to make up a fairy tale to explain where babies come from. But even a child as young as three who has a pregnant mother or aunt may have a suspicion of where the baby is growing from observing the woman's figure and from bits of overheard conversation. It's likely to mystify and worry him to have his parent nervously telling him something different from what he suspects is the truth. Even if he doesn't suspect anything at three, he is surely going to find out when he's five or seven or nine. It's better not to start him off wrong and have him later decide that you're untrustworthy. If he finds that you didn't tell him the truth, it puts a barrier between you and makes him uneasy. He's less likely to ask you other questions later. Another reason for telling the truth at three is that children at this age are satisfied with simple answers. You get practice and build a foundation for the harder questions that come later.

Sometimes small children who have been told where the baby is growing confuse parents by talking as if they also believe the stork theory. Or they may mix up two or three theories at the same time. This is natural. Small children believe part of everything they hear, because they have such vivid imaginations. They don't try, as grown-ups do, to find the one right answer and get rid of the wrong ones. Also, children can't learn anything from one telling. They learn a little at a time, and come back with the same question until they feel sure that they've got it straight. Then, at every new stage of development, they're ready for a bit more detail.

Be prepared to be surprised. Probably your child's questions won't come in exactly the form or at the moment you expect. You might visualize a scene at bedtime when your child is in a confidential mood. Actually, the question is more likely to be popped in the middle of the grocery store or while you are talking on the street with a pregnant neighbor. If it does, try to curb that impulse to shush your child. Answer on the spot if you can. If that is impossible, say casually, "I'll tell you later."

Don't make too solemn an occasion of it. When children ask you why the grass is green or why dogs have tails, you answer in an offhand way that gives them the feeling that it is the most natural thing in the world. Try to get the same spirit of naturalness into your answers about the facts of life. Remember that even if this subject is charged with feeling and embarrassment for you, it is a matter of simple curiosity to children.

Other questions—"What does the father do about it?" or "Is Aunt Susie (who is single) going to have a baby?"—may not come until children are four or five or older, unless they observe animals or have friends with baby brothers or sisters. Then you can explain that the seed comes out of the father's penis and goes into the uterus, a special place different from the stomach, where the baby will grow. It may be some time before they can visualize this situation. When they are ready for that, you can mention something in your own words about loving and embracing.

The child who hasn't asked. What about the child who has reached the age of four or five or more and hasn't asked any questions at all? Parents sometimes assume that this means the child has never thought of these questions. But it's more likely that the child has gotten the feeling, whether the parents meant to give it or not, that these matters are embarrassing. You can be on the lookout for indirect questions and hints and little jokes that a child uses to test out parents' reactions.

For example, a child of seven who is not "supposed" to know anything about pregnancy may keep calling attention to his mother's large abdomen in a half-embarrassed, half-joking way. Here is a good chance for the parents to explain. A little girl who is at the stage of wondering why she isn't made like a boy sometimes makes valiant efforts to urinate standing up. There are occasions almost every day, in a child's conversation about humans and animals, when a parent can help a child ask what she wants to know, and to give her a reassuring explanation, even though she hasn't asked a direct question.

How schools can help. Many schools make a point of letting children in kindergarten or first grade take care of animals, such as rabbits, guinea pigs, or mice. This gives them an opportunity to become familiar with all sides of animal life—feeding, fighting, mating, birth, and suckling of the young. It is easier in some ways to learn these facts in an impersonal situation, and it supplements what children have learned from their parents. But what they find out in school, they probably want to discuss and clear up further at home.

By the fifth grade, it's good to have biology taught in a simple way, including a discussion of reproduction. At least some of the girls in the class are entering puberty and need some accurate knowledge of what is happening. The discussion from a somewhat scientific point of view in school should help the child to bring it up more personally at home. Teaching and talking about sex in a reasonable and factual manner does not make children more prone to act in sexually irresponsible ways; just the contrary.

HOW SEXUALITY DEVELOPS

We are sexual beings from the day we're born. It's in our nature. Exactly how that nature is expressed depends on family, cultural, and social values. In the United States, there is a long tradition of puritanical and repressive attitudes toward sex. Other cultures embrace sexuality as a part of life.

Sensuality and sexuality. Sensuality refers to taking pleasure in the physical senses. Sexuality focuses on specific body parts. Babies are sensual creatures. They take uninhibited pleasure in their whole bodies, especially in the mouth and skin. They eat with gusto, smacking their lips when full, raising a ruckus when hungry. They delight in being held, stroked, kissed, tickled, and massaged. The pleasure principle reigns supreme.

Over time, infants may begin to learn that certain emotions and ideas are off-limits. If an infant who is rubbing her genitals is told, "No! Don't do that! That's nasty!" she begins to associate that sensation with disapproval. A nursing toddler may discover at some point, and with some unhappiness, that he can't just pull out his mother's breast whenever he wants it. While prohibitions may put a stop to certain behaviors, the desire for pleasure does not vanish.

As children grow, they need to bring their physical urges into line with social rules. They learn, for example, that it's okay to pick your nose or to scratch certain parts of the body, but not when other people are watching. An understanding of the idea of privacy develops gradually. A young child will say, "I want my privacy," in the bathroom, but will happily romp around the house with nothing on. Usually by the time they enter first grade, children understand privacy more or less as adults do.

Masturbation. Between four and eight months of age, infants discover their genitals. They do this the same way they discover their fingers and toes—through random exploration. From time to time, they intentionally rub their genitals, because it feels good.

By eighteen to thirty months, children are becoming aware of genital differences. This awareness centers on the boy's penis and the girl's lack of one. This is how children see it, until they learn that girls have a vagina and a uterus in which to grow babies, which boys lack. This natural interest in the genitals may lead to more masturbation.

Masturbation can take different forms. In addition to stroking their genitals with their hands, children may rub their thighs together, rhythmically rock back and forth, or make pelvic thrusting motions while sitting on the arm of a couch or chair or lying on a favorite stuffed animal. Children at this age will also stroke their genitals to comfort themselves when they're tense or frightened (a behavior seen in other primate species as well).

Most school-age children continue to masturbate, although less openly and less often. Some masturbate a lot, some only a little. Apart from occasional skin irritation, masturbation doesn't cause any medical or psychological problems, unless children are punished severely or made to feel ashamed.

Early sexual curiosity. Preschool-age boys and girls are often openly interested in each other's bodies and, if permitted, will spontaneously engage in show-and-touch. "Playing doctor" helps to satisfy sexual curiosity; it's not a sign of sexual abuse or inappropriate overstimulation. Among school-age children, comparing penis size among boys and appearance and size of the clitoris among girls is normal, part of the general process of seeing how you measure up to your peers. Some healthy children engage in these sorts of investigations; others don't.

How much modesty in the home? Standards of modesty vary from home to home. It's common for young children of both sexes to sometimes see each other undressed at home, at the beach, and in the bathroom of a preschool. There is no reason to think that this exposure has any ill effects. Children are interested in each other's bodies just as they are curious about many things in the world around them.

When young children regularly see their parents naked, however, it sometimes raises anxiety. The main reason is that young children's feelings for their parents are so intense. A boy loves his mother much more than he loves any little girl. He feels much more envy of his father than he feels toward any boy. So the sight of his mother naked may be overstimulating, and the chance to compare himself unfavorably with his father every day may make him feel inadequate. Sometimes a boy can be so envious that he feels like doing something violent to his dad. Nudist fathers sometimes relate how their three- and four-year-old sons make snatching gestures at the father's penis during morning shaving; then the boy feels guilty and fearful. A little girl who regularly sees her father nude also may be too stimulated.

This isn't to say that all children are upset by parental nudity. Many aren't, especially if the parents have a wholesome naturalness and aren't being naked in a lascivious or showy way. Yet we don't always know the effect on the child, so it's probably wise for parents to keep reasonably covered once their children turn two and a half or three. Before that, it's helpful if children can accompany their parents into the bathroom, so they can see what the toilet is for.

Occasionally a parent is caught off guard when a curious child comes into the bathroom. The parent shouldn't then act shocked or angry. It's only necessary to say, "Will you wait outside until I get dressed?" A good time to start insisting on your own privacy is when you begin to feel uncomfortable with your child seeing you naked. If you're uncomfortable, your child will sense it, and feel uncomfortable himself.

After the age of six or seven, most children begin to want a little more privacy for themselves, at least at times, and they are also much more capable of managing toileting and hygiene on their own. At this point, it makes sense to respect children's appropriate requests for privacy.

Unwanted touching. As children begin to grasp the concept of privacy, they can be taught about acceptable ways to touch others, and which kinds of touches are *not* okay. They need to know to resist unwanted touching or other harassment firmly and loudly, and to tell a parent or other trusted adult. If the person who made them uncomfortable threatens them that telling will result in an awful consequence (getting taken away, for example), then they must *certainly* tell. You can reinforce these core lessons from time to time by drawing your child's attention to stories of brave people who are changing the world by speaking out against abuse. (See page 695 for more on sexual abuse.)

Girls and puberty. It's best if the subject of puberty comes up before the first changes appear. In girls this is usually around age ten, but it can be as early as eight. Girls starting puberty need to know that during the next two years their breasts will develop, hair will grow in their pubic area and under the arms, they'll shoot up in height and weight, and their skin will become oilier and possibly prone to pimples. Toward the end of the two years they'll probably have their first menstrual period (see page 199).

Talking about periods, some mothers emphasize what a curse they can be; others emphasize how delicate a girl becomes at such times and how careful she must be. Neither approach really helps. Knowing that menstruation prepares the uterus for growing a baby at least takes the mystery away, and links the discomfort to a powerful (latent) ability.

A matter-of-fact approach is reasonable. Girls and women can live perfectly healthy, normal, vigorous lives right through their menstrual periods. It is only the occasional girl who has cramps severe enough to keep her out of activities, and there are good treatments for them. During the months she is waiting for her first period, giving the child a box of sanitary pads (and one to carry with her, to be prepared) helps put her in the right mood. It makes her feel that she is grown-up and ready to deal with life, rather than waiting for life to do something to her.

Boys and puberty. Boys need to be told about puberty before it starts, usually around age twelve but sometimes as early as ten (see page 199). You should explain about the naturalness of erections and nocturnal emissions. Nocturnal emissions, which are also called wet dreams, are an ejaculation of seminal fluid from the prostate gland during sleep, often in the course of a dream of a sexual nature. Parents who know that nocturnal emissions are certain to occur and that boys will at times feel a strong urge to masturbate will sometimes tell the boy that these things are not harmful as long as they don't happen too often. The trouble is that adolescents easily become worried about their sexuality, easily imagine they are abnormal. Being told that "this much is normal, that much is abnormal" is apt to make them more anxious. Boys need to be told that it's equally normal to have many or few nocturnal emissions, and that some perfectly normal boys have none at all.

TALKING WITH TEENS ABOUT SEX

Does sex education encourage sex? Many parents are afraid that talking about sex with their teenagers will encourage sex. It doesn't. If anything, the more children learn about sexuality from talking with their parents and teachers and reading accurate books, the less they feel compelled to try to find out for themselves. Taking the mystery away from sex makes it less appealing to a teen, not more. Learning about abstinence—that is, effective ways to say "No, thank you"—is also helpful. But there is good evidence from many studies that abstinence education alone doesn't reduce irresponsible and risky sex. To be effective, education about sex and sexuality has to encompass everything, including the biology of reproduction and contraception, the way sex is sold in the media, emotional and spiritual aspects of sex, religious and other values, and abstinence.

Talk about sex often. With adolescents, just as with younger children, it's best for talk about sex to come up naturally from time to time rather than in one big solemn lecture. It's easiest to talk with a teenager about sex if sex has been an open topic of conversation all along. One way to make sex a routine part of conversation is to comment on the sexual images that are everywhere on the Internet, on television, and in newspapers and magazines. If your seventh grader knows that you are comfortable talking about sex, then he won't be freaked out when you talk with him about sex when he's a freshman and sophomore in high school.

A good time to talk about sex is when you're in the car together, perhaps driving your child to some fun activity. Having scenery to look at can help you both feel less self-conscious, and the car makes it hard for your teen to get up and walk away. These discussions should include talking about contraception, with specifics about both the boy's and girl's responsibilities. If you just can't get comfortable enough to talk about sex with your teenager, it's important to find another adult whom you both trust who can.

Go beyond fear. One mistake that is easy to make is to concentrate on the dangerous aspects of sex. Of course, the child who is moving into adolescence should know that intercourse can cause pregnancy and that promiscuity breeds infections. For some, the fear of negative consequences will help them make wise decisions. But teens are constituted to believe that nothing bad can happen to them. For most teens, horror stories about AIDS and unwanted babies won't have much impact.

More than just warnings, teens need guidance in thinking through the psychological and relationship aspects of sex. What hopes or fears are motivating them? Do they see having sex as their ticket of admission into the popular crowd, or as a way to cement a tenuous relationship? Are they giving in to pressure or making an independent decision? Are they being honest and open in their relationships, or manipulative? Though advice is important, teens aren't usually great at listening to it. To help them think through the decisions they have to make, you should plan to do more listening than talking.

Teens are more likely to make good decisions—to avoid reckless promiscuity or put off sex altogether—if they have a solid foundation of self-respect, and if they have positive prospects for college or careers to look forward to. Wise parents help their children make small decisions all through the growing-up years, about how to choose their friends, how to spend their time, and how to do the right thing. The common sense and values children learn in this way help them to navigate the rocky shoals of adolescent sex.

GENDER NONCONFORMITY AND
SEXUAL PREFERENCES

In cultures with rigid sex roles, few things matter more than being born a girl or a boy. This is still true for us in the United States, but less so with each passing year. And as the power of gender wanes, possibilities open up for nonbinary genders, a spectrum of genders, or no gender at all. For the children who fit into these newer categories, the freedom to be who they are is everything; and for everyone else, the acceptance of diverse possibilities enriches and liberates.

Social attitudes toward sexual attractions are also bending toward freedom. Some people are attracted to the opposite sex (heterosexuality), whereas others are attracted to the same sex (homosexuality), to both males and females (bisexuality), or to an even broader group of people (that is, pansexuality). Still others may express little or no sexual attraction to anyone (asexuality). Gender and sexual preference are different: The first has to do with who you *are*; the second has to do with the people who inspire romantic feelings in you. Sexual "preference" is probably a poor choice of words, though, because we know that neither gender nor hetero- or homosexuality are matters of choice. Both arise from structures in the brain that are not chosen, but that come into being as the brain develops. The exact mechanisms aren't known, but it's clear that choice—whether a child's or a parent's—is not part of the process.

Neither is education. Children don't learn their genders or sexual leanings from their parents. Children raised by same-sex parents aren't any more likely to grow up homosexual than are the children of heterosexual ones. Nor are they more likely to suffer from mental illness, or to be geniuses, for that matter. The quality of parenting doesn't have much to do with it; biology runs the show.

This being the case, parents can't reasonably feel responsible for their children's gender identities or for their sexual leanings. They also shouldn't worry that open discussion about sexuality or gender will somehow give children permission to take on nonmainstream identities. Children will, or will not, depending on how their brains are made. This is something parents don't get to choose.

Parents *can* choose, however, to understand, accept, and support their children, whatever courses their brains steer them to. The choice to accept and support is critical to a child's happiness, and possibly to her survival: The rate of suicide is frighteningly high among LGBT youth, but not so high when they know that their parents stand behind them.

How gender identity develops. By age two, most children can tell you their gender, but their ideas about what that means aren't fully formed. Early on, for example, it's common for boys to think that they can have babies, and for girls to think that they ought to have penises. Such wishes are simply a sign of the young child's belief that anything is possible—if you want a penis, well, you can *have* a penis!

Sigmund Freud built an elaborate theory around the idea of penis envy, a theory most psychologists now reject. Little girls might well envy some of the privileges their male counterparts enjoy, such as peeing standing up and being allowed to play rough. By the same token, little boys might envy girls' access to lipstick and high heels. (Certainly, in societies that value boys over girls—as was the case in Freud's Vienna—this inequity might inspire envy, reasonably enough.)

Children do identify themselves with their parents and, if the relationship is warm, seek to grow up like them. But they don't only model themselves on the same-sex parent. They try on the roles and styles of many people they love and look up to. Dr. Spock recalls learning how to care for children by watching his mother (who had five more after him). I had a similar experience, except that my mother, who taught pre-school for forty years, had *hundreds* of children.

Society's unwritten laws for little boy and girls don't need to be obeyed. It's normal for little boys to want to play with dolls and for little girls to want to play with cars, and it's quite all right to let them. There is no harm in boys and girls wearing unisex clothes—jeans and T-shirts—if that's what they want. As for chores, it's good for boys and girls to be given the same tasks. Boys can do as much bed making, room cleaning, and dishwashing as their sisters. And girls can take part in yard work and car washing. This isn't to say that boys and girls can't swap certain chores or that it all has to come out exactly even, only that there shouldn't be discrimination in the assignments.

Gender fluidity and transgender. Children are typically assigned their sex according to their genitals or given genetic testing if there's a question. However, a person's gender is not just about anatomy or even chromosomes. Gender is mostly about a person's internal sense of self as male, female, both, or neither.

Gender is a product of the brain. Conveniently, most children's genitals and other parts agree with their brains; but this isn't always so. Just a few years ago, the standard psychiatry handbook labeled brain-body disagreements as "gender-identity disorder." The new name, "gender dysphoria," avoids the harmful notion that children in this situation have a disease. Related terms are "gender diverse," "gender nonconforming," "gender expansive," and others. All this terminology should become less important as society comes to accept gender fluidity as just a fact of life.

"Transgender" applies to children who have a persistent and strong belief that their body gender is wrong. This conviction arises from the biology of the brain; it's not the result of parenting good or bad. A young boy who wants to put on a dress and lipstick is most likely just playing mommy. A boy who insists that he's really a girl, and becomes upset whenever forced to wear pants, and keeps this up year after year, may be transgender. A girl who plays rough and likes to wear pants is probably a tomboy (or, actually, just a kid!). A girl who year after year insists that she is really a *he*, who becomes upset anytime she's made to wear a dress, and who only enjoys boy-typical play, may be transgender.

Such convictions often arise in early childhood and sometimes disappear in a few years. If they persist through puberty, they're much less likely to fade away. Efforts to "re-educate" such children are futile and cruel. Most major medical centers have specialized programs to help transgender children and their parents deal with the challenges of making certain, making plans, and undergoing a thoughtful transition (go to drspock.com). These programs bring comfort to families that might otherwise suffer greatly; their value is hard to overstate.

When parents think that their little boy is effeminate or their little girl is too masculine, they may wonder whether the child will grow up to be homosexual. Because of prevailing prejudices against homosexuality, this idea makes many parents anxious. But sexual orientation and gender identity are separate issues. While many gender-expansive children do grow up to be homosexual, many do not. With all of these issues, it's parents' willingness to understand and support their children that makes positive long-term outcomes possible.

Homosexuality and homophobia. Experts have a hard time determining how common homosexuality is, because there is still so much stigma attached to it. Also, the distinction between gay and straight is not as clear-cut as one might think. Quite a few people who identify themselves as straight have, or have had, sexual relations with people of their own gender. Some are bisexual; others feel homosexual attraction but only engage in heterosexual behavior. Human sexuality, like so much else, falls along a continuum. According to most published reports, between 5 and 20 percent of U.S. adults could be classified as homosexual. Whether you go with the lower or the higher estimates, the point is, that's *a lot* of people.

Some parents fear that contact with gay or lesbian teachers may cause children to become gay, but a child's sexual orientation can't be changed in this way. Rather, the evidence shows that a person's basic or primary sexual orientation is set early in development, beginning in the womb.

If your child asks about gays and lesbians, or even if you're just talking about sex in general, you can explain quite simply that some men and women fall in love with and live with people of the same sex. If homosexuality is considered a sin in your family's religion, you will need to handle the issue with special sensitivity, since there is a chance that your own child may grow up to be homosexual. In that case, you will want to have talked about the issue in such a way that your child feels comfortable confiding in you and seeking your support, and is not overcome with shame.

Homophobia can kill. A child with same-sex attractions who grows up in a family or culture that condemns homosexuality is at high risk for serious mental and physical health problems. Teens whose families reject their homosexuality report severe depression more than six times as often as their heterosexual peers, and attempt suicide more than eight times as often.

THE MEDIA

The electronic genie grants three wishes: infinite information, constant communication, and endless entertainment. But these magical gifts have a dark side: distraction, dependence, and social isolation. Rather than serving us, the electronics take over. As parents, we're in a bind. On one hand, we can't deny our children access to the digital world; on the other hand, we know that the territory is potentially dangerous. We're trying to lead our children across a minefield without a map.

Actually, the situation with media isn't that much different than the rest of parenting: lots of promise, lots of uncertainty. In the end, you have to trust yourself, your knowledge of your children, your protective instincts. I can't give you a prescription to follow, but I'll share some experiences and some recommendations that make sense to me.

Infants and electronics. If you plop an infant down in front of a TV, he'll stare at it and might seem interested. Actually, he's just mesmerized by the shifting colors and sounds. We know that babies aren't following the stories, because they're just as happy staring at random colors. Looking at videos takes no effort, and as a result the brain circuits that create effortful attention (the frontal lobes) aren't activated. Probably for this reason, children who consume lots of electronic videos show less ability to attend to things like picture books, or other people talking to them, that do require concentration.

A lot of marketing goes into convincing parents that their children need electronics to learn. It's a lie. In Silicon Valley, for example, many successful tech-savvy parents limit their children's access to screens, and instead make sure they have lots of three-dimensional learning opportunities. Young children, in particular, learn best when they are free to use all their senses to figure out how things (and other people) work.

The American Academy of Pediatrics recommends very limited if any exposure to electronic screens for children under age two. The one exception is video chats with family members (like grandparents, or parents deployed overseas). Because these chats involve real people who are responding to the baby the way family members do, they are more like in-person interactions than prerecorded shows or computer games.

For older toddlers and young children, the Academy recommends no more than an hour a day. Video or TV viewing should be with a parent right there, talking with the child about what's happening on-screen. It's the human interaction that's valuable; the electronics are just a prop. In other words, you should use electronics to bring your baby and you close, not come between you.

Watch TV with your child. The idea is to help your child to make sense of the world in a more realistic and wholesome way and to see TV for the fantasy it is. As these lessons are learned, your child can become immunized against wholesale acceptance of the media's messages.

When you watch together, you can comment on whether what you've just seen bears any resemblance to the real world. If you've just watched a fight where someone gets punched and merely shrugs it off, you can say, "That punch in the nose must have really hurt. Don't you think it did? Television isn't at all like real life, is it?" This teaches your child to empathize with the victim of violence, rather than identify with the perpetrator. When viewing a commercial, you might comment, "Do you think what they are saying is true? I think they just want you to buy their product." You want your child to view commercials for what they are and to understand their manipulative intent. When viewing a scene with impersonal sexual content, you can comment, "That's not what it's like in real life at all. Usually that happens after people have known each other for a long time and really love each other."

TV in the bedroom. When a child can't fall asleep, well-meaning parents turn on the TV to keep him calm in bed. Pretty soon he can *only* fall asleep when the TV is on. After a while he begins waking in the middle of the night and turning on the TV for an hour or two. In the morning he's cranky, then can't pay attention in school. The parents feel stuck; if they take the TV out of the bedroom they have a miserable and sleepless child on their hands. If they don't, the midnight TV viewing ruins the child's days.

TV in the bedroom is a good example of a solution that becomes a problem. Many addictions fit this description: Alcoholism often starts as a solution to being socially uncomfortable and opioid addiction as a solution to pain. Both solutions grow into problems that are worse than the problems they solved.

The simple answer is take the TV out of the bedroom. Expect some pushback (tantrums, sleepless nights); it won't last forever. This still leaves the problem of how to help your child fall asleep comfortably at a reasonable time. The key is to build a connection in your child's brain between lying down in bed and falling asleep, a healthy habit (see page 774). The first step is to establish that a bed is for sleeping. Watching TV happens somewhere else.

Do you need a television? Very few parents choose to live entirely without TV. But the ones who do always seem happy with that decision. Children who never get into the habit of watching television don't miss it. They simply fill their days with other activities. Parents often think that television makes their lives easier because it keeps their children occupied for blocks of time. But when you figure in all the hours spent arguing about how much children can watch and what shows they can and cannot watch, then add in the hassles of getting the children to stop watching so they can do homework or chores, it probably takes less effort to not have a television at all. Even just dropping the cable subscription can make a difference, not only in the family budget, but also in your quality of life.

Addicted to the game. My behavior clinic is full of children glued to handheld video games. A parent tells me about her child's problems with inattention and anger. Meanwhile, the child (who is sitting two feet away) is in another world altogether, absorbed in the game. I ask, "What triggers the anger?" "It's when I try to take away the game!"

The child's behavior may seem controlling or manipulative. But it's really the game that is in control. The child responds in anger because he feels that he *has* to keep playing, that the parent is trying to take away something he *needs*. For some children, gaming becomes an addiction: Nothing holds their attention except the game, and without it they suffer from painful boredom. The mere thought of going without their game sends them into a panic. Certain games exert particularly strong control because of the fascination of fantasy violence, or because there are other players online who apply peer pressure. These games are best avoided entirely (go to drspock.com for a list of more positive games).

The fact that stopping the game is so traumatic is what tells you that gaming has turned from a pleasure to a compulsion. Parents have to set limits on gaming. This works best if you take control from the start: Impose time limits, take the game away when you want to or need to, and make it clear that the game belongs to you. If your child protests too loudly or too long, he loses access to the game that day. He has to show that he's not a slave to the game, by accepting your control over it.

You can assert your control at any time, even if your child has gotten into the habit of gaming all day every day, even if a well-meaning relative has given him a game as a present. You are still the boss. You are acting not out of malice, but out of love, to protect your child from falling into a habit that can quickly undermine his health and happiness. When you stop the game, you need to help your child shift to another activity that is fun and rewarding. When games are filling a vacuum, it makes stopping even harder.

Secondhand screens. We know about the dangers of secondhand cigarette smoke. In a similar way, parental overuse of electronics can harm nearby children, a problem I think of as "secondhand screens." Babies and young children are naturally social. They're wired to capture their parents' attention by cooing and babbling, smiling, reaching, and eventually pointing and saying words. In today's digital world, though, these attempts to communicate may be met with an unresponsive parent whose focus has been grabbed by social media. When this happens over and over, the child may give up even trying to interact.

No one knows the long-term effects of secondhand screens, but you can see the short-term effects in any park or subway. The parent or babysitter stares at the cell phone, and the baby stares into space looking lifeless and depressed. For a baby, it's less distressing to just shut down than to be ignored while trying to interact. Ignoring a child is a form of punishment, after all. (I don't mean to say that you have to instantly respond to every peep out of your baby's mouth, but don't let your cell phone send your baby an unintended message.)

Teens, screens, and sex. We have all read the stories of young kids who visit chat rooms, get seduced by strangers, then get sold into sex slavery. More often, what really happens is not quite as dramatic, but bad enough. Teens meet older people in chat rooms and get into wildly unequal (and illegal) sexual relationships.

Teens who have warm and supportive parents are less likely to be trapped in this way. Open discussions about sex, and how sex, money, and power get mixed up in our society, may also help. It's reasonable, too, to create the expectation that you want to see where your child is going online. This can work if you and your child have a relationship of mutual trust. For example, your child might take you for a tour of her social media world. And you might also explore together some of the potentially tempting, and maybe dangerous, chat rooms. Your role is to provide calm, reasonable, and supportive information. It doesn't help to flip out. Also, it doesn't help to spy on your child. If you do, you undermine your child's ability to trust you as a wise ally. And if you can't trust your child, that's a serious problem that needs work, maybe therapy. Online spying isn't the answer.

Here are some commonsense rules children need to learn:

1. Never post personal information—your address, your phone number, or the name of your school—or send it to anyone you haven't already met in person.

2. Never tell anyone else your password. Although chat room correspondents may seem like your friends, they are really strangers. You need to be as careful with these strangers as with those you meet on the street.

3. If a message makes you feel uncomfortable in any way, stop and tell an adult.

4. Use good "netiquette"—treat people with politeness and consideration. Inappropriate or rude communications are not acceptable, even if you're anonymous.

5. Only post comments or pictures that you'd be comfortable showing to your principal or your grandmother.

Once it's posted, you lose control of the material, because someone else can copy it and pass it along. Deleting material from your page doesn't delete it from the online world.

Online pornography. Before your child goes online alone, talk about what she's likely to find. Explain that pornography is a business: Some adults pay money to see pictures of other adults naked. Help your child understand what's wrong with this mix of commerce and sexuality. Let your child know what you expect her to do if she runs across a sex site (leave the site, turn off the computer, tell you). Talk with teens about pornography's damaging effects on the people who make it—they are often victims of sexual abuse or addicts supporting their habits—and on people who try to model their own sex lives after it.

Remember, talking about sex doesn't make children engage in it (see page 642). Instead, when you can discuss sex in a matter-of-fact way, it takes away some of the thrill of mystery that so often surrounds the topic. Also, you let your child know that you are approachable and askable.

Pornography can capture a teen's imagination and distort a young person's ideas about sexual intimacy. Any teen with access to the Internet and a closed door has almost certainly wandered into the back alleys of porn. If you have a teen or preteen child, you should probably take a look around those ugly districts yourself, just to know what's there. Then, as part of your ongoing discussions about sex, let your child know your thoughts. My own take is that human bodies are not bad, sex is not bad, but pornography is sex without emotion or human connection, fueled by desperation and money. It's a symptom of injustice and oppression in the world.

If you can bear to do it, and if you think it's best, look at some porn sites together with your teen. At least that way the sites are not mysterious and forbidden (and therefore alluring). Also, your teen can hear your humane voice speaking out against the pornographers' siren song. Then, with your teen's full awareness, put blocking software in place to keep your teen out of the pornographic cesspool. Just like you don't leave cigarettes lying around the house, or dishes of candy for that matter, it's unwise to make access to porn too easy. For teenage boys, in particular, the allure of impersonal fantasy sex is hardwired, not simply something that can be shut off by a lecture or even by healthy communication. Consider buying some books or magazines that aren't quite as potently toxic as the online poison, but that still meet a teen's hormone-driven needs.

Screens and socialization. One of the very best things about the Internet is that it allows people to create communities over distance. Support groups for rare and not-so-rare medical conditions—Williams syndrome, Down syndrome, cystic fibrosis, and hundreds more—are wonderful helps for so many families (go to drspock.com).

For many children who have difficulty making social connections in the everyday world, the Internet also opens doors to social engagement. But it shouldn't be a substitute for in-person friendships. A teen who claims to be content to go home, close his door, and commune with online gaming pals needs more in life. He needs help from parents, teachers, and perhaps professionals, to feel comfortable enough in the real world to connect with three-dimensional peers.

More on media and children. This topic could fill whole books. Go to drspock.com for links to trustworthy information, The American Academy of Pediatrics posts many valuable articles and parent guides, for example.

DIFFERENT TYPES OF FAMILIES

As our society has opened up, we've learned that children can thrive in many different types of families: families with one parent, families with two mommies or two daddies, and many other variations. The freedom to create families outside the traditional mold means that more people can now devote their hearts and talents to the raising of children.

ADOPTION

Reasons to adopt. A couple should decide to adopt only if both of them love children and very much want a child. All children, whether biological or adopted, need to feel that they belong to their parents and are loved deeply and forever. An adopted child can easily sense a lack of love. She's looking for it, having been through one or more previous separations. She knows that she was given up for some reason by her biological parents, and she may fear secretly that her adoptive parents might someday give her up, too.

You can see why it's a mistake to adopt when only one parent wants to, or when the parents are thinking of it for practical reasons, such as to have someone to take care of them in their old age, or to salvage a failing marriage. Adoption for these reasons is unfair.

Parents sometimes consider adopting to provide a sibling for their only child. It's a good idea to talk this over with a mental health professional or the adoption agency before proceeding. The adopted child is apt to feel like an outsider, and if the parents lean over backward to show affection for the newcomer, it may upset rather than help their biological child.

There can be pitfalls, too, in adopting to "replace" a child who has died. Parents need time to work out their grief. It's not fair to ask one individual to play the part of another; a child is bound to fail at the job of being a ghost. She should not be reminded of what the other child did, or be compared with her either out loud or in the parents' minds. Let her be herself.

At what age should a child be adopted? For the child's sake, the younger the better. Even though early placement is not possible for thousands of youngsters living in foster homes and institutions, these older children can also be successfully adopted. The agency will help older children and parents decide if adoption is right for them.

Adopt through a good agency. Probably the most important advice is to arrange the adoption through a first-rate agency. It is always risky for the adopting parents to deal directly with the biological parents or with an inexperienced third person. This leaves the way open for the biological parents to change their minds. Even when the law stands in the way of the biological parents, the conflict can ruin the happiness of the adopting family and undermine the security of the child.

A good agency will help the biological mother and relatives to make the right decision in the first place about whether or not to give the baby up. Wise agencies and the laws in many states require a period of adjustment before an adoption becomes final. A skilled agency worker can help the family through this period. All state health departments have a section that licenses adoption agencies, and that can help you find a qualified one.

Gray-market adoptions. Most of the children waiting to be adopted are older. This means that people who want to adopt babies or very young children may have to wait a long time. It's often quicker to adopt a baby through a lawyer or doctor, rather than going through an adoption agency. A lot of people think they won't have any trouble if they get a "gray-market" baby this way, as opposed to a black-market baby who is clearly being adopted without any legal procedures at all. But gray-market adoptions also can lead to trouble, both legal and emotional, when, for example, the biological mother decides that she wants the baby back.

Children with special needs. Now that more unmarried parents are keeping their children, fewer very young infants are available for adoption. Many older children still need parents, however, as do sibling groups and children with chronic medical or behavioral conditions. These children are as much in need of love and can be as rewarding to parents as any other child. Older children may have already lived in other foster homes. Fearing another rejection, they may act out, testing to see if once again they will be sent away. With support and clear expectations, adopting such children can be especially rewarding.

Nontraditional parents. In the past, most adoption agencies would only consider married, heterosexual couples without biological children. Now many agencies welcome single parents, parents in committed gay and lesbian partnerships or marriages, parents whose race is different from the child's, and others. Childhood passes quickly, and a permanent parent *now* is of more value than the possibility of two parents some time in the future. Furthermore, agencies have learned that when it comes to adopting successfully, a family's outward characteristics matter less than the character of the hopeful parent or parents.

Open adoption. In recent years, it has become increasingly common for the adoptive parents to exchange information with the birth parent or parents. They may even meet. Sometimes the birth mother can choose which of several possible adoptive parents she prefers. And in some cases an arrangement is made for the birth mother to keep up with the child—for example, receiving a snapshot of the child and a yearly letter from the adoptive parents.

Openness can work well for all parties involved. Many children seem to be able to handle having both a birth mother and "a mother who takes care of me." Knowing their birth mother spares children the pain of wondering, "What is she like? What would she think of me?" Even if the reality is sad—the mother may have serious problems of her own, for example—it may be less disturbing to the child than an idealized (or demonized) fantasy.

Telling the child. When should a child be told she is adopted? She's sure to find out sooner or later from someone, no matter how carefully the parents think they are keeping the secret. It's a disturbing experience for an older child or an adult to discover suddenly that she is adopted.

The news shouldn't be saved for any definite age. From the beginning, parents should let the adoption come up naturally in their conversations with each other, with the child, and with their acquaintances. This way, the child can ask questions whenever the subject begins to interest her. She finds out what adoption means bit by bit, as she gains understanding.

Some adopting parents make the mistake of trying to keep the adoption secret; others err in the opposite direction by stressing it too much. If they go too earnestly at the job of explaining to the child that she's adopted, she may begin to wonder, "What's wrong with being adopted, anyway?" But if they accept the adoption as naturally as they accept the color of the child's hair, they won't have to make a secret of it or keep reminding her of it.

Answering children's questions. Let's say that a child around three hears her mother explaining to a new acquaintance that she is adopted, and asks, "What's 'adopted,' Mommy?" The mother might answer, "A long time ago I wanted very much to have a little baby girl to love and take care of. So I went to a place where there were a lot of babies, and they brought me a baby, and it was you. And I said, 'Oh, this is just exactly the baby that I want. I want to adopt her and take her home to keep forever.' And that's how I adopted you." This makes a good beginning because it emphasizes the positive side of the adoption, the fact that the mother received just what she wanted. The story will delight the child, and she'll want to hear it many times.

Children who have been adopted at an older age will need a different approach. They may have memories of their biological and foster parents. Agencies should help both the child and the new parents handle this. It is important to realize that questions will surface repeatedly during different stages of this child's life. They should be answered as simply and honestly as possible. Parents should allow the child to freely express her feelings and fears.

Between the ages of three and four, an adopted child may want to know where babies come from (see page 632). It is best to answer truthfully but simply enough so that the three-year-old can understand easily. But when you explain that babies grow inside the mother's abdomen, it makes the child wonder how this fits in with the story of picking her out at the agency. Maybe then, or months later, she asks, "Did I grow inside you?" Then you can explain, simply and casually, that she grew inside another mother before she was adopted.

Eventually a child will raise the more difficult question of why her biological parents gave her up. To imply that they didn't want her would shake her confidence. Any sort of made-up reason may bother her later in some unexpected way. Perhaps the best answer and nearest to the truth might be, "I don't know why they couldn't take care of you, but I'm sure they wanted to." While your child is digesting this idea, she needs to hear that she's always going to be yours now.

Information about the birth parents. At some point, most adopted children want to know about their biological parents. Adoption agencies used to reveal only vague generalities, and completely concealed their identities. Today the courts may compel an agency to reveal the identity of the biological parents. If a visit follows, the outcome may be helpful or disturbing. A child's demands to meet her biological parents should be discussed with the adoption agency, and with the adoptive parents. The decision is one that deserves careful thought.

The adopted child must belong completely. An adopted child may harbor the secret fear that her adoptive parents will someday give her up, just as her biological parents did. Adoptive parents have to keep this possibility in mind, and never, under any circumstances, say or hint that the idea has crossed their minds. While they should be ready to let her know that she is theirs forever at any time the question seems to enter her mind, the thing that gives the adopted child the greatest security is being loved, wholeheartedly and naturally.

International adoption. Each year, families in the United States adopt thousands of infants and young children who were born elsewhere. Adoption takes place across other borders, too, all over the world. The process is complicated by politics, nationalism, and concerns about cultural identity. From the children's point of view, it often brings great improvements in health and happiness and the chance to grow up in a loving family.

There are many challenges. Children often arrive malnourished, missing immunizations, and with other medical conditions—issues that are usually dealt with easily. However, many also have developmental and emotional issues that can be harder to treat.

Many internationally adopted children have lived in institutions that barely met their physical and emotional needs. The longer a child has lived in an orphanage or similar institution, the greater the chance of lasting physical, intellectual, and emotional damage. Others have had to endure the pain of separation from loving foster parents.

Still, most internationally adopted children grow up to be emotionally as well as physically healthy. Early on, nearly all show signs of delayed growth and development, but most catch up within two or three years.

A lot depends on changing historical and political conditions. A country might rule, for example, that foreigners can adopt only children with severe physical disabilities. A few months later, though, the law may change. Because of these variables, an adoption agency that specializes in international adoptions and has country-specific experience is essential.

Internationally adopted children often look different from their adoptive parents, and may face insensitive comments or outright prejudice. For children old enough to speak and who don't know English, the trauma of suddenly not being able to communicate adds to the stress of the adoption. Because the children's biological heritage links them to a different culture, their relationship to that culture becomes an issue for the parents to grapple with when the children are young, and for the children themselves when they are older.

For many parents, adopting from a different country has political and ethical implications, too. The parents understand that they have benefited, in part, from the terrible conditions in the child's country of origin. Some families translate these concerns into action, perhaps by sending money and supplies to help other children who were left behind.

Many children adopted from overseas end up doing wonderfully, but some do not. Developmental-behavioral pediatricians and other experts can help parents weigh the risks. Only the parents know how much uncertainty they can bear.

Parents who choose to raise a child who may end up with severe problems are brave. But parents have also acted courageously who search their souls and decide that they cannot follow that path.

SINGLE-PARENT FAMILIES

Being a single parent makes a tough job that much tougher. You don't have a supportive partner to ease the relentless day-to-day responsibilities of raising children. Everybody and everything depends on you. You don't get a real break or vacation. If you are the only breadwinner, financial worries add to your burden. It's much harder to get ahead at work. It sometimes feels as if you just don't have enough physical and emotional energy to keep it all going.

At any given time, about one-quarter of the children in the United States live in single-parent homes. Over their lifetimes more than half of all children will spend some time in a single-parent household, either because of divorce or because their parents never married. Most single parents are mothers, and many have incomes below the federal poverty line.

Being a single parent is no picnic, but it does have its rewards. You and your children may achieve a special closeness. When things go well—as they often do—there can be a great sense of accomplishment.

Pitfalls of single parenting. One potential pitfall is an unwillingness to set firm limits. Many single parents feel guilty because their children are not growing up with two parents. They worry that their children are missing something essential, and they regret not being able to spend more time with their children. The temptation is strong for parents to indulge their child, giving in to the child's every whim. This isn't helpful.

Another pitfall for single parents is to treat their children as their best friends, telling them their deepest feelings. A single parent will sometimes have her school-age child sleep with her, not because the child is frightened or lonely, but because the parent wants company. Children can take on extra chores and provide some emotional support to a distressed parent, but they shouldn't take on an adult role. They need to be kids, with their own circle of friends, and their own hobbies and interests. For their part, single mothers need to feel okay about cultivating their own friendships, apart from their children.

The mother as single parent. It would be foolish to say that a father's absence makes no difference to a child. But if the job is handled well, the child can grow up well-adjusted. The mother's spirit matters a lot. A single mother may feel lonely, tied down, or cross at times, and she will sometimes take her feelings out on the child. This is natural and won't hurt him too much. But at the same time, she needs to have a life of her own, and not feel guilty about it. Getting help from friends and family is crucial. If there is a kind man among the helpers—an uncle or grandfather or adult friend—the child can have the experience of learning from a man and looking up to him. Single mothers with money do better, because they can buy help; but more often than not, poverty complicates the problem.

The father as single parent. For single fathers, although money may be less of an issue, nurturing may be a challenge.

Many men have been brought up believing that being a nurturing person is soft and therefore feminine. They find it hard, at least at first, to provide the gentle comforting and cuddling that children need, especially young children. But with time and experience, they can certainly rise to the task. Single fathers seek out nurturing women—aunts, grandmothers, or friends—who can become important in the lives of their children.

The betraying parent. For children in single-parent families, one of the most painful things is to look forward to time with the nonresident parent, and then the parent fails to show up. This happens to many children, repeatedly. Each betrayal leads to a cascade of anger: anger at the absent parent; guilt about that anger; self-blame ("If only I was a better kid . . ."); anger at the custodial parent; anger at the world. Underneath, children often hold on to the toxic idea that the betrayal is somehow their fault; it makes them hate themselves and everyone else. Nonresident parents who make promises to show up and then don't keep them break their children's hearts. The other parent, the one who looks after the child every day, is left trying to mend the wound.

For the mother in this situation—and it usually is a mother—the best thing to tell a child may be, "I don't know why your father didn't show up, but I know it's not your fault. He's doing this for his own reasons, which I don't understand. But I know that it has nothing to do with you, and there's nothing either of us can do about it. It makes me angry." This message—and the hug that follows—needs repeating over and over. Sometimes a professional counselor or therapist can help a child handle his real, understandable fury at the absent parent.

STEPFAMILIES

It's no accident that so many fairy tales have an evil stepmother or stepfather as the villain. After a separation, divorce, or death, a child may form an especially close and possessive bond with the remaining parent. Then along comes a stranger who takes away the parent's heart, bed, and at least half of the parent's attention. The child cannot help resenting this intruder, no matter how hard the stepparent tries to form a good relationship.

The hostility gets under the stepparent's skin and he is likely to feel the urge to respond in kind. The new relationship between the adults quickly becomes strained because it feels like a no-win, either-or choice. It's helpful for a stepparent to remember that these problems are common, maybe inevitable, and not necessarily a reflection of their worth or of the eventual outcome of the relationship. The tension may persist for months or years. In other situations, the new parent may be much more easily accepted.

Dr. Spock recalled his own stepparenting experience: "Years ago, with what I thought was great wisdom, I wrote a magazine article about stepparenting. Then in 1976 I became a stepfather and realized that I was quite incapable of following my own advice. I had advised stepparents to strictly avoid trying to be disciplinarians, but I kept reproaching my eleven-year-old stepdaughter for her consistent rudeness, and I kept trying to make her conform to a few rules of mine. This was one of the most painful relationships I ever experienced, and the one that taught me the most."

Why is stepparenting so hard? There are plenty of good reasons why life in a stepfamily is stressful, at least initially:

✦ *Loss.* By the time they enter a stepfamily, most children will have experienced significant loss: the loss of a parent, and perhaps the loss of friends because of a move. This sense of loss affects a child's early response to the new stepparent.

✦ *Loyalty issues.* The child may wonder, "Who are my parents now? If I show affection to my stepparent, does it mean I can't or shouldn't love the parent who is no longer with me? How can I split my affections?"

✦ *Loss of control.* No child ever makes the decision to have a stepfamily; the decision is made for him by adults. He feels buffeted by forces and people over whom he has no control.

✦ *Stepsiblings.* All of these stresses can be made worse by the presence of stepsiblings. The child wonders, "What if my mother or father loves my stepbrother more than me? Why do I have to share my possessions, or my room, with this complete stranger?"

Positive aspect of stepfamilies. While difficult beginnings are common, most family members eventually adapt to the new circumstance. Children often establish close, long-lasting relationships with stepparents and stepsiblings. After all, each has the shared experience of a disrupted and reconstituted family, and each is devoted to the same person, who is the child's biological parent. Children can also fruitfully divide their time between two families, each with a biological parent and a stepparent. For a child who is flexible and well supported, this "dual citizenship" of living in two separate families can be enriching.

Tips for stepparenting. There are some general principles that may be helpful. The first is for the parents to agree ahead of time on how they'll handle the children and to have realistic expectations of what the new family will be like. It is better for a stepparent to avoid moving into the guiding and correcting role of a full parent too soon. A stepparent who tries to enforce such things as chores, bedtime, and curfews too soon is sure to be judged as a harsh intruder, even if enforcing the same rules as the natural parent.

On the other hand, it's not good for parents to be submissive when the stepchild intrudes into their territory, for instance, and abuses one parent's possessions. The parent should set a limit in a friendly but firm way: "I don't like it when you hurt yourself or your things, and I don't like it when you hurt my things, either." You can't make an issue of every hostile look; you'd be grouchy all day. So ignore the small slights and save your comments for major infractions of the rules.

It's important for the parents to understand that children need plenty of time to get used to the new arrangement. At the same time, it helps for parents to be consistent about family expectations regarding bedtime, chores, and homework.

When to seek help. Too often, the stresses that come along with stepparenting end up straining marriages to the breaking point. It's wise to seek professional help early, rather than waiting for the problems to grow. The help may take the form of guidance or direction for the parents on how to proceed;

marital or family therapy; or individual counseling for one or more of the children. Stepparent groups, available through many community child guidance centers, can be helpful, too. For more on stepfamilies, see Divorce (page 703).

GAY AND LESBIAN PARENTS

Same-sex marriage is now the law of the land! In the United States, perhaps one-third of gay and lesbian couples are involved in parenting, and more than two million children live with one or more LGBT parent. The experience of children in nontraditional families depends on where they live. Some communities are accepting. In others, parents may feel isolated and vulnerable, even now.

Effects on children. There have been many studies looking at the development of children of gay and lesbian parents, and the results all line up: There are no significant differences between children raised by heterosexual parents and those raised by gay or lesbian parents. What matters is not the parents' gender or sexual orientation but how loving and nurturing they are. Since gay men and women can be as warm and caring (or as dysfunctional) as heterosexual parents, it is not surprising that the mental health of their children is comparable.

Compared to children in heterosexual households, the children of gay and lesbian parents are equally likely to play with same-sex peers when they are in grade school and to choose opposite-sex romantic partners when they are older. As a group, they are more tolerant of different sexual orientations and more sensitive to minority status. They are less likely to be victims of sexual abuse. Surprisingly, perhaps, they are no more likely to be teased at school than other children.

Finding support. There are many books written for gay and lesbian parents that you might find useful, as well as national support groups (go to drspock.com). Many communities offer support groups for children (and parents) to share their experiences with others in similar circumstances. There are also some terrific books for children that address issues of gay and lesbian families.

Help for heterosexuals. Awareness about gay and lesbian parents has grown so much in recent years that many heterosexual parents feel comfortable with the issue. But others still have concerns. Will it be confusing to a child with a mommy and daddy to be friends with a child who has two mommies or two daddies? I think the answer is simply no. Children are remarkably able to accept plain facts when they are presented plainly.

What *can* be confusing is when a child is taught that homosexuality is wrong, and then meets parents who seem to be very nice and who have great kids, and who turn out to be gay or lesbian. In that case, the child may have a hard time reconciling what she knows from firsthand experience with what she has been told is true.

Opposition to gay and lesbian parenting often arises from the fear that such parenting fosters homosexuality (it doesn't), or from a religious conviction that homosexuality is sinful. Such doctrines put tremendous pressure on children who do not fit the heterosexual mold, and put them at risk for a range of mental health problems, including suicide. Parents may struggle to reconcile their faith with their need to provide love and security to their children (see page 645 on sexuality and gender).

The emergence of gay and lesbian families gives you an opportunity to teach your child about different types of families and to value what is really important: kindness, consideration, and warmth. These lessons will serve your child well in our increasingly diverse world.

CHILDREN WITH
SPECIAL NEEDS

Who are these children? In the past it was common to label a child by the name of his condition—a "Down syndrome child" or an "autistic child." Now the "child" comes first, and we talk about a child with a disability rather than a disabled child. Changing how we talk changes how we think. Children with special health care needs are, first and foremost, children. They have all the same needs for love, acceptance, freedom, fun, friendship, challenge, and participation in society as other children, and some special needs as well.

A wide range of children fall under this heading. They include children with common medical conditions such as asthma and diabetes; those with moderately uncommon conditions such as Down syndrome and cystic fibrosis; and those with rare conditions such as phenylketonuria. Among them are children with complications of prematurity such as cerebral palsy, deafness, or blindness; children whose brains have been damaged by trauma or infection; and children with physical malformations such as cleft palate, dwarfism, or disfiguring birthmarks. Altogether, there are probably three thousand different conditions that comprise special health care needs.

Each condition carries its own set of problems and therapies. And, of course, the children who have these conditions and their families all have their unique strengths and weaknesses, so that it is unrealistic to talk about children with disabilities as though they were a single large group. Still, there are some common issues.

COPING WITHIN THE FAMILY

Early responses. Grief is normal. Parents have to mourn the loss of the healthy child they had, or the perfect child they imagined, before they can accept the real child they have now. Grief often starts with denial, then switches to anger; it may involve bargaining (making deals with God, for example), or shade into depression. Finally, with luck and effort, there is acceptance and the ability to take action, confront obstacles, celebrate victories, and in general to find meaning in what fate has decreed. The idea that grief happens in stages isn't quite right. All of these different reactions come and go, like clouds overhead. So you may find yourself feeling angry or depressed for no apparent reason—at the supermarket, say—until you realize that your grief has picked this time to reemerge.

Grief becomes worrisome when a father or mother becomes locked in with no room to move—the parent who cannot acknowledge the reality of the child's circumstances; who is angry at everybody all the time; or who is so depressed that it's hard to get out of bed or to enjoy normal pleasures. Although such responses are common early on, it's concerning if they persist month after month. It's normal to need to be alone for a time, but it's not healthy to stay isolated. Grief weakens when it's shared. The ability to grieve together with a partner, friends, family, or a professional is a strong sign of resilience. People are not meant to suffer alone.

Another common reaction is guilt. A parent thinks, "It must be something I did wrong," and dwells endlessly on what that might have been. The problem with guilt is that it leaves no way forward. Preoccupation with the past saps the energy that a parent needs to cope with the present. Guilt can even become a handy excuse: "It's all my fault, so I can't be expected to do anything about it." Don't fall into this trap, and if your partner has fallen in, confront him and drag him out.

Different parents cope differently. One parent tries to learn everything possible about her child's condition; another puts all her trust in an expert. One parent shows a lot of emotion; another puts on a stoic face and may seem cold. One wants to talk; another craves silence. One parent blames himself and becomes depressed; another blames others, or the world at large, and becomes furious. One feels hopeless; another dives into political advocacy.

It's important to be aware of these potential differences in style and look past them to the underlying reality, which is that both parents care deeply. It may take conscious effort, sometimes with the help of a professional, for parents to understand and accept each other's different coping styles. Without that, the pain of emotional isolation can amplify the difficulty of caring for a child with special needs.

Specialization. It often happens that one parent specializes in the care of the child with the disability, going to all the appointments and support group meetings and learning everything about the condition. At the same time, the other parent—often the father—may feel more and more left out, and less and less comfortable taking care of the child. The father may also find that he has less and less to say to the mother, who is wrapped up in the world of the disability. The marriage can suffer.

The best way to avoid this trap is for both parents to participate in caring for the child with special needs. If one parent stays home with the child during the day, the parent with the out-of-home job should make sure that he or she cares for the child for blocks of time after work and on weekends, and takes time off from work now and then to go to appointments and meetings. It may seem unfair—after all, the parent with the job is probably working hard all day long, too, and deserves to relax—but unfair or not, it's really necessary if parents are to stay together and function as a team.

Save time for siblings. If a child's special needs become the sole focus for the family, the other siblings are bound to feel resentment. They may wonder why it takes a problem to engage their parents' attention. Some start to cause trouble themselves, as if to say, "Hey, I'm your child, too." Others become hyper-responsible "little adults." They may demand perfection of themselves, as though that could somehow make up for their sibling's lack of perfection and win their parents' love.

All children have needs, even if they aren't "special needs." Many times a school play or softball game may have to take a back seat to an emergency medical appointment. But it's good if *sometimes* the routine doctor's appointment is what ends up being rescheduled. A typically developing sibling who doesn't demand attention may need individual attention offered, or even insisted on at times. A child's often unspoken resolution to "not make any demands" is a problem to be dealt with.

That said, it can be helpful to offer to involve healthy siblings, if they wish, in some of a child's evaluation or therapy sessions. This takes some of the mystery out of the attention the child with special needs is receiving. But if a sibling doesn't want to tag along to the clinic or the therapist's office, honor that preference when you can. A child who feels he has some say in the matter is much more likely to offer his assistance freely and with a good heart.

Siblings need to hear, many times, that the special challenges in the family are nobody's fault; neither the child with the complex condition, nor anyone else, is to blame.

It isn't easy being the sibling of a child with special needs. But it can be a positive experience, teaching empathy and compassion, tolerance for differences among people, courage, and resilience. Many pediatricians have siblings with special needs; I doubt this is just a coincidence.

Nurture your adult relationships. Your relationship with your spouse requires care and attention. The statistics are thought-provoking: Under the strain of a severely disabled child, about a third of marriages crumble, a third stay the same, and a third grow stronger. Growth requires open communication and mutual trust. Most of all, it takes a commitment to invest energy in the relationship itself. Friendships and ties to the community also need cultivating. You need and deserve to have a life beyond your child's special needs.

In practical terms, this means finding respite: someone to take care of a child for a time so that you can go to a movie, do some shopping, or visit friends. Respite can come from professional agencies, friends, one's church or synagogue, and family. Don't feel that you should never leave your child. She needs to learn to separate from you, just as any child does, and you need to feel comfortable when she is in the care of others. For many parents, it also means continuing a professional career and arranging for others to step in to share the work of caring for a child's special needs.

There is no perfect way to be a parent of a child with special needs. There are always trade-offs: Sometimes you just need to get away for your own peace of mind; sometimes you feel that you're neglecting one family member while you attend to the needs of another; sometimes you feel as if you're just not up to the task. This is all par for the course; you can't do it all. The good news is that you don't need to. Perfection is a trap: Good enough much of the time, with failure now and then that you move past, and the ability to treasure small victories, is what success looks like.

TAKING ACTION

Having a child with special health care needs can bring on helplessness and despair. The antidote to those feelings is to take action. Learn all you can about your child's condition. The more you understand about it, the less mysterious it will be, the better you will be able to understand the doctors, and the more you will be able to help the teachers and therapists. Connect with the national organizations that deal with this problem; read books; talk to professionals and other parents.

A medical home. A child with special health care needs benefits if she has a medical team that understands her condition, knows the available medical and social service resources, and can coordinate her care. For children with very complicated conditions—spina bifida for example, or cystic fibrosis—the medical team may involve several different medical specialists, nurses, therapists, and others. In this situation, especially, it's worth seeking out and cultivating a long-standing relationship with a particular doctor on the team who knows you and your child well, and who you can trust.

Parent support groups. Parent groups can provide education, tips for finding the best doctors and therapists, and personal support. There are national organizations for most medical and developmental conditions, and many local groups as well. Some are listed in the Resource Guide (see page 887), or you can find them online, at your local library, or through your child's doctor.

Advocate for your child. You may find that you have to negotiate with various professionals and bureaucracies. The school system may not offer a program that meets your child's special needs. Insurance companies may balk at paying for certain tests or therapies. Your community might not offer services and opportunities your child needs and deserves.

In these cases, an insistent, knowledgeable parental voice can make a difference. Seek out local, state, or national organizations whose purpose is to educate and empower parents to be effective advocates. Ask your child's doctor, or go through the national organizations listed at drspock.com.

Don't be discouraged if your first efforts meet resistance. Over time you'll become more and more effective. You also don't have to do it alone. The only voice more powerful than that of a persistent parent is the voice of a *group* of persistent parents. Join up with a national coalition of parents to make your single voice part of a chorus to influence legislators and the courts.

Many communities and religious groups rally in support of their members with special needs. Introduce your child to your neighbors, to people in your place of worship, to school leaders. Help them to understand your child's needs, abilities, and special gifts. Insist that your child has the right to participate in all aspects of community life, and that your child will greatly enrich the community in the process.

STRESSES AND TRAUMAS

Ordinary life for a child in the twenty-first century can be extraordinarily stressful. Television beams terrorism, earthquakes, and wars into the home. Threats are everywhere: global warming, wars, the police (for some children more than others). Politics threaten—especially in our polarized era. Some dangers are real, but many are the product of overheated coverage. For example, child abduction has not skyrocketed, although news coverage of it has. Fear is a daily intrusion.

Some stresses are common: the temporary absence of a parent, or the more lasting separation of divorce; a serious illness; a death. Economic instability—with insecure food resources and unstable housing—adds to the strains many children feel. Some traumas are extreme, such as physical and sexual abuse, or the death of a parent. Domestic violence terrifies children, even if they are not physically harmed themselves.

When you think about all this, what is remarkable is that so many children grow up strong, loving, and optimistic. This resilience comes from a powerful inner drive toward happiness and health and from relationships—or even a single relationship—with adults who care for them and believe in them.

THE MEANING OF STRESS

Stress is physical. Under stress, the body releases adrenaline and cortisol to boost concentration and endurance (think of doing a long, hard math test). Higher levels of adrenaline trigger the flight-or-fight response (think of being attacked by a vicious dog). The heart races, blood pressure and blood sugar skyrocket, muscles tense, digestion and other noncritical functions shut down, concentration narrows to a pinpoint focus, and time moves slowly.

Stress changes the brain. A severe stress forges a special neural connection between the stressor and the stress response system. If the same stimulus shows up again—perhaps it was a mugger in a face mask—the fight-or-flight response is faster and stronger; so fast that it can occur even before the conscious brain notices what's going on. This special connection, however, also means that anything like the original threatening stimulus—a completely harmless face mask, for example—can trigger an inappropriate stress response.

This is what happens in people with post-traumatic stress disorder, or PTSD. PTSD, sometimes called shell shock when it affects soldiers, can also plague children who have experienced violence or other severe trauma. In the full syndrome, along with an exaggerated fight-or-flight reaction, children can experience terrifying memories of the trauma while awake or asleep; they may attempt to avoid anything that might trigger those memories; and they may experience a feeling of numbness or unreality. Problems with learning, eating, sleeping, and getting along with others are common.

Vulnerability to stress. Some children are unusually vulnerable to stress. Even as babies, they respond to any new person or thing with a stronger physiologic reaction. In preschool they tend to be more cautious or shy, taking longer to feel comfortable in any new situation, and they're prone to fears and other anxiety-related problems. This vulnerability to stress is inborn; it often runs in families, and scientists are finding the responsible genes. Stress-vulnerable children are more likely to develop symptoms in response to any severe stressor, such as being chased by a dog or living through an earthquake.

If your child seems unusually sensitive to stress, you can help him develop coping skills by exposing him only to stresses that he can handle. For example, you might decide to turn off the television when the news is all about a war or a tornado, and instead talk about the situation over dinner—a much less intense exposure. Each time your child succeeds in handling a mildly stressful situation, his coping skills and confidence grow. For example, a child might learn to remember a list of five people who keep him safe (Mommy, Daddy, Grandma, firemen, the mayor . . .). Even young children can learn to use slow, controlled breathing to trigger relaxation, and to notice when their bodies are feeling calmer.

Stress in the long term. Childhood traumas can last a lifetime and cross generations. In large studies, the more childhood traumatic events a person has experienced, the higher the rate of long-term health problems, both physical (obesity, hypertension) and mental (anxiety and depression, addiction). Some of these outcomes are related to chronic overproduction of the stress hormone cortisol.

When traumatized children become parents themselves,

many overreact to their children's upsets and protests, making it hard for them to calm their children down. Others, having learned to ignore their own emotional responses, turn a blind eye when their children are distressed. New awareness of the effects of so-called toxic stress are leading to better identification and treatment.

TERRORISM AND DISASTERS

September 11, 2001, awakened the United States to terrorism, a stark fact of life that was already well known in many other places. (Children who were five and six years old on 9/11 are now of the age to be parents themselves. Some of you may remember that day, and the weeks and months that followed.)

Children who experience large-scale destruction, either directly or through repeated exposure to graphic images on television, are likely to show signs of stress. After 9/11, for example, preschool children across the country drew pictures of airplanes in flames, or built towers out of blocks and crashed toy airplanes into them. Play of this kind is one way that young children take control of frightening realities. A sign of healthy coping is that the child eventually begins to create happy endings. The airplane lands safely; the building doesn't fall down; the child comes away looking relieved.

The play of a child who has been traumatized is different: The planes continue to crash, the buildings collapse over and over, and the child comes away exhausted and even more worried than before. This kind of repetitive, compulsive play is a sign that a child needs the help of a skilled psychologist or therapist.

Responding to disasters. Disasters, both natural and man-made, threaten the basic contract between parents and children, which is that parents will keep their children safe. So it is very important that parents reassure their children that the adults are doing whatever needs to be done to make sure no one else is hurt. Parents also need to shield their children from being further traumatized by repeated exposure to televised images of the event. As hard as it was to turn off the television after 9/11 or during coverage of more recent battles and disasters, that is exactly what wise parents did.

The reason for a child's anxiety may be different from what you'd expect; a good general rule is to listen carefully to your child first, then try to answer the specific questions or concerns your child has. Children take security from familiar surroundings and routines, so a quick return to the comforting patterns of everyday life—breakfast, school, the bedtime story—is also very helpful.

Finally, it's important to pay attention to your own stress responses. Children follow their parents' lead. If your emotional foundation has been shaken, your child will pick up on it. It helps to tell your child how you are feeling in simple terms, so that your child knows what is upsetting you (otherwise he's likely to imagine that *he* is). Your child does not have to know everything; it's better to seek support from a peer or professional. Look to friends, family members, clergy, or others in the community. If all have been traumatized by the same event, outside help will be needed.

In the immediate aftermath of a disaster, problems with eating, sleeping, paying attention, and behaving are common, in parents and children. These should get better over time, with noticeable improvement by about six months. If stress symptoms aren't following this expected pattern, then talk with a professional who has been trained to treat trauma.

DOMESTIC VIOLENCE

Every family has disagreements. Sometimes arguments turn into shouting, then threats, pushing, hitting, and more extreme violence. Children who witness these scenes often suffer psychological damage, even if they aren't physically harmed. More often than not the attacker is the father. During the fight the child may cower in a corner, feeling terrified, enraged, and powerless. Afterward he's apt to become clingy and afraid to let his mother out of his sight. Still later he may appear to change sides, taking on the characteristics of the abuser. He hits his mother and showers her with the same curses that his father used. Psychologists call this behavior identification with the aggressor; it's a sign of emotional trauma.

The children may also become aggressive toward others, even strangers who seem to them somehow threatening. They may have problems sleeping and paying attention in school; they may grow poorly because these children are constantly afraid, and being frightened takes your appetite away. Child abuse and domestic violence often go together.

What you can do. The first and most important thing is that the violence must stop. This often means that the mother and children leave the home, a very hard decision. (Although I mention mothers here because they are most likely to be the victims, men can be victims of domestic violence as well.) The National Domestic Violence Hotline, (800) 799-7233, is a twenty-four-hour source for immediate help and referral to a program or shelter in your area. The website of the National Coalition Against Domestic Violence, www.ncadv.org, provides specific information to help you stop the violence, find safety, make legal plans, and get support (click on "Protect Yourself," then "Getting Help"). Children who have behavior problems as a result of exposure to domestic violence often need professional help to get past the trauma and recover their ability to feel safe and enjoy life.

PHYSICAL ABUSE AND NEGLECT

Anger at children. Most parents get angry enough at their children once in a great while to want to hit them. You may feel angry at a baby who continues to cry for what seems like hours when you have done everything possible in the way of comforting her, or at a child who has broken some precious possession right after you have asked him to put it down. Your rage boils up, but in most cases you control yourself. You may feel ashamed and embarrassed afterward. If you often get so angry, talk with your own doctor or your child's. Frequent anger can be a symptom of depression. Depression is very common in parents of young children, and it can be treated.

The roots of child abuse. Abuse and neglect refer to actions that threaten or fail to protect a child's basic physical and emotional well-being. Children who have physical or mental disabilities or special needs are also more vulnerable to abuse. Anything that increases stress in a family—such as poverty, addiction, and mental illness—increases the risk. But children from all backgrounds and classes are affected. Many abusive adults were abused, neglected, or molested when they were children. As parents they may replay long-ago traumas, now taking the abuser's role. This doesn't happen all the time; overall about one-third of children who are victims of abuse grow up to be abusers themselves.

Laws against abuse. Under U.S. federal law, parents and other caregivers must meet minimal standards for protecting children's safety and health. The precise definitions of abuse and neglect vary from state to state. Every state has a child protection system responsible for identifying and investigating possible abuse. Doctors, teachers, and other professionals are required by law to report possible cases; other people can also file reports. In any given year, reports are filed on behalf of roughly one out of twenty children, most often for suspected neglect. In most cases, investigators don't confirm the suspicions. Among confirmed cases, perhaps one in five results in the child being taken out of the home.

Internationally, the United Nations Convention on the Rights of the Child gives children the right to be spared from physical or mental violence, injury, abuse, neglect, and sexual exploitation. (Although 192 countries have signed this international convention, the United States has not.) Many other developed countries have lower rates of child abuse and neglect than the United States, probably because these countries provide greater supports to families such as universal health care and paid parental leave. We need to do a better job of preventing abuse and neglect, not just outlawing it.

Physical abuse and culture. In many parts of the world, slapping, spanking, and whipping are considered good parenting. In other countries, increasingly, these practices are illegal.

The United States occupies a middle ground: Spanking is still accepted in many communities, but physical punishment that leaves bruises or scars often gets reported. The fear that children may be taken away paralyzes some parents. One mother told me, "My children don't respect me, because they know there is nothing I can do!" In fact, there are many things parents can do that do not involve inflicting physical pain (see page 601).

Spanking may be "cultural," but cultures change all the time. Decades ago, nothing was thought of husbands beating their wives. Earlier yet, it was considered honorable to kill somebody who insulted you. Spanking should go the way of wife beating and dueling.

Other cultural practices may be mistaken for abuse. One example is cupping, a common practice in Southeast Asia that involves placing a warmed glass over the child's skin. As the air in the glass cools, it sucks the skin into the glass, raising a welt. I'm told it hurts, but the purpose of this treatment is not to punish but rather to take away illness.

SEXUAL ABUSE

Abductions of children by strangers make the news, but by far most sexual molesters are people the child knows, such as family members, stepparents, friends of the family, or babysitters. Sexual abuse happens to both boys and girls.

What to tell children. The goal is a child who is safe, but not scared of every stranger who passes on the street. A good maxim is "Talk with people, but don't go with them." As a sensible precaution, children should learn never to accept candy or a ride from somebody who isn't a family member of friend of the family, or to let such a person walk them places.

Young children ages three to six can learn to say no if an older child tries to touch their private parts. The topic can come up while bathing and toileting, activities where parents normally touch children's sensitive areas, or in response to a question, or after a child has been discovered "playing doctor." Repetition helps. You can add, "Sometimes a grown-up may want to touch you, or may want you to touch his private parts, but you should not. Tell him you don't want him to. Then tell me. It won't be your fault." This last is mentioned because children often hide these incidents since they feel guilty, especially if the molester is a relative or family friend.

When to suspect. Sexual abuse is difficult for parents to suspect and for doctors to diagnose, because shame, guilt, and embarrassment lead to silence and because there usually are no physical signs. If there is genital or rectal pain, bleeding, bruising, or signs of infection, you should seek medical evaluation. It's important to know that most mild vaginal infections in girls before puberty are not a result of sexual abuse.

Children who have been sexually abused often exhibit inappropriate sexual behaviors, such as imitating adult sex acts in front of (or with) other children. This is very different from normal sexual exploration, playing doctor or "You show me yours, and I'll show you mine." A child who masturbates compulsively or publicly may be replaying traumatic experiences.

Other behaviors associated with sexual abuse are less specific, including withdrawal, excessive anger or aggression, running away from home, fears (especially of situations related to the abuse), changes in appetite, sleep disturbances, a recent onset of bed-wetting or soiling, poor concentration, or a decline in school performance. Of course, these behavior changes can occur for many reasons, and most often they are *not* signs of sexual abuse. The point is to keep the possibility of sexual abuse in mind but not to obsess about it.

Getting help. If you suspect sexual abuse, call your child's doctor. In many cities, there are specialized teams of doctors, psychologists, and social workers who evaluate children who may have been victims of sexual abuse. The point of these evaluations is to find out if abuse occurred and to gather evidence that can be used in court to convict the abuser, all without further traumatizing the child. Part of the evaluation is also to check for any medical problems, such as infection, that may need treatment.

Sexually abused children often struggle with feelings of shame and guilt. Parents can help by frequent reassurance that the child is not at fault, and that the parent will make sure that the abuse never happens again. It is crucially important that a child who has been a victim sees that her parents are standing up for her and doing everything they can to protect her in the future.

Any child who has been the victim of sexual abuse needs psychological evaluation. Treatment can often be brief, but it may need to be repeated later on because issues related to the abuse are bound to resurface. Psychological recovery from sexual abuse is possible but often takes years.

DEATH

A fact of life. It might be a goldfish or a grandfather, but in just about every childhood something or somebody dies. Children have questions about death, and it's better if parents answer them than if the children are left to come up with their own theories. Honesty and simplicity are best. Like sex, the topic of death comes up naturally in everyday life. Children are curious. Is that bird lying on the ground dead, or just resting? How could you find out? If something is dead, can it become un-dead? Why do grown-ups look serious and sad whenever they talk about somebody who died?

Helping young children understand death. In the preschool years, children's ideas about death are influenced by the magical tendencies of their thinking. Children this age are apt to believe, for example, that death is reversible and that the dead person will come back someday. (People who go away to another city sometimes come back; why not people who go away to death?)

They tend to feel responsible for everything that happens in their world, including death, and may fear punishment for unkind thoughts they had about the dead person or animal. They may view death as catching, like a cold, and worry that someone else will soon die.

Since this is the age when children take everything quite literally, it's especially important not to refer to death as "going to sleep." Many children will then become terrified of going to sleep or else think that somebody should just wake up Grandpa.

Young children think in very concrete terms: "How will

Uncle Bob breathe if he's in the ground?" Parents can help a child by being equally concrete: "Uncle Bob won't breathe anymore. He also won't eat with us anymore or brush his teeth. Being dead means that your body stops working completely; you can't move or do anything. Once you are dead, you cannot become un-dead." Young children need to hear, sometimes several times, that they in no way caused the death.

Even children as young as three or four can understand that death is a part of the life cycle. Things and people have beginnings, they start small, they grow up, they get old, and they die. That is how things work. Several good picture books talk about death with gentleness and clarity; go to drspock .com.

Death and faith. All religions provide explanations of death. Whether these involve heaven and hell, reincarnation, or spirits moving about the earth, I think it is important for parents to clarify to their children that these beliefs are built on faith, which is a special way of understanding the world. Children need to learn to treasure their own faith, while at the same time accepting that other people's faiths may lead them to see things differently.

Funerals. Many parents wonder whether to allow a young child to attend the funeral of a relative or close family friend. Most children from the age of three onward can attend a funeral and perhaps accompany the family to the cemetery for the burial, as long as they want to and the parents prepare them for what will happen. Children get from funerals what adults do: a confirmation of death's reality, and a chance to say goodbye in the company of friends and family.

It's important that an adult whom the child knows well stays with the child the whole time to offer comfort, answer questions, and take the child home if he becomes too upset.

Dealing with grief. Some children show their grief by crying; others may become hyperactive or clingy; others may seem unaffected, although later it becomes clear that they were also grieving. Parents can help their child deal with grief by acknowledging that the death of a friend or grandparent is very sad and that it is sad to know that that person won't be coming back. As a parent, you do not need to pretend that you yourself are not upset or sad. By letting your child see that you have strong feelings, you make it okay for the child to accept her own feelings, too. By handling your feelings appropriately—for example, by talking about them—you teach your child how to deal with sadness and grief.

If a child asks about your dying. Probably the scariest thing for a child is the death of a parent. If there has been a death recently that has affected your family, or if your child asks you earnestly about death, you can assume that underlying it is the concern that you might die.

Here some simple reassurance is in order. You can state that you are not going to die until your child is all grown up and (if you're lucky) has children of his or her own. Then, when you are a very old grandparent, it will be time for you to die. Most children are comforted by having this terrifying event put off into an unimaginably distant future. They know they aren't grown-ups yet, so they don't have to fear your dying. Although you can't be absolutely certain that you will live that long, this is not the time to go into all of the possibilities. Your confident promise to stay alive is the reassurance your child needs.

SEPARATION FROM A PARENT

Children draw their sense of security from their relationships with their parents. When young children have to be separated from a parent, even for a relatively short time, the stress of the separation can cause lasting difficulties. In a young child's mind, "only a few days" can seem like forever.

Traumatic separations. If a mother goes away for a number of weeks—to care for an ailing relative, for instance—her baby of six to eight months is likely to go into a depression, especially if the mother has been the only caretaker up to that time. The baby becomes visibly depressed. She loses her appetite, lies on her back rolling her head from side to side, and no longer tries to explore her surroundings.

At around two years of age, separation from the mother no longer produces depression; instead it results in anxiety. Commonly a mother is called out of town by an emergency or decides to take an all-day job without preparing the child for the change to out-of-home care, or perhaps a child has to stay alone in the hospital for several days.

The child may seem fine while the mother is away, but when she returns all the pent-up anxiety breaks out into the open. The child rushes to cling to her mother and cries out in alarm whenever her mother goes into the next room. At bedtime she clings to her mother with a grip of steel and can't be put down. If the mother finally gets free and heads for the door, the child unhesitatingly scrambles over the side of the crib, though she has never dared do this before, and rushes after her. It's a truly heartrending picture of panic. If the mother succeeds in getting the child to stay in her crib, the baby may sit up all night.

Instead of becoming clingy, a child may punish her mother by refusing to recognize her when they are reunited. When she decides to recognize her mother again, she may scream at her in rage or begin hitting her. A father's sudden absence can trigger the same behaviors, if the father is the main caregiver.

What you can do. For a younger child, try to keep the separation as short as possible. Have a family member, rather than a stranger, take care of the child. Tape a photo of the absent parent where it can be seen from the crib. Have an article of the parent's clothing for the child to cuddle with (beware, though, of suffocation risks with infants). Make a tape recording of the parent telling favorite stories or singing favorite songs.

For older children, make a calendar and check off each day until the parent returns; talk about what you'll all do together then; have frequent telephone or video calls. For separations that are months in length, tie the parent's return to an expected change in the seasons or to another milestone the child will recognize. So instead of saying "Daddy will be back in June," say, "First we'll have winter; then the weather will warm up and flowers will start coming out; and after that, Daddy will be home." Read stories about families that have to be apart but then come together again (my favorite is the classic *Make Way for Ducklings,* by Robert McCloskey). If the date of the parent's return is uncertain (as when one parent serves in the military overseas), it is even more important to exchange letters, phone calls, and emails, to remember what you did when you were all together and talk about the good times to come. Video phone calls can be a godsend.

DIVORCE

Divorce now ends roughly one half of marriages. You can read about friendly divorce in fiction and see examples of it in movies, but in real life most separations and divorces involve two people who are angry with each other. Divorce is often very hard on children. In most cases, it brings with it lowered living standards; often children have to move away from friends and school; parents are often upset or depressed, making them less able to support their children; children may blame themselves (unrealistically) for the breakup and may feel that they cannot be loyal to one parent without being disloyal to the other. On the plus side, divorce may release children from a household made toxic by anger or violence. On the negative side, the emotional fallout can damage children for decades.

Stages of separation. Divorce is a milestone in a process that typically stretches over years. The end of the marriage may begin with a gradual buildup of differences and grievances, or with a sudden rupture due to violence or infidelity. If the buildup is slow, children may endure months of confusing, anxiety-provoking silences or full-throated battles; there may be interludes when everything seems fine, only to fall apart again. The parents are likely to be as confused and worried as their children. There may be separations and reconciliations. Finally it becomes clear that the marriage is beyond saving. Later, the actual divorce begins.

Recovery from the divorce also follows a typical sequence. After a period of disruption and uncertainty, things fall into a routine of regular visits or moving back and forth between households. The children eventually let go of their hopes that their parents will reunite; the parents recover from their emotional shock and begin to rebuild their social lives. At some point the children may acquire stepparents and perhaps stepsiblings as well; it may be a joyful development or a stressful one.

This sequence plays out, with variations, a million times a year. Some children acquire emotional scars, but many come through the process well. That says a lot about children's resilience and parents' will for their children to thrive, even though their marriages have died.

Marriage counseling. When a marriage is in trouble but before it's past hope, it makes sense for parents to give marriage counseling or family therapy an honest try. It's best, of course, if both husband and wife go into counseling on a regular basis. Even if one spouse refuses to acknowledge his or her role in the conflict, it may still be worthwhile for the other to get counseling on whether and how to save the marriage. After all, there were strong positive attractions in the beginning, and some divorced people say later that they wish they had tried harder to solve the problems and make a go of it.

Telling the children. Children are always aware of and disturbed by conflicts between their parents, whether or not divorce is being considered. It is good for them to feel that they can discuss these situations with their parents. They need to get a more sensible picture than their morbid imaginations may suggest. Also, they need to believe in both their parents in order to grow up believing in themselves. For this reason, it's wise for the parents to avoid bitterly heaping blame, which is a natural temptation. Instead, they can explain their quarrels in general terms, making it clear that they are trying to work things out so that everyone in the family can be happier.

It is wise to keep children from hearing the word "divorce" shouted in anger. When the parents are certain that they cannot make the marriage work, the coming divorce should be discussed with the children, not just once but again and again. To young children the world consists of the family, which to them is mainly the father and mother. Breaking up the family is like the end of the world. So the divorce has to be explained much more carefully to them than it would be to an adult.

Children's concerns are often specific and concrete. They want to know where they will live and with whom, where they will go to school, what will happen to the parent who moves away. They need to hear over and over that both of their parents will always love them, and that it wasn't anything they did that made their parents divorce (young children are egocentric and will imagine that their own actions are to blame). They need many opportunities to ask their questions, and they need patient answers at a level they can understand. Parents might be tempted to give too much information; it's better to listen carefully and try to answer just what the child is asking.

Emotional responses. In one famous study, children under six most often showed fears of abandonment, sleep problems, the return of bed-wetting and temper tantrums, and aggressive outbursts. Children of seven and eight expressed sorrow and feelings of aloneness. Nine- and ten-year-olds were more understanding about the realities of divorce, but they expressed hostility toward one or both parents and complained about stomachaches and headaches. Adolescents spoke of the painfulness of the divorce and of their sadness, anger, and shame. Some had trouble developing romantic relationships.

The best way to help children is to give them regular opportunities to talk about their feelings and to reassure them that it's okay to feel the way they do. When parents are in too much pain themselves to be able to have these discussions, it's important to find a professional counselor whom the children can see regularly; counseling for parents helps, too.

Parents' reactions. The parent who gains custody of the children—often the mother—usually finds the first year or two after divorce very difficult. The children are more tense, demanding, and complaining. The mother is apt to feel tired out from working at a job and caring for the home and the children single-handedly. She may miss adult companionship, including the social and romantic attention of men. Worst of all, most mothers say, is the fear that they will not be able to earn a satisfactory living and run the family. This is a realistic fear, as poverty often follows on the heels of divorce. Fathers who get custody of their children have similar problems, although the prospect of poverty is often less stark.

As for the noncustodial parent, studies show that newly divorced fathers are miserable much of the time. If they get involved in casual affairs, they soon find that these are shallow and meaningless. They are unhappy not to be consulted about both important and unimportant plans for the children. They miss the company of their children. Even more, they miss having their children ask them for advice or for permission, which is part of what a father is for. Their children's weekend visits often settle into a routine of fast food and movies, which may satisfy the children's needs for pleasure but not their need for a real relationship. Fathers and children may also find conversation difficult in this new situation.

Custody. After several decades in which custody was routinely awarded to the mother unless she was clearly unfit, courts are increasingly seeing fathers as capable of assuming primary responsibility for their children.

Many factors are more important than the sex of the custodial parent: Who has been providing most of the care? This is especially relevant for babies and small children who will badly miss their accustomed caregiver. What kind of relationship does each child have to each parent? What is each one's expressed preference, especially in later childhood and adolescence? How important is it for each child to live with a brother or sister?

When a child or teen finds tensions building with the custodial parent, she may start thinking that the grass is greener on the other side. Sometimes it is better for this child to live with the other parent, at least for a while. But a child who moves back and forth several times may be trying to leave her problems behind rather than solve them. It's better to try to get to the bottom of what's troubling her.

Joint custody. In the past it has usually been assumed that the divorcing parents will be adversaries with regard to custody, child support, alimony, and property settlement. The more this battling attitude can be avoided, the better for the children. Joint custody keeps the noncustodial parent (more frequently the father) from getting the short end of the stick in visitation rights and, even more important, keeps him from feeling divorced from his children, a feeling that often leads to a gradual withdrawal from contact with the children.

When speaking of joint custody, some lawyers and parents mean an equal sharing of the children, such as four days with one, three with the other, or one week with one and then a week with the other. This may or may not be practical for the parents or comfortable for the children. School-age children have to keep going to the same school, and children in day care or attending preschool should continue at the same facilities. Children like routines, and need them.

It's more positive to see joint custody as embodying a spirit of cooperation between the divorced parents with regard to the children's welfare. This means first and foremost that they consult with each other about plans, decisions, and responses to the children's major requests, so that neither parent feels left out. (It may be helpful to have a counselor, one who knows the children, to help the parents come to some decisions.) The second priority is to share the children's time in such a way that each parent keeps in touch with them as closely as possible, which will depend on such factors as the distance between the parents' homes, the capacity of the dwellings, the location of the school, and the preferences of the children as they grow older. Obviously, if one parent moves across the continent, the visits will have to come at vacation times, though the parent can still keep in touch electronically, by phone, or by exchanging letters.

Joint physical custody is when children split their time between parents; joint legal custody means that both parents have a say in major decisions in the child's life, involving such things as school, camp, and religious matters. In either case, joint custody can have significant positive ramifications if the parents can work together for the benefit of their children. In general, children have a better social, psychological, and academic adjustment when both parents remain involved in their lives.

Visitation. Five days with the mother and weekends with the father has a practical sound and is a common schedule, but the mother may well want some weekend time with the children, when she can be more relaxed, and the father may want an occasional weekend without them. Similar considerations may apply to school vacations. As the children get older, friends, sports, or other activities may draw them to one home or the other. So any schedule requires flexibility.

It is vital that nonresident parents not casually break their appointments for visits. Children are hurt when they get the impression that other obligations are more important. They lose faith in the negligent parent and in their own worth. If appointments have to be canceled, this should be done ahead of time and substitutions made if possible. Most important of all is that the nonresident parent should not break contact frequently or erratically.

Some noncustodial fathers and mothers feel shy or awkward when visitation time comes. They often respond by simply providing treats—meals out, excursions, trips to the movies or to sporting events. There is nothing wrong with these occasionally, but parents shouldn't think of treats as essential on every visit; such behavior would signal that they are afraid of silences, and it will make these treats more obligatory every week.

The children's visits can generally be as relaxed and as humdrum as staying in their regular home. That means opportunities for activities such as reading, doing homework, bicycling, roller skating on the sidewalk, shooting baskets, playing ball, fishing, or working on hobbies such as model building, stamp collecting, or carpentry. Parents can participate in those activities they enjoy, which provide ideal opportunities for casual conversation.

Younger children are often irritable when they make the transitions from one parent to the other. Especially on their return from a visit with the noncustodial parent, children may be cranky from tiredness. Sometimes it's simply that the child is having difficulty shifting gears moving out of one setting and into another. Each departure and return may remind the child, at least subconsciously, of the original departure of the nonresident parent. Parents can help by being patient during the transitions, by being absolutely reliable about time and place of pickup or drop-off, and by trying to keep these exchanges as free of conflict as possible.

Grandparents after a divorce. It's also important for the children to maintain as much contact with their grandparents as they had before the divorce. It can be very difficult to stay in touch with the parents of your ex-spouse, especially if you or they feel hurt or angry. Sometimes the custodial parent may say, "The children can see your parents during their visitation time with you. I won't have anything to do with your parents." But birthdays, holidays, and special occasions are never so conveniently arranged. Try to remember that grandparents can often be a great source of support and continuity for the children, so keeping in touch will be worth the extra effort. The grandparents' own emotional need to stay in touch with their grandchildren should also be respected.

Avoid trying to bias the children. It's vital that one parent not try to discredit or even criticize the other to the children, though this is a great temptation. Both parents feel a little guilty about the failure of the marriage, at least unconsciously. If they can get their friends, relatives, and children to agree that the ex-spouse is at fault, they can lessen the guilt. So they are tempted to tell the worst possible stories about their ex, leaving out any mention of their own contribution. The trouble is that children sense that they are made up of both parents, and if they come to accept the idea that one was a scoundrel, they assume that they've inherited some of that. Besides, they naturally want to retain two parents and be loved by both. It makes them feel uncomfortably disloyal to listen to criticism. It's equally painful for children if one parent involves them in keeping secrets from the other parent.

By adolescence, children know that all people have imperfections, and they are not so deeply affected by the faults of their parents, though they can be very critical. Let them find the faults for themselves. It's no good for one parent to try to win the children's allegiance by criticizing the other. Teenagers are prone to turn hot and cold on a slight provocation. When they become angry at the parent they've favored, they may do an about-face and decide that all the unfavorable things they've heard in the past about the other parent were unfair and untrue. Both parents will have the best chance of retaining their children's love for the long haul if they let them love both, believe in both, and spend time with both.

It's a mistake for either parent to grill the children about what happened while they were visiting the other parent. This only makes children uneasy, and in the end it may backfire and make them resent the querying parent.

Dating for the parent. Children whose parents have been recently divorced usually think of them as still married and want them to get back together. They often feel that dating represents faithlessness on the part of their parent and an unwelcome intrusion on the part of the date. So it is best for parents to go slowly and be tactful in introducing their dates to their children.

Let the fact that the divorce is permanent sink in for a number of months. Be alert to the children's remarks. After a while you can bring up the topic of your loneliness and drop the idea that you may want to have a friend to date. It's not that you are allowing your children to control your life forever; you are simply letting them know that dating is a possibility, and doing so in a way that is more comfortable for them than being presented with a person in the flesh.

If you are a mother who has been living with young children who rarely or never see their father, they may beg you to marry and give them another daddy. Nonetheless, they're likely to become jealous as soon as they see the growing closeness between you and a man. A similar thing happens to a father who's had custody of his young children. Don't be surprised by your children's strong and contradictory feelings.

Long-term effects on children. Children who have been through a divorce never come out untouched, but many go on to have happy, fulfilled lives. Others struggle for a long time with feelings of anger, loss, or uncertainty. Children who are able to continue to have loving relationships with both parents do the best. Where this is not possible, help over the years from professional counselors or therapists can make recovery possible.

Common Developmental and Behavioral Challenges

ACTING OUT

TEMPER TANTRUMS

Why tantrums? Almost all children have temper tantrums between one and three years. They're developing a sense of their own will and individuality. When they're thwarted, they know it and feel angry. Yet they don't usually attack the parent who has interfered with them; instead, they kick the floor. Perhaps the grown-up is too big, and too important to the child.

When feelings of fury boil up, young children often aren't able to contain or control them. The loss of self-control adds to the upset. Being out of control in this way makes children feel cut off from the people they love and rely on. It's a scary, awful feeling.

The typical tantrum lasts between thirty seconds and a couple of minutes, rarely more than five minutes. It seems like much longer. At the end, a child often feels sad and wants comforting.

It's normal for children to feel upset at times, and to express their feelings in dramatic ways. See pages 126 and 141 for more on typical tantrums in young children.

You can't dodge all temper tantrums. Sometimes you can see a tantrum coming and head it off by redirecting your child to a less frustrating activity. But you can't always respond quickly enough. When the storm breaks, try to respond calmly. Getting angry yourself only forces her to keep up her end of the fight. Don't argue with her, because she's in no mood to listen to reason. Don't try to mollify your child by giving him something, *anything*, to stop crying; this just teaches him that yelling and screaming are what it takes to get what he wants. On the other hand, if what your child wants is something that you would have been happy to give him if you'd only understood soon enough (say, another piece of apple, or just a few minutes more with a favorite toy), it's fine to admit your mistake, and give it to him. You're not "giving in"; you're just being reasonable.

One child cools off quickest if the parent simply goes about her business, perhaps with a friendly word of support: "I know you'll feel better in a little bit." Another, more upset and less in control of her emotions, needs to be picked up and held. Close physical contact and the feeling of being contained helps this child feel less scared and more connected. As soon as the worst of the storm has passed, both of these children could use a hug and kiss to show that the connection with their parent is strong again, and then a suggestion of something fun to do.

It's embarrassing to have a child throw a tantrum on a busy sidewalk. Pick her up gently, with a grin if you can manage one, and take her to a quiet spot where you can both cool off in private. Any parent watching will know what is going on and feel sympathetic. The key is your ability to handle your child's upset without getting too upset yourself. It's bad enough when one person loses emotional control; it's really awful when two people do!

Frequent tantrums. A child who has frequent temper tantrums may have inborn traits of temperament that increase frustration. For example, she may be very sensitive to any change in temperature or sound, or to the feel of different clothes on the skin. One child has a tantrum every time her parents put her socks on unless the seams at the toes are in exactly the right place. Another child has the trait of high persistence. Once she gets started doing something, it's very hard to tear her away. Later on this child might excel in school, where high persistence often earns high grades. But in a young child, the persistence guarantees a couple of tantrums a day.

Another temperament trait that results in frequent tantrums is high intensity of expression. Children with this trait are very dramatic. When they're happy, they shout with glee; when they're upset, they wail in despair. Another kind of tantrum-prone child is very sensitive to new people and places. It takes this child several minutes before he feels comfortable. If he's pushed to join the group before he's ready, he may break down into a tantrum.

If your child is having frequent temper tantrums, ask yourself the following questions: Does she have plenty of chances to play freely outdoors? Are there things for her to push and pull and climb on there? Indoors, has she enough things to play with, and is the house childproofed? Do you, without realizing it, arouse balkiness by telling her to come and get her shirt on instead of slipping it on without comment? When you know that she needs to use the toilet, do you find yourself asking her if she wants to go to the bathroom instead of leading her there? When you have to interrupt her play to get her indoors or to meals, do you give her a minute or two to finish up and find a good stopping place? Do you get her mind on something pleasant that you're about to do? When you see a storm brewing, do you meet it head-on, grimly, or do you distract her with something else?

Learned tantrums. Some children have learned that tantrums are the best way to get what they want or to avoid unpleasant tasks. It can be hard to sort out these manipulative tantrums from tantrums caused by frustration, hunger, tiredness, or fear. One hint is that manipulative tantrums tend to stop right away once the child gets what he wants. Another hint is that the child may work up to the tantrum by whining in a demanding way. The answer to these tantrums, of course, is for parents to stand firm. When they say, "No more cookies now," they shouldn't change their mind two minutes later in response to a tantrum.

To make this strategy work, you have to pick your battles carefully. If you feel strongly that cookies before dinner are a bad idea, then by all means lay down a "no cookies" rule, and stick to it. But if you don't feel very strongly about cookies, consider saying yes *before* the tantrum, because if you wait until after the tantrum to say yes, you end up rewarding your child for having a tantrum. That just results in more tantrums.

Many children throw tantrums about cookies, but rarely when it comes to getting buckled into their car seats. Why? Because their parents are absolutely consistent when it comes to the car seats, so the children know there is no point in challenging that rule.

Tantrums and language delay. Delayed language development often goes with tantrums, frequently in boys. A child may become frustrated because he can't make his needs and wants known. He may feel cut off from other children and adults. When he's upset, he can't use words to express his frustrations; he can only act out his rage.

As children grow older, they learn to talk to themselves to calm themselves down. If you think about it, you probably talk to yourself, too, either out loud or silently, when you need to calm down or reassure yourself. A child who has underdeveloped language skills can't use this powerful means of self-comforting and self-control. So negative emotions are more likely to blow up into tantrums.

Children with limited language skills often need to be picked up and held; this helps them regain control. Other children, when they're very upset or scared, temporarily lose their language abilities and also need physical comforting.

Tantrums as a sign of other problems. By age four or five, most children are down to the rare tantrum, maybe one a week. But one child in five continues to have tantrums that occur three or more times a day, or long tantrums that regularly persist for more than fifteen minutes.

Causes of frequent tantrums in older children include developmental problems, such as intellectual disabilities, autism, or learning disabilities. Chronic medical problems, such as allergies, eczema, or constipation may decrease a child's frustration tolerance. Certain medications may put children on edge. When children have been seriously ill, parents often have a hard time setting limits. Frequent tantrums may be the unhappy result.

A child who regularly hits or bites himself or other people while having a tantrum is showing signs of serious emotional upset. When in doubt, use your own feelings as a guide. If you find your child's tantrums annoying or sometimes amusing (although you should not let your child see this), then you're probably handling them just fine. If you find yourself feeling angry, ashamed, or upset by your child's tantrums, or if you worry that you might lose control yourself, then there is a real problem. Anytime tantrums are not responding to basic good parenting and the passage of time, it makes sense to seek the help of an experienced professional.

SWEARING AND BACK TALK

Potty talk. Many four-year-olds revel in bathroom words. They cheerfully insult each other with expressions like "You great big poop" and "I'll flush you down the toilet," and think they are very witty and bold. This is a normal phase that passes soon.

Young children who continue to delight in naughty words are often those whose parents express shock and dismay, and threaten dire consequences. The child thinks: "Hey, this is a pretty good way to stir things up. This is fun! This gives me power over my parents!" This excitement outweighs any unhappiness she might feel about making her parents angry.

The easiest way to stop a young child from using naughty words is to simply ignore them, or say something very low-key, such as "You know, I don't like that kind of talk." If their words float out into space and nothing comes back, children are apt to lose interest.

School-age swearing. As they grow older, children learn swear words from their friends, if not from siblings, parents, or media. They swear to show that they are worldly-wise and not afraid to be a little bad.

What's a good parent to do? As with the three- or four-year-old, it's better not to act horribly shocked. For timid children, seeing that their parents are shocked has too strong an effect; it worries them and makes them afraid to be around children who use bad words. But most children who find they have shocked their parents are delighted, at least secretly. Some of them go on cussing endlessly at home, hoping to get the same rise. Others, stopped at home by threats, use their bad language elsewhere. The point is that when you show children that they have the power to scandalize the whole world, it's like handing them a cannon and telling them, "For goodness' sake, don't set it off."

On the other hand, you don't have to sit mute and just take it. You can tell your child firmly that you and most people don't like to hear those words. End of discussion. If your child persists, in a challenging way, you can use a time-out as a reasonable consequence, or subtract 25¢ from the allowance for each infraction.

Teenagers. Some teenagers liberally interject curse words into their conversations. Expletives serve multiple purposes: to express disgust or contempt (a common feeling in many teens), to underline the importance of the topic, to discharge emotion, or to show disdain for what they think of as arbitrary and old-fashioned societal taboos. But cursing at this age mainly serves as a mark of belonging to one's peer group.

You will lose any debate about whether swearing is good or bad. Your child already knows that some behaviors make you unhappy. But it is reasonable for you to request that your teen limit his swearing to times when it won't offend others or prove harmful to himself—for example, no swearing in your presence, no swearing in front of his little brother, and no swearing at school. As with younger children, if you make a big deal about the swearing, you will probably only end up giving your teen an easy way to assert independence and feel powerful. With teens, in particular, it works best to focus on what they are saying, rather than on how they are saying it.

Back talk. Young children talk back to test limits and assert power. It can also be an effective diversionary tactic: If your mom gets upset about the back talk, she might forget that she just asked you to wash the dishes. Even if she remembers in the end, a few minutes of sassing can delay the dishes, which is also a "win" of a kind.

So with back talk, stay calm and focused on the real issue. Let your child know that you have heard her, but then make sure that your rules still stand: "I know you don't want to stop now, but it's time to pick up," while helping the child to get started picking up.

Sometimes children aren't aware that they're being rude; they think they're being clever. A clear, unemotional statement often works best: "When you talk to me in that tone of voice, it makes me feel that you don't respect me, and that makes me angry." Another approach is to ask the child what he meant by his tone of voice: "Were you meaning to sound sarcastic just now? I just want to be sure I really understand what you want to tell me." An appeal to fairness ("I don't use put-downs when I talk to you; so it isn't fair for you to put me down") is often more effective, in the long run, than a resort to force ("Say that again and I'll wash your mouth out!").

BITING

Biting babies. It's natural for a baby to try now and then to take a bite out of a parent's cheek. Their teething makes them want to bite anyway, and when they feel tired they're even more in the mood for it. It doesn't mean much, either, when a child of between one and two bites another child, whether it's in a friendly or angry spirit. Children at that age can't express complex feelings in words, so biting is a way to communicate.

Also, it's hard for them to put themselves in another's shoes. They might recall the unpleasant feeling of *being* bitten, but still not grasp that someone else feels more or less the same thing when they, the babies, are the biters. That kind of perspective shifting develops over a period of years.

A parent or other caregiver can say firmly, "That hurts! Be gentle," and then put the child down on the floor briefly or remove him from the playgroup for a moment. The idea is simply to give him the message that this behavior makes you unhappy, even if he is too young to understand exactly why.

Toddlers and preschoolers who bite. If biting is a problem between ages two and three, you need to know if it's connected to other issues. How is your child getting along otherwise? If he's tense or unhappy much of the time and keeps biting other children for no good reason, that's concerning. Perhaps he is being disciplined or restricted too much at home and is frantic and high-strung. Perhaps he has had too little chance to get used to other children and imagines them to be dangerous and threatening. Perhaps he is jealous of a baby at home and carries over the fear and resentment to all other small children, as if they were competitors, too. When biting is accompanied by many other aggressive and worrisome behaviors, it's the underlying problem, rather than the biting itself, that deserves attention.

More often, however, biters are model citizens in other respects, and the biting is a normal developmental challenge, not the mark of a psychological problem. Even the gentlest of children can go through a brief biting phase.

What to do about biting. If you can, prevent biting before it starts. Are there predictable times it occurs? If so, a little more adult supervision during those times may be quite useful. Is your child often frustrated because he is the least competent member of his playgroup? Consider changing his daily routine, and be sure to give him lots of positive attention when he is behaving well.

When you see your child's frustration growing, try to redirect him to another activity. If your child is old enough, you can discuss the problem at another time and ask him to help you think about how it hurts and what else he could do when he has the urge to bite.

Some children only get their parents' full attention after they've broken something or bitten someone. It's much more effective to give your child attention in response to positive behaviors.

If the biting has already occurred, it's helpful to attend to the child who was bitten first, and ignore the biter. After comforting the victim, give your child the firm message that biting makes you unhappy. Tell him not to do it again. Then sit with him for a few minutes while the message sinks in. Avoid long lectures.

Bite back? If you've been bitten by an infant or a toddler, don't bite back. Biting a child to show him how it feels usually breeds anger rather than empathy. With a young child, if you bite hard enough to hurt, you can cause injury and you certainly cause fear. If you only bite gently, your child might think you're playing a game and answer with a new bite of his own. (The same goes for hitting, slapping, or pinching.)

The best response is to keep from being bitten in the first place. When your toddler gets that gleam in his eye, draw back or hold your child at a distance. Show him that you don't like biting and won't let it happen. If you're too slow and the biting has already happened, use your face and voice to show you are hurt, and put your baby down for a few seconds. Losing your attention is punishment enough to teach a young child.

Biting after three. Two developments tend to put an end to biting around age three: better language and stronger impulse control. The message you've been repeating for years, "Use your words," starts to sink in. (Remember, though, all children act younger when they're tired, hungry, or stressed.) If biting keeps up, it may be a sign of a bigger developmental or behavioral problem. It's worth a discussion with your child's doctor.

MESSINESS, DAWDLING, AND WHINING

MESSINESS

Let them get dirty sometimes. Children love to get dirty, and it's good for them. They love to dig in earth and sand, wade in mud puddles, and splash in the sink. They want to roll in the grass and squeeze mud in their hands. When they have the chance to do these delightful things, it enriches their spirit and makes them warmer people, just the way beautiful music or falling in love improves adults.

Small children who are always sternly warned against getting their clothes dirty or making a mess, and who take these warnings to heart, might become inhibited and mistrustful of the things they enjoy. If they become really timid about dirt, it can also make them too cautious in other ways, and can keep them from developing into the free, warm, life-loving people they were meant to be.

I don't mean to give the impression that you must always let your children make any kind of mess that strikes their fancy. But when you do have to stop them, don't try to scare them or disgust them; just substitute something else a little more practical. If they want to make mud pies when they have their Sunday clothes on, have them change into old clothes first. If they get hold of an old brush and want to paint the house, set them to work with a pail of water for "paint" on the garage or a bathroom floor.

Messes around the house. Once children are old enough to make messes, they're old enough to start learning to pick up. They need a lot of help at first; later, they can take on more of the task themselves. A child who leaves messes may have learned that someone else—Mommy, perhaps—cleans up. This child needs to hear clear, consistent expectations. Another child is simply overwhelmed. He needs help organizing the task into manageable pieces: "First, find all the wooden blocks and put them in the block box."

If children refuse to clean up their messes, it's reasonable for them to lose the privilege for a few days of playing with the toys that they left around. If you have to pick up the toys, they're going to be "stored" where they can't be gotten. If you've stored away a lot of your child's toys, there are simply fewer toys around to trip over. Toys stored for longer periods become almost new again when they come out of the closet, and therefore much more fun for a while.

The messy room. A child's bedroom is a different story. If a child has her own room, it's good for her to experience the consequences of her messiness. From a parent's point of view, that may mean keeping quiet about a level of disorder that would be unacceptable in the public parts of the home. Setting aside vermin, fire hazards, and a floor so cluttered that it's impossible to walk, a messy room harms no one but its occupant. A child who always has to search around for her favorite pants or socks that match eventually learns to put things where they belong.

Giving your child responsibility doesn't mean that you can't remind her gently from time to time about the room, or even offer to help out. After a certain level of messiness, many children simply don't know where to start. But the problem belongs to your child, and so should the solution.

Messy bedrooms rank high in the complaints I hear from parents. When messy room is the lead-off complaint, I always wonder, "Is that *all*?" A mess lover who in other respects is growing up happy and terrific is not, in my mind, a reason for concern. She'll grow up eventually, and either decide to keep her home neat or not.

DAWDLING

After you watch a parent trying to jump-start a dawdling child in the morning, you vow that you'll never get in that fix. The parent urges him, warns him, and scolds him to get out of bed, get washed, get dressed, eat his breakfast, start for school. It's exhausting.

All children tend to slow down when doing tasks that aren't fun. Some are more easily distracted and thus less goal-directed than others. In response to constant pushing by their parents, they become habitual dawdlers. It's easy to fall into the habit of prodding children, but it can build up an absentminded balkiness in them. Parents feel they have to nag or the child won't get anywhere. The child assumes that there's no reason to move until the parent's irritation reaches a certain point. It becomes a vicious circle.

Early teaching. Young children function best when they follow routines. For everyday tasks such as getting up in the morning or getting ready to go outside, it helps them to do the same steps in the same order each time. If you've ever watched snack time at a well-run preschool, you know how efficient young children can be when they are running through familiar patterns. As soon as your child begins to remember the routine on his own, step out of the picture. When he slips back and forgets, lead again.

When he goes to school, let him think of it as his job to get there on time. It may be better to quietly allow him to be late once or twice and find out for himself how sorry he feels. A child hates to miss things even more than his parent hates to have him miss them. That's the best prod to move him along.

Dealing with dawdling. An older child who dawdles may be disorganized or distractible. She starts out with the intention of getting dressed, but on the way to her dresser she finds a toy that needs playing with, a doll that has to be put to bed, and a book that needs reading. Fifteen minutes later, she's still in pajamas, happily playing.

One strategy is to help the child make a chart, using pictures or words (if she can read and write), outlining the different steps that must be done to, say, get ready for school in the morning. Cover the list in clear plastic, so that the child can use a dry-erase marker to check off each step as she completes it. Set a timer, and let her try to get through her list before it dings. Give her a simple reward for "beating the clock." The best rewards follow naturally; in this case, getting dressed and ready on time without having to be nagged means that there is time for a few minutes of reading aloud (by you), video gaming, or even television before it's time to leave for school.

If you have to, you can stand over your child and dictate every step of the process. This will annoy both of you at first. Next, dictate two steps at the same time: "Okay, now brush your teeth and wash your face." Once your child is doing two steps independently, give her three, and so on, until she's got the whole sequence down.

Before you start this process, talk with your child about what you are going to do. Think of it as skill building, like learning to play the piano. Chart your progress daily, so you can watch together as learning takes place. Once your child has conquered one difficult sequence, she'll be able to approach future learning challenges with ever greater confidence. "Remember how we solved the getting-ready problem? Now let's work on bedtime."

WHINING

The whining habit. Young children whine when they're tired or uncomfortable and when they're working themselves up to a tantrum. A few children get into the habit of whining all day for a variety of reasons: to get special treats or privileges, because they're bored or jealous, or because things aren't going just right. They seem constantly dissatisfied and unhappy, and they make those around them miserable as well. There's a quality to their whining not just of distress but also of coercion: They're going to keep it up until you give them what they want.

A child who persistently whines at one parent—her mother, say—may act much more grown-up with her father and at school. Often, too, a parent who has two or more children will only put up with whining in one. Whining is part of their relationship. The child's demanding and complaining and the parent's resisting, pleading, yelling, and (often) giving in follow a predictable pattern. Neither seems to be able to break the cycle.

What to do about whining. There are definite, practical steps you can take if your child is a habitual whiner. First, ask yourself whether your attitude is feeding the whining. You may be using some expression of evasiveness, hesitation, submissiveness, or guilt, mixed with the inevitable irritability that comes from feeling victimized. If you can't see any uncertainty in your behavior, ask yourself how you may be unwittingly rewarding the whining—for example, by paying too much attention to it or by finally giving in to stop the onslaught.

If your child whines for special privileges, the solution is to make as many rules as necessary to cover all the usual pleas and then stick to them with determination and consistency. Bedtime is always to be at a certain hour; only certain television programs may be viewed; friends may be invited for a meal or an overnight only at a certain frequency. These are the family rules, etched in stone by benevolent dictators. There are just no arguments about them. At first, when you stop giving in to the whining, you can expect it to get worse for a while. Then, after you have held your ground, it will go away.

If your child whines that he has nothing to do, it's smarter not to be drawn into suggesting lots of possible activities. A child in this mood will shoot each one down, scornfully and with relish. Instead, toss the responsibility back to your child: "Well, I've got a ton of work to do, but then I'm going to do some fun stuff afterward." In other words, "Follow my example: find things to do for yourself. Don't expect me to amuse you or argue with you."

You can tell your child that you only respond to requests made in a normal tone of voice. Or you can say simply, "Please stop whining right now!" If your child persists in annoying you and threatens to make you miserable unless you give in, you can impose a time-out.

It's fine to give children reasons: "We're not having pizza for dinner because we just had pizza for lunch" or "We have to go home now so we can take our naps." But often parents just have to make a decision and children just have to live with it. "We're not buying that toy today, because we're not buying toys today." Confident parents don't engage in endless arguments with their children about the limits they've set. If allowed, children will keep these conversations going forever and probably out-negotiate the parent at every turn. State your case, set your limits, and end the conversation pleasantly but decisively.

It's fine for children to ask for something special occasionally, and fine for parents to give freely what they ask for, as long as they think the request is reasonable. But it's also important for children to learn to accept "No" or "Not today" as an answer. Demanding whining is a sign that your child still needs to learn this important lesson. If you catch yourself feeling bad about being tough on your child or wondering if you aren't somehow hurting him by not giving in to his demands, remind yourself that your child is strong (strong enough to make your life miserable at times), and that a strong parent is what your child needs in order to move forward. Saying no is an act of love.

HABITS

THUMB-SUCKING

The sucking urge. Sucking is how babies get nourishment, and it also helps them relieve physical and emotional tension. Babies who nurse more tend to thumb-suck less, because they're already getting plenty of sucking. Some babies need more sucking than others. One baby only nurses fifteen minutes at a time and yet never puts a thumb in her mouth. Another baby takes twenty on each bottle, and still needs more sucking time. Some begin to thumb-suck in the delivery room and keep at it. Other thumb-suck early but soon give it up.

(Thumb-sucking is different from the thumb, finger, and hand chewing that almost all babies do once they begin to teethe. During his teething periods, the baby who is a thumb-sucker is sucking one minute and chewing another.)

After about six months, babies thumb-suck for different reasons: to comfort themselves; when they're bored or frustrated; to put themselves to sleep. When a baby can't make a go of things at a more grown-up level, she falls back on earlier behavior, a time when sucking was her chief joy. It's rare for a child beyond the age of a few months to begin to thumb-suck for the first time.

Thumb-sucking by itself is not a sign of unhappiness,

maladjustment, or lack of love. In fact, most thumb-suckers are very happy children; children who are severely deprived of affection don't usually thumb-suck.

When is sucking a problem? If a child is sucking a great deal of the time instead of playing, parents should ask themselves whether there is anything they ought to do so that she won't need to comfort herself so much. Another child may be bored from not seeing enough of other children or from not having enough things to play with. Or perhaps she has to sit in her playpen for hours.

A boy of a year and a half may be at loggerheads with his mother all day if she is always stopping him from doing the things that fascinate him instead of diverting him to playthings that are permissible. Another boy has children to play with and freedom to do things at home, but he's too timid to throw himself into these activities. He thumb-sucks while he watches. The point of these examples is only to make it clear that if anything needs to be done for excessive thumb-sucking, it is to make the child's life more satisfying.

Sometimes in an older child, thumb-sucking is simply a habit, a pattern of behavior that repeats for no good reason. The child wants to stop, but his fingers seem to end up in his mouth of their own accord; he's not really aware that he's doing it.

Health effects of thumb-sucking. The physical problems caused by thumb-sucking are mild. Thickened skin on the favorite thumb or finger is common and goes away on its own. Minor infections around the fingernail are usually easy to treat. The worst problems are orthodontic. It is true that thumb-sucking often pushes the upper front baby teeth forward and the lower teeth back. How much the teeth are displaced will depend on how much the child sucks her thumb and, even more, on what position she holds her thumb in. But dentists point out that this tilting of the baby teeth has no effect on the permanent teeth, which begin coming in at about six years of age. In other words, if a child gives up thumb-sucking before six years of age, as happens in a great majority of cases, there is very little danger of displacing the permanent teeth.

Preventing thumb-sucking. You don't need to be concerned when babies suck their thumbs for only a few minutes before their feeding time. They are probably doing this only because they're hungry. It's when babies suck their thumbs as soon as their feeding is over or when they suck a lot between feedings that you might think of ways to satisfy the sucking craving.

If your baby begins to suck her thumb or finger or hand, it's best not to stop her directly but to try to give her more opportunity to suck at the breast, the bottle, or the pacifier. If your baby hasn't been a confirmed thumb-sucker from birth, the most effective method by far to prevent the habit is the ample use of the pacifier in the first three months. If you're bottle-feeding, think about using a nipple with a smaller hole, so your baby gets to do a lot of sucking during feeding. If you're breastfeeding, think about letting your baby nurse longer, even after she's gotten most of the milk she needs.

With a thumb-sucker, it's better to go slowly in omitting feedings. It's not just the length of each feeding but also the frequency of feedings over twenty-four hours that determines whether a baby satisfies the sucking instinct. So, if a baby is still thumb-sucking even though you have made each breast- or bottle-feeding last as long as possible, it is sensible to go slowly in dropping other feedings. For example, if a three-month-old baby seems willing to sleep through the late-evening feeding at the parents' bedtime but is doing a good deal of thumb-sucking, you might wait a while longer before dropping the late-evening feeding—perhaps a couple of months, provided the baby is still willing to drink when awakened.

Methods that don't work. Why not tie babies' arms down to keep them from thumb-sucking? This would cause them a great deal of frustration, which could produce new problems. Furthermore, tying down the hands usually doesn't cure the baby who is thumb-sucking a lot, because it doesn't respond to the baby's need for more sucking. A few despairing parents use elbow splints or put bad-tasting liquid on the baby's thumbs, not just for days but for months. And the day they take off the restraint or stop the liquid on the thumb, the thumb pops back in the mouth.

The only time bitter-tasting liquids can be helpful is for the very motivated older child who just needs something to alert him when his thumb goes into his mouth unconsciously. The child should be in charge of painting his own thumbs. Success is much more likely if he feels in control of the process.

Breaking the habit. Elbow splints, mitts, and bad-tasting stuff on the thumb won't stop the habit any more often in older children than they do in small babies. These approaches may even prolong the habit by setting up a power struggle between the determined sucker and his parents. The same applies to scolding a child or pulling his thumb out of his mouth. What about the common ploy of handing a child a toy when he starts to thumb-suck? It certainly is sound to have enough interesting things around for him to play with so that he won't be bored. But if every time his thumb goes in the mouth you jump toward him and poke an old toy into his hands, he'll soon catch on.

What about bribery? If your child is one of the rare ones who is still thumb-sucking at the age of five and you are beginning to worry about what it will do to the permanent teeth when they come in, you will have a fair chance of succeeding if the bribe is a good one. A girl of four or five who wants to get over her thumb-sucking may be helped by having her fingernails painted like an older girl's. But practically no child of two or three has the willpower to deny an instinct for the sake of a reward. You're apt to make a fuss and get nowhere.

If your child is thumb-sucking, see to it that his life is good. In the long run it will help him if you remind him that someday he will be grown-up enough to stop. This friendly encouragement makes him want to stop as soon as he is able. But don't nag him.

Most important of all, try to stop thinking about it. If you keep on worrying, even though you resolve to say nothing, the child will feel your tension and react against it. Remember that thumb-sucking goes away all by itself in time. In the overwhelming majority of cases, it is over before the adult teeth appear. It doesn't go away steadily, though. It decreases rapidly for a while, and then comes back partway during an illness or when the child has a difficult adjustment to make.

Eventually it disappears for good. It rarely stops before three years. It usually peters out between three and six.

Some dentists use metal wires attached to the upper teeth to make thumb-sucking not only unpleasant but virtually impossible. This measure should be a last resort. Not only is it expensive, but it takes all control away from the child at an age when it's important for children to feel that they can be in control of their bodies.

OTHER INFANT HABITS

Stroking and hair pulling. Babies who suck their thumbs past the age of one often do some kind of stroking at the same time. One little boy rubs or plucks a piece of blanket, a diaper, a silk cloth, or a woolly toy. Another rubs his earlobe or twists a lock of his hair. Still another wants to hold a piece of cloth right up close to his face and perhaps stroke his nose or lip with a free finger. These motions seem to replay how younger babies gently touch their mother's skin or clothing when they nurse.

When a baby gets into the habit of twisting and tugging on strands of his own hair, the result can be unattractive bald spots. Parents often worry, because they think of hair pulling as a sign of emotional distress (as it is for older children). But for babies, it's just a habit. The best treatment is simply to cut the hair short so that there is nothing for the baby to grab hold of for a while. By the time the hair grows back, the habit is usually gone.

Ruminating. A small number of babies suck and chew on their tongues until their last meal comes up, a practice known as ruminating. Some cases begin when thumb-sucking babies have their arms restrained; they turn to sucking their tongues instead. It's best to give these babies their thumbs back before the ruminating becomes a habit, and to make sure they have enough companionship, play, and affection. Rumination may signal unusually high tension between infants and their parents. Professional guidance can help.

RHYTHMIC HABITS

Body rocking, head banging. From eight months to about four years, many children rock their bodies and bang their heads. A baby lying in her crib may roll her head from side to side or get up on all fours and jounce back and forth against her heels. With each forward movement her head may hit against the crib; it looks painful, but it clearly isn't. It's never hard enough to cause brain injury, but it sometimes raises a lump. A baby sitting on a couch will rock hard against the back and let it bounce her forward again.

You see these self-comforting behaviors when young children are sleepy, bored, or upset, or in response to physical discomfort from teething, for example, or an ear infection. Perhaps they're an attempt to reproduce the experience of being rocked and carried by a parent.

The same movements, especially head banging, occur frequently and intensely in some children who are emotionally neglected or physically abused, and in some with autism or other developmental disorders. Let your child's doctor know if these behaviors happen regularly.

NAIL-BITING

What it means. Sometimes nail-biting is a sign of tenseness; sometimes it's just a habit. Nail-biting is more common in relatively high-strung children who are inclined to worry a lot, and it tends to run in families. Children often bite their nails when they are anxious—for instance, while waiting to be called on in school or while watching a scary movie.

A good general approach is to find out what some of the pressures on your child are and try to relieve them. Is she being urged, corrected, warned, or scolded too much? Are your expectations for schoolwork and extracurricular achievements too high, or are her own self-imposed expectations? Is she getting along with peers? Ask her teachers what they see in the classroom and the lunchroom. If movie, radio, and TV violence makes her jittery, it's wise to make such programs off-limits. (Actually, that's probably best for all children.)

Prevention strategies. School-age children are often motivated to stop nail-biting because they sense disapproval from peers or because they want nicer-looking nails. You can support this positive motivation by offering suggestions. But it's best to let your child be in charge of the campaign. The problem belongs to your child, and the solution should, too.

Nagging or punishing nail-biters usually doesn't stop them for longer than half a minute, because they seldom realize they are doing it. In the long run, it may increase their tension or encourage them to think of the biting as their parents' problem, not their own. Bitter liquid on the nails can work, if the child asks for it as a way to remind himself that he wants to stop the nail-biting. But if it's put on against his will, the child is bound to think he's being punished. That only gives him another thing to feel tense about and may prolong the habit.

Take a broader view. If your child is otherwise reasonably happy and relaxed, you don't need to make too much of nail-biting. But when nail-biting is one of a host of worrisome behaviors, then it makes sense to seek professional help. It is the cause of the child's anxiety, not the nail-biting itself, that should be of greatest concern.

STUTTERING

What causes stuttering? Between two and three years of age, almost every young child goes through a period when talking is an effort and the words sometimes don't come out right; they may repeat words, or hesitate and then rush ahead too fast. This is all part of normal speech development. About one child in twenty has more difficulty talking, repeating many words or parts of words, lengthening some and entirely blocking others; some also tense up the muscles in their faces. Fortunately, mild to moderate stuttering like this usually goes away by itself.

We don't really know what causes persistent stuttering. Like many other speech and language problems, it's much more common in boys than girls; and it often runs in families. Brain-scan studies have found some differences in the size of certain brain areas in adults who stutter. It used to be thought that stuttering was caused by stress. That makes sense, because children who stutter almost always stutter more when they are under stress. But many children experience severe stresses without ever stuttering, and many who stutter are otherwise quite well-adjusted.

A tongue tie (when the fold of skin that runs from the middle of the underside of the tongue to the floor of the mouth appears to be too short to allow free movement of the tongue) has nothing to do with stuttering.

How to help. When your child talks to you, give him your full attention so that he doesn't get frantic. Let a couple of seconds go by before responding. Pause often. Be natural; you don't have to talk so slowly that it's weird. Help others in the family talk in the same relaxed, unpressured way. Stuttering gets worse when children feel they only have a few seconds to make themselves heard. Instead, make it a family rule that everyone takes turns and gives the others time to express themselves.

Telling a child to slow down or asking him to repeat himself often just increases his self-consciousness, making the stuttering worse. Instead, respond to what the child is saying rather than to how he says it. Don't grill your child by asking question after question; instead, take turns talking and listening.

Anything you can do to lower your child's stress level is likely to help. Does he have enough chances to play with other children? Does he have toys and equipment enough, indoors and out? When you're playing with him, let him take the lead. Play quietly sometimes, simply doing things without necessarily talking at the same time. A regular daily schedule, less pressure to perform, and less rushing around are all helpful. If your child was upset by being separated from you for a number of days, try to avoid further separations for a couple of months. If you think you have been talking to him or urging him to talk too much, try to train yourself out of it.

When to get help. Since most children who stutter get better on their own, it can be hard to know when to refer a child for special help. A good rule of thumb is to get help right away for severe stuttering and for any stuttering that hasn't shown signs of getting better after about four to six months.

When is stuttering severe? In severe stuttering, the child stutters pretty much all the time, even when relaxed; he's very self-conscious and may avoid speaking altogether; there's usually a lot of muscle tension in the face, and the voice pitch may go up (another sign of tension). When you're with a child who has a severe stuttering problem, you probably feel tense yourself. Trust your instincts: If a child's speech difficulty makes you feel uncomfortable, that's a sign to get help.

With severe stuttering, get help from a trained speech and language pathologist, the sooner the better (see the Resource Guide, page 899). There are special techniques to teach a child to speak more fluently. Even if speech therapy can't fix a child's stuttering, it may keep it from getting worse. A good therapist can help the child and the family understand the problem and adapt to it in healthy ways.

TOILET TRAINING, SOILING, AND BED-WETTING

READINESS FOR TOILET TRAINING

First, relax. Lots of parents feel anxious about the whole business. Maybe you've heard about children who can't get into child care because they're still in diapers, or about five-year-olds who refuse to use the toilet. In reality, you probably have nothing to worry about. Most children learn how to use the potty sometime between age two and a half and three and a half. Generally speaking, babies themselves gradually gain control of their own bowels and bladders as they grow. Their natural drive to grow up is as important as any efforts you make.

Timing isn't critical. Some children start training as early as eighteen months, others as late as thirty-six. As a group, those who start younger don't finish any sooner. Girls usually do finish a couple of months before boys. Parents are wise to avoid the extremes. Harsh punishments often backfire, while a completely hands-off approach runs the risk that your child will decide that diapers are the way to go. It's best to steer a middle course and adjust your training to your child's motivation and level of maturity.

Toileting and development. Toilet training normally happens around the time when young children are beginning to get a sense of themselves as individuals. At this age, around two or three, they want independence and control over everything they do. They are just learning that some things belong to them, and that they can decide whether to keep those things or give them away. They're fascinated by what comes out of them and pleased by their own growing mastery over when it comes out and where it goes.

Learning to use the toilet gives children control of parts of the body that previously functioned automatically. This new control makes them feel proud, so proud at first that they may try to perform every few minutes. In learning to use the toilet, they are accepting the first serious responsibility assigned to them by their parents. Successful cooperation on this project gives parents and children new confidence in each other. The child who previously enjoyed making messes with food and BMs now begins to take satisfaction in cleanliness.

Of course, toileting means the end of dirty diapers! That's important, all right. But toilet training also plays a part in the formation of a child's character. Children come to prefer clean hands, clean clothes, and (to some extent) a neat home and an orderly way of doing business. If you take advantage of your child's natural desire to become more grown-up and self-sufficient, the process will be a lot easier.

Early toilet training. In the first year, a baby shows very little awareness of bowel function. When her rectum becomes full, particularly after a meal when the intestines are active, the stool presses against the inner valve of the anus and causes it to open somewhat. This stimulates a squeezing, pushing-down action of the abdominal muscles. The baby, in other words, does not decide to push the way an older child or adult does;

it happens automatically. The bladder also works on autopilot in much the same way.

Even though small babies can't consciously control when they go, they can be trained to urinate and move their bowels on cue. Early training was common in the United States and Europe a few generations ago, and is still standard practice in many parts of the world where diapers are scarce. The process is simple enough. The mother senses when the baby is about to have a BM (often a few minutes after the baby has eaten) and sits the baby on a toilet or potty. Over time, the baby comes to associate sitting on the potty with relaxing his anal opening.

A similar technique can be used to train a baby to urinate on cue. When the mother senses that the baby is about to urinate, she holds the baby in a particular position (over a sink, for example), and makes a "psssh" sound. The baby learns to link the position, sound, and act of passing urine. After that, if the mother holds the baby in the right position and makes the right sound, the child urinates by reflex.

This process is truly toilet *training* rather than learning, because the baby is not conscious of what she herself is doing, at least not at first. It takes a lot of attention and persistence to train a child in this manner, and it's important that the parent remain calm and positive. If the parent becomes frustrated or impatient, the negative emotion is bound to become linked, in the child's mind, with the act of being put on the potty—just what you don't want to have happen.

Bowel control between twelve and eighteen months. At this age children gradually become conscious of when a bowel movement occurs. They may pause in their playing or change facial expression momentarily, though they are nowhere near ready to notify a parent.

As they gaze fondly at their BM in their diaper, they are likely to develop distinctly possessive feelings for it. They are proud of it as a fascinating personal creation. They may sniff the smell appreciatively, as they have been taught to sniff a flower. Such positive pride in the movement and its smell and the enjoyment of messing in it if the opportunity arises are characteristic reactions of this period.

One aspect of this possessiveness, as parents who have succeeded in catching movements have discovered early in the second year, is a reluctance about giving up the BM to the potty and to the parent. Another aspect is anxiety about seeing the BM flushed away in the toilet; to some small children this is as disturbing as if they saw their arm being sucked down the toilet.

Later, after about eighteen months, a child's possessive feelings toward his BMs naturally give way to a preference for being clean. You don't need to teach a child to be disgusted by body functions. The natural preference for being clean helps motivate a child to become trained and stay trained.

Indirect signs of readiness. Beginning in the second year, other aspects of readiness appear that we don't ordinarily associate with toilet training. Children now feel an impulse to give presents, and take great satisfaction from this—though they usually want them right back again. Their contradictory feelings may show in the way they hold out one of their toys to a visitor but refuse to let go of it. It's at this age that children become fascinated with putting things in containers and watching them disappear and reappear. Toddlers take great pride in learning any skill that they can carry out independently, and they enjoy being praised for their accomplishment. They gradually imitate more and more of the activities of their parents and older brothers and sisters. This drive can play an important part in training.

Balking. Often, a child who took to the idea of using the potty seat early in the second year will back off suddenly. He sits down willingly but doesn't have a BM. Then, right after getting up, he moves his bowels in a corner of the room or in his pants. Parents sometimes say, "I think my child has forgotten what it's all about."

I don't believe children forget that easily. I think that their possessive feelings about their BMs have become temporarily stronger and that they are simply unwilling to give them up. Early in the second year they have an increasing urge to do everything for themselves, in their own way, and toileting may seem too much like the parents' scheme. So they hold the movement in, at least until they can get away from the seat, which symbolizes giving it up and giving in.

If this resistance persists for many weeks, children may hold back not only when on the seat but for the rest of the day if they can manage it. This is a psychological type of constipation. Balking can occur at almost any point in the toilet-training process, but it is more apt to occur between twelve and eighteen months, rather than later. Balking may be a signal for you to wait at least a few months, in order to let your child feel that it is he who has decided to control his bowels and bladder, rather than that he is giving in to parental demands.

Readiness between eighteen and twenty-four months. At this age, most children show more definite signs of readiness. They often show a new desire to please the parents and fulfill their expectations—very helpful for toilet training. They begin to take great pride in learning any skill that they can carry out independently, and they enjoy being praised for their accomplishments. They gain the idea that certain things belong in certain places, and they begin to take interest in putting away their toys and clothes.

Body awareness is increasing, so they have a greater sense of when a movement is coming or being passed. They may stop playing for a few seconds, or they may act a bit uncomfortable afterward. They may make a sign or sound to the parent to indicate that the diaper is soiled, as if asking to be cleaned up. You can help by gently reminding your child to tell you if he has had a BM. At first he may tell you when it's already too late. But with practice, he'll notice the feeling of pressure in the rectum that signals that a BM is ready. Without this body awareness, it's hard to learn to use the toilet independently.

In addition, children's ability to move around is now much improved. They can walk and climb almost anywhere, and certainly can get onto the potty chair and sit steadily. They are able to pull their diaper or pants down by themselves.

A child who has arrived at these developmental milestones is probably ready to learn the fine art of bowel and bladder control.

A GENTLE TRAINING APPROACH

Training without force. If you wait until they are ready, children can learn to use the potty without being forced. Training children when they are ready makes the whole process more relaxed and pleasant, without a power struggle. Children who train this way often end up feeling quite proud of themselves, and ready to take on the next developmental challenge. In the 1950s, T. Berry Brazelton showed that these children rarely develop bed-wetting and soiling problems. Such problems were quite common among children who had been subjected to the harsher and more controlling training approaches that were then standard practice.

Following this gentle approach, most children are out of diapers somewhere around age two and a half, and dry at night at around age three to four. This works because children decide of their own free will to gain control over their bladder and bowels when they feel able, because they want to be grown-up. You need to be patient and wait for the signals that your child is ready.

Once you do decide to go ahead, at about age two to two and a half, your attitude is always the same—a consistent, kind expectation that your child will use the toilet as older children and adults do. When your child is successful, give mild praise—sharing pleasure, but not jumping up and down as though the achievement were truly extraordinary (remember, it's what you expect). When your child has a setback or refuses to comply, let him know that you're still confident he'll get the hang of it pretty soon. Anger and criticism have no role in this campaign.

The adult toilet or a potty seat? You can buy child-size toilet seats that fit over the regular adult seats. But these put the child high up in the air—an uncomfortable position in which to try to relax and let go. You'll need to find a seat with footrests, and get a sturdy step stool so your child can climb up by himself.

A better solution is to use a child's small plastic potty. Children feel friendlier toward a small piece of furniture that is their own and on which they can sit down by themselves. Their feet stay on the floor, and there is no height to make them feel insecure. For boys, don't use the urine guard that comes with the seat. All too often, it hurts a boy when he is getting on or off. Then he won't use the seat again.

The first stage. To begin, let your child become familiar with the potty, without any pressure to perform. If you allow your child see you use the toilet, he'll know what it's for and may want to mimic this grown-up activity. You can use tactful suggestions and flattery, but don't show disapproval for failure. If your child does sit on the potty, don't try to make him stay any longer than he wants to; that's a sure way to make the potty seem like a punishment. Let him get used to the seat for at least a few weeks as an interesting piece of furniture to sit on with all his clothes on if he wishes, rather than as a contraption to take his BMs away.

The second stage. When your child has accepted the seat, you can suggest casually that he use it with the lid up for BMs, the way his parents use the toilet seat. Pretend that it doesn't matter much to you. Children at this age are easily alarmed by being hurried or pushed into an unfamiliar situation. You can show how you sit on the grown-up toilet seat, and he can sit on his potty while you are sitting on the toilet.

Let your child get up and leave the seat immediately if he wants. The experience of sitting will be helpful, no matter how brief it is. The child should think of sitting on the seat not in any sense as an imprisonment but as a voluntary ritual carried out with pride.

If the child has not been willing to sit down without diapers, allow a week or so before suggesting it again.

You can explain again how Mommy and Daddy, and perhaps one or two of the child's older acquaintances, use their toilet that way. It often helps to have your child watch a friend perform. (If he has an older brother or sister, he will probably already have watched.)

After the idea of depositing the BM or urine in the potty has been discussed a couple of times, you can take off the child's diaper at a time when a movement is most likely, lead him to the seat, and suggest he try it. It is okay to use praise or small rewards to encourage your child to sit, but don't spend a lot of time urging or pushing him if he doesn't want to. Try another time or another day. Someday, when the BM does go into the potty, he'll understand better and may want to cooperate.

After a BM in the diaper, lead the child to the seat and show him the BM while you put it in the potty. Explain again that Mommy and Daddy sit on their seat to have their BMs, that he has his own seat, and that someday he will do his BM in it just like them.

If you have had no success in catching a movement or urination, drop the business for a few weeks and then try gently again. Take an upbeat attitude without making it a big deal or applying a lot of pressure.

At this stage, don't flush the BM from the diaper down the toilet until the child has lost interest and gone on to something else. Most one- to two-year-olds are fascinated with the flushing at first and want to do it themselves. But later some of them become frightened by the violent way the water flushes the movement away, and they become afraid to sit on the seat. They probably fear that they might fall in and be swirled away in a watery rush. Until two and a half years, it's a good idea to empty the potty and flush the toilet after the child has left the room.

The third stage. When your child begins to be interested and cooperative, take him to the seat two or three times a day, especially if he gives the slightest signal of readiness to urinate or have a BM. Even if a boy just has to urinate, I recommend that he sit rather than stand at this stage. If he manages to pass some urine or BM in the right place, praise him for being so grown-up—"just like Daddy" or Mommy, brother, sister, or admired friend—but don't overdo it. At this age a child doesn't like to be too compliant.

When you're sure your child is ready for the next step—going by himself—let him play for periods without any clothes on from the waist down. Put the potty seat nearby, indoors or out, explaining that this is so that he can go all by himself. If he is not resistant, you can remind him every hour or so that he may want to go all by himself. If he gets bored or resistant or has an accident, put him back in diapers and wait.

Is this the right method for you? As you know from visiting the bookstore, there is now a small industry in books about toilet training. Many of them promise fast results. Why wait patiently when you can get the process over with right away? Why not just tell your child what you want him to do, and expect him to do it?

If your child is very obedient, a simple demand for potty performance might work. However, if your child often resists your demands, toileting can easily become the focus of a power struggle.

This is a struggle that you are bound to lose. Young children are more powerful than their parents when it comes to two things: what goes into their bodies and what comes out. If a child is determined not to eat the food that's in front of him or to hold on to his bowel movements, there isn't a lot a parent can do about it. When a child holds back, the bowel movements often become hard and dried out, and therefore painful to pass. The child then has a new motivation to resist the toilet—and so the problem just gets worse.

Many parents feel they have to train their children early so that the children can begin day care. However, day care providers are often quite experienced with toilet training and can be a great help. This is a perfect example of a developmental challenge that is easier to tackle when parents and day care providers work as a team.

Among the many techniques for quick toilet training, one is actually research-proven. Psychologists Nathan Azrin and Richard Foxx described their method in detail in the book *Toilet Training in Less than a Day*. I suspect, however, that many parents find the instructions hard to follow, particularly since real-life children don't always respond the way they're supposed to. Resistance and tantrums can be a problem. The approach might work best when parents have an experienced professional available to coach them through it.

Fear of painfully hard movements. Sometimes a child has a spell of unusually hard movements that are painful to pass.

Collections of small, hard pellets are rarely painful. It's usually the hard movement in one large piece with a wide diameter that is to blame. As it passes, this movement may tear a tiny slit, or fissure, in the edge of the stretched anus, which may bleed a little. (If you notice blood in your baby's diaper, let the doctor know about it.) Each time another movement passes it opens the fissure again. This is quite painful, and may keep the fissure from healing for weeks.

You can easily see how a child who has once been hurt may develop an aversion to having BMs. If the child does succeed in holding back the movement for several days, it is more likely to come out large and hard. A vicious cycle develops, leading to worse and worse constipation.

Constipation is the number one cause of toileting refusal in young children. The key is to take care of the constipation before trying to make any progress toileting. During this process, it helps to keep reassuring the child that you know he is worried that the next BM will hurt the way the previous one did, but that he doesn't need to worry anymore because you are going to make sure the poop stays soft. If constipation is severe, you'll probably need a doctor's help to deal with the problem (see page 504).

BLADDER CONTROL

Simultaneous bowel and bladder control. One of the advantages of the gentle approach described above is that when children feel ready to control themselves, they usually achieve bowel and bladder control almost simultaneously. By twenty-four to thirty months, most children have enough body awareness and physical control; once they decide they want to be grown-up in these respects, very little special effort is required on the parents' part.

Attitudes toward BMs and urine. Children rarely make an issue of daytime urination. It seems that urine doesn't matter to them as a possession the way BMs do. Also, with BMs, if a child holds on long enough, the urge to empty the rectum tends to pass. With urine, the urge to go just gets stronger over time.

Bladder function tends to mature by itself. The bladder empties itself frequently in the first year. But by fifteen to eighteen months it begins to retain urine for a couple of hours, even though no training has been started. In fact, an occasional baby becomes spontaneously dry at night by a year of age. The bladder retains urine for longer periods during sleep than during wakefulness, and dryness may be discovered after a two-hour nap months before daytime control is achieved.

There may continue to be occasional accidental wettings in the daytime for several months after children have gained general control of urine. Usually, it's because a child is too busy playing to stop to go to the toilet.

Easily removed pants. When your child can successfully control his BMs and bladder, put him in pants that he can pull down by himself. This further step toward independence will lessen the chance of backsliding. But don't use pants before the child is generally succeeding: They won't do any good, and you'll have wasted their value as a mark of independence. Pull-Ups probably slow down the process of toilet training by giving children the gratification of being out of diapers without having done the work to master their bodily functions. Also, they're so absorbent, they remove the sensation of wetness that normally motivates a child to use the potty.

Inability to urinate away from home. It sometimes happens that a child around two has become so well trained to his own potty chair or toilet seat that he can't perform anywhere else. You can't urge him or scold him into it. He will probably wet his pants eventually. If he does, he may need reassurance that he hasn't done anything wrong; he's still learning. Keep this possibility in mind when you take him traveling, and bring along his own seat if necessary, and some changes of clothing.

If he is painfully full and can't let go, and you're visiting at a friend's home or staying at a hotel, try having your child sit in a warm bath for half an hour, letting him know it's okay to urinate in the bathtub.

It's good to get a child used to urinating in different places early. There are portable urinals for boys and for girls to which they can become accustomed at home and which can then be taken along when they visit. Some children are more comfortable in diapers when they're away from home, so you may want to give them that choice.

Standing up to urinate. Parents are sometimes worried because a two-year-old boy won't urinate standing up. It's fine for boys to sit down to urinate until they are comfortable on the potty. The longer they sit for urinating, the less likely they are to miss the toilet. A boy is bound to get the idea sooner or later when he sees his father or older boys standing.

Staying dry at night. Many parents assume that children learn to stay dry through the night only because the parent takes him to the toilet late in the evening. They ask, "Now that he is reasonably dry in the daytime, when should I begin to toilet train him at night?" This is a mistaken idea, making night dryness sound like too much of a job. It's closer to the facts to say that a child just naturally becomes dry at night when his bladder becomes mature enough, provided he isn't nervous or rebellious. It helps a little if the parents share in children's pride when they begin to have dry nights.

Most children become dry at night at around three years of age, although roughly one in five still wets the bed at age five. Boys tend to be later than girls, high-strung children later than relaxed ones. Slowness in becoming dry at night is often a family trait.

Teach proper wiping and handwashing. When your daughter shows an interest in wiping, you'll have to negotiate letting her wipe first with you finishing up until she can do a complete job by herself. This is the time to start teaching little girls to wipe from front to back to prevent bladder infections. Boys often need help with hygiene, too.

Handwashing is part of going to the bathroom. A step stool helps young children reach the sink. Little hands need small bars of soap, the size you find in hotel bathrooms. To wash effectively takes at least twenty seconds of brisk rubbing with soap suds, a fairly long time. To help make the time pass pleasantly, and to get your child into the habit of washing for long enough, make up a song to sing while washing, or tell a story about each finger. It takes about twenty seconds to sing the ABCs once or "Happy Birthday" twice.

SETBACKS IN BOWEL AND BLADDER CONTROL

Expect setbacks. Mastery occurs in little steps for most children. Emotional upsets, illness, traveling, and a new baby can all cause setbacks even in a child who seemed fully trained. Scolding and punishing don't help. When accidents occur, reassure your child that he'll regain control soon. It's a mistake to make too big a deal of it. (Once a child has been dry for a good many months, a change to regular wetting could be caused by a bladder infection or diabetes; see page 520.)

Backsliding on BMs. Many children refuse to have their BMs on the potty after they have trained themselves for urine; this happens more often to boys. They may hide in a corner when they have to have a BM, or insist on having a diaper on. Some appear afraid of the toilet. Constipation is a common problem, and in fact precedes the toileting refusal more often than not; this needs to be taken care of as a first priority (see page 501).

It can be terribly frustrating to parents, who know that their child *could* use the potty if only he *would*. Sticker charts, rewards, threats, bribes, and pleading are all likely to fail. What works—once you have made certain that your child is passing soft bowel movements daily—is to remove all the pressure for potty performance and give your child back his diapers or Pull-Ups. Let him know that you're confident he'll be able to use the potty when he's ready to, and leave it at that. This approach works within a matter of a few months in the great majority of cases. If toileting refusal continues past four years of age, it's best to consult with a pediatrician or psychologist who is experienced in helping families with toilet-training problems.

SOILING

Normal accidents. It's normal for a young child to have an occasional accident. The child may have forgotten to wipe well, or he may have been so busy playing that he ignored the feeling of fullness in his rectum until it was too late. The answer for these problems is a gentle reminder about wiping and making it a habit to take a toilet break a couple of times a day. For a very busy child, it helps to have a small box of picture books or special toys in the bathroom, so there's something to do while sitting on the potty for a few minutes.

Soiling in the older child. After about age four, soiling is a more serious problem. In the typical case, a school-age boy who has been using the toilet normally for years begins passing stool in his underpants. What is bewildering to the family is that he barely seems to notice it has happened and claims to have had no sensation of passing the stool; what's more, he denies smelling it.

Of course, other children notice the odor and may tease the child or shun him. Then soiling becomes a psychological and social emergency. Children with this problem often pretend they don't care about it, but they are simply trying to protect themselves from the distressing reality. The medical term for this problem is "encopresis."

In most cases, encopresis is the result of severe constipation. As the stool sits in the colon it forms chunks of dry, clay-like material that build up, stretching the rectum and the muscles that hold the anus closed. The overstretched muscles lose function, and the child loses the sensation of fullness and the ability to hold stool in. Liquid stool sneaks out of the partly open anus, and smaller chunks may come out without the child noticing. As for not smelling the stool, that's because people normally can't smell their own body odors (bad breath, for example).

The treatment is, first and foremost, to take care of the constipation. It is also very important to explain to the child what is going on and why he is not to blame. Exercises to strengthen the abdominal muscles (for more effective pushing) and regularly scheduled time on the toilet help the child pass stool every day and give him a way to exert some control over the situation. No one in the household should be allowed to shame, embarrass, or criticize the child, on the general principle that family is about supporting each other, never hurting. The most helpful attitude is "we're all in it together," with child, parent, and doctor playing on the same team.

Rarely, soiling occurs without constipation. The child passes normal BMs in his pants, rather than stains or chunks. This form of encopresis is more likely to reflect an emotional disturbance or a response to severe stress. A child behavior professional can help.

BED-WETTING

Everybody wets the bed until they learn how to stay dry. Most girls have mastered nighttime dryness by about four, most boys by five. No one knows for sure why girls develop earlier. At age eight, about 8 percent of children—one in twelve—still wet the bed. So if you have a third grader who wets the bed, you can reassure him that there is most likely at least one other child in his classroom who has the same problem.

Bed-wetting patterns. A child who has never consistently been dry at night has what doctors call *primary nocturnal enuresis*. This is the most common pattern. The causes and treatments are discussed below and on the following pages.

Less commonly, a child who has been dry at night for several months suddenly starts wetting again. Doctors call this pattern *secondary nocturnal enuresis* and look for medical causes such as bladder infections and diabetes. Sometimes a young child starts bed-wetting again in response to a normal stress. It could be the birth of a sibling, a move, or some other change. In these cases, patience and reassurance often do the trick. In a few weeks, the child feels better and is able to take charge of nighttime dryness again. Severe psychological stress such as sexual abuse can also cause a child to start wetting; it's important to keep this in mind, but understand that other, less concerning causes are more likely.

A third pattern involves daytime wetting. A child may have continual dampness in the underpants, may pass urine with coughing or laughing, may drink a lot and pass large quantities of urine, or may have frequent urges but not pass much at any given time. All of these symptoms call for medical assessment.

Causes of bed-wetting. With primary nocturnal enuresis, when a child has never learned to stay dry at night, there is rarely a medical cause to be treated. The problem is often inherited. If both parents wet the bed into late childhood or adolescence, their children are very likely to have the same problem. Many people think that children who wet the bed are especially deep sleepers, but research doesn't consistently find this. Most children who wet the bed do not appear to have smaller bladders than other children, but their bladders may be more prone to empty themselves before they are completely full.

It's very common for a child with bed-wetting to have constipation. The lower part of the bladder sits right next to the rectum. A rectum that is packed full of hard stool makes it difficult for the urine to get out, and forces the bladder to squeeze extra hard. The result is an overactive bladder that contracts in response to a small amount of urine. Attempts to treat the bed-wetting without first dealing with the constipation often fail. Treating the constipation often fixes the problem (see page 501).

Mainly, though, the cause of bed-wetting is simply that the child has not yet learned how to stay dry at night. In any given year, out of seven school-age children who wet the bed, one will become dry on his own. For the other six, there are effective ways to speed the process along.

Learning to stay dry. Staying dry is like learning to ride a bicycle. Once the brain has learned to balance the bike, you don't have to think consciously about it anymore; you simply hop on and ride. It's the same with staying dry. Once the brain has been trained, you simply fall asleep. The autopilot does the rest.

Holding in urine involves the action of two separate muscles. The outer muscle is under conscious control: It's the one you tighten up when you're trying to hold on until you get to the next rest stop. The inner muscle is under unconscious control: It's the one that keeps you dry without your having to think about it all the time. As the bladder fills up with urine, it sends nerve signals to the brain. The brain then sends back signals that tell the inner valve to stay closed; if the bladder is full enough, the brain creates an uncomfortable feeling that tells you to find a bathroom or (if you're asleep) that wakes you up. For children, learning to stay dry at night is a matter of learning to notice the signals coming from their bladders, even while they're asleep. People notice all sorts of things while asleep. They notice changes in temperature, uncomfortable body positions, and if they're about to roll off the side of the bed. Parents, of course, notice every little sound coming from their baby's room.

It helps children to know about these things—brain training, bicycles, muscles that hold in urine, signals from the bladder—when they decide they want to be dry at night.

Treatments for bed-wetting. Commonsense treatments include reminding your child not to drink a lot in the hour or two before bedtime and putting a night-light in the hall so it's easy for her to get to the bathroom. Some parents insist that their child not drink anything at all after dinner, but this more drastic measure is often uncomfortable for the child and rarely works anyhow. Avoiding caffeine-containing drinks such as colas and tea also makes sense, since these increase urine production.

Children who have wet the bed for years get used to sleeping on damp sheets. They need to get used to the feeling of a dry bed so that they'll be motivated to keep it that way. A good strategy is to make up your child's bed like a sandwich: Put down a plastic mattress cover, then a cloth sheet, then another plastic sheet, then a final cloth sheet. If the child wakes up in a damp bed, he can simply pull off the top sheet and the plastic one under it, put on a pair of dry pajamas, and climb back into a warm, dry bed. In the morning, the child can help with the laundry and remake the sandwich bed for the following night. Taking responsibility in this way helps a child realize that the bed-wetting is *his* problem to solve, not simply an annoyance to his parents.

Medications for bed-wetting include imipramine and desmopressin (DDAVP). Both of these medications can be quite effective in temporarily decreasing bed-wetting, but there are disadvantages. Both are dangerous when taken in overdose. Desmopressin is expensive. And neither actually solves the problem. Once a child stops taking the medication, bed-wetting often resumes.

Brain training is a better solution. The child learns to visualize his bladder filling up with urine, then sending an instant message or a tweet to the brain. Some children like to imagine a little person at a monitor up there. When the message comes in that the bladder is full, the little person jumps up and rings a bell, waking the child up.

Children who visualize this scene several times as they are falling asleep often find that they wake up while the bed is still dry. This isn't magic. Our thoughts when we sleep incorporate what we've been thinking about during the day. So a vivid memory of an imagined bladder alert, then a trip to the bathroom and a happy return to a dry bed, really can change a child's sleep pattern. (Parents have all had the experience of putting a sick child to bed, then waking at every tiny cough or sneeze.) Psychologists and behavioral pediatricians who are trained in hypnotherapy often help children control their bed-wetting using this imaginative approach.

Another learning technique involves the use of a bed-wetting alarm. These devices use an electronic sensor to detect the presence of urine, then buzz, beep, or vibrate to wake the child up. The child learns to rouse at the very first sign of wetting, and then begins to rouse a few seconds *before* the urine flows. Bed-wetting alarms can lead to dryness in nearly three-quarters of children after a month or two of use, and in most cases the improvement is permanent. Inexpensive bed-wetting alarms cost less than one month of desmopressin, and you only have to buy one. Sometimes the alarms are combined with visualization or medication.

A major advantage of approaches based on learning rather than medication is that they let a child take credit for solving his own problem. The next time he faces a difficult challenge, you can remind him of his past success. In this way, bed-wetting becomes an opportunity for growth.

SLEEP PROBLEMS

NIGHT TERRORS AND SLEEPWALKING

Crying in the night. A child of three or four sits up in bed, eyes wide-open, crying or talking in a confused way. When his parents go to comfort him, he struggles and cries louder. After ten or twenty minutes he settles down. In the morning he's just fine.

This is a typical night terror, upsetting, but only harmful to the tired and worried parents. The child may seem terrified, but he isn't dreaming: Night terrors have no plots (no monsters). His eyes are wide-open, but his brain waves still read "asleep," and it's actually hard to wake him up. Unless his parents do wake him mid-terror, he won't have any memory of the event.

Night terrors usually happen in the first half of the night, when most deep sleep takes place. They seem to be caused by the immaturity of the brain, and most children grow out of them by age five or six. They may increase when a child feels stressed, when starting in a new school for example, or when parents are arguing a lot. So it's reasonable to lower stress if possible. If the night terrors happen at about the same time each night, you may be able to wake your child a few minutes *before* the night terror. Doing this resets the sleep cycle, and often prevents the terror. Sometimes medication helps.

Sleepwalking and sleep talking. These problems have a lot in common with night terrors. They start with the child in deep sleep, and the child has no memory of them when she awakens. They're not dangerous in themselves, but sleepwalking can lead to injury if a child stumbles into something or falls downstairs. Safety gates or even a latch on the child's bedroom door may be what it takes to keep a child safe. Medicine is rarely needed or helpful.

INSOMNIA

Difficulty falling asleep. Young children often fight sleep because they don't want to say goodbye to all the exciting things in the world, or because they are uncomfortable separating from their parents at bedtime. Bedtime resistance can also be simply an annoying habit.

In older children and teens, the most common cause of insomnia is television in the bedroom (see page 653). At first the television may seem to make falling asleep easier, but it quickly becomes a habit that is hard to break. Rather than relaxing into restful sleep, the child stays awake until he simply cannot hold his eyes open any longer, well past the point of normal tiredness.

The best treatment for this problem is to keep television out of the bedroom. If the TV has already become a bedtime habit, you can expect an angry child at first, but this is no time to waver or give in. To wean a child from television dependence, try reading aloud or using recorded books. The child can listen with her eyes closed and drift off to sleep to a familiar story or soothing music.

Medication can induce sleep in children, but the benefits tend to be short-lived. Many parents give their children melatonin for sleep, because it has the reputation of being entirely safe. Obvious side effects are rare, although some children get nightmares. However, other important negative effects are starting to show up in the research. It's best to avoid medication unless it's truly needed. Doctors may prescribe medication for the insomnia that is part of another condition, such as ADHD.

Retraining for sleep. A better approach starts with a bedtime routine. Children are creatures of habit, and the routine—same events, same order, starting with a bath, and ending with kisses—creates a healthy habit (see page 127). Over time, the act of lying down in bed becomes linked in the brain with falling asleep.

Going to sleep is like the program your computer runs when it shuts down; it's a series of steps, not just switching off the power. If a tired child lies down in bed and suddenly feels wide awake, that means that the wrong "program" is being triggered.

To retrain the brain, don't let the child lie in bed awake for long. After about five to ten minutes, get him up out of bed and have him do something quiet (listening to a story, for example) in a different room. When his eyes grow heavy, have him lie down in bed again. Repeat this until he falls asleep within a few minutes of lying down. With repetition over a few nights, the brain will connect lying down with falling asleep, and the healthy sequence (lie down, get comfortable, fall asleep) will happen on the first try. This approach works well for adults, too.

Midnight waking. Children who wake in the middle of the night and can't fall back asleep have a different form of insomnia. In young children, the problem is often a habit. The child has gotten used to being rocked to sleep, or falling asleep sucking on a milk bottle (awful for the teeth—see page 454). When she wakes up and there's nobody to rock her or no bottle, she just can't fall asleep, no matter how tired she is.

In an older child, depression may interfere with sleep; chronic medical conditions such as allergies may also be at fault. Children can suffer from restless legs syndrome, with leg pains and sleeplessness. A few children wake in the middle of the night and eat compulsively.

For young children, teach them to fall asleep on their own at bedtime. Kiss them good night when they are still drowsy, not yet completely asleep. After they've learned to soothe themselves into sleep at bedtime, it's easy for them to do the same thing in the middle of the night.

For older children, search for new sources of stress. It could be something as serious as bullying in school or as innocent as wanting to be friends with someone who isn't interested; reduce the stress if you can. Stick to a predictable bedtime routine: television off a good hour or two in advance, bath, pajamas, brushing the teeth, stories, prayers if they are part of your family tradition, kisses. Protect your child from disturbing television images, whether from horror shows, kids' cartoons, or the news. Substitute stories that are interesting, but not scary (go to drspock.com for suggestions). Try to have peaceful evenings at home. If these commonsense approaches don't help, ask your child's doctor to make certain there is no medical cause for the problem.

DISORDERS OF FEEDING AND EATING

FEEDING PROBLEMS

How feeding problems start. Nearly all babies are born with enough drive to eat to keep them fueled and gaining weight at the proper rate. But they also have the instinct to resist food if they feel pressured, and the ability to feel disgusted by any food after a single unpleasant experience. What's more, their appetites change all the time. For a while a child may feel like eating squash or a new breakfast cereal, but next month the same foods disgust her. Some appetites stay big despite illness and unhappiness, but others are more moderate and easily affected by health and spirits.

You can see how feeding problems might begin at different stages in a child's development. Some babies become balky in their early months if their parents push them to finish their bottles, even if they feel full (think how uncomfortable it is to overeat). Some develop problems when the first spoon foods are introduced. They may have a hard time learning to swallow solids without gagging. After eighteen months, many become more picky because their weight gain naturally slows down; because they're more opinionated; and perhaps because of teething. Urging toddlers to eat usually stifles their appetites, and it may take months for the appetite to return. A common time for eating problems to begin is at the end of an illness. If an anxious parent begins pushing food before the child is ready, the pressure may quickly increase the child's disgust, which can then become a fixed feature.

Not all eating problems start with parental pressure. A child may stop eating because of jealousy of a new baby or worries of many kinds. But whatever the original cause, the parents' anxiety and urging usually make the problem worse and keep the child's appetite from returning.

Parents' feelings. It's the rare parent who can remain unemotional about a child's feeding problems. If your child eats poorly, it's natural to imagine that everyone thinks you're a bad parent, and to feel angry at the same little person you are worried about. Food refusal can seem willful, as though your baby went on hunger strike to punish you. You may also remember your own childhood struggles with eating (these issues often run in families); or perhaps you're upset by the fact that your child is the only one in the entire family who has ever refused food.

Maybe the worst thing about feeding problems is that you feel scared for your child's health, and powerless over something you think you ought to be able to control. In fact, it's rare for serious malnutrition to result from a child's picky eating habits, and controlling a child's food intake is much, much easier said than done. Working together with a supportive physician can relieve some of the pressure and worry, and can also let you know that you are not uniquely incapable. Many feeding problems are hard for doctors, too!

Treating feeding problems. The aim is not to *make* the child eat, but to let her natural appetite come to the surface so that she *wants* to eat. Try not to talk about her eating, either threateningly or encouragingly. Don't praise her for taking an unusually large amount or look disappointed when she eats little. With practice, you should be able to stop thinking about it. That's real progress. When your child feels no more pressure, she can pay attention to her own appetite.

It may take weeks for a child's timid appetite to come back. She needs a chance to slowly forget all the unpleasant associations with mealtime. You don't want your child to eat because she has been beaten in a fight, whether you have been forcing her or taking her food away. You want her to eat because she feels like eating.

Start by offering the foods she likes best. You want her mouth to water when she comes to meals, so much so that she can hardly wait to begin. As a first step, for two or three months, serve only the wholesome foods she likes best, omitting all the foods that she actively dislikes and offering as balanced a diet as possible.

The ultra-picky child. A parent might say, "Those children who dislike just one type of food aren't real problems. Why, my child likes only peanut butter, bananas, oranges, and soda pop. Once in a while he'll take a slice of white bread or a couple of teaspoons of peas. He refuses to touch anything else."

This is a more difficult feeding problem, but the principle is the same. You could serve him sliced bananas and a slice of enriched bread for breakfast; a bit of peanut butter, two teaspoons of peas, and an orange for lunch; a slice of enriched bread and more banana for supper. Let him have seconds or thirds of any of the foods if he asks for them. Give him a multivitamin as nutritional insurance. Serve different combinations of this diet for days. Hold firm on soft drinks and other junk foods; if his stomach is awash with syrup, it takes away what little appetite he has for more valuable foods.

If at the end of a couple of months he is looking forward to his meals, add a couple of teaspoons (no more) of some food that he sometimes used to eat (not one he hated). Don't mention the new addition. Don't comment, whether he eats it or leaves it. Offer this food again in a couple of weeks, and meanwhile try another. How quickly you add new foods will depend on how his appetite is improving and how he's taking to the new foods.

Make no distinctions between foods. Let him eat four helpings of one food and none of another if that's what he prefers, as long as the food is wholesome. If he wants none of the main course but does want dessert, let him have dessert in a perfectly matter-of-fact way. If you say, "No dessert until you've finished your vegetables," you further take away his appetite for the vegetable or the main course and you increase his desire for desserts. This result is the opposite of what you want. The best way to handle the dessert problem is to serve fruit every night except one or two, when you offer ice cream or something baked as a special treat. If he only eats the sweeter desserts, let him; he'll come around in time.

It's not that you want children to go on eating lopsided meals forever. But if they have a feeding problem and are already suspicious of some foods, your best chance of having them come back to a reasonable balance is to let them feel that you do not care one way or the other about what they eat.

It's a great mistake for the parent to insist that children who have feeding problems eat "just a taste" of a food they are suspicious of, as a matter of duty. If they have to eat anything that disgusts them, even slightly, it lessens the chance that they will ever change their minds and like it. And it lowers their enjoyment of mealtimes and their general appetite for all foods. Certainly never make them eat at the next meal food that they refused at the last meal. That's looking for trouble.

Serve less than they will eat, not more. For a child who is eating poorly, serve small portions. If you heap her plate high, you'll remind her of how much she is going to refuse and you'll depress her appetite. But if you give her a first helping that is less than she is going to eat, that will encourage her to think, "That isn't enough!"

You want her to have that attitude. You want her to think of food as something she is eager for. If she has a really small appetite, serve her miniature portions: a teaspoon of beans, a teaspoon of vegetables, a teaspoon of rice or potatoes. When she finishes, don't say eagerly, "Do you want some more?" Let her ask, even if it takes several days of miniature portions to give her the idea. It's a good idea to serve the miniature portions on a very small plate, so that the child doesn't feel humiliated by sitting in front of tiny portions of food on a huge plate.

Stay in the room. If you can be sociable and relaxed and get your mind off the food, it's fine to stay, whether or not you are eating your own meal. Otherwise, it may be better for you to retire from the picture at the child's mealtime—not crossly, not suddenly, but tactfully and gradually, a little more each day, so that he doesn't notice the change, or busy yourself with other cooking or cleaning, so that you aren't hovering over your child. Pleasant companionship is what you're aiming for.

No acts, bribes, or threats. Certainly, you shouldn't bribe your child to eat: a little story for every mouthful, or a promise to stand on your head if he finishes his spinach. Although this kind of persuasion may seem effective at the beginning, in the long run it dampens a child's appetite more and more. Also, you have to keep upping the ante to get the same result, and end up putting on an exhausting act for five mouthfuls.

Don't ask a child to eat to earn his dessert, a piece of candy, a gold star, or any other prize. Don't ask him to eat for Aunt Minnie, to make his mother or father happy, to grow big and strong, to keep from getting sick, or to clean his plate. Children should not be threatened with physical punishment or loss of privileges in an attempt to get them to eat.

It's reasonable for a child to be expected to come to meals on time, to be pleasant to other diners, to refrain from making disparaging remarks about the food or declaring what she doesn't like, and to eat with the table manners that are reasonable for her age. It's fine for the parents to take her preferences into account as much as is possible (considering the rest of the family) in planning meals, or to ask her occasionally what she would like, as a treat. But it's bad for her to get the idea that she's the only one to be considered. It's sensible to put a limit on sugar, candy, soda, cake, and the other less wholesome foods. All this can be done without argument as long as you act as if you know what you're doing.

NEEDING TO BE FED

Should the parents feed a poor eater? A child who is given proper encouragement will take over his own feeding at somewhere between twelve and eighteen months. But if the parents have continued to feed him until age two or three or four, probably with a lot of urging, it won't solve the problem simply to tell him, "Now feed yourself."

By this time, the child has no desire to feed himself; he takes being fed for granted. To him, being fed is a sign of his parents' love and concern. If they stop suddenly, it hurts his feelings and makes him resentful. He is liable to stop eating altogether for two or three days—and that's longer than any parents can sit by and do nothing. When they feed him again, he has a new grudge against them. When they try another time to give up feeding him, he knows his strength and their weakness.

A child of two or more should be feeding himself as soon as possible. But getting him to do it is a delicate matter that may take several weeks. You mustn't give him the impression that you are taking a privilege away. You want him to take over because he wants to.

Serve him his favorite foods, meal after meal and day after day. When you set the dish in front of him, go to the kitchen or into the next room for a minute or two, as if you had forgotten something. Stay away a little longer each day. Come back and feed him cheerfully with no comments, whether or not he has eaten anything in your absence. If he gets impatient while you are in the next room and calls you to come and feed him, come right away with a friendly apology. He probably won't progress steadily. In a week or two he may get to the point of self-feeding at one meal and insisting that you feed him at others. Don't argue at all during this process. If he eats only one food, don't urge him to try another. If he seems pleased with himself for doing a good job of self-feeding, compliment him on being a big boy, but don't be so enthusiastic that he gets suspicious.

Suppose for a week or so you have left him alone with good food for as long as ten or fifteen minutes and he's eaten nothing. Then you ought to make him hungrier. Gradually, over three or four days, cut down to half what you customarily feed him. This should make him so eager that he can't help starting to feed himself, provided you are being tactful and friendly.

By the time the child is regularly feeding himself as much as half a meal, it's time to encourage him to leave the table rather than you feeding him the rest of the meal. Never mind if he has left some of his foods. His hunger will build up and soon make him eat more. If you go on feeding him the last half of the meal, he may never take over the whole job. Just say, "I guess you've had enough." If he asks you to feed him some more, give him two or three more mouthfuls to be agreeable and then suggest casually that he's through.

After he has taken over completely for a couple of weeks, don't slip back into the habit of feeding him again. If someday he's very tired and says, "Feed me," give him a few spoonfuls absentmindedly, and then say something about his not being very hungry. A parent who has worried for months or years about a child's eating, who spoon-fed him much too long and finally let him feed himself, has a great temptation to go back to feeding him the first time he loses his appetite or is sick. Then the job has to be done all over again.

GAGGING

Some children gag easily; some hardly ever gag. Children who have spent a long time in the intensive care unit as newborns often show special difficulties managing textured foods. These early difficulties can set children up for persistent gagging problems.

The child beyond the age of a year who can't tolerate anything but pureed food has usually been fed forcibly, or at least urged vigorously. It isn't so much that she can't stand lumps. What makes her gag is having them pushed into her. The parents of gagging children usually say, "It's a funny thing. She can swallow lumps all right if it's something she likes very much. She can even swallow big chunks of meat that she bites off the bone."

There are three steps in curing a child who gags. The first is to encourage her to feed herself completely (see the section preceding). The second is to get her over her suspicion of foods in general. The third is to go unusually slowly in coarsening the consistency of her food. Let her go for weeks or even months, if necessary, on pureed foods, until she has lost all fear of eating and is really enjoying it. Don't even serve her meats, for instance, during this time if she cannot enjoy them finely ground.

In other words, go only as fast as the child can comfortably take it. A few babies have such sensitive throats that they gag even on pureed foods. In some of these cases, the cause seems to be the pasty consistency of the food. Try diluting it a little with milk or water. Or try chopping vegetables and fruits finely without mashing them.

In most hospitals there are speech and language pathologists or occupational therapists who specialize in problems of gagging and swallowing. Working with one of these specialists can be very helpful.

THIN CHILDREN

Many thin children come from thin stock on one or both sides of the family. They eat well, aren't sickly, aren't nervous; they just never want to eat much. Other children are thin because their appetites have been taken away by too much parental pressure, or for other nervous reasons. Children who constantly worry about monsters, death, or a parent's going away, for example, may lose their appetites. Angry arguments or physical fighting between parents can have the same effect. The jealous younger sister who is driving herself all day long to keep up with an older sibling burns up a lot of energy and gives herself no peace at mealtime, either. A tense child is made thin via a two-way process: The appetite is kept down, and the restlessness uses up extra energy.

Hunger. Many children throughout the world are malnourished because their parents can't find or afford the proper food. Even in the United States, as many as one child in four regularly experiences days or weeks when he can't count on having enough to eat. Food insecurity interferes with children's growth, and plays havoc with their ability to learn in school. Hungry children can be overweight if the only foods the family can afford are low-cost, high-calorie, low-nutrient ones. With wages rising slower than expenses, more and more self-sufficient and hardworking people need food assistance.

Illness. Doctors monitor children's growth at each checkup. Children who become thin during an acute illness usually recover their weight promptly once they get better. A pattern of poor weight gain over time should trigger a search for causes. Among the causes of weight loss are diabetes (which also produces excessive hunger and thirst and frequent urination), serious family tensions, tumors, intestinal diseases, and obsession with the need to diet.

Feeding a thin child. A healthy child may stay thin despite a large appetite. In many of these cases, the child prefers relatively low-calorie foods, like vegetables and fruit, and shies away from rich desserts. If your child doesn't seem to have any kind of problem, has been slender since infancy, but gains a reasonable amount of weight every year, relax: He's meant to be that way. If you've gotten caught up in a power struggle with your child over feeding, try to take the pressure off your child and yourself.

Thin children whose stomachs never seem to want to take much at a time may need to eat between meals. That doesn't mean constant snacking, which tends to blunt the appetite (as dieters who eat tiny portions all day long know). It means three meals and three snacks: breakfast; midmorning snack; lunch; afternoon snack; dinner; bedtime snack. It's tempting to give a thin child high-calorie, low-nutrition junk food, either as a bribe or to have the comfort of seeing him eat something. But it's better to offer foods with more nutritional value than just calories. Some low-volume, high-nutrition foods are nuts and nut butters, avocado, olives, dried fruits, and oils.

OBESITY

Parents have to walk a fine line. On the one hand, everyone knows that obesity causes serious medical problems: hypertension, heart disease, diabetes, cancer, knee pain, back pain, sleep apnea, asthma attacks, and social rejection. No parent wants any of this for her child. On the other hand, constant reminders, shaming, and food restrictions drive many children to overeat as an act of defiance. Compliant children who buy into their parents' obesity anxiety may become uptight and unhappy around food, and risk developing eating disorders. What parents need is a rational, informed, and relaxed approach to prevent and respond to overweight and obesity.

What is obesity? Without getting too technical, it's reasonable to think of obesity as simply an unhealthy excess of fat. It's hard to measure body fat precisely, but a combination of height and weight called the body mass index (BMI) gives a pretty good estimate. The U.S. Centers for Disease Control publishes normal values for BMI for boys and girls at different ages, based on measurements of thousands of children made several years ago. Pediatricians define obesity as a BMI higher than ninety-five out of one hundred of these index children, matched for age and sex. In the years since the normal BMI values were established, children as a whole have gotten heavier, so that now nearly 20 percent of school-age children have BMIs above the ninety-fifth percentile on the standard charts, in the obese range.

Practically speaking, that means that a child who has a normal BMI, according to the charts, probably looks skinny in comparison to the other children in the neighborhood. A child who is visibly overweight most likely falls into the obese range on the charts, and many children who seem to be of normal size do, too.

BMI is the standard measure, but it does not tell the whole story. Athletic children may have high BMIs if they are very muscular. BMI isn't usually calculated for infants, which is a good thing, because young babies should be fat. Plump babies often grow up to be lean children and adults. But by age six or seven, when children are normally at their thinnest, a child who is obese is unlikely to simply grow out of the condition. By adolescence, obesity is usually a lifelong problem.

What causes obesity? Genes play a leading role. Rarely, a single malfunctioning or missing gene causes obesity all by itself. Much more often, obesity is the result of dozens of genes, which each play a small role. Some increase appetite or decrease the sense of fullness; others turn down the metabolism, reduce fidgeting (which burns energy), or increase the efficiency with which the body lays on fat. Everyone has some "fat genes," but unlucky people who inherit more than their share are much more likely to end up overweight. This is one reason that obesity tends to run in families.

It's not only which genes you inherit, but also which ones are turned on. Undernutrition early in life can switch on genes that cause the body to retain fat, and these genes stay active from then on. This effect can start even before birth, so that babies who are born small often grow into adults who are too large. Chemicals in the environment can also mimic hormones that control genes that ultimately affect weight (see page 17). Genes carried in the billions of bacteria that populate our intestines also play a role in obesity. Antibiotics taken for illnesses, or fed to animals that then are eaten by people, also can promote obesity, perhaps by affecting these bacteria.

Other causes are there for all to see. Watch an hour of children's TV and you'll experience dozens of ads for highly-processed, high-calorie foods. The price tag for all of this marketing has been estimated at more than $10 billion a year, and that's not counting ads on websites, social media, and apps for children. All those ad dollars translate into processed foods bought and consumed by children. Fast-food outlets are strategically located near schools. Purveyors of soda locate their vending machines *in* schools, if they're allowed to.

Obesity and poverty go hand in hand. It takes resources to push back against the tide of fast food, food ads, commercial culture, and pressure-filled days that drag so many children toward obesity. Families with funds live in areas where it's safe to walk and ride bikes, where grocers sell fresh fruits and vegetables; where the playgrounds are safe, schools have physical education, and after-school programs are plentiful and high-quality.

One cause that many people focus on—a lack of willpower—turns out to be less important. Children with obesity aren't as a rule any lazier or less disciplined than other children, and telling a child to "just say no" doesn't help, nor do threats and dire predictions. Reciting a list of maladies, like the list that started off this chapter, doesn't help children lose weight or keep it off; it just makes them anxious and sad.

What parents can do. Early choices affect the odds of being obese. It helps when mothers eat well, avoid excess stress, and keep a healthy weight during pregnancy (see page 16). Breastfeeding for six months or longer also lowers the risk of obesity.

You can choose to feed your family a diet based mainly or entirely on plants (vegans and vegetarians have lower rates of obesity than meat eaters). You can take the money you save on meats and buy pesticide-free fruits and vegetables, while making your home a "no-buy zone" for foods that are highly processed and high in fats and refined sugar (especially high-fructose corn syrup).

You can make healthy activities part of your family's lifestyle. Make time for hiking, biking, or working out together; cut back on TV and other screens, or do without them entirely; enjoy pleasant family dinners together. The key to making all this happen is parental leadership, and leading by example. If obesity runs in your family, it's especially important for you to choose a healthy lifestyle for yourself and your children. If there are members of your family who are thin, remember that healthy eating and exercise are good for all children, not just those who are overweight.

Don't single out your weight-challenged child; make health-wise decisions for the whole family. Control the quality of the food you serve, keep healthier foods plentiful and varied, but make and buy smaller amounts of richer food. When it comes to high-cal foods, such as ice cream, buy small amounts and plan for them to be eaten in one sitting; don't buy the economy size and hope that it will last. Don't forbid your child from certain foods, but do keep them physically distant. A donut in the store a mile away is much less appealing than one on the kitchen counter. Don't expect willpower to solve the problem, but do set up the home environment to be maximally supportive.

With teens, you can't dictate; you have to work as partners. Ask your teen if it would be most helpful for you to give him tactful reminders, or if he would prefer you to keep quiet. If he chooses "keep quiet," try your best to honor his wish, however hard that may be. Teens appreciate having a voice. They usually don't mind asking for help, as long as they feel it is not being thrust upon them.

Obesity is complex, so treatments need to be comprehensive. Effective teams often include doctors, nutritionists, psychologists, recreation therapists, teachers, coaches, and others.

Extreme measures. There is no end to diets and pills that claim to make weight loss easy. None of them works over time, and some are dangerous. Ultra-low-carbohydrate diets aren't any better, in the long run, than sensible eating. These and other diets that cut out whole classes of nutrients pose a real risk of interfering with normal growth and development.

The most thoroughly studied weight-loss medications can claim at best a reduction of 5 percent or 10 percent in the weight of obese adults, and less is known about their effects in children. Stimulant medications prescribed for ADHD often cause weight loss, but it comes right back once the medication stops. These medications should only be used for ADHD. The side effects of other weight-loss medications can be severe. Pills are almost never the solution.

Finally, weight-loss surgery is increasingly being offered to extremely obese teens. It's still available only in specialized centers, however, and only to children who meet strict criteria, and it's enormously expensive and somewhat dangerous. Most important, for the surgery to work, the child has to stick to a regimen of healthy eating and exercise for life; otherwise the weight will come back.

EATING DISORDERS

As early as age ten or eleven, it's common for girls to believe that they should diet. Many boys, for their part, seek unnaturally sculpted muscles. Eating disorders—anorexia nervosa and bulimia—are a serious concern.

The main feature of anorexia is compulsive dieting with severe weight loss, while bulimia involves out-of-control eating (bingeing) followed by self-induced vomiting, laxative abuse, or other extreme measures to limit weight gain. Together, these disorders affect somewhere between 2 percent and 9 percent of women in the United States, mainly in their teens and early adult years (the actual numbers are hard to know, since people with eating disorders often hide them). Among people with eating disorders, about one in ten is male.

Our culture is body-obsessed. Why some people develop eating disorders and others don't is still a mystery. Science has identified some of the genes that put children at risk, along with adverse experiences, perfectionism, and stress.

Addicted to thinness. One way to look at eating disorders is as a form of addiction. Eating disorders may start out as something that seems positive—losing weight, getting in shape—but then the addiction takes over. Just as the alcoholic is always thinking about how to get his next drink, the anorexic is always thinking about how to lose the next few ounces, and the bulimic is always resolving to escape the destructive binge-purge cycle.

A person with an eating disorder cannot simply decide to stop having the disorder. While some women say that they have overcome eating disorders on their own, most require professional treatment, often by a team including physicians, psychologists, nutritionists, and others. Recovery is rarely quick or easy, but people *can* recover.

Psychological changes. Anorexia nervosa is about more than just dieting too much. A girl or woman with anorexia nervosa believes that she is overweight, even though she is obviously too thin. An extreme fear of gaining weight dominates her thoughts; being fat is the worst possible fate she can imagine. In medical terms, "anorexia" refers to a loss of appetite. But many people with anorexia nervosa are hungry all the time. They often obsess about food, cooking elaborate meals that they do not eat. Some exercise compulsively—two or three times a day.

People who develop anorexia may be outwardly successful—earning good grades, for example—but often feel inwardly inadequate. They may have trouble expressing emotions, particularly anger. They tend to feel that they are not in control of most aspects of their lives, but that weight loss is something they *can* control. People with the disorder may alienate their friends and family, who see the person's self-destructive behavior but cannot talk them out of it.

Physical changes. In anorexia, the abnormal loss of body fat drives hormone levels down, and menstrual periods cease or don't start. (Males with anorexia also have abnormal sex hormone levels.) As the malnutrition worsens, the bones lose calcium; there is damage to organs throughout the body, including the heart. About one in ten people with anorexia nervosa dies as a result of the disease. In bulimia, frequent vomiting damages the teeth and affects blood chemistry.

Treatment. Because anorexia is a complex disorder, with physical, psychological, and nutritional components, it is best treated by teams that include psychologists, psychiatrists, family therapists, and nutritionists. The first priority is weight gain. People who are severely underweight typically need to be hospitalized to ensure that they put on pounds safely. Psychotherapy focuses on helping the person change how she thinks about her body and what it means to be attractive and successful. She needs to learn to express her feelings in nondestructive ways. Medication can help treat depression or other psychiatric problems.

Preventing eating disorders. If your child is overweight, talk about being healthy rather than about losing weight. Make sensible eating and exercise a whole-family affair. Pressure on a child to slim down usually backfires, leading to overeating, but it can also trigger an eating disorder in a child who is driven to please.

Respect your child's natural body type. If your child has a medium build, let her know that you approve. There's little to be gained from trying to reshape your child. As parents, we absorb the same thin-is-beautiful message that is everywhere in our culture. It's important that we keep these attitudes to ourselves.

Never tease your child about being chunky or pudgy. You don't mean harm, of course, but joking like this can hurt. Children take the message to heart, and the idea develops that they really do need to diet. And if your child is naturally slender, don't go on and on about how wonderful it is to be thin. Naturally thin children may be at increased risk of developing anorexia nervosa because it is easier for their bodies to burn calories. If they receive a lot of praise or admiration for being thin (or if their sibling does), the temptation to embrace thinness as an end in itself can be strong.

Talk with your children about how TV, movies, and print advertisements glorify thinness. "Look at that actress," you might say. "She's really thin! Most real people who are healthy aren't that skinny." It's up to you to counteract the attempt by businesses to sell their products by promoting an unrealistic and unhealthy ideal of beauty. Even children's cartoons embrace the unattainable: tiny waists and large breasts in female characters; huge shoulders and chests in males. Protecting children from this harmful ideal is a good reason—one of many!—for limiting or eliminating TV viewing for young children.

Pay attention to hints that your child is thinking a lot about weight. If she seems fascinated by fashion models or rail-thin celebrities, try to encourage other interests—for example, art or music. If she begins talking about dieting, change the focus, if you can, to being healthy rather than getting thin. Even for children who are chunky, dieting is rarely the best answer. Aim instead for healthy eating and enjoyable physical activity.

Pay special attention if your child is involved in ballet or in sports like gymnastics or wrestling, because of the importance of weight limits. For children and teenagers, coaches should see it as their first duty to ensure that their young athletes are healthy. They should not be suggesting weight-loss diets, and should work with parents to watch for signs of unhealthy dieting.

A child who develops an eating disorder is often a perfectionist. He may be more successful than his classmates but less happy. With such a child, try to lower the pressure to succeed. Steer your child toward team sports, because these activities tend to put children under less pressure. If your child takes dance or music lessons, look for a teacher who emphasizes joyful self-expression rather than perfect technique. Appreciate your child's good grades, but be sure to openly recognize other things about her as well—her good sense or her loyalty to friends, for example—so she learns that high grades are not the most important thing about her.

Examine your own behavior. If you are constantly dieting, you're teaching your child that weight is something to be fought and controlled. If you do need to lose weight, it's probably best to make your diet part of a comprehensive plan to lead a healthier life, not just something you're doing to look good. Focusing on good health is a better message for your child and will probably be more effective in the long run for you, too.

SIBLING RIVALRY

JEALOUSY AND CLOSENESS

There is bound to be some jealousy between siblings. If it is not severe, it probably helps children to grow up to be more tolerant, independent, and generous. One way children learn to deal with their jealous feelings is to take on some of the nurturing qualities of their parents. In many families, jealousy gets turned into friendly competition, mutual support, and loyalty.

You might also know other families where the children never really liked each other very much, and may not have much to do with each other even as adults. Parents affect how sibling relationships develop, and luck also plays a role. Some siblings naturally enjoy each other's company—they'd be friends even if they weren't from the same family. Other siblings start out with very different personalities—one likes noise and excitement, while the other craves peace and quiet—and so have a harder time getting along.

Equal love, different treatment. In a general way, the more agreeably parents get along with each other, the less sibling jealousy there is. When all the children are satisfied with the warm affection they receive, they have less reason to begrudge the attention their parents give to their brothers and sisters.

What makes each child secure in the family is the feeling that his parents love him and accept him for who he is.

Parents can love their children equally without treating them exactly the same. A useful principle is "We all get what we need—and sometimes we all need different things." A younger child needs an earlier bedtime. An older child needs more responsibility for chores and more freedom.

When parents or relatives treat different children *equally* rather than individually, jealousy often intensifies. A harassed mother who is trying hard to treat her jealous children with perfect justice may say, "Now, Susie, here's a little red fire engine for you. And Tommie, here is one exactly like it for you." Each child then, instead of being satisfied, suspiciously examines both toys to see if there is any difference between the two. It's as if the mother said, "I bought this for you so you wouldn't complain that I was favoring your brother," instead of implying that "I bought this for you because I knew you'd like it."

Avoid comparisons and "typecasting." The fewer comparisons, complimentary or uncomplimentary, between siblings the better. Saying to a child, "Why can't you be polite like your sister?" makes him resent his sister and the very idea of politeness. If you say to an adolescent girl, "Never mind if you don't have dates like your sister. You're much smarter than she is, and that's what counts," it belittles her unhappiness at not having dates and implies she should not be feeling what, in fact, she is feeling. This is a setup for further rivalry.

It is tempting for parents to typecast their children. One child is "my little rebel," while the other is "the angel." The first child may begin to believe that she always has to buck authority or risk losing her identity in the family. And even though the "good child" may sometimes feel like doing something naughty, she may fear that she has to continue to play her assigned role or risk losing her parents' love. And she may resent the "rebel" for having a freedom she lacks.

Sibling fights. It generally works better if parents keep out of most of the fights between children who can stand up for themselves. When parents concentrate on pinning the blame, it leaves one warrior feeling more jealous.

To a greater or lesser degree, children's jealous squabbles come about because each would like to be favored by the parents. When parents are quick to take sides, in the sense of trying to decide who is right and who is wrong, it encourages the children to fight again soon. The fight then becomes a tournament to see who can win Mom's allegiance, at least this time. Each wants to win the parents' favor and see the other scolded.

If you do feel you have to break up a fight—to protect life and limb, to prevent rank injustice, or simply to restore quiet—it's better simply to demand an end to the hostilities, refuse to listen to arguments, act uninterested in who is right and who is wrong (unless a flagrant foul has been committed), concentrate on what's to be done next, and let bygones be bygones. You could suggest a compromise; distraction might save the day; or the children might need to be separated.

Older children who are left to take care of their younger brothers and sisters may resort to threats or violence to establish their control. In these situations, you may need to put someone else in charge (a hired sitter or an adult relative, for example), or enroll the children in an after-school program or child care center. When sibling fighting is severe and getting worse, family therapy may be needed.

THE MANY FACES OF JEALOUSY

Recognizing sibling jealousy with a new baby. If a child picks up a large block and hits the baby with it, the mother knows well enough that it's jealousy. But another child is more polite. He simply observes the baby without much enthusiasm or comment. One child focuses all his resentment against his mother, grimly digging the ashes out of the fireplace and sprinkling them over the living room rug in a quiet, businesslike way. Another with a different makeup mopes and becomes dependent, loses his joy in the sandpile and his blocks, and follows his mother around, holding on to the hem of her skirt and sucking his thumb.

Occasionally you see a small child whose jealousy is turned inside out. He becomes preoccupied with the baby. When he sees a dog, all he can think of to say is, "Baby likes the dog." When he sees his friends riding trikes, he says, "Baby has a tricycle, too." In this circumstance, some parents might say, "We found that we didn't have to worry about jealousy at all. Johnny is so fond of the new baby." It is fine when a child shows love for the baby, but this doesn't mean that jealousy isn't there. It may show up in indirect ways or only in special circumstances. He may hug the baby just a little too tightly. Perhaps he's fond of her indoors but is rude when strangers admire her on the street. A child may show no rivalry for months until one day the baby creeps over to one of his toys and grabs it. Sometimes this change of feeling comes on the day the baby begins to walk.

Being oversolicitous of the baby is just another way of coping with the stress. At its root is the same cauldron of mixed feelings—love and jealousy—that drive other children to regress or indulge in wrathful fits. It's wise to go on the assumption that there is always some jealousy and some affection, whether they both show on the surface or not. The job is not to ignore the jealousy, forcibly suppress it, or make the child feel deeply ashamed about it, but to help the feelings of affection to come out on top.

Handling different kinds of jealousy. When the child physically attacks the baby, a parent's natural impulse is to act shocked and shame him. This doesn't work out well for two reasons. He dislikes the baby because he's afraid his parents are going to love her instead of him. When they threaten not to love him anymore, it makes him feel more worried and cruel inside. Shaming also may make him bottle up his feelings of jealousy, which do more harm to his spirit and last longer if suppressed than if allowed to stay out in the open.

As a parent in this situation, you have three jobs: to protect the baby, to show the older child that he is not permitted to put his mean feelings into action, and to reassure him that you still love him and that he is really a good boy. When you see him advancing on the baby with a grim look on his face and a weapon in his hand, obviously you must grab him and tell him firmly that he can't hurt the baby. (Whenever he succeeds in being cruel, it makes him feel guilty and more upset inside.)

This situation gives you an opportunity to teach your child that his feelings are understandable and acceptable; it is the acting on those feelings that is not permitted. You can turn your grab into a hug and say, "I know how you feel some-times, Johnny. You wish there weren't any baby around here for Mommy and Daddy to take care of. But don't you worry, we love you just the same." If he can realize at a moment like this that his parents accept his angry feelings (but not his angry actions) and still love him, it is the best proof that he doesn't need to worry.

As for the child who intentionally spreads dirt around the living room, it's natural for you to feel angry, and you will probably scold him. But if you realize that he acted from de-spair and anxiety, you may later feel like reassuring him. Try to remember what may have happened that sent him over the edge.

Withdrawal is concerning. The child who mopes in his jeal-ousy needs affection, reassurance, and drawing out even more than the child who eases his feelings by being naughty. With the child who doesn't dare show directly what's bothering him, it may actually help him to feel better if you can say under-standingly, "I know that sometimes you feel mad at the baby and angry with me because I take care of her." If he doesn't respond after a while, consider hiring a temporary helper for the baby if you can afford one, and see if he can recover his old zest for life through more individual attention for a short while.

It is worthwhile to consult a children's psychiatrist or psy-chologist, or a pediatrician with special expertise in child be-havior and development, about the child who cannot seem to get over his jealousy, whether it takes the form of constantly misbehaving or moping or being obsessed with the baby. The therapist may be able to draw the jealousy to the surface so that the child can realize what's worrying him and get it off his chest.

If the jealousy comes out strongly only after the baby is old enough to begin grabbing the older child's toys, it may help a great deal to give him a room of his own, where he can feel that he and his toys are safe from interference. If a separate room is out of the question, find a big chest or cupboard for his things, one with a latch that the baby can't work. Not only does this protect his toys, but having a latch that only he can operate gives him a great sense of importance and control. (Beware of toy chests with heavy lids, however, as these are sometimes a cause of serious injury.)

Sharing toys. Should you make an older child share her toys with the baby? If you do, chances are her resentment will grow, even if she does what you tell her to. Instead, suggest that she give the baby a plaything that she has outgrown. This may appeal to her pride in her relative maturity. It lets her demonstrate a generosity of spirit toward the baby that is not really there. But true generosity starts when a child feels secure, loved, and loving. It doesn't help to force a child to share when she's feeling insecure and selfish; it just deepens her insecurity.

Generally speaking, jealousy of the baby is strongest in the child under five, because he is more dependent on his parents and has fewer interests outside the family circle. The child of six or more is drawing away a little from his parents and building a position for himself among his friends and teachers. Being pushed out of the limelight at home doesn't hurt so much. It would be a mistake, though, to think that jealousy doesn't exist in the older child. He, too, needs consideration and visible reminders of love from parents, particularly in the beginning. The older child who is unusually sensitive or who has not found his place in the outside world may need just as much protection as the average small child.

Stepchildren whose relationships in the family might be shaky anyway may need extra help and reassurance. Even the adolescent girl, with her growing desire to be a woman, may be unconsciously envious of her mother's new parenthood or pregnancy. Teens often seem scandalized to learn that their parents have a sex life. A typical remark is "I thought my parents were beyond that sort of thing."

Feeling guilty doesn't help. There's one caution to add here that may sound contradictory. Conscientious parents sometimes worry so much about jealousy and try so hard to prevent it that they make the older child less secure rather than more so. They may reach the point where they feel positively guilty about having a new baby, feel ashamed to be caught paying any attention to her, and fall all over themselves trying to appease the older child. If a child finds that his parents are uneasy and apologetic toward him, it makes him uneasy, too. His parents' guilty behavior reinforces his own suspicion that there is dirty work afoot and inclines him to be meaner to both baby and parents. In other words, the parents should be as tactful as possible with the older child but should not be worried, apologetic, submissive, or lacking in self-respect.

JEALOUSY OF THE NEW BABY

If you want to understand how a firstborn feels toward the new baby, imagine this scenario: Your partner comes home one day with another woman and says to you: "Dear, I love you as much as I always have, but now this person is going to live with us, too. By the way, she is also going to take up a lot of my time and attention because I'm crazy about her and she is more helpless and needy than you are anyway. Isn't that wonderful? Aren't you delighted?"

Feelings of rivalry are often more intense in a firstborn child, because he has been used to the spotlight and has had no competition. A later child has had to share his parents' attention since his birth. He can see that he's still just one of the children. This doesn't mean that second and third children don't feel rivalry. They do.

The first weeks and months. No matter how well you've prepared your older child (see page 24), the first weeks and months call for tactful parenting: Don't act too excited about the new baby; don't gloat over her; don't talk about her all the time; as far as is convenient, take care of her while the older one is not around; fit in her bath and some of her feedings when he is outdoors or taking his nap.

Many young children feel the greatest jealousy when they see their mother feeding the baby (with *their* breast, no less!). If your older one is around when you feed the baby, he should be allowed in freely; it's okay for him to take a try at the breast or a bottle. But if he is playing happily downstairs, don't attract his attention to what's going on. The goal is not to avoid rivalrous feelings altogether—that is impossible—but rather to minimize them in the first weeks, when the awful reality of the situation for the older sibling is beginning to sink in.

It's a little sad to see an older child trying a bottle out of envy of the baby. He thinks it's going to be heaven. But when he gets up his courage to take a suck, disappointment spreads over his face. It's just milk, after all, coming slowly, and it has a rubber taste. He may want a bottle off and on for a few weeks, but there's not much risk that he'll want to go on with it forever if his parents give it to him willingly and if they do other things to help him learn to deal with his jealousy.

Other people play a part in jealousy, too. When a family member walks into the house, he should suppress the impulse to ask the child, "How's the baby today?" Better to act as if he has forgotten there is a baby, sit down, and pass the time of day. Later he can drift over to have a look at the baby when the older one is interested in something else.

Grandparents who make a big fuss over the baby can be a problem, too. If the grandfather meets the older sibling in the front hall with a big package tied up in satin ribbon, and says, "Where's that darling baby sister of yours? I've brought her a present," the brother's joy at seeing his granddad turns to bitterness. If parents don't know a visitor well enough to coach her in how to act, they can keep a box of inexpensive presents handy and produce one for the older child every time a visitor comes with a gift for the baby.

Helping your child feel more grown-up. Playing with dolls may be a great solace to the older child, whether girl or boy, while the mother cares for the baby. He wants to warm his doll's bottle just the way his mother does and have reasonable facsimiles of the clothing and equipment that his mother uses. But doll play shouldn't take the place of having the child help care for the real baby; it should only supplement it.

A great majority of young children react to a baby's arrival by yearning to be a baby again, at least part of the time. This developmental regression is quite normal. They may, for example, lose ground in toilet training and begin to wet or soil themselves. They may lapse into baby talk and act helpless about doing things for themselves.

It's fine to play along with this craving to be a baby, when the impulse is very strong. You might even good-naturedly carry your child up to his room and undress him, as a friendly game. Then he can see that he is not being denied these experiences, which he imagines are delightful but which may prove disappointing.

The drive to continue to grow and develop usually soon overtakes the wish to be a baby again. You can help by not paying too much attention to the baby wishes, and instead appealing, most of the time, to the side of your child that wants to grow up. You can remind him of how big, strong, smart, or skillful he is, how much more he is able to do than the baby. That's not to say that you should be constantly giving him overenthusiastic sales pitches, but you should remember to hand him a sincere compliment whenever it is appropriate.

At the same time, don't push him too hard to be a grown-up. After all, if you are constantly calling all the things that your older child temporarily yearns to do "babyish" and all the things that he's temporarily reluctant to do "grown-up," he can only conclude that he wants to be a baby.

It's also important to avoid making direct comparisons that imply that you prefer the older child to the baby. To feel that he is favored may gratify a child temporarily, but in the long run he will feel insecure with parents who are partial, because he worries that they might change their preference. The parents should, of course, let their love for the baby be evident. But all the same, it is very helpful to give the older child chances to feel proud of his maturity and to remember that there are lots of disadvantages to being a baby.

Turning rivalry into helpfulness. One of the ways in which a young child tries to get over the pain of having a younger rival is to act as if he himself is no longer competing in the same league as the baby. Instead, he becomes a third parent. When he's feeling very angry with the baby, he may act the role of the disapproving parent. But when he's feeling more secure, he can be the kind of parent you are, one who teaches the baby how to do things, who gives him toys, wants to assist in feeding and bathing, comforts him when he's miserable, and protects him from dangers.

You can assist his role-playing by suggesting how he can help you at times when it wouldn't occur to him, and by showing real appreciation for his efforts. Sometimes it's not even pretend help: Parents of twins, who are often desperate for assistance in caregiving, are frequently amazed to find how much help they received from a child as young as three years with tasks like fetching a bath towel, a diaper, or a bottle from the refrigerator.

A small child almost always wants to hold the baby, and parents are apt to hesitate for fear he may drop her. But if the child sits on the floor (on a carpet or blanket), in a large stuffed chair, or in the middle of a bed, there's little risk, even if the baby is dropped.

In such ways the parents can help a child to actually transform resentment into cooperation and genuine altruism. The stresses and strains of coping with a new sibling can stimulate new skills in conflict resolution, cooperation, and sharing. Learning to cope with the challenges of not being the only show in town is a lesson that can pay off all through life.

SIBLINGS WITH SPECIAL NEEDS

If the new baby has a problem—colic, say, or any illness—she'll naturally suck up an even greater share of parental attention. For the older child, a little extra reassurance that his parents love him just as much as before, even though they're worried about the baby, will go a long way. It may be helpful for the parents to divide their chores to be sure that one parent is always available to the older child. He'll also need to be reassured that nothing he thought or did is responsible for the baby being sick. Remember that young children are prone to think that everything that happens in the world is because of them.

Children with autism or other special needs place extraordinary demands on their parents (see page 680), and also on their siblings. With all of the intense focus going to the neediest child, a healthy sibling could easily imagine that he is unimportant; resent his brother or sister for monopolizing the parents; then despise himself for resenting the helpless sibling.

It's good for a healthy child to help out in the care of a sibling with special needs. But the healthy child has needs of his own: to have friends, play baseball, take piano lessons, and just goof off. And the healthy child needs at least some of the parents' time all to himself.

Meeting the special needs of one child and the everyday needs of his siblings puts heavy demands on parents and on a marriage. There will be times when *someone's* needs aren't met. The point is, it shouldn't always be the healthy child who has to make that sacrifice. Finding the right balance is tough. It may be that you need help from relatives, friends, professionals, and community programs. Don't be afraid to ask for it.

Among the siblings of children with special needs, a certain number grow up angry or sad, burdened with emotional or behavioral problems. Many others, however, develop maturity, generosity, perspective, and a sense of purpose that serve them well throughout life.

ANXIETY AND DEPRESSION

I t's natural, when your child is sad or scared, to try to make everything better. At the same time, you need to realize that sadness, worry, and even fear are normal, healthy emotions. When we love something, we feel sad when we lose it. Sadness teaches us to keep the things and people we love close. Fear warns us about danger. Worries are plans to prevent loss and sadness. Healthy children feel sad and worried sometimes, but they have the tools and supports they need to keep negative emotions from taking over.

Anxiety and depression are what happens when the losses are too big, or the supports and coping tools are too weak. It's not always obvious when normal sadness and fear cross the line into depression and anxiety disorders. The sections that follow can help you make the call, and get the needed help.

ANXIETY

Anxiety disorders are more common than depression, and even more common than ADHD (which, sometimes, every child seems to have!). The key feature that sets off anxiety disorders from normal worries is *interference with everyday functioning.*

For example, one little boy is afraid of dogs, and whenever he passes a dog on the sidewalk he stands on the other side of his mom and grips her hand tight. He sometimes has dreams with scary dogs in them. Over time, though, he meets some nice dogs and begins to feel a little more comfortable, at least with the ones he knows. These are normal fears.

Another little boy is *very* afraid of dogs. He cries when he sees a dog a half block away (even a nice dog, on a leash), and makes his mom cross to the other side of the street. Some days he refuses to go outside, because outside is where dogs are. His well-meaning parents invite a very nice dog over, and he completely loses it, screaming uncontrollably. Even a story-book about a dog is too upsetting. For this boy, dogs trigger a powerful fear that makes normal living impossible. He has a dog phobia, and needs treatment.

Types of anxiety. Anxiety disorders take different forms in children. Many children have exaggerated fears of specific things, such as dogs (as in the example above), insects, or bad weather. Fears of monsters under the bed, the dark, and ghosts are very common, and usually normal (see page 152). But very intense fears, for example of being alone in a room at home, even during the day, may signal a disorder.

Here are some more examples: An eight-year-old boy may worry that something bad will happen to his mother while he is away at school, to the point that he can't concentrate on his lessons (separation anxiety). A ten-year-old girl is so terrified she will be called on in class that she throws up (performance anxiety). A twelve-year-old simply worries all the time, about everything. He can't sleep, and his body aches from the tension (generalized anxiety).

Less common anxiety disorders include panic attacks, where a teenager suddenly has the intense feeling that he can't breathe, is dying, or is going crazy. If he's had one of these attacks in an elevator, for example, he may refuse to ride in elevators for fear that he'll have another attack. If he's had an attack anywhere outside home, he may avoid leaving home for fear of another attack (agoraphobia).

Obsessive-compulsive disorder (OCD) is a form of anxiety in which a child engages in rituals—turning the lights off and on a certain number of times, or washing her hands repeatedly—in response to the feeling that something dreadful will happen if she doesn't. Once the ritual is done, the fear subsides for a bit, but it always comes back, often stronger and stronger.

A surprising number of children have a dread of talking to people outside the family. At home they chat away normally, but if a stranger comes to visit, they immediately fall silent. At school they may be so silent that their teachers think they are seriously delayed. A normally shy or slow-to-warm-up child feels comfortable eventually. A child with selective mutism doesn't. Attempts to bribe, pressure, or entice her to talk just add to the anxiety and make the problem worse. Specialized therapy can help, however.

In some children, anxiety looks like aggression. An eight-year-old boy overturns his desk in school and gets sent home. He does this again and again, until someone realizes that he *wants* to be sent home, because it eases his anxiety at being away from his mother. Another child has meltdowns over what seem to be minor issues—getting her peanut butter sandwich on the wrong bread, or getting a problem wrong on a worksheet. She yells, clenches her teeth, and breaks her pencils. For this anxious child, anything that goes wrong is a disaster of major proportions. The answer isn't a time-out or another punishment; it's figuring out how to turn down the anxiety.

What causes anxiety disorders. For many children, the tendency to respond with anxiety to anything new, different, or vaguely scary is inherited (see pages 122 and 152). Researchers have focused on genes that control the brain systems that normally turn anxiety off and on.

Along with genetics, anxiety disorders can be triggered by stressful or traumatic experiences. At one extreme are children who undergo life-threatening trauma in wars, street violence, domestic violence, tornadoes, floods, and earthquakes. At the other extreme are children whose anxiety is triggered by more everyday stresses, such as getting vaccinations (needle phobia), and being teased in school. These children may have inherited more than their fair share of the anxiety-leaning genes, and it only takes a little stress to tip them over into an anxiety disorder.

Since anxiety disorders run in families, many anxious children have overly anxious parents. Parents can sometimes teach their children to feel anxious, without really meaning to create a problem. For example, a parent may warn a child over and over never to talk with strangers, because children get abducted by strangers all the time and "then you'll never see me again, ever!" The fear is unrealistic (stranger abductions are very rare, despite daily sensational news reports), but the anxiety is real!

Treatments for anxiety. The first step in treatment is a thorough assessment. Some rare medical conditions can look like anxiety, or cause it. For example, a strep throat or other infection can trigger the sudden appearance of obsessive behaviors in a previously well child. In other children, there is a pattern of anxious responses going back to early childhood. Careful probing often identifies other family members with anxiety problems. The assessment may uncover learning problems, sleep problems, or other emotional concerns that also need treatment. Blood tests can't make the diagnosis of anxiety, but they can rule out medical conditions such as hyperthyroid that can trigger anxiety. Brain scans aren't helpful.

The main treatment for anxiety disorders is a particular form of therapy called cognitive behavioral therapy, or CBT. The idea is simple and powerful. The child learns how to relax, using a combination of breathing, muscle control, and imagining (see drspock.com for more on relaxation, and how to teach your child and learn it yourself). Children are, as a rule, better imaginers than are grown-ups, so they have a natural advantage here! Next, under the guidance of the therapist, the child begins a program of gradually exposing himself to whatever it is that is making him anxious, first by imagining, and then in real life. At each step of the way, the child controls his anxiety by using his relaxation skills, until he is able to face what used to scare him. The therapist acts like a coach, and the child like a kid learning a new skill (something kids do all the time). One word of warning here: Not all therapists have been trained in CBT. It's worth finding one who has been.

Along with CBT, some children benefit from medication for anxiety. But medicine doesn't give children skills, and anxiety tends to be lifelong. So medicine shouldn't be the only treatment. A child psychiatrist or developmental-behavioral pediatrician will know how to prescribe and monitor medication.

It's important, too, to deal with the triggers. If anxiety is driven by too-high expectations regarding academic or athletic performance, comparisons with a super-successful sibling, tormenting classmates, or real dangers in the community or instability at home, it's up to the parent to help confront these issues. Often when a parent's anxiety comes under better control, the child improves as well. A very powerful treatment is the parent's confidence in the child. "This anxiety is a tough problem, but I *know* that we'll be able to tackle it together, and you'll be able to come out on top."

DEPRESSION

When to suspect depression. A child with depression doesn't always look sad. A very young child might appear listless and stop eating. A school-age child might develop stomachaches or headaches and miss school. (The first thing to do, of course, is to have the doctor check for other illnesses.) A child with depression might be irritable, constantly angered by the littlest things.

Like depressed adults, children with depression lose interest in doing things they used to think were fun; nothing excites them. They may lose energy and the ability to concentrate on schoolwork. Grades often drop. They often eat and sleep much more than usual, although sometimes the opposite occurs. If you question the child gently, she might admit that she thinks she is to blame for everything being bad, and she is sure that things can never get better; she may have thought of killing herself.

One form of depression starts at a particular time. A child is doing well, and then all of a sudden grades drop and the child loses interest in friends and hobbies. Another form limps on, month after month and year after year. The child is just never really happy; he slogs through life without gusto. Either type can get better if it's recognized and treated.

What causes depression? Like anxiety, depression runs in families. Many of the same genes that set children up for anxiety also increase the risk of depression. As with anxiety, loss also plays a role. Losing a parent to death, or desertion, is a powerful depression trigger. So are the deaths of siblings, grandparents, and even well-loved pets. Smaller losses, such as moving away from friends, can also play a role. Knowing about genes and loss can alert you to think about depression if your child is at risk.

Some other helpful facts: Boys and girls are equally affected when they are young; among adolescents, depression is more likely in girls. Teenage boys, when they are depressed, are at especially high risk of killing themselves, particularly if they drink or take drugs. The method of choice is often a gun. Locking up guns and ammunition separately helps, but a resourceful teen can overcome that obstacle. It's safest to not have guns in the home (see page 397).

Bipolar disorder. Rarely, an older child bounces between periods of depression and periods of extremely high energy during which he feels superhumanly happy, attractive, intelligent, and strong. This is the profile of manic-depressive or bipolar disorder. Younger children may also have bipolar disorder, although the symptoms are somewhat different and harder to pin down. One clue is extremely violent tantrums that go on and on. If there is also a history of bipolar disorder in the family, a child psychiatrist will think carefully about the possibility that the child has inherited the disorder. ADHD can look similar and needs to be treated differently; so it's important to consult with an experienced psychiatrist.

Treatments for depression. Hopelessness is a symptom of depression, so one of the first goals of treatment is to convince parents and children that depression can be treated. It does get better!

Treatment starts with a thorough assessment, to identify key symptoms, risk factors (genes, losses) and triggers, and to exclude medical conditions that need treatment (hypothyroid or sleep disorders, for example). Two specific forms of talk therapy—cognitive behavioral therapy and interpersonal therapy—work well. It's important to find a clinician who is well trained in these therapies. If you've been referred to a therapist, or if you're searching for one, you can ask specifically about what approaches the therapist plans to take, and about the therapist's training and credentials. A good therapist will not be offended.

Medications can also help, but they shouldn't be the only treatment; effective talk therapy comes first. Antidepressant medications are not risk-free, so plan on reading and talking with your child's doctor or psychiatrist. The most commonly used antidepressants all come with a warning that they may trigger suicidal thoughts. This is terrifying, but it shouldn't hold you back. The risk is *thoughts,* not suicide itself. In fact, when some countries banned the use of these medications, the number of actual suicides rose steeply. In other words, if a child needs an antidepressant medication, it's safer for the child to take the medication than not to.

In any case, you don't need to decide about medication right away; the most important thing is to think about the possibility of depression, and to talk with your child's doctor. Depression is treatable, and even if it comes back (as it sometimes does), it can be treated again. Many people who are living happy lives can tell you that they went through a period of depression in the past. It's reasonable, and very helpful, to keep this hope in mind.

HYPERACTIVITY (ADHD)

What is hyperactivity? It's normal for young children to have boundless energy and no common sense. Lots of three-year-olds have a hard time sitting quietly through an entire picture book. Many four-year-olds act first and think later. Even at five, sustained attention to things that aren't really very engaging, like picking up toys and most skill-and-drill worksheets, is the exception, not the rule.

When people use the term "hyperactivity" to refer to a behavioral disorder, they are referring to attention deficit hyperactivity disorder, or ADHD. According to the standard definition (which changes a bit with each new edition of the American Psychiatric Association handbook), ADHD includes three main parts: inattention, impulsivity, and hyperactivity. Inattention is defined as very low ability to focus and sustain attention to dull or difficult tasks. Impulsivity is doing whatever comes to mind without considering the consequences of one's actions first. Hyperactivity is an unusually high need to run around, or to have some part of the body (hands, feet, mouth) in constant motion, even when it's appropriate to be still. When these problems interfere seriously with a child's life, when they're persistent and occur in multiple settings (home, school, neighborhood), the diagnosis of ADHD is likely. A child who is doing okay in school and at home does not have ADHD, even if he has endless energy, clowns around in class, or daydreams a lot.

ADHD is very hard on children and families. The children constantly get into trouble; their teachers scold them and blame them for every disruption; their parents find themselves shouting and punishing much more than they would like; their friendships don't usually last. Sadness, loneliness, resentment, and anger often follow.

ADHD, inattentive presentation. Some children have problems with attention, without too much hyperactivity or impulsiveness. For them, the diagnosis of ADHD, inattentive presentation, or ADHD-I, might fit. This terminology is awkward, since "hyperactivity" is in the title but the children are not hyperactive. Some people prefer to use "ADD," omitting the "H." But other people use "ADD" to mean the same thing as "ADHD." The newest official manual uses "AD/HD," with the slash meant to signify *either* attention deficit *or* hyperactivity. I'm sticking with "ADHD."

Whatever you call it, these children have a real problem. Their minds wander or get stuck on irrelevant details; they miss what's important; they're often disorganized and easily distracted. They may read well, but forget everything they've just read; do their homework but forget to turn it in; lose things all the time; daydream a lot. The consequences— failing grades, frustrated parents, self-blame—can be severe. But the problem often goes unrecognized because the children aren't disruptive; they may even be unusually quiet. Experts are still unsure if ADHD-I is really a subtype of ADHD, or something different. So if you're a little confused, you are not alone.

Does ADHD exist? Nearly every professional agrees that there are *some* children who are extremely hyperactive, impulsive, and inattentive as the result of a malfunction of the control and attention circuits in the brain. Using the standard psychiatric definition, a large number of children in the United States—somewhere between 5 percent and 10 percent—have ADHD. The number seems to grow every year, but no one is certain whether this is because more and more children have problems with brain development, or because more and more professionals are able to recognize the condition; or maybe it's both.

One problem with the diagnosis of ADHD is that it relies on parents and teachers answering questions that are open to differing interpretations. For example, one of the criteria is that a child "often has difficulty organizing tasks and activities." But the terms "often," "difficulty," and "tasks and activities" aren't defined. Does "often" mean twice a day, or all day long? Is fixing a bicycle—something many children with ADHD do quite handily—a "task," or does that term only apply to schoolwork? Schoolwork is *supposed* to be challenging. If a child is having difficulty completing her advanced calculus homework, does that count? It's not surprising that teachers and parents often don't agree in their assessments of whether a particular child is hyperactive. There is no completely objective way to make the diagnosis.

So although it is clear that there are many children who are struggling in school and at home, and whose problems fit the description of ADHD, it's not clear how many of them have abnormal brains. I suspect that many of them—especially the younger ones—have brains that are perfectly healthy but simply are not well suited to doing what we now require all children to do, namely, sit still, listen, and follow directions for paper-and-pencil tasks all day long.

Does poor parenting cause ADHD? There's no evidence that it does. Some parents of children with ADHD have excellent parenting skills; many have average skills; and a few have limited skills. A child who has never learned to take no for an answer or to wait for what he wants can look like he has ADHD. But most children with ADHD grow up with reasonable limits and discipline, yet do not learn to control themselves normally.

Things that look like ADHD. Just because a child has the symptoms of ADHD, it doesn't mean that he has the disorder. Sleep problems can cause inattentiveness (see Sleep Apnea, page 485). So can a form of epilepsy that causes a child to black out for a few seconds many times a day. Other causes include medications taken for allergies or other reasons; problems with eyesight or hearing; and emotional problems such as anxiety or depression. Children can fail to pay attention to a school curriculum that is much too hard (why bother?) or much too easy (boring!). Often there are several different problems going on at once: emotional and learning problems, stressful homes, out-of-control classrooms. An experienced pediatrician or behavioral expert can help sort all this out.

A positive response to ADHD medication doesn't prove that the problem is ADHD. Medications for ADHD improve attention in most people, regardless of whether or not they have ADHD. These medications may also make some conditions worse. Or they may fool parents and doctors into thinking that they are helping, when the real issue is not being addressed. For example, a child with a learning disability may sit quietly when he takes ADHD medication, but still not learn well. So it is very important that parents and doctors take time and care when diagnosing ADHD.

ADHD or bipolar disorder. Increasingly, school-age children are being diagnosed with bipolar disorder, which used to be called manic depression. In adults, this condition is marked by well-defined episodes of elevated energy and mood (mania) alternating with decreased energy and mood (depression). In children, these cycles may be very short, and the manic phase can appear as extreme anger. It takes an experienced clinician to tell if the problem is severe tantrums, ADHD with impulsive anger, irritable depression (now sometimes termed "DMDD," for disruptive mood dysregulation disorder), or truly bipolar disorder.

The medications for bipolar disorder tend to be powerful, with potent side effects, including dramatic weight gain and diabetes. Medications in this class should only be prescribed by doctors who have special training, such as child psychiatrists or developmental-behavioral pediatricians.

How doctors diagnose ADHD. There is no blood test or brain scan to diagnosis ADHD. A doctor diagnosing ADHD should obtain information from at least one parent and one teacher, either by interview or through questionnaires or written descriptions. The doctor should review the child's developmental and psychiatric history, review the family history, interview the child, do a thorough physical and developmental examination, and consider all of the possible conditions that could look like ADHD, or that can accompany ADHD. A doctor who makes a diagnosis of ADHD after spending fifteen minutes with a child is not giving state-of-the-art care.

Often, a pediatrician or family doctor will work together with a psychologist or psychiatrist to diagnose ADHD. The process may involve psychological testing and a detailed learning assessment.

Treatments for ADHD. There are many kinds of treatment available to children with ADHD. While many children do end up taking medication, the diagnosis of ADHD does *not* automatically mean that a child has to be on medication. One of the most important treatments is education. As the parent of a child with ADHD, you need to know a lot about the condition, more than what's in this book (see the Resource Guide and go to drspock.com). A child with ADHD, too, needs to understand what's going on in her brain, what situations are especially difficult, and what things help her to function at her best.

Counseling can help children cope with problems brought on by the ADHD, such as difficulty making friends and dealing with frustration, and with the learning problems and behavior problems that often go along with ADHD. For example, many children with ADHD have dyslexia as well (see page 835), which requires special education. Pretty much every child with ADHD has problems with organization. Routines at home help days go more smoothly. For example, once a child knows that finished homework always goes back in the folder right away and the book bag always goes on the bench by the back door, mornings can become much less rushed and stressful. Many schools offer organizational coaching by a trained counselor. Some of the most highly (and consciously) organized people are adults who have learned to cope with their ADHD.

Even though ADHD is pretty common, a family dealing with ADHD can feel alone and stressed. Like any chronic medical or developmental condition, ADHD can strain a marriage. Wise parents keep their eyes out for warning signs (less communication, less physical affection) and address the issues head-on, communicating more, and getting counseling if necessary. All children need and deserve happy parents.

Medications for ADHD. Decades of research show that medication is the most effective treatment for the core symptoms of ADHD. The medications most often used to treat ADHD are stimulants. Stimulants work well for nearly eight out of ten children with ADHD who take them. Stimulants increase alertness by stimulating parts of the brain that are active during focused attention; mainly the parts in front, under the forehead. In this, they work a lot like strong coffee. Also like caffeine, stimulants cause the heart to beat faster and can create a feeling of being wired.

The two main stimulants are methylphenidate (the medication in Ritalin, Concerta, and Metadate, among others) and amphetamine (the medication in Adderall, Dextrostat, Dexedrine, and others). Other kinds of medication besides stimulants are sometimes used for ADHD. Stimulants are sometimes confused with tranquilizers or narcotics, but they are very different in what they do and how they affect the brain.

It's a mistake to tell a child that ADHD medication is "a

vitamin." Children know when they are being lied to! I explain that the medication helps the brain to focus, like eyeglasses that help the eyes to focus. I tell the child honestly that stimulants help activate the control circuits in the brain, "so you can be more in control of yourself." Children want to be the bosses of their own bodies, not ruled by random impulses.

Are stimulants safe? Many parents are afraid to use medication to treat ADHD. It's reasonable to have concerns about any medication that affects how a child's brain works, especially if the child may take it for many years. However, many of the fears that parents have are based on misinformation. For example, it does not appear that stimulants are addictive the way drugs such as heroin or cocaine are. Children who suddenly stop taking stimulants do not develop cravings or long-term withdrawal symptoms. Some people do abuse stimulants to get high, but children who take stimulants to treat ADHD report feeling calmed down by the medication, not jazzed up.

Children with ADHD do go on to develop alcoholism and other addictions more often than other children, but I don't think the medication is to blame. Instead, children with ADHD may turn to alcohol or drugs as a way to deal with feelings of sadness and hopelessness that result from their endless troubles in school, at home, and with peers. Medication treatment for ADHD may make it *less* likely that teens will abuse illegal drugs or commit suicide in an impulsive moment of despair.

Stimulants do have side effects, such as stomachaches, headaches, decreased appetite, and sometimes sleep problems. But for the most part, these are mild and go away after a dose adjustment. Children taking stimulants should not be spacey or act like zombies. These are symptoms of overdosing. A key to the safe use of medication—any medication—is close monitoring. Children on medication for ADHD should see the doctor at least four times a year, more often in the beginning while adjusting the dose. I know medication is working when I ask a child how it makes him feel, and he responds, "I feel like myself."

Children who start medication for ADHD do not have to stay on it for their entire lives, although many do choose to continue through adolescence. As children get older, their physical hyperactivity tends to diminish, but their difficulty focusing often continues, and medication continues to help them. People with ADHD can do well off medication if they learn how to exercise a great deal of self-discipline. Many people with ADHD choose jobs that keep them very physically and mentally busy.

What happens to children with ADHD? With good medical care and education, children with ADHD should be able to succeed. As they grow, the traits that caused them so much trouble in school—spontaneity, energy, the ability to think about three things at once—may serve them very well in the workplace. Once, a successful software salesman, the father of one of my patients, told me that he had ADHD. "Actually," he said, "*all* of us in the office have it; we need it to do this job!"

How can you tell if your approach to ADHD is working? Your child has a reasonably accurate view of his strengths and weaknesses, and accepts what he sees. He tries hard, and gives himself credit for trying. He has friends, and is somebody you not only love, but also *like*. A child who feels rejected, and who deep down believes that he *deserves* to be rejected, needs more help. Over time, loneliness and self-hatred are among the most painful and harmful by-products of untreated ADHD.

What you can do. If you think your child might have ADHD, talk with your child's doctor, or find another professional who can help you. The Resource Guide (see pages 894–95) and the website drspock.com list parent support organizations that can be very helpful. The more you know, the better you'll be able to work with doctors, teachers, and other professionals to support your child's healthy development.

LEARNING DISABILITIES

When a child is struggling in school, it's important to look for a learning disability. Learning disabilities (LDs) are subtle brain problems that affect academic functions: reading, writing, calculating, listening, and others. Many children—perhaps one in seven—have a learning disability. LDs don't show up on standard CT scans or MRIs, but they're easy to spot with simple testing if you know what you're looking for. Identifying LDs opens the door to accommodation, remediation, and success.

Understanding LDs. Consider the normal unevenness in talents. One child is great in writing but poor in math; another is strong in science but weak in foreign languages. Learning disabilities occur when the unevenness is so severe that a child fails at one or more subjects, even while she may do fine or excel in other subjects. It's common to see, for example, a child who is excellent in math and has a fine artistic eye but whose reading skills are a year or more delayed.

It's important to understand that LDs and intelligence are separate issues. Children with LDs can have IQ scores that are high, average, or low. Many geniuses (Einstein, Edison, and a long list of others) had dyslexia, which is an LD that impairs reading. A child with a cognitive disability (see page 843) can also have an LD, and may need patient and skilled intervention to make progress.

LDs are not the only problems that affect learning. Hearing and vision deficits can, obviously. Any illness that causes a child to miss a lot of school or to feel exhausted while in school can also. Some medications interfere. A skilled medical and developmental assessment is a must.

What it feels like to have an LD. Children with an LD know that there is something wrong with them, but may not have an idea of what it could be. Their teachers and parents tell them to try harder, and sometimes, through very great effort, they have some success. For example, a child might spend five hours on a thirty-minute homework assignment. He does well, but he's simply not able to work that hard day after day. His teacher is pleased, but she doesn't see why he shouldn't always perform up to the level he is capable of. Instead of recognizing his extraordinary effort, she's likely to think he's lazy. Understandably, the child might come to resent the teacher because she is impossible to please.

You can see how what starts as a learning disability can easily morph into an emotional or behavioral problem. Some children choose to be class clowns or to rebel against class discipline as a way of drawing attention away from their academic weaknesses. In their view, it is better to be "bad" than to be "stupid." Other children suffer in silence. They try to disappear in class, never speaking up. They lie that they don't have homework. They may act out their frustration or try to preserve their dignity by getting into fights. Each misdeed confirms the judgment that they are "bad."

Dyslexia. By far, the most common LD involves reading and spelling. Dyslexia makes up about 80 percent of all LDs, affecting as many as 15 percent of all children. It is largely genetic: if both parents have it, chances are better than fifty-fifty that their child will, too. It's more common in boys, by about two to one.

The signs of dyslexia change over time and vary from child to child. Very young children who begin to babble later or with less variety of sounds than normal children may grow up to have dyslexia, as may toddlers who are late talkers. A child who is not talking well by age five has a high chance of showing reading problems.

In kindergarten and early grade school, children with dyslexia struggle to connect letters with sounds. They may know the alphabet song, but they can't tell you the sounds that the different letters make (they often have a hard time remembering the names of the letters, too, even though they can sign them). Rhyming, which requires sensitivity to the sounds that make up words, is often very hard for them. If they do learn to read a few words, it's because they have memorized them whole; they don't have the ability to sound out the letters and then put the sounds back together to make words.

Children with dyslexia often reverse letters, and confuse letters that look alike (*b*'s and *d*'s and *p*'s, for example). It's a common misconception, however, that letter reversal is the defining feature of dyslexia. Up to age seven, letter reversals are common in *all* children. Children with dyslexia also tend to mix up whole words when they are talking, or struggle to think of names for common objects (like doorknobs or nostrils).

Most children with dyslexia eventually learn how to read. However, they tend to read slowly and with difficulty. They may miss the point of what they've read because it takes so much effort for them to decode the words. Tests are a special hardship because it takes them so long to read the instructions. If they go at their own pace, they complete the first half of the questions, then run out of time; if they rush to get through the whole test, they end up making lots of errors because they haven't read and understood the questions. However, if they're tested verbally, they often demonstrate a strong knowledge of the topic. (Children with dyslexia should have non-timed tests as part of their individual education plans.) Even as grown-ups, they rarely read for pleasure, although if they are very interested in a book, they may plow through it.

Often, children and adults with dyslexia have special abilities, part of the uneven brain development I described earlier. Frequently they are extremely creative and brilliant visual thinkers. There's a long list of outstanding scientists, entrepreneurs, and artists who are thought to have had dyslexia. There's a wonderful picture book about a girl with dyslexia and how she struggles in school. It's called *Thank You, Mr. Falker*, written and illustrated by Patricia Polacco, who herself has dyslexia. Dyslexia doesn't have to limit a child's life chances; it may even expand them.

Most scientists agree that the problems underlying dyslexia are mainly in the parts of the brain that process the sounds of the language. Despite the fact that reading requires seeing, most children with reading problems see perfectly well. (Some optometrists have claimed that they can cure dyslexia with eye exercises, but the evidence for this is weak.)

The treatments for dyslexia that have been shown to be effective all involve training the brain to connect speech sounds with letters, and to combine the individual sounds into words. The most well-known of these programs are probably Orton-Gillingham and Lindamood-Bell, but there are several others, all similar in their approach. If your child has dyslexia, it's worth seeking a tutor or program that uses one of these tried-and-true approaches.

With dyslexia, as with other learning disabilities, the most important first step is to recognize the problem, give it a name, and help the child understand that it is not a matter of laziness or stupidity, but rather something that, with work, can be overcome. *Overcoming Dyslexia* by Sally Shaywitz, MD, is a readable and authoritative guide.

Other learning disabilities. Every ability needed to succeed academically has a corresponding disability. This is a partial list of academic abilities and what happens when they are lacking:

- *Reading.* Children need to be able to connect written symbols (letters and groups of letters) with the sounds they represent. Then they need to connect those sounds together and link them to words they know. Problems handling word sounds underlie most cases of dyslexia.

- *Writing.* Children have to be able to form all of the letters automatically—that is, without thinking about their shapes. If they have to stop and think about each letter, their writing will be slow and choppy and they will not be able to keep up with writing assignments.

+ *Math.* The ability to handle basic math processes—addition and subtraction—is related to an underlying ability to visualize things in space and gauge their quantity. Children with problems in this area may have what's called *dyscalculia,* a specific learning disability for math.

+ *Memory.* Skills involved in memory include taking information in, holding on to it, and finding it again in response to queries such as "Who invented the lightbulb?" Problems with any of these memory processes—intake, storage, or retrieval—can cause a learning disability.

+ *Other skills.* There are many specific skills that can become problem areas, such as understanding or expressing spoken language, keeping things in order (sequencing), rapid recall, controlling complex muscle movements, and so on. Often a child has difficulty with more than one particular skill (and may have strengths in other areas).

LD assessments. The assessment for a learning disability begins with finding out what a child knows in specific subject areas, how accurately and quickly he can read, and the level of his math skills. The tests that answer these questions are called achievement tests.

The LD assessment also tries to determine the child's

strengths and weaknesses when it comes to learning. To do this, psychologists give an IQ test. There are several IQ tests in wide use: the Wechsler, Stanford-Binet, and Kaufman tests, for example. All involve puzzles and questions that, in theory, reveal how well the child can make use of visual and verbal information to solve problems. IQ is a pretty good predictor of how well a child will do on a standard school curriculum. IQ is important, but it's a mistake to treat a single test score as though it were a full description of a child's thinking ability.

In fact, IQ testing is just the beginning. There is an entire field called neuropsychology devoted to testing how people go about using information of different sorts. The very best LD assessments may include several hours of testing by a neuropsychologist, looking at such mental processes as short-term and long-term memory, sequencing, maintaining and shifting attention, inferential thinking, motor planning, comprehension of complex grammar, and so on. The goal of this sort of test battery is to pinpoint the particular learning processes that are slow or weak, in order to strengthen them or help the child compensate for them using other learning strategies.

LD in the law. Since the 1970s, there has been a string of federal laws that spell out the responsibilities of schools for teaching children with special needs. The latest of these is the Individuals with Disabilities Education Act (IDEA) of 1990, which has been revised and reissued several times since then. IDEA covers the full range of medical and developmental diagnoses, including ADHD, dyslexia, and speech and language conditions, all of which are very common. It also covers severe vision and hearing impairments and neurological problems such as cerebral palsy, as well as many mental and emotional problems. Any problem that makes it impossible for a child to function successfully in a typical classroom comes under IDEA.

The essence of IDEA is that every child has a right to a "free and appropriate public education in the least restrictive environment." Take a close look at this sentence. "Free" means that a combination of local, state, and federal money pays for the education. "Appropriate" means that the child gets what he needs in order to be able to learn. If he needs an expensive hearing aid or a special chair to support his body, he should get those things. If he needs an aide in order to function in the classroom, the law says that the school has to provide one. "Least restrictive environment" means that a child should not be sent off to a separate place, away from his classmates, just because he has a disability. It used to be common practice, for example, to send all the children who were not "normal" to a single "special needs" classroom. Today that would be considered a violation.

Under IDEA, parents have the right to request an evaluation if they think their child might have an LD; the evaluation must be completed by the school within ninety days. The evaluation, referred to as a multi-factored evaluation (MFE), generates an education team report (ETR) covering multiple areas of functioning. The ETR is compiled by a team including a school psychologist, the child's teacher, and other professionals such as a speech and language pathologist and audiologist. If the team concludes that the child meets the state's criteria for an LD, it writes an individualized education plan (IEP). The IEP sets the educational goals for the child, specifies the special education services the school will provide, and lays out how the school will gauge whether or not the interventions have been successful. By law, parents have to be included in the process and have to sign off on the conclusions; if they disagree at any point, they can appeal.

Under a separate federal law, children who don't qualify for special education may still have a right to special accommodations in school. For example, children with ADHD who do not meet the criteria for an LD may still qualify for special help under Section 504 of the Rehabilitation Act of 1973 (a "504 plan" for short; go to drspock.com). Parent support organizations listed in the Resource Guide provide much more information on the legal aspects of LDs.

Treatments for learning disabilities. The first and most important treatment for a learning disability is for everyone to acknowledge that it exists. Once that happens, teachers and parents can recognize how hard the child is really working, and praise the effort rather than criticizing the outcome. Children need to hear that they are not stupid; they have a problem that they need to work on, but they don't have to deal with it alone. With the help of parents and teachers, things can get better.

Specific educational treatments depend on the type of LD. For dyslexia, the most effective treatments center on intensive teaching of letters and the sounds they make. The child may use all of his senses, for example, feeling wooden letters, cutting them out of paper, and making them out of cookie dough and then tasting them. In addition to attacking the problem head-on, special educators teach children how to work around learning difficulties. A child who struggles with reading might listen to books on tape; a child with extremely poor handwriting might type some of his writing assignments on the computer. Just as critically, teachers also help children focus on and develop their strengths. For more information on LDs, you can begin with the sources listed in the Resource Guide (see page 889).

INTELLECTUAL DISABILITY

Labels and stigma. Over the years, people have used many different terms to describe children and adults whose intellectual abilities are significantly below average: "slow," "delayed," "cognitively impaired," and "mentally retarded." These terms have taken on a heavy load of stigma, to the point that they are now insults. The new term is "intellectual disability" (ID). In addition to changing the words we use, we need to change how we think about this problem. It's not a cause for shame, to be hidden away. ID is one of many conditions that make it difficult for people to function without special assistance. When they receive that assistance, they can participate in all aspects of society; love and be loved; and contribute to their communities.

What the diagnosis means. With any developmental milestone, some children reach it sooner, some later. A child who takes much longer than most may be developmentally delayed; the label doesn't say anything about why the delay exists or what it means for the future. Many children with developmental delays eventually catch up without any input from therapists or other professionals.

When milestones in several areas—language, movement, and play, for example—are all very late, the child is more likely to need special help, and may never fully catch up in some respects. A child with ID typically learns and develops many skills at a slower rate than most other children. Young children with more severe delays, or with medical conditions that are known to affect brain development, may be diagnosed with ID within the first year or two of life, but others may not be diagnosed until later.

To be diagnosed with ID, a child must typically score extremely low on a standardized intelligence test administered by a qualified professional. Also—and just as important—the child must show real-world disability; that is, inability to carry out everyday activities such as self-care (feeding, grooming, dressing), communicating needs and ideas, and getting around in an age-appropriate manner. Standardized adaptive behavior questionnaires help these judgments to be as objective as possible.

In the past, children were categorized as having mild, moderate, or severe ID on the basis of their IQ score. Now the focus is more on the amount of support a child needs. Does the child need special support only some of the time, in some situations (for example, in school), or most of the time, in most settings? Instead of being just a label, the diagnosis of ID becomes a description of the kind and intensity of help a child needs to make progress and get along in life.

Causes of ID. When intellectual disability is severe, it's often possible to find an underlying cause. Examples include rubella (German measles) or Zika, both viral infections that can cause brain damage prenatally, but only cause mild illness in older children. Inherited metabolic errors such as phenylketonuria cause ID unless they're identified and treated early in life. ID is part of many genetic conditions, such as Down syndrome (see page 857).

When ID is mild, however, it is often impossible to pin down a cause. We know that many different things can affect the developing brain, such as exposure to lead or mercury, or malnutrition early in life. Prenatal alcohol exposure is the most common and preventable cause of ID. Cigarette smoking during pregnancy can have similar, if less dramatic, effects.

Children with mild ID often come from homes that provide relatively little intellectual stimulation. In these cases, we know that high-quality, early intervention and preschool programs can make a big difference in the child's intellectual development. Encouraging parents to read aloud to their babies and giving them picture books to get them started also increases young children's language development, a key component of IQ (see page 568). The brain is a very adaptable organ; given the right stimulation, it can blossom in surprising ways.

What children with ID need. Like all children, children with ID need stimulation and challenges that fit their level of ability, even if that means challenges that are below the child's chronological age. For example, a child of seven or eight may need opportunities to play make-believe, while his typically developing age-mates have moved on to board games. Children with ID need playmates they can enjoy and keep up with, even if they are much younger. In school, they need to be placed in classes where they can feel that they belong and can accomplish something. Like all children, when they are given challenges that match their abilities, they delight in learning.

Parents of a typically developing child don't have to ask an expert to find out his interests. They simply watch him playing and sense what else might appeal to him. They observe what he is trying to learn and help him tactfully. The same should hold true for a child with intellectual disability: You watch to see what he enjoys. You get him the playthings that are sensible. You help him locate the children he has fun with—every day, if possible. You teach him the skills he wants assistance with.

Early intervention. Under federal law, every state is required to have a system in place to coordinate early intervention (EI) services for children with ID and other special needs. The state-funded coordinating agency is supposed to work with the parents to create an individual family service plan (IFSP) that spells out the needs of the child and family, and how they will be met. The EI law specifically recognizes that children exist in families, and that in order to meet a child's needs, the whole family has to be taken into consideration. In addition to the usual therapies (occupational, physical, and speech and language), the IFSP could include respite services, or other needed supports. The EI agency should help families find and pay for these services either through private insurance or through publicly funded programs.

IDEA and special education. After age three, children with ID have specific educational rights under the Individuals with Disabilities Education Act (IDEA, see page 839).

In the past, it was believed that children with ID should

from the start be sent to special day schools in their own communities or, if none was available, to specialized boarding schools. Now, more and more, educators strive to integrate children with disabilities into mainstream school activities. When it's done well, mainstreaming benefits all children, both those with disabilities and those without. When it's done poorly, without adequate provision for children's special needs, it can mean simply that a child with special needs does not have his needs met and therefore does not learn. IDEA gives parents the power to ensure that their children are educated appropriately.

The child with more severe ID. A child who at eighteen months is still unable to sit up and shows little ability to interact with people or things presents more complicated problems. She will have to be cared for like a baby for a long time. Whether this occurs at home or in a residential setting depends on the degree of disability, the temperament of the child, and the ability of the family to meet her needs and manage the strains involved in caring for her. In the past, the assumption was that children with intellectual disability would all be sent to special schools. Now the assumption is that children with ID will live at home and attend regular schools with the supports they need.

Adolescence and the transition to adulthood. As teens, children with ID face the same conflicting desires and fears that bedevil and enchant other adolescents, but with added challenges. If they require adult supervision, it will be harder for them to socialize in typical teen ways, hanging out or going to a movie. And it may be difficult for them to understand the social rules that govern relationships between the sexes. It doesn't help that many people assume that a person with intellectual impairments doesn't, or shouldn't, have sexual feelings. Early and continuing education about sexuality and human relationships is especially important for children with intellectual disability.

Parents also worry about what happens next, when their child with a disability has to find a place in the world. By law, schools are required to provide special education to children through age twenty-one or beyond. Most communities have programs to help young adults make the transition to further training, appropriate jobs, and suitable living arrangements. Throughout the teen years, the process of setting educational and life goals and evaluating them serves a double purpose: it ensures that children with ID receive the help they need, and it encourages them to take control, as much as they can, of their own destinies.

See drspock.com for more on community, legal, and financial supports for children and adults with ID.

Many useful and dignified jobs can be performed well by people who have less than average intelligence. It's the right of every individual to grow up well-enough adjusted and well-enough trained to be able to handle the best job that she has the capability to do.

AUTISM

Growing awareness. With the rate of autism now over one in a hundred, and even higher among boys, nearly everybody knows a family affected by autism. This dark cloud has a silver lining: Awareness about autism is also at an all-time high, and the fear and shame associated with the diagnosis have begun to recede.

People now understand that autism is caused by abnormal development of the brain, not bad parenting. We know that early, intensive special education can help children with autism learn to communicate and think more flexibly. With greater availability of high-quality treatment programs, professionals are making the diagnosis at earlier and earlier ages, greatly improving children's lives.

What is autism? Children with autism have problems in three main areas: communication, relationships, and unusual interests, behaviors, and sensations. Although many typically developing children have difficulties in one or another of these areas, it is the overall pattern of problems that constitutes autism.

Communication. Children with autism don't use language

for the usual purposes of sharing ideas, understanding what others are thinking, and making social connections. Or rather, they need to be taught to do this; it doesn't come naturally. They may not babble at the expected time (around six to twelve months) and often are late to say words. If they do speak, they may repeat words meaninglessly, sometimes reciting long scripts memorized from TV shows or commercials, but they can't carry on a normal conversation. Children with autism also have problems with nonverbal communication. They don't typically use eye contact to show that they are listening, or point to things to show that they find them interesting.

Relationships. The old idea is that children with autism are completely cut off socially ("autism" comes from a word that means "self"). It turns out that's not quite right. While they are often content to entertain themselves, children with autism do seek relationships with the people closest to them, but often in odd ways, such as backing up into a parent as a way to request a hug. Infants with autism may not cuddle like other babies or reach out to be picked up; some are upset by tickle games or games such as "s-o-o-o big" that most babies find delightful. Older children often ignore peers or interact in unwanted ways because they can't read the social cues that mean "I'm ready to play now" or "Leave me alone." Teens with autism often feel confused by and excluded from the typical social world, but also feel lonely and wish for closeness.

Interests, behaviors, and sensations. Many children with autism are fascinated by mechanical things and develop very particular interests. Many love trains; others assemble extensive collections of specific objects, or learn everything there is to know about obscure subjects. They often repeat the same behaviors over and over. One child lines up toy cars in the same order, or perpetually flicks the lights off and on. Another child puts a disk into the DVD player and takes it out again, for hours at a time. Any attempt to change the routine may trigger a tantrum. Spinning objects often seem to hold a special fascination. Children with autism often spin their own bodies, flap or twist their hands, or rock back and forth repetitively. They may react unexpectedly to sounds, odors, or touch. For example, many love the feeling of being held tightly, but hate being touched lightly. A child might scream loudly over and over, but cover his ears in distress at the sound of a flushing toilet or a siren a block away.

The range of autistic problems. Experts recognize a spectrum of autistic disorders. At the mild end, a child may appear merely odd or quirky. Such children can function pretty well in most settings—for example, in a classroom where the teacher knows what's going on and can provide extra support. Other children need support throughout the day, and even then may show lots of distress related to their autism.

Many children with autism also have intellectual disability (ID, see page 843), although others have normal intelligence or are gifted. Very bright children with autism often learn to read very early (*hyperlexia*), although they may not understand the words they're saying. Savants, like the Dustin Hoffman character in *Rain Man,* may be capable of amazing mental feats. People with autism who also have ID suffer greatly from the combination of problems. Language abilities also vary along a spectrum. People with autism who have strong language skills—a condition which used to be called *Asperger's syndrome*—may function well as adults, particularly in technical fields. People who have both autism and very weak language skills tend to show more behavior problems and suffer more social isolation as a result of the combination of disorders.

Autism terminology keeps changing. Old terms include "Asperger's," "high-functioning autism," and "PDD-NOS" (for "pervasive developmental disorder, not otherwise specified"). Now everything is *autism spectrum disorder* (ASD), with or without intellectual and language disability, and graded by degree of severity. It's helpful to remember that the diagnosis, whatever it is, isn't nearly as important as the *child*. There is so much more to any individual child than is carried in the diagnostic label. Some children with autism are happy-go-lucky and love music; some are more grumpy and find solace in bright colors. Some love dogs; some prefer cats, or goldfish.

Compared with neurotypical children, children with autism are more vulnerable to other brain-based disorders, such as epilepsy, depression, ADHD, and anxiety. An attentive doctor will stay alert for such conditions, and treat them as needed.

What causes autism? There's strong evidence that genetics plays an important role. Autism runs in families, and it's not uncommon for siblings to share the diagnosis. Older age of mothers' or fathers' is linked to autism, perhaps because the likelihood of adverse changes to genes increases with age. Environmental exposures to certain pesticides or other industrial chemicals may also contribute. Nobody knows for sure. It's certain, however, that "bad" or "cold" parenting is not part of the equation.

One theory that makes sense to me is that autism affects the way the brain processes information coming in from the senses, something like a television set with bad reception. Some of the signal gets through okay, other bits are distorted, and other bits are lost altogether. It's possible that the core difficulties in autism—with communication, relationships, and behaviors—are responses to these mixed-up signals, the child's attempt to cope with a confusing and frightening world.

Some of the more dramatic symptoms, such as violent temper tantrums, might be expressions of the extreme frustration and unhappiness that come from being cut off from other people. The love of spinning, another common symptom, might reflect abnormalities in the child's vestibular sense, the sense that normally controls balance. Children with autism may avoid eye contact, because the human face provides too much information all at once—something the child finds overwhelming and upsetting. Or it may be that children with autism lack the ability to make sense of the information conveyed in facial expressions, an ability that typically developing children acquire very early in life (or perhaps they are born with it). In this case, children with autism avoid eye contact not because it is upsetting but because it isn't interesting; it doesn't tell them anything. New research suggests that this may be the case.

If autism distorts the way a child sees, hears, feels, and tastes, then all of the everyday sensations that normally connect children with their parents—shared glances, cuddling, music—might instead set the child with autism apart. The challenge in treating autism is to get past the garbled sensory input and connect with the child, overcome the child's defensive behaviors, and teach the child the skills to communicate ideas and feelings.

Early signs of autism. Early detection of autism greatly improves the outlook. Very early in infancy, parents may have a vague feeling that something just isn't right. Looking back later, they may realize that their baby didn't gaze into their eyes or engage in babbled "conversations" like other infants. Other early signs include, by twelve months, not pointing at objects using the pointer finger to direct the parent's attention; by fifteen months, not using any words to communicate wants or simple ideas; or by two years, not putting two words together to make simple sentences. None of these warning signs is diagnostic for autism (hearing loss, other developmental problems, and variations of normal development sometimes look the same). Still, if you notice any of them, you should seek a developmental evaluation for your child and not simply accept reassurance that he will "grow out of it."

Therapies for autism. We don't have a cure for autism, but we definitely have effective treatments, more and more each year. The sooner treatment begins, the better the outcome.

The mainstay of autism therapy is early, intensive education with a focus on communication. Programs that have been shown to improve children's language and relationship skills usually involve effort several hours a day, several days a week. Applied behavior analysis (ABA) is the best-researched treatment approach; professionals trained to provide this specialized therapy may identify themselves as Board Certified Behavior Analysts (BCBAs). Children may be involved in more than one program and may also have tutors or hired assistants with varying levels of training working with them. A number of disciplines, including speech and language therapy, physical therapy, and occupational therapy, can contribute to the total treatment package.

Given the great intensity of this effort, it is common for one parent to devote all of her time to the care and education of the child with autism. Finding a balance so that others in the family also stay involved and all family relationships are nurtured is a critical challenge (see page 681).

No medication has been found to cure autism. Various medications are used, however, to reduce symptoms of rage, anxiety, or obsessiveness, which may make family life intolerable or interfere with the child's education. Many parents turn to complementary and alternative medicine looking for a cure. There they find many theories and therapies. Many children are put on gluten-free, dairy-free diets and given large doses of B vitamins. Such dietary changes are difficult to maintain but not dangerous. In some cases, parents see real improvements. More often, though, improvement is mild or short-lived.

More controversial are treatments that involve giving children medications intended to rid the body of heavy metals such as mercury. Chelation therapy, as this approach is called, is costly, often painful, potentially dangerous, and utterly unproven. Parents are right to want to do everything possible for their children who have autism. But they need to keep in mind the medical dictum "First, do no harm."

Parents of a child with autism need to learn a great deal to manage their child's education. The Resource Guide on page 895 lists some reliable starting points.

DOWN SYNDROME AND
OTHER GENETIC DISORDERS

I t's amazing, given the thousands of genes that need to be transmitted across generations and copied over and over during development, that genetic disorders are as rare as they are. One of the most common and most recognizable is Down syndrome, named after a nineteenth-century doctor. The other term for this disorder, trisomy 21, refers to the cause, a third copy of chromosome 21, or, in some cases, an extra chunk of that chromosome. This section focuses on Down syndrome, but much of the information applies to other genetic disorders as well.

What is Down syndrome? A child born with Down syndrome faces a range of developmental challenges and medical illnesses. Early on, feeding problems and developmental delays are common, along with heart problems, problems with hearing and vision, ear and sinus infections, obstructive sleep apnea (see page 485), low thyroid hormone, constipation, spinal instability, and more. Intellectual disability ranges from mild to severe. The children grow slowly, and as they age, they face increased risks of leukemia and Alzheimer's. Many children with Down syndrome are friendly and happy, but some are irritable and many suffer from anxiety and depression. Any particular child may have none, a few, or many of these problems.

About one child in seven hundred is born with Down syndrome, making it common as genetic disorders go. As a woman ages, the chances that one of her eggs will contain an extra chromosome 21 rises, and with it the chance of having a child with Down syndrome. By age thirty-five, a mother has one chance in 250 of having a child with Down syndrome.

Testing for Down syndrome. Prenatal blood tests can warn of the possibility of Down syndrome, and tests of the amniotic fluid (amniocentesis) or part of the placenta (chorionic villus sampling) can confirm the diagnosis as early as the first trimester. *All* pregnant women should be able to get prenatal testing if they want it, and most obstetricians recommend it for all mothers age thirty-five and over. At birth, physical features may raise the possibility of Down syndrome, but a final diagnosis depends on a blood test that may take a week or two to get back from the lab.

Treatment. Genetic disorders work in different ways, and some conditions can be cured by diet or specific nutrients. In phenylketonuria, for example, the body is unable to break down phenylalanine, and a diet that cuts out nearly all of that substance is curative.

For Down syndrome, there is no known cure. However, treatments to deal with the various illnesses caused by the genetic error are very important; for example, looking closely for heart disease and leukemia. Children with Down syndrome benefit from having a committed doctor who can help parents anticipate the various health issues that are bound to come up, and access the specialists and therapists they need. It's worth the effort to find a doctor who has special expertise and experience working with children with disabilities, and with Down syndrome in particular.

Educational planning should be tailored to a child's particular interests, temperament, and learning style. This is true for all children, of course, but it's especially critical for children with Down syndrome. Inclusion in regular classes often works well but usually requires special support from a knowledgeable educational specialist or school psychologist (see page 898).

Children with Down syndrome and other genetic disorders do best when parents, doctors, and teachers work together, with parents leading the team. Participation in a parent support group can give parents the information and encouragement they need to be effective in that role (see the Resource Guide, page 898).

GETTING HELP

WHY PEOPLE SEEK HELP

Back in the nineteenth century, psychiatrists mostly treated people who were deemed insane. That stigma still keeps many from seeking help. But child mental health professionals are trained to treat problems early, before they grow out of control. There's no reason to wait until a child is severely disturbed before seeking behavioral health care, any more than there is to wait until he is in a desperate condition from pneumonia before going to the doctor.

FIRST STEPS

A child's primary care doctor is often the best place to start. If that's not an option, look in the telephone book or an online directory under "Family Services," "Counseling," or "Mental Health." Most communities have agencies to provide behavioral health services for children. Religious leaders may provide counseling themselves, or can refer you to other professionals. Or you can call a hospital nearby and ask the switchboard to connect you with the right department.

Depending on your particular needs, one type of professional might be better than another. The paragraphs below give brief descriptions of many of those most likely to be of help. See the Resource Guide (page 895) for the professional societies for each discipline, where you can often find a listing of their members in your area.

Family social service agencies. Most cities have at least one family social service agency, and larger cities often have several. Although agencies may identify themselves with a particular religion (Catholic or Jewish, for example), all provide services regardless of a family's faith. These organizations are staffed by social workers trained to help parents with most family problems: child management, marital adjustment, budgeting, chronic illness, housing, and finding jobs and medical care. They often have consultants—psychiatrists or psychologists— who help with the more difficult cases.

Many parents have grown up with the idea that social agencies are for destitute people only. The truth is just the opposite: The modern family agency is just as glad to assist families who can afford to pay a fee (or carry private insurance) as it is to lend a hand to those who can't.

TYPES OF THERAPY

It's important to realize that there are many different types of therapy. Most therapy doesn't involve lying on a couch and talking about your dreams while a bearded psychoanalyst takes notes. Insight-oriented therapies attempt to bring patients to a deeper understand of their personal histories and motivations, including early childhood experiences. But cognitive behavioral therapy (CBT) focuses on the here and now, seeking to change behavior by changing how patients think about themselves and others. CBT can be surprisingly powerful. For example, a child suffering from depression can learn to recognize the negative, overly critical thoughts he repeats to himself, and to substitute more realistic and hopeful ones. Thoughts and emotions are linked; when one changes, the other does, too.

Young children, who have a hard time putting feelings into words, often benefit from play therapy. Older children may benefit from art therapy or narrative therapy, in which they learn to create stories that help them cope. For children with problematic behaviors, a behavioral approach, focusing on identifying triggers and consequences of negative and positive behaviors, can be very effective. Most behavior therapies include a component of parent training; that is, specific instructions and coaching to help parents intervene effectively to change their children's behavior.

Family therapy can often be extremely helpful, sometimes in combination with one of these individual approaches. There are many options out there. When you are considering starting to work with a therapist, ask about the therapeutic approach to make certain it is something that feels comfortable to you.

CHOOSING A PROFESSIONAL

Ask friends and family for a recommendation. Talk with the professional before bringing your child and see how you feel. It's important that both you and your child feel comfortable. Many community-based services are provided free or on a sliding scale. Private insurance providers may offer limited choices; it's wise to find out exactly what mental health benefits your plan allows before you begin treatment.

Developmental-behavioral pediatricians (DBPeds). These are doctors who have done the usual pediatrics training plus three more years studying and taking care of children with developmental and behavioral problems. Some specialize mainly in developmental problems, such as intellectual disability or autism; others in problems of behavior, such as bed-wetting or ADHD. It's appropriate to ask about a particular doctor's training and expertise.

Most DBPeds have experience in assessing and treating common behavioral and emotional problems of children. Like psychiatrists, they are trained in the use of medications to treat behavior, although certain very severe problems, such as bipolar disorder, are probably best handled by psychiatrists. Many DBPeds work closely with nurse practitioners, who are RNs with additional training in clinical care. They often prescribe commonly used medications such as stimulants for ADHD.

Psychiatrists. These are medical doctors who specialize in mental and emotional disorders. A child and adolescent psychiatrist has additional training in handling the particular problems of children and adolescents. Psychiatrists often work as part of a team, prescribing medications, while other professionals— psychologists or social workers, for example—provide counseling or talk therapy. Certain severe conditions, such as anorexia nervosa, bipolar disorder, and major depression, are probably best treated with the help of a child psychiatrist.

Psychologists. Psychologists who work with children are trained to assess and treat problems of learning, behavior, and emotion; many also provide testing for intelligence, academic achievement, and autism. Some specialize in the problems of children facing chronic medical illnesses and repeated hospitalizations, often in collaboration with Child Life professionals. Psychologists are often the best resource for cognitive behavioral therapy (CBT) to treat anxiety or depression in children. To be a licensed psychologist, a person must have earned a PhD and have done a clinical internship (worked with clients under the supervision of a seasoned therapist). Psychologists generally don't prescribe medication, but often work with doctors or nurses who do.

Social workers. These professionals have had at least two years of classroom and clinic training after college, leading to a master's degree. To earn an LCSW (licensed clinical social worker) degree, a master's-level candidate must provide counseling or therapy to clients under supervision and pass a state licensing examination. Social workers can evaluate a child, his family, and his school situation and can treat behavioral problems in both the child and the family. Many social workers also have advanced training in family therapy.

Psychoanalysts. These are psychiatrists, psychologists, or other mental health professionals who treat emotional problems through exploration of unconscious conflicts and defenses as they have developed over time, and through the patient's relationship with the analyst. Child psychoanalysts (like psychologists) often use play and art to communicate with their young patients, and they often work with the parents as well. Legitimate psychoanalysts have advanced degrees, have studied psychoanalysis and undergone psychoanalysis themselves, and have worked under supervision for years. However, there is no national licensing of these professionals, and anyone can legally call himself or herself a psychoanalyst. So it's important to look carefully at a person's credentials before entering into psychoanalytic treatment.

Family therapists. The main insight of family therapy is that everyone in the family is connected to everyone else. A child's difficult behavior often causes difficulties in the family as a whole, and problems in the family often result in troubled behavior in a particular child. Frequently the best way to improve the child's behavior is to help the whole family function better.

Family therapists can be psychologists, psychiatrists, social workers, or other professionals who have completed additional training in family therapy. Most states have licensing requirements that include at least a master's degree, two years of family therapy practice under close supervision, and a standardized exam.

Licensed professional counselors and school counselors. The qualifications for a professional counselor in most states are a master's degree in counseling and either two or three years of supervised practice—between two thousand and four thousand hours. School counselors are specially trained to provide counseling in schools. The training to become a licensed professional counselor (LPC) or school counselor is similar in scope to the training of many family therapists or master's-level psychologists.

Speech and language, occupational, and physical therapists. Therapists in these fields can be exceptionally helpful in the assessment and treatment of children with both developmental and behavioral difficulties. All apply a variety of techniques involving education, specialized exercises, and hands-on manipulation. The best of these therapists also work with parents to help them continue the treatments in between sessions. There is a fair amount of overlap between these professions in terms of the problems they address and the techniques they employ. This makes sense, because when it comes to children, all of the systems—moving, playing, handling objects, paying attention, eating, and communicating—are interconnected. Training for these professions involves at least a master's degree and passing a state board examination, and many have further advanced training.

WORKING TOGETHER

Parents should plan to work closely with the professionals they choose. Some therapists limit a parent's involvement to bringing the child and taking him home again. Most, however, invite parents to take a much more active role.

It's reasonable, early on, to talk with the professional about the main goals of the therapy. Ask what specific changes you should expect to see and when. Then, from time to time, check in and see if you are getting where you hoped to be. For specific issues such as bed-wetting or tantrums, a few sessions may be all that's needed; other problems may take longer. Often children and parents benefit from working with the same professional on and off over a period of years.

One advantage of clarifying your expectations early on is that it can help you make good decisions if things are not going well. You can't expect instant changes regarding problems that have developed over a long time, and problems often seem to get worse before they get better. Once you've chosen a professional to work with, it makes sense to stick with that person for a time, even if there are periods of uncertainty. On the other hand, if months have gone by without positive change and your expectation was that changes would appear, it's appropriate—necessary, really—that you talk with the therapist about trying a new approach, or a new therapist.

A setback, even a change from one professional to another, is not the end of the world. What's most important is that you and your child continue to believe that things can get better. In the long run, an attitude of hopeful activism is most likely to bring about the needed growth.

COMMON MEDICATIONS
FOR CHILDREN

MEDICATION SAFETY

All medications should be treated with respect. Prescription drugs can have powerful side effects. But over-the-counter medications can also be dangerous, especially if a child takes an overdose. Notably, some common cough and cold medicines have been found to be unsafe in children, sometimes even deadly—yet they are readily available without prescription and packaged for older children and adults. With *any* medication, be sure to follow the dosing directions on the bottle. In general, the younger the child, the more cautious you need to be. Follow these commonsense guides to lower the risk:

+ Give medications, whether prescription or not, only on a doctor's advice.

+ Keep medications in a locked cabinet or drawer. Even timid children have been known to climb up to high cabinets or shelves when curiosity drives them.

+ Don't put your trust in childproof caps. They will slow a persistent child down, but they might not stop her.

+ Tell your child that the medication is medicine, not candy.

+ Pay special attention when you have visitors who might be carrying medications with them, or when you and your child visit others' homes. A handbag left sitting on a low table is a tempting target for a toddler.

At times of stress, or when your daily routine undergoes a change, think about medications, cleaning supplies, and other household hazards in general.

PRESCRIBING TERMINOLOGY

When doctors write prescriptions, they use a shorthand that can be confusing. When they say take one pill twice daily ("BID" in doctorese), they mean one pill every twelve hours. For example, you could take one dose at 8:00 a.m. and another at 8:00 p.m.

Three times a day (TID) means every eight hours (for example, 8:00 a.m., 4:00 p.m., and midnight); four times a day (QID) is every six hours (8:00 a.m., 2:00 p.m., 8:00 p.m., and 2:00 a.m.). "PRN" means "as needed." "PO" means "by mouth." A prescription that reads, "Take one tab PRN PO QID," means you *may*—but aren't required to—take one tablet as often as every six hours.

Measurements may also need translating. The instructions that come with over-the-counter medicines speak of teaspoons, tablespoons, ounces, or occasionally capfuls. But prescriptions are likely to be written in milliliters (ml) and milligrams (mg). A standard teaspoon equals five milliliters, a tablespoon equals fifteen milliliters, and an ounce equals thirty milliliters. A doctor who instructs you to give "one teaspoon three times a day" wants you to give five milliliters every eight hours. Since the teaspoons in your home may not hold exactly five milliliters, it's safer to use a medicine cup or an oral syringe in order to get the dose right.

The reason it's good to be familiar with these terms is that you can ask questions. If the doctor tells you to take one tablet three times a day, then writes "BID" on the prescription, you should ask about that. If the doctor writes "QID," and you're not sure whether you should give the medicine every six hours on the button, even if it means waking your baby, you should ask. Be sure you understand the instructions before you leave the office. Ask the pharmacist, too. You can't be too careful.

GLOSSARY OF COMMON MEDICATIONS

A basic knowledge of a few frequently used drugs can help you treat these common complaints with confidence. But giving medication to a child can be a confusing business. Drug companies complicate things by giving medications multiple names. There's the trade name you probably know (Tylenol, for instance), and the generic name—often unpronounceable—that identifies the active ingredient (acetaminophen, in this case). Many over-the-counter drugs contain several active ingredients. A medicine for allergy, cough, and cold symptoms may contain brompheniramine, dextromethorphan, and pseudoephedrine; each does something different. When you give your child a spoonful of medicine, it's not always easy to know just what you're giving.

To clear things up a bit, the guide that follows lists the generic names for some of the most common medications and tells what each medication is supposed to do. Many commonly used medications fall into a few categories—antibiotics, antihistamines, and anti-inflammatory medications, for example. Information about those drugs is grouped under the applicable categories.

The purpose of this guide is not to replace the advice of

doctors or pharmacists. It is to help you better communicate with them. So when the doctor says, "Let's give her some ibuprofen for that sore shoulder," you can be thinking, "Oh, Motrin; we already tried that."

The following guide includes only a fraction of the drugs used today. For a more complete listing, look online at www.medlineplus.gov and click on "Drugs and Supplements." That site also has a helpful online tutorial on understanding medical jargon, a glossary of medical terms, and other helpful information.

This guide includes only *some* of the most common side effects for the medications listed. The package inserts that come with prescription drugs list many more. Any medication can trigger an unpleasant or dangerous side effect. Any unexpected, unpleasant symptom that shows up after taking a medication is a side effect until proven otherwise.

Acetaminophen

(over the counter) *Trade names:* Tylenol, Tempra.

Effects: See Nonsteroidal anti-inflammatories. Acetaminophen reduces fever and pain.

Side effects: In large overdoses, causes serious liver disease. Ask the doctor if you are giving it for more than a couple of days.

Acetylsalicylic acid (Aspirin)

(over the counter) *Trade names:* Bayer, Ecotrin, many others.

Effects: See Nonsteroidal anti-inflammatories.

Side effects: Use only under doctor's guidance. In children, aspirin can cause life-threatening liver disease (Reye's syndrome).

Advil

(over the counter) See Ibuprofen.

Albuterol

(prescription only in the U.S.) *Trade names:* Proventil, Ventolin.

    Effects: See Bronchodilators.

Amoxicillin

(prescription only in the U.S.) *Trade names:* Amoxil, Trimox.

    Effects: See Antibiotics. Amoxicillin is often the first-line treatment for ear infections.

Amoxicillin clavulanate

(prescription only in the U.S.) *Trade name:* Augmentin.

    Effects: See Antibiotics. Often the second choice if amoxicillin fails because of drug resistance.

    Side effects: More likely than amoxicillin to cause stomach upset, diarrhea.

Amoxil

(over the counter) See Amoxicillin.

Antibiotics

(prescription only in the U.S.)

    Effects: Antibiotics kill bacteria; not helpful in common viral infections, such as colds.

    Side effects: In infants, especially, look for signs of thrush or candidal diaper rash; stomach upset, rashes are common.

Antihistamines

(mainly over the counter) *Trade names:* Benadryl, Atarax, Claritin, Zyrtec.

Effects: These drugs block the action of histamine, a major component of allergic reactions. Used commonly to treat hay fever, hives, other allergic rashes, etc.

Side effects: In young children, often cause hyper or over-excited response; in older children, sedation or drowsiness. Claritin and Zyrtec are examples of newer (and more expensive) versions of antihistamines. They don't block histamine any better, but may cause fewer side effects. Antihistamines are often sold as part of combination medications containing decongestants and other medications, which may be unsafe for young children.

Antivirals

(most are prescription only)

Effects: May shorten symptoms of some viral infections, such as oral herpes (cold sores) and influenza.

Side effects: Various, including stomach and intestinal upset, and allergic reactions that can be serious.

Augmentin

(prescription only in the U.S.) *Effects:* See Amoxicillin clavulanate.

Azithromycin

(prescription only in the U.S.) *Trade names:* Zithromax, Zmax.

Effects: See Antibiotics; this drug is similar to erythromycin but requires fewer daily doses (and costs much more).

Side effects: Stomach upset, mainly.

Bacitracin ointment

(over the counter) *Trade names:* Neosporin, Polysporin.

Effects: A mild antibiotic that can be applied to the skin (topical).

Side effects: Rare.

Beclomethasone nasal inhalation

(prescription only in the U.S.) *Trade names:* Vancenase, Beconase.

Effects: See Corticosteroids, inhaled. Nasal corticosteroids reduce symptoms of hay fever.

Side effects: Rare when used as directed.

Benzocaine

(over the counter) *Trade name:* Anbesol.

Effects: Dulls pain sensation (anesthetic). However, effects wear off with repeated use.

Side effects: Stinging or burning feeling. Overdose can cause heart rhythm disturbances.

Bisacodyl

(over the counter) *Trade name:* Dulcolax.

Effects: Stimulates the intestines to contract and propel feces forward.

Side effects: Cramping, diarrhea.

Brompheniramine

(over the counter) *Trade names:* Dimetapp, Robitussin.

Effects: See Antihistamines.

Bronchodilators

(prescription only in the U.S.)

   Effects: Combat tightness of the bronchial tubes caused by asthma.

   Side effects: Increase in heart rate and blood pressure, nervousness, jitters, anxiety, nightmares, and other behavior changes.

Chlorpheniramine

(over the counter) *Trade names:* Actifed, Sudafed, Triaminic.

   Effects: See Antihistamines.

Clemastine

(over the counter)

   Effects: See Antihistamines.

Clotrimazole cream or ointment

(over the counter) *Trade name:* Lotrimin.

   Effects: Kills the fungi that cause ringworm and some diaper rashes, as well as athlete's foot.

   Side effects: Rare.

Corticosteroids, inhaled

(prescription only in the U.S.)

   Effects: Inhaled corticosteroids are the best medications for reducing inflammation in the lungs caused by asthma.

   Side effects: With overuse or misuse, enough corticosteroid is absorbed into the body to produce serious side effects; talk with the doctor about how to avoid them.

Corticosteroids, topical

(over the counter or prescription)

Effects: Corticosteroid creams, ointments, and lotions reduce itching and inflammation of the skin; especially useful for eczema and some allergic reactions. There is a range of strengths.

Side effects: Thinning of the skin, lightening of pigment, absorption of medicine into the body; all are worse with stronger corticosteroids used over larger areas for longer periods of time. Use of lower strength preparations for short periods is usually safe.

Co-trimoxazole

(prescription only in the U.S.) *Trade name:* Bactrim.

Effects: An antibiotic, often used for bladder infections; no longer used for ear infections (see Antibiotics).

Side effects: Stomach upset; call a doctor if paleness, rash, itching, or other new symptoms appear.

Cromolyn

(prescription only in the U.S.) *Trade name:* Intal.

Effects: Reduces inflammation in the lungs in asthma; not as powerful as inhaled corticosteroids.

Side effects: Rare.

Decongestants

(over the counter) *Trade names:* Actifed, Triaminic, Sudafed; anything labeled "decongestant."

Effects: These medications cause blood vessels in the nose to contract, so the nose makes less mucus.

Side effects: Can be severe in young children under age

four, or even deadly. Since these medications aren't effective in any case, it's best to avoid them, or use only on a doctor's advice. They often cause an increase in heart rate and blood pressure; nervousness, jitters, anxiety, nightmares, and other behavior changes. After a couple of days, the body often adjusts, so the medications no longer work. Be especially careful when taking with other medications that may have similar side effects, such as stimulants.

Dextromethorphan

(over the counter) *Trade names:* Robitussin, Delsym, Coricidin and many others.

Effects: Supposed to suppress the cough reflex, but effectiveness is slight or perhaps nonexistent.

Side effects: Can be severe in young children; not safe under age four; use only under doctor's guidance in any child. Be aware, too, of other medications combined with the cough suppressant; all can have serious side effects.

Diphenhydramine

(over the counter or prescription) *Trade name:* Benadryl.

Effects: See Antihistamines.

Docusate

(over the counter) *Trade names:* Dulcolax, Colace.

Effects: A stool softener; not absorbed by the body.

Side effects: Diarrhea, vomiting, allergic reactions.

Erythromycin

(prescription only in the U.S.) *Trade name:* EryPed.

> *Effects:* An antibiotic, often used when penicillin allergy is present.
>
> *Side effects:* Upset stomach, mainly.

Ferrous sulfate, ferrous fumarate

(over the counter or prescription) *Trade names:* Fer-In-Sol, Feosol, Slow Fe, et al.

> *Effects:* Iron preparations; combat anemia caused by iron deficiency.
>
> *Side effects:* In overdose, iron is extremely dangerous, causing ulcers and other problems. Be careful with these medicines.

Flunisolide oral inhalation

(prescription only in the U.S.) *Trade name:* AeroBid.

> *Effects:* See Corticosteroids, inhaled.

Fluticasone nasal inhalation

(prescription only in the U.S.) *Trade name:* Flonase.

> *Effects:* See Corticosteroids, inhaled.

Fluticasone oral inhalation

(prescription only in the U.S.) *Trade name:* Flovent.

> *Effects:* See Corticosteroids, inhaled.

Guaifenesin

(over the counter) *Trade names:* Robitussin, Sudafed.

> *Effects:* An expectorant, supposed to loosen mucus to make it easier to cough up.
>
> *Side effects:* Rare, but it is often combined with other medications (e.g., decongestants) that may have severe side effects.

Hydrocortisone cream or ointment

(over the counter) *Trade name:* Cortizone.

Effects: See Corticosteroids, topical. Hydrocortisone 0.5 percent and 1 percent are fairly weak, good for minor itching rashes, with few side effects.

Side effects: Like all corticosteroids, side effects increase with higher dose and longer use; check with the doctor.

Hydroxyzine

(over the counter) *Trade name:* Atarax.

Effects: See Antihistamines.

Ibuprofen

(over the counter) *Trade names:* Advil, Motrin, Pediaprofen.

Effects: See Nonsteroidal anti-inflammatories. Ibuprofen is good for aches and pains.

Side effects: Stomach upset, especially in high doses. Overdose is dangerous.

Ketoconazole lotion or cream

(over the counter) *Trade name:* Nizoral.

Effects: Kills the fungi that cause ringworm and some diaper rashes.

Side effects: Rare.

Loperamide

(over the counter or prescription) *Trade name:* Imodium.

Effects: Reduces diarrhea by reducing contractions in the intestines.

Side effects: Bloating, stomach pains.

Loratadine
(over the counter) *Trade name:* Claritin.
> *Effects:* See Antihistamines. Loratadine may cause less drowsiness than older (far cheaper) antihistamines.
> *Side effects:* Rarely headache, dry mouth, drowsiness, or hyper behavior.

Metoclopramide
(prescription only in the U.S.) *Trade name:* Reglan.
> *Effects:* Reduces acid reflux from the stomach by strengthening the sphincter muscle that closes off the top of the stomach.
> *Side effects:* Drowsiness, restlessness, nausea, constipation, diarrhea.

Miconazole
(over the counter) *Trade name:* Desenex.
> *Effects:* Kills the fungi that cause athlete's foot and other rashes.
> *Side effects:* Rare.

Montelukast
(prescription only in the U.S.) *Trade name:* Singulair.
> *Effects:* Reduces inflammation in the lungs in asthma.
> *Side effects:* Headache, dizziness, upset stomach.

Motrin
(over the counter)
> *Effects:* See Ibuprofen.

Mupirocin ointment

(prescription only in the U.S.) *Trade name:* Bactroban.

    Effects: Kills bacteria that commonly cause skin infections.

    Side effects: Rare.

Naproxen

(over the counter or prescription) *Trade name:* Aleve.

    Effects: See Nonsteroidal anti-inflammatories. Naproxen is good for aches and pains.

    Side effects: Stomach upset, especially at high doses. Dangerous in overdose. Take with food; talk to the doctor if taking for more than a day or two.

Nonsteroidal anti-inflammatories (NSAIDs)

(over the counter or prescription) Examples include acetaminophen, ibuprofen, naproxen, and others.

    Effects: These medications reduce inflammation in muscles and joints, lower fever, reduce pain.

    Side effects: All can cause stomach upset, especially at higher doses; overdose can be very dangerous. Talk with your doctor if using at high doses or for long periods of time.

Omeprazole

(over the counter and prescription) *Trade name:* Prilosec.

    Effects: Reduces stomach acid; often used to treat reflux (GERD).

    Side effects: Headache, rash, vomiting, vitamin deficiency.

Oral rehydration solutions

(over the counter) *Trade names:* Pedialyte, Oralyte, Hydralyte, and others.

Effects: Used to prevent dehydration in children who are losing water through vomiting and diarrhea, these solutions consist mainly of water, salt, potassium, and different kinds of sugar in the right proportions, so that as much water as possible is absorbed from the intestines into the bloodstream. Flavored varieties and ice pops work well, too.
Side effects: None. However, a child who is having a lot of vomiting and diarrhea should be under a doctor's supervision. It's possible to become dehydrated even while taking one of these rehydration solutions.

Penicillin

(prescription only in the U.S.) *Trade name:* none; often called "Pen VK."
Effects: See Antibiotics. Penicillin by mouth or penicillin by injection is the first-line treatment for strep throat.
Side effects: Allergic reactions, usually a rash with little itchy bumps, are common; more serious allergic reactions are rare but do happen. Notify your doctor if your child is allergic.

Phenylephrine

(over the counter) *Trade names:* Neo-Synephrine, Alka-Seltzer Plus.
Effects: See Decongestants.
Side effects: Not safe in young children; use only on doctor's advice.

Polymyxin B

(over the counter) *Trade name:* Neosporin.
Effects: A mild antibiotic that can be applied to the skin (topical).
Side effects: Rare.

Pseudoephedrine

(over the counter) *Trade names:* PediaCare products, Sudafed, and others.

> *Effects:* See Decongestants.
>
> *Side effects:* Not safe in young children; use only on doctor's advice.

Pyrethrins and Pyrethrum

(over the counter) *Trade names:* RID, Nix, and others.

> *Effects:* These medications kill head lice.
>
> *Side effects:* Rare.

Ranitidine

(over the counter) *Trade name:* Zantac.

> *Effects:* Reduces stomach acid, reducing heartburn (a symptom of acid reflux).
>
> *Side effects:* Headache, dizziness, constipation, stomach pain.

Tylenol

(over the counter)

> *Effects:* See Acetaminophen.

RESOURCE GUIDE

It's easy to be overwhelmed by the universe of online information and hard to know what to rely on. This guide lists reliable and informative government and nonprofit sites (website names ending in .gov and .org, rather than .com). Most of the sites include articles for parents, guides to further reading, and directories of local groups and professionals; many also have interactive discussion groups and special features for children and teens. Most of the sites have Spanish-language sections as well as English.

You'll need access to the Internet, which is available through most public libraries. For those who cannot go online, the guide includes telephone numbers as well; some are for hotlines, others are for the main office of the organization.

To help you find what you need, the list is organized according to the major sections of this book, then alphabetically within each section. There are too many sites to include in these pages. You can find more listings, along with other helpful information, at drspock.com.

A word of caution: Even for well-respected sites, there is no guarantee that all of the information on them is accurate. Check the authorship before you read the article. Every article should list the author and his or her qualifications. Is the author someone you'd trust to advise you about your child? You should also be able to see when the article was last updated. Articles that are outdated or that don't tell you when they were written aren't as trustworthy. Finally, you have to use your own common sense: If something you read seems wrong or suspect, look at other sites and sources, or ask your child's doctor.

YOUR CHILD, AGE BY AGE

Child care. The National Association of Child Care Resource and Referral Agencies (NACCRRA) provides information on child care, and links to local agencies that provide referrals to high-quality infant and child care: www.childcareaware.org, (703) 341-4100.

College planning and funding. The U.S. Department of Education provides information on choosing and paying for college: www.studentaid.ed.gov, (800) 4-FED-AID (433-3243).

Doulas. If you are pregnant or planning a pregnancy, find out about the benefits of doulas at DONA International: www.dona.org, (888) 788-DONA (3662).

Emotional development and care. Zero to Three is a well-respected nonprofit that provides information for parents and professionals about young children's emotional development. The organization was founded many years ago by leading doctors and researchers, and continues to support excellent research, policy, and education. There's a large selection of wonderful materials to help parents raise emotionally healthy children. Zero to Three is also a leader in early childhood education: www.zerotothree.org, (800) 899-4301.

Gifted children. National Association for Gifted Children: www.nagc.org, (202) 785-4268.

Learning disabilities. The Learning Disabilities Association of America is a good source of information on learning disabilities and special education, with local groups nationally: www.ldanatl.org, (412) 341-1515. Also see LD Online: www.ld online.org, (703) 998-2600 (WETA public broadcasting is the parent organization); the Council for Exceptional Children: www.cec.sped.org, (888) 232-7733.

Parent involvement in schools. The National Parent Teacher Association (PTA) is a good resource for information on parent involvement, examples of successful programs, and local groups: www.pta.org, (800) 307-4PTA (307-4782).

FEEDING AND NUTRITION

Breastfeeding. A reliable source for information, individual support, and groups is La Leche League: www.llli.org, (800) LALECHE (525-3243).

General nutrition. For solid information on food and nutrition, start with www.nutrition.gov, run by the U.S. Department of Agriculture. You'll find, among other things, links to the U.S. Nutrient Database, which lists the nutrient makeup of nearly every food. Another good source is the

Academy of Nutrition and Dietetics: www.eatright.org, (800) 877-1600.

Healthy eating on a budget. The Iowa State University Extension has a creative interactive site that teaches how you can save money and eat better: http://www.extension.iastate.edu /foodsavings.

Vegetarian eating and nutrition. For well-researched information on nutrition and health, as well as creative recipes, visit the Physicians Committee for Responsible Medicine: www .pcrm.org, (202) 686-2210.

HEALTH AND SAFETY

All conditions. Maybe the best source for basic medical information—definitions of medical terms and facts about illnesses and medications—is MedlinePlus, a service of the U.S. National Library of Medicine: medlineplus.gov, (888) FIND-NLM (346-3656). There is an easy-to-use medical dictionary and a helpful tutorial on how to make sense of medical jargon. The alphabetical list of drugs and supplements is complete and well organized. The medical encyclopedia provides short but accurate articles on most topics.

Another reliable and helpful set of health information is at www.cdc.gov, (800) CDC-INFO (232-4636), the website of the U.S. Centers for Disease Control and Prevention. The CDC publishes information on infectious diseases and epidemics, as well as growth charts, dental health, safety, nutrition, emergency preparedness, travel medicine, and a host of other important topics.

Also, see the listings for KidsHealth, and the American Academy of Pediatrics, below in the section on Raising Mentally Healthy Children.

Asthma and allergy. Asthma and Allergy Foundation of America: www.aafa.org, (800) 7-ASTHMA (727-8462); American Academy of Allergy, Asthma and Immunology: www.aaaai.org, (414) 272-6071.

First aid, CPR training. The American Red Cross provides training, information on preparedness, and opportunities to be helpful across the globe: www.redcross.org, (800) 773-2767.

Food allergies and anaphylaxis. Food Allergy Research and Education: www.foodallergy.org, (800) 929-4040.

Medications. For facts about medications, their uses, and possible side effects, see medlineplus.gov.

Oral (dental) health. The National Institute of Dental and Craniofacial Research has parent-friendly information: www.nidcr.nih.gov, and click on the "Health Info," (866) 232-4528.

Poison control hotline. A good number to have taped next to the telephone: (800) 222-1222. More information is at www.poison.org. (The site has catchy jingles to help you memorize the number—worth a listen!)

RAISING MENTALLY HEALTHY CHILDREN

All conditions: children's health and behavior. For clear and reliable information about all aspects of children's health and behavior, see KidsHealth: www.kidshealth.org. The articles are written in plain language, but they give enough detail to be helpful. Although the writers are not named, the articles are reviewed by named doctors or psychologists whose credentials are published; you can also see the date of the latest update. There are separate sections for kids and teens, which are fun but still informative. There is a helpful Spanish-language option throughout the site. The number for the parent organization, the Nemours Foundation, is (904) 697-4100.

The American Academy of Pediatrics (AAP) runs a large website: www.aap.org, (847) 434-4000. The AAP is the main professional group for pediatricians, and it writes the guidelines that define good pediatric care. A lot of the information on the AAP site is intended for doctors and other health professionals, but the home page has a link to articles for parents on a range of topics, including immunizations and injury prevention, and many issues in the areas of behavior and mental health.

Adoption. Information is available at www.childwelfare.gov, (800) 394-3366; under "Topics," click on "Adoption." Also, North American Council on Adoptable Children: www.nacac .org, (651) 644-3036.

Advocacy. The Children's Defense Fund advocates to improve the lives of children in many ways. The site gives you many ways to become active: www.childrensdefense.org, (800) CDF-1200 (233-1200).

Alcoholism. Alcoholics Anonymous supports people getting free of alcoholism; Al-Anon and Alateen help families and children cope with alcoholism: www.aa.org, (212) 870-3400; www.alanon.alateen.org, (888) 425-2666.

Bullying. Stop Bullying Now, www.stopbullyingnow.gov, is a project of the U.S. Department of Health and Human Services. The site has a wonderful section for children, and includes information on cyberbullying and many materials to use with schools.

Child abuse prevention. Parents Anonymous supports parents who are seeking positive and nonviolent ways to raise their children: www.parentsanonymous.org, (909) 621-6184.

Domestic violence. The website of the National Coalition Against Domestic Violence, www.ncadv.org, provides practical information to help victims of abuse find safety; most of the pages have a button that navigates away from the site instantly, making it less likely a victim will be caught using the site. The national domestic violence hotline is (800) 799-SAFE (7233); TTY (800) 787-3224.

Environment and environmental health. The Natural Resources Defense Council (NRDC) has a very helpful section on living green, with information on how to minimize waste and environmental hazards in everyday life: www.nrdc.org, (212) 727-2700.

Foster families. National Foster Parent Association, www .nfpainc.org, (800) 557-5238.

Gay and lesbian parents. Parents, Families and Friends of Lesbians and Gays (PFLAG) provides information to help families adapt to and support a gay, lesbian, or transgender child: www.pflag.org, (202) 467-8180. Also see the Family Equality Council: www.familyequality.org, (646) 880-3005.

Grandparenting. American Association of Retired Persons (AARP) Grandparent Information Center: www.aarp.org /relationships/grandparenting, (888) OUR-AARP (687-2277).

Service. UNICEF: www.unicef.org, (212) 686-5522, and www.unicefusa.org (800) 367-5437. Save the Children also provides many ways for you and your children to become involved in helping others around the world: www.savethechildren .org, (800) 728-3843.

Single parents. For local support groups, see Parents Without Partners: www.parentswithoutpartners.org, (800) 637-7974.

Social justice. The Southern Poverty Law Center provides tools to teach children to value diversity and speak up for justice; the site is mainly for professionals, but the magazine *Teaching Tolerance* is well worth a look: www.tolerance.org, (888) 414-7752.

COMMON DEVELOPMENTAL AND BEHAVIORAL CHALLENGES

ADHD. A large national organization, Children and Adults with Attention-Deficit/Hyperactivity Disorder (CHADD) provides information, advocacy, and parent support groups:

www.chadd.org, (800) 233-4050. Also, LD Online: www
.ldonline.org, (703) 998-2600 (WETA public broadcasting is
the parent organization).

Autism. The Autism Society is a very large organization
with local chapters all over: www.autism-society.org, (800)
3-AUTISM (328-8476).

Eating disorders. The National Association of Anorexia Nervosa and Associated Disorders (ANAD): www.anad.org, (630)
577-1333. There is also a helpline: (630) 577-1330.

Mental health, all topics. The National Institute of Mental
Health provides a wealth of information on ADHD, anxiety,
depression, and many other mental health issues for parents
and children. Check out "Health Topics" at www.nimh.nih
.gov, (866) 615-6464.

GETTING HELP

Mental health professionals. The sites below all offer directories of doctors, counselors, or therapists; some are more
complete than others. Before searching online, a better first
step is often to ask your child's doctor for a personal recommendation.

   American Academy of Child and Adolescent Psychiatry. Information on ADHD, depression, anxiety, and other common
child mental health problems. There is a computerized listing of psychiatrists, with limited information: www.aacap.org,
(202) 966-7300.

   American Association for Marriage and Family Therapy.

Search for family therapists in your area: www.aamft.org, (703) 838-9808.

American Psychoanalytic Association. Learn about psychoanalysis, and search for analysts in your area: www.apsa.org, (212) 752-0450.

American Psychological Association. The website includes a Psychology Help Center with information on many different topics for both adults and children, as well as a directory of psychologists: www.apa.org, (800) 374-2721.

Psychology Today, the popular magazine, runs a well-organized website with local listings of many psychologists, counselors, family therapists, and similar professionals: www.psychologytoday.org.

The Society for Developmental and Behavioral Pediatrics (SDBP): www.sdbp.org. Developmental-behavioral pediatricians aren't psychologists or psychiatrists, but they have special training in helping parents and children deal with many different medical and behavioral challenges.

CHILDREN WITH SPECIAL NEEDS

There are organizations that provide support for children and families affected by virtually every condition. What follows is only a partial listing.

Autism. See Autism Society of America (page 895) and Easter Seals (pages 897–98).

Blindness. American Council of the Blind: www.acb.org, (800) 424-8666; American Foundation for the Blind: www.afb.org, (800) 232-5463; National Federation of the Blind and National Organization of Parents of Blind Children: www.nfb.org, (410) 659-9314.

Brain injury. Brain Injury Association of America: www .biausa.org, (800) 444-6443.

Cerebral palsy. United Cerebral Palsy: www.ucp.org, (800) 872-5827. Click on "Explore Resources" and then "For Parents and Families," or go directly to www.mychildwithoutlimits .org, a rich resource for education and supports, not limited to cerebral palsy.

Cystic fibrosis. Cystic Fibrosis Foundation: www.cff.org, (800) FIGHT-CF (344-4823).

Deaf-blind. National Center on Deaf-Blindness: www.national db.org, (503) 838-8754.

Deafness. National Institute on Deafness and Other Communication Disorders: www.nidcd.nih.gov, (800) 241-1044, a branch of the National Institutes of Health, provides solid information; the Alexander Graham Bell Association for the Deaf and Hard of Hearing: www.agbell.org, (202) 337-5220, advocates for services for children and adults.

Developmental delay. See www.mychildwithoutlimits.org.

Diabetes. American Diabetes Association: www.diabetes.org, (800) DIABETES (342-2383).

Disabilities. Easter Seals provides developmental services, including therapies, home-based and center-based education, camps, and medical services, in most communities: www.easter seals.com, (800) 221-6827. A good overall resource is the Council for Exceptional Children: www.cec.sped.org, (888) 232-7733.

Down syndrome. The National Down Syndrome Society (NDSS), with information and a directory of local support groups: www.ndss.org, (800) 221-4602. The National Down Syndrome Congress (a different organization) has local chapters and excellent annual conventions: www.ndsccenter.org.

Dyslexia. International Dyslexia Association: www.interdys .org, (410) 296-0232.

Epilepsy. Epilepsy Foundation of America: www.epilepsy .com, (800) 332-1000.

Fetal alcohol syndrome. National Organization on Fetal Alcohol Syndrome: www.nofas.org, (202) 785-4585.

Fragile X. National Fragile X Foundation: fragilex.org, (800) 688-8765. This site provides a great deal of information and support for children and adults affected by fragile X, as well as for professionals.

Intellectual disability. The largest national organization serving children and families with intellectual disabilities is The Arc, www.thearc.org, (800) 433-5255.

Lead poisoning. The U.S. Environmental Protection Agency (EPA) provides information on lead, including safe cleanup:

www.epa.gov/lead. There is also a lead hotline: (800) 424-LEAD (424-5323).

Muscular dystrophy. The Muscular Dystrophy Association provides information for families, programs, support groups, and more: www.mda.org, (800) 572-1717.

Rare disorders. NORD, the National Organization for Rare Disorders, provides information on more than a thousand rare and genetic disorders, along with networking and publications: www.rarediseases.org, (800) 999-6673.

Selective mutism. Selective Mutism Group, Childhood Anxiety Network: www.selectivemutism.org. The FAQ section is particularly helpful, and there are resources for finding clinicians skilled in treating SM.

Sickle cell. Sickle Cell Disease Association of America (SCDAA): www.sicklecelldisease.org, (800) 421-8453.

Spina bifida. Spina Bifida Association: www.spinabifida association.org, (800) 621-3141.

Stuttering. The Stuttering Foundation: www.stutteringhelp .org, (800) 992-9392.

Tourette's disorder (also called Tourette's syndrome). Tourette Association of America: www.tsa-usa.org, (718) 224-2999.

INDEX

Abuse, child. *See* Child abuse
 and neglect
Accidents, 382
 See also Injuries, preventing
Acetaminophen (Tylenol), 351,
 354, 378, 450, 528, 873,
 874, 884
Acetylsalicylic acid (aspirin), 354,
 389, 437, 482, 528, 874
Acid reflux, 519
 See also Gastroesophageal
 reflux disease
Acne
 in adolescents, 224–225, 228
 in babies, 108–109
Acquired immune deficiency
 syndrome. *See* AIDS
ACT, 217–218
Acting out, 717–727
 See also Biting behavior;
 Temper tantrums

back talk, 724
potty talk, 722
school-age swearing, 722–723
swearing by teenagers, 723–
 724
Adderall, 829
Adenoids, 362, 363, 485, 486
ADHD (attention deficit
 hyperactivity disorder),
 191, 195, 196, 502, 545,
 551, 775, 793, 813, 820,
 823–832, 852
bipolar disorder and, 827
defined, 823–824
diagnosing, 825–826, 827–
 828
inattentive, 824–825
learning disabilities and, 191,
 827
medications for, 826–827,
 829–831

ADHD (*cont.*):

   other conditions that look
     like, 826–827

   parenting and, 826

   resources for, 894–895

   three parts of, 823–824

   treatments for, 828–832

Adolescence (twelve to
    eighteen), 197–228

   See also Puberty

   acne in, 224–225, 228

   after-school time and, 591

   alcohol in, 207, 208, 398

   appearance as important in,
    204

   challenges of, 197–198

   chores and family
    participation in, 224

   civil behavior in, 224

   confidential medical care in,
    223

   defiance in, 221–222

   diet and nutrition in, 199,
    225–226

   early (twelve to fourteen),
    202–206

   exercise and, 227

   friendships and social life in,
    202, 203–204

   health issues in, 224–228

   idealism in, 197, 210, 211, 226

   identity formation in, 210–211

   independence, freedom, and
    limits in, 197, 203, 206,
    210, 211, 220, 591

   late (eighteen to twenty-one),
    210–211

   middle (fifteen to seventeen),
    206–210

   parental strategies for dealing
    with, 220–224

   and parents' history as
    teenagers, 207–208

   parents' judgments about
    allowing activities of, 222–
    223

   physical development in,
    198–202

   respect in, 220–221

   risky behaviors in, 198, 207–
    208

   safety rules and, 220, 223

   school and, 197

   sex education and, 642–644

   sexuality in, 197, 205, 208–
    209

   sexual preferences and, 205–
    206, 209–210

   sleep and, 227

   suicide in, 223–224, 398

   swearing in, 723–724

   work and, 208, 210

Adoption, 661–669

   age at, 662

agency for, 662–663

answering children's questions about, 665–666

belonging in, 667

of children with special needs, 663

gray-market, 663

information about birth parents, 666–667

international, 7–8, 667–669

nontraditional parents and, 664

open, 664

reasons for, 661–662

to "replace" a child who has died, 662

resources for, 892

telling child about, 664–665

Adrenaline, 688

Advil. *See* Ibuprofen

AIDS (acquired immune deficiency syndrome), 279, 526–527, 644

HIV, 67, 279, 526–527

talking about, 526–527

Airbags, 402, 404

Airplanes, 404–405

Albuterol, 875

Alcohol, 553, 830

adolescents and, 207, 208, 398, 563

breastfeeding and, 261–262

prenatal exposure to, 845, 898

resources for, 893, 898

Allergic reactions

anaphylaxis, 438, 891

first aid for, 438

hives, 438, 492

Allergies, 53, 247, 465, 471, 776, 826

eczema and, 489

food, 53, 304–305, 306, 323, 891

nasal, 486–488, 489

preventing, 488

resources for, 891

seasonal, 486

Allowances, 177

Almond milk, 128, 260, 324

Alpha-linolenic acid (ALA), 314

Aluminum, 282

Alzheimer's, 282

American Academy of Family Physicians, 375

American Academy of Pediatrics (AAP), 247, 297, 343, 375, 652

American Dietetic Association, 320

Amino acids, 315

Amoxicillin, 358, 464, 875

Amoxicillin clavulanate, 875

Amphetamine, 829

Anaphylaxis, 438, 891

Anesthesia, 364–365
Angel's kisses, 72
Anger in child, 612–613
Anger in parent, 2, 85, 86,
    139–140, 622–625, 693
    admitting, 624–625
    help for, 139, 625
Animal bites
    first aid for, 424–425
    preventing, 420–421
Animals, fear of, 154–155, 814
Ankles, 517
Anorexia nervosa, 226, 793–796
Anterior cruciate ligament
    (ACL), 412
Antibiotics, 358, 464, 473,
    790, 875
    for ear infections, 470–471
    resistance to, 464, 470, 471
Antidepressants, 820–821
Antihistamines, 425, 465, 487–
    488, 876
Antivirals, 876
Anxiety, 519, 545, 813, 826, 852
    See also Fears; Separation
        anxiety
    aggression and, 815–816
    compulsions and, 179–180
    with strangers, 99–100, 117,
        123–124
Anxiety disorders, 813–818
    causes of, 816

obsessive-compulsive
    disorder, 545, 815
    treatments for, 816–818
    types of, 814–816
AP (Advanced Placement) tests,
    218
Appendicitis, 358, 498
Appetite, 128, 245, 288
    feeding problems and, 777–
        778, 779, 787, 788
Asperger's syndrome, 851, 852
Aspirin (acetylsalicylic acid), 354,
    389, 437, 482, 528, 874
Asthma, 113, 323, 462, 482–
    485, 551
    care for, 484–485
    causes of, 483
    identifying, 482–483
    resources for, 891
    symptoms of, 347
    treatment for, 483–484
Atopy, 489
Attention deficit hyperactivity
    disorder. See ADHD
Augmentin, 875
Autism, 78–79, 195, 503, 811,
    849–855
    awareness about, 849
    causes of, 852–853
    defined, 849–851
    early signs of, 854
    intellectual disability and, 851

interests, behaviors, and
    sensations in, 850–851
language and, 849–850, 851–
    852
range of problems in, 851–852
relationships and, 850
resources for, 895, 896
therapies for, 854–855
vaccines and, 374–375
Autism spectrum disorder
    (ASD), 852
Azithromycin, 876

Baby blues, 41–42
Baby bottles, 34
    See also Bottle-feeding;
        Formula-feeding
    clogged nipple holes, 288
    heating in the microwave,
        285–286
    propping when feeding, 286,
        396
    size of nipple holes, 287–288,
        290
    taking to bed, 291, 294–295,
        776
    weaning from, 291–295
Baby carriers, 27–28, 30, 71
Baby food
    making your own, 306
    ready-made, 306–307
Baby powder, 33, 64, 109

Babyproofing. See
    Childproofing
Babysitters, 86, 582–583, 591–
    592
    See also Child care
    concerns about, 583–584
Bacitracin ointment, 877
Back injuries, 434
Backpacks, 30, 409
Back talk, 724
Bacteria, 24, 108, 224, 304,
    350, 424, 506, 790
    in meat, 304, 328, 506
    tooth decay and, 291, 292,
        451, 453, 454
    vaccines and, 369, 374
Balloons, 396
Baseball, 411, 458
Bassinets, 28, 52
Baths, bathing, 140
    equipment for, 29
    fear of, 123
    getting ready for, 62–63
    lotions and, 64
    navel and, 61, 64
    for newborns, 61–64
    soaps and shampoos for, 33,
        62–64, 107
    sponge baths, 61–62
    tub, 61, 63–64
    water temperature in, 29, 63,
        388

Bathtub, drowning in, 384

Beans and legumes, 303–304, 307, 316, 317, 326, 327, 332

Beclomethasone nasal inhalation, 877

Bedding
blankets, 28, 51, 70
mattresses, 28, 29

Bedtime
See also Sleep
routines for, 82, 127, 573, 775, 776
separation anxiety at, 136–137

Bed-wetting, 766–771
causes of, 767–768
fear of, 137–138
learning to stay dry, 768–769
patterns of, 767
treatments for, 769–771

Bees, 419, 425

Behavioral problems, 834
See also Acting out; Therapy

Benadryl (diphenhydramine), 487–488, 880

Benzocaine, 877

Bicycles, 382, 407–409
helmets for riding, 382, 407–408, 409

Bilirubin, 73

Bipolar disorder (manic-depressive disorder), 545, 819–820, 827

Birth
children and, 25
delivery, 18, 25, 35–36
doulas for, 18–19, 22, 888
emotional responses to, 35–36
father's role in, 18–19, 35
parents' sexual relations after, 43
planning, 18–19
skin-to-skin contact following, 249–250

Birth control, 228

Birth defects, 318, 371

Birthmarks, 72–73

Birth order and spacing, influence of, 547–548

Bisacodyl, 877

Bites
See also Insect bites and stings
animal, first aid for, 424–425
dog, preventing, 420–421
human, 424–425

Biting behavior, 721–722, 725–727
after age three, 727
in babies, 725
biting back, 727
how to handle, 726
in toddlers and preschoolers, 725–726

Biting nails, 744–745

Bladder, 520–521
  See also Urination
  constipation and, 502
  infections of, 520
Bladder control, 760–763
  See also Bed-wetting
  pants and, 761–762
  setbacks in, 764
  simultaneous with bowel
    control, 760–761
  staying dry at night, 763
Blankets, 28, 51, 70
Bleach, 389–390
Bleeding, blood
  in bowel movements, 60, 61,
    106, 348
  first aid for, 426–427
  minor wounds, 426
  nosebleeds, 427
  severe wounds, 426–427
  in urine, 348
  in vomit, 348
Blindness, 896–897
Blisters, 109
  burns with, 429
  impetigo, 110, 492–493
  on newborns, 72–73
  rash with, 108
Blood. See Bleeding, blood
Body control, 92
Body differences and injury,
  worries about

  in adolescents, 202–203
  in preschoolers, 156–159
Body mass index (BMI), 789
Body odor, 201
Body rocking habit, 743
Body temperature. See
  Temperature, body
Boils, 493
Bonding, 35–36, 39
Bones, 432–433, 516–518
  broken, splinting for, 433–
    434
  broken wrists, 433
  calcium intake and, 316–317,
    324
  cow's milk and, 316–317,
    324
  and elbow injury in toddlers,
    432
  fractures of, 432–434
  growing pains and, 516–517
  growth of, 200, 202, 260
  osteoporosis and, 316, 320
  vitamin D and, 319
Books
  See also Reading aloud
  benefits of, 576–577
  nonracist and nonsexist,
    577
  taking care of, 568, 569,
    571–572
Booster seats, 403–404

Bottle-feeding
  See also Feeding in the first year; Formula-feeding
  with breast milk, 258, 268–269, 274, 276, 279
  teething and, 238
Botulism, 454, 465, 466
Bowel movements (BMs)
  See also Constipation; Diarrhea; Toilet training
  accidents and stool leakage, 503, 765–766
  blood in, 60, 61, 106, 348
  in breast-fed babies, 254
  child's attitude toward, 752, 761
  color of, 60, 73, 107, 302
  fiber and, 502, 503
  meconium, 58
  mucus in, 60–61, 302
  in newborns, 58–61
  straining with, 59–60
  undigested food in, 302, 303
Bowlegs, toeing in, and toeing out, 97–99
BPA, 281, 282
Brain, 44, 86, 93, 112, 128, 240, 314, 372, 435
  anxiety disorders and, 816
  autism and, 849, 853
  body temperature and, 351
  experience and, 555–556
  gender and, 645–646, 647–648
  growth and development of, 13, 16, 32, 106, 143, 247, 556–557
  infection of, 371
  injury to, resources for, 897
  intellectual disability and, 844–845
  intelligence and, 564–565
  learning and, 555–558
  puberty and, 199
  stress and, 688
  synapses in, 556, 557
Bran, 503
Brazelton, T. Berry, 755
Bread, 308, 313, 315, 327, 334, 503
  toast, 308, 329
Breast cancer, 247, 324
Breastfeeding, 19–20, 80, 92, 247–278, 299
  See also Feeding in the first year
  baby's behavior in, 254–255
  baby's bowel movements and, 59
  baby's refusal to nurse, 237–238
  benefits of, 247–249, 471
  bottle-feeding combined with, 250

bottle-feeding versus, 247

breast engorgement and, 272–273

breast shape and, 19, 248, 259–260

breast size and, 259

challenges in, 270–274

crying and, 257–258

difficult behaviors in, 255–256

exercise and, 259

first days of, 249–250

frequency of, 252–254

friends and relatives and, 250–251

and fussing at the breast, 270

getting help for, 252

getting started, 249–256

how long to nurse at each feeding, 253

hunger and, 51, 253, 257–258

interval between feedings, 232–233

lactation consultants for, 21–22, 249, 252, 254, 259, 267

latching on, 253, 266, 271

letdown reflex, 253, 263

medications and, 258, 262, 279

milk supply concerns, 51

mother's and father's mixed feelings about, 248

mother's diet during, 52, 88, 260–261

mother's health and, 258–263

mother's illness and, 274

menstruation and, 238, 262–263

night feedings, 251

nipple biting and, 270

nipple care and, 267

nipples, flat or inverted, 259, 271–272

nipples, sore or cracked, 253, 267, 271

one or both breasts, 254

pain during, 271

plugged milk ducts and, 273

positions for, 263–265, 271

practical and personal benefits of, 247–249

pregnancy likelihood during, 262–263

prenatal consultation for, 21–22

resources for, 889

sexual feelings from, 248–249

sucking in, 266–267

techniques for, 263–267

tips for success, 249

as tiring for the mother, 262

weaning from, 274, 275–278

weight gain and, 256–257

working mother and, 267–269

Breast growth in puberty, 198–200

Breast infection, 273

Breast milk, 80, 279, 297, 299

  benefits of, 247

  bottle-feeding with, 258, 268–269, 274, 276, 279

  colostrum, 252

  manual expression of, 269–270

  nutrients in, 239, 317

  pumped, 34, 258, 268, 270

  supply concerns, 251–252, 256–258

Breasts, swollen

  in adolescent boys, 201

  in newborns, 74

Breathing, rescue, 443–444

Breathing problems, 113–114

  See also Asthma; Choking; Croup

  breath-holding spells, 113–114

  bronchiolitis, 479–480

  bronchitis, 479

  epiglottitis, 477, 478

  labored breathing, 347

  in newborns, 73–74

  noisy breathing, 113, 347

  rapid breathing, 347

  snoring and obstructive sleep apnea, 485–486

  stridor, 113, 347, 477

  when to call the doctor, 347

Brompheniramine, 877

Bronchiolitis, 479–480

Bronchitis, 479

Bronchodilators, 483–484, 878

Bulimia, 226, 793–794, 795

Bullying, 174–175, 191, 548, 776

  resources for, 893

Burns

  with blisters, 429

  electrical, 429, 458

  first aid for, 428–429

  preventing, 386–389

  scalding, 29, 387

  severity of, 428

  sunburn, 416–417, 428

Burping, 53, 104, 286

Caffeine, 331, 509

Calcium, 226, 260, 316–317, 450, 502

  sources of, 324–325, 330

Calories, 312, 313, 321

Campylobacter, 505

Cancer, 311, 320, 322, 324, 371, 372, 476

  breast, 247, 324

  breastfeeding and, 247

  cervical, 372

  skin, 71, 416

  testicular, 524

Candida, 108
Candy, 309, 313, 330
Carbohydrates, 311, 312
Caregivers. *See* Child care
Carriages, 30
Carriers, 27–28, 30, 71
Carrier seats, bicycle, 409
Cars, injuries and, 382, 401
    airbags and, 402, 404
    driveways and, 407
    to pedestrians, 405–407
    preventing, 401–404
Car seats, 382, 401–402
    booster seats, 403–404
    for infants, 27–28, 38, 52, 402
    for toddlers, 403
Cat litter, 17
Cause and effect, 560
Celiac disease (CD), 327, 328,
    357, 509–510
Cell phones, 134, 174, 179,
    335, 656
Celsius, 353
    See also Thermometers
Centers for Disease Control
    (CDC), 375, 378, 789,
    890
Cereals, 240, 245, 294, 332
    introducing, 300–301, 302,
    307
Cerebral palsy, 897
Cervical cancer, 372

Cesarean birth, 35, 252
Chat rooms, 656
Cheating, 178–179
Chemicals, toxic, 16–17, 199
Chest pain, 519
Chewing gum, 453, 470
Chicken pox (varicella), 372,
    376, 528
Chicken soup, 356, 465–466
Child abuse and neglect, 693–
    695
    See also Sexual abuse
    and anger at children, 693
    laws against, 694
    physical, and cultural
        differences, 694–695
    resources for, 893
    roots of, 693–694
Childbirth. *See* Birth
Child care, 40, 579–595
    after-school, 590–591
    alternatives, 581–588
    arrangements in the first year,
        581
    calls and visits to programs,
        588–589
    carefulness in caregiver, 583
    choosing a program, 588–
        590
    concerns about caregivers,
        583–584
    continuity of, 537

Child care, (*cont.*):
   day care centers, 584–585
   disposition of caregiver, 582
   education of caregiver, 583
   effects on children, 535–537, 586–587
   experience of caregiver, 582–583
   family day care, 585–586
   by father, 580
   favoritism in, 584
   finding a program, 588
   by grandparents, 86, 584, 629
   group size and, 589–590
   in-home (babysitters), 86, 582–583, 591–592
   language differences and, 583
   licensing and accreditation of, 585, 589
   and maturity of caregiver, 592
   as partnership, 587–588
   preschool versus, 159–160
   quality of, 587
   by relatives, 584
   resources for, 888
   work schedules and, 581–582
Child Care Aware, 588
Childproofing, 118–119, 382, 390–391
   See also Injuries, preventing
Chlorpheniramine, 878

Choking, 382
   first aid for, 439–444
   on food, 308–310, 396
   Heimlich maneuver for, 442–443
   preventing, 143, 395–396
   and size of objects, 395–396
   swallowed objects and, 435–436, 439
   on toys, 395–396
   unable to cough or breathe, 439–443
Cholesterol, 305, 314–315, 316, 330
Chores, 176, 177, 224, 647
Cigarettes and secondhand smoke, 17, 48, 207, 208, 261, 386, 389, 462, 467, 471, 524, 563–564, 845
Circumcision, 67–68, 520
Clemastine, 878
Cliques, 174
Clothing, 110, 140
   caps, 32
   flame-retardant, 32, 388
   for newborns, 31–33, 69
   onesies, 28, 31–32
   preschoolers and, 161
   putting on and taking off, 69–70
   shoes, 101–102
Clotrimazole, 878

Clubs and cliques, 174

Cognitive behavioral therapy
    (CBT), 817, 862–863, 865

Colds, 38, 113, 294, 319, 459–
    467, 414, 459–467, 468
    aspirin for, 354
    complications of, 461–462
    described, 459–461
    fever in, 461–462
    medicines for, 360, 464–465
    preventing, 466–467
    things that look like colds but
        aren't, 462
    treatment for, 463–466

Cold weather, 414–415, 467

Colic, 90, 237
    crying and, 84–89
    defined, 85
    help for parents, 88–89
    medical evaluation of, 86–87
    remedies for, 87–88
    responding to, 85–86

Colitis, 509

Collarbone, broken, 434

Collections, 170

College, 210, 211–220
    academic majors and, 214
    choosing, 211–216
    costs, financial aid, loans, and
        saving for, 213, 218–220
    diversity and, 214–215
    entrance exams for, 217–218

extracurricular activities and,
    214

high school guidance
    counselors and, 216–217

location and, 213–214

religious identification and,
    214

resources for, 888

school reputation and, 215

school size and, 213

types of schools, 212–213

College Board, 218

Colostrum, 252

Compulsions, 179–180

Concerta, 829

Coneflower (echinacea), 465

Concussions, 435

Conjunctivitis (pinkeye), 112,
    515–516

Conscience, 171, 180

Constipation, 316, 496–497,
    501–505
    development of, 501
    encopresis and, 503, 765–766
    in first year, 106
    infant formulas and, 283
    lifestyle and, 502, 503–504
    in newborns, 59, 60, 61
    problems caused by, 502–503
    toilet training and, 759–760
    treatments for, 503–505
    urination and, 502, 520

Consumer Product Safety Commission, 395–396, 400, 412–413

Contagious illnesses, isolation for, 360–361

Contraception, 228, 643

Convulsions. *See* Seizures and convulsions

Cookies, 332

Corticosteroids
inhaled, 878
topical, 879

Cortisol, 467, 688, 689

Co-trimoxazole, 879

Cough, 462
in bronchitis, 479
in croup, 476, 477
swallowed objects and, 435–436, 439
See also Whooping cough

Cough medicines, 464–465, 466, 479

Cow's milk. *See* Milk, cow's

CPAP (continuous positive airway pressure), 486

Cradle, 28, 31

Cradle cap, 110

Creams and lotions, 33, 64

Creeping and crawling, 31, 93, 95–96

Crib death. *See* Sudden infant death syndrome

Cribs, 28–29, 31
toys and mobiles, 79, 560

Criticism, 539, 543, 604
effective, 603

Crohn's disease, 509

Cromolyn, 879

Croup, 113, 476–478
spasmodic, 477
treatment for, 477–478
what it looks like, 476–477

Crying, 2, 50–54
colic and, 84–89
fussy, 50, 51
hunger and, 51
reasons for, 37, 50–54
spoiling and, 37, 53
tips for comforting, 54

Cupping, 695

Cups
See also Weaning from bottle to cup
sippy, 293

Curiosity, 117, 150–151, 191–192, 193
See also Exploration

Cuts and scratches, first aid for, 423–424

Cystic fibrosis (CF), 357, 509, 897

Cysts, in mouth, 111

Cytomegalovirus (CMV), 17

Dairy products, 226, 240, 241, 304, 316–318, 320, 321, 329–330
  See also Milk, cow's
  concerns about, 323
  during illness, 356
Dark, fear of, 154
Dawdling, 124, 731–733
Day care
  See also child care
  centers, 584–585
  family, 585–586
Deafness, 897
Death, 698–701
  See also Sudden infant death syndrome
  explaining to children, 152, 155–156, 698–699
  funerals, 699–700
  grief following, 700
  of parent, child's fear of, 700–701
  religious faith and, 699
Decongestants, 465, 879–880
DEET, 418–419
Defiance, 221–222
Dehydration, 348, 355–356, 505, 508, 521
  rehydration solutions for, 356, 508, 884–885
Delivery, 18
  See also Birth
  breastfeeding and, 249

cesarean, 35, 252
children's involvement in, 25
emotional responses to, 35–36
planning, 18–19
Dental issues. *See* Teeth; Teeth, care of; Teeth, injuries to; Teething
Depression, 813, 818–821, 826, 852
  See also Suicide
  anger and, 625, 693
  bipolar disorder, 545, 819–820, 827
  causes of, 819
  in children and adolescents, 196, 224, 398, 548–549, 551, 776, 818–821
  homosexuality and, 650
  postpartum, 41–42
  signs of, 818–819
  treatments for, 820–821
Desmopressin (DDAVP), 770, 771
Development, physical, 92–99
  milestones in, 77–78
Developmental-behavioral pediatricians, 864
Developmental disorders, 161, 195
Dexedrine, 829
Dextromethorphan, 465, 880
Dextrostat, 829
DHA, 314

Diabetes, 357, 897

Diaper rash, 107–108, 522

Diapers, diapering, 52, 55–58, 144

cleaning baby, 55

cloth diapers, 52, 55–57

disposable diapers, 55–57

equipment for changing baby, 29

folding a diaper, 56–57

ointments and, 33, 108

squirming while being changed, 94–95

washing diapers, 58

when to change diapers, 55

Diaper wipes, 55, 107–108

Diarrhea, 53, 356, 371

apple-juice, 508–509

chronic, diseases causing, 509–510

in first year, 106–107

from food poisoning, 506, 507

from infections, 60, 505–506

persistent, 508–509

rash from, 108

vomiting with, 506

when to call the doctor, 348

Diet

See also Breastfeeding; Formula-feeding; Nutrition; Solid foods, starting; Vegetarian diets

of Dr. Spock, 320–325

fiber in, 261, 313, 316, 502, 503

low-fat, 240–241

typical North American, 311

Diphenhydramine (Benadryl), 487–488, 880

Diphtheria, 370, 376, 475

Disabilities

See also Intellectual disability; Learning disabilities; Special needs, children with

resources for, 897–898

Disasters, 690–692

Discipline, 597–625

See also Limits, setting; Punishment; Rewards

and asking child instead of telling, 613–614

behavior modification and, 604

at child care programs, 589

confusion about, 618–619

defined, 597–598

distractibility and redirection in, 125, 605, 614

firmness and consistency in, 600–601

good, 598–599

guilt and, 619–621

ineffective, 598

permissiveness and, 599, 616–621

positive expectations in, 604
reasons in, 614–616
rules in, 598, 601–602
in school, 184, 185
shying away from, 617–618
sticking to convictions in, 600
strict versus casual, 599
and talking about
    expectations, 604
threats in, 606–607
warnings in, 614, 615
Diseases. *See* Illness, chronic;
    Illnesses, common
    childhood
Disruptive mood dysregulation
    disorder (DMDD), 827
Divorce, 703–713
    and biasing children against
        other parent, 711–712
    children's concerns about, 705
    custody after, 707–709
    emotional responses to, 705–706
    grandparents and, 710–711
    long-term effects of, 713
    marriage counseling, 704
    parents' dating after, 712
    parents' reactions in, 706–707
    stages of separation, 703–704
    telling children about, 704–705
    visitation and, 709–710
Doctor, 20, 104, 252, 343–345,
    861

asking questions of, 344
breastfeeding and, 21–22
checkups with, 343–344
child's reactions to, 99, 141
choosing, 20–22
continuity of care and, 21
developmental milestones
    and, 78
disagreements with, 344–345
"getting to know you" visit
    with, 20–21
liking and trusting, 18, 345
second opinions and, 345
sexual questioning and, 209–
    210
telephone calls to, 345–349
Docusate, 880
Dog bites
    first aid for, 424–425
    preventing, 420–421
Dogs, 420
    fear of, 154–155, 814
Domestic violence, 16, 692–693
    resources for, 893
    stopping, 692–693
Doulas, 18–19, 22, 888
Down syndrome, 845, 857–859
    defined, 857–858
    resources for, 898
    testing for, 858
    treatment for, 858–859
Driveways, 407

Dropping and throwing things, 125–126
food, 126, 129
Drowning, 382, 384
preventing, 384–386
Drug abuse, 198, 207, 208, 262, 398, 553, 591, 830
DTaP vaccine, 376, 423, 475
Dyscalculia, 838
Dyslexia, 833–834, 835–837, 841
resources for, 898

Ear infections, 238, 291, 372, 467–472
antibiotics for, 470–471
middle-ear effusion and, 471–472
otitis media, 461, 468–472
pain in, 469–470
preventing, 471
ruptured eardrum and, 469
swimmer's ear, 472
Ears and hearing, 134, 191, 467–468, 826
earwax, 472
hearing test, 472
of newborns, 44–45, 64–65
objects in ear, 430–431
Eating disorders, 227, 793–798
as addiction, 794
anorexia nervosa, 226, 793–795, 796

bulimia, 226, 793–794, 795
preventing, 796–798
resources for, 895
sports and, 412, 797
Echinacea, 465
E. coli, 304, 505, 506
Eczema, 109, 247, 305, 323, 488–491
allergies and, 489
appearance of, 488–489
treatment for, 490–491
Education, 182
See also College; School
economic disparities and, 183–184
Eggs, 226, 239, 317, 321, 330
allergies to, 304
introducing, 305
Elbow injuries, 432
Electrical injuries, 429, 458
Electronics, 80, 135
cell phones, 134, 174, 179, 335, 656
children's dependence on, 179, 654–655
infants and, 651–652
parents' overuse of, 656
Emergencies. See First aid and emergencies
Emotional needs of children, 533–577
resources for, 888–889

self-esteem, 543–545
Emotions
  See also Anger; Depression;
    Fears; Guilt
  of father, 14–16, 40–43
  learning and, 557–558
  of mother, 14–15, 40–43
Encopresis, 503, 765–766
Enemas, 60
Environment, 552
  chemicals in, 199
  diapers and, 55
  nature, 550–552
  resources for, 893
EPA, 314
Epiglottitis, 477, 478
Epilepsy, 512, 826, 852
  resources for, 898
EpiPen (epinephrine), 438
Epstein-Barr virus, 475
Erythema toxicum, 109
Erythromycin, 881
Estrogen, 199
Exercise
  adolescents and, 227
  breast-feeding and, 259
  constipation and, 502, 503
Exploration, 2, 134, 551
  safety and, 117–121, 381
Eye problems, 111–112, 514–
    516, 826
  blocked tear duct, 111

conjunctivitis (pinkeye), 112,
    515–516
crossed eyes, 112, 514
harmful fluids in eye, 437–438
lazy eye, 112
nearsightedness (myopia),
    514–515
objects in the eye, 431
ointments and drops for,
    360
reasons to see a doctor, 514
styes, 516
walleyes, 514
Eyes and vision, 92, 191
  behaviors that affect vision,
    516
  eye-hand coordination, 92
  eye protection, 411, 417
  in newborns, 45, 64–65

Fahrenheit, 353
  See also Thermometers
Fainting, 519
Falls, 382
  See also Head injuries
  playgrounds and, 409–410
  preventing injuries from,
    398–399
  rolling over and, 93–94, 435
  stairs and, 399
  walkers and, 30, 103, 399
  from windows, 399

Families, 661–677
  See also Adoption; Gay and
    lesbian parents; Parents;
    Single-parent families;
    Stepfamilies
  birth order dynamics in,
    547–548
  challenges and, 7–9
  global mobility and, 8–9
Family and Medical Leave Act
    (FMLA), 580
Family day care, 585–586
Family social service agencies, 862
Family therapists, 866
Fathers, 541–542
  childbirth and, 18–19, 24
  child care by, 580
  and child's favoritism toward
    mother, 142
  domestic violence and, 16
  family leave for, 580
  feelings of, 14–16, 40–43
  gender awareness and, 146–147,
    538–539
  parenting responsibility in,
    541–542
  as single parents, 670–671
Fatigue
  in babies, 53
  in preschoolers, 165–166
Fats and oils, 240–241, 311,
    313–314, 320, 321, 329

cholesterol, 305, 314–315,
    316, 330
  infants and low-fat diets, 241
  omega-3 fatty acids, 314,
    323, 328
  omega-6 fatty acids, 314
  saturated, 313–314, 315,
    328, 330
  unsaturated, 313–314
  trans fats, 313–314, 329
FDA (Food and Drug
    Administration), 281
Fears, 814
  See also Anxiety
  of animals, 154–155
  of bath, 123
  of bedtime separation, 136–137
  of body differences and
    injury, 156–159, 202–203
  of the dark, 154
  of death, 152, 155–156
  helping child cope with, 138–
    139, 153–154
  imaginary worries, 152–153
  lying and, 178
  at one year, 122–124
  overprotectiveness and, 139–140
  play and, 153
  in preschoolers, 152–156
  of sounds and sights, 122
  of strangers, 99–100, 117,
    123–124

tantrums and, 141

in two-year-olds, 136–140

of water, 155

of wetting the bed, 137–138

Feeding and eating

See also Breastfeeding; Bottle-
feeding; Feeding and eating
problems; Feeding in the
first year; Meals; Nutrition;
Solid foods, starting

appetite changes, 128, 245

choking prevention and,
308–310

food choices and fads, 143–144

independence in, 81, 140

as learning experience, 128–129

planning for, during
pregnancy, 19–20

playing with food, 81, 245–
246

preschoolers and, 161

resources for, 889–890

socializing and, 129

spoons and, 81, 241–242,
243

toddlers and, 128–129

weight and growth and, 128

Feeding and eating problems,
152, 777–798

See also Eating disorders

bribes, threats, and acts as
persuasion in, 782–783

development of, 777–778

gagging, 785–786

illness and, 356–357

needing to be fed, 783–785

parents' feelings about, 778

pickiness, 779–781

and serving less than they will
eat, not more, 781

and staying in the room, 782

teething and, 238

thinness, 786–788

throwing food, 126, 129

treating, 779

Feeding in the first year, 38, 46,
231–246

See also Bottle-feeding;
Breastfeeding; Hunger

baby's needs and, 231–232

cereal in, 245

changes and challenges in,
244–246

choosiness in, 245

decisions in, 80–81, 231

emotional closeness and, 81

getting enough and gaining
weight, 236–238

giving up control, 242–244

independence in, 81

making messes and, 241

night feedings, 234–235, 251

refusing vegetables, 244–245

schedules for, 232–234

Feeding in the first year (*cont.*):
  self-feeding, 241–244
  slowing down after six
    months, 244
  table manners and, 244
  when to feed, 232–235
Feelings. *See* Emotions
Feet
  bowlegs, toeing in, and toeing
    out, 97–99
  flat, 517
  pain in, 517
  shoes for, 101–102
Ferrous sulfate, ferrous
    fumarate, 881
Fetal development, 13–14
Fever, 53, 346–347, 349–355,
    357, 370, 371, 372
  See also Thermometers
  aspirin and, 354
  cause of, 351
  colds with, 461–462
  how long to keep taking
    temperature, 353
  joint pain with, 518
  in newborns, 346
  normal body temperature
    fluctuations versus, 349–351
  seizures with, 353–354, 513
  taking temperature and, 351–
    353
  treatment for, 354–355

Fever, scarlet, 474–475
Fiber, 261, 313, 316, 502, 503
Fire, 386–389
  See also Burns
Fireworks, 421
First aid and emergencies, 423–
    445
  allergic reactions, 438
  bites, 424–425
  bleeding, 426–427
  burns, 428–429
  choking, 439–444
  convulsions and seizures, 439
  cuts and scratches, 423–424
  elbow injury in toddlers, 432
  electrical injuries, 429
  emergency telephone
    numbers, 444
  equipment for, 445
  fractures, 432–434
  harmful fluids in eye, 437–
    438
  head injuries, 435
  Heimlich maneuver, 442–
    443
  insect bites, 425
  kit for, 444–445
  neck and back injuries, 434
  nosebleeds, 427
  objects in nose or ears, 430–
    431
  objects in the eye, 431

poisons, 436–438

rescue breathing, 443–444

resources for, 891

skin infections, 430

splinters, 424

sprains and strains, 431–432

swallowed objects, 435–436, 439

First year (birth to about three months). *See* Newborns

First year (four to twelve months), 77–114

See also Feeding and eating

breathing troubles in, 113–114

caring for your baby in, 79–80

car seats and, 52

common physical issues in, 104–114

constipation in, 106

crying and colic in, 84–89

developmental milestones in, 77–78

diarrhea in, 106–107

electronics in, 80

eye troubles in, 111–112

growth in, 82

hiccups in, 104

learning and exploration in, 77

mealtime behavior in, 81

mouth troubles in, 110–111

physical development in, 92–99

play in, 79–80

playpens in, 31, 102–103

rashes in, 107–110

shoes in, 101–102

sleep in, 82–84

spitting up and vomiting in, 104–106

spoiling in, 79, 89–92

strangers and, 99–101

swings and, 29–30, 103

when to call the doctor, 104

Fish, 17, 261, 304, 305, 314, 316, 317, 322, 328–329, 332

mercury in, 17, 328, 395

Fish oils, 314

Flame retardants, 17, 32, 388

Flaxseed, 314

Flowers, poisonous, 392

Flu

See also Influenza

stomach, 60, 505–506

Flunisolide oral inhalation, 881

Fluoride, 24, 240, 451–452, 456

Fluticasone nasal or oral inhalation, 881

Fontanel, 38, 65–66

Food
  allergies to, 53, 304–305,
    306, 323, 891
  choking on, 308–310, 396
  poisoning from, 506, 507
  See also Feeding and eating;
    Nutrition; *specific food types*
Football, 411
Formula-feeding, 19, 20, 34,
    80–81, 247, 279–295,
    297, 299
  See also Feeding and eating;
    Feeding in the first year
  amount of formula in, 280
  baby half-finishing, 289–290
  basics of, 280
  bottle propping and, 286,
    396
  bowel movements and, 59
  breastfeeding combined with,
    250
  breastfeeding versus, 247
  changing formula, 52–53, 88,
    105
  choosing formula, 279–283
  clogged nipple holes and, 288
  cow's-milk formula, 281
  do-it-yourself formulas, 281
  equipment for, 34
  and falling asleep, 289, 290
  falling asleep with bottle in
    mouth, 291, 776

  fussing and, 290
  getting babies to take more,
    288–289
  giving the bottle, 285–286
  heating a bottle in the
    microwave, 285–286
  iron in formula, 106, 240,
    281, 283, 317
  liquid, concentrate, and
    powder formulas, 282
  love in, 286
  mixing and diluting formula,
    280, 282
  nipple hole size and, 287–
    288, 290
  overfeeding, 287
  position for, 286, 471
  preparing formula, 279–283
  problems with, 286–291
  reasons for, 279
  saving and refrigerating
    formula, 283–284
  soy-based formula, 281–282
  specialized formulas, 281–
    282
  spitting up and, 287
  sterilizing, 280, 282, 284–286
  teething and, 238
  temperature of, 282, 285–286
  vitamin D in, 71, 239
  washing equipment, 284
  weaning from, 291–295

Fourth of July, 421

Fractures, 432–434

Fragile X, 898

Freud, Sigmund, 646–647

Friendships, 174, 203–204

   see also Social lives of children

Frostbite, 414

Fruit juices, 106, 251, 331

   diarrhea and, 508–509

   prune, 60, 106, 302, 303

Fruits, 226, 240, 245, 261,

   316, 329, 332, 336

   bowel movements and, 502,

   503

   introducing, 300, 301, 302–

   303, 307, 308

   phytochemicals in, 320

   prunes, 60, 106, 302, 303,

   307, 503

Funerals, 699–700

Gagging, 785–786

Games, 169–170, 178–179,

   561

Gastroenteritis (stomach

   infections), 60, 505–506

Gastroesophageal reflux disease

   (GERD), 52, 53, 105,

   506–507

Gay and lesbian parents, 7, 540,

   645, 675–677

   adoption and, 664

   effects on children, 676

   heterosexual parents' concerns

     about, 676–677

   resources for, 894

   support for, 676

Gender differences and roles,

   537–541, 645

   child's awareness of, 146–147,

   157–159, 538–539, 631,

   638

   chores and, 176, 647

   cultural changes and, 537–538

Gender dysphoria, 648

Gender identity, 538

   See also Sexual orientation

   brain and, 645–646, 647–648

   development of, 646–647

   gender fluidity and

     transgender, 647–649

   nonconformity, 645–650

   parents and, 645–646

   suicide and, 646, 650

Gender of unborn baby, 15, 17

Genes, 13, 545–546

   anxiety disorders and, 816

   experience and, 555–556

   mental health problems and,

   545–546

   obesity and, 789–790

Genetic disorders, 845, 857–859

   See also Down syndrome

   phenylketonuria, 845, 858

Genital problems, 520–523
sore on penis, 521–522
testicle, 523–524
vaginal discharge, 522–523
warts, 372
Genitals
child's awareness of gender
differences in, 157–159,
638
gender assignment and, 647
masturbation, 205, 637,
638–639, 642
terms for, 632
GERD. *See* Gastroesophageal
reflux disease
German measles (rubella), 371,
376, 844–845
Glucose, 313
Gluten, 327–328, 509–510
Glyphosate, 261
Grains, 226, 245, 261, 297,
311, 313, 316, 317, 326–
328, 332, 335, 336, 502
See also Cereals
Grandparents, 22, 337, 627–630
as caregivers, 86, 584, 629
and divorce of parents, 710–
711
medications of, 383, 391
as parents (custodial
grandparents), 630
resources for, 894

sibling rivalry and, 808
tensions between parents and,
627–629
Greenfield, Marjorie, 268
Grief
over death, 700
in parents of special needs
children, 680–681
Groups
cliques, 174
common-interest, 172
Growing pains, 516–517
Growth, 82, 128
Guaifenesin, 881
Guilt, 5, 36, 86, 139
anger and, 624
baby's gender and, 15
and child with special needs,
681
discipline and, 619–621
labor and delivery and, 35
Gum, 453, 470
Guns, 223–224, 397–398, 819
Gymnastics, 412, 797

Habits, 737–747
See also Stuttering; Thumb-
sucking
compulsions, 179–180
nail-biting, 744–745
nervous, 179–181
rhythmic, 743

ruminating, 742–743
stroking and hair pulling, 742
Halloween, 421–422
Handedness, 93
Hands, using, 92–93
Handwashing, 131, 361, 466, 763
Harnesses, 121
Hay fever, 486
Headaches, 371, 372, 510–511
migraine, 511
when to call the doctor, 510
Head banging habit, 743
Head injuries
concussion in, 435
first aid for, 435
from sports, 410–411
when to call the doctor, 348
Head lice, 495
Hearing. See Ears and hearing
Heartburn, 53
Heart disease, 128, 143, 247, 311, 314, 315, 320, 323
Heart murmurs, 518–519
Heart problems, 518–519
Heat cramps, 415
Heat exhaustion, 415
Heat rash, 415
Heat stroke, 415
Heavy metals, 17, 261, 328–329
See also Lead poisoning; Mercury

Heimlich maneuver, 442–443
Helmets
bicycle, 382, 407–408, 409
multisport, 412–413
Help, psychological. See Therapy
Hepatitis A, 371, 376
Hepatitis B, 371, 376
Heredity. See Genes
Hernias
groin, 523–524
umbilical, 74
Hib (Haemophilus influenzae type B), 371, 373, 376, 478
Hiccups, 104
High chairs, 94
Hip pain, 517
HIV (human immunodeficiency virus), 67, 279, 526–527
See also AIDS
Hives (urticaria), 438, 492
Homecoming of newborn, 25–26
preparation for, 22–24
Home safety
See also Childproofing
equipment for, 386, 400–401
Homework, 189–191
Homosexuality, 205–206, 209–210, 538, 645, 649–650, 677
homophobia and, 205, 649–650

Homosexual parents. *See* Gay and lesbian parents

Honey, 454, 465, 466

Hookworms, 500

Hormones, 13, 39
  birthmarks and, 72
  breastfeeding and, 247–248, 249, 253
  in foods, 324, 328
  infant formulas and, 282
  oxytocin, 247–248, 249, 263, 271
  puberty and, 199
  and swollen breasts in newborns, 74
  and vaginal discharge in newborns, 75

Hormone treatments, 202

Hospitalization, 362–366
  anesthesia in, 364–365
  late reactions to, 365–366
  parental visits and, 365
  preview programs and, 363
  when and what to tell your child about, 363–364
  worries about, 362–363

Hot weather, 415–416

Housework, 22

HPV (human papillomavirus), 372, 376

Humidifiers, 69, 463–464

Hunger, 288, 299, 787

breastfeeding and, 51, 253, 257–258

Hydroceles, 523–524

Hydrocortisone cream or ointment, 882

Hydroxyzine, 882

Hyperactivity, 823–824
  See also ADHD

Hyperlexia, 851

Hyperpigmentation, 72

Hypertrophic cardiomyopathy (HCM), 519

Hypothermia, 414

Hypothyroidism, 501

Ibuprofen, 354, 882, 884
  RICE, 517

Illnesses, common childhood, 459–529
  See also specific illnesses and symptoms
  caring for a sick child, 366–368
  contagious, isolation for, 360–361
  diet during, 355–357
  feeding problems at end of, 357
  getting back to normal after, 367–368
  giving medicine, 358–360
  limiting spread of, 361

Imaginary friends, 151
Imaginary worries, 152–153
Imagination, 134, 150–151, 550, 576
Imipramine, 770
Imitation
learning by, 133–134
of parents, 145–146, 599
Immunizations, 369–380
autism and, 374–375
body comfort during shots, 378
boosters, 377
distracting child during shots, 379–380
giving child choices during shots, 379
helping child cope with shots, 378–380
herd immunity and, 372
historical perspective on, 369
how vaccines are made, 374
how vaccines work, 369–372
illnesses prevented by, 370–372
medications for pain of, 378
mercury in, 374
primary series of, 377
record-keeping for, 378
risks of, 373–375
safety of, 374
schedule for, 375–378
side effects of, 373
talking to child about, 379
Vaccine Information Statements, 375
weighing risks and benefits of, 373
Impetigo, 110, 492–493
Impulsivity, 823–824
See also ADHD
Inattention, 823–824, 826
See also ADHD
Independence, 152–153
in adolescence, 197, 203, 206, 210, 211, 220, 591
in school-age children, 170–172
in toddlers, 116–117
in two-year-olds, 137
Individuals with Disabilities Education Act (IDEA), 839–841, 846–847
Individuation, 115
Infants. See First year (four to twelve months); Newborns
Infections, 247, 317, 372
See also Ear infections; Intestinal infections
bladder and kidney, 520
breast (mastitis), 273
stomach, 60, 505–506
skin, 430
yeast (thrush), 110–111

Inflammatory bowel disease
(IBD), 375, 509
Influenza (flu), 372, 462, 481–482
aspirin for, 354, 528
H1N1 "swine flu," 481
preventing, 481–482
symptoms of, 481
treatment for, 482
vaccine for, 372, 377, 481,
482
Injuries, preventing, 381–422
See also Choking; Poisons,
poisoning
"accidents" and, 382
air travel and, 404–405
bicycles and, 407–408
car rides and, 401–404
child's age and, 382
cold weather, 414–415
dog bites, 420–421
in driveways, 407
falls, 398–399
from fire, smoke, and burns,
386–389
from fireworks, 421
guns and, 223–224, 397–
398, 819
at Halloween, 421–422
at home, 383–401
home safety equipment, 386,
400–401
hot weather, 415–416

insect bites, 418–420
to mouth and teeth, 457–458
outside the home, 401–409
playground, 409–410
principles of, 382–383
from sports, 410–413, 458
strangulation, 397, 409
in streets, 405–407
stressful times and, 383
suffocation, 70, 382, 397
sun safety, 71
supervision and, 383
toys and, 400
Injuries, treatment for. See First
aid and emergencies
In-line skating, 412–413, 458
Insect bites and stings
bee stings, 419, 425
first aid for, 425
preventing, 418–420
Insecticides, 17
Insect repellents, 418–419
Insomnia, 774–776
difficulty falling asleep, 774–
775
midnight waking, 775–776
Institute of Medicine, 502
Insulin, 313
Intellectual disability (ID),
843–848
in adolescence and
adulthood, 847–848

autism and, 851
causes of, 844–845
diagnosis of, 843–844
early intervention and, 846
labels and stigma around, 843
laws and, 846
resources for, 898
severe, 847
what children need, 845–846
Intelligence
See also Thinking
brain and, 564–565
IQ tests, 227, 392, 564, 833,
839, 844
learning disabilities and, 833–
834
multiple intelligences, 564–
565
International Board Certified
Lactation Consultant
(IBCLC), 252
International Childbirth
Education Association, 252
Internet, 553
pornography on, 658–659
safety and, 656–658
social connection and, 660
Intestinal infections, 60, 505–
506
appendicitis, 358, 498
Intestinal parasites (worms),
499–501

Intestines
hernias and, 523–524
obstruction in, 499
Intussusception, 499
Iodine (antiseptic), 429
Iodine (dietary), 317, 330–331
IPV polio vaccine, 376
IQ tests, 227, 392, 564, 833,
839, 844
Iron, 106, 240, 261, 300, 317,
322, 323, 393
in breast milk, 317
in formulas, 106, 240, 281,
283, 317
sources of, 317, 322
supplements, 317, 389, 881
in vegetarian diets, 322
Irritable bowel syndrome (IBS),
509
It's Not Forsythia, It's for Me
(Needlman), 163
IUDs (intrauterine devices),
228

Jaundice, 73
Joints, 516–518
sprains and strains, 431–432

Ketoconazole lotion or cream,
882
Kidney infections, 520
Kindergarten. *See* Preschool

Kitty litter, 17
Knee pain, 517

Labor. *See* Delivery
Laboratory Schools, 163
Lactation consultants, 21–22,
    249, 252, 254, 259, 267
Lactose, 323
La Leche League, 252
Language, 536, 556
    See also Reading aloud
    autism and, 849–850, 851–852
    books in teaching, 570–571
    bilingual families, 9, 567
    caregiver and, 583
    delay in, and tantrums, 720–
        721
    two-year-olds and, 134, 135
    understanding words, 560
Language therapists, 866–867
Latchkey children, 590–591
Laxatives, 60, 226, 436, 505, 793
Lead poisoning, 17, 382, 392–
        395, 501
    from paint, 23, 28–29, 80,
        392–394, 450
    from water, 284–285, 393, 394
    resources for, 898–899
Leads, wrist, 121
Learning
    See also Thinking
    brain and, 555–558

electronics and, 135
emotion and, 557–558
imitation and, 133–134
multiple intelligences and,
    564–565
preschool and, 160
styles of, 572
two-year-olds and, 134
Learning disabilities (LDs),
    191, 833–842
    See also Dyslexia
    ADHD and, 191, 827
    assessment of, 838–839
    intelligence and, 833–834
    laws and, 839–841
    lead poisoning and, 382,
        392
    resources for, 889
    treatments for, 841–842
    understanding, 833–834
    what it feels like to have,
        834–835
Left-handedness, 93
Lesbian parents. *See* Gay and
    lesbian parents
Libraries, 574
Lice, head, 495
Licensed clinical social worker
    (LCSW), 865
Licensed professional counselor
    (LPC), 866
Lidocaine, 450

Limits, setting, 544
  for adolescents, 206, 220, 591
  firmness and friendliness and, 611–612
  love and, 533–534
  single parents and, 669–670
  tips for, 611–616
  for toddlers, 119–121
  for two-year-olds, 140–141
Linoleic acid (LA), 314
Listening skills, 576
Literacy, 183, 566
  learning to read, 186–187
  See also Reading aloud
Lockjaw (tetanus), 370, 376, 423
Loperamide, 882
Loratadine, 883
Lotions and creams, 33, 64
Love, 544, 618–619
  for baby, 15
  bonding and, 35–36, 39
  enjoying, 544
  limits and, 533–534
Lycopene, 320
Lying, 177–178
Lyme disease, 419
Lymph nodes, swollen, 476

Make-believe play, 151, 153, 169, 576
Manic-depressive disorder. *See* Bipolar disorder

Manners, 621–622
  school-age children and, 171–172
  table manners, 129, 161, 171, 244, 545, 603
  two-year-olds and, 134
  for young children, 622
Margarine, 329
Marriage counseling, 704
Mastitis, 273
Masturbation, 205, 637, 638–639, 642
Matches, 388
Maternity leave, 40, 579–580
Math, 177, 190, 838
Mattresses, 28, 29
MCV (meningococcus vaccine), 376
Meals, 335, 451
  behavior at, 81
  breakfast, 333
  dinner, 333–334
  lunch, 333, 334
  simple, 332–335
  at six to twelve months, 307–310
  snacks between, 143, 226, 337–339, 451
  suggested, 332–334
  table manners and, 129, 161, 171, 244, 545
Measles, 370–371, 375, 376

Measles, German (rubella), 371, 376, 844–845

Measles, mumps and rubella vaccine (MMR), 374, 376

Meatless dishes, 322

Meats, 226, 241, 261, 304, 309, 315–318, 320–322, 328, 332, 502
ground beef, 328
preparation and cooking of, 304, 322, 328, 506

Meconium, 58

Media, 651–660
See also Electronics; Internet; Television

Medical issues, 343–368
See also Doctor; Hospitalization; Illnesses, common childhood; specific issues

Medical supplies, 33–34

Medications, 358–360, 826, 869–871
See also Antibiotics
administering, 358–359
breastfeeding and, 258, 262, 279
for colds, 360
generic prescriptions, 360
glossary of, 873–886
left-over, 358
over-the-counter, 360
pill-taking fears, 359

poisoning from, 383, 390, 391, 392
prescribing terminology for, 870–871
resources for, 891
safety with, 869–970

Medline Plus, 890

Melanin, 416

Melatonin, 774–775

Memory skills, 838

Meningitis, 371, 372

Meningococcal disease, 371

Meningococcus vaccine (MCV), 376

Menstruation, 228
breastfeeding and, 238, 262–263
in puberty, 198, 200, 641–642

Mental health
See also Therapy
adolescence and, 198
hereditary influences on, 545–546
neighborhood and peer influences on, 548–549
resources for, 892–894, 895–896

Mercury, 395
in fish, 17, 328, 395
in glass thermometers, 33, 352, 395
in vaccines, 374

Messiness, 729–731
  around the house, 730–731
  messy room, 731
Metadate, 829
Methylphenidate, 829
Metoclopramide, 883
Miconazole, 883
Microwave use, 285–286
Midwives, 18, 20
Migraine headaches, 511
Milestones, developmental,
    77–78
Milia, 108
Milk, breast. See Breastfeeding;
    Breast milk
Milk, cow's, 128, 143, 226,
    240, 245, 281, 305, 329–
    330, 466
  bone health and, 316, 317,
    324
  breastfeeding and, 260
  calcium and, 324, 330
  concerns about, 81, 323–324
  cow's-milk formula versus,
    281
  iron needs and, 323
  sensitivities to, 60–61, 323,
    502
Milk, nondairy
  almond, 128, 260, 324
  soy, 128, 260, 261, 281, 324
Milk stains, 104–105

Milk sugar (lactose), 323
Mineral oil, 33, 64, 504
Minerals, 261, 297, 316–318
    See also Calcium; Iron
  iodine, 317, 330–331
  zinc, 261, 317, 465
MMR (measles, mumps, and
    rubella) vaccine, 374, 376
Mold, 23
Moles, 72
Money and allowances, 177
Mononucleosis, 475
Montelukast, 883
Mosquitoes, 384, 419
  West Nile virus and, 528
  Zika virus and, 17, 419, 529
Mothers
  feelings of, 14–15, 40–43
  gender awareness and, 146–
    147, 538–539
  as single parents, 670
Mothers, working. See Working
    parents
Motion, need for, 52
Motivations of others, child's
    figuring out, 562
Motrin. See Ibuprofen
Mouth guards for sports, 411,
    458
Mouthing objects, 79–80
  first aid for swallowed objects,
    435–436, 439

Mouth problems, 110–111
See also Teeth, care of; Teeth, injuries to
cysts, 111
swelling, and anaphylaxis, 438
thrush, 110–111
MRSA, 493
Mucus
in bowel movement, 60–61, 302
in nose, 33–34, 65, 69, 113, 347, 475
in nose, bulb suction for, 463
in vagina, 75
Mumps, 371, 376
Mupirocin ointment, 884
Muscular dystrophy, 899
Mutism, selective, 155, 815, 899
Mycoplasma, 462
Myopia, 514–515

Nail-biting, 744–745
Nails, cutting, 33, 65
Naproxen, 884
Naps, 47, 83, 126–127, 151, 165
National Association for the Education of Young Children (NAEYC), 589
National Coalition Against Domestic Violence, 693
National Domestic Violence Hotline, 692–693

National Education Association, 189–190
National Highway Traffic Safety Administration, 402
National Parent Teacher Association, 189–190, 889
National Poison Control Center hotline, 348, 390, 392, 436, 437, 444, 891
National Research Council, 187
Natural world, 550–552
Nature versus nurture, 6–7
Navels of newborns, 61, 64, 66, 74
Nearsightedness, 514–515
Neck injuries, 434
Negativism, 115–116, 140–141
Nervous habits, 179–180
tics, 180–181
Newborns (birth to about three months), 35–76, 534
bathing, 61–64
being with, 44
birthmarks on, 72–73
blue fingers and toes in, 73
body parts of, 64–68
bonding with, 35–36, 39
bowel movements in, 58–61
breast swelling in, 74
breathing problems in, 73–74
buying things before birth of, 26–34

caring for, 44–45

car seats for, 38, 52

challenges of, 36–37

checklist of things you'll need
    for, 27

clothing for, 31–33, 69

common concerns, 72–76

ears, eyes, mouth, and nose
    of, 64–65

extra help and, 22

fever in, 346

fontanel (soft spot) of, 38,
    65–66

homecoming, preparation for,
    22–24

individuality of, 45

jaundice in, 73

meeting needs of, 37–38

nail trimming, 33, 65

navel of, 61, 64, 66, 74

penis of, 55, 67

reading to, 568

room temperature for, 48,
    68–69, 70

senses of, 44–45

sleep and, 38, 46–49

spoiling and, 37, 53

startles and jittery movements
    in, 75–76

sun exposure and, 71

temperature and fresh air for,
    70–71

touch and, 38–39, 51–52

umbilical hernia in, 74

undescended testicles in, 75

vaginal discharge in, 75

visitors and, 23

working mothers and, 39–40

worries about, 38, 40

Night feedings, 234–235

Nightmares, 149, 152

Night terrors, 152, 773, 774

9/11 attacks, 690, 691

Nitrate salts, 24

No, saying, 120–121, 140–141

Nocturnal emissions (wet
    dreams), 205, 642

Nonsteroidal anti-
    inflammatories (NSAIDS),
    884

Nose

    allergies, 486–488, 489

    allergy treatments, 487–488

    blowing, 361, 466

    mucus in, 33–34, 65, 69,
        113, 347, 475

    mucus in, bulb suction for,
        463

    of newborns, 64–65

    nosebleeds, 427

    nose drops and, 463

    objects in, 430–431

Nose syringe, 33–34

Nudity, parental, 639–640

Nurse home visits, 22–23

Nurse practitioners, 20, 343

Nursery school. *See* Preschool

Nursing. *See* Breastfeeding

Nutrition, 311–339, 393

　See also Diet; *specific food types and nutrients;* Solid foods, starting

　adolescents and, 199, 225–226

　calories, 312, 313, 321

　fundamentals of, 311–320

　healthy eating habits, establishing, 312, 322

　resources for, 889–890

　teeth and, 450–451

　tips for happy eating, 335–339

　two-year-olds and, 143–144

　what to cook, 326–332

Nuts and nut butters, 304, 305, 309, 314, 317, 321, 329

　peanut, 304, 305, 309, 315, 327, 396

Oats, 316, 327

Obesity, 201, 227, 247, 311, 319, 320, 486, 551, 553, 788–793

　causes of, 789–791

　defined, 789

　extreme measures for, 792–793

　poverty and, 787, 790–791

　what parents can do about, 791–792

Object permanence, 559

Obsessive-compulsive disorder (OCD), 545, 815

Obstetricians, 18, 20

Occupational therapists, 866–867

Oils, baby, 33, 64

Oils in diet. *See* Fats and oils

Ointments, 33, 108

Omega-3 fatty acids, 314, 323, 328

Omega-6 fatty acids, 314

Omeprazole, 884

Oral rehydration solutions, 356, 508, 884–885

Orphanages, 535–536

Osgood-Schlatter disease, 517

Osteoporosis, 316, 320

Otitis externa, 472

Otitis media, 461, 468–472

　See also Ear infections

Outdoor play, 551

Overprotectiveness, 139–140

Overstimulation, 54

Overweight, 502, 787

　See also Obesity

Oxytocin, 247–248, 249, 263, 271

Pacifiers, 34, 250, 287

Pain

growing pains, 516–517

when to call the doctor, 347–348

Panic attacks, 815

Parasites, intestinal (worms), 499–501

Parenting

  See also Discipline

  and accepting the child you have, 6–7

  ADHD and, 826

  authoritative, 618–619

  autism and, 849, 852

  avoiding sibling comparisons and typecasting, 800–801

  building child's self-esteem, 543–545

  community choice and, 549

  effects of early care, 535–537

  family types and challenges, 7–9

  giving children equal love but different treatment, 799–800

  global mobility and, 8–9

  goals and expectations in, 3, 7

  how much to tell child about their own early behavior, 207–208

  learning, 2–3

  nature versus nurture and, 6–7

  overprotectiveness, 139–140

  respect and, 220–221, 544–545

  self-sacrifice in, 5

  special-needs children and, 9

  styles of, 618–619

  and thinking about own childhood and parents, 2, 8, 9

  and trusting yourself, 1–3

Parents

  See also Anger in parent; Fathers; Gay and lesbian parents; Mothers; Single-parent families

  child as best friend of, 670

  children's imitation of, 145–146, 599

  children's romantic feelings toward, 147–150, 152, 639–640

  competitive feelings between children and, 539–540

  conflicts between, 134

  favoritism of one child for one parent, 142–143

  and feeling differently about each child, 547

  feelings of, 2, 85–86

  and gender identity of children, 645–646

  needs of, 3–5

  nudity and modesty of, 639–640

Parents (*cont.*):
preschoolers' devotion to, 145–147
relationship between, 5
school and, 188–189, 889
sexual relationship between, 5, 43
teachers and, 188, 192, 193–194
Parents and Friends of Lesbians and Gays (PFLAG), 210
Parking lots, 405
PCV13 (pneumococcus vaccine), 376
Peanuts and peanut butter, 304, 305, 309, 315, 327, 396
Pedestrian safety, 405–407
Pediatrician. *See* Doctor
Peekaboo, 559, 569
Peers, 172, 548–549
See also Social lives of children
Penicillin, 885
Penis
adolescence and, 201
circumcision, 67–68, 520
diapering and, 55
foreskin of, 67
of newborns, 55, 67
sores on, 521–522
Penis envy theory, 646
Peritonitis, 498
Permissiveness, 599, 616–621
Personality. *See* Temperament

and personality
Pertussis (whooping cough), 370, 374, 462
Pesticides, 199, 261
Phenylephrine, 885
Phenylketonuria, 845, 858
Phones, 134, 174, 179, 335
Phthalates, 17
Physical education, 187–188
Physical therapists, 866–867
Physician. *See* Doctor
Physicians' assistants (PAs), 343
Phytochemicals, 320
Phytoestrogens, 282
Piaget, Jean, 558, 560–561, 563, 564
Pimples. *See* Acne
Pinkeye (conjunctivitis), 112, 515–516
Pinworms, 499–501
Plants, poisonous, 392
poison ivy, 493
Plastic bags, 397
Play
fears and, 153
in first year, 79–80
games, 169–170, 178–179, 561
make-believe, 151, 153, 169, 576
outdoor, 551
preschoolers and, 151, 153
two-year-olds and, 135

Playgrounds, 409–410

"Playing doctor," 639, 696

Playpens, 31, 102–103

Pneumococcus, pneumococcal disease, 372, 461

Pneumococcus vaccine, 376

Pneumonia, 350, 370, 372, 461, 480–481

Poison ivy, 493

Poisons, poisoning, 119, 381
  See also Lead poisoning; Mercury
  first aid for, 436–438
  food poisoning, 506, 507
  medications, 383, 390, 391, 392
  plants and flowers, 392, 493
  poison control hotline, 348, 390, 392, 436, 437, 444, 891
  preventing injuries from, 389–392
  skin contact with, 437

Polio (poliomyelitis), 369, 371, 376

Politeness. See Manners

Political activism and social justice, 550, 894

Polymyxin B, 885

Pool safety, 385

Popularity, 172, 173–174
  clubs and cliques, 174

unpopular children, 172, 194–196, 548–549, 612

Pornography, 658–659

Postpartum depression, 41–42

Post-traumatic stress disorder (PTSD), 688

Posture, 181–182

Potty talk, 722

Poverty, 183, 706
  overweight and, 787, 790–791

Powders, 33, 64, 109

Praise, 543–544, 565, 602, 604
  effective, 603

Pregnancy, 13–34
  chemical exposure during, 16–17
  choosing baby's doctor during, 20–22
  consulting with doctor before, 16
  father's feelings during, 14–16
  fetal development, 13–14
  helping siblings cope with, 24–26
  likelihood of, during breastfeeding, 262–263
  mixed feelings about, 14–15
  planning during, 16–20
  prenatal care, 17–18
  preparing for baby's homecoming, 22–24

Preschool, 138, 139, 159–167
  child care versus, 159–160
  first days at, 164–165
  pressures in, 166–167
  reactions at home, 165–166
  readiness for, 160–161
  as school, 159
  siblings' starting before baby's
    arrival, 24–25
  what children learn in, 162–163
Preschoolers (three to five
    years), 145–167
  biting by, 725–726
  body differences and injury,
    worries about, 156–159
  curiosity and imagination in,
    150–151
  devotion to parents in, 145–147
  fascination with babies in, 147
  fears in, 152–156
  gender awareness in, 146–
    147, 157–159
  reading with, 572–575
  romantic feelings toward
    parents, 147–150, 152,
    639–640
  separation anxiety in, 165
  sleep and, 151–152
  and television and videos,
    151, 152, 153
Prickly heat, 109–110
Protein, 297, 311, 312, 313, 315

  requirements for, 315
  vegetarian sources of, 303–
    304, 322
Prunes and prune juice, 60,
    106, 302, 303, 307, 503
Pseudoephedrine, 465, 886
Psychiatrists, 864
Psychoanalysts, 865–866
Psychologists, 864–865
PTA, 188, 189–190, 889
Puberty, 197, 198–202
  age of, 199, 200, 201
  in boys, 199, 200–202, 642
  in girls, 198–200, 641–642
Pubic hair, 200, 201
Public Health Service, 375
Punishment, 597, 601–611
  See also Discipline
  natural or logical, 610
  necessity of, 605–606
  nonphysical, 608–609
  overreliance on, 610–611
  physical (spanking), 589,
    597, 607–608, 694–695
  rewards and, 602–603
  time-outs, 608–610
Pyloric stenosis, 507
Pyrethrins and Pyrethrum, 886

Rabies, 425
Ranitidine, 886
Rashes, 53, 107, 491–494

See also Eczema
on body, 109–110
chicken pox, 372, 376, 528
cradle cap (seborrhea), 110
dangerous, 491–492
diaper rash, 107–108, 522
diarrhea and, 108
on face, 108–109
heat rash, 415
hives, 438, 492
impetigo, 110, 492–493
measles, 370–371, 375, 376
newborns and, 64
poison ivy, 493
prickly heat, 109–110
ringworm, 494
roseola, 350
scabies, 493–494
on scalp, 109–110
scarlet fever, 474–475
when to call the doctor, 108, 348–349
Reactive airways disease, 483
Reading and literacy, 183, 566
dyslexia and, 833–834, 835–837, 841
learning, 186–187
Reading aloud, 566–577
with babies, 568–569
bilingual families and, 567
to older children, 575–577
to preschoolers, 572–575

to toddlers, 569–571
vocabulary and, 569, 573, 576
Rebellion, 171–172, 220
Red Cross, 439, 592, 891
Rehydration solutions, 356, 508, 884–885
Relationships, 2, 534–535
See also Social lives of children
early, 534–537
trust and, 534–535, 536
Religion, 8, 156, 631, 649, 677
college and, 214
death and, 699
Repetition, 557
Rescue breathing, 443–444
Resource guide, 887–899
Respect, 220–221, 544–545
Respiratory distress, 347
Respiratory syncytial virus (RSV), 479–480
Rewards, 601–603, 611
See also Praise
punishments and, 602–603
Reye's syndrome, 354, 372, 482, 528
Rheumatic fever, 473
Rhinovirus, 460
RICE (rest, ibuprofen, cold, and elevation), 517
Ringworm, 494

Risk, 207, 381
  See also Safety
  adolescents and, 198, 207–208
  exploration and, 118
  and false sense of danger, 553–554
  importance of, 553–555
  sex and, 198, 207
Ritalin, 829
Rocking your baby, 51–52, 254
Rolling over and falling, 93–94, 435
Room for new baby, 24, 48
Roseola, 350
Rotavirus, 371, 374, 376, 377, 508
Roughage. *See* Fiber
Roundworms, 500
Routines, 732
  bedtime, 82, 127, 573, 775, 776
RSV (respiratory syncytial virus), 479–480
Rubella (German measles), 371, 376, 844–845
Ruminating, 742–743
RV (rotavirus vaccine), 376, 377

Safety, 141, 381
  See also Childproofing;
    Injuries, preventing;
    Poisons, poisoning; Risk

  exploration and, 117–121, 381
  Internet and, 656–658
  mouthing objects and, 79–80
  overprotectiveness and, 139
  rules for adolescents, 220, 223
  and setting limits, 119–121, 206, 220
  toys and, 400
  walkers and, 30, 97, 103, 399
Salmonella, 505, 506
Salt, 297, 306, 320, 330–331
  iodine in, 317, 330–331
  sodium in, 317–318
Same-sex parents. *See* Gay and lesbian parents
SAT, 217–218
Scabies, 493–494
Scald burns, 29, 387
Scalp
  bathing, 64
  lice on, 495
  rash on, 109–110
  ringworm and, 494
Scarlet fever, 474–475
School, 548–549
  See also College; Preschool; Teachers
  adolescents in, 197
  discipline in, 184, 185
  homework, 189–191
  outside world and, 184–185

parents and, 188–189, 889

physical education in, 187–188

purpose of, 182–183

sex education and, 636–637

sleep needs and, 227

success in, 182–191

School, problems in, 191–194

   See also Bullying; Learning
     disabilities

   causes of, 191–192

   help outside of school for,
     193

   and parents as child's
     advocate, 188–189

   and repeating a grade, 192–193

   school's help with, 185–186

   talking with child about,
     192–193

   unpopularity, 172, 194–196,
     548–549, 612

School-age children (six
     through eleven years), 169–
     196

   allowance for, 177

   bad manners in, 171–172

   cheating by, 178–179

   and children turning into
     kids, 169

   chores for, 176, 177, 647

   common behavior concerns,
     177–182

   compulsions in, 179–180

home life of, 176–177

independence from parents,
   170–172

lying by, 177–178

outside world and, 169–172

posture of, 181–182

rules and order valued by,
   169–170, 179

social lives of, 172–175

swearing by, 722–723

tics in, 180–181

School counselor, 866

Scoliosis, 518

Scratches and cuts, first aid for,
   423–424

Scrotum, 523–524

Seats, infant, 29–30, 38, 52

Seborrhea, 110

Seeds, 314, 329

Seizures and convulsions, 370,
   511–514

   See also Epilepsy

   breath-holding and, 113

   causes of, 512–513

   fever and, 353–354, 513

   first aid for, 439, 513–514

   medical intervention for, 514

   tonic-clonic (grand mal),
     511, 513–514

   twitching as possible sign of,
     76

   types of, 511–512

Selective mutism, 155, 815, 899

Self-esteem, 543–545

Senses, 44–45, 122, 135

Separation, 701–703

   returning to work, 39–40,
      579–580

   traumatic, 701–702

Separation anxiety, 122, 126,
      814

   at bedtime, 136–137

   in preschoolers, 165

   used by child for control, 138

September 11 attacks, 690, 691

Sex education, 209, 631–637,
     658

   abstinence, 209, 643

   adolescents and, 642–644

   awareness of genital
     differences, 157–159, 638

   for babies, 632

   and child not asking
     questions, 636

   children's questions and,
     632–636

   concentrating on dangerous
     aspects in, 644

   in early childhood, 631–632

   as encouraging sex, 642–643

   gender differences, 146–147,
     157–159

   school's role in, 636–637

   stork fable and, 634–635

   television and, 653

   and terms for body parts, 632

Sex roles. *See* Gender differences
   and roles

Sexual abuse, 522, 695–697

   getting help for, 697

   what to tell children about,
     695–696

   when to suspect, 696–697

Sexuality, 631–650

   See also Puberty

   adolescents and, 197, 205,
     208–209

   contraception and, 228, 643

   development of, 637–642

   early curiosity, 639

   Internet safety and, 656–658

   masturbation, 205, 637,
     638–639, 642

   modesty in the home and,
     639–640

   pornography and, 658–659

   risky behaviors and, 198,
     207, 591, 643

   sensuality and, 637–638

   spiritual side of, 631

   unwanted touching and, 641

Sexual orientation, 205–206,
     538, 645–650

   See also Homosexuality

Sexual relationship between
     parents, 5, 43

Shaking a baby, 86
Sharing, 135, 563, 805–806
Shigella, 505
Shocks, electrical, 429
Shoes, 101–102
Sibling rivalry, 547, 799–812
   jealousy of the new baby, 802–810
   other family members and, 808
   parental guilt about, 806
   parental intervention and,
     803–804
   and sharing toys, 805–806
   turning into helpfulness, 810
   withdrawal and, 804–805
Siblings
   birth order and spacing of,
     547–548
   of children with special
     needs, 682–683, 811–812
   comparing and typecasting,
     800–801
   fights between, 801–802
   helping prepare for new baby,
     24–26
   influence of, 547
   relationships between, 799
   rivalry, 799–812
   stepsiblings, 673, 704
SIDS. See Sudden infant death
   syndrome
Single-parent families, 540–
   541, 669–671

adoption and, 664
betraying parent and, 671
concerns with, 669–670
father as parent, 670–671
mother as parent, 670
resources for, 894
Sinusitis, 461, 462
Sitting up, 93, 94
Skateboarding, 412–413,
   458
Skin cancer, 71, 416
Skin color
   blue, 73
   sun and, 416
   yellow or orange, 73, 302
Skin conditions
   See also Blisters; Rashes
   boils, 493
   head lice, 495
   infections, 430
   of newborns, 64
   poison contact, 437
   warts, 494
Sledding, 413
Sleep, 28–29
   See also Sudden infant death
     syndrome
   adolescents and, 227
   amount needed, 47
   on back versus stomach, 49
   bedtime routines, 82, 127,
     573, 775, 776

Sleep (*cont.*):
bedtime separation anxiety, 136–137
changes in, 83
clothing for, 31, 32
co-sleeping, 48, 138–139
cribs and bassinets, 28–29
early waking, 83
fatigue and, 53
in first year, 82–84
habits of, 47–48
location for, 48
naps, 47, 83, 126–127, 151, 165
newborns and, 38, 46–49
night feedings and, 234–235
noise and, 48
parents' work hours and, 84
preschoolers and, 151–152
safety tips for, 49
school and, 227
and sorting out day and night, 46–47
taking a bottle to bed, 291, 294–295, 776
toddlers and, 126–127
wet dreams during, 205, 642
Sleep problems, 84, 191, 319, 773–776, 826
See also Insomnia
nightmares, 149, 152
night terrors, 152, 773, 774
obstructive sleep apnea, 485–486
retraining for sleep, 775
sleepwalking and sleep talking, 774
Sleep sacks, 28, 70
Smallpox, 369
Smegma, 67
Smoking. *See* Cigarettes and secondhand smoke
Snacks, 143, 226, 337–339, 451
Sneezing, 113
Snoring, 485–486
Soap, 33, 62–64, 107
antibacterial, 33, 361
handwashing, 131, 361
Soccer, 411–412
Social lives of children, 172–175
in adolescence, 202, 203–204
bullying, 174–175, 191, 548
clubs and cliques, 174
friendships, 174, 203–204
importance of peers, 172
popularity, 172, 173–174
unpopular children, 172, 194–196, 548–549, 612
Social workers, 865
Sodium, 317–318
See also Salt
Soft spot (fontanel), 38, 65–66

Solid foods, starting, 275, 297–310
  allergy triggers and, 304–305
  before or after milk, 298
  cereals, 300–301, 302, 307
  choking hazards, 308–310
  commercial baby foods, 306–307
  eggs, 305
  finger foods, 308
  food preferences and, 297
  fruits, 300, 301, 302–303, 307, 308, 311
  high-protein vegetarian foods, 303–304
  homemade baby food, 306
  how to introduce foods, 299–300
  lumpy and chopped food, 307–308
  meat, 304, 309
  mixed dinners in jars, 306
  order of foods in, 300
  six to twelve months, meals at, 307–310
  spoon foods, 297, 298, 308.
    See also Solid foods, starting
  spoon types and, 298–299
  timing of, 298
  tongue thrust reflex and, 298
  vegetables, 297, 300, 301–302, 307, 308
  when and how to begin, 297–307
Sorbitol, 453
Sore throats, 473–476
  scarlet fever, 474–475
  strep throat, 461, 473–474
Soups, 334
  chicken, 356, 465–466
Soy products, 304, 314, 315, 327
  soy-based formula, 281–282
  soy milk, 128, 260, 261, 281, 324
  tofu, 304, 307, 308, 322, 327, 329
Space heaters, 387, 388
Spanking, 589, 597, 607–608, 694–695
Sparklers, 421
Special needs, children with, 9, 679–686
  adopting, 663
  advocating for your child, 685–686
  coping within the family, 680–684
  early responses to, 680–681
  medical home for, 684–685
  and nurturing adult relationships, 683–684
  parents' coping styles and, 681
  parents' specialization and, 681–682
  parent support groups and, 685

Special needs, children with (*cont.*):
  resources for, 896–899
  siblings and, 682–683
  taking action for, 684–686
  types of conditions, 679
Speech. *See* Talking
Speech therapists, 866–867
Spina bifida, 318, 899
Spinal cord injuries, 434
Spine, curvature of, 518
Spitting up, 104–106
  See also Vomiting
  from overfeeding, 287
  when to call the doctor, 105–106
Splinters, 424
Splinting, 433–434
Spock, Benjamin, v, xxv, xxvi,
    551, 619, 647
  on appreciating children, 533
  on competitiveness and
    expectations, 539
  diet of, v, 320–325
  on HIV, 527
  on immunization, 369
  on sexuality, 631
  on stepparenting, 672
  on teeth, 447
  on values, 549–550
Spoiling, 611–612
  caring for sick child and, 366
  discipline and, 599
  how to unspoil, 90–92
  in first year, 79, 89–92
  newborns, 37, 53
  working parents and, 595
Sponge baths, 61–62
Spoon foods, 297, 298, 308
Spoons, 81, 241–242, 243,
    244, 298–299
Sports injuries, 410–413, 458, 517
Sprains, 431–432
Stairs, preventing falls down, 399
Standing up, 93, 96–97
Staphylococcus, 492, 493
Starches, 245, 312–313
Startling, 75–76, 85
Stepfamilies, 672–675, 704
  concerns with, 672–673
  parenting tips for, 674
  positive aspects of, 673–674
  siblings in, 673, 704
  when to seek help, 674–675
Stimulants, 829–831
Stomachaches and stomach
  problems, 358, 495–501
  See also Colic; Constipation;
    Diarrhea; Vomiting
  appendicitis, 358, 498
  common causes of, 496–497
  infections, 60, 505–506
  stress and, 497–498
  when to call the doctor, 495–
    496
Stork bites, 72

Stork fable, 634–635

Strains, 431–432

Strangers
  anxiety about, 99–100, 117, 123–124
  infants' reactions to, 99–101
  manners and, 622

Strangulation, 397, 409

Strawberry marks, 72

Street safety, 405–407

Strep throat, 461, 473–474
  scarlet fever, 474–475

Streptococcus, 492

Stresses and traumas, 467, 521, 687–713, 776
  See also Child abuse and neglect; Death; Divorce; Domestic violence; Separation; Sexual abuse
  anxiety disorders and, 816
  brain and, 688
  headaches and, 510
  lasting effects of, 689–690
  meaning of stress, 688–690
  physical effects of, 688
  PTSD, 688
  stomachaches and, 497–498
  terrorism and disasters, 690–692
  vulnerability to, 689

Stridor, 113, 347, 477

Strollers, 30, 118

Stuttering, 161, 745–747
  causes of, 745–746
  help for, 746–747
  resources for, 899

Styes, 516

Substance abuse, 198, 207, 208, 398, 553, 591, 830

Sucking, 92
  in breastfeeding, 266–267
  instinct and craving for, 51, 232, 737

Sucking blisters (type of blister), 72–73

Sucking thumb. *See* Thumb-sucking

Sudden infant death syndrome (SIDS; crib death), 34, 48, 49, 69, 507, 524–525
  responses to, 524–525
  talking about, 525

Suffocation, 70, 382, 397

Sugar and sweets, 226, 297, 306–309, 311, 312–313, 316, 320, 330, 331–332
  illness and, 355, 356
  taming a sweet tooth, 337
  tooth decay and, 451, 453, 454

Sugar water, 106

Suicide, 818, 819, 830
  adolescents and, 223–224, 398
  antidepressants and, 820–821
  LGBT youth and, 646, 650

Sun
  newborns and, 71
  safety in, 71, 416–418
  sunburn, 416–417, 428
  sunglasses, 417–418
  sunscreen, 71, 417
  vitamin D and, 71, 226, 239,
    260, 319, 321
Suppositories, 60
Surgery, 362
  See also Hospitalization
Swaddling, 51–52, 254
Swallowed objects, first aid for,
  435–436, 439
Swearing, 722–724
Swimmer's ear, 472
Swimming lessons, 386
Swings, infant, 29–30, 52, 103
Swollen glands, 476

Table manners, 129, 161, 171,
  244, 545, 603
Talcum powder, 33, 64, 109
Talking, 78
  See also Stuttering
  articulation, 161
  fear of (selective mutism),
    155, 815, 899
  two-year-olds and, 134
Tantrums. See Temper tantrums
Teachers, 182
  bullying and, 175

dislike between child and, 194
parents and, 188, 192, 193–194
Tear duct, blocked, 111
Teenage years. See Adolescence
Teeth, 447–458
  baby, 447–448, 739
  development of, 447–449
  layers of, 456
  permanent, 448–449, 739
  thumb-sucking and, 738–739
Teeth, care of, 450–452
  brushing, 454–455
  chewing gum, 453
  dental varnish and sealants,
    456
  dentist visits, 452
  flossing, 455–456
  fluoride, 24, 240, 451–452,
    456
  nutrition, 450–451
  parents with bad teeth, 453–
    454
  resources for, 891
  toothbrush for, 454–455, 458
  tooth decay (cavities), 451,
    453–454
  tooth decay from bottles and
    sipping, 291, 292, 295,
    454
  toothpaste, 451, 452
Teeth, injuries to, 456–457
  cracked teeth, 456–457

knocked out of mouth (avulsed), 457

loosened teeth, 457

preventing, 457–458

Teething, 270, 294, 449–450, 737

biscuits for, 308

feeding and, 238

gels for, 450

help for, 449–450

rings for, 449

symptoms of, 449

Television, 576, 651–653

in bedroom, 653–654, 774

limits on viewing, 574

not having, 654

obesity and, 790, 791

preschoolers and, 151, 153

sexual or violent content on, 653

watching with your child, 652–653

Temperament and personality, 6, 7, 45, 93

heredity and, 546

siblings and, 547

Temperature, body, 351

See also Fever; Thermometers

Fahrenheit and centigrade (Celsius) equivalents, 353

newborns and, 38

normal variations in, 349–351

Temperature, room, 48, 68–69, 70

Temperature, water, 29, 63

Temper tantrums, 717–722

fear and, 141

frequent, 719–720

language delay and, 720–721

manipulative, 720

reasons for, 717, 721–722

responding to, 717–718

as sign of other problems, 721–722

in toddlers, 126

in two-year-olds, 141–142

"Terrible twos," 115, 133

Terrorism, 690–692

Testicles, 201, 523–524

undescended, 75

Testosterone, 199

Tetanus (lockjaw), 370, 376, 423

Therapy, 861–868

for anger, 139, 625

choosing a professional for, 863–867

for postpartum depression, 42

resources for, 895–896

types of, 862–863

unpopular children and, 196

working together in, 867–868

Thermometers, 33, 351–353
  glass, 33, 352, 395
  taking rectal temperature,
    351–352
  Fahrenheit and centigrade
    (Celsius) equivalents, 353
Thinking, 558–565
  abstract, 197, 558, 561, 562–
    563
  concrete operations, 561–
    562, 563
  formal operations, 563
  preoperational, 560–561
  sensorimotor, 559–560
Thinness, 786–788
Threadworms, 499–500
Throat problems
  See also Breathing problems;
    Croup
  diphtheria, 370, 376, 475
  epiglottitis, 477, 478
  mononucleosis, 475
  scarlet fever, 474–475
  sore throat, 473–476
  strep throat, 461, 473–474
  swelling, and anaphylaxis, 438
Throwing things, 125–126
  food, 126, 129
Thrush, 110–111
Thumb-sucking, 737–742
  breaking the habit of, 740–742
  health effects of, 738–739

  meaning of, 737–738
  methods that don't work for,
    740
  preventing, 739–740
  ruminating and, 743
Ticks (biting pests), 419–420
Tics, 180–181
Time-outs, 608–610
Time with child, 593–595
  quality and quantity of, 593–
    594
  single parents and, 669–670
  special, 594
  spoiling and, 595
Toddlers (twelve to twenty-four
    months), 115–131
  See also Toilet training
  biting by, 725–726
  challenging behaviors in,
    124–126
  difficulty stopping fun
    activities, 124–125
  distraction as discipline
    technique with, 125, 605
  dropping and throwing
    things, 125–126, 129
  eating and nutrition for, 128–
    129
  elbow injuries in, 432
  exploration by, 117–121, 122
  fears at around one year,
    122–124

harness or wrist lead for, 121

independence in, 116–117

negativism in, 115–116

outgoingness in, 117

reading to, 569–571

safety and, 117–121

setting limits with, 119–121

sleep issues with, 126–127

Toeing in and toeing out, 97–99

Tofu, 261, 304, 307, 308, 322, 325, 327, 329

Toilet training, 130–131, 152, 749–771

See also Bladder control

adult toilet versus potty seat in, 755–756

balking at, 753

development and, 749–750

early, 750–751

gentle approach to, 754–759

handwashing and, 131

hard bowel movements and, 759–760

learning about the potty, 130

pants and, 761–762

preschoolers and, 161

readiness for, 130, 749–754

setbacks in, 764

soiling, 765–766

terms used with child in, 131

Toilet Training in Less Than a Day (Azrin and Foxx), 130, 759

two-year-olds and, 144

wiping and handwashing in, 763

Toiletries, 33–34

Tongue, sucking and chewing on, 742–743

Tonsils, 362, 473, 474, 485

Touch, importance of, 38–39, 51–52

Tourette's disorder (Tourette's syndrome), 181

resources for, 899

Toxoplasmosis, 17

Toy chest, 400

Toys, sharing of, 135, 805–806

Toy safety, 400

choking hazards, 395–396

Transgender people, 647–649

Traumas. See Stresses and traumas

Trembles, 75–76

Trick-or-treating, 421–422

Trust, 534–535, 536

Tuberculosis (TB), 527–528

Twitching, 76

Two-year-olds, 133–144

See also Toilet training

challenging behaviors in, 140–143

diet and nutrition for, 143–144

favoritism toward one parent, 142–143

Two-year-olds (*cont.*):
  fears and worries of, 136–140
  language and, 134, 135
  learning in, 133–134
  negativism in, 140–141
  play and, 135
  setting limits with, 140–141
  temper tantrums in, 141–142
  "terrible twos," 115, 133
Tylenol. *See* Acetaminophen

Ulcerative colitis, 509
Ultrasounds, 13, 15, 17, 92
Ultraviolet (UV) exposure, 416–417
Umbilical hernia, 74
UNICEF, 421, 894
United Nations Convention on the Rights of the Child, 694
University of Chicago, 163
Unpopular children, 172, 194–196, 548–549, 612
Urinary tract problems, 520–523
  bladder and kidney infections, 520
  frequent urination, 502, 520–521
  inability to urinate away from home, 762
  infrequent urination, 521
  painful urination in girls, 522
Urination, 254

  See also Bladder control
  concern about wetting the bed, 137–138
  constipation and, 502, 520
  standing up for, 762
  training a baby to urinate on cue, 751
Urine
  blood in, 348
  child's attitude toward, 761
  color of, 239, 302, 355
  dehydration and, 508
Urticaria (hives), 438, 492
Uterus, 248

Vaccinations. *See* Immunizations
Vagina
  bathing, 64
  discharge from, 75, 522–523
Values, 549–550
Vaporizers and humidifiers, 69, 463–464
Varicella (chicken pox), 372, 376, 528
Vegan diets, 226, 239, 317, 318, 320, 321
Vegetables, 226, 240, 261, 311, 313, 316, 326–327, 332, 502
  bacteria in, 506
  child's refusal of, 244–245
  corn, 326–327

green leafy, 314, 316, 317, 326
introducing, 297, 300, 301–302, 307, 308
phytochemicals in, 320
temporary substitutes for, 336–337
Vegetarian diets, 226, 319, 321
  introducing high-protein foods in, 303–304
  iron in, 322
  lacto-ovo, 321
  resources for, 890
  vegan, 226, 239, 317, 318, 320, 321
Video chats, 652
  See also Skype, FaceTime, 594
Videos and video games, 151, 152, 153, 179, 553, 651–652, 654–655
Violence, 9
  See also Domestic violence
  on television, 653
  terrorism and disasters, 690–692
Viruses, 23
  vaccines and, 369, 374
Vision. See Eyes and vision
Vitamins, 239–240, 318–319
  breastfeeding and, 260, 261
  colds and, 465
  megadoses of, 319
  multivitamins, 16, 239, 240, 317, 318, 321, 337

toxicity and, 319, 389
vitamin A, 318, 319
vitamin B_1 (thiamine), 318
vitamin B_2 (riboflavin), 318
vitamin B_3 (niacin), 318, 319
vitamin B_6 (pyridoxine), 318, 319
vitamin B_9 (folic acid; folate), 16, 17, 318
vitamin B_{12} (cobalamin), 239, 240, 318, 321, 330
vitamin C (ascorbic acid), 305, 318–319, 331, 450, 465
vitamin D, 71, 226, 239, 240, 260, 319, 321, 330, 450, 502
vitamin E, 319
vitamin K, 319
Vomiting, 53, 237, 348, 372
  blood in, 348
  diarrhea with, 506
  in first year, 104–106
  food poisoning and, 506, 507
  GERD and, 52, 53, 105, 506–507
  overfeeding and, 287
  when to call the doctor, 105–106, 348
  without diarrhea, 506–507
Vomiting, forcing
  bulimia, 226, 793–794, 795
  swallowed object and, 436

Walkers, 29–30, 97, 103, 399

Walking, 93, 97, 101

Warts, 494
genital, 372

Wasps, 419

Water, drinking, 313, 331
for babies, 238–239
dietary needs, 502
fluoride in, 24, 240, 451, 452
lead in, 284–285, 393, 394
for nursing mothers, 251

Water, fear of, 155

Water, well, 23–24

Water heater, temperature and,
29, 387

Water safety and drowning
prevention, 382, 384–386

Weaning
agreement in, 275
mother's hesitation in, 277–
278
sudden, 276

Weaning from bottle to cup,
128, 291–295
changing from formula to
water, 295
and emotional attachment to
bottle, 295
getting used to the cup, 292–
293
gradual, 293–294
optimal age for, 292

parental concerns about,
295
preventing problems with,
294–295
reluctant weaners, 294
signs of readiness for,
291–292
sippy cups and, 293
timing of, 291–292

Weaning from breastfeeding,
128, 274, 275–278
to bottle, 274, 275–276
to cup, 277–278

Weight, 82, 252
See also Obesity
overweight, 502, 787
thinness, 252, 786–788

Weight gain, 226, 252, 254
average, for babies, 236
breastfeeding and,
256–257
fat babies, 237
and feeding in the first year,
236–238
how often to weigh, 237
slow, 237

Well water, 23–24

West Nile virus, 418, 528

Wet dreams, 205, 642

Whining, 142, 720, 734–736

Whooping cough (pertussis),
370, 374, 462

WIC (Women, Infants, and Children) nutrition program, 252
Windows, falls from, 399
Wipes, 55, 107–108
Work
  adolescents and, 208, 210
  chores, 176, 177, 224, 647
Working parents
  See also Child care
  breastfeeding and, 267–269
  child's bedtime and, 84
  returning to work, 39–40, 579–580
  schedule and, 581–582
  spoiling and, 595
  and time spent with child, 594

World Health Organization, 247
Worms, 499–501
Wounds, first aid for, 426–427
Wrist leads, 121
Wrists, broken, 433
Writing skills, 837–838

Xylitol, 453, 470

Yeast
  diaper rash caused by candida, 108
  thrush, 110–111

Zika virus, 17, 418, 419, 529, 844–845
Zinc, 261, 317, 465